Michael Tomlin
1972

The Early History of Malawi

Edited by Bridglal Pachai

Professor of History
Chancellor College
University of Malawi

Longman

LONGMAN GROUP LIMITED
London
Associated companies, branches and
representatives throughout the world

First published 1972

ISBN 0 582 64090.3 paper
ISBN 0 582 64089.X cased

Printed in England by
THE BARLEYMAN PRESS
Bristol

Contents

Illustrations

Plates

Acknowledgements

Grateful thanks are due to the Chancellor of the University of Malawi, His Excellency the President of the Republic of Malawi, Dr H. Kamuzu Banda for opening the History Conference and for addressing it; to the Vice-Chancellor, Dr Ian Michael, and the former Principal of Chancellor College, Professor John Utting, for encouragement and help; to the contributors of the various chapters and the bodies which funded their travelling expenses; to the British Council, Blantyre, for part payment of the travelling expenses of a contributor; to the Director, United States Information Services, Blantyre for photocopying facilities; to Professor George Shepperson for many kindly services; to Professor Phillip V. Tobias for producing a paper under extreme pressure; to Professor Agnew and Mr James Lupoka for assistance with maps; to my wife and my children for putting up with the rigours of checking scripts; to Miss Mercy Kasambara, Chancellor College, History Department Secretary, for typing the scripts; and, finally, to my colleagues Leroy Vail, Robin Palmer and Martin Chanock for splendid all-round team work.

B. Pachai

The editor and publishers would like to express their gratitude to the following for permission to reproduce photographs: to the Director of the Livingstone Museum, Zambia for Fig. 1.6, which also appears on the cover; to the Society of Malawi for Figs 5.1, 9.2 and 20.1; to the Museum of Malawi for Figs 5.3 and 5.6; to Methuen and Co. Ltd for Fig. 16.2; to the Radio Times Hulton Picture Library for Figs 18.1 and 18.2; to the Department of Information, Government of Malawi for Figs 12.3 and 12.4; to Rev. Tom Colvin, C.C.A.P., Blantyre, for Fig. 23.1. Figs 1.2, 1.3, 1.4, 1.5 and 12.2 were taken by the contributors and Figs 23.2 and 23.3 by the editor.

We are grateful to the following for permission to reproduce copyright material: to Mrs Agnes Avery for extracts from a letter of Norman Leys to the Secretary of State for the Colonies; Edinburgh University Library for various extracts from missionary letters in the Shepperson Collection; Methuen and Co. Ltd for extracts from *British Central Africa* by H. H. Johnston; Missionari d'Africa, Rome for extracts from the *Mponda Mission Diary*; the Controller of Her Majesty's Stationery Office for extracts from *C.O. 525–66 Nyasaland 1916 Vol. 1 Nyasaland Native Rising* and William Thomson Phelps Stokes Fund for an extract from *Education in Africa* by Jesse Jones.

vii

Abbreviations

RNLB	Rhodesian Native Labour Bureau
WNLA	Witwatersrand Native Labour Association
F.O.	Foreign Office
C.O.	Colonial Office
B.C.G.A.	British Cotton Growing Association
B & E.A.	Blantyre and East Africa Company
N.E.A.	North-Eastern Rhodesia
B.C.A.G.	British Central Africa Gazette
J.A.H.	Journal of African History
RSEA	Records of South-Eastern Africa
CHCAP	Conference on the History of Central African Peoples
P.R.O.	Public Record Office, London
A.H.U.	Arquivo Historico Ultramarino, Lisbon
C.P.	Confidential Print

Note on Place Names

Reference is made in this book to the following places whose names have either since changed or are now spelt differently.

Old name	Present name
Florence Bay	Chitimba
Fort Johnston	Mangochi
Cholo	Thyolo
Mlanje	Mulanje
Fort Jameson	Chipata
Rumpi	Rumphi
Deep Bay	Chilumba

Biographical Notes

1	Professor Swanzie Agnew	Professor of Geography, University of Malawi, Chancellor College.
2	Dr Edward A. Alpers	Assistant Professor of History, University of California, Los Angeles.
3	Professor Eric Axelson	Professor of History, University of Cape Town.
4	Mr Colin A. Baker	Principal, Institute of Public Administration, University of Malawi.
5	Dr Martin L. Chanock	Lecturer in History, University of Malawi, Chancellor College.
6	Professor J. Desmond Clark	Professor of African Prehistoric Archaeology, University of California, Berkeley.
7	Mr P. A. Cole-King	Director of Antiquities, Malawi.
8	Dr A. J. Dachs	Lecturer in History, University of Rhodesia.
9	Rev. Philip Elston	Chaplain and History Teacher, Malosa Secondary School, Malawi. Post-graduate student, University of Malawi, Chancellor College.
10	Dr B. S. Krishnamurthy	Senior Lecturer in History, University of Zambia.
11	Dr Harry W. Langworthy	Lecturer in History, University of Zambia (now at Cleveland State University).
12	Dr Ian Linden	Lecturer in Biology, University of Malawi, Chancellor College.
13	Dr Hugh W. Macmillan	Ph.D. graduate, University of Edinburgh.
14	Dr K. J. McCracken	Lecturer in History, University of Stirling, Scotland.
15	Dr George Nurse	Medical Superintendent, St Michael's Hospital, Batlharos, Kuruman, South

	Africa (formerly Senior Medical Officer, Witwatersrand Native Labour Association, Lilongwe).
16 Professor B. Pachai	Professor of History, University of Malawi, Chancellor College (Editor).
17 Dr Robin H. Palmer	Lecturer in History, University of Malawi, Chancellor College.
18 Mr J. L. Pretorius	Literature Secretary of Nkhoma Synod, C.C.A.P. Training Officer for Christian Literature Association of Malawi.
19 Mr Keith R. Robinson	Formerly of Historical Monuments Commission, Rhodesia.
20 Rev. Dr J. M. Schoffeleers	Principal, Catechetical Training Centre, Likulezi, Malawi.
21 Professor George Shepperson	Professor of Commonwealth and American History, University of Edinburgh.
22 Professor Phillip V. Tobias	Professor of Anatomy, Witwatersrand University, Johannesburg.
23 Mr H. Leroy Vail	Lecturer in History, University of Malawi, Chancellor College.
24 Professor Monica Wilson	Professor of Social Anthropology, University of Cape Town.

Introduction

Ever since the name *Maravi* was first inserted in a Portuguese map in 1546, numerous writings have appeared giving general accounts of the land and the peoples associated with it. These accounts by travellers, missionaries and traders, civil servants, soldiers and journalists, have all tended to draw attention to the historical circumstances of their time and place. Naturally, the people wrote about the things they saw, did and visualized in the context of their day. Put together, or even looked at separately, the writings constitute a valuable introduction to an understanding of local and regional history.

Many things happened in 1546. Martin Luther, for example, died in Germany and the ruler Askia Ishak I was attempting to hold back the further decline of the Songhai empire in the Western Sudan. Both these events, one European and the other African, are important to the student of history in Malawi. But of greater importance, to him, in the first place, is a good grasp of the main outlines of the history of his own country. Where detailed local histories are not available the story of man's achievements and failures in the outside world becomes less meaningful. There is no justification for ignoring the charity which begins at home.

The study and the writing of history are themselves inseparable from the emergence of vigorous and viable nationhood. It is not unusual, then, that with the attainment of independence, Malawi started her own university in 1965. Before this, the Federation of the Rhodesias and Nyasaland, with a status of a different kind, had started a University College in Salisbury in 1956.

Before this last date, the local history of Malawi and of many of her neighbours was little more than an intellectual curiosity in which a few interested persons were engaged. Desmond Clark tells us that no 'archaeologist set foot in Malawi before 1950, as far as I know, and no systematic investigation began before 1965'.[1]

The same may be said of history with a few exceptions, namely, the studies on Nyasaland and North-Eastern Rhodesia undertaken in the 1940s by Norman H. Pollock and A. J. Hanna, neither of whom visited the country during the course of their researches.[2] Their works are, none the less, valuable. In the 1950s four notable scholars devoted their energies to aspects of Nyasaland history. They were Roland Oliver, George Shepperson, Thomas Price and Margaret Read.[3]

The scholarship and the publications of the 1940s and the 1950s were based on assumptions and premises that have since been considerably revised. Benedetto Croce's remark that all history is contemporary history recognized the different mental equipment of scholars in different periods.[4] This equipment includes assumptions and attitudes, the kind of questions that historians ask, and the types of historical movements they study and write about.

In the 1960s the colonial heritage was still with us. Generations who had been brought up under colonial régimes had become colonial-oriented through force of habit and constant exposure. School syllabuses were replete with *1066 and all that*. The metropolitan royal families, institutions, wars, treaties and empires were studied stolidly and solemnly. Colonial conquerors and administrators were generally regarded as belonging to another world. Their standards were projected as being out of reach, unattainable. When a band of Blantyre missionaries, white and black, from Nyasaland started their classes in Mozambique with *God save the Queen* in 1897, it was the fashionable thing to do. When they had the audacity to do it in Portuguese territory it was more than an audacious act. It was an act of carrying the flag.

In Malawi, the old flag came down in 1964 but the many who had served it both from within and without were still around. Transition to independence is both a matter of tangibles and intangibles. A whole host of peoples and circumstances must combine to make the transition and what follows it real and meaningful. The voice of the politician has to be buttressed by the pen of the historian. If, as Croce says, history should 'vibrate in the historian's mind', the era which commenced with the attainment of independence heralded a new approach and a new set of guiding principles to match the contemporary scene.

For the historian in the new African university it was not simply a case of exchanging new lamps for old or even of pouring new wine into old bottles. A first major consideration was that of drawing the right balance between the African and the non-African areas for study. Even if the balance could be struck, there was the related problem of teaching material. Though there were many books on Malawi and her neighbours written by missionaries, traders, explorers and administrators, perhaps enough to refute Hegel's remarks made in 1831 that 'Africans were a people without a history',[6] and repeated in other ways by Professors Trevor-Roper and A. P. Newton,[7] they were not of the quality, quantity, depth or variety upon which serious scholarship could continue to draw. They were written, too, for a particular audience. What was worse, as Mr Vail points out in this volume, some were directed at perpetuating certain myths.[8]

A beginning had therefore to be made by writing on various aspects of local history. This, as many would bear witness, has not been an easy task. Historical material has not always been easy to obtain. Historians have not always been able to stay long enough to complete their assignments. Funds have often been limited and priorities have had to be worked out and respected. All in all, however, the picture is not a gloomy one even if the problems were numerous.

We have referred to the first serious consideration of drawing up the right balance between the different areas of historical studies. There is another aspect to this exercise of 'redressing the balance'. This lies in the concept of restoration, of the restoration or reassertion of the African personality and the African past. In the new exercise this has sometimes been seen as a crusade to re-echo the African Voice.[9] It is right and proper that the African Voice should be heard where it was stifled before but it is equally right that it should be heard in the context of the drama and alongside the other actors. When one set of assumptions gives way to another, it is to be expected that the later assumptions will themselves be questioned. This represents the continuation of the historical exercise. It is fitting, therefore, that certain articles in this volume, which makes its appearance early in the 1970s, should question the assumptions and the accomplishments of the 1960s.

This is not to say that the sixties have been unproductive in local or regional histories in Central Africa. On the contrary, this decade will go down as one of valuable pioneering work. In September 1960 the Leverhulme Inter-Collegiate History Conference was held at the University College of Rhodesia and Nyasaland 'to make a sort of interim survey of the progress and difficulties of research, writing and teaching in African History'.[10]

In May 1963 the seventeenth conference of the Rhodes-Livingstone Institute (later to become the Institute of Social Research of the University of Zambia) was convened to discuss the history of the Central African people.[11]

Two History workshop sessions were held in 1967 primarily for the benefit of secondary school teachers of History, the first of these was held at Dar es Salaam in January[12] and the second at Blantyre in June-July.[13]

In July 1968 a History Conference was held at the University of Zambia under the sponsorship of the University of California at Los Angeles. The main thrust of this conference was, in the words of Professor Leonard Thompson, to look at the 'forgotten factor in Southern African history', viz., 'the history of the African peoples themselves before they were subjected to white over-rule'.[14]

Within a decade, considerable gaps have been closed or narrowed down; new ones have been discovered and old ones are being re-examined. In the historiography of Malawi recent doctoral theses by John McCracken, Andrew Ross, Roderick Macdonald, Matthew Schoffeleers, Roger Tangri and Hugh Macmillan, among others, have produced new material and interpretations on the Livingstonia Mission, the Blantyre Mission, African education, the Mang'anja, modern political movements, and the African Lakes Corporation, respectively.

The present volume derives from a conference on the early history of Malawi held at Blantyre under the auspices of the University of Malawi from 20 July to 24 July 1970. It was opened by His Excellency the President of Malawi, Dr H. Kamuzu Banda in his capacity as Chancellor of the University of Malawi. Twenty papers were presented. In addition to these, contributions from the following persons have been gratefully received and included: Professor Phillip V. Tobias of the University of Witwatersrand; Professor J. Desmond Clark of the University of California at Berkeley, Mr K. R. Robinson and Dr H. W. Macmillan.

Three special points should be made about the conference itself. The first is that whereas some participants have worked on aspects of Malawi history, archaeology and anthropology for upwards of twenty years, others newly arrived in the country have had less than twenty months to be initiated in Malawi history. They had no access to the National Archives during this time, a handicap which, as far as all the present members of the History Department, Chancellor College, are concerned, happily no longer exists. This has been one of the most rewarding outcomes of the conference and augurs well for future research and scholarship in Malawi.

The second point is that in addition to the reinforcement and new insights introduced by a number of complementary disciplines at the conference and in this volume, a refreshing feature was the contribution of the non-professionals: a minister of religion, now a post-graduate student of the University of Malawi; a son of a missionary who is himself developing into a fine scholar; a medical man, who has spent many years in this country, have, all three of them, enriched the conference and this volume by their contributions. Professor Shepperson was right in reminding the delegates that the rôle of the 'amateur' should not be underrated.

The third point is a stock-taking of where we stand in the task of promoting Malawi history. This point is concerned with the past, and present and the future and is adequately covered in the final resolution which was adopted at the closing session of the conference:

'The delegates to the International Conference on the early history of Malawi wish to express their appreciation of the significance of this meeting. They have been reminded of the remarkable richness and potentiality of Malawi history. They admire the results already achieved by the researches of the staff of the University and other scholars resident in Malawi. In the discussions of the Conference a number of new directions for inquiry have been raised and there has been some discussion of priorities, for example the urgent importance of folklore collection. The delegates of the Conference have expressed their hope that these discussions will be developed in a report on historical research and writing in and about Malawi to be drawn up by a committee of local and other scholars and accompanied by a survey of source material available for Malawi history. The delegates to the International Conference express their profound hope that students of Malawi history will enjoy the widest access to the archival and field resources without which these exciting potentialities cannot be fulfilled.'

New tasks lie ahead and these will have to be tackled with resolution and speed. For the moment, this volume is being presented as the first instalment of a greater commitment. It comprises twenty-four chapters in all. In order to give readers an idea of the ground covered in these chapters a brief synopsis follows, beginning with the opening chapter by Professor Tobias.

Professor Tobias begins with a review of what is known about the antiquity of man in Africa. The various discoveries in Africa of specimens belonging to the group of creatures termed *Australopithecinae* have yielded proof of the animal origins of man. Africa has thus made a significant contribution to knowledge on the evolution of man, to which have been added other discoveries which serve to illuminate the phases of man's development. Professor Tobias describes the four major stages of 'hominization', viz., *Australopithecus*, *Homo habilis*, *Homo erectus* and *Homo sapiens*, with appropriate illustrations and states that on the strength of present evidence it is possible to say that the first two of these stages were 'enacted only in Africa'. The author then leads on to a historical survey of archaeological research in Malawi, drawing attention to the pioneering work in this field both in the period before 1950 when very little systematic work was done and in the period after 1950, the most significant achievements of which were recorded in the last decade. Professor Tobias notes the sequence of Late Stone Age sites in Malawi and elsewhere in Central Africa. In Malawi, these have been excavated at Fingira (revealing stone artefacts dating from 3,530 to 3,350 years before the present, found in association with human skeletons which have been characterized as belonging to the Khoisan people), Hora Mountain, Mikolongwe Hill, and the Livingstonia Plateau. The earliest date obtained so far from any of these Late Stone Age sites (in one of the nine rock shelters of Hora Mountain) is some 12,000 years older than the Fingira date given above, while the latest date (Nyika) is about 2,000 years ago or about the time when Malawi entered the Iron Age. In this chapter, the author gives a coverage of man's antiquity as well as a résumé of the Stone and Iron Age periods, the last two anticipating, briefly yet usefully, chapters 2 and 4 by Desmond Clark and Keith Robinson respectively, two of the notable pioneers in Malawi archaeology.

In chapter 2, Professor Clark reviews the prehistoric origins of Malawi history in order to remind us that the personality of a country is no less than the full picture of its historic and prehistoric past. This picture is arrived at with the aid of oral, written and tangible sources in which the tools and techniques of anthropology and archaeology are of considerable help to the historian. Though the greater part of man's history during the Stone Age, according to Professor Clark, covers a span of some two and a half million years man's cultural advance has been most pronounced over the past 600,000 years only. In Malawi, no human remains dateable to this latter period have been found as yet, though faunal remains have been found in the Karonga district going back to some three to four million years. Somewhat less ancient are the fossilized elephant remains also found in Karonga together with a variety of tools used in the exercise of dismembering the elephant dated at between 50,000 and 100,000 years ago. The first human remains in Malawi have been assigned to the 'Later Stone Age' in the period 8000 B.C. up to A.D. 200. During this period the 'Akafula' hunters, short and robust, spread themselves over a wide area, possibly speaking a 'click' language at some stage.

This chapter is followed by a geographical account by Professor Swanzie

Agnew (chapter 3) in which our notions of migration and settlement patterns are improved by an understanding of how and why Malawi attracted people in large numbers in the first place; the routes that were followed through the wasp-waist of Central Africa, and through the Luangwa depression as well as other routes. The factors for population growth and formation of permanent settlements were present in the form of good land and plentiful water. Similar factors had given rise to the importance of places like Kisi, Ivuna and Kalambo, all in the neighbourhood of Malawi, where important Iron-Age sites have been discovered. At Ivuna the presence of cattle was dated to the thirteenth century (chapter 9) and the existence of a tsetse-free corridor into Malawi facilitated the entry of pastoralists. In addition to the entry of people and domestic animals, food plants and other cultural influences filtered in as well. Because of helpful environmental factors, Professor Agnew sees Malawi as the 'cross-roads between the different cultural regions of eastern, central and southern Africa'.

The Iron Age in Malawi is the subject matter of chapter 4, for which the earliest date (third century A.D.) was obtained from charcoal deposits in the Phopo Hill area of Lake Kazuni. The pottery associated with the Iron-Age settlements of Northern Malawi appears, according to Mr Robinson, to have closer affinities with early Iron Age pottery from Uganda and Kenya rather than with Zambia, though certain elements are related to the Gokomere pottery of Rhodesia and Zambia. The earliest date in the southern region (fourth century A.D.) was obtained at Nkope Bay at Cape Maclear and the Bwanje river area of Ncheu. Until July 1970 there was no evidence of coastal trade associated with this period but in that month a single blue glass bead and half a cowrie shell were discovered in a sealed deposition containing Nkope type ware. These were unearthed in excavations at Matope. On the other hand, Kisi pottery dated eleventh century A.D. and Mbande Hill pottery dated fifteenth century A.D. are examples of movements between the area east of Livingstone Mountains and the Karonga district. On the basis of Iron Age settlements, Mr Robinson submits a tentative hypothesis that some of the first early Iron Age immigrants entered Malawi from the north, travelling on both sides of the lake. He also raises the interesting proposition that the relationship between the Gokomere ware of Rhodesia and the Nkope ware of Southern Malawi could mean either that it represents development in the pottery industry itself as the people migrated southwards or that it implies contact with a related group of people who were already making their pottery in the Gokomere tradition.

After the Iron Age sequence we come to chapter 5 in which Mr Cole-King looks at the issues of transport and communication. He observes that the obvious north-south line of the Rift valley seems not to have been used much until the latter half of the nineteenth century, though about eight east-west trade routes cut across it. The north-south line was, of course, used as a migration route (chapters 3 and 4). Dr Livingstone's travels drew attention to the feasibility of using the Shire waterway to link with the lake in spite of the gap of some forty miles created by cataracts. The explorer minimized the difficulties of this waterway (see also chapter 20) and thus left behind him, what the author prefers to label, the Livingstone myth.[15]

After the first five chapters which deal primarily with archaeological and geographical questions, we are introduced, in chapter 6, to Rev. Dr Schoffeleers' examination of two issues, viz., the composition of the people, within the Chewa[16]-speaking cluster, who were traditionally identified by the name *Malawi* or *Maravi*, and the factors which distinguished them from other members of the cluster. Using oral traditions, corroborated by evidence obtained after examining place names, the author suggests that the name was first associated with the Phiri clan but, adding to this information after using ethnographic sources, Dr Schoffeleers argues that the Chewa-speakers had two names, of which the *generic* name was always *Maravi* or *Malawi* and the specific name was a different one, the difference owing its existence to traditional clan organization. The author concludes that the name was associated, as we have noted, with the Phiri clan and that it ceased to be used commonly after the 1850 invasions by other peoples when the Phiri lost much of their previous lands. The position of the Phiri rulers was further strengthened by their use of fire as a symbol of royal status.

In the next chapter (chapter 7), Dr Langworthy reviews Chewa political organization in the precolonial era and refers to the factors which tended towards decentralization of the political authority of the Chewa king, Kalonga, his famous kinsman, Undi, as well as the tributary kings. Vacant kingly or chiefly positions were filled from within separate matrilineages by a process of selection in which local councillors and headmen decided upon their choice; the senior king did not select the candidate though he could influence the choice or otherwise delimit the area of a subordinate. Chewa political loyalties were in the first instance due to the lineage of the office-holder and afterwards to his 'subjects'. Within this framework, described as 'successful decentralization of authority', the author gives an account of the Kalonga's relations with members of his own family; his relations with subordinates; his ritual and religious roles; his judicial, economic and military services. The Kalonga's main power derived from the operation of reciprocal services in exchange for goods or labour services received. For as long as the Chewa kings controlled trade, this reciprocal relationship survived in spite of the inherent decentralizing tendencies in the Chewa political system. When the substance in the pool of economic wealth was no longer redistributed by the Kalonga, decentralization became accentuated and a number of territorial kingdoms emerged. The products of decentralization themselves, these kingdoms, with the exception of that of Mwase Kasungu, failed to adapt their system to meet the challenges of external agents in the nineteenth century.

The third of the chapters to deal, though peripherally, with Chewa history (chapter 8) concerns itself with dating the phenomenon of Chewa migration. Dr Nurse uses linguistic evidence, written Portuguese sources and archaeological evidence to piece together information on the early history of the Lolo people, an offshoot of the main Lomwe cluster. Of the Lolo group, the two main parts are the Kokhola and the Cuabo. The thrust of this chapter is to construct a possible date for the separation of the Lolo speakers from the Lomwe proper and to account, similarly, for the first contact of the Lolo with the Maravi. Dr Nurse arrives at the tentative conclusion that the Lomwe had begun to separate from the Makua around A.D. 800; by about A.D. 1200, the vanguard of the Lolo had already made contact with the Maravi. The author veers to the argument that the changes introduced in pottery types during the second phase of the Iron Age in Malawi (see chapter 4) which began about A.D. 1100 were due to the arrival of an early group of Maravi peoples. It is possible that it was this early group whom the Lolo first met on their southward march towards the Zambezi. The Lolo, Dr Nurse tells us, were not a people with any dynamic history of their own; they did not, for example, have a centralized political system. But a study of them is, nevertheless, instructive in throwing 'some light on more assertive peoples', like the Zimba and the Maravi.

With three chapters on the early central and southern peoples of Malawi (chapters 6, 7 and 8) we pass on to the northern parts of the country. In chapter 9 Professor Monica Wilson deals with the arrival of the Nyakyusa chiefs in the Rungwe valley and the Kyungu of the Ngonde at Mbande Hill some time during the fifteenth century, only to find earlier groups already settled in these regions. In the area in which the Kyungu settled the earlier inhabitants were Tumbuka-speakers; Nyiha; Nyamwanga; Iwa and others. Before settling in Karonga the Kyungu is known to have visited Bisa country. This raises a question about the date of arrival of the Bisa in Zambia and neighbouring territory. Another of the points raised by Professor Wilson concerns the Tumbuka. If they followed patrilineal descent and inheritance (see chapter 10), the author argues that they must have affinities with the Nyiha and other Corridor peoples to the north as well as with the matrilineal Maravi to the south. The introduction of cattle into the Corridor area altered forms of marriage as well as rules of inheritance and descent. Excavations at Ivuna have revealed that cattle were present there from the thirteenth century. Trade was one of the most important activities in most of the Corridor area. Oral traditions and archaeological finds have combined to produce evidence that trade existed before the coming of Kyungu in the fifteenth century. Professor Wilson argues, even if this is not conceded in some quarters, that ivory formed the basis of trade in Kyungu's country from the time of the arrival of the first Kyungu in the fifteenth century. The author ends with a plea for further investigations into a number of aspects of the history, culture and economic activities of the corridor peoples, including the influence of the Kisi pot markets of Pupangandu and the extent of Bisa trade to the coast.

In the second of the chapters on Northern Malawi (chapter 10), Mr Vail examines the history of the Tumbuka-speaking peoples with a view to evaluating two commonly-held myths, viz., that the Chikulamayembe dynasty in the post-*Balowoka* period was instrumental in uniting these peoples and that the Ngoni in Northern Malawi later destroyed this dynasty, replacing it completely with Ngoni rule. Mr Vail argues that to postulate a historical unity for all the Tumbuka-speaking peoples is to start from the wrong premises. He sees cultural differences between the northern sector peopled most probably by immigrants from the patrilineal areas in Southern Tanzania

xxii

and North-Eastern Zambia or late-comers from the west who adopted the patrilineal system, and the southern sector made up of a mixture of matrilineal peoples from the west and autochthones probably related to the Chewa peoples. Mr Vail's researches into Tumbuka history continue. With further inquiries into linguistic differences, aided by detailed clan histories, a fuller picture will emerge in due course. For the present, the chapter is a timely reminder that certain outmoded generalities are inaccurate. One of these concerns itself with the term *Tumbuka* itself. The Tumbuka-speaking peoples are not necessarily the same as the Tumbuka-proper of the pre-*Balowoka* period.

If our knowledge of Tumbuka history is only now beginning to fall into place, that of Yao history is far from satisfactory. Though connected with much of Malawi's history in the eighteenth and nineteenth centuries no detailed study has yet emerged to supplement the pioneering work of the Yao historian Yohanna Abdallah, *Chikala cha Wayao* (1919) recently reprinted by Cass. In the short chapter (chapter 11) on the Yao, Dr Alpers, who has himself researched and written widely on the Yao outside Malawi,[17] gives a timely warning that the Yao should not be looked upon as an undifferentiated ethnic group responding as such to the challenges of the time. They settled in different parts of central and southern Malawi among various neighbours. The pulls and pressures against them were not identical. The only common end result was that four groups of them eventually settled in Malawi during the second half of the nineteenth century. Dr Alpers suggests points for future research on such aspects as their relationship with the Maravi peoples prior to Yao entry in Malawi; the effects of the Makua-Lomwe raids on the Yao; the Muslim factor, including the rôles of different Muslim brotherhoods. Yao history must soon receive the attention it deserves and, in addition to the points suggested by the author, various others may be added such as their relationship with the Chewa, the Lomwe, the Ngoni, the Administration, the Christian and pagan institutions in the land as well as their economic, military and religious rôles.

The Yao represent one of the nineteenth century invaders of Malawi. The other were the Ngoni, the subject matter of the next three chapters. In chapter 12 the Ngoni of Malawi are treated as a whole. Internal and external politics are seen as an interplay of various factors. The author sees the Ngoni political system as exemplified in the position of the paramount chief and the relations between him and his peers as one of the strengthening features of Ngoni society. Except among the southern Ngoni for a short while, there were no civil wars among the main Ngoni segments. With relative stability in leadership, they were able to encounter African as well as non-African pressures with a great measure of success. The Ngoni who settled among the Tumbuka proper had no difficulty in establishing themselves quickly over a people with no long traditions of territorial chieftainships. Those who settled among the Chewa in the central and southern parts encountered no opposition from these non-martial peoples with the singular exception of Mwase Kasungu. In the north, the Tonga, and in the south, the Yao, offered the stiffest opposition. Against African opponents the Ngoni resorted to war but against European traders, missionaries and administrators they resorted to negotiation and compromise and finally capitulated, either peacefully or under protest but never violently as had their cousins in Matabeleland.

In chapter 13, Dr McCracken deals with the impact of Christianity on Northern Ngoniland, which gives rise to the emergence of a Christian elite as well as to new ideas. But even if Christianity contributed to the internal changes wrought in Ngoni society, internal tensions within the society were of greater import in directing the Ngoni response. The author sees these tensions as the consequence of various developments: the relative freedom of captives to live as before under their own chiefs; the tensions between the Jere rulers and the non-Jere councillors and those between the paramount chief and his Jere peers. Given that these internal tensions did exist, it is not clear whether the position of the paramount chief was seriously threatened. Whether these tensions constituted a dialogue of dissent or, as in the case of the Maseko Ngoni, the bedrock of disunity, the fact remains that the Northern Ngoni remained basically united.

This was not the case with the Maseko Ngoni who owed their dominance, in the first place, to a well-trained army. In chapter 14 Dr Linden argues that it was, paradoxically, the conservatism of the war divisions and their refusal to come to terms with more modern methods of warfare, that undermined this dominance. This factor, together with the recurring civil wars between the two Ngoni divisions; the divisive effects of Yao tactics, militarism and slaving activities; and the disruptive nature of British non-official and official influence, all combined during the years 1870–1900 to change the martial nature of Maseko society.

The three chapters on the Ngoni introduce us, *inter alia*, to the British involvement in African politics in Malawi. In chapter 15 we see another European involvement, that of the Portuguese. In spite of their very meagre financial and manpower resources, the Portuguese government made a number of bids in the last quarter of the nineteenth century to occupy southern Malawi. In chapter 15, Professor Axelson gives a summary of the main events in this episode from 1875 to 1890. Had the governor-general of Mozambique acted on the secret instructions sent to him before the arrival of the Livingstonia Mission in 1875, the Shire river would have come under Portuguese control. But even after the entry of this mission the Portuguese carried forward their half-hearted attempts to retrieve the position. With opposition from many quarters they nonetheless pushed forward with expeditions into the interior. In the end they failed to shake off the British. If anything, the expeditions served to mobilize the British into action and the end result was the establishment of a British Protectorate.

One of the many things about the British that the Portuguese resented was their transportation of arms and ammunition on Portuguese waters for use in interior wars. One such war was the Arab war in Karonga. This war combines a number of aspects of Malawi history, including the Islamic factor and imperialism. It is useful to include, as the subject matter of chapter 16, a note from Dr Macmillan on the origins of this war. Some of the questions asked in this chapter have been asked, for example, in the context of the 1915 rising. Was Chilembwe motivated by personal feelings or by a series of 'irritations'? Was the rising an anti-colonial movement stimulated by Yao aspirations? An Ngonde historian and educationalist has argued that it was not Mlozi but his subordinate, Kopa Kopa whose murder of an Ngonde named Fumbuka brought about a series of alliances which led to the war.[18] In this chapter, Dr Macmillan puts forward the view that the Arab war was not fought because of commercial rivalry; nor does he find evidence to support the view that it was due to a series of irritations. He sees it more as an Arab conspiracy to take over the area and calls for further investigations into the roles of Mlozi, Salim bin Nasur, Kabunda and Ramathan. This, of course, implies an investigation in the geographical area of Karonga as well as among the Senga of north-eastern Zambia.

In the Arab war the British encountered groups which resisted British intrusion; they found, too, a number of groups who were prepared to collaborate with them for different reasons. In chapter 17 the politics of collaboration is the theme Dr Dachs develops. He reminds us of a common tendency on the part of historians, especially in African history, to polarize their treatment of the politics of confrontation into divisions of subjugation and resistance. There is, he argues, an equally important division which represents a middle course between the extremes: that of collaboration. The author gives examples of how and why collaborators practised the creed of accommodation. It was not always the weapon of the weak. Harry Johnston's policy of divide and rule between the years 1891 and 1896 provided a fertile ground for the proponents of collaboration.

In chapter 18, Dr Palmer looks at the advent of European rule in Rhodesia and Malawi in the opening years of the 1890s. Both countries provided identical or related problems for the new rulers but the ways in which these problems were tackled by those placed in charge of the political administrations were largely different. The results of the policies pursued produced differences as well as similarities. In this chapter Dr Palmer analyzes the factors responsible for the situations that emerged. He begins by considering the personalities of the men on the spot, Jameson and Johnston; their disparate financial resources; their contrasting ideologies. While Jameson was content to exploit the situation in Rhodesia without destroying tribal authority, Johnston operated the other way round. The author compares these two administrators and their administrations within the framework of issues concerned with taxation, labour and land. The comparison is instructive and serves as a reminder that colonial policies are best studied outside the restricted limits set by monistic concepts.

Having been introduced to the Johnston administration from a comparative angle in the previous chapter, the next chapter (19) looks more closely at the structure and development of Johnston's administration. Local policies are best understood when the terms of reference of administrators, resources, personnel and problems are all considered as essential determinants. It is a well-known fact that Johnston's administration, and for that matter succeeding administrations, was hamstrung by financial limitations. There were other limitations, too, which Mr Baker reviews in this chapter.[19] Administrative history complements legal and constitutional history. By all accounts, Harry Hamilton Johnston was a remarkable man; his term of office, as Mr Baker shows, for all its questionable policies, left behind it what James Stewart described at the time as 'good administrative results'.

Johnston was severely criticized by the Scottish missionaries for many of his policies. One mission which was otherwise kindly disposed to him criticized his policy towards the Yao. This was the Anglican Mission, more correctly known as the Universities' Mission to Central Africa at the time. Rev. Elston introduces aspects of the work of this mission in chapter 20. While the Livingstonia Mission and the Blantyre Mission have been the subject of historical researches in recent times,[20] the U.M.C.A. has not been studied. Rev. Elston reviews the first unsuccessful attempt of this mission to launch its work in Malawi, describing the failure as 'traumatic in its effect' and important for an understanding of later developments and policies. The author considers three aspects of the U.M.C.A. contribution up to 1914: medical work, education and evangelism. He is, of course, conscious that at this stage he is 'giving more of an "official history",' rather than 'critical comment upon that history'. As his own researches continue the obvious gaps concerning the African response—relationship with other missions as well as with the Administration, for example—will no doubt be narrowed down. The U.M.C.A. was placed in a most advantageous position to comment on the Yao and the numerous articles in *The Nyasa News* and in *Central Africa*, both of which were publications of the mission itself, are sources of important information on the Yao who the U.M.C.A. claimed were little understood and much maligned.

The second of the chapters on mission histories in this volume appears in chapter 21 in which Mr J. L. Pretorius traces the history of the Dutch Reformed Church Mission between 1889 and 1914. The settlement of this mission among the Ngoni in the central region drew it into Ngoni-Administration politics (see also chapter 12). Mr Pretorius shows how this mission acted in almost the same way as the Blantyre Mission further south, as a critic of the Administration in such matters as the collection of hut tax. Another significant aspect of this mission was its emphasis on the development of the rural economy. The author describes this development which was based on the expansion of village schools, village industries and village agriculture. The work of the mission in Zambia and Portuguese East Africa is reviewed very briefly and it is hoped that the rich material on the D.R.C.M. in various places in Central and Southern Africa will be published in due course through the continuing researches of Mr Pretorius and others.

One of the D.R.C.M.'s interests was in matters connected with land and labour, both of which it considered to be the prime wealth of Malawi. It was, of course, not alone in this assumption. It is no exaggeration to claim that land and labour represent the pillars of recent Malawi history upon which numerous subjects are hung. In chapter 22 Dr Krishnamurthy analyzes these two pillars of economic consequence. With regard to the first, he argues that the dichotomy of interests, European and African, prevented the Administration from taking a clear line of action. For the most part it was held that economic development was dependent upon European enterprise. The private estates became the questionable preserves of European estate owners; Crown lands, too, by 1914, were deemed to be suitable mainly for European settlement. For as long as Africans were looked upon as subsistence farmers, the Administration saw no need to grant them large acreages of what was in any case their own land. On the second issue, that of labour, there was, again, a conflict of interests. Labour was essential for the success of European enterprise as it was for African subsistence or cash economy. The author argues that it was not shortage of labour but the failure to regulate it satisfactorily that contributed to the labour 'problem'. Various factors are advanced to explain this failure.

The land and labour problems of Malawi were vigorously mentioned as some of the grievances that found their expression in the Chilembwe rising of 1915. In the penultimate chapter of this volume (chapter 23) the co-author of the monumental work of the Nyasaland rising of 1915 looks at the historiographical attempts made by Africans as well as Europeans during the twenty years that followed the rising to explain the events connected with it. Professor Shepperson has himself often stressed the contribution of the non-professional historian. It was singularly appropriate that when the subject matter of this chapter was presented to the conference one such person, the Rev. Wylie Pilgrim Chigamba (whose own memoirs are at present being written), adorned the conference with his presence and skilful narration, drawing from the experience which earned him seven lashes and a five-year prison sentence. With the evidence presented to the Commission of Inquiry which was set up after the rising now available in the Public Record Office, London, the oral and written statements of Chigamba's contemporaries are now available for the first time. From among these, Professor Shepperson selects the testimonies of Robertson Namate, Stephen Kundecha, Harry Kambwiri Matecheta, M. M. Chisuse and Elliot Kamwana, all of whom have helped in different ways to make history in Malawi. The views of Wallace Kampingo (passed on to George Simeon Mwase in Zomba prison), Archdeacon Glossop (U.M.C.A.), S. S. Murray (European civil servant) and Dr Norman Leys (Government Medical Officer) are also presented by the author.

Professor Shepperson's historiographical essay marks yet another contribution to historical scholarship. In the context of this volume it leads us on to other questions of historiographical import with which the volume closes. In the final chapter, Dr Chanock makes a plea that historians should not overemphasize 'unilinear development and directional change'. Relating this tendency to Malawi history, the author argues that to understand historical processes 'we need to look at what has happened without interpreting it in the light of what we would like to come about.' In their search for historical continuity, historians have become preoccupied, Dr Chanock argues, with mission-induced industrialization and education, processes which affected the few but not the masses. 'The heart of the transformatory process', according to the author, 'lies elsewhere. It lies in the villages with the gradual change from a "subsistence" to a market oriented peasantry'. In this process certain aspects of village life were not affected: headmen and lesser chiefs continued to exercise age-old authority even when the colonial regime wrought changes among the top flight of traditional rulers; respect for seniority in age persisted; respect for discipline survived. Dr Chanock's closing argument is not that there is no validity in what has been achieved so far by the historians but that in looking at the phenomena of development and change, the gaze must be along more paths than one: 'The colonial government created not one set of clerks but two.' Unilinear development tends to look at the one only.

Whichever way historians and students gaze, the path of Malawi history, at this stage, has many blind or dim alleys awaiting illumination.

The chapters which follow this introduction attempt to give a coverage of the early history of Malawi as a contribution towards this illumination.

B. Pachai,
Editor.
Blantyre, December 1970.

FOOTNOTES

1 Clark, J. D., 'Digging for History,' *Society of Malawi Journal*, XXII, 1, 1969, 58.

2 Pollock, N. H., *Nyasaland and North-Eastern Rhodesia*, Ph.D. thesis, University of Pennsylvania, 1948, published in 1971 by Duquesne Press, U.S.A. Hanna, A. J., *The Beginnings of Nyasaland and North-Eastern Rhodesia, 1859–1895*, Ph.D. thesis, University of London, 1948, published by O.U.P., 1956.

3 Oliver, R., *The Missionary Factor in East Africa*, Longmans, 1952, and *Sir Harry Johnston and the Scramble for Africa*, Chatto and Windus, 1957. Shepperson, G. and Price, T., *Independent African, John Chilembwe and the Origins, Setting and Significance of the Nyasaland Rising of 1915*, Edinburgh University Press, 1958, reprinted 1963.
Read, M., *The Ngoni of Nyasaland*, O.U.P., 1956; *Children of their Fathers*, Methuen, 1959.

4 Collingwood, R. G., *The Idea of History*, Oxford, 1956, 202.

5 Pachai, B., (ed.) *The Memoirs of Lewis Mataka Bandawe, M.B.E. Malawian evangelist, scholar and civil servant*, Nkhoma, 1971.

6 Hodgkin, T., *Nigerian Perspectives*, O.U.P., 1960, 18.

7 Fage, J. D., *On the Nature of African History*, Inaugural lecture, University of Birmingham, 1965, 2–3.

8 Chapter 10.

9 See for example the *African Voice* series under the general editorship of Professors B. A. Ogot and T. O. Ranger. The first in the series was by T. O. Ranger, *The African Voice in Southern Rhodesia*, Heinemann, 1970.

10 *Historians in Tropical Africa*, Proceedings of the Inter-Collegiate History Conference, 1960, 1.

11 The results of the conference were published in Stokes, E. and Brown, R., (eds) *The Zambesian Past. Studies in Central African History*, Manchester University Press, 1965.

12 Ranger, T. O. (ed.) *Aspects of Central African History*, Heinemann, 1968.

13 A mimeographed booklet entitled *Malawi Past and Present* edited by Pachai, B., Smith, G. W. and Tangri, R. K. was produced. This has now been published in slightly revised form by the Christian Literature Association of Malawi, Nkhoma Mission, 1971.

14 Thompson, L. M., (ed.) *African Societies in Southern Africa,* Heinemann, 1969, 1.

15 See also C. A. Baker, 'Malawi's early road systems', *Society of Malawi Journal*, XXIV, 1, January 1971.

16 According to Bruwer the name Chewa is derived from the ancient verb root *Chewa* from which the neutral form *ku-ceuka* still survives. The ancient form is no longer used but it continues to survive in the proverb *Umcewe mwana angapsye*. ('Look behind you, the child might get burnt' or simply 'keep an eye on what's happening behind your back.')
I am grateful to Mr J. L. Pretorius for the reference from Bruwer, J. P. van S., *Die Gesin Onder die Moederregtelike Acewa*, M.A. thesis, University of Pretoria, 1949, 6.

17 E. A. Alpers, *The Role of the Yao in the development of trade in East-Central Africa, 1698–c.1850*, Ph.D., University of London, 1966.
'Trade, State, and Society among the Yao in the Nineteenth Century,' *Journal of African History*, X, 3, 1969, 405–420.

18 Rev. Amon Mwakasungula, *Thank You, Scotland*, Unpublished manuscript with the Editor.

19 This is part of a larger study by the author entitled *Johnston's Administration: A History of the British Central Africa Administration, 1891–1896*, Government Printer, Zomba, 1971.

20 Notably by K. J. McCracken, *Livingstonia Mission and the Evolution of Malawi, 1875–1939*, Ph.D. thesis, Cambridge, 1967 and A. C. Ross, *The Origins and Development of the Church of Scotland Mission, Blantyre, Nyasaland, 1875–1926*, Ph.D. thesis, University of Edinburgh, 1968.

1 The Men who came before Malawian History

Phillip V. Tobias

There is no sharp dividing line between history and prehistory. On the contrary, continuity is the keynote in our studies of the past. Often, indeed, the two phases of man's early records have existed side by side: while history was being written down on the East African coastline by travellers, missionaries and entrepreneurs, no written records were being kept further afield and prehistory was being enacted. Thus, we can recognize an overlapping of prehistory and history for some centuries, perhaps even for a millennium or two. To this phase of the immediate past, the name protohistoric period is often applied.

Scholars have probed the roots of Malawian history back into the proto-historic past. They have found that, with deeper delving, fewer and fewer written records were available; more and more was it necessary to depend upon oral tradition, the material culture, the languages men speak and spoke, to draw inferences about the comings and goings, the identity and way of life, of early inhabitants. Such evidence takes us deep into the Iron Age of the early Malawian agriculturalists and even into the antecedent Later Stone Age of the hunters and food-gatherers.

By that time, our written records are silent; men's spoken languages and folklore are mute—and only the material evidence unravelled by the archaeologist's spade continues the story back beyond the protohistoric into the prehistoric.

It is my task to set the stage for the study of Malawian history by summarizing the events of its prehistory. In the account which follows, I shall lean heavily on the work of many others, but mostly of Professor J. Desmond Clark. In his former capacity as Curator and then Director of the National Museum of Zambia (then the Rhodes-Livingstone Museum) in Livingstone, and in his present capacity as Professor of African Prehistoric Archaeology at the University of California, Berkeley, he has done most to place Malawi on the archaeological map.

The present review—which does not even claim to be a critical appraisal —basks in the reflection of Dr Clark's and his collaborators' original researches in Malawian prehistory.

In addition, I owe a debt to such earlier workers as F. Dixey, Rodney Wood, Cullen Young, and C. van Riet Lowe, and more recent observers like W. H. J. Rangeley, R. R. Inskeep, C. Vance Haynes, J. E. Mawby, V. Eggers, G. Cole, J. Yellen, B. Sandelowsky, K. R. Robinson, P. A. Cole-King, and L. H. Wells, and to the reviews for this territory of Brian M. Fagan and H. J. Deacon. Furthermore, Miss Beatrice H. Sandelowsky (now Mrs W. Pendleton) has generously allowed me to read her unpublished and as yet incomplete doctoral dissertation on *Later Stone Age Assemblages from Malawi and their Technologies*.

Perhaps it is appropriate in a work of this nature to begin with a brief review of our knowledge of the antiquity of man in Africa. Then we shall survey the history of archaeological exploration in Malawi.

THE ANTIQUITY OF MAN IN AFRICA

'It is . . . probable that Africa was formerly inhabited by extinct apes closely allied to the gorilla and chimpanzee; and as these two species are now man's nearest allies, it is somewhat more probable that our early progenitors lived on the African continent than elsewhere.'[1]

Nearly a century has elapsed since Darwin wrote those prophetic words. At that time, only Europe had yielded any fossils bearing on the antiquity of man. The turn of Asia was to come a score of years later with the discovery of *Pithecanthropus erectus* at Trinil in Java by a Dutch surgeon, Eugene Dubois, in 1891. This proved to be the fore-runner of a series of discoveries in Indonesia and China, which were to throw light on a major chapter of human evolution. The Asian fossils are dated by most workers to the middle part of the Pleistocene epoch and may have spanned the period from about 750,000 to about 300,000 years ago. When one turns to Africa, however, more than fifty years were to elapse before any concrete verification of Darwin's prediction was to emerge. True, fossil mammals were brought to light in north-west Africa by a number of French scientists, notably Thomas and Pomel, as early as the second half of the nineteenth century. But it was not until the first decades of the present century that the equatorial and southern parts of the continent came to be explored palaeontologically.

The earliest discoveries of fossils attributable to the human family (*Hominidae* or hominids) were those of several Algerian sites (1886/8–1921), Olduvai hominid 1 from Tanganyika (1913), Boskop in the Transvaal (1913), Bromhead's site in Kenya (1913) and Broken Hill in Zambia, then Northern Rhodesia (1921). Although morphologically interesting and highly diverse from one another, these sets of remains were clearly hominid in character.

Much more equivocal was the skull of a child recovered by R. A. Dart from Taung (then called Taungs) in the Cape Province in 1924 (Fig. 1.1). From the beginning Dart regarded the individual represented by this very

2

1.1 The most important sites at which discoveries of fossil hominids have been made in Africa (up to 1968)

well preserved skull as an ape with a number of man-like departures. He made it the type of a new genus and species, *Australopithecus africanus* (the southern ape of Africa). The animated controversy which followed lasted for a quarter of a century. Only the discovery of further specimens, as well as meticulous anatomical and odontological studies,[2] gradually convinced scientists that the group of creatures embraced by the term, *Australopithecinae*, had an excellent claim to be regarded as hominids, rather than as aberrant pongids (members of the *Pongidae* or family of the apes). Thus, it has come to be recognized that Africa has made a crucial contribution to the study of human origins: in the judgment of most workers, it has yielded the essential proof of the animal

3

origins of man. In this way, Darwin's old prediction has been borne out in the last forty-odd years.

The australopithecine chapter of hominid evolution is not the only important part of the story written in Africa. For many other discoveries have been made, especially over the last fifteen years, illuminating both earlier and later phases of man's development (Fig. 1.1). It is probably no exaggeration to claim that, with more workers, more funds, more energy and more interest than ever before being deployed in the task of digging up man's past in Africa, the resulting spate of recent discoveries has more than doubled the amount of evidence available. The new remains have come from Algeria, Morocco, Cyrenaica, Chad, the Sudan, Ethiopia, Kenya, Uganda, Tanzania and South Africa. Together, the African relics comprise a major proportion of the world's total evidence bearing on the antiquity of man.

These discoveries have enabled a two-pronged attack to be made on the problem of man's ancestry. Firstly, by direct study of the hominid skeletal remains, much has been learnt about the appearance, posture and gait, brain size and form, and bodily functions of the early hominids. Secondly, by study of the ecology and of the implemental and other cultural remains accompanying the hominid fossils, it has been possible to reconstruct a picture of the behaviour and of the dependence upon culture of man's putative ancestors.

From these discoveries of prehistoric remains, it is possible to recognize several major stages of hominization.

(i) *Australopithecus* (Fig. 1.2): This genus comprises members of the family of man known to have existed at least from Upper Pliocene to Middle Pleistocene times. Small-brained and upright-walking, the australopithecines were tool-makers. Bone, tooth and horn seem to have provided one source of raw material for their implemental activities. In addition, they may have begun utilizing stone as a raw material, but opinion is divided on whether they went so far as to master the rather more complex set of manoeuvres necessary for manufacturing implements of a specific archaeological culture, such as the Oldowan Culture.

(ii) *Homo habilis* (Fig. 1.3): a rather shadowy stage marked the emergence of the first members of the genus *Homo*. Evidence is accumulating that, in the Lower Pleistocene, some of the early hominid populations, though still essentially australopithecine in structure, underwent an increase of about fifty per cent in brain-size. The populations with this larger brain seem to have been responsible for the first systematic, cultural, stone tool-making. The earliest expression of this cultural propensity is known as the Oldowan Culture and is especially well-known from Olduvai Gorge, Northern Tanzania.

(iii) *Homo erectus* (Fig. 1.4): this later species is essentially a Middle Pleistocene phenomenon of man. Brain-size has become still bigger, body-size and form have approached closely to those of modern man. Cultural activities have become regular and consistent; indeed it seems that Man has come to depend on his cultural skills, including, in places, the mastery of fire, for his very survival. The African Acheulian Culture typifies Man's cultural achievements in Africa during much of this time.

(iv) *Homo sapiens* (Fig. 1.5): late in the Middle Pleistocene, the modern

4

species of man makes its appearance, and attains its heyday in the Upper Pleistocene and Holocene. Anatomical transformation of earlier hominids to modern human form is virtually complete. Cultural dependence is firmly established: with it goes cultural diversity, adaptability and versatility. The divergence of man into numerous populations adapted to a variety of geographical and ecological situations is a feature of human evolution up to fairly recently—then to give way to an ongoing phase of cultural and physical convergence.

At the level of each of these four stages of hominization, Africa has made vital contributions to our understanding of human evolution (Fig. 1.6). Indeed, there is evidence to suggest that the first two major stages were enacted only in Africa. If this is correct, Africa has a justifiable claim to being the cradle of mankind.

HISTORICAL SURVEY OF ARCHAEOLOGICAL RESEARCH IN MALAWI

Let us now make a brief historical survey of researches in Malawi to see which of the major stages of the human story are represented in the record.

The history of prehistory in Malawi divides itself conveniently into two phases: the twenty-year period between the two World Wars and the twenty years since 1950.

1 *The Period between the Wars*

Little systematic work characterized this era: it was a time of accidental discoveries and limited reconnaissance. Nyasaland of the day had no National Museum and no prehistorians. An early record is that of Cullen Young[3] who reported on some bow stands lying in chiefs' graves in West Nyasaland. These iron objects were later described by Fagan[4] as the most easterly examples of Congo tool forms then known.

Encouraged by the late Professor C. van Riet Lowe, Director of the Bureau of Archaeology (later the Archaeological Survey) of the Union of South Africa, Rodney C. Wood collected stone implements from a number of localities, mainly in Northern Nyasaland, in the 1930s.[5, 6] He brought to light evidence of a later phase of the Sangoan Culture and of Later Stone Age remains.[5, 7] Among the numerous artefacts sent by Wood to Lowe in Johannesburg were a variety of bored stones, collected especially in the high ridge and plateau country in the north.[6] Today, such stones of very diverse sizes are known to be concentrated on the Nyika and the Vipya Plateau, as well as in neighbouring territories like Zambia and the Katanga, and more emote parts of Africa like Ethiopia and Nigeria. Although their uses were probably varied, it is believed that some of them were connected with a simple vegecultural stage of development of the Later Stone Age and earliest metal-using groups of these parts of Africa.[6]

Among Wood's most important discoveries were a later Middle Stone Age site at the Mwenerondo Mission some five miles due south of Karonga. The site comprises an eroded former terrace of Lake Malawi, at the base of the foothills limiting the low lying plain at the north-west end of the Lake. As J. D. Clark[7] has indicated, this region is a cul-de-sac, shut in by the Lake on the east and mountains on the north and south. The terrace is about 100 feet above the present lake level and, according to Wood, can be traced for some twelve miles south of Mwenerondo.

Throughout the twelve-mile stretch of beach, there is a wealth of stone implements in fresh, unrolled condition. The beach seems to have possessed an abundance of raw material. It was probably in the nature of 'a vast factory site and camping ground'. Collections from here were sent to the Archaeological Survey in Johannesburg, the National Museum of Southern Rhodesia in Bulawayo, and the Rhodes-Livingstone Museum in Livingstone; they were later identified as belonging to the late Middle Stone Age and to be of Sangoan tradition.[7] Clark believed the manufacturers were a relatively isolated group who perpetuated the Sangoan tradition in the North Nyasa plain, as well as in the Luangwa Valley of Zambia, long after it had been largely obscured by new developments on the Zambian plateau to the west and north-west.

Perhaps the most systematic and significant work done in this field between the wars was that of Dr F. Dixey who was Director of the Geological Survey of Nyasaland in the 1920s and 1930s. He studied the age and the succession of Great Rift Valley deposits and faulting, as episodes in the formation of Lake Malawi. The lake deposits on the north Malawi plain were identified as belonging to three major stages of the Pleistocene geological epoch, namely, the Lower, Middle and Upper Pleistocene. From some of the deposits he recovered extinct animal bones of a kind usually attributed to the African Middle Pleistocene. He also discovered some very primitive stone tools made from pebbles or water-rolled stones. This seems to provide us with the very earliest evidence available of human inhabitation of Malawi.

2 The Recent Period of Archaeological Investigation, 1950–1970

The post-war era began with an invitation from the Nyasaland Government to J. Desmond Clark in 1950 to investigate certain rock-painting sites in the central and northern parts of the territory. Paintings were traced in several shelters. Excavations in two of them revealed Later Stone Age industries classified as belonging to the same L.S.A. culture as that found in the northern half of Zambia—the Nachikufan. What is more, one of the rock-shelters, situated on Hora Mountain, some miles north of Mzimba, yielded two human skeletons.[9] These were in fact 'the first human remains of determinable physical type from a Nachikufan deposit'.[10]

In 1958, following reports from Mrs A. C. J. Doel, owner of a property on Nkudzi Bay on the west shore of Lake Malawi some thirty miles north of Fort Johnston, and from the late Mr W. H. J. Rangeley, then Provincial Commissioner at Blantyre, R. R. Inskeep visited and partly excavated a proto-

6

historic cemetery on Mrs Doel's property. The twelve burials located in a small test area provided a wealth of well associated ethnographic material of the later Iron Age. These included many pots, iron tools, beads and other imported objects, testifying that trade with the coast was well-developed at the time. 'There seems little reason to doubt that the Nkudzi cemetery was a nineteenth century burial ground of a Nyanja group.'[11]

In the 1960s, the work gathered pace and, for the first time, something approaching systematic reconnaissance, study and excavation was embarked upon, largely under the inspiration and leadership of Desmond Clark. Building on the earlier work of F. Dixey, Clark in 1963 led a University of California team in a survey of the Lake Malawi Rift.[12] This was followed by a geological, palaeontological and archaeological programme in 1965–66, during which the University of California team studied not only the Malawi Rift, but also the Rungwe volcanic massif and the Southern Rukwa basin.[13] The Lake Beds in the Karonga District were closely scrutinized and the fossilized animal bones and stone cultural remains in the beds were identified. As a result, much light was thrown on the stratigraphic sequence and fauna from the lake beds.

The major deposits exposed are divided into three sedimentary units, which have been informally designated the Chiwondo, Chitimwe and Karonga formations.[14]

The oldest formation is the Chiwondo and it consists mainly of lacustrine mudstones, marls and tuffs. The vertebrate animal remains are largely of extinct genera and species belonging to the period which extends from approximately the junction between two major geological epochs, the Pliocene and the Pleistocene, up to the middle Pleistocene. Despite intensive searching, no signs of occupation by hominids (members of the family of man) were found in the Chiwondo formation: neither hominid skeletal remains nor cultural material came to light—although hominid inhabitation of other parts of the sub-continent is well known from this early time period (c.2–3 million years up to c.750,000 years before the present).

Overlying the Chiwondo Beds unconformably are the gravels and sand of the Chitimwe Formation, which seem to have been deposited during and after a period of widespread erosion. The lower part of the Chitimwe Forma-tion contains rolled artefacts (products of human workmanship) suggesting an age of Middle to early Upper Pleistocene times. In this part of the Chitimwe, a most interesting elephant kill site was excavated close to the village of Mwanganda, about five miles west of Karonga.[15] Most of the bones exposed by the archaeologists at this site belong to a single elephant, with a few teeth and other parts of a hippopotamus and a giraffe. Scattered around and under the bones were stone implements of what was evidently a butchery tool-kit of the time. The nature of the bones and their juxtaposition with the artefacts provided clear evidence of intentional bone-breaking by man. As in several other such occurrences, it seems permissible to conclude that at such sites with only a single carcase, or a few at most, 'human butchering practices generally resulted in the disarticulation, dispersal and differential fracture of the bones of the large food animals. It would seem also that they were butchered at the place where they were killed or where the carcase was found.'[16]

The upper Chitimwe Beds include gravel layers with which are associated more advanced expressions of palaeolithic culture. These occurrences are classified as early Middle Stone Age or possibly Sangoan in the lower gravels, and as definitive Middle Stone Age in the overlying sands. In 1965, V. Eggers excavated an M.S.A. site (U.C./A Ch1A) and in 1966, another one, the Chaminade School site, was excavated by G. Cole. The analysis of the material from these sites is at present under way.[17]

In the topmost levels of the Chitimwe Sands are occurrences of Later Stone Age artefacts which were excavated in 1965 by J. Yellen. Charcoal from these beds has been dated to about 3,500 years ago and onwards. These dates have been corroborated by dates obtained by B. H. Sandelowsky and K. R. Robinson[18] for the Later Stone Age deposit in a rock shelter on Fingira Hill near the south-west end of the Nyika. Other dates obtained by Sandelowsky[19] in a series of excavations of L.S.A. deposits range from about 3,500 to about 2,100 years before the present.

Some Iron Age material, too, occurs in the uppermost part of the Chitimwe Formation.[15]

The third of the sedimentary units associated with the Malawi Rift, provisionally dubbed the Karonga Formation, consists of alluvium dateable to the most recent geological epoch, the Holocene.[15]

The investigation of the Malawian Later Stone Age spread far beyond the Chitimwe Beds. In the south, L.S.A. material has been found on Cape Maclear, the promontory at the tip of a peninsula jutting into the southern end of Lake Malawi.[20] Clark and Cole-King found numerous artefacts on the site of the Old Livingstonia Mission. In 1969, I located some additional remnants there, during a brief visit to Cape Maclear made possible by the generosity of Dr George Nurse.[21] Cole-King records that Clark found quartz artefacts in a rock shelter some 200 feet up the north-east side of Nkhunguni Hill and in a few eroded areas beside the Fort Johnston Road. One such area, near the Mwalawamphini (a huge granite boulder not far from Cape Maclear itself), had been noted by F. de Guingand[22] as a possible Middle Stone Age site, a possibility which J. D. Clark confirmed on his visit there with Cole-King in 1968.[20] A large rock shelter (Mwalawolemba) on Mikolongwe Hill in the south was explored by Cole-King with two test trenches and a test pit in 1966: although poor in quality and preservation, the recovered material seems to be an expression of an L.S.A. industry.[23]

Other L.S.A. occurrences in the south are reported from Malowa Rock Shelter in the Shire Highlands,[24] and suggested from 'Tax Defaulters' Shelter' on Chiunda Hill in east Kasupe District, between Lake Malombe and Lake Chilwa.[25]

The most thorough and systematic work on the L.S.A. of Malawi is that which grew directly out of the University of California field programme in 1966. Apart from the Fingira Cave excavation,[18] most of the work remains unpublished and I have been fortunate in learning about it directly from Mrs Beatrice Sandelowsky-Pendleton and from her doctoral dissertation.

Perhaps the most important of this series of excavations was that made at

Fingira Hill by Sandelowsky and Robinson in 1966.

A rock shelter with paintings on Fingira Hill had been noted by the late W. H. J. Rangeley. Along with Mr John Grieg, the Forest Officer for the Northern Region, J. D. Clark visited the shelter in 1966. Although the paintings were disappointing, stone artefacts were found in the cave floor. The subsequent excavation by Sandelowsky and Robinson yielded an abundance of L.S.A. implements, dating from 3,530 to 3,350 years before present. Well associated with the cultural material were the scattered remains of a few human skeletons of adults and children, including an intact human skull and a virtually complete human skeleton lying supine and spreadeagled in curious fashion over large rocks near the cave mouth. According to D. R. Brothwell, the remains represent 'short statured individuals who would "fit" as early Khoisan people [belonging to] the broader Bush/Negro category'.[26]

A comparative study is indicated and is much needed on the several L.S.A. human remains now available from Central Africa. Apart from the Hora and Fingira remains from Malawi, these include human skeletons excavated by C. Gabel[27] from Gwisho (Lochinvar) in the Central Kafue Basin of Zambia, remains from Chipongwe south of Lusaka,[28] part of the back of a skull from Leopard's Hill Cave near Lusaka,[29] unpublished human skeletons recovered by D. Phillipson at the Thandwe Shelter in the Eastern Province of Zambia and which the author has been invited to study, and (probably L.S.A.) the Bushmanoid skull 7418 excavated by K. R. Robinson[30] from a shelter at Chitura Rocks, Nyabombgwe river, Inyanga District of (Southern) Rhodesia.[31]

Other excavations of L.S.A. deposits were of Mwalawolemba Shelter on Mikolongwe Hill in southern Malawi,[32] the Chowo Rock Shelter on the Nyika Plateau, the Homestead Shelter on the eastern slopes of the Livingstonia Plateau, an open site at the village of Kafyenyengo north of the Homestead Shelter, about a mile and a half north of Manchewe Falls, and the rock-shelter known as Hora/5 on Hora Mountain (an inselberg on the Mzimba Plain) a few miles north of the town of Mzimba.[19]

The remaining burst of activity in the 1960s has been into the Iron Age of Malawi.[33] As recently as 1961, Fagan could write, '. . . little is known about the earliest Iron Workers in the territory, beyond some oral tradition'.[34] Yet, such progress was chalked up during the 1960s that, by 1969, Deacon was able to state: 'The work of Robinson has shown the considerable potential for Iron Age studies in Malawi and this country occupies an important area of Central Africa which has hitherto been terra incognita for the Iron Age researchers.'[35]

Since the events of the Iron Age in Malawi have formed a major topic of discussion at this conference, it is not proposed to deal with them in any detail here. The only point which I shall emphasize is the timing of the supersession of the L.S.A. by the Iron Age. In a word, what evidence do we have of the date at which iron workers entered Malawi and began to replace the pre-existing Later Stone Age culture?

From the L.S.A. sites excavated in Malawi, we have a number of carbon-14 dates. Some idea of the duration of the L.S.A. is provided by an early date

9

for a charcoal sample taken between 20 and 28 inches below the surface of the cave deposit in Hora/7.[36] For this sample, the Gulbenkian Radio-Carbon Dating Laboratory in Salisbury, Rhodesia, obtained a date of 16,680± 180 B.P. (before present) or 14,730 ± 180 B.C. (Sample SR-145). Now this date is older by some 12,000 years than the other L.S.A. dates available from Malawi. Moreover, according to Sandelowsky,[19] the cultural remains from this part of the Hora/7 deposit differ from those associated with younger dates in Malawian L.S.A. deposits. Sandelowsky identified a number of cultural features—such as the presence of stone points, the preponderance of discoid cores and faceted striking platforms—characteristic of industrial complexes of the Middle Stone Age and Second Intermediate, which preceded the Later Stone Age. Hence it might be inferred tentatively that the Hora/7 occurrence just precedes the beginning of the Later Stone Age proper. This would tally with evidence from Zambia that the Later Stone Age there covered a time span of over 10,000 years.[19]

The *latest* dates so far obtained for L.S.A. deposits in Malawi are just over 2,000 years B.P. For example, charcoal from a rock shelter near Chowo Rock on the Nyika gave a date of about 175 ± 120 B.C. (Sample SR-127). The level from which this sample was taken contained only Stone Age material, although higher levels in the deposit contained Iron Age materials along with stone implements. Hence, the layer from which the carbon was obtained probably represents a final phase, or the end, of the Later Stone Age.[37] Comparable dates are available from Zambia and Tanzania.

Thereafter, evidence presents itself that Iron Age cultural traits were introduced into Malawi from about 2,000 years ago. Some early dates of Malawian Iron Age remains are:—

A.D. 295 ± 95 (SR-128) —Phopo Hill Iron Age Site (test 1) in the Rumpi Area, verging on the foothills of the Nyika Plateau.

A.D. 205 ± 170 (SR-148)—Phopo Hill Iron Age Site (test 3).

A.D. 360 ± 120 (SR-174)—Nkope Bay (layer 3, test 5), about twenty-five miles north of Fort Johnston on the eastern shore of the Cape Maclear Peninsula.[38]

It seems clear that there was an overlap of L.S.A. and Iron Age traits for some centuries,[24] but as the evidence from Zambia and Malawi indicates, 'Wherever Iron Age and Stone Age traits are found together, stone implements disappear very soon after the contact, while the Iron Age traits persist unchanged.'[19] Nevertheless, isolated L.S.A. survivals into the present day are known.[39]

Details of the period of change in Malawi and other parts of south-central Africa are becoming increasingly well-documented.[40] With the present intensification of researches, it seems likely that before long we shall possess a relatively detailed human history in Malawi over the last 2,000 years.

One result of all this work is that, late in the summer of 1968, Dr J. D. Clark did a two-month survey of Malawi sites for U.N.E.S.C.O.,[41] with the establishment of an Antiquities Department in view:[42] this important development has materialized under the directorship of Mr P. A. Cole-King.

As for the men themselves, the record remains sparse. Human skeletal remains are available from only four sites to date: Hora Mountain, Fingira Hill, Nkudzi Bay and Matope Court on the Upper Shire river. The first two sets of bones date from the Later Stone Age: they represent populations inhabiting Malawi before the arrival of the first iron workers. They are unequivocally the skeletons of representatives of the modern species of man, *Homo sapiens*. As far as their population traits go, they are compatible with the Khoisan group of Southern Africa, though Wells[10] has recognized in the Hora skulls features which align them with skeletons from Ngorongoro in Northern Tanganyika and from Nakuru in Kenya: the characters common to these groups of skulls, in turn, are reminiscent of the Caucasoid or Erythriote peoples to be found in the Horn of Africa and dubbed 'African Mediterranean' by Briggs.[43] Perhaps, the Hora skulls are linked with the diffusion into south-central Africa of an African Mediterranean people, which blended with some of the prior Khoisanoid (Bushman and/or Hottentot) inhabitants.[10]

Another group of human skeletal remains are those which Inskeep excavated from a nineteenth-century graveyard at Nkudzi Bay. Essentially, they would be closely akin to the present-day inhabitants of Malawi.

Finally, unpublished bones which are apparently human have come to light from one of the cast pits at Matope Court on the Upper Shire river.[44]

Before 3–4,000 years ago, although a long record of lithicultural remains is available from Malawi, there are as yet no bony remains of the men themselves. From within the territory, no skeletons of any of the earlier forms of mankind have been found, such as the African version of Neandertal man (often called *Homo sapiens rhodesiensis*), nor of *Homo erectus*, *Homo habilis* or *Australopithecus*, the kinds of hominid who lived in Africa at earlier and earlier times, even back to five million years ago.

Summary

Of the four major stages of hominization defined at the outset, we have seen that Malawi has so far yielded human cultural remains ascribable to the latest two stages only. The following table summarizes in a very oversimplified form the representation of the four stages in the Malawian geological, palaeontological and archaeological record.

The table shows that, on present evidence, it would seem reasonable to infer that hominids did not penetrate into the Malawian area until the third stage of hominization. However, it cannot be too strongly emphasized that this is a provisional inference only. These are still early days in the archaeological exploration of Malawi. With the first two stages of hominization represented both to the north and to the south-west, and with deposits dateable to these early stages known to be present in Malawi, it may well be only a matter of time before this inference is upset, and the presence of first and second stage hominids in Malawi is revealed. Deposits of the right age are present. Conditions are very suitable for preservation in many areas. Only patient searching and systematic excavation will answer the question whether Malawi did not

	Deposits of appropriate age present	Cultural remains present	Human skeletal remains present
First stage (*Australopithecus*, Upper Pliocene-Middle Pleistocene, cultural beginnings)	+	−	−
Second stage (*Homo habilis*, Lower to Middle Pleistocene, Oldowan Culture)	+	−	−
Third stage (*Homo erectus*, Middle Pleistocene, African Acheulian)	+	+	−
Fourth stage (*Homo sapiens*, Late Middle Pleistocene to Holocene, 'Sangoan', 'Middle Stone Age', 'Later Stone Age', 'Iron Age')	+	+	+

become suitable for hominid habitation before the late Middle Pleistocene, or whether Man's venturesome forebears had indeed penetrated to Malawi, as they had to the Transvaal and even to the Cape Province, by the Lower Pleistocene. Malawi lies in a crucial position, foursquare between the East African Rift Valley deposits and the Transvaal dolomitic limestone caves. It may yet bring to light important discoveries which will help bridge the gap between these two great prehistoric provinces.

Acknowledgements

I express my gratitude to Professor Bridge Pachai, Mr K. R. Robinson, Mrs Beatrice Sandelowsky-Pendleton, Dr R. J. Mason, Mrs E. Hibbett, Miss C. J. Orkin, Mr A. R. Hughes and Miss D. Rosenblatt.

FOOTNOTES

1 Darwin, Charles, *The Descent of Man*, 1871.

2 Further specimens were discovered by R. Broom and J. T. Robinson at

Sterkfontein, Kromdraai and Swartkrans in the Transvaal; by R. A. Dart and his collaborators at Makapansgat in the Transvaal; by L. Kohl-Larsen at Garusi in Tanzania; and by L. S. B. and M. D. Leakey and their helpers at Olduvai Gorge and Peninj in Tanzania. See also W. E. Le Gros Clark, (1947) 'Observations on the anatomy of the fossil *Australopithecinae*', *J. Anat.*, **81**, 300–33; (1950) 'South African fossil hominids', *Nature, London*, **165**, 893–4; (1950) 'New palaeontological evidence bearing on the evolution of the Hominoidea', *Q.J. Geol. Soc. Lond.*, **105**, 225–64; (1952) 'A note on certain cranial indices of the Sterkfontein skull No. 5', *Amer. J. Phys. Anthrop.*, **10**, 119–21; (1952) 'Hominid characters of the australopithecine dentition', *J. Roy. Anthrop. Inst.*, **80**, 37–54. For an odontological study, see J. T. Robinson (1956) 'The dentition of the *Australopithecinae*', *Transv. Mus. Mem.*, **9**.

3 Young, T. C. (1929) 'A note of iron objects of unknown origin from Northern Nyasaland', *Man*, p. 147. Cited in Fagan, B. M. (1961) 'Pre-European iron-working in Central Africa with special reference to Northern Rhodesia', *J. Afr. Hist.*, **2**, 199–200.

4 Fagan, B. M. op. cit.

5 Clark, J. D. 'A review of prehistoric research in Northern Rhodesia and Nyasaland', in *Proc. III Pan-African Congress on Prehistory, Livingstone 1955*. Chatto and Windus, 1957. pp. 412–32.

6 Clark, J. D. (1962) 'Beyond South Africa', *S. Afr. Archaeol. Bull.*, Supplement, **17**, 68–77.

7 Clark, J. D. (1954) 'Upper Sangoan industries from Northern Nyasaland and the Luangwa Valley: a case of environmental differentiation', *S. Afr. J. Sci.*, **50**, 201–8.

8 Lowe, C. van Riet (1940) 'Bored stones in Nyasaland', *S. Afr. J. Sci.*, **37**, 320–6.

9 Clark, J. D. (1956) 'Prehistory in Nyasaland', *The Nyasaland Journal*, **9**, No. 1.

10 Wells, L. H. 'Late Stone Age human types in Central Africa' in *Proc. III Pan-African Congress on Prehistory, Livingstone 1955*. Chatto and Windus, 1957. pp. 183–5.

11 Inskeep R. R. (1965) 'Preliminary investigation of a Proto-historic cemetery at Nkudzi Bay, Malawi', *National Museums of Zambia, Special Paper*, 34.

12 Clark, J. D., Stephens, E. A. and Coryndon, S. C. (1966), 'Pleistocene

fossiliferous lake beds of the Malawi (Nyasa) Rift: a preliminary report', in *Amer. Anthrop. special publication: Recent studies in Palaeo-anthropology* (eds J. D. Clark and F. C. Howell), **68** (2), 16–87.

13 Deacon, H. J. (1969) 'South Africa', *Cowa Survey: Reports on Old World Archaeology, Area 13*, **4**, 1–15. Clark, J. D. and Haynes, C. V. (1970) 'An elephant butchery site at Mwanganda's village, Karonga, Malawi, and its relevance for Palaeolithic archaeology', *World Archaeology* **1** (3), 390–411. Clark, J. D., Haynes, C. V. and Mawby, J. E. (1971) 'Interim report on palaeo-anthropological investigations in the Lake Malawi Rift', *Proc. VI Pan-African Congress on Prehistory and Quaternary Studies, Dakar, 1967.*

14 Clark and Haynes, op. cit.; Clark, Haynes and Mawby, op. cit.; Clark, J. D., Stephens, E. A. and Coryndon, S. C. op. cit.

15 Clark and Haynes, op. cit.

16 Clark and Haynes, op. cit., 409.

17 Deacon, H. J. op. cit.

18 Sandelowsky, B. H. and Robinson, K. R. (1968) *Fingira: Preliminary Report*. Malawi Government, Department of Antiquities, **3**, 1–6.

19 Sandelowsky, B. H. (1971) *Later Stone Age assemblages from Malawi and their technologies*. Ph.D. dissertation to be submitted to the University of California, Berkeley.

20 Cole-King, P. A. (1968) *Cape Maclear*. Malawi Government, Department of Antiquities, **4**.

21 I was paying my first visit to Malawi, in order to represent the University of the Witwatersrand, Johannesburg, at the first Degree Congregation of the University of Malawi at Limbe (24 July 1969) and to participate in the First Science Conference of the International Biological Programme, Malawi (25 and 26 July 1969).

22 Guingand, F. de (1953) *African Assignment*, 89–90.

23 Sandelowsky (1971) op. cit.; Cole-King, P. A. (1968) *Mwalawolemba on Mikolongwe Hill*. Malawi Government, Department of Antiquities, **1**.

24 Denbow, J. and Ainsworth, R. (1969) *Malowa Rock Shelter: Report on preliminary excavation*. Malawi Government, Department of Antiquities, **7**, 1–13.

25 Klass, L. (1969) *Investigations, mainly of hill sites, carried out in Chief*

Nyambi's Area, Kasupe District. Malawi Government, Department of Antiquities, **7**, 35–46.

26 Sandelowsky, B. H. and Robinson, K. R. (1968) op. cit.; Sandelowsky, B. H. (1971) op. cit.

27 Gabel, C. (1962) 'Human crania from the Later Stone Age of the Central Kafue Basin, Northern Rhodesia', *S. Afr. J. Sci.*, **58**, 307–14; (1963) 'Lochinvar Mound: a Later Stone Age composite in the Kafue Basin', *S. Afr. Archaeol. Bull.*, **18**, 40–8; (1963) 'Further human remains from the Central African Later Stone Age', *Man*, **63**, 38–43; (1965) *Stone Age Hunters of the Kafue.* Boston, University Press, 1–118.

28 Clark, J. D. and Toerien, M. J. (1955) 'Human skeletal and cultural material from a deep cave at Chipongwe, Northern Rhodesia', *S. Afr. Archaeol. Bull.*, **10**, 107–16; Wells, L. H. (1950) 'Fossil Man in Northern Rhodesia', in *The Stone Age Cultures of Northern Rhodesia.* Cape Town, South African Archaeological Society, 143–52.

29 Wells, L. H. (1950) op. cit.

30 Robinson, K. R. (1958) 'Some Stone Age sites in Inyanga District', in *Inyanga: Prehistoric Settlements in Southern Rhodesia*, by R. Summers. Cambridge University Press, 270–309.

31 Tobias, P. V. (1958) 'Skeletal remains from Inyanga', in Summers, *Prehistoric Settlements*, op. cit., 159–72.

32 Cole-King (1968) *Mwalawolemba*, op. cit.

33 Robinson, K. R. (1966) 'A preliminary report on the recent archaeology of Ngonde, Northern Malawi', *J. Afr. Hist.*, **7** (2), 169–88; (1970) *The Iron Age of the Southern Lake Area of Malawi*, Malawi Government, Department of Antiquities, **8**, 1–131; Robinson, K. R. and Sandelowsky, B. H. (1969) 'The Iron Age of Northern Malawi: recent work', *Azania*, **3**, 1–40.

34 Fagan, B. M., op. cit., 207.

35 Deacon, H. J., op. cit., 2.

36 Hora/7 is one of the nine rock shelters on, or at the foot of Hora Mountain which were located by J. D. Clark (1956, op. cit.) and Robinson and Sandelowsky (1969, op cit.).

37 Sandelowsky (1971) op. cit.; Robinson and Sandelowsky (1969), op. cit.

38 Robinson, K. R. (1970) op cit.; Robinson and Sandelowsky (1969) op. cit.

39 McCalman, R. and Grobbelaar, B. J. (1965) 'Preliminary report of two stone-working Ova-Tjimba groups in the northern Kaokoveld of South West Africa', *Cimbebasia*, **13**, 1–39.

40 Fagan (1961) op. cit.; (1963) 'The Iron Age sequence in the Southern Province of Northern Rhodesia', *J. Afr. Hist.*, **4** (2), 157–177; (1967) 'The Iron Age peoples of Zambia and Malawi', in *Background to Evolution in Africa*, eds W. W. Bishop and J. D. Clark, Chicago, University Press, 659–686; (1967) *Iron Age Cultures in Zambia I: Kalomo and Kangila*, Chatto and Windus, 1–270; (1965) *Southern Africa*, Thames and Hudson, 1–222; Hiernaux, J. (1968) 'Bantu expansion: the evidence from physical anthropology confronted with linguistic and archaeological evidence', *J. Afr. Hist.*, **9** (4), 505–15; Robinson and Sandelowsky (1969) op. cit.; Fagan, B. M., Phillipson, D. W. and Daniels, S. G. H. (1969) *Iron Age Cultures in Zambia II: Dambwa, Ingombwe Ileda and the Tonga*, Chatto and Windus, 1–270; Clark, J. D. 'Research in African Prehistory, 1966–67, and the programme at Berkeley', *Palaeoecology of Africa*, **4**, 133–5; Clark, J. D. (1970) *The Prehistory of Africa*, Thames and Hudson, 1–302; Robinson (1970) op. cit.; Robinson, K. R. (1969) *The Early Iron Age in Malawi*. Malawi Government, Department of Antiquities, **6**.

41 Clark, J. D. (1968) *Malawi Antiquities Programme*, U.N.E.S.C.O. Publication 872/BMS.RD/CLT, Paris.

42 Gabel, C. (1969) 'African Archaeology in the United States, 1968', *African Studies Bull.*, **12** (1), 27–33.

43 Briggs, L. C. (1954) *The Stone Age Races of Northwest Africa*. American School of Prehistoric Research, Peabody Museum, Harvard University, **18**, 1–98.

44 K. R. Robinson: personal communication to the author.

2 Prehistoric Origins

J. Desmond Clark

All behaviour derives from environmental influences and the freedom of choice and expression that these provide. The personality of a country, therefore, and the national characteristics of its inhabitants stem directly from the past events which, whether by circumstance or design, have combined to mould the people into what they are today. Traditional customs and beliefs, dress, architectural features, food habits, relationships with neighbouring peoples and many other social and economic factors, as well as the blending of ethnic elements in the physical make-up of the population itself, are the outcome of the sequence of events that lies within the historic and prehistoric past.

Culture and personality are intimately interwoven with the past and a knowledge of the events that make up this background is essential for understanding and improving human relationships today. Pride in the historic past and the cultural and political achievements documented therein is, therefore, readily understandable and an important factor in producing a balanced and stable society. History is compounded from many sources—written, oral, tangible—so that the surviving evidence of past achievements, in the form of architectural monuments or traditional arts, forms a significant and inseparable part of a country's national heritage and for this reason most peoples have taken steps to ensure that such evidence is preserved for posterity.

In sub-Saharan Africa, where many materials do not long survive in a tropical climate, the role of the archaeologist becomes all the more important since his specialist knowledge alone can reconstruct the past from the often insignificant evidence that has been preserved. His task is made all the more important by reason of the paucity of written documents, especially in the interior parts of the sub-continent where documents only became common from the middle of the last century. Prior to this, such records as exist in the writings of Arabs or European sailors, soldiers and travellers, in no way provide any continuity and are generally ambiguous in their meaning and in the geographical location of the places or peoples to which they refer. They do provide, however, especially where there is chronological certainty, a

17

framework within which the history of earlier centuries can be reconstructed by using other means.

One of the most important of these additional sources is oral tradition which, through genealogies and king lists and the recording of important events, can, if properly analysed, carry back the story 200, 300 and, though more rarely, 400 years further into the past. Traditions handed down by word of mouth necessarily become compressed, however, and it is often unwise to accept the chronology they suggest without confirmation from other sources. There are, however, special cases where the traditional history relates to powerful political and religious authorities, such as were the Luba, Lunda, Tutsi or Hima kingdoms, where the responsibilities for preserving and transmitting the traditional history were more strictly or specifically provided for.

Another source of information comes from anthropology, from a knowledge of the techniques and practices found among the different tribal elements and of the material culture that is associated with these. Pottery forms, decoration and techniques of manufacture, methods of smelting iron or copper, agricultural practices or hunting techniques, building methods and many other activities that can be seen today, preserve by their survival the basis for interpreting and reconstructing many of the features uncovered by archaeological excavation and so help to throw light on the unrecorded past.

Yet another source of historical data is provided by comparative linguistics. The relationships between the various languages and dialects of Bantu and the study of cognates and related word roots are providing a relative chronology for the separation of ethnic units, for the determination of the degree of relationship between others and details of the social and economic structure of societies ancestral to those of the present day. Here again, one is no nearer an absolute chronology from linguistics than from oral tradition and for this it is also necessary to turn to the archaeologist working in conjunction with colleagues in the natural and human sciences.

The development in 1950 of the radiocarbon method of dating has revolutionized knowledge of human prehistory over the past 40,000 years. It is especially important in the chronology it provides for the last 2,000 years during which time the ancestors of the present-day African peoples make their appearance. Other dating methods extend the time-scale back considerably further and, where a sufficient number of diachronic and synchronic dates has been obtained, there is no reason to doubt the validity of the chronology that they provide within the range of error of the chronometric dating method that is used. Also, where two or more discrete archaeological aggregates are in stratigraphic relationship, the chronological and cultural sequence can be clearly established.

As the following brief description will show, however, a knowledge of the physical features and ecology of Malawi is essential to an understanding of the archaeological and historical record that is emerging and of the significance of the geographical position of this country for the history and prehistory of southern Africa generally.[1]

The phisycal geography of Malawi is dominated by the Rift Valley and the huge, deep freshwater lake that lies within it. Lake Malawi is 360 miles long.

from 10–15 miles wide and c.2,500 feet deep. Since its mean surface water elevation is 1,550 feet above sea level, the deepest part of the lake extends about 1,000 feet below the level of the sea.

The political boundaries of Malawi have in part been drawn with regard to the watershed of the lake and its only outlet—the Shire river—at the southern end. The country thus embraces an extensive area of the high interior plateau of Central Africa to the west and south. This is divided into western and eastern, or south-eastern, sections by the low-lying trough, the extension of the Rift Valley, between the south end of the Lake in the north and the Zambezi Valley in the south (see Fig. 3.6).

To the east, as also at the north end, Malawi's boundaries have been dictated more by political than by geographical or ethnic considerations and only the south-eastern parts of the watershed on the east side of the lake and the closed drainage basin of Lake Chilwa on the south-eastern section of the plateau, lie within the borders of Malawi.

Steep, sometimes precipitous escarpments form the boundary of the Rift on its eastern and western sides and the low-lying land bounding the lake itself is often not more than two or three miles in width. Sometimes, however, the rift scarp plunges with hardly a break almost sheer into and below the water. In other places, as in the vincinity of Nkhotakota or in the north-west at Karonga, the approach to the lake is easier and the escarpment further removed from the shoreline so that the area of rich alluvial soils is more extensive and attains several miles in width.

West of the lake the tableland has a general elevation of between 3,000 and 4,000 feet with ridges and plateaux that may rise to as much as 8,000 feet on the Nyika in the north. There are also innumerable lesser rocky hills and kopjies in many of which are rock shelters and caves which preserve evidence of a late prehistoric rock art tradition. This elevated region supports a ubiquitous growth of *Brachystegia* woodland, except on the higher ridges and plateaux where man-induced grasslands are steadily encroaching upon evergreen montane forest now mostly found as relicts lining the stream courses and in other protected and favourable refuges. Also in the Central Region between Ncheu and Lilongwe, grassland and thornbush already predominated over woodland by the time the first European missionaries arrived.

The plateau area to the east of the Rift in southern Malawi (known as the Shire Highlands) has an elevation of only 2,000 to 3,000 feet though, again, many rock-strewn hills and ridges rise for several hundred feet above the undulating surface. The most impressive of these are the isolated massifs of Zomba (7,000 feet) and Mlanje (10,000 feet) Mountains. The vegetation pattern of the western plateau is repeated here except that montane and lowland evergreen forest species form relict patches in many of the higher sheltered parts.

The plateau climate is generally cool and stimulating, being induced mostly by a summer rainfall that derives from the north-east and reaches very heavy proportions (over 64 inches (1,625 mm)) in the south-east, round Mlanje and in the north and north-west, round Nkhata Bay and on the territorial boundary with Tanzania. By contrast, the land within the Rift is hot and supports, where this has not been cut out for gardens, a thornbush and lowland thicket which may be almost impenetrable. At the southern end of the country the altitude is only some 200 feet above sea level.

Both the red and brown soils of the plateau and the black soils of the lowlands produce excellent crops and must have been a very important factor in bringing about the early settlement of the country by Iron Age peoples.

The wild life is—or was—as numerous and varied as in other parts of the southern African savanna and provided one of the richest environments anywhere in the world for hunting and gathering peoples. In addition, Lake Malawi and the smaller, shallower lakes of Malombe, Chilwa and Chiuta provide, in their fish population, an important source of protein.

Malawi is a land of topographical and climatic contrasts—plateaux ridges, steep escarpments and varied lowlands—highly attractive to both cultivators and mixed farmers. Particular importance attaches to the absence of tsetse fly from much of the plateau region and large parts of the lake shore and Lower river. These thus provided a favourable route for cattle herdsmen moving from northern Zambia and Tanzania, in the north, to the Zambezi and across to Rhodesia, in the south (see Fig. 3.4).

The main access routes for people moving into the country are across the Lake from the east, from where came traders from the coast; from the south up the Shire river from the Zambezi Valley; from the west from the Katanga across the Zambia plateau and the Luangwa Valley; and from the north along the watersheds of the rivers draining to the Indian Ocean lakes of Tanganyika and Rukwa, and of the Congo system which could thus have given access to peoples coming from the east coast, Tanzania, the south-eastern Congo or the East African lakes.

Within Malawi itself the ease or difficulty of access to the lake shore was always of importance and the earliest farming populations probably settled the agricultural lands of the lake shore and Lower river south of Nkhotakota from the western plateau.

It certainly calls for no surprise that a country so rich in natural resources constituted from early times an invitation to settlement from so many directions, as research is now showing.

The prehistoric past of the human race, before man's discovery of how to use metals and when stone was his main raw material for tools and weapons is known as the Stone Age. In Africa south of the Sahara this is normally divided into three periods: Earlier, Middle and Later. The Stone Age was immensely long (c.2·6 million years), covering by far the greater part of man's history. Cultural advance during this time was at first extremely slow becoming increasingly more rapid during the Middle and then the Later Stone Ages, that is to say, during only the past 60,000 years of human history.

In Malawi we have so far not been successful in finding evidence of man's presence before the end of the Middle or beginning of the Later Pleistocene period, though very interesting fossil material occurs which dates to the earlier Pleistocene some two million or more years ago.[2] At the north-west end of Lake Malawi in Karonga district, is a unique series of sediments named the

Chiwondo Beds.[3] These preserve archaic Pleistocene fossil fauna that represent the animals living on the shores and within the waters of the lake some two million years ago.

These beds were the subject of study and excavation by the University of California team in 1965, 1966 and 1968.[4] The faunal assemblage is comparable to that from sediments dating to the earlier part of the Lower Pleistocene in the Victoria, Baringo and Rudolph lake basins in Kenya and Ethiopia, on the one hand and, on the other, to that from old, brecciated deposits in limestone caves in South Africa. The faunal assemblages from the east African sites are now believed to date between 3·2 million and 4·2 million years before the present.

At both the east African and the South African sites the remains of early hominids (Australopithecines) have been found but without stone tools though these appear in the geological record c.2·6 million years ago.[5] The Chiwondo Beds are similarly without artifacts but, in spite of intensive search, no hominid remains have yet been recovered from them. This may be due to the scarcity of beach and terrestrial deposits in the Chiwondo Beds and it may be that further search will bring more of these to light. The fossils recovered are of considerable significance, however, since they represent the only evidence of Lower Pleistocene fauna from the whole of south central Africa and provide the link between the east and South African faunal assemblages. The Karonga sites provide the southernmost known limit for some east African genera and species and the northernmost limit for some of the South African forms.

The fauna shows that the environment of the lake shore at that time was more open than it is today and, like the east and South African thornbush country and grassland, supported several different kinds of elephant, black and white rhino, giraffe and antlered giraffe, several different kinds of pig including giant forms, many bovids, gazelles, three-toed horses and ostrich as well as hippopotamus (large and pygmy), crocodiles, water tortoises and fish in the lake. Small rodents, carnivores and primates are conspicuous by their extreme rarity.

Other localities on the western and southern parts of the lake shore (e.g. Nkhata Bay, Nkhotakota, Lake Malombe and Cape Maclear) have been examined for similar sediments and fossils but without success and it would appear that it is in Karonga district only that the earlier Pleistocene sediments and fossils are preserved.

Middle Pleistocene sediments appear to be completely absent from the Rift or other parts of the country with the result that evidence of the Earlier Stone Age Acheulian Industrial Complex is almost entirely lacking. While the earlier Acheulian is preserved in the large river valleys of the Zambezi and Congo tributaries, this Industrial Complex is nowhere common until later or Upper Acheulian times, shortly before or at the beginning of the Upper Pleistocene.

It is not surprising that it is absent from the Malawi plateau areas which embrace the higher parts of the watersheds, but its absence from the Rift Valley was not expected. The reason is probably to be found in the sequence of earth movements—faulting and other events—that brought Lake Malawi to its present level and depth and the Middle Pleistocene sediments that should overlie and immediately post-date the Chiwondo Beds are probably now further to the east and beneath the present surface of the lake.

At several points down the west and east sides of the lake, however, high level benches exist and it may be that a search of these for residual gravels and other sediments will produce part of the missing evidence. Also, examination of the lower parts of both walls of the Rift south of the lake down to the Cholo Escarpment should be carried out for both Middle and Later Pleistocene sediments.

The oldest clear evidence of man's presence in Malawi is found in the Rift in a small collection of very rolled, and so derived, artifacts from the lower part of a group of sediments known as the Chitimwe Beds in Karonga district; from an elephant butchery site at the base of the Chitimwe Beds near Karonga; and from the basal gravel in the Upper Pleistocene alluvial sequence in the Linthipe river at Linthipe on the plateau.

The choppers and flake tools in the lower Chitimwe conglomerates may be late Middle or early Upper Pleistocene in age, but the most interesting and important of these assemblages is the butchery site (Mwanganda's) which yielded a complete tool-kit (choppers, scrapers, knives) for dismembering and cutting up the beast. These were found lying in association with the fossilized elephant remains that would be between 50,000 and 100,000 years old.[6] Up to now this find is unique but there is no reason to suppose that other sites in undisturbed context with fossils will not be found when a systematic search of the Later Pleistocene alluvial deposits in the larger river valleys on the plateau and of the lake basins of Chilwa and Chiuta, of the confines of the Vwaza Marsh and of the Shire Valley is carried out.

The Linthipe river find is particularly encouraging since these are the first Earlier Stone Age implements from the plateau itself. Although the artifacts are not especially good examples of the stone worker's art, they nevertheless comprise a handaxe on a flake, the lower half of a cleaver, a crude biface and a large trimmed flake, all made of hard quartzitic rock from the Basement Series.

The general sequence to be found in this and most of the other river valleys studied (Shire (Chikwawa); Bu (Kasungu/Nkhota Kota road bridge); Changalembe; Lisangadzi; Kasitu; Nyanyangu; etc.) shows two separate aggradation terraces. The older and higher of the two is composed of two successive alluvial deposits separated by a disconformity, and each with a gravel at the base. The lithology of these alluvial deposits closely resembles that found in similar circumstances in other parts of south central Africa. Thus, the sediments of the older terrace of the Malawi rivers are equated with the Alluvium IIa and IIb of the Zambian and Rhodesian rivers; the lower terrace equates with Alluvium III in these countries. The basal gravel of the IIa Alluvium often contains Upper Acheulian and Sangoan artifacts and the gravel at the base of Alluvium IIb contains Middle Stone Age implements.

With the exceptions referred to above and isolated artifacts from the

Alluvium IIb gravels, the Malawi valley deposits have produced few finds. This is not because they do not exist but because the systematic investigation of the deposits has yet to be made. When this is carried out in the Linthipe and other river valleys—such as that of the Onzi at Nkhotakota—further Upper Acheulian assemblages are likely to be found. Also the presence of carbonate nodules in the form of kunkar in the IIa Alluvium is encouraging for the preservation of associated fossils.

In contrast to the extreme paucity of material from Earlier Stone Age times, artifacts from the Middle Stone Age occur widely over the whole of the north-western part of the lake shore, from the Songwe river in the north to Florence Bay in the south. These date between about 50,000 and 10,000 years ago. They are preserved in the middle and upper parts of the Chitimwe Beds—gravels, grits and sands representing riverine and fan deposits— between the escarpment and the lake shore.

The earlier part of the Middle Stone Age is not well known but for the later stages several sealed workshop and occupation surfaces have been un-covered. These have produced an abundance of artifacts and the distribution patterns provide important evidence of working techniques, activities and general behaviour. Later Middle Stone Age artifacts have also been collected from Chikale Beach (Nkhata Bay) Nkhotakota, the Livingstonia plateau (and perhaps the Nyika), Hora Mountain and the Shire at Chikwawa and Liwonde. The specimens from Hora were from an excavated rock shelter.

The Middle Stone Age appears to be more common in the north than in the centre and south but this is probably because more investigation has been carried out in the north than elsewhere. It is most probable that open sites will be found in the Central Region and, in particular, the lower layers in caves and rock shelters such as those at Diwa Hill, Chencherere Hill and Mphunzi Mountain in Dedza district may be expected to contain later Middle Stone Age assemblages.

No skeletal remains of this age are known from Malawi.

Much more is known about the Later Stone Age occupants of Malawi than about those of earlier times on the basis of excavations in caves, rock shelters and on open sites.[7, 8] Dates already obtained show that the Later Stone Age in Malawi ranges in time from about 8,000 B.C. up to $\pm$ A.D. 200. Oral tradition also suggests that it further extends into comparatively recent times with the Akafula hunters and gatherers who were found occupying much of the plateau country and valleys by the Maravi on their arrival, probably in the late fifteenth or early sixteenth century A.D.[9] In isolated pockets these people may have survived into the last 200 years.

Most of the excavated sites lie in the north of the country—back from the lake shore in Karonga district, on the Livingstonia plateau, on the Nyika and at Hora Mountain. However, excavations at Mphunzi and Mikolongwe extend our knowledge to the southern parts of the country also.

In Karonga district an unlimited supply of hard quartzite cobbles provided a source of raw material that was regularly used, while at Mikolongwe dolerite was also employed. The main raw material, however, was quartz in its crystal-line and semi-crystalline forms. From these rocks small, microlithic artifacts

23

were made and used as the cutting and working parts of hunting weapons and domestic equipment. Other implements included heavier cutting and scraping tools, grindstones, pestles and rubbers and the bored stone for weighting a digging stick or a spring trap.

The Malawi Later Stone Age can already be divided into two contemporary phases—a north-western, lake shore phase where a greater number of large tools are present and a plateau phase, best known from the rock shelter sites of Fingira Hill and Chowo on the Nyika. Here many trapeze and lunate shaped microliths are found with small scraping tools, adzes, the polished axe, grinding and rubbing equipment and an interesting industry of bone arrow points and awls. There was also much pigment and the back wall of the shelter had been painted. Subsequent survey and excavation on the Nyika have shown that almost every hill and ridge carries the tell-tale scatter of worked quartz and shows that this plateau has been a regular hunting ground since at least the third millennium B.C. on the basis of radiocarbon dates from the lower levels at Fingira Cave.[10]

Painted rock shelters and caves are most common in Mzimba, Lilongwe and Dedza districts and it is certain that very many more remain to be discovered.[11] There seems to be little doubt that most of this art is to be associated with the Later Stone Age population, though this has not yet been proved with certainty for Malawi. The earlier stages all comprise schematic motifs— circles, stars, gridirons, ladders, parallel lines and more complicated linear and curvilinear designs that belong to the central African schematic art tradition which separates the east African naturalistic tradition from that south of the Zambezi.

These designs are usually executed in red paint of various hues and later in red and white or white alone. Several styles recognized in Zambia are present in Malawi also. Paintings situated in caves are often comparatively well preserved but those in shelters are generally badly exfoliated. Some of the best of the paintings are found at Mphunzi, Diwa Hill and Mikolongwe. These styles are overlain by a later, semi-naturalistic series of anthropomorphic or zoomorphic figures in white which are probably the work of Iron Age cultivators and may be connected with initiation ritual. The latest art is in black (charcoal) and comprises geometric designs (Diwa Hill) and poorly drawn human figures (Homestead Shelter, Livingstonia).[8] It is unfortunate that up to now little of this art has been traced, analysed or reproduced.

The Hora (1950) and Fingira (1967) excavations produced human skeletal remains. Two burials were found at the former and at least one burial and scattered bones from several individuals at the latter.[12] These show that the physical type associated with the Later Stone Age assemblages in the northern parts of the territory was short, robustly built and exhibited both Negroid and some Bushmanoid characteristics. There is indeed no reason to suppose that this physical type does not still manifest itself from time to time at the present day and form a basic element of the population of Malawi. Oral tradition provides some information on the appearance and technical abilities of the Akafula hunters[9] while linguistic studies by Nurse[13] indicate that it is possible that they spoke a Bushman 'click' language.

The earliest cultivators who were also metal-workers, occupied the plateau and Rift about the middle of the second century, A.D. Excavations carried out by Robinson[14] show that the northern and southern parts of the country, both the plateau and the Rift, were occupied about the same time. Any movement of population that accompanied the appearance of the new economy and technology must have been comparatively rapid and the tsetse fly, if it was present in the country at that time, must have been restricted to insignificant pockets of bush.

More research at selected localities is necessary before it is possible to show what happened to the indigenous, stone-using, hunting/gathering peoples but it seems most probable that a significant element was incorporated within the gene pool from which the present-day population derives. The hunters and gatherers certainly occupied some of the most favourable micro-environments in the continent though it is probable that they were never numerous by present-day standards.

Movement by Iron Age cultivators and stock owners is likely to have been a steady but gradual process by small, rather than large, groups who were welcomed because of the new food sources and improved technical skills they brought with them. Their need for land for cultivation and herding would not have conflicted with the requirements of the hunters and such evidence as exists suggests an amiable symbiotic relationship between the two groups. Hunting remained a very important part of the economic pattern but added to this were the advantages of domestic plants and animals which encouraged the growth of larger and permanent settlements. Only much later, from the sixteenth century onwards, did competition for land and other resources lead to major conflict among the tribal populations of Malawi and by this time most of the old prehistoric peoples had elected to change the hunting/gathering, stone-using way of life for the advantages of the new economy. Whether this reflects the true nature of these revolutionary changes, only further work will show but it serves as a model that fits such evidence as we possess at present and is, therefore, capable of being tested.

Archaeology can be seen, therefore, to be of fundamental importance for writing the history of the indigenous peoples of Malawi, just as it is for Zambia, the east African countries or South Africa and, of course, for the prehistoric past of Europe or any other country.

Excavation of settlement sites, burials, special activity sites such as those connected with metal-working, pot-making, hunting or fishing, can provide specific knowledge of social and economic customs and even of political systems, of ethnic and cultural relationships, migration, hybridization or extinction, all of which can now be dated in terms of years. What archaeology alone cannot provide, or only in very rare instances, are connections with individuals or specific events. Even this difficulty can often be overcome by correlation of the evidence from excavation with that from the oral or written record.

Each of these sources of data, therefore—oral tradition, comparative linguistics, manuscript documents, ethnology and, above all, archaeology— has an important contribution to make to African history and the basis of this knowledge will only come from the objective sharing of information and the integration of the findings that each of these sources can provide or corroborate. As yet, such interdisciplinary research has barely begun, though the realization of the need for it to be undertaken has been general among scholars and others working towards the elucidation and cognizant of the importance of a long history to the modern people of Africa.

FOOTNOTES

1 Pike, J. G. and Rimmington, G. T. (1965) *Malawi: A Geographical Study.* O.U.P.

2 Clark, J. D., Stephens, E. A. and Coryndon, S. C. (1966) 'Pleistocene fossiliferous lake beds of the Malawi (Nyasa) Rift: a preliminary report', *Amer. Anthrop.*, **68** (2), pp. 46–87.

3 Dixey, F. (1927) 'The tertiary and post-tertiary lacustrine sediments of Nyasa Rift Valley', *Q. J. Geol. Soc. Lond.* **83** (3).

4 Clark, J. D., Haynes, C. V., Mawby, J. E. and Gautier, A., in press, *Interim report on palaeo-anthropological investigations in the Lake Malawi Rift*, Quaternaria, Rome.

5 Leakey, M. D. (1970) 'Early Artefacts from the Koobi Fora area', *Nature*, **226**, 228–30.

6 Clark, J. D. and Haynes, C. V. (1970) 'An elephant butchery site at Mwanganda's village, Karonga, Malawi and its relevance for Palaeolithic archaeology', *World Archaeol.*, **1** (3), 390–411.

7 Clark, J. D. (1959) 'Prehistory in Nyasaland', *Nyasa. J.*, **9** (1), 92–119.

8 Robinson, K. R. and Sandelowsky, B. H. (1969) 'The Iron Age of northern Malawi: recent work', *Azania*, **3**.

9 Rangeley, W. H. J. (1963) 'The earliest inhabitants of Nyasaland', *Nyasa. J.*, **16** (2).

10 Sandelowsky, B. H. and Robinson, K. R. (1968) *Fingira: a Preliminary Report*. Government of Malawi, Department of Antiquities, **3**.

11 Clark, J. D. (1959) 'Rock Art of Nyasaland', in *The Rock Art of the Federation of Rhodesia and Nyasaland*, ed. Summers. National Publications Trust, Salisbury. 163–221; Metcalfe, M. (1956) 'Some rock paintings in Nyasaland', *Nyasa. J.*, **9** (1), 58–71.

12 Wells, L. H. (1957) 'Late Stone Age human types in Central Africa', in *Prehistory: the Third Pan-African Congress, Livingstone (1955)*, eds J. D. Clark and S. Cole. Chatto and Windus, 183–5. And D. R. Brothwell, personal communication to the author.

13 Nurse, G. T. (1968) 'Bush roots and Nyanja ideophones', *Soc. Malawi J.*, **21**.

14 Robinson, K. R. (1970) *The Iron Age of the Southern Lake Area of Malawi*. Government of Malawi, Department of Antiquities, **8**.

3 Environment and History: the Malawian setting

Swanzie Agnew

The purpose of this paper is to examine the geographical position of Malawi with particular reference to the physical barriers by which it is surrounded; to consider how far these barriers have been the cause of Malawi becoming an area of transition between the main cultural regions of eastern, central and southern Africa; and also to consider the special environmental factors which account for Malawi having one of the highest population densities in Africa south of the Sahara.

Malawi has a land area of 36,324 square miles, excluding lake waters, and a population, at the time of the 1966 census, of four million people (Fig. 3.1). It is bordered by Lake Malawi on the east from the northern frontier to about as far south as Fort Johnston and straddles the Shire and Lake Chilwa lowlands further to the south.

Lake Malawi, which is the last of the great lakes of the African Rift Valley system, occupies a position where the Rift Valley has swung due south and is within 400 miles of the Indian Ocean. The Shire river which flows out of the lake follows the line of the rift until its confluence with the Zambezi, 100 miles upstream from the labyrinthine distributaries of the Zambezi delta.

The Zambezi valley occupies the first major trough to have broken through the highlands of East Africa and to lie transversely across the Rift valley. Upstream from its confluence with the Shire river, the Zambezi narrows and from Tete to the Victoria Falls it divides the Central African plateaux by its deep gorges and its hot and unhealthy valley. A north-easterly projection of the Zambezi trough is the Luangwa tectonic depression which interrupts the eastward continuation of the Central African plateau.

Much of the Luangwa floor and bordering escarpments is waterless in the dry season and the plentiful game provide hosts for the tsetse. Towards the head of the Luangwa trough the valleys rise in altitude and open out where they cross the 4,000 to 5,000 foot plateau of Central Africa before they again narrow towards the headwaters of the streams within the highlands of northern Malawi, while to the west of the Luangwa depression the fault-line excarpment of the Muchinga mountains gradually disappears as it merges with the plateau watershed.

28

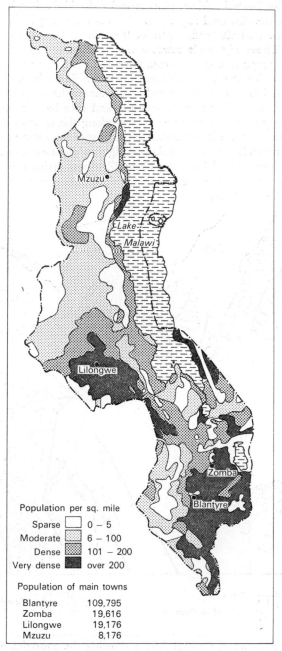

Population per sq. mile

Sparse	☐	0 – 5
Moderate	▨	6 – 100
Dense	▨	101 – 200
Very dense	■	over 200

Population of main towns

Blantyre	109,795
Zomba	19,616
Lilongwe	19,176
Mzuzu	8,176

3.1 Population density in Malawi

Between the Central African plateau and Lake Malawi and encircling the lake head are the dissected highlands of the north rising to above 7,000 feet over extensive summit levels such as the Nyika, Poroto and Livingstone Mountains. These highlands narrow the isthmus of land between Lakes Malawi and Tanganyika and between these and the Rukwa rift. This isthmus is the bridge which spans the rift furrow between East Africa and the smooth Congo/Zambezi divide and it has aptly been named the wasp-waist of Central Africa (Fig. 3.2). Coming from East Africa and once having passed over this bridge, the way is open either to continue along the crest of the Muchinga escarpment and to move into Zambia to the west of the Luangwa trough or to turn southwards and to enter the Malawian highlands to the east of the Luangwa.

Migration into Malawi from the Congo/Zambezi divide came either from

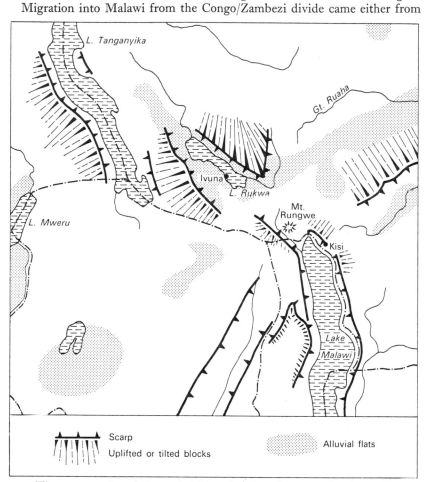

3.2 The wasp-waist of Central Africa showing the constricted passageway between Central Africa and East Africa and the northern gateway into Malawi. (Redrawn and adapted from A. Warren, *Africa in Transition*, Eds Hodder and Harris, Methuen, 1967.)

the west across the shallow head of the Luangwa depression, or from the north over the Chitipa plain and then southwards passing to the west of the Nyika massif. The Nyika highlands isolated the lowlands at the head of Lake Malawi from the effect of these migrations and within that enclave the peoples developed cultural ties to the north of Lake Malawi rather than with the groups inhabiting the plateau (Fig. 3.3).

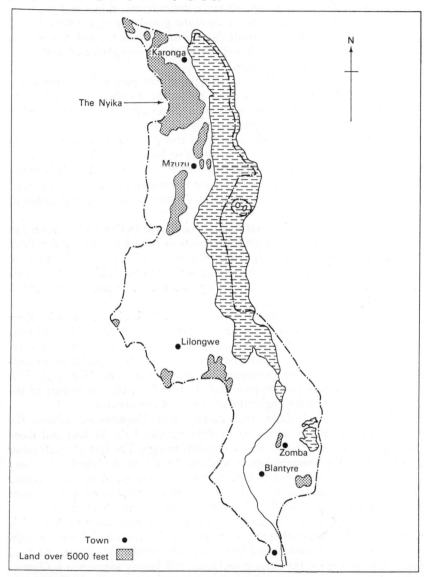

3.3 Highlands and escarpments separating the Karonga enclave and the lake-shore littoral from the interior plateau

31

In contrast with the ease of entry into Malawi from the Congo/Zambezi divide, the Zambezi valley is a formidable barrier to communication between Central and Southern Africa. To reach the uplands of Malawi from the south, the most feasible route is across the Zambezi to the east of its confluence with the Luangwa. From the high plateau of Rhodesia there is a swift descent along the tsetse-free corridor of the Mazoe and Ruenya valleys to the Zambezi floor. Near Zumbo and for some distance downstream, ridges and spurs on the north bank lead upwards to the montane grasslands of the Kirk Range along the Malawian border. A route further to the west through the present Eastern Province of Zambia debouches into the grassy glades of Malawi to the west of the Dzalanyama Range.

These grassland areas which are so suitable for pastoralists became the heartland of the Ngoni invaders from across the Zambezi, a heartland to which groups of these invaders either returned or attempted to return after further abortive northward migrations.

Although the Zambezi is an obstacle to traffic between country lying to the north and south of the river, it is navigable for small craft as far as Tete, 250 miles from its mouth, and the Shire river which flows into it between Tete and the sea is also navigable for small craft from its confluence with the Zambezi to the Murchison rapids at Chikwawa which is a distance of about 100 miles.

It was by these waterways that Arab, Swahili and Indian traders sought to explore and exploit the commercial prospects on both banks of the Zambezi. And it was by these waterways, too, that the British and the Portuguese sought to establish and extend their spheres of influence. This latter development was accelerated when David Livingstone reached Lake Malawi for the first time in September 1859.

Extensive areas of the country between Lake Malawi and the Shire river on the west and the Indian Ocean on the east consist of tsetse-infested bush-land (Fig. 3.4). Moreover, until about the middle of the nineteenth century, the Rovuma river was the frontier between the Afro-Asian maritime civiliza-tion to the north and the Portuguese Empire to the south (Fig. 3.5). This combination of circumstances protected Malawi from the full impact of the slave trade until after the beginning of the nineteenth century.

Malawi's western frontier with Zambia and Moçambique follows the watershed between the river systems draining into Lake Malawi and those flowing away towards the Luangwa/Zambezi trough. The fact of the frontier running along the watershed gives a physical unity to the lakeside territory of Malawi which, on account of its location and the set of the surrounding physical barriers, is marginal to the cultures of eastern, central and southern Africa and largely isolated from influences from the outside (Fig. 3.6).

As in other parts of Africa, the distribution of population in Malawi is uneven. Heavily dissected country or inaccessible scarped highlands remain thinly populated or unoccupied but where constraints are absent and food production is assured the rural population, still largely supported by home-grown foods, amounts to 100 to 300 persons per square mile, while in some peri-urban areas associated with modern economic activities the population

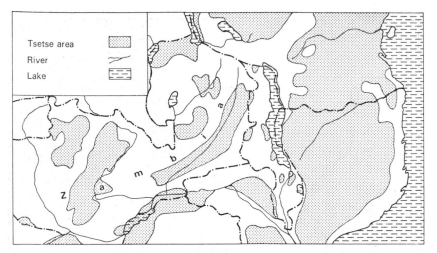

3.4 The distribution of tsetse is governed by a number of factors. Areas densely populated and cleared for agriculture, edaphic grasslands, and altitudes higher than 5,000 feet are generally less infested than woodland areas harbouring game as hosts.

rises to as much as 1,000 per square mile (Fig. 3.1).

If the principle of geographic momentum is accepted, it is reasonable to assume that the region occupied by present-day Malawi has long had a greater concentration of population than many neighbouring areas. This is a consequence of the exceptionally favourable environment offered by a lakeshore situation where all but 5 per cent of the land area has at least thirty inches of rainfall a year. This is the minimum amount required for secure dry land farming in Central Africa[1] (Fig. 3.7).

The presence of several lakes and the rapid changes in altitude over short distances, for example from 150 feet in the Lower Shire valley to over 8,000 feet on the Nyika and Mount Mlanje, gives rise to a diversity of climates and a variety of ecosystems. In so small a land area as Malawi, fifty-three natural regions have been identified and mapped.[2]

The occurrence of so many different but closely adjacent environments has always presented opportunities to draw upon the resources offered by different kinds of flora and fauna and to exploit production cycles at different periods of the year. Such an environment must always have been favourable to the survival and increase of both hunter/gatherer societies and agricultural communities.

The most propitious surroundings for fostering population growth and the early development of permanent settlement are found where the two environments of land and water meet. Here, too, water communication favours the exchange of goods over long distances. This is illustrated by the remains of important Iron Age sites which have been found at Kisii on the north-east shore of Lake Malawi, Ivuna on Lake Rukwa, and Kalambo near the southern-

<figure>

Portuguese

Arabs

</figure>

3.5 Lake Malawi and the Shire River territory in relation to the coastal spheres of influence of the Arabs and the Portuguese, 1880. (Adapted and redrawn from J. Duffy, *Portugal in Africa*, Penguin, 1962.)

most point of Lake Tanganyika.[3] The establishment of the Ngonde kingdom which lasted from the fifteenth to the nineteenth centuries in an area that is now the north-eastern borderland of Malawi was also probably due to its having control of the northern shores of Lake Malawi[4] and command of a trade route into the interior.[5]

It is important to note the difference between the two types of lakes characteristic of Africa, both of which are represented in Malawi. One type is a deep linear lake lying in the down-faulted segments of the African rift

3.6 (opposite) The trends and patterns of the major river systems within the Lake Malawi/Shire Rift Valley basin have had a bearing on directing migratory movements southwards and towards the grasslands of the western watershed, i.e. movement was initiated from the lakeshore.

34

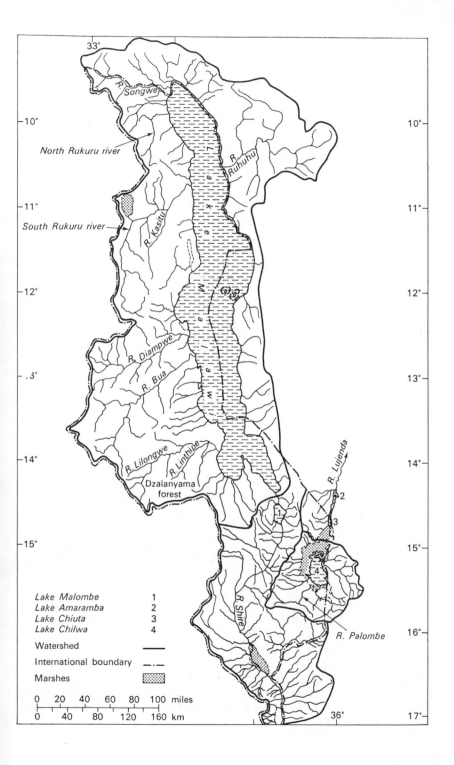

Lake Malombe — 1
Lake Amaramba — 2
Lake Chiuta — 3
Lake Chilwa — 4

Watershed
International boundary
Marshes

0   20   40   60   80   100 miles
0   40   80   120   160 km

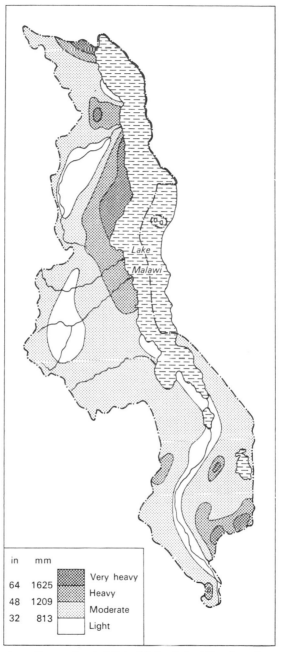

in	mm		
64	1625		Very heavy
48	1209		Heavy
32	813		Moderate
			Light

3.7 Distribution of annual rainfall in Malawi showing that the greater part of the country receives more than 30 inches of rainfall, the minimum amount required for secure dry land farming. (Adapted and redrawn from Collins – Longman *Atlas for Malawi*.)

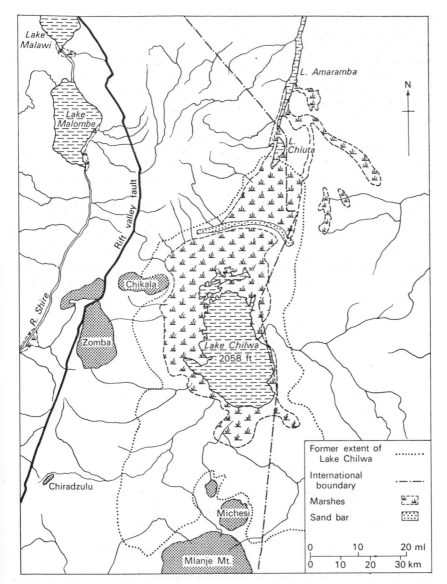

Map legend:

Former extent of Lake Chilwa	....
International boundary	—·—·—
Marshes	
Sand bar	

Scale:
0 — 10 — 20 ml
0 — 10 — 20 — 30 km

Map labels: Lake Malawi, Lake Malombe, Rift valley fault, R. Shire, L. Amaramba, L. Chiuta, Chikala, Zomba, Lake Chilwa 2058 ft, Chiradzulu, Michesi, Mlanje Mt., N

3.8   Lake Chilwa Basin is an example of a basin lake in the process of sedimentation offering a lacustrine environment in the midst of the savannah woodlands of the plateau.

system, of which Lake Malawi is an example. Lake Malawi is the third largest lake in Africa and has the appearance of an inland sea. The other type of lake is shallow and occupies saucer-shaped depressions warping the smooth African shield, a typical example being Lake Chilwa which comprises 1,000

37

square miles of marshland and shallow open water (Fig. 3.8). While Lake Malawi has played a formative role in the history of the region, Lake Chilwa merely offered the advantages of a lacustrine environment interrupting, and encircled by, the deciduous woodlands of the Central African plateau. It is also possible that these shallow basin lakes and the marshlands, such as those in the Lower Shire valley, may have become places of refuge for hunter/fisher groups who were displaced by incoming cattle keepers and the first agriculturalists.

The permanent settlements which grew up in the favourable environments near the lakes contrasted very markedly with the pattern of life in the plateau woodlands where the alternation of wet and dry seasons and the ecological brittleness of the environment enforced a system of shifting agriculture with accompanying ephemeral settlements.

The type of movement associated with peoples engaged in shifting agriculture in the plateau environment can be depicted in simple models usually taken to demonstrate the theory of diffusion of innovations.[6] The mode of diffusion away from an original centre, which occurs among subsistence cultivators as the natural fertility of the soils they are working becomes exhausted, is illustrated in Fig. 3.9a. The movement of a larger group of

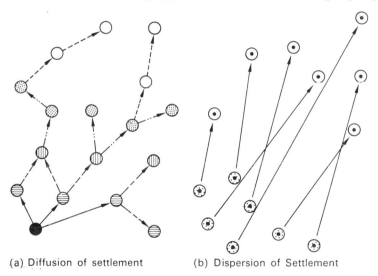

(a) Diffusion of settlement   (b) Dispersion of Settlement

3.9 Expansion of original settlement in the woodlands of East Central Africa, either by (a) diffusion related to the shifting nature of the agricultural system or (b) dispersion in the face of hazard and catastrophe. (Adapted from P. R. Gould, *Assoc. of Amer. Geog.*, Resource Paper No. 4, 1969.)

people from one place to another, usually in response to intolerable restraints such as pressure from an incoming alien group, persistent slave raiding, a deteriorating environment, famine, epidemic disease, or intrusion by tsetse is demonstrated in Fig. 3.9b. The slow movements (diffusion) of a lineage

38

group differ markedly from the migration (dispersion) of a large number of people such as a whole clan or tribe, but both types of movement led to the rapid occupation of large areas of the plateau lands of southern Africa.[7]

The spread of the agricultural communities through the woodlands of present-day Malawi did not lead to a weakening of group cohesion, as might have been expected, because of two important factors which prevented this from happening.

The first, a cultural factor, was the mystical power of the chiefs of the Maravi people who alone could intercede for them with the High God (Mulungu) to send rain or to ward off disasters such as epidemic diseases.[8]

The second factor, an environmental one, was the location of dry season water supplies or of water retentive alluvial soils. This factor led to movements of diffusion or dispersal following the valleys. Now the rivers draining into Lake Malawi belong to north and north-east trending systems and, since the expansion of settlement has been predominantly southwards, dispersion from either the north or from the shores of Lake Malawi would therefore have led up the valleys towards the broad-lobed *dambos* or marshlands of the headwaters of the rivers.[9] The low plateau interfluves between the separate drainage basins made for easy intercommunication while, within each valley, a network of paths would have established communal solidity, but where the rivers plunge down the escarpments in steep courses or by inaccessible gorges, an abrupt break occurs separating the inhabitants of the plateau from those of the Rift Valley and these groups tended to grow apart.

It was therefore singularly appropriate that the original rain-shrine at Kaphiri-Ntiwa in the Dzalanyama range, which is traditionally the place where the first men and animals descended from heaven,[10] should have stood at the geographical frontier between the marsh-filled headwaters of the rivers of the Lake Malawi drainage system of the plateau and the swift flowing, rock-bedded streams which run southwards to the Zambezi and Shire low-lands.

Migratory movements down the Wankurumadzi and other southward flowing rivers were beyond the sphere of influence of the shrines of the spirits of the Central Maravi, and the people who moved southwards into the Lower Shire valley and who later became known as the Mang'anja founded their own shrine of 'Mbona on the west bank of the Shire river not far from Nsanje.

Although there were factors which helped to maintain cultural continuity in the plateau environment, the actual course of events was one continuous succession of changes in settlement in response of shifting agriculture, in contrast to the permanence of settlement and the solidarity of societies characteristic of major riverine and some lacustrine environments.[11]

The Dzalanyama range has been regarded as the line of separation between the Chewa and Mang'anja groups of the Maravi, and the rift escarpment as a zone of separation between the plateau and the lakeshore peoples, but a more readily identifiable and precise barrier is Lake Malawi which, measuring 350 miles in length and between ten and fifty miles in width, must be considered to have been an important factor in the control of movement and

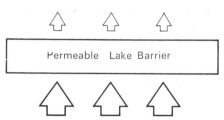

3.10 A permeable lake barrier demonstrating the retarding effect on the passage of ideas or movement of people from one shore to the other. (Adapted from P. R. Gould, *Assoc. of Amer. Geog.*, Resource Paper No. 4, 1969.)

settlement.

Gould describes the role a lake can play as a *permeable* barrier which retards the passage of ideas and allows only some of them to reach the far shore[12] (Fig. 3.10). It can be shown that a lake also acts as a permeable barrier to a migrating people in so far as only a certain number of them are able to make the crossing and to establish themselves on the far side. An example of this is found in the oral tradition of the Henga people where much is made of the difficulties that confronted them when they reached the eastern shore of Lake Malawi during their migration westward down the Ruhuhu basin and of the courage and determination required of those who made the crossing of the lake by canoe, a feat which earned their leader the honorific titles of *Mlowoka* and *Nguluka*,[13] the latter title not to be confused with the founder of the

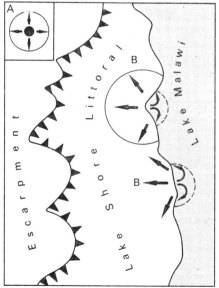

3.11 Diffusion of innovation from an unrestricted land centre (inset diagram A) and a centre placed at the lakeshore, B. The radius of adoption is greater in B than in A. (Adapted and redrawn from P. R. Gould, *Assoc. of Amer. Geog.*, Resource Paper No. 4, 1969.)

Chikulamayembe dynasty.

A lake can also influence the process of diffusion and strengthen cultural ties within a community when a centre of innovation arises close to a lakeshore. This is illustrated in Fig. 3.11 taken from Gould.[14] In this diagram the pattern of diffusion of an innovation from an unrestricted land centre is depicted at A; while the spread of an innovation from a centre located at a lakeshore, where the radius of diffusion is increased on the landward side to a far greater extent than would have been the case had the water not acted as a barrier to movement, is illustrated at B. At B there is, as it were, a concentration of energy in a smaller sector and therefore a wider radius of impact.

Where numerical facts have been available it has been demonstrated statistically that these patterns of diffusion of innovation can be accepted as being valid. It is therefore reasonable to assume that similar patterns of diffusion were part of the process by which a number of separate ethnic groups merged to form the Tonga people of the Nkata Bay area.

Community of interest undoubtedly developed amongst the Tonga as a result of the ease of communication by water between their closely spaced lake-shore settlements. Inland from the littoral plain the uninhabited escarpment formed a barrier which prevented dispersion of settlement and helped to maintain the state of isolation needed to produce tribal cohesion and the growth of ethnic individuality. The Tonga adopted cassava as their staple diet, a common practice among fisher-folk in Central Africa, and the high yields obtained from this crop were sufficient to support their steadily growing sedentary population. Thus a lakeside situation not only fostered permanent settlement but also offered conditions favourable for the development of tribal bonds.

When considering the nature of barriers in relation to the influence they may have exerted upon paths of dispersion and upon cultural evolution, it may be assumed that the pattern of river systems, but not necessarily their present channels, have remained virtually unchanged for the last 20,000 to 40,000 years. During the same period the major landforms, including those of the Rift Valley, may also be supposed to have been largely the same as they are at present but this is not necessarily so for such features as plant associations, the underground water table level which in turn affects the availability of water in the dry season, or fluctuations in the flow of rivers or the size and level of lakes. These are affected by variations in rainfall linked to periodic changes in climate.

It cannot be presumed that the climate, in particular the average temperature and mean annual rainfall, were the same in the past as they are today. The Pleistocene period consisted of a series of wet and dry phases which correspond with marked fluctuations in climate. These pluvials and interpluvials are believed to be correlated but not necessarily coincident in time, with the glacials and interglacials of the northern hemisphere.

It has been estimated that fluctuations in rainfall in Rhodesia during the Pleistocene epoch ranged from 50 per cent to 150 per cent of the present annual average. The same range of variation may have occurred in Malawi but, considering its more easterly position, periodic falls in the amount of

41

rainfall to the lower end of the range would have had less serious effects than on the interior plateau.[15]

Variation in temperature, together with greater or lesser persistence of cloud cover, would have affected the distribution of plant associations. There is evidence to show that during the well documented Gamblian Pluvial, which lasted in East Africa from about 40,000 to 12,000 B.P., temperatures

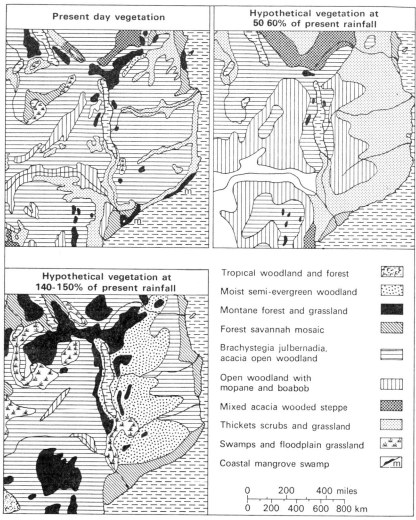

3.12 Presumed changes in plant association types as compared with present-day vegetation in East Central Africa, were the mean annual rainfall to be decreased to 50–60% or increased to 140–150% of the present-day rainfall. (Adapted and redrawn from H. B. S. Cooke, *Ecology in South Africa*, Ed. Davis, Junk, 1964.)

fell by about 5°C and montane plant communities descended some 500 metres from their former heights.[16]

Hypothetical reconstructions of the vegetation in southern Africa[17] for climatic periods during which the mean annual rainfall was between fifty and sixty per cent and between 140 and 150 per cent of what it is today (Fig. 3.12) show Malawi to have had very different vegetations from those of the plateau lands further west. In periods of greater aridity the presumed ecological conditions in Malawi were noticeably more favourable than they were in the surrounding areas. In periods of higher rainfall the spread of evergreen forest may have made human settlement more difficult except to those specialized forest groups who had learned to adapt themselves to these conditions; nevertheless, deductions drawn from the conditions prevailing in Malawi in the periods of differing rainfall make it appear likely that during both periods the density of population was higher in the area than in adjacent territories.

Summers maintains that the advance or retreat of lowland and montane forest, plateau savanna woodland, and mopane/baobab associations in response to changes in the amount of annual rainfall over prolonged periods has had important effects on the sequence and distribution of prehistoric cultures and he has attempted to demonstrate that this has been the case in Rhodesia from the Early Stone Age to the present time.[18]

It is now generally recognized that the presence or absence of mopane woodland which is subject to heavy infestation by tsetse has always to a very great extent influenced movement and settlement in Africa. Tsetse are carriers of organisms which transmit nagana to domestic animals and sleeping sickness to man. The organisms which cause nagana are ubiquitous and therefore all tsetse can transmit this disease to domestic stock. The organisms which infect man with sleeping sickness are limited in their distribution. Hence, in many places, it is possible for man to live in contact with tsetse but it is never possible for domestic stock to do so because, if tsetse are present, transmission of nagana always occurs.[19] It follows that agriculturalists who did not keep any domestic stock had a greater choice of land and freedom of movement than cattle herders. The latter, moving southwards across Central Africa through the main tsetse belt, were compelled to follow corridors of less badly infested land. One such avenue led through the gateway from East Africa into Central Africa by way of the Fipa plateau, then south through the highlands of Malawi and onwards to the Zambezi valley between Tete and Zumbo where the tsetse belt appears to have narrowed opposite the Mazoe valley which Summers maintains was occasionally free from fly, as is believed to have been the case at least in the early nineteenth century.

The same corridor was used by some of the Ngoni during their northward migrations from South Africa. It was a result of contact with the pastoral Ngoni during their northward movements, and by virtue of large areas of the country in which they were living being free from tsetse, that the Chewa and Tumbuka peoples became cattle keepers. The fact of their becoming cattle keepers set the Chewa and Tumbuka apart from those other groups, such as the Yao and Lomwe, who came into Malawi as woodland agriculturalists with no experience or understanding of cattle.

43

It is a very striking fact that the main traditional crops of Malawi were here growing in a region which was either margiual to or outside their main areas of distribution in Africa. Let us take a few examples from the distribution maps compiled by Murdock [20]

Cassava or manioc is an important crop in two major areas, one being the

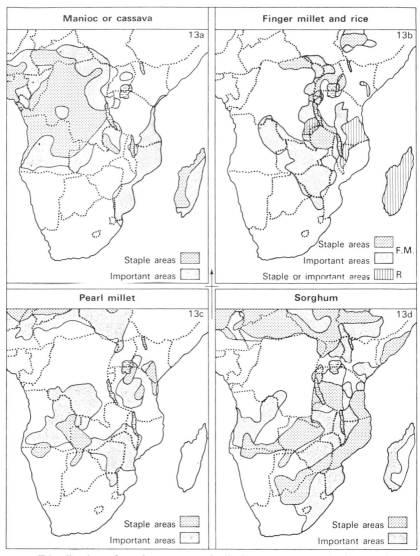

3.13 Distribution of staple or economically important crops in South, Central and East Africa. (Adapted, with permission, from the *Geographical Review*, Vol. 50, 1960, copyrighted by the American Geographical Society of New York.)

region of the Congo basin, and the other the lowlands of the East African coast extending inland to include the low-lying country of southern Tanzania and Moçambique as far as the eastern shore of Lake Malawi with an extension along the western and northern shores of the lake from about Nkhata Bay northwards (Fig. 3.13a).

Rice has been grown in Madagascar since the early centuries of the Christian era and was introduced to the adjacent continent of Africa by the Arabs at a very much later date. It is now an important crop in parts of Egypt, West Africa, the Congo, Kenya and also in a large area extending north-westwards, westwards and south-westwards from the coast between Kilwa and Cape Delgado into Tanzania, Mozambique and Malawi (Fig. 3.13b).

Thus, both cassava and rice appear to have spread into Malawi by diffusion from the lowlands of the East African coast.

Bulrush-millet or pearl-millet is an important crop in the Sudanic belt from the Atlantic coast to the Nile valley and along the course of the Nile into Upper Egypt; in the semi-arid central plateau of Tanzania; and in the Zambezi basin with extensions into the south-western Congo, the Angolan highlands, and the eastern highlands of Rhodesia. The area in which bulrush-millet is economically important includes the southern lowlands of Malawi as part of the lower Zambezi cropping system (Fig. 3.13c).

Sorghum which is indigenous to Africa and the leading crop of the continent as a whole is widely distributed in Egypt and throughout the summer rainfall areas of tropical and sub-tropical Africa excepting the rain forest belt. In Malawi, however, sorghum is of economic importance in the Lower Shire valley only, while eleusine or finger-millet is, or was until very recently, the main crop in the plateau areas of the country (Fig. 3.13d).

Eleusine or finger-millet is extensively grown in parts of Ethiopia and in the highlands lying to the east and south of the Congo basin and throughout Rhodesia into the northern Transvaal. It is a particularly important crop in the environs of Lakes Victoria and Tanganyika and in the plateau lands of Malawi (Fig. 3.13b) giving place to sorghum and bulrush-millet in the drier southern lowlands of Malawi.

Maize has now displaced the traditionally important crops in most parts of Malawi and other staples have kept their importance in three areas only. Cassava is still the staple diet of the people living along the northern shores of Lake Malawi; bulrush-millet continues to be grown in the Lower Shire valley, probably because its returns are more reliable than those of maize in this area of low rainfall; and eleusine is still a favoured crop in the area of thinly populated woodlands north of Rumpi.

The widespread adoption of maize as the chief agricultural crop in Malawi is in contrast to Zambia where maize is grown largely as a secondary green vegetable except where population densities are high, as in the case of the cattle-keeping Tonga of the Southern Province and the Ngoni-Chewa of the Eastern Province.

In Zambia it is claimed[21] that there has been a resistance to the adoption of maize as the main crop in many traditional systems of agriculture because of a higher demand in the standard of soil fertility, the restricted planting period, the unreliability of yield in marginal conditions and the labour needed in preparing the meal from the seed.

This accords with M. P. Miracle's research which revealed that until well into the present century maize was not the mainstay of the diet in the bulk of the areas in East and Central Africa where it is now of major importance.

While the rapid dietary change in Malawi can be explained by cultural contacts with Arab slavers, Ngoni overlords, European settlers and the early development of migratory labour to the white dominions of Southern Africa, yet one is tempted to accept Sir Joseph Hutchinson's thesis that pressure on land arising from a rapid increase or concentration of rural population ultimately results in the intensification of agricultural systems.[23]

Unquestionably, maize demands a more careful selection of soils and higher agronomic practices than are needed for ashbed cultivation of finger millet, the broadcasting of rice in seasonally inundated alluvial land or the vegetative planting of cassava on mounds.

Moreover it is within the major maize growing areas that one can see further intensification of production in the adoption of crop rotation by the cultivation of tobacco and groundnuts primarily as cash crops alternately with maize for subsistence needs.

It is evident that Malawi has received her main food plants from a diversity of regions beyond her own borders, including the East African highlands, the lowlands of the East African coast, the lower Zambezi valley, southern Africa and, very likely, the Congo basin. That so many and diverse crops were able to thrive in so small an area as that of Malawi is illustrative of the advantages offered by the great variety of environments which are encountered in Malawi and have given to the country the broad resource base that has enabled it always to support higher population densities than any of the neighbouring territories.

The fact of Malawi having received its most important food plants from so many different surrounding areas illustrates very clearly that the position it occupies is, as it were, that of a cross-roads between the different cultural regions of eastern, central and southern Africa.

Since 1891, however, when Malawi was declared to be a British Protectorate, communications and trade relations have been developed predominantly with countries lying to the east and south.

A railroad connecting Malawi with Beira and with the Rhodesian line and railway system at Dondo, eighteen miles from Beira, was opened in 1922 and a new railway line, opened in 1970, now connects Malawi with the port of Nacala which is 700 miles north of Beira.

Partly on account of transport facilities and for other historical reasons, Malawi obtains many of her imports from or through Rhodesia and the Republic of South Africa. Moreover, many Malawians work in Rhodesia and South Africa where there are at present more employment opportunities than in their own country and where migrant labour from Malawi is encouraged.

In view of Malawi's geographical position and the orientation of the modern communications systems that link her with the outside world, it has followed naturally that she has developed close ties and economic relations with

46

Mozambique, Rhodesia and South Africa.

But with the impending move of the capital, now at Zomba, and of the international airport, now at Blantyre, to Lilongwe in the Central Region, the completion of the lakeside road, the rapid development of road communications throughout the length of the land, the opening of new industrial plants in all the Regions, and the improvements in agriculture and stock-breeding that are now taking place and leading to larger surpluses being available for export, it is to be expected that greatly increased trade and commercial relations and social intercourse with countries lying to the north and west of Malawi will follow.

The early historical connections of Malawi with Central and East Africa are thus likely to be reaffirmed and its position as a cross-roads between separate cultural and economic areas re-emphasized.

FOOTNOTES

1 J. G. Pike and G. T. Rimmington, *Malawi: A Geographical Study* (London, 1965), 17.

2 Swanzie Agnew and M. Stubbs, eds *Malawi in Maps* (to be published by the University of London Press Ltd, 1971).

3 B. Fagan, 'Early trade and raw materials in South Central Africa', *J. Afr. Hist.*, 10 (1) 1969, 1–13. Fagan discusses the importance of the salt trade of Ivuna on Lake Rukwa which has continued from at least the period of the Iron Age villages (A.D. 1215 ± 100 to A.D. 1410 ± 100) to the present day. For salt making near Lake Chilwa see E. Gray, 'Notes on the salt-making industry of the Nyanja people near Lake Chilwa', *S. Afr. J. Sci.*, 41, 1945, 459; and G. Chikwapulo in *The Malawian Geographer*, (2), 1969.

4 K. R. Robinson, 'A preliminary report on the recent archaeology of Ngonde, Northern Malawi', *J. Afr. Hist.*, 7, (2) 1966, 169–88.

5 Monica Wilson, 'Changes in social structure in Southern Africa: the relevance of kinship studies to the historian', in *African Societies in Southern Africa*, ed. L. Thompson (London, 1969), 71–86.

6 P. R. Gould, 'Spatial Diffusion', *Association of American Geographers, Resource Paper No. 4* (Washington, 1969).

7 Gould, 'Spatial Diffusion'.

8 J. M. Schoffeleers, 'M'bona the guardian-spirit of the Mang'anja'. Unpublished B. Litt. thesis of the University of Oxford, 1966, 54.

9 The marshes or *dambos* of the headwaters in the Congo-Zambezi divide

and between the Luangwa river and Lake Malawi drainage systems are one of the most remarkable features in Africa and are of great ecological importance.

10 J. M. Schoffeleers, 'M'bona', op. cit.

11 The location of such capitals and important sites as Sanga on Lake Kisale in the Lualaba valley, Kazembe's capital of the Bemba Kingdom on the Luapula river, the M'bona shrine in the Lower Shire valley, and the Portuguese station at Tete on the Zambezi illustrates the strength and stability derived from riverine situations.

12 P. R. Gould, 'Spatial Diffusion', op. cit.

13 A. Mhango, 'The History of the Henga People', History Seminar Paper, 1969–70, Chancellor College, University of Malawi, 4.

14 P. R. Gould, 'Spatial Diffusion', op. cit.

15 G. Bond, *Past Climates in Central Africa*, Inaugural Lecture, University College of Rhodesia and Nyasaland (London, 1962), 1–34.

16 E. Van Zinderen Bakker, 'Pollen analysis and its contribution to the palaeontology of the Quaternary in Southern Africa', *Ecology in South Africa*, ed. D. H. S. Davis (The Hague, 1964), 24–34.

17 H. B. S. Cooke, 'The Pleistocene environment in Southern Africa', *Ecology in South Africa*, ed. D. H. S. Davis (The Hague, 1964), 1–23.

18 R. Summers, 'Environment and Culture in Southern Rhodesia', Proceedings American Philosophical Society, Vol. 104, No. 3 (1960), pp. 267–291.

19 J. P. Glasgow, *The Distribution and Abundance of Tsetse* (London, 1963), 1.

20 G. P. Murdock, 'Staple Subsistence Crops of Africa', *The Geographical Review* (1960), 523–40.

21 G. Kay, *A Social Geography of Zambia* (London, 1965), p. 55.

22 M. P. Miracle, 'The Introduction and Spread of Maize in Africa', *J. Afr. Hist.* 6 (1) 1965, 39–55.

23 J. Hutchinson, 'Land and Human Population' *The Listener*, (September 1966), pp. 303–11.

24 J. W. B. Perry, 'The Evolution of the Transport Network of Malawi'. Unpublished B. Litt. thesis, University of Oxford, 1967, 19.

4 The Iron Age in Malawi: A brief account of recent work

K. R. Robinson

K. R. Robinson

I INTRODUCTION

The intention of this paper is to state as clearly and briefly as possible the results of Iron Age investigations undertaken in Malawi during the last five years.[1]

The main areas covered are as follows:

1 *Northern Region*

   (a) An area based on Karonga with the Songwe river and Florence Bay (Chitimba) as the northern and southern limits.
   (b) Livingstonia and the Nyika.
   (c) The Rumpi district, including Lake Kazuni on the south Rukuru.

2 *Southern Region*

   (a) The Cape Maclear peninsula and Fort Johnston.
   (b) The Bwanje river valley including the escarpment to the west of it.

   It will be apparent that there is a gap of some 300 km between the northern and southern fields which requires to be investigated. In addition, as yet no work has been done south of a line drawn from Fort Johnston to Ncheu. In short, most of the investigations have been in the vicinity of Lake Malawi.

   Archaeological investigation may be said to consist of three phases. First, reconnaissance and discovery of sites, second, the testing of selected sites for stratigraphy, diagnostic finds such as pottery and charcoal for dating, and, finally, more extensive excavation where this is considered justifiable. In Malawi the third phase has not yet been attempted as far as the Iron Age is concerned, but a beginning has been made with the first and second phases.

Erosion

Widespread sheet erosion and gullying has removed nearly all trace of occupation deposit in some areas, leaving quantities of pottery of varying date lying on a natural denuded surface. Much of the erosion is almost certainly due to the practice of hoe cultivation along streams and rivers over a considerable period.

II SUMMARY OF SITES AND THE ARCHAEOLOGICAL EVIDENCE EARLY IRON AGE (NORTHERN REGION)

Mwavarambo, Karonga District

Pottery which has affinities with known Early Iron Age ware was first recovered in lands ridged for cassava near Mwavarambo village on the Lufilya river north of Karonga.[2] Unfortunately no good undisturbed site was located anywhere in the area. (Fig. 4.1).

The fabric of Mwavarambo ware tends to be thick in proportion to the size of the vessel. A sooty black to reddish finish is usual but graphite burnish sometimes occurs on bowls.

The pots (Fig. 4.2a, b, f) are usually globular with rather wide everted rims which are frequently undecorated, but in some instances there is a thickened rim-band, and this is sometimes decorated with incised hatching or more rarely comb stamping. Lips may be notched or nicked, but no instances of fluted, channelled or bevelled lips were recovered on either pots or bowls. Decoration below the rim or on the shoulder usually consists of two or three grooves or channels running round the vessel. These may be combined with simple motifs formed by point impressions, comb stamping or incision. Incised cross-hatching also occurs. The bowls tend to be hemispherical or deep with in-turned rims some of which are decorated with comb stamping or incised motifs.

No finds other than pottery were recovered, and no conventional excavation was possible.

The affinities of this pottery appear to lie with the Early Iron Age Complex to the north in Tanzania and south-east Kenya, and possibly to some extent with Kalambo, but the occasional presence of thickened and decorated rim-bands is reminiscent of the Gokomere pottery tradition in Rhodesia and Zambia.

Charcoal samples obtained at a depth of twenty to thirty-six cm have been dated A.D. 1065 ± 80 (U.C.L.A.—1289) and 1295 ± 80 (U.C.L.A.—1242). These dates may indicate a late survival for this type of ware, but in view of the disturbed conditions at the site, and the presence of a Later Iron Age occupation level in the area, it is thought that the dates may not apply to the Mwavarambo ware.

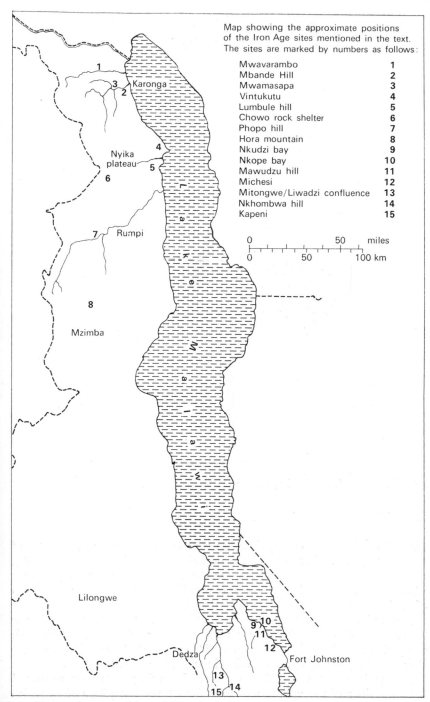

Map showing the approximate positions of the Iron Age sites mentioned in the text. The sites are marked by numbers as follows:

Mwavarambo	1
Mbande Hill	2
Mwamasapa	3
Vintukutu	4
Lumbule hill	5
Chowo rock shelter	6
Phopo hill	7
Hora mountain	8
Nkudzi bay	9
Nkope bay	10
Mawudzu hill	11
Michesi	12
Mitongwe/Liwadzi confluence	13
Nkhombwa hill	14
Kapeni	15

4.1 Approximate position of Iron Age sites

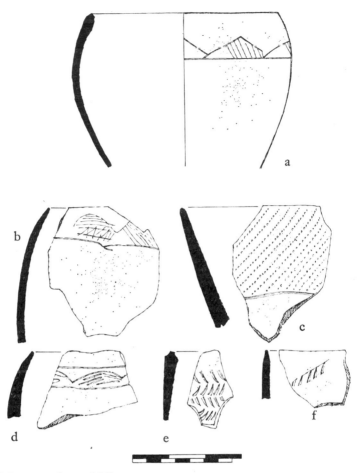

4.2   Mwavarambo and Nkope ware

Phopo Hill: Lake Kazuni

Phopo Hill lies about twenty-four km west of the administrative centre of
Rumpi (Fig. 4.1). Near the outlet from Lake Kazuni there is a road bridge
crossing the south Rukuru river, and in the river bed near this bridge sherds
which appeared to be of early type were noted in 1967.[3] Eventually their place
of origin was traced to some 300 m further down stream at a point where the
high river bank has been much eroded, and midden material exposed in the
upper levels of the bank. At this point erosion gullies have cut through
occupation deposits which cover much of the gently sloping land between the
river and Phopo Hill, an area varying in width from 100 to 200 m.

   Pottery, iron slag, tuyere fragments and bone fragments were recovered
from the sides of the gullies, and later from three test pits, one of which

reached the depth of three m. Fragments of burnt daga (mud) showed the imprints of sticks set close together and suggesting the remains of circular dwellings constructed of wood and daga.

Iron smelting was an important activity at Phopo as shown by the large slag heaps and the presence of iron at depth. Faunal remains include fish and game animals.

The pottery closely resembles Mwavarambo ware, both with regard to the vessel forms and decoration. Channelled decoration appears to have been better executed on the Phopo pottery than on that from Mwavarambo, but the quantity of material from the latter site available for comparison is distinctly limited. Lips are sometimes grooved or channelled.

Shell disc beads averaging five mm in diameter occurred throughout the deposits. There were no glass beads.

Charcoal samples obtained from the test pits have given the following radiocarbon dates:

Test 1, 60 cm depth   A.D. 295 ± 95 (SR-128)
Test 2, 30–45 cm depth   A.D. 505 ± 120 (SR-161)
Test 3, 50–66 cm depth   A.D. 205 ± 170 (SR-148)

These dates clearly indicate an occupation of the site during the third century A.D.

Lumbule Hill: Livingstonia

Lumbule Hill is located approximately 3 km north of the Manchewe Falls, Livingstonia (Fig. 4.1). The country is hilly and well watered.

Pottery[4] similar to that from Phopo was recovered at the depth of from 30–60 cm below the surface. The top 20 cm of deposit contained later pottery which is probably of early Phoka origin.

A radiocarbon date has been obtained from charcoal contained in a small pit sunk into natural bedrock and associated with typical Phopo Hill ware as follows:

Test 1, 60–90 cm depth (in pit)   A.D. 565 ± 100 (SR-147).

There was evidence of iron and smelting. No beads were recovered.

Nyika

Sherds of Phopo/Mwavarambo type were recovered from a rock shelter near Chowo Rock (Fig. 4.1) at a height of about 2,000 m above sea level, and suggests the possibility that there may be a connection between this Early Iron Age pottery and the ancient iron workings which exist in the area.[5]

Mwavarambo, Phopo, Lumbule and the Chowo Rock shelter are at present the only known Early Iron Age sites in the northern region of Malawi, but there are almost certainly many others. The pottery from all four sites appears to be very closely related.

Early Iron Age pottery from northern Malawi (Mwavarambo/Phopo Hill wares) appears to have its closest affinities with material to the north of it, namely the Early Iron Age pottery complex of Uganda and Kenya. It does not seem to be closely related to Zambian material west of the Luangwa valley, and the chevron in false relief is not included among the decorative motifs. On the other hand it contains some elements which are reminiscent of the Gokomere pottery tradition of Rhodesia and Southern Zambia.

Vintukutu, Deep Bay (Chilumba)

This site is situated on the edge of the eroded scarp which runs more or less parallel with the lake. Sherds occurred at a depth of 20–25 cm below the surface.

The amount of pottery recovered was small because of the limited size of the excavation. The fabric is thin throughout. Most of the sherds represent bowls, the majority of which are deep with slightly in-turned rims. Two sherds belong to carinated bowls. The pots were also sometimes carinated, others were simple shouldered pots. The usual methods of decoration was by incision. Cross-hatched narrow bands or triangles on the shoulder or below the rim are common, but comb stamping is also represented, in one instance combined with raised nicked ribs. There is also a single example of a grooved curvilinear pattern.

This pottery has been listed among the Mwamasapa variants.[6] There is, however, no great resemblance to Mwamasapa ware, on the other hand it is closer to the latter than to the Mwavarambo or Phopo Hill wares.

Charcoal associated with the sherds has been dated as follows:

A.D. 850 ± 80 (U.C.L.A.—1299)

This date includes the site within our arbitrary upper limit for the Early Iron Age, namely, A.D. 1000.

The date for this site as yet stands alone and must, therefore, be regarded with caution. One of the most striking differences between Vintukutu ware and known Early Iron Age wares is the comparative thinness of fabric in the former. This may mark the introduction of a new pottery fashion into Malawi which continued in one form or another up to recent times.

The affinities of Vintukutu ware are at present uncertain, but there appears to be some resemblance to Kapeni ware in the south.

III EARLY IRON AGE (SOUTHERN REGION)

Nkope Bay: Cape Maclear

The Early Iron Age site at Nkope (Fig. 4.1) covers a considerable area along the edge of Lake Malawi, extending inland as far as the base of Nkope Hill, a distance of some 300 m. Sherds were first noticed eroding out of the bank leading down to the lake shore. The early occupation level is completely sealed below up to sixty cm of deposit containing evidence of later occupation. A total of nine test pits were dug.

Worked iron and evidence of iron smelting was well represented, and copper was also known to the early Iron Age inhabitants.

Faunal remains[7] indicate that hunting and fishing were important activities. The soft shelled turtle was consumed in fair quantities.

The main importance of this site lies in the occupation deposit which contains three definite occupation levels each marked by a distinctive type of pottery, which, taken in the order of their deposition, have been named Nkope, Mawudzu and Nkudzi ware respectively.

Nkope ware[8] has much in common with the Early Iron Age pottery of northern Malawi, but there are some differences to be noted between the northern and southern material as might be expected in view of the distance between them of about 300 km. The wide un-thickened and usually un-decorated type of pot rim, common in the Mwavarambo/Phopo pottery, is rare at Nkope where rims tend to be of the narrow thickened variety, usually decorated, and in this they resemble the Gokomere tradition in Rhodesia (Fig. 4.2, c, d, e, g, h, i).

In the bowls there are also differences. In many of the Nkope bowls, for instance, the in-turned type of rim is much accentuated and usually decorated with fluting. (Fig. 4.2,i). This type of bowl rim closely resembles material described from Kwale in south-east Kenya.[9]

It is important, however, to bear in mind the fact that the Nkope bowls which resemble those from Kwale are simply developed examples of a type of bowl already present at both Mwavarambo and Phopo in the north, and also the fact that pottery similar to Kwale ware has been found in central Tanzania.[10] Therefore a common origin appears more likely than any direct links between the Nkope and Kwale material. In other bowls the rim is thickened and flattened in a manner reminiscent of Ziwa ware from Inyanga, Rhodesia.[11] Apart from these details vessel forms vary remarkably little from north to south.

With regard to decoration, grooving or channelling on the lip of pots is a feature occurring throughout all the material. It is also true to say that comb stamped decoration on the pot rims is more frequent in the Nkope pottery than further north.

At Nkope the presence of microlithic material associated with sherds at the lowest level strongly suggests that the site was occupied by Later Stone Age hunters before the arrival of the makers of Nkope ware. It is also possible that the Stone Age people remained in the vicinity for some time after this event.

Charcoal samples have been dated as follows:

Test 3, 60–80 cm   A.D. 775 ± 100 (SR-175)
Test 5, 50–70 cm   A.D. 360 ± 120 (SR-174)

Test pits dug immediately south of Nkopola Hill (Fig. 4.1) within the fenced area occupied by the M.A.L.D.E.C.O. Fisheries clearly proved a pottery sequence similar to that described at Nkope.

Nkope ware has also been noted at at least seven other sites in the Cape Maclear peninsula, while a couple of sherds were picked up well inland from the bed of the Lisangadzi river near Mtoli village. Sherds have also been found on the eastern shore of the lake at Moto village, almost opposite to Michesi (Fig. 4.1). All these sites suggest an economy similar to that which was practised at Nkope.

The Bwanje River Area and the Western Escarpment

In 1969 it was decided to investigate the upper Bwanje river valley centred on Sharpevale, and including the escarpment to the west of the river. This area is about fifty km south-west of Nkope.

Sheet erosion and gullying made it difficult to find suitable occupation deposits, but for the same reasons pottery of all periods was comparatively easy to find. The main Early Iron Age sites are shown in Fig. 4.1. Most of them are located in the low country at about the 150 m level, as a rule on the upper reaches of a river not far from the point where it emerges from the foothills of the escarpment. Such a situation ensured a permanent supply of running water and fertile silty soil.

The site at the Mitongwe/Liwadzi confluence was excavated. There was an occupation deposit approximately one m in thickness containing pottery, bone, iron and charcoal. The bone is difficult to identify in detail because of its fragmentary nature, but most of it represents large game animals. The pottery appears to be identical with that from the lower levels at Nkope, but the finer types of bowls with in-turned and fluted rims may be absent.[12] The overall impression gained is that the Mitongwe pottery is intended for hard usage, and less for ceremonial purposes than the Nkope material.

Nkope ware extends well west of the peninsula as far as the plateau in the vicinity of Kambironjo mountain, but the most permanent sites appear to have been in the low country at the foot of the escarpment, and on the lake shore. It must be emphasized, however, that research over a wider area, including Lilongwe and the central region as a whole, may produce evidence which will modify this picture to some extent.

A charcoal sample from the Mitongwe/Liwadzi site has been dated as follows:

Test 2, 135 cm depth   A.D. 370 ± 60 (SR-209)

Economy and Trade in the Early Iron Age of Malawi

Until 1970 no evidence of coastal trade such as the presence of glass beads or other imports had been recovered from any Early Iron Age site in Malawi.

In July 1970, however, a single blue glass bead and half a cowrie shell were taken from well sealed deposits containing pottery of Nkope type during excavations at Matope on the upper Shire (the evidence is as yet unpublished). These finds are not unexpected in view of similar imports recovered at Mabveni and other early sites in Rhodesia.

No direct evidence of agriculture in the form of seed has been recovered, but grindstone fragments, iron hoe fragments and a preference for good fertile soil are indirect evidence that cultivation by hoe was practised.

So far there is no definite evidence of domestic stock such as sheep or cattle.[13]

The evidence for iron smelting and working is very strong, and it is probable that large furnaces were constructed. Copper may also have been smelted.

Hunting and fishing were major pursuits, and the emphasis appears to have been on whichever form of game or fish was most easily killed.

Lake or river-side sites were preferred, but some occupation may have occurred on the higher ground such as the Nyika and near Kambironjo mountain in the south, in view of isolated finds of pottery.

IV   LATER IRON AGE (NORTHERN REGION)

Mwamasapa: Karonga District

Mwamasapa village is located about fifteen km west of Karonga on the south bank of the north Rukuru river. The evidence[14] from this site, and also from the related site at Mwenepera, suggests that the type of dwelling represented by the buried remains of wood and daga structures was probably a conical wooden framework covered with daga and perhaps grass. Such dwellings are still known to the Phoka of the Nyika, and to the Nyiha of southern Tanzania.

Pottery, iron, glass beads and charred seeds of sorghum were recovered from below the hut remains at a depth of sixty cm below the surface.

The beads resemble some of those which have been recovered from Leopard's Kopje, phase 2 sites in Rhodesia, c. eighth to ninth century.[15]

The pottery[16] is entirely different from any of the Early Iron Age wares. The fabric is thin, the pot forms are mainly of gourd-shaped or necked vessels with poorly defined shoulders, and with no eversion or thickening of the rim. Decoration is almost entirely confined to rounded impressions[17] placed close together, probably applied by the use of some form of comb. Bands of these impressions were formed on the necks of pots and below the rims of bowls; the lower edge was usually scalloped and edged by grooving. The lip is also frequently decorated (Fig. 4.3a–d).

Associated with the typical Mwamasapa ware are sherds and pot fragments which are believed to be of Kisi origin. Both the clay and finish strongly support the view that the present day Kisi custom of bringing pottery across the lake from their home below the Livingstone mountains to Ngonde for

57

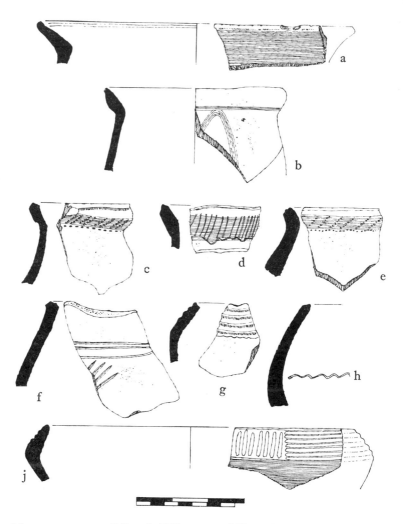

4.3 Mwamasapa ware, Mbande Hill ware and Kapeni ware

exchange for grain may be of ancient origin.

Radiocarbon dates for charcoal samples obtained from below hut daga fragments are as follows:

Test 2, 46–60 cm   A.D. 1090 ± 80 (U.C.L.A.—1239)
Test 5, 46–60 cm   A.D. 1190 ± 80 (U.C.L.A.—1243)

A sample from Mwenepera:

Square A, 30–36 cm   A.D. 1240 ± 80 (U.C.L.A.—1244)

An excavation, located on the south bank of the north Rukuru river, north-east of the Court House, exposed thirty cm of occupation deposit which contained pottery, iron, slag, daga lumps and charcoal. There was natural sterile earth below thirty cm.

The pottery,[18] although showing some similarity to Mwamasapa ware, possesses features absent in the latter material. These include a pot with a flared neck and a carinated shoulder, a slightly thickened and cross-hatched rim sherd, and a more geometric element in the decoration.

Charcoal recovered from this deposit has been dated as follows:

Test A, 15–30 cm   A.D. 1450 $\pm$ 80 or 1600 (U.C.L.A.—1245)

The earlier date appears more likely in view of the fact that the adjoining area near the Court House shows evidence of occupation by the makers of Mbande Hill ware.

An important site containing similar pottery to that of Mbande Court is located at Mulinda's village near Mwavarambo, and there are also several others.

Mwamasapa ware, although dated slightly later than Vintukutu ware, may in fact be partially contemporaneous with it. Although the two types of pottery differ with regard to vessel forms and method of decoration, there is an overall similarity due to the mutual preference for a thin-walled vessel with no thickening of the rim, features which separate both types of ware from the Mwavarambo/Phopo pottery tradition. Some Mwamasapa variants, such as the material from Mbande Court, may perhaps represent some mixing of Vintukutu and Mwamasapa traditions, and the comparatively late date for Mbande Court (1450 $\pm$ 80) allows sufficient time for this to have occurred.

Pottery has been described which was associated with hut remains and a grave of a known Phoka ancestor at Kafyenyengo village, Livingstonia.[19] The sherds bear a general resemblance to both Mwamasapa and Vintukutu material, and may be mixed. Very obviously this is an area which requires further investigation.

Pottery from the upper levels of a rock shelter near Chowo Rock on the Nyika[20] may be related to some of the Kafyenyengo pottery. Associated glass beads suggest a late eighteenth or early nineteenth century date.

An excavation in a rock shelter on Hora Mountain in the Mzimba district produced a number of sherds which were mixed with white quartz artifacts of Later Stone Age type below twenty cm. At forty cm sherds ceased and there were quartz artifacts only. A radiocarbon date of B.C. 14, 730 $\pm$ 180 (SR-145) was obtained for charcoal collected from the base of the Iron Age deposit, this date is thought to refer to the Stone Age occupation levels which underlay the pottery horizon, and which may be a form of Later Middle Stone Age.

The bulk of the pottery is probably of early Tumbuka origin, but there are three small sherds from the lower levels which are perhaps Early Iron Age. More work is required in order to connect this material with other pottery occurrences.

This hill is about thirteen km west of Karonga on the south bank of the north Rukuru, and near Mpata Gap (Fig. 4.1). Mbande Hill is said to have been first occupied by an elephant-hunting Fipa known as Simbobwe who came from the north. This man and his followers were driven out by the first of the Ngonde chiefs whose dynastic title is *Kyungu*. This line of chiefs had its origin in the Kinga country at the north-eastern end of Lake Malawi. The early Kyungus lived with their wives inside an enclosure on the hill summit. Their power to begin with was mainly of a spiritual nature, an important aspect of which was rain-making.[21]

Large fragments of ceremonial bowls and other vessels were recovered from the hill summit, on the surface or buried below humus.[22]

A trench dug adjacent to an earthwork on the summit exposed 60 cm of midden deposit below which was natural pebbly earth. The finds include pottery, glass beads, worked iron and copper, shell and bone fragments. A piece of blue and white porcelain resembling examples from Rhodesian ruins such as Khami dated c.1573–1619, was recovered from an eroded slope in the vicinity.

The glass beads closely resemble beads from the later deposits at Zimbabwe.

The pottery[23] consists for the most part of hemispherical to sub-spherical pots and bowls. As a rule the outside of the vessel is scored all over with lines scratched or grooved into the damp clay, and in some instances the inside has been treated in a similar manner. Other forms of decoration are confined to incised cross-hatching, point impressions and moulded nipples or bosses, and there is one example of a pierced lug (Fig. 4.3e, f).

All this material appears to have strong affinities with pottery made by the Kinga and Kisi, in fact some of it may have been imported as the clay resembles in appearance that in known Kisi wares.

Mbande Hill ware is distinctive and easily recognized in the field. It invariably overlies deposits containing Mwamasapa ware or variants when these are present. In short, it was intrusive into an area where pottery of Vintukutu/Mwamasapa traditions were already established. It is safe, therefore, to attribute the latter wares to the ancestors of groups found by the first Kyungu, among whom were probably Fipa, Nyika and other peoples of northern origin.

There are numerous sites in the Karonga district which contain typical Mbande Hill ware; they occur along the rivers and flank the lake shore and as a rule they are marked by the presence of large baobab trees.

Charcoal samples from the trench dug on Mbande Hill summit have been dated as follows:

Test 1, A. 46–60 cm   A.D. 1410 ± 80 (U.C.L.A.—1236)
Test 1, A. 0–30 cm   A.D. 1680 or 1500 ± 80 (U.C.L.A.—1246)

Kapeni Hill, Nyanyangu River

This site is located on the north bank of the Nyanyangu river, a tributary of the Bwanje, and almost opposite Kapeni Hill (Fig. 4.1).

The excavation of the remains of a pole and daga structure produced a quantity of pottery, some of it in large fragments and much of it extremely weathered.[24] With the exception of iron slag and tuyere fragments, sherds were the only finds. There was a very limited amount of charcoal from below the daga and pottery.

The clay is usually full of quartz grit, but some of the vessels show evidence of superior finish, particularly the bowls which may be burnished with graphite or ochre. The pots are mainly globular with short vertical, concave or flared necks, but there are also carinated pots. Bowls are usually deep with sharply in-turned rims forming a carination near the mouth of the vessel. There are also shallower bowls which are carinated at their greatest diameter. Open-mouthed hemispherical bowls are also represented.

The decoration is frequently bold, but some of the vessels demonstrate considerable neatness and care. Incision, grooving and point impressions are the usual methods of decoration. Rims are often nicked. Moulded bosses and ring bases are also features (Fig. 4.3g–j).

Two radiocarbon dates have been received recently for this pottery:

Kapeni Hill site, test 3: 1235 ± 75 (SR-221)

Nkhombwa Hill site, test 1: 1375 ± 75 (SR-220)

These dates confirm the archaeological evidence which suggests the period A.D. 1000–1400. There would appear to be some affinity between Kapeni pottery and that from the northern Early Iron Age sites such as Phopo Hill, and Mwavarambo. There are also possible affinities with early Natal coastal pottery, a matter which requires further investigation.

Kapeni ware has also been found at a number of other places in the Bwanje river area, but the only other definite occupation site besides Kapeni as yet recorded is at Nkhombwa Hill within the confluence of the Nyanyangu and Bwanje rivers.

Mawudzu Hill: Cape Maclear

This site is located on the eastern side of the Cape Maclear peninsula, some thirty km north of Fort Johnston (Fig. 4.1).

Excavations produced evidence of only one occupation period excluding surface material attributable to the present day inhabitants and their immediate forbears.[25]

The occupation deposit proved to have a maximum depth of one m. It contained pottery, bone, shell charcoal and a few stone pounders. Glass beads, iron and copper were recovered from a shallow deposit on the hill summit.

With regard to the pottery,[26] the fabric of the vessels is usually rather thin and contains coarse grits. The vessel forms are simple, pots may be spherical with a constricted mouth, shouldered with a conical or concave neck, or open mouthed and more or less U-shaped. The latter may be large, measuring up to fifty cm in height by forty cm across the mouth. Bases may be rounded or flattened. Decoration is usually confined to the neck or shoulder. Impressed and incised chevrons or scallops are common motifs. A dentate pattern in false relief is also known. Decoration frequently occurs to a limited extent on the inside of bowls (Fig. 4.4a–f).

The glass beads are mainly Indian red cylinders.

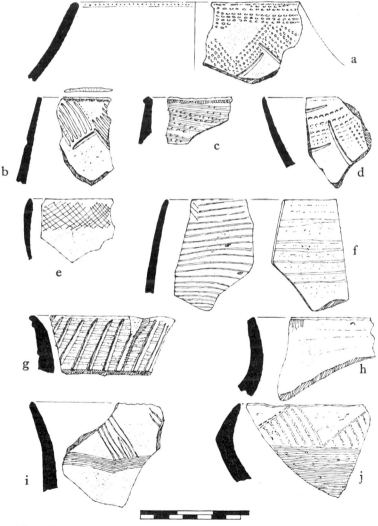

4.4   Mawudzu ware

A charcoal sample from Mawudzu Hill has been dated as follows:

Test 1, 40–50 cm   A.D. 1480 ± 95 (SR-178)

Identical material was recovered from above the Early Iron Age levels at Nkope and Michesi. In addition, Mawudzu ware was collected from numerous sites all over the Cape Maclear peninsula, the eastern shore of Lake Malawi and the western shore of Lake Malombe.

Mawuduzi Variants

Investigations in 1969, centred on Mitongwe Estate near Sharpevale, has shown that pottery which is basically similar to the Mawudzu Hill material is widespread in the area, some fifty km south-west of Mawudzu Hill.[27] It occurs in the Bwanje valley, in the foothills of the escarpment, and as far west as the Livulezi river which marks the limit of our reconnaissance.

While Mawudzu ware shows some typological affinities with the northern Later Iron Age wares, as might be expected there are considerable differences between the northern and southern material. Some of these may be due to the influence of the Kapeni pot makers, for instance the pedestal based pot or bowl is common to both Kapeni and Mawudzu pottery.

At this stage all that can be concluded with reasonable certainty is that Mawudzu ware belongs to the period of Maravi dominance, and is to be associated with Nyanja groups who were living at the southern end of the lake.

VI RECENT IRON AGE (ALL AREAS)

In the Karonga district it appears that pottery similar to Mbande Hill ware was in general use by the Ngonde until comparatively recent times. Today, however, Henga, Wemba and Mambwe influences seem to predominate. Kisi pots from across the lake may also be found at nearly every dwelling.

Further south in the Rumpi district, Livingstonia and on the Nyika modern Tumbuka fashions are usual.[28] The Phoka near Manchewe Falls, Livingstonia, make pots which differ slightly in form from those made by the Tumbuka, but the decoration is very similar in both types of pottery. A striking feature in modern Tumbuka pots is the extreme form of everted rim. Pottery believed to be of old Tumbuka manufacture does not show this feature.[29]

The type of pottery excavated at Nkudzi Bay[30] occurs all over the Cape Maclear peninsula, but mainly on the lake. Sites containing this Nkudzi ware also extend to the Bwanje river valley, the escarpment and the plateau. These latter sites are said to have been occupied by the Wisa (Bisa) who were also living on the lake together with Nyanja people early in the nineteenth century.[31] Inskeep[32] has remarked on resemblances between the Nkudzi Bay pottery and Venda pottery. There are also some points in common between some of the

Nkudzi vessels and the polychrome ware from Khami Ruins in south-western Rhodesia.[33]

In the Cape Maclear/Fort Johnston areas modern pottery has adopted Yao fashions to a large extent,[04] and this also applies to some extent to the Bwanje valley and adjacent areas, except that in the latter there is also Nguni influence. Some of the early Ngoni sites contain pots scored all over the outside and sometimes in the inside, rather like the early Ngonde pottery from Mbande Hill. Possibly this is evidence of contact between the Maseko Ngoni and northern pot makers during the former's stay in the north during the early part of the nineteenth century.

That this seems likely is supported by a recent article by G. T. Nurse[35] in which contacts between the Maseko Ngoni and the Matengo of the Songea area of southern Tanzania are mentioned. This event, or a similar one, could explain the presence of a northern trait so far south.

Migration and/or Diffusion: Tentative Deductions

As previously stated,[36] the available evidence may indicate that some of the first Early Iron Age immigrants to enter Malawi did so from the north, perhaps by way of the Songwe valley. Groups may have travelled down both sides of Lake Malawi. The possibility that the lake itself was used by at least some of the immigrants seems worth considering. Although there is as yet no direct evidence that this did happen, it was an obvious choice for people who may already have been used to lakes and rivers. Evidence from Nkope shows that the inhabitants were well able to exploit the lake for food which would have been difficult without canoes.

An important question would appear to be: does the increase in Gokomere characteristics in the southern material (Nkope ware) indicate a development within the pottery industry as time went on and the people migrated further south, or does it imply contact with a different but perhaps related group of people already making their pottery in the Gokomere tradition?

No work has yet been done along the lower Shire and the Zambezi valley east of Zumbo, but in view of the Dambwa sites higher up the Zambezi which contain wares closely related to Gokomere[37] and the presence of Ziwa ware in the north-eastern part of Rhodesia, it would not be surprising if Gokomere variants are eventually found in the lower Zambezi valley.

To the east of Lake Malawi the position is unknown except for the fact that Nkope ware exists on the eastern shore of the lake. The country between the lake and the eastern seaboard may prove to be of vital importance in the understanding of the Early Iron Age of Malawi.

An origin west of Lake Tanganyika has been suggested for the Early Iron Age immigrants into Zambia,[38] and attention has been drawn to the fact that in Zambia regional differentiation in the Early Iron Age pottery occurs from the earliest period, the conclusion being that a number of different, but perhaps related, groups may have arrived in the country over a period of several centuries. In Malawi it would appear that an area east of Luangwa valley, and centred on Lake Malawi, was occupied during the first few centuries A.D. by

64

people who, although perhaps related to contemporaneous groups in Zambia, may have become divided from them by geographical and ecological factors.

Much has been written on the origin and diffusion of the Early Iron Age of Central, East and Southern Africa as represented by the dimple-based and channelled wares.[39] It is evident, however, that the archaeological evidence from West Africa and other vital areas is still scanty and therefore it appears advisable to keep an open mind on this question.

With regard to central and southern Africa of which Malawi forms a part, our main concern at present is how the various Early and Later Iron Age groups arrived in their respective geographical areas, and when. This is a particularly tricky problem in view of the uniformity displayed by the radio-carbon dates for all the areas which include the Congo, Uganda, Kenya, Tanzania, Malawi, Zambia and Rhodesia.

A northern origin for Mwamasapa ware has also been suggested. Since first expressing this view[40] pottery has been illustrated from Ivuna in southern Tanzania.[41] This material, although certainly not identical with any of the Later Iron Age pottery from Malawi, does possess some features in common with both the Mwamasapa ware and variants, and the later wares from Living-stonia and Chowo rock shelter on the Nyika.[42]

Again, the archaeological evidence does not yet warrant any assumptions with regard to possible movements of the Kapeni and Mawudzu pot makers.

With regard to Nkudzi ware, Bisa influence from the northwest suggests a Luba/Lunda origin.

An attempt has been made to distinguish industries and phases in the Iron Age of northern Malawi[43] but it is probable that revision will become neces-sary as more evidence accumulates. So far as the southern lake area is concerned, in my opinion it would be premature to venture on any form of classification at present, and this should remain the position until the central and southern areas of the country have received thorough investigation. A provisional chronological chart is given in the table below.

Systematic work by ethnologists and ethno-historians is required in order to obtain a full understanding of the Later Iron Age period in Malawi.

	A Northern Malawi	B Nyika and Livingstonia	C South Rukuru at Lake Kazuni	D Southern end of Lake Malawi	Possible affinities with material elsewhere
Recent	Ngonde	Tumbuka/Phoka	Ngoni	Ngoni Yao Nkudzi	{Luba-Lunda (D) {Venda
	Mbande Hill 1680 ± 80				
Later Iron	Mbande Court 1450 ± 80 Mbande Hill 1410 ± 80			Mawudzu 1480 ± 95 {Nkhombwa 1375 ± 75 {Kapeni 1235 ± 75	{Leopards Kopje {Mapungubwe M$_2$ (D) {Phopo Hill {?Natal coastal (D)
Age	?Mwavarambo 1065 ± 80 Mwamasapa 1190 ± 80 Mwamasapa 1090 ± 80	Mwamasapa Variants	Mwamasapa Variants		
Early Iron		Vintukutu 850 ± 80 Lumbule 565 ± 100	Phopo 505 ± 120 Phopo 295 ± 95 Phopo 205 ± 170	Nkope 775 ± 100 Mitongwe 370 ± 60 Nkope 360 ± 120	{Gokomere {Kwale, south-east Kenya (D)
Age	?Mwavarambo				

Tentative chronology based on the known radiocarbon dates, and on the archaeological evidence. All dates are A.D.

1 Reference is made in the text to published reports in which the excavations have been described, and the pottery fully illustrated. The illustrations in this report are only intended to give the reader a very general idea of the material mentioned.

2 Robinson, K. R. (1966) 'A preliminary report on the recent archaeology of Ngonde, northern Malawi', *J. Afr. Hist.* **7** (2), 185, Figs 2 and 3.

3 Robinson, K. R. and Sandelowsky, B. H. (1968) 'The Iron Age of northern Malawi: recent work', *Azania*, **3**, Figs 12–14.

4 Ibid., Fig. 14, nos. 1–3.

5 Ibid., 27.

6 Robinson and Sandelowsky (1968) op. cit., 25.

7 Speed, E. (1970) 'Report on the Nkope faunal remains', in Robinson, K. R. (1970) *The Iron Age of the Southern Lake Area of Malawi: recent work*. Government of Malawi, Department of Antiquities.

8 Robinson (1970) op. cit., Figs. 11–16.

9 Soper, R. (1967) 'Kwale: an early Iron Age site in South-eastern Kenya', *Azania*, **2**.

10 Smolla, G. (1957) 'Prähistorische Keramic aus Ostafrika', *Tribus*. n.f. Band 6, 1956, pp. 35–64.
Pottery said to resemble the Sandaweland material described by Smolla has been discovered recently in the Uvinza area of Tanzania, in the lowest levels at salt-working sites which have been dated A.D. 420–160 (N—463) and A.D. 590 ± 200 (N—465) (J. E. G. Sutton and A. Roberts, 'Uvinza and its salt industry'. *Azania* 3, 1969, 45–86 and D. W. Phillipson, 'Notes on the later prehistoric radiocarbon chronology of eastern and southern Africa'. *J. Afr. Hist.*, **1**, 1970, 1–15). Uvinza is located about 50 km east of Lake Tanganyika near Ujiji.

11 Summers, R. (1958) *Inyanga*, C.U.P.

12 Robinson (1970) op. cit.

13 Fragmentary Bovid remains were recovered from Test 1, Phopo Hill excavations, firm identification was not possible and there is no evidence to prove that domestic cattle are represented (unpublished report 'Faunal remains from Phopo Hill' by C. K. Brain and E. A. Speed. I am indebted

to Mrs B. H. Pendleton (née Sandelowsky) for this piece of information).

14 Robinson (1966) op. cit.

15 Ibid., 182.

16 Ibid., 179, Figs 4–6.

17 In some instances it is possible that the seeds of millet or sorghum have been impressed into the damp clay to produce these impressions.

18 Robinson (1966) op. cit., 184–5 and Fig. 6, nos. 37–9.

19 Robinson and Sandelowsky (1968) op. cit., 16–19, nos. 5–16.

20 Ibid., 22, Fig. 20, nos. 1–6.

21 Wilson, G. (1939) *The Constitution of Ngonde.* The Rhodes-Livingstone Papers, 3. The Rhodes-Livingstone Institute, Livingstone, Zambia.

22 Robinson (1966) op. cit., 172–8.

23 Ibid., pp. 175–6, Figs 7 and 8.

24 Robinson (1970) op. cit., Figs 27–30.

25 Ibid.

26 Ibid., Figs 17–21.

27 Ibid., Figs 32–3.

28 Robinson and Sandelowsky (1968) op. cit., Fig. 19 and Fig. 20, nos. 7–10.

29 Ibid., Fig. 11.

30 Inskeep, R. R. (1965) *Preliminary Investigation of the Proto-Historic Cemetery at Nkudzi Bay, Malawi.* National Museums of Zambia, special paper.

31 Tindall, P. (1965) 'Historical Background' in Preliminary Investigation of a Proto-Historic Cemetery at Nkudzi Bay, Malawi, National Museums of Zambia, special paper, 28.

32 Inskeep, R. R. (1965) op. cit. and (1969) 'The Archaeological Background', in *Oxford History of South Africa, Vol. 1*, eds Monica Wilson and Leonard Thompson, 37.

33 Robinson, K. R. (1959) *Khami Ruins* C.U.P.

34 Ibid., Fig. 23.

35 Nurse, G. T. (1969) *The Matengo Settlement*, Government of Malawi, Department of Antiquities, 7, 21–3.

36 Robinson (1966) op. cit. and (1968) op. cit.

37 Fagan, M. B., Phillipson, D. W. and Daniels, S. G. H. (1969) *Iron Age Cultures in Zambia, Vol. 2* Chatto and Windus, Figs. 6–22.

38 Phillipson, D. (1968) 'The Early Iron Age in Zambia: regional variants and some tentative conclusions', *J. Afr. His.* **9** (2), 208.

39 Clark, J. D. (1967) 'A record of early agriculture and metallurgy in Africa from archaeological sources', in *Reconstructing African Culture History*, eds C. Gabel and N. R. Bennett. Boston University Press. Clark, J. D. (1970) *The Prehistory of Africa*. Thames and Hudson. Posnansky, M. (1968) 'Bantu Genesis—archaeological reflexions', *J. Afr. Hist.* **9** (1). Hiernaux, J. (1968) 'Bantu expansion: the evidence from physical anthropology confronted with linguistic and archaeological evidence', *J. Afr. Hist.*, **9** (4). Huffman, T. (1969) 'The Early Iron Age and the spread of the Bantu', *S. Afr. Archaeol. Bull.*, 25.

40 Robinson (1966) op. cit.

41 Fagan, B. and Yellen, J. E. (1968) *Inventaria Archaeologics Africana: Tanzania TAI: Iruna 1968*. Musée Royal de l'Afrique Centrale, Belgium.

42 Robinson and Sandelowsky (1968) op. cit., Figs 17, 18 and Fig. 20 nos. 1–6.

43 Ibid.

5 Transport and Communication in Malawi to 1891, with a summary to 1918

P. A. Cole-King

I   INTRODUCTION AND EARLY HISTORY

Up to the present the progress of mankind has been bound by the limitations of time and space. Whether freedom from these limitations is a matter for the afterlife, beyond the fringe of human endeavour, or is merely a matter of scientific development, only the future can tell. The story of transport and communication is the story of how man, who cannot exist without making contact with his fellows, has learned to reduce his limitations, each stage of his development being marked by improvement in his ability to move himself, his ideas and his goods, from A. to B. In English the words *transport* and *communication* have numerous shades of meaning which frequently overlap, but they may be reduced simply to this: movement of people, movement of ideas, movement of goods.

Man is a land animal equipped with two basic means of communication, walking and talking. He can also adapt slightly to water though his swimming abilities compare unfavourably with those of the aquatic animals. In the air he can move very swiftly, but in one direction only. Man's great advantage over all other living things lies in his capacity to make use of mechanical devices to improve his natural abilities. So, today, we see the basic walking and talking of our distant Stone Age ancestors transformed into moon rockets and televized commentaries on World Cup football.

The earliest men whose remains have so far been found in Malawi lived between 50,000 and 100,000 years ago at the beginning of that long period of history known as the Stone Age. Progress in all fields of human activity during this period was extremely slow and it was not until around A.D 300., when the first Iron Age farmers were settling in Malawi, that it began to accelerate towards the Space Age pace of the past hundred years. Transport in the Stone Age was simple: men moved on foot from place to place, as dictated by the needs of finding a livelihood by hunting and gathering, and they carried their few belongings with them. Whenever groups of people moved about between their hunting grounds and their homes, in caves or roughly made shelters, they made tracks or used the tracks made by the animals they hunted. Because it was easier to follow existing tracks than to push through virgin bush the tracks tended to be consolidated by constant use. They may be reckoned as the

70

first roads and their use the first development in communications.

The second development also occurred during the Stone Age, the discovery of the buoyant properties of wood and the use of floating logs to cross stretches of water. A further probable development was the lashing together of several logs to form a raft.

The simple tracks which served the needs of the Stone Age were constantly shifting with the shifting population and it was not until the migration of the first Iron Age farmers around 300 A.D. that what I shall call the traditional system of communication in Malawi began to emerge. This has largely been replaced from the middle of nineteenth century by what I call the modern system. The Bantu migration, of which the first Iron Age farmers in Malawi were a part, was in itself a major feat of transport and communication spread over many hundreds of years and covering thousands of miles. Its effect in Malawi was gradually to populate the country, from around A.D. 300 to A.D. 1600, with iron-working and pottery-making agriculturalists who assimilated the Stone Age hunters and established a comparatively advanced and settled society. The traditional system which they evolved consisted of a network of tracks connecting each village with the next throughout the country together with a few major routes, principally for trade, lying east-west across the line of Lake Malawi and the Shire river. The modern system, in contrast, is based on a main trade route lying north-south along the line of lake and river with an ever-increasing number of roads replacing the old inter-village tracks.

II   THE TRADITIONAL SYSTEM

Whereas the people of the Stone Age appear to have lived in isolated groups which had little need to contact one another, the Iron Age farmers were organized under chiefs holding sway over a number of more or less scattered villages with whom contact was necessary to maintain cohesion. Furthermore the settlements, if they may be called such, of Stone Age people were probably only inhabited for weeks or months at a time, whereas the villages of the early Malawi farmers were semi-permanent, lasting so many years until the soil in the neighbourhood became exhausted by cultivation and necessitated a change of locality. The need for contact and the semi-permanent nature of villages resulted in the growth of a well-defined and well-used system of paths between them.

The only first hand sources of information available on the period of the traditional system are occasional Portuguese records, such as those of Bocarro, 1616; Lacerda, 1798; Gamitto, 1831; and the diaries of Livingstone and Kirk, 1859–63. Most of these come right at the end of the period, Livingstone in fact being largely responsible for the beginnings of the Modern System, but their records of what they saw are almost certainly valid in general terms for hundreds of years before their visits.

Livingstone was often pictured by his romantic admirers in distant Victorian England as hacking his way through impenetrable jungle on his journeys. In fact he went 'tramping along with a steady heavy tread, which kept one in

71

mind that he had walked across Africa',[1] using the long-established local tracks which he describes in some detail:

'We always follow the native paths, though they are generally not more than fifteen inches broad, and so often have deep little holes in them, made for the purpose of setting traps for small animals, and are so much obscured by the long grass, that one has to keep one's eyes on the ground more than is pleasant. In spite, however, of all drawbacks, it is vastly more easy to travel on these tracks, than to go straight over uncultivated ground, or virgin forest. A path usually leads to some village, though sometimes it turns out to be a mere game track leading nowhere.'[2]

And again:

'The only roads are footpaths worn by the feet of the natives into hollows a few inches deep, and about fifteen to eighteen inches wide, winding from village to village, as if made by believers in the curved line being that of beauty.'[3]

In the light of the comments of Livingstone (and others) on the twisty nature of Malawi paths, it is perhaps only fair to point out that some forty years later G. K. Chesterton was moved to write 'The rolling English drunkard made the rolling English road'. All the records, however, of early travellers in Malawi from Bocarro to Livingstone made it clear that guides were a necessity to avoid getting lost in the complexity of local communications.

Obstacles in Africa seem generally to be avoided rather than removed and this leads to the devious nature of the paths rather than any lack of sobriety on the part of those who made them. Rivers, however, cannot be avoided and certain places become recognized as crossing places owing to their shallowness and narrowness. Gamitto, on his journey from Tete to Kazembe's in 1831, which took him along the line of the watershed between the Luangwa-Zambezi and Lake Malawi-Shire through Maravi country, that is nowadays north western Mozambique and the Mchinji District of Malawi, noted the use of cut down trees to bridge streams and both he and Lacerda, 1798, recorded the use of bamboo bridges by the Maravi. Gamitto, a careful observer who recorded details of several ethnic groups in the course of his journey, states that they were the only people who made bridges. It is interesting to note that apparently all Central African languages have borrowed the Chichewa word for a bridge, *ulalo*, which supports the view that early Malawians were the only bridge builders in the area. Gamitto tried crossing one of the bamboo bridges and he regarded them as dangerous structures, an opinion evidently shared by their makers who 'are very careful in securing them, though they do not cross them unless it is absolutely essential'.[4] Gamitto also noted people crossing rivers in canoes made of pieces of bark sewn together with twine or in wooden dugouts.[5]

Apart from the inter-village network of paths the other feature of the traditional system in Malawi was its trade routes. Livingstone remarked on the local trade between villages in things like iron, tobacco, salt and skins and in

72

particular the trade between the hills where baskets and nets were made and the lakeshore where they were exchanged for fish.[6] All this implies carriage of goods on recognized local routes. But there were also main routes covering hundreds of miles for trade between the interior and the coast. These main routes ran roughly northeast-southwest across the rift formation of lake Malawi and the Shire river, partly because the areas of supply and demand lay east and west of one another, on the coast and on the interior plateau, and partly because the general line of waterways in this part of Africa, apart from the rift, is towards the Indian Ocean, the natural line of paths being along the ridges of higher ground between rivers.

Along these east-west trade routes cloth, guns and beads were carried by head load to be exchanged in the interior for ivory, copper, and, later, slaves, who also conveniently helped to solve the return transport problem (see Fig. 5.1). The east coast trade was only gradually extended to the interior and how early it reached Malawi and the lake it is not yet possible to say with certainty though there have been suggestions of some time around the twelfth century A.D.

The obvious north south line of the Rift valley, Lake Malawi and the Shire river, connecting with the Zambezi and the Indian Ocean seems not to have been used as a trade route, apart from limited trade in the lower Shire region nearest to the Zambezi, until the latter half of the nineteenth century, though its existence was recorded by a Portuguese, Fr Manoel Godinho, in 1663. Gamitto, in 1831, expressed uncertainty as to whether 'Lake Marave . . . has communication with the sea' and does not seem very clear as to whether it was a lake or an enormous river that he was talking about, but he made it clear that it lay as a barrier across existing east-west routes, being approached from the east by coast Arabs and from the west by

'Bisa who are today the merchants of these regions . . . Embarking in canoes it is necessary to sleep two nights on islands, with which (the lake) is sprinkled, before arriving on the third day in the afternoon on the opposite shore . . .'[7]

This is evidently a reference to the crossing between Bandawe, Chizumulu island, Likoma island and Cobue. Gamitto suggested that efforts should be made to organize expeditions to locate the lake, buy canoes, load them with goods and then sail them 'downstream' to its connection, if any, with the ocean, thus opening up a valuable route for Portuguese trade. No one heeded the suggestion and it was left to Livingstone to open up the route from the Zambezi end.

The principal rift crossings on the east-west trade routes were: around the north end of Lake Malawi; Bandawe to Cobue; Nkhota Kota to Mtengula (but probably not earlier than the nineteenth century); several places in the Senga bay area to Cape Ngombo; around the south end of the lake across the Shire near Fort Johnston; several river crossings below lake Malombe; the Chikwawa neighbourhood; Chiromo (See Fig. 5.2).

The Portuguese traveller, Gaspar Bocarro, on his celebrated journey from

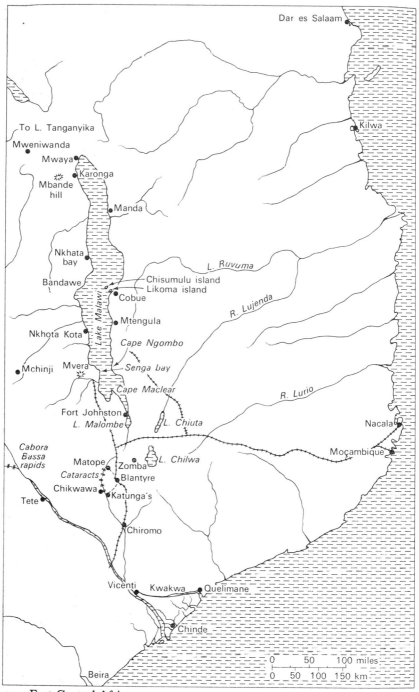

5.2   East Central Africa

Tete to Kilwa in 1616 followed what must have been a well-used route. It is difficult to interpret from the account of his journey exactly where he crossed the rift but it was probably in the neighbourhood of Lake Malombe. His passage from place to place was handled in a business-like manner by all concerned, suggesting that important travellers were no rarity, and copper from mines near Tete was accepted as payment for guides and safe passage throughout, plus the usual gifts to chiefs and headmen.[8] Two hundred years later travelling conditions seem to have deteriorated in one respect for both Lacerda and Gamitto note the frequency of highway robbery in certain areas, the remedy for which was armed escort.[9] Among the Maravi people different means of protection were employed. Chiefs and headmen travelled with magic tail-switches which were used at crossroads to sprinkle the ways they were not taking so that they might not be followed by enemies. Ordinary men going on a long journey obtained medicine from a witch-doctor which guaranteed protection only as long as they had no contact with women on their journey. The unfortunate traveller had thus to make the difficult choice between sex and safety.[10]

Although the Malawi rift valley seems to have lain across trade routes rather than being used as such itself, it did furnish a line for migration. There are traditions that some elements of the Maravi people came from the north, down the eastern side of Lake Malawi, one being that

'Mwase of Likoma, his people and their companions left Mwaya on the northern shore of lake Malawi in a big canoe known by the name of "Lumbila" and reached Manda . . . Kwambe . . . Unga. One day Lunga, Mwase's relation, went fishing in his small canoe . . . until he came to a solitary island in the lake . . . and found that there were no people . . . Returning to Unga, Lunga told us of his discovery . . . and we left for Likoma in our canoe "Lumbila".'[11]

The use of dugout canoes on the waterways of Malawi is mentioned by Portuguese writers in the sixteenth century, but it is probably safe to assume that canoe building was part of the comparatively advanced knowledge of the earliest Iron Age immigrants who were settled on the lakeshore by the fourth century A.D. It is known that they practised fishing and had iron tools; so it is likely that they made proper fishing craft. It is also possible that the Later Stone Age people, whose traces are also abundant on the lakeshore, had discovered how to hollow out tree trunks using fire and stone adzes.

In 1861 Livingstone recorded dugout canoes making regular lake crossings at what he estimated to be a speed of three miles per hour or more,[12] and Kirk describes seeing them near Senga bay:

'September 12th. Blowing a gale from the North . . . Two canoes full of goods and people have set out to cross the Lake. Those paddling stand up, like the landsmen of the interior. They make the canoes go at a great rate and the swell today makes no difference to them.'[13]

As in the case of the network of footpaths already mentioned it is known that there had been a regular canoe traffic across the lake for several hundred years previous to Livingstone's and Kirk's observations.

The introduction of Arab dhows to the lake was probably comparatively late. Tradition states that chief Chikulamayembe crossed the lake in what may have been the first dhow to be built there in imitation of the Zanzibar craft.[14] The wording of Livingstone's remark, on his first visit to Nkhota Kota in 1859, that 'Two enterprising Arabs had built a dhow, and were running her, crowded with slaves, regularly across the Lake',[15] suggests that even at this date it was by no means a common occurrence. Two years later, when he returned to Nkhota Kota, there were two dhows operating and Jumbe, the self-styled Sultan of the place, was engaged in building a third.

> 'This new one was fifty feet long, twelve feet broad and five feet deep. The planks were of a wood like teak, here called *Timbati*, and the timbers of a closer grained wood called *Msoro*.'[16]

Canoes were a feature of the Shire, but appear to have been used only locally for fishing and crossing the river until the advent of Livingstone and the later missionaries and travellers, all of whom found it possible to hire numbers of canoes to undertake the transport of themselves and their supplies over long distances. A traveller in 1884, W. Montagu Kerr, was evidently undecided on the merits of this mode of travel, first finding 'the inaction of canoeing more trying to the system than marching' and then later that 'there was an undoubted charm about this canoe life'.[17] Dr James Stewart, missionary of the Free Church of Scotland, commented primly on the stalwart individuals who propelled the canoes on their long journeys:

> 'The canoe men relieve the tedium of the paddle by singing. There is little in their songs. Anything serves for a rhyme. Sometimes the songs are not remarkable for their purity.'[18]

Apart from canoes, the only vehicles in use during the period of the traditional system seem to have been men themselves and *machilas*. The use of men for the transport of goods is obvious, but they also seem to have been used to carry their superiors. Gamitto, when he was in what is now Mchinji District, was visited by chief Mkanda 'old and stout but well proportioned' who 'came and visited our camp carried on a negro's back'.[19] The machila or palanquin (see Fig. 5.3), a device consisting of a hammock slung on poles in which a traveller is borne by porters, was probably restricted to African chiefs and European travellers. Bocarro, in 1616, did not apparently use one, but Lacerda records being carried in one for several days when he was sick[20] and they had probably been used for some time by the Portuguese. Livingstone and the early Scottish missionaries to Malawi seem to have felt that walking was a suitably humble means of progress, but the members of Consul Elton's expedition in 1877 had no such ideas, regarding machilas as of 'the greatest use to the African traveller', by which, of course, was meant the

76

European traveller in Africa.[21]

Communication of ideas is basically a matter of language, a subject outside the scope of what is normally understood by 'transport and communications'. Transport of ideas beyond the range of speech does come within that scope and can be summarized as far as the earlier period is concerned in terms of messengers, travelling more or less long distances on foot, and drums. The use of drums, to transmit messages from village to village, as well as for ritual or musical purposes, probably goes right back to the first Iron Age farmers or even earlier. It is the origin of the name of the hill *Mvera*—place of hearing— from which Chiwere's warriors would listen for the summons to arms drummed out from the chief's headquarters. Drum messages could repel as well as attract. Tradition has it that the first Kyungu of the Ngonde reached the sacred Mbande hill near Karonga by stealth and then scattered his enemies by beating his drum from the top.[22]

III   BEGINNINGS OF THE MODERN SYSTEM

Livingstone's visits to Malawi, as well as providing a large part of our knowledge of what the traditional system of communication in Malawi was like also heralded the modern system. It was he who showed that although the Shire river was blocked by forty miles of cataracts it still provided a feasible route to the lake and his visits paved the way for the succeeding missionaries, traders, planters and finally administrators, all of whom made use of the north-south line of the lake and the Shire river, connecting with the Zambezi and Indian Ocean. The traditional east-west pattern of trade routes, which had largely degenerated into slave routes, were deliberately put out of use firstly by the moral persuasion of the missionaries, backed by opportunity for alternative forms of trade, and, finally, after 1891, by the armed forces of the administration.

The 1858–64 Zambezi Expedition led by Livingstone, was sent by the British government to open up routes to the interior of Africa for exploration and trade. Having discovered that the Zambezi was blocked for navigation by the Cabora Bassa rapids, Livingstone turned his attention to the Shire and reports that it led to a great inland lake, only to discover on sailing up it in his steamer *Ma Robert* in January 1859 that once again navigation was blocked by cataracts. In August of the same year he returned and travelled overland past the cataracts, finding that they extended some forty miles, after which the Shire river was again navigable. He reached the lake on September 16th and although not the first European to reach it he was the first to give it the publicity it deserves. After this first visit he concluded that from the lake.

'Water carriage exists by the Shire and Zambezi all the way to England, with the single exception of a portage of about thirty five miles past the Murchison Cataracts, along which a road of less than forty miles could be made at trifling expense.'[23]

Two years later he returned in a new steamer, the *Pioneer*, and this time overcame the 'portage' by carrying past the cataracts a sail-cum-rowing boat in which he went along the upper Shire to the lake and up its western shore to a point near Nkhata Bay where he was forced to turn back. It was left to the Livingstonia missionaries, fourteen years later, to complete the first circumnavigation of the lake.[24]

Livingstone was much impressed with the suitability of the lakeshore for European settlement, especially the 'magnificent harbour' at Cape Maclear, and of the value of the lake as an inland waterway. Early in 1863 he acted on his idea of four years earlier and began clearing a road northwards from his base at the junction of the Mwambezi and the Shire, half a mile below the first cataract, along which he planned to carry, in wagons, the sections of a small steamer, the *Lady Nyassa*, specially ordered from Britain to his specification. The plan was to take it to pieces and transport it to the lake. The work proved harder than he expected. When only some six miles of road were completed the expedition was recalled by the British Government, but not before Livingstone had had some success in taking a mule-cart as far as the Mkulumadzi stream and driving an ox-cart over the less rugged country south of his base.[25] Livingstone seems to have preferred to minimize the difficulties of access to the lake in his writings, so as not to deter others from following his footsteps, thereby creating what might be termed the Livingstone myth of a workable waterway to the interior. Possibly many of the traders and settlers of the last quarter of the nineteenth century would have been deterred had they had a true picture of the hazards of navigation on the Zambezi and lower Shire, as well as of the more obvious barrier of cataracts. The waterway was workable, but only to a limited extent and its limitations had to be overcome with a railway before any real development in commerce could begin.

Livingstone's basic idea of taking a dismantled boat past the cataracts for reassembly on the upper Shire was first proved possible by the Livingstone Search Expedition led by E. D. Young, R.N., formerly in charge of the *Pioneer*, which came to Malawi in 1867 to investigate reports of the great traveller's murder somewhere on the shores of the lake. A small sectional steel sailing boat, appropriately named the *Search*, was brought out (see Fig. 5.4), proved successful and enabled the members of the expedition to show that the rumours of Livingstone's murder were untrue. Experience with the *Search* was to prove invaluable to Young in 1875, two years after Livingstone's death, when he was called on to lead the first party of missionaries of the Free Church of Scotland which was sent out to found the Livingstonia Mission, in memory of the explorer, on the shore of the lake he had made known to the world. The missionaries were equipped with a small steamer, the *Ilala*, built in sections largely according to Young's ideas, with which to keep open their lines of communication from the lake to the upper end of the cataracts. Several hundred porters were employed to carry the *Ilala* and the mission stores and equipment past the cataracts, after which the ship was reassembled and then sailed to Cape Maclear where the mission settled. Young commented:

5.4 Transportation of the *Search*: pieces carried by porters over some thirty to forty miles of bush country. (Adapted from a drawing by courtesy of the Museum of Malawi.)

'It may be that things will so develop that the road used by us from the coast will eventually become the trade route to the interior. . . . The first stage must be from the Kongone (mouth of the Zambezi) to Matiti, and for this purpose a small and handy shallow draught steamer can be employed, not drawing more than twenty four inches of water, and built on the American principle with "hindwheel" propulsion. The second stage will be the portage to the head of the Cataracts, a difficult matter now, but to be shorn of most of its weariness by the construction of a good road; and then for the upper waters and the Lake itself, a steamer of twice the *Ilala*'s proportions should be brought into use.'[26]

Young's forecast contributed to the Livingstone myth and also proved accurate for the waterway, though it was twenty years before stern-paddle steamers were brought into use on the lower river, but the essential "good road' never materialized in the form intended by Livingstone or Young. Shortly after their arrival at Cape Maclear, Young and Dr Robert Laws, the future head of the mission, completed the first recorded circumnavigation of Lake Malawi which Livingstone had had to abandon fourteen years earlier.

With the establishment of Livingstonia at Cape Maclear and the missionaries' need of the waterway as their only means of outside communication, the scheme for a forty mile road beside the cataracts might well have been attempted, especially if the work of the mission on the lake expanded and was followed by traders and settlers leading to the development of the lake area as a whole. But quite incidentally the Established Church of Scotland missionaries effectively scotched the possibility of the road when they founded Blantyre in 1876, only a year after Livingstonia. Blantyre was soon seen as the natural staging post for a loop road some seventy miles in length, bypassing the cataracts by a more feasible route than that beside the cataracts themselves, albeit longer. From 1877–9 the resources of the two missions were combined in making the road, from the lower Shire, just below modern Chikwawa through Blantyre to Matope on the upper Shire to serve the interests of both. The section from the lower Shire to Blantyre probably the first true road in Malawi, if road is taken to mean a way deliberately constructed between A and B rather than a way which has come into being through constant usage. The architect of the road was James Stewart, a civil engineer from India who devoted his career to the Livingstonia Mission.

The position of Blantyre as a communications centre was strengthened in 1878 by the arrival of John and Frederick Moir, joint managers of the recently formed Livingstonia Central Africa Company, later the African Lakes Company and nowadays the African Lakes Corporation. The company was founded largely by the interests supporting the Livingstonia Mission with the object of following up missionary work with legitimate trade and opening up a route from the Indian Ocean to Lake Tanganyika. The joint managers were to

'superintend the route between Quilimane on the coast via Blantyre and Lake Nyasa, to circumnavigate the Lake, and to start a branch line up the Zambezi to Tete, and other lines (into Lake Tanganyika) as they might open up.'[27]

The Moirs, although their Free Church enterprise might seem to have a natural base at Livingstonia on the lake, decided to make Blantyre, the home of the Established Church mission, their headquarters for the practical reason that, being comparatively accessible to the lower Shire and the outside world, to the Shire highlands and to the upper Shire and the lake, it was a better trading centre than anywhere on the lake itself. For transport on the Zambezi and lower Shire the Moirs brought out a small side-paddle steamer, the *Lady Nyassa II*, named after Livingstone's unsuccessful vessel, and in 1882 the Company took over the *Ilala* from the Livingstonia mission for use as a trading vessel on Lake Malawi and the upper Shire, except when needed by the mission. These solitary vessels were augmented by the arrival of the *James Stevenson*, for service on the lower Shire in 1887 and of the *Domira*, for the lake in 1889. There were also several smaller boats and barges.

Between them, the Scottish mission and the African Lakes Company, established a line of stations along the Zambezi, the Shire and the lake, starting from Quelimane and going to Vicenti, Katunga's, (A.L.C.) Blantyre, (Established Church) Matope, (A.L.C.) Cape Maclear, (Free Church) Bandawe, (Free Church) Karonga (A.L.C.) and Mweniwanda (Free Church) in the north, all except Blantyre and Mweniwanda being actually beside the waterway. The African Lakes Company station at Katunga's, a few miles below modern Chikwawa on the east bank of the Shire, was the main 'port' of the country from which Stewart's road led up the escarpment to Blantyre. From Blantyre the road went to Matope at the head of the cataracts. For the first few miles from Katunga's.

'A 10-feet wide road was made at one time, and has been hoed occasionally, but it is generally so overgrown with grass as to render it almost invisible.'[28]

So Buchanan described Stewart's road in 1885 and went on to tell of the gradients of one in five to one in ten on the escarpment itself which involved a climb of 3,000 feet in fourteen miles. Later the Company attempted to reduce the hardships of the journey by importing donkeys and horses for the use of travellers on those sections of the route from Katunga's to Matope that were not infested with tsetse fly.[29] The road from Chikwawa (Katunga's) to Blantyre has been altered several times since it was first made but it still follows Stewart's original layout to a large extent, a tribute to his skill.[30]

In the north, the Stevenson road, a project to connect Lake Malawi with Lake Tanganyika, ran inland from Karonga through Mweniwanda. The road was begun in 1881, financed to begin with by James Stevenson, Chairman of the Company. Its construction was supervised at first by James Stewart, who died in 1883 after several miles of the road had been completed. The first consignment of parts for the London Missionary Society's steamer *Good News*, having been transported all along the difficult route from Quelimane, was on its way to Lake Tanganyika. The Stevenson road made slow progress following Stewart's death. McEwan, his successor, also died on the job, and it was not until many years later that it was eventually completed for wagon traffic by the British South Africa Company.[31]

Another steamer which was brought to Lake Malawi along the difficult route from Quelimane was the Universities' Mission steamer *Charles Janson* in 1884–5. It travelled in the usual sections and a young African teacher, Augustine Ambali, was with the carriers on the climb from Katunga's to Blantyre. Ambali described the trip as follows:

> 'I walked from Katunga's and I started in early morning with the men who carry the iron plates and the boiler and it was very hard work to climb the hill between Katunga's and Blantyre, it was hard job to do it. . .[32]

A piece of almost British understatement.

Once away from water the only means of travelling generally available to the early missionaries and traders was on foot or by machila, and as has already been noted, the latter was seemingly out of favour with the missions, only coming into its own after 1891 and the arrival of administrators who liked to travel on someone else's feet. For anyone going on a journey there was usually 'a whole army of guides, servants, carriers, soldiers and camp-followers' ready to be hired for a few yards of calico.[33] Carriers, *tenga-tenga*, were the only means of moving supplies and equipment and allocation of loads could be a problem, as Henry Rowley of the Universities' Mission found in 1861:

> 'Some of the burdens were larger than others, some lighter, and the clamour and contention before each man was satisfied with his particular load was amusing.'[34]

The line of mission and trading stations along the waterway formed the main trade artery around which the modern system of communications and the state of Malawi have grown up. By 1891, when a British Protectorate was declared over the area of what is now Malawi, none of the missionaries, planters or traders making up the largely British expatriate community had established themselves very far from the waterway. In consequence the agreements on their respective spheres of influence made in the interests of their nationals between Britain, Portugal and Germany, prior to the Protectorate declaration, left Malawi as a long narrow country, hugging the line of lake and river which Africans had always regarded as an obstacle to their east-west trade but which was the lifeline of the Europeans.

It has been suggested that if it were not for the cataracts on the Shire river the waterways of Malawi would have provided the means for considerable economic growth from an early date. This view ignores the added difficulty of access from the sea to the Zambezi. The delta of the Zambezi is a low-lying, swampy area, presenting a uniform appearance when viewed from the sea, making its seven mouths hard to locate. Once found, there is still the problem of sand bars which can make it both difficult and dangerous to arrange the transhipment of goods and passengers from ocean going liners to river boats.

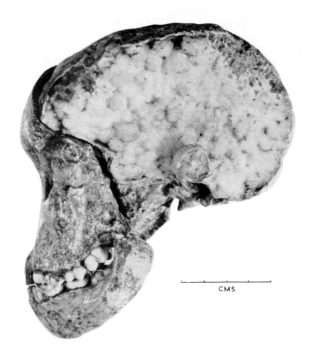

CMS

1.2 Left lateral view of skull and natural endocranial cast of *Australopithecus africanus* from Taung in the Cape Province of South Africa. The endocast is coated with a layer of crystalline lime or calcite. The almost completely erupted permanent upper first molar is clearly seen; also the small deciduous canine. Note the very slight degree of protrusion of the jaws (prognathism) and the absence of a chin on the mandible.

This specimen was the first discovered member of the australopithecines: it was described by Professor Raymond A. Dart in 1925. At this early stage in hominid evolution, these creatures had already set themselves apart from members of the ape family in a number of anatomical features. Probably, too, they had embarked upon implemental activities which ultimately provided their main means of coping with the challenges of their environment.

A

B

C

CMS

CMS

CMS

Facing page, top: 1.3   Three views of the reconstructed parietal bones of the cranial vault of Olduvai hominid 7, the type specimen of *Homo habilis.* A – from above; B – oblique anterior view of the biparietal arch; C – posterior view of the biparietal arch, together with an artificial plaster endocranial cast in position. The volume of the part-endocast is 363 cubic centimetres, from which the total endocranial capacity has been estimated as about 657 cc. From these bones and other parts of the same skeleton, we know that the individual represented was a juvenile: when the capacity of his brain-case is corrected to the probable adult value, a size of 684 cc is obtained. This size of brain-case is about half as big again as the average size for *Australopithecus africanus* skulls so far discovered.

These bones of the type specimen of *Homo habilis* were found in Bed I in the famous prehistoric site of Olduvai Gorge on the Serengeti Plain of northern Tanzania. The evidence suggests that at this stage of their evolution, African hominids developed stone tool-making activities to a set and regular pattern, the earliest manifestation of which is called the Olduvai Culture.

Facing page, bottom: 1.4   The beautifully preserved cranium of Olduvai hominid 9, from the upper part of Bed II, Olduvai Gorge, in Tanzania. The specimen has been identified as belonging to a member of the extinct species, *Homo erectus,* which lived in Asia, Africa and, probably, Europe during the Middle Pleistocene. This specimen possesses one of the largest brow-ridges ever encountered in a hominid cranium. The endocranial capacity has been estimated to be 1,000 cc. This type of man was probably responsible for making the hand-axes and other stone tools of the 'African Acheulian Culture'.

Above: 1.5   A fragment of a human lower jaw-bone from the Cave of Hearths, Makapansgat, Transvaal. The specimen was found in a hand-axe layer, representing the latter part of the African Acheulian Culture, and dating from the earlier part of the Upper Pleistocene. Neandertaloid features are present, which align this South African Stone Age individual with some of the later hand-axe makers of North-West Africa. There is a poorly developed bony chin and the front surface of the jaw retreats. There is evidence to suggest that this individual was congenitally lacking a wisdom tooth (3rd molar). The owner of this jaw has been classified as *Homo sapiens rhodesiensis.*

5.1 An ivory caravan of the African Lakes Company, 1896

5.3 A *machila*

Livingstone used the Kongone mouth, which was at that time usually adequate for vessels of small draught, and he was followed there by the 1867 Search Expedition and the first party of Livingstonia missionaries in 1875. The first Blantyre mission party in 1876 went to Quelimane which gave comparatively good access to the river Kwakwa. The Kwakwa, however, was not a mouth of the Zambezi, its upper reaches being separated from that river by a few miles of swampy land. Only when the Zambezi flooded was there a temporary channel across the swamp connecting it to the Kwakwa. At other times it was necessary to trans-ship goods and passengers the short distance overland from one river to the other. The Moir brothers in 1878 used the Kwakwa route and, apart from occasional uses of the Kongone, it became the recognized route to Blantyre and the lake, the inconvenience of the land portage being considered more than offset by the accessibility of the Kwakwa to the Indian Ocean. The Moirs had to wait until March 1879 before floods opened the temporary channel and allowed them to take their paddle steamer *Lady Nyasa II* from the Kwakwa to the Zambezi where she stayed, carriage on the Kwakwa subsequently being done by canoe and houseboat.[35]

The transfer of people and goods overland from one river to the other was nevertheless a serious handicap to communication particularly as there was another overland section to face at Blantyre. In 1888 David Rankin, who by his own amusing account had suffered much on the river section of his first journey to Blantyre five years earlier, set out to explore the whole Zambezi delta to see if there was any good access, financed by the Royal Scottish Geographical Society. From information gathered from a Portuguese planter in the area, Rankin found the Chinde mouth, with adequate depth of water over the sand bar and easy access to the main channel of the Zambezi, early in 1889 and soon after his return to England he announced his discovery in *The Times*. A survey ship, H.M.S. *Stork*, was sent out to verify the position and, drawing thirteen feet of water, passed comfortably into the Zambezi in July. On board was H. H. Johnston, British Consul for Portuguese East Africa, on his way to Lake Malawi to conclude treaties with those chiefs desirous of friendly relations with Britain, an obvious prelude to protectorate.[36] Johnston seems, on this, his first visit, to have found something of Livingstone's enthusiasm for the possibilities of the lake. On his return to England he wrote of Cape Maclear that it was 'destined perhaps to become the great English capital on Nyasa'.[37] In 1891, when agreements between the Powers had been reached, Johnston returned, this time as Commissioner and Consul-General for the new British Protectorate. He made Zomba the capital. He had proceeded from Chinde up the Zambezi in a small gunboat paddle-steamer, H.M.S. *Herald*, which together with her sister-ship H.M.S. *Mosquito* was placed on the river, now recognized as an international waterway, to look after British interests. Subsequently Chinde, both the Portuguese settlement and the British concession, became a flourishing port, the gateway, until it was outdated by the railway, to central Africa.[38]

The year 1891 marks the turning point between the traditional and the modern systems of communication in Malawi. From then on, the modern system, founded on the line of waterway opened up by Livingstone and his successors, began to develop. The trade routes of the traditional system which had degenerated into slave routes were eliminated by force and the traditional network of paths began to be supplemented, and in part replaced, by roads linking the centres of administration which themselves resulted in a shifting of focus of local life. Without going into details of trade it is clear that the obstacles in the lake and river route to the Indian Ocean were enough to prevent any proper expansion, especially when the level of water in the Shire began to decline in the 1890s making it increasingly difficult for even the flat-bottomed paddle-steamers to navigate.

One of the less fortunate legacies of the colonial era is that the boundaries of modern African states are determined by nineteenth century agreements made between European powers according to the pattern of how their nationals had happened to settle in various areas. These agreements were often made without consideration of African ethnic groups which were divided as a result. In the case of Malawi, the pattern of European (largely British) settlement followed closely the only line of communication available, a north-south line of lake and river. Hence the boundaries of the British Protectorate made it a long narrow country lying along that line. Factors of transport and communication made Malawi the shape that it is and this shape has in turn determined the further development of communications. The main trunk roads today run north-south and the railway similarly follows the line of lake and river.

IV   SUMMARY OF DEVELOPMENTS 1891–1918

The full story of developments in the modern system of transport and communications in Malawi, from the setting up of the Protectorate to the end of the First World War, is beyond the scope of this paper, so only the main points will be outlined.[39] The declaration of a British Protectorate over the country, itself largely the result of increasing British interests, in turn stimulated further development, encouraged new settlers and made it necessary to raise revenue to help towards the cost of administration. Although, by modern standards, the amount of economic growth was small during the 1890s it became increasingly evident that the transport system based on the Shire river route was inadequate. The lake, with several natural harbours, was good for communications but only within its own limits. The problem of access to Malawi was accentuated from about 1895 onwards, when one of the long periodic falls in the level of the lake began to affect the level of the Shire so that first Katunga's and later Chiromo became inaccessible to paddle steamers.

In a paper presented to the British Association at Edinburgh in 1892 John Buchanan had stated that

'. . . I wish merely to ventilate a railway scheme for British Central Africa which has been in my mind for years. It is simply that we should construct a railway from the Shire to Lake Nyasa, making Chiromo at the mouth of the

Ruo our starting point, and subsequently another line to connect Nyasa and Tanganyika. For the first project alone a sum of about £500,000 would be necessary. It seems a large sum, but we may as well look the matter in the face at once, for a few years hence the money will have to be forthcoming.'[40]

His views were shared by the whole commercial and administrative community. Surveys were carried out of a possible route to connect Blantyre with the lower Shire in which the African Lakes Corporation took the lead but it was through the initiative of Eugene Sharrer, a British subject of German origin, that the Shire Highlands Railway Company was formed, its prospectus being first published in the British Central Africa Gazette on 1 December 1895. Sharrer had considerable trading and landholding interests in the Protectorate amongst which he had acquired most of the land over which the proposed railway would run and which he was to make available to the company. Disagreement and delay, however, followed the floating of the company and it was not until December, 1902 that the contract for the construction of the railway was signed and work begun in 1903. Originally the line was planned to run to Blantyre from Mapalera, thirty miles upstream from Chiromo, then it was rerouted from Chiromo, but by the time work actually began the level of the Shire was such that Chiromo itself was largely inaccessible and thirty miles of line had first to be built downstream to Port Herald (Nsanje) before materials could be brought up to start the main section to Blantyre. The whole railway was not officially opened until 31 March 1908, though completed sections had been in use before that.

With the opening of the Shire Highlands Railway, satisfactory transport of goods and passengers was available from Blantyre to Port Herald from where steamers still operated on the Shire and Zambezi to Chinde, the ocean port. Continuing irregularities in the river level made Port Herald an unreliable terminal and in 1915 an extension, called the Central African Railway, was opened from Port Herald to Chindio on the Zambezi, thus providing an alternative to the Shire. To complete this summary, the Portuguese opened a line from Beira to Muracca, opposite Chindio, in 1922 so that apart from a short ferry trip across the Zambezi there was now a direct rail link between Blantyre and Beira. In 1935 the Zambezi railway bridge completed the direct link. The previous year the railway had been extended north from Blantyre to Salima near the shore of Lake Malawi.

It will be noted that the Malawi railway system, planned as it originally was to bypass the unnavigable stretches of the river route, perpetuated the north-south alignment of the main trade artery. The latest development in Malawi's communications, however, the Nacala rail link, follows approximately the line of one of the old east-west traditional trade routes, and it seems fitting to include some observations on the harbour at Nacala made by H. O'Neill, British Consul to Mozambique, in 1885, long before there was any thought of Nacala being of possible benefit to Malawi:

'In the beginning of 1883, I had occasion to visit the coast which lies between Mozambique and Fernao Veloso bays, and I availed myself of the oppor-

85

tunity to make a rough survey of Nakala, the southern arm of the latter bay.

'This splendid port has not, as far as I can discover, been yet brought to light, although it is without doubt one of, if not the finest, port of the East African Coast. In the British Admiralty charts it is utterly unmarked, and I have only seen an attempt to portray it in a Portuguese map once shown me at Ibo. . . . Except at its southern extremity, which ends in a huge tidal Khor overrun with mangrove bush, Nakala presents, along almost its whole length, coast lines of considerable beauty. . . . In a recent report (1884) of Captain Augusto Castilho, a distinguished Portuguese Naval Officer, now Governor-General of Mozambique, he speaks of Nakala in the following enthusiastic terms:- (1) "one of the finest harbours of the coast. . ." (2) "in which hundreds of the largest ships might ride out with security the most violent tempests". . . . Again in another part of the same report . . . Captain Castilho repeats "Nakala is one of the best harbours of the globe".'[41]

Alongside the development of the railway was that of the modern system of roads, the basis of which in the southern part of the country was laid during the term of office of Harry Johnston, from 1891–96. One of the first tasks of his administration was to establish posts or *bomas* at strategic points, such as Fort Lister, Fort Anderson (Mlanje), Mpimbi, Liwonde or Fort Johnston, many of which were on former east-west slave routes, to control chiefs resisting the imposition of an alien administration. Roads were made to connect these bomas with the three main centres, Zomba, Blantyre and Chiromo, and they were generally planned as straight as the terrain would allow, seldom following the traditional paths. 'Roads' is an exaggerated term to apply to these early routes which were little more than cleared tracks fit for bicycles or small carts and liable to be washed out and overgrown in the wet season.

The Blantyre-Zomba road was the first to be brought up to macadamized standard in the early years of the present century, at the same time as the road system was being extended through the central part of the country to the north, linking up the more remote bomas, such as Ncheu, Dedza and Lilongwe, and reaching Karonga in 1909. During the 1914–18 war the need to keep open supply lines to the troops in the north, operating in German East Africa, resulted in big improvements to the main road north as far as Dedza which was brought up to motor vehicle standard, at least in the dry season. Another legacy of the war was a number of surplus vehicles which were afterwards sold off to contractors who used them to operate transport services for goods and the mails.

Motor cars and lorries were few and far between before 1914, chiefly because of road conditions, though motor cycles were becoming popular, there being some 200 in use by 1910. Motor transport was mostly used by Europeans but bicycles, the first of which, a 'penny-farthing' was introduced by Fred Moir about 1883, were being used by Malawians who could afford them. Two wheeled hand-carts resembling rickshaws and known by the local name of *garetta* (see Fig. 5.5) were extensively used for European travel as were the slower *machilas*. Efforts to overcome the problems of road transport before

86

5.5 A *bush car*. (Adapted from a photograph by courtesy of the Museum of Malawi.)

1900 included the use of ox-carts, steam traction engines and a monorail, but only the first named met with any success. Until the end of the First World War, porterage by head load was the cheapest, most reliable, and most widely used form of road transport.

Prior to 1891 there was no regular postal system, the early missionaries and settlers sending their mail by runner to the nearest Portuguese station for stamping and onward delivery to Europe. The first post office, and for many years the main sorting office, was opened at Chiromo in 1891 (see fig. 5.6) and was quickly followed by other offices at the new administration bomas as they were built. Typical figures quoted in the *British Central Africa Gazette* in February, 1894, show that a busy post office like Blantyre was handling some 3,300 letters per month whereas a small one like Fort Lister only 130 or so. External mail went by river to or from Chiromo, internal mail being distributed on foot except for stations along the lakeshore. After the railway was opened the mail was brought to Limbe, which became the main sorting office, but mail carriers continued to be used for internal distribution until after 1918.

The other important development in communication which took place during the early years of the Protectorate was the telegraph. Cecil Rhodes had conceived the idea of a line linking the Cape to Cairo (together with a similar idea for a railway) and in 1893 his African Transcontinental Telegraph Company began working on a line linking Blantyre with Salisbury, which was already linked to Capetown and the outside world. The line was to go across Portuguese territory through Tete to Chikwawa and on to Blantyre. The Blantyre-Chikwawa section was opened in September 1894, and soon afterwards extended to Tete. Thereafter progress was delayed by difficulties with the Portuguese and by the Mashonaland Rising of 1896 and it was not until April 1898, that Blantyre was finally connected with Capetown and the outside world by an alternative line through Umtali. Meanwhile, progress had been made on the line north from Blantyre which reached Zomba in July 1896, Fort Johnston in 1897 and Karonga the year after. Alongside the telegraph system telephone communication made little progress. A few private lines were in existence in Blantyre in the 1890s and Zomba had its own telephone system by 1904 but it was not until ten years after the war that a start was made on a proper telephone service.

To sum up, the Nyasaland Protectorate had by 1918 acquired the basis of the modern system of communications, consisting of a main rail and river route in and out of the country for goods and passengers, telegraphic and postal communication with the rest of the world and a road network linking the administrative centres within the country. A hint of the future had also been given by the visit of a military aeroplane to Fort Johnston in 1916.

FOOTNOTES

1 Goodwin, H., *Memoir of Bishop Mackenzie*, 1864, 323.

2 Livingstone, D. C., *Narrative of an Expedition to the Zambezi and its Tributaries*, 1865, 469.

3 Livingstone, *Narrative*, 534.

4 Gamitto, A. C. P., *King Kazembe*, translated by I. Cunnison, 1960, 49–50.

5 Gamitto, *Kazembe*, 82.

6 Livingstone, *Narrative*, 113.

7 Gamitto, *Kazembe*, 64–5.

8 Theal, G. M. *Records of South Eastern Africa*, 3, 1899, 414–9.

9 Burton, R. F. (Compiler) *The Lands of Cazembe*, 1879, 68 and 73; Gamitto, *Kazembe*, 68 and 89.

10 Gamitto, *Kazembe*, 77–8.

11 'A Short History of Mwase of Likoma Island and his Tribe the Mphli Tribe,' (Manuscript loaned to the writer in 1969.).

12 Livingstone, *Narrative*, 198.

13 Foskett, R. (Ed.) *The Zambezi Journal and Letters of Dr. John Kirk*, 1965, 372.

14 Nyirenda, S., 'History of the Tumbuka Henga People', reprinted from *Bantu Studies*, 1931, 6.

15 Livingstone, *Narrative*, 390.

16 Livingstone, *Narrative*, 512.

17 Montagu Kerr, W. *The Far Interior*, 1884, Vol. II, 244 and 260.

18 Wallis, J. P. R. (Ed.), *The Zambezi Journal of James Stewart.*

19 Gamitto, *Kazembe*, 118.

20 Burton, *Cazembe*, 75.

21 Elton, J. F., *Travels and Researches*, 1879, 244.

22 Wilson, G. *The Constitution of Ngonde*, 1939, 10.

23 Livingstone, *Narrative*, 129.

24 Young, E. D. *Nyassa*, 1879, 92–131.

25 Wallis, J. P. R. (Ed.) *The Zambezi Expedition of David Livingstone*, (1956) 238–42.

26 Young, *Nyassa*, 42–3.

27 Moir, F. M. *After Livingstone*, 1923, 8–9.,

28 Buchanan, J., *The Shire Highlands*, 1885, 36.

29 Murray, A. C., *Nyasaland en Mijne Ondervindingen aldaar*, 1897, 75 and 81.

30 Sclater, B. L., 'Routes and Districts in Southern Nyasaland,' *The Geographical Journal*, November, 1893, 412.

31 Fotheringham, L. M., *Adventures in Nyasaland*, 1891, 6–10; Moir, *Livingstone*, 65–7.

32 Ambali, A., *Thirty Years in Nyasaland*, 1931, 23.

33 Drummond, H., *Tropical Africa*, 33.

34 Rowley, H., *The Story of the Universities' Mission to Central Africa*, 1866, 131.

35 Moir, *Livingstone*, 30.

36 Rankin, D., *The Zambezi Basin and Nyasaland*, 1893, 217–32; Johnston, H. H., *British Central Africa*, (1897), 79 and 82.

37 Johnston, H. H., *Livingstone and the Exploration of Central Africa*, 1891, 111.

38 Sclater, 'Routes', 403–4.

39 The writer is working on a detailed study which it is hoped to publish in due course.

40 John Buchanan, 'The Industrial Development of Nyasaland', *Geograph. J.*, March, 1893, 253.

41 O'Neill, H., 'Some Remarks upon Nakala'. *Proceedings of the Royal Geographical Society*, 1885, 373–5.

6 The Meaning and Use of the Name *Malawi* in Oral Traditions and Precolonial Documents

J. M. Schoffeleers

In this paper[1] we shall put ourselves two distinct questions. The first is: which people within the Chewa speaking cluster were traditionally indicated by the name *Malawi* or Maravi?[2] The second: why were they thus distinguished from other members of that cluster?

The material has been arranged in two sections corresponding to these questions. The first contains an examination of a number of traditional accounts on the origin of the name, which has the etymological meaning of *fire flames*, and on the identity of the people thus indicated. These appear to have been people of the Phiri clan, who are further identified as a group of invaders who initially established themselves on the south-western lake shore. Since this preliminary identification is fundamental to the issue under discussion, additional evidence will be adduced from the field of topography and ethnography.

In the second section the values and functions symbolized by the Phiri's relationship to fire will be examined. Here, I shall discuss the role of fire in Chewa myth and ritual as a symbol of transition and as a symbol of royal power. This will allow us to phrase in everyday terms the association of the Phiri people with fire.

I THE IDENTITY OF THE MARAVI

Oral History and the Origin of the Name Malawi

Two well-known traditions about the origin of the name are mentioned in an official publication issued on the occasion of the country's obtaining independent status in 1964.[3] The first says that *malawi* is the Chichewa word for *flames*, and that it came to be adopted by a band of ancestral immigrants when for the first time they looked down from the surrounding high plateaux onto Lake Malawi, 'which shimmered like flames in the sunshine'. The same publication records a second tradition which tells us that the newcomers found the rich grasslands round the lake afire and that they derived their name from this.

A third story, not mentioned in the above publication, is that recorded by S. Y. Ntara in his collection of Chewa oral history. He interprets malawi as 'hot, low-lying land', this meaning being derived from the vibrations of hot air which 'look like flames of fire'. He adds that the name refers in the first place to that part of the lake shore which stretches between the Linthipe river in the north and the modern township of Fort Johnston in the south, this being the area where the Maravi immigrants initially settled.[4]

Acknowledgement should also be made of a theory proposed by T. Price who suggests that the flames referred to may have been those of the smelting fires of iron workers.[5] The author himself admits, however, that he has found no corroboration in oral history for his theory, and I shall therefore treat it separately.

All three popular traditions mentioned above are based on an identical and generally accepted etymology of the name which conveys the idea of fire flames or the optical illusion of flames caused by heat or light. Apart from this, however, they have some other points in common. One is their reference to the lake, the other their reference to ancestral migrations. Thus, they provide us with a preliminary answer to the question of Maravi identity: they were immigrants, who were somehow associated with fire, and who settled on the lake shore.

There is a second strain of traditions, which do not purport to explain the origin of the name, but nonetheless associate fire with a wave of migrations. These traditions, a number of which I recorded among the Mang'anja of the Chikwawa District, tell us how, on their way south, one section of the immigrants who bore the name of Phiri, trekked over the hills, whereas the others kept to the valleys. So that they might not lose sight of each other, the Phiri were in the habit of setting the grass on the hills alight. Yet other versions, obtained from the same area, mention that the Phiri introduced fire to the country whose inhabitants, until then, had eaten their food raw. A similar tradition is found in the lake shore area where it is said that the Phiri immigrants gave the autochthonous population fried fish to eat, which they were not used to, and which consequently caused them to vomit.[6]

A number of differences appear to exist with respect to the first strain of traditions. First, the immigrants are said to have belonged to the Phiri clan. Second, these Phiri brought fire rather than just seeing or finding it. This particular difference relates to a third one which is the appearance on the scene of another group of people, distinct from the Phiri, with whom contact is established by means of fire. This again relates to a different focal event: it is not the name-taking which is central to the story but the effect which the possession or introduction of fire has on the other group. Finally, it should be noted that all traditions of the first strain locate the central event in the lake shore area, whereas those of the second strain mention different locations.

It would appear that the two strains mentioned relate in reality to the same broad event but that they represent respectively the traditions of the invaders and those of the autochthonous people among whom they settled.[7] This would lead us to the conclusion that the Maravi mentioned in some of these traditions are identical to the Phiri figuring in the others. However, as we cannot draw such a conclusion from the stories themselves, we shall have to find other sources for further corroboration. Since we have seen that the name 'Malawi' was used to indicate places and people, the appropriate areas to look for further evidence seem to be those indicated by topography and ethnography.

Topographic uses of the name Malawi

Topographically, the name Malawi is or has been used to indicate the south-western lake area as well as three categories of places, i.e. ancient settlements, hills and royal shrines. Each of these categories will be discussed separately, and possible connections between them and the Phiri will be examined.

There is substantial evidence that Malawi, as the name for a district, was particularly applied to the south-western lake area. I have already quoted Ntara to this effect, but the same opinion has been expressed by Rangeley and Price, and local investigations have confirmed that to this day the inhabitants of the area south and north of the Nkadzipulu stream regard their area as the original Malawi.[8] This view seems to have been shared by some of the early travellers for there is extant a map which indicates the south-western lake area as 'the kingdom of Maravi, the principal kingdom of the Bororos', the latter name being used in those days as a kind of generic indication for the peoples north of the lower Zambezi.[9] It is in this area that the principal ruler Karonga made his first headquarters which also bore the name Malawi.

The earliest known document indicating this is a letter written in 1624 by the Jesuit missionary Luis (Luigi) Mariano, resident at Tete, to his religious superior in Goa. The name Malawi (Maravj) occurs no less than six times throughout Mariano's letter as that of the capital of a Chief Muzura, which he located at some point half a league from the south-western lake shore.[10] This Muzura has been identified by modern historians as one of the Karonga paramounts, who were known to the seventeenth century Portuguese as the principal rulers of the Empire of Malawi. Mariano, who had not been to the lake himself, had drawn up his report from interviews with a number of travellers. One such, by the name of Gaspar Bocarro, had been there in 1616, some eight years before Mariano's letter was written, but his report appeared much later.[11] He too, mentions Malawi (Maravy) as Muzura's capital, although in his report its location is somewhat further away from the lake. Subsequent maps, however, all locate the capital Malawi in the area indicated by Mariano. Whatever its precise location, there is little or no doubt that the capital of the Karonga rulers was in the south-western lake district and known by the name Malawi.

Another capital known by that name was that of Kaphwiti, the first paramount of the Mang'anja. He had broken away from the Karonga at some time before the sixteenth century and had established himself to the south-west on

93

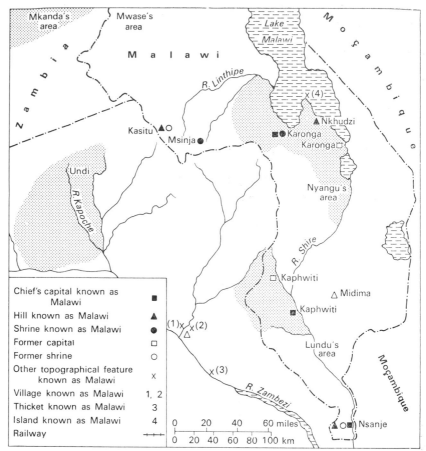

Chief's capital known as Malawi ■
Hill known as Malawi ▲
Shrine known as Malawi ●
Former capital □
Former shrine ○
Other topographical feature known as Malawi ×
Village known as Malawi 1, 2
Thicket known as Malawi 3
Island known as Malawi 4
Railway ++++

6.1   Topographic and ethnographic occurrence of the name *Malawi*

the banks of the Wamkurumadzi river, a tributary of the Shire.

There are two points to be made here: the first is that both rulers were Phiri clansmen, which suggests that the name was particularly used to indicate Phiri settlements. This is explicitly confirmed by Ntara's important statement that the Phiri were in the habit of calling their settlements Malawi.[12] The second point is that both capitals had an alternative name, that of the Karonga being Mankhamba, and that of Kaphwiti being Khumbo. It would appear therefore that Phiri settlements were known both by the generic name Malawi and by a proper name. In the political and ethnic upheavals which followed at later periods the proper name tended to survive so that on modern maps we find, for instance, Mankhamba instead of Malawi.

There are at least four hills or mountains within the boundaries of present day Malawi known by that name. From north to south these are in the Kasitu section of the Dzalanyama Range west of Dedza; in the Nkhudzi Bay area

94

south of Cape Maclear; along the Midima road a few miles south-east of the city of Blantyre; and in the lower Shire valley south of Nsanje township. Here again, it appears that there exist definite associations with the Phiri clan which are of a semantic, historical and religious order.

First, the Chichewa word for hill is *phiri*. Second, in the accounts of oral history the Phiri are constantly referred to as 'the people of the hills', their name being variously derived from the fact that they are said to have camped on hills, trekked over hills or built their settlements on hills. Third, it has been established in three of the four instances mentioned above, that these hills were sacred to ancestral worship, and that two of these definitely belonged to the Phiri clan.

The two shrines referred to as being definitively Phiri are those of Msinja near the Dzalanyama range and of Khulubvi near Nsanje. The foundation of the former is ascribed either to the second Karonga or to the first Undi who ruled over the western section of the Maravi peoples.[13] The Khulubvi shrine near Nsanje is said to have been established by the Kaphwiti paramounts at a time when their power still extended to the north bank of the Zambezi. At a later date it was taken over by the Lundu chiefs after they had supplanted the Kaphwitis in the southern part of their paramountcy. A third instance of a Phiri cult area known by the name Malawi is that of the sacred grove of the deceased Karongas on the north bank of the Nkadzipulu stream.[14] The important point again is that all four royal houses mentioned belong to the Phiri clan, and it may be stated, by way of general conclusion, that there is every evidence of a constant association of the name Malawi in its topographical sense with that clan.

Ethnographic occurrence of the name Malawi

The name Malawi as an ethnic designation has been used in different senses from the earliest documents onwards. It has sometimes been used as a blanket term for all the peoples living between the Zambezi and the southern part of the lake, and as such it was interchangeable with the designation *Bororo*. But it was also realized that there were groups within this agglomeration which could be called the Maravi proper. Thus we have seen how an eighteenth century map mentions the south-western lake area as 'the kingdom of Maravi, the principal kingdom of the Bororos'.

Gamitto was the first of the modern ethnographers to define the Maravi proper. According to him they were the people living east of the Shombwe stream in the present day Moçambique. He distinguishes these Maravi from the Chewa living to the west of them and the Mang'anja whom he placed to the north.[15] The Livingstone expedition's identification of the Maravi is equally important. After some initial confusion they were gradually able to assert the existence of two groups of Maravi proper: one in the triangle formed by the west bank of the Shire and the south bank of the Wamkurumadzi river, who were under the leadership of Kaphwiti; the other in the area between Mt Dedza and the lake shore, the traditional land of the Karongas where

Rebman, too, had located the Maravi some fifteen years earlier.[16] Both Gamitto and Livingstone recognized the historical, linguistic and cultural unity of these Maravi with the other Chewa-speaking peoples, although Gamitto was of the opinion that the Yao, Makua and Lomwe also belonged to them.

It will be noted that these three groups of Maravi were found in the areas of three of the most important Phiri chiefs, which again suggests an association with the Phiri clan. But in all three areas as well as in a fourth not yet mentioned, the chiefdom of Mkanda in Zambia, the same populations now refer to themselves by other names: those of the south-western lake shore are now known as Nyanja, those of Undi and Mkanda as Chewa, and those of Kaphwiti as Mang'anja. It would therefore seem that a change of name has taken place, and in two or three areas we may even pinpoint with some precision the time when this change occurred. Thus the inhabitants of the chiefdom of Mkanda were known to Lacerda in 1798 as Maravi and to Gamitto in 1831 as Chewa.[17] Again, in the thirty-odd years which elapsed between Livingstone's travels and Sir Harry Johnston's writings the name seems to have virtually disappeared from the lower Shire and lake areas, for he writes that Maravi as an ethnic name was nearly extinct in those days.[18] What ought we to make of this?

It has sometimes been suggested that the entire Chewa-speaking population once referred to itself as Maravi, and that the present ethnic designations originated with a later and rather recent fragmentation of the mother body.[19] This, to me, seems to be an oversimplification of the facts. For one thing, we have some evidence in Portuguese documents of the seventeenth century that the present ethnic designations were already used at that time. The names Nyanja and Mang'anja occur already, although it is not quite clear whether they were also used as ethnic names.[20] Oral history, on the other hand, is much more emphatic. The Nyanja and Mang'anja state that they were called *Chipeta* before they took their present names, and by way of proof they point to a rock in the old Mang'anja land in which M'bona, their guardian spirit, is said to have carved his tribal tattoos when he arrived there from the north. Elsewhere, I have tried to define the tattoo episode as one of the earliest M'bona traditions, probably antedating the arrival of the Kaphwitis in the fifteenth century.[21] Even if the episode belongs to a later tradition, it must have originated before the close of the sixteenth century, when the third and last M'bona was murdered by Lundu.

The available evidence then points to the existence of specific ethnic designations long before Lacerda's travels, and it appears therefore that the Chewa-speaking peoples were once known by two names: a specific and a generic one, the latter being Maravi. It also seems that the ethnic designation Maravi gradually faded away and had almost disappeared in Sir Harry Johnston's time. However, the question remains whether the Chewa speakers as a whole ever referred to themselves as Maravi. In my opinion this has never been the case. Instead each Chewa-speaking tribe seems to have consisted of two sections: the Maravi and the non-Maravi; and this distinction seems to have been based on their traditional clan organization. I shall try to clarify this

96

point with reference to the situation in the Chikwawa District.

The traditional inhabitants of this district are the Mang'anja. However, we have seen how Livingstone found that in the triangle formed by the Shire and the Wamkurumadzi Rivers north of the Chikwawa Boma the Mang'anja referred to themselves as Maravi. On the other hand, both Livingstone and Kirk state that on the opposite bank of the Shire there were only Mang'anja and no Maravi.[22] Why this distinction within one and the same ethnic group? The answer may be provided by the distribution of clans.

The Chikwawa District has a very high percentage of Phiri and Banda clansmen. An examination of the baptismal records of the Chikwawa Mission for the period 1918–28 reveals that, of the 1,300 persons registered, forty per cent were Phiri and twenty-two per cent Banda, the remaining thirty-eight per cent being shared among forty-seven other clans, none of which accounted for more than four per cent of the total. A factor of the utmost importance is that the majority of Phiri in these registers came from the north-western part of the district, which was Livingstone's Maravi district. The tentative conclusion, then, is that the Phiri Mang'anja referred to themselves as Maravi, whereas the other sections always called themselves Mang'anja. This conclusion is supported by the evidence adduced in the topographic section, and, if it is correct, it may explain why some of the related peoples were also known by two different names, and why, in particular, Lacerda referred to Mkanda's people as Maravi, while Gamitto knew them as Chewa. The definitions seem to have depended on the area in which the information was obtained. If the area were predominantly Phiri, the answer to the ethnic question may have been Maravi, whereas in non-Phiri areas the answer given may have been the proper ethnic name.

One last question remains: why did the Phiri cease to call themselves Maravi? Here I venture the opinion that this was due to the breaking down of the traditional clan organization as a result of the post-1850 invasions and the subsequent alienation of much of the land of the Phiri clan.

II   THE SYMBOLISM OF FIRE

If the hypothesis that the Phiri were called Maravi or 'people of the fire flames' in contrast to the non-Phiri holds true, the question arises why this association with fire was so forcibly and consistently made?

The Phiri, who were Iron Age people, may have come to Malawi as early as the fourteenth century.[23] According to Professor Desmond Clark the use of fire dates from the end of the Earlier Stone Age. He further maintains that its knowledge spread to southern Africa in the late Chelles-Acheul times, and that by the time of the first Intermediate Stone Age it must have been almost universal.[24] The pre-Phiri inhabitants of the country were, therefore, people who, from time immemorial, had known the use of fire. Yet, some traditions about the Phiri suggest, and others clearly state, that they were the ones who *introduced* it. It would therefore appear that their mastership of fire is to be regarded as a kind of symbolic statement about some other reality, and I would like to suggest two things in particular as the historical contents of this statement. First, the appearance of fire in these stories characterizes the advent of the Phiri as an important transition in the history of the Chewa speakers. Secondly, it indicates the effect of this transition to have been the establishment of the Phiri as the new ruling class. This theory is based, on the one hand, on the specific function of fire in myths and transition rites, and, on the other hand, on the role of fire as a symbol of royal status.

Fire as a Symbol of Transition

In the main transition rites of the Chewa speakers burning marks the close of the marginal period in which persons pass from one condition to another and during which they are in a state of incompleteness and vulnerability. This is most clearly visible in the life cycle rites of puberty and death, at the completion of which the huts of the initiates and of the deceased are burnt together with some objects left over from the past stage. Both events were traditionally solemnized by the sacred *nyau* mimes which in their turn are brought to a close by the burning of the zoomorphic structures which envelop the performers during the dance.[25]

Similarly, the function of fire as a transitional symbol is vividly brought out by the primal myth of the Chewa peoples. In this myth fire appears as the agent which radically changed the primal condition of the cosmos. It relates how at first spirits and animals were living peacefully together with man, at a time when agriculture was still the only way of obtaining food. One day, however, man accidentally invented fire, which spread to the surrounding grasslands and drove the spirits and the animals away. God, who also had to flee, proclaimed that, because of this evil deed, man should die and join him on high. From that day onwards there was hostility between men and animals. Man set about hunting the animals of the bush, and the animals took revenge by afflicting unprotected hunters with a mystical disease causing madness and death.[26]

The primal myth may be regarded as a reflection on the seasonal cycle in Malawi, which is marked by a wet and a dry period. The main occupation during the wet season is agriculture. The dry period is, particularly towards its close, characterized by bush and grass fires which flare up everywhere. In days gone by parts of the forest were often set alight by hunters in order to trap game. Here again, fire functions as a transitional symbol dividing two periods which are contrasted with each other in terms of the climatic and the occupational cycle.

The final puberty and death rituals mentioned above, which are usually performed during the dry season, are lent cosmic significance by the performance of the *nyau* ceremony which, from the religious viewpoint, is to be regarded as a re-enactment of the primal myth. Thus, the major changes of the human life cycle are drawn into the perspective of the climatic cycle, and, conversely, the burning of the land appears to derive part of its symbolic

5.6 Chiromo Post Office. The photograph shows Nyasaland's first post office, opened in 1891, with the first postmaster, H. C. Marshall, in his *machila*

9.2 Phoka cave dwellers near Khondwe, Mount Waller (Chombe), 1895

12.2   Hora Mountain

12.3   Inkosi Amon Mtwalo (1873–1970) and his wife Emily Nhlane. Behind them are Petros Moyo, Mopo Jere and Charles Chinula

12.4   Inkosi ya Makosi, M'Mbelwa II

16.2 Mlozi

1.6 Skeleton found on the Hora Mountain

significance from the human transition rites.

It seems, therefore, that in view of its parallels with the primal myth and the transition ceremonies, we are justified in interpreting the finding or introduction of fire by the Phiri as a symbolic statement about the beginning of a new era. More specifically, the Phiri era was characterized by the establishment of new dynasties which for one thing seem to have put greater emphasis on the permanency of the chief's tenure of office than the ones preceding them. In local oral traditions this change of governmental organization is expressed in terms of sexual polarity, as a change from female to male leadership.[27]

Since it is one of this paper's contentions that the theme of fire in the migration stories of the Maravi also refers to their coming in the capacity of rulers, I shall now briefly examine the function of fire as a royal symbol.

Fire as a Symbol of Royal Power

In the context of royal rituals fire appears to symbolize the role of the living rulers as the source of fertility and order, and that of the deceased chiefs as the providers of rain.

The chief in Chewa mythology is often portrayed as the custodian of fire. This is, for instance, brought out by a tradition recovered at Nambuma about Undi. The story relates how Undi lived in a hive-shaped structure, the roof of which descended to the ground. In this hut he kept a perpetual fire which he fed day and night with pieces of reed mats cut by himself. These mats were the ones on which girls had been anointed at the conclusion of their pubertal ceremonies, and they were considered a symbol of fertility.[28] Undi's action as described in this tradition may therefore be regarded as a ritual which he had to perform for the benefit of his country.

When the chief died, the royal fire was quenched and only relighted when his heir succeeded to the office. A general state of disorder ensued during which people could rob and plunder at will and molest travellers, as was witnessed by Gamitto.[29] By so doing the people were ritually returning to the state the country was in before the coming of the local dynasty, and the quenching of the royal fire marked a period in which the normal functioning of the chief's office had been interrupted.

Fire was also regarded as a symbolic representation of the deceased chiefs and their power of providing rain. The bush and grass fires which flare up everywhere during the dry season and the dense smoke which they produce are, in the context of the primal myth, associated with the ascent of the royal spirits to the sky. Smoke clouds are thought to be converted into rain clouds, and when these have been formed, the spirits descend again with the rains as in the primordial times. The climatic cycle is thus conceived of as a giant twofold movement, in which the royal spirits alternate between the sky and the earth to ensure a regular rainfall.[30] This idea is well illustrated by a ceremony at the Phiri shrine of Bunda Hill where the officials ritually set fire to the hill every year in the month of September in order 'to call the rains'.[31] The name 'Malawi', thus, also refers to the royal spirits under the aspect of fire and rain-giving, and it may therefore be considered as an archaic name

99

for such spirits.[32] This was vividly brought home to me one day when I was looking at the Malawi Hill near Nsanje. I asked three men who were standing at the road side why the hill was called Malawi, and their spontaneous answer was, '*Nanga si mizimu?*' (Is it not because of the spirits?). Cult areas seem therefore to have been called Malawi not only because of Phiri ownership, but also because of the Phiri spirits to which they were sacred.

This reference to royal rituals, however brief, may suffice for our purpose. It suggests that fire was thought of as symbolically expressive of the chief's personal existence—fire disappears with the old chief and returns with his successor—and of his main functions in respect of the promotion of order and fertility.

At this point I may perhaps take up Price's theory that the name Malawi may have referred to the smelting furnaces which at one time abounded in the country. Traditions in the Chikwawa area maintain that they were controlled by the Phiri chiefs, in other words by the Maravi. There is as yet no further evidence to support this view, but, if it is correct, there would indeed be a demonstrable connection between the name Malawi and the smelting furnaces, although in quite another sense than the one proposed by Price.

III   SUMMARY

It appears that the name Malawi has been used in the past by the Chewa peoples to indicate members of the Phiri clan as well as districts, settlements and cult centres particularly associated with that clan. Data supporting this view has been obtained from the fields of oral history, topography and ethnography.

With regard to the meaning of the name, it has been stated in agreement with every known tradition and opinion that the primary idea conveyed is that of fire flames. Further, it has been shown from the evidence of oral traditions that the Phiri invaders were explicitly associated with fire, or more particularly, that they were reputed to have brought fire to this country. As this statement was seen to be historically incorrect, its message has then been analyzed in terms of the symbolism of fire. Fire appeared to have two symbolic functions relevant to the subject under consideration. One of these is that fire in myth and ritual marks the division between two well-defined periods and the end of a state of disorder and danger. By the same token, its reputed introduction by the Phiri has been interpreted in terms of the introduction of a new order, radically different from the one preceding it. In the traditional political context fire seems to have been an important royal symbol, and its association with the Phiri has been interpreted as a statement about their coming to the country in the capacity of rulers.

1 Part of the material for this paper was collected during a period of field research in 1966–67, financed by the Nuffield Foundation, London, to whom grateful acknowledgement is made.

2 In this paper the spelling 'Malawi' will be used whenever the name occurs in a general context and when it is used as a geographic designation; 'Maravi' will be written when the name is used in an ethnographic sense.

3 Malawi Government, *A Portrait of Malawi*, (Zomba, 1964), 4.

4 S. Y. Ntara, *Mbiri ya Achewa*, (Limbe, 1965), 20.

5 T. Price, 'The Meaning of Mang'anja', *Nyasa. J.*, **16**, (1), 1963, 74–7.

6 Personal communication by Dr F. Mnthali, Univ. of Malawi.

7 J. M. Schoffeleers, 'The Theme of Fire in Some Chewa Migration Stories: a Case for Structural Analysis', (In preparation).

8 W. H. J. Rangeley, 'Makewana the Mother of All People', *Nyasa. J.*,, **10** (2), 1952, 32; T. Price, 'More about the Maravi', *Afr. Stud.*, **11** (2) 1952, 76. The views of these two authors are confirmed by Dr I. Linden, University of Malawi, who has recently conducted research in the area.

9 A facsimile of this map, dated 1772, in *Portrait of Malawi*, 13.

10 L. Mariano (1624) in G. Beccari, *Rerum Aethiopicarum Scriptores Occidentales*, (Rome, 1912), XII, 112–14.

11 G. M. Theal, *Records of South-Eastern Africa*, (London, 1898–1903), III, 416.

12 Ntara, *Mbiri*, 20; Thornton, a member of the Livingstone expedition, noted the existence of two settlements called 'Malawi' on the north bank of the Zambezi opposite Tete, but he gives no further details; cf. E. C. Tabler (ed.), *The Zambezi Papers of Richard Thornton*, (London, 1963), I, 96, 97, 201.

13 The Karonga tradition is in Ntara, *Mbiri*, 13; that of Undi in Rangeley, 'Makewana', 32–3. The present officials accept neither version, insisting that its foundation should be attributed to the first Makewana (Interview, October, 1969).

14 W. H. J. Rangeley, 'M'bona the Rain Maker', *Nyasa. J.*, **6** (1), 1953, 9; Livingstone also mentions a thicket by the name of 'Malawi' on the north

bank of the Zambezi, below Tete, and Kirk, one of his companions, noted a little island 'Malawi' off Cape Maclear, but neither author provides further details; cf. J. P. R. Wallis ed., *The Zambezi Expedition of David Livingstone*, (London, 1956), I, 176; R. Foskett ed., *The Zambezi Journal and Letters of Dr. John Kirk*, (Edinburgh, 1965), I, 368, 369.

15 A. C. P. Gamitto, *O Muata Cazembe*, (Lisbon, 1854); this and the following references are to the English translation by I. Cunnison, entitled *King Kazembe*, (Lisbon, 1960); the reference here is to vol. I, 63.

16 J. Rebman, *Dictionary of the Kiniasa Language*, (Basle, 1877), introduction; Wallis ed., *Livingstone*, 96, 173, 189, 194, 319; Foskett ed., *Kirk*, 117, 172, 353, 363.

17 R. F. Burton, ed., *The Lands of Kazembe*, (London, 1873), 76; Gamitto, *King Kazembe*, I, 62.

18 H. H. Johnston, *British Central Africa*, (London, 1897), 59.

19 E. H. Lane Poole, *The Native Tribes of the Eastern Province of N. Rhodesia*, (Lusaka, 1938),34; T. C. Young, 'The Idea of God in Northern Nyasaland', in E. W. Smith ed., *African Ideas of God*, (London, 1950), 37; M. G. Marwick, 'History and Tradition in East-Central Africa through the eyes of the Northern-Rhodesian Chewa', *J. Afr. Hist.*, 4, 1963, 378.

20 M. G. Theal, *Records*, III, 361, 416; VII, 266.

21 J. M. Schoffeleers, 'The History and Political Role of the M'bona Cult Among the Mang'anja', Dar es Salaam—UCLA Conference on the History of African Religions, (Dar es Salaam, June 1970).

22 Wallis, ed., *Livingstone*, 173; Foskett, ed., *Kirk*, 363.

23 E. Alpers, 'The Mutapa and Malawi Political Systems', in T. O. Ranger, ed., *Aspects of Central African History*, (London, 1968), 19. Abraham's view of a kin relationship between the Mbire clan Soko-Chirongo and the Maravi clan Phiri-Chirongo, quoted by Alpers in this context, may find some lexicologic corroboration in R. S. Rattray, *Some Folk-Lore Stories and Songs in Chinyanja*, (London, 1917), 175–6. Rattray states that the food taboo of the Phiri was the flesh of the baboon, whose archaic name he renders as *soko*. A southern lake shore myth explaining the origin of the Phiri clan also relates this event in the context of a quarrel between a baboon and a wild pig. In consequence of this quarrel the animals separated for ever, the baboon taking the name of 'Phiri' for himself and retiring to the hills.

24 J. D. Clark, *The Prehistory of South Africa*, (Penguin, 1959), 104, 105,

25 A detailed description of these rites in J. M. Schoffeleers, Symbolic and Social Aspects of Mang'anja Religion, (Ph.D. dissertation, Oxford, 1968).

26 J. M. Schoffeleers, 'A Theology of Bush-fires', Paper read to the Philosophical Society of Malawi (publication forthcoming).

27 Ntara, Mbiri, (1950, ed.), 34; an identical statement was made in the most emphatic manner by the Msinja officials (Interview, October 1969).

28 Manuscript by the late Father Darot, (Nambuma, 1930).

29 Gamitto, King Kazembe, I, 102, 103; Mary Tew, The Peoples of the Lake Nyasa Region, (London, 1950), 14, 15.

30 Schoffeleers, 'Bush-fires'.

31 Interview September 1969.

32 This has first been recognized by R. Von Sicard, Ngoma Lungundu, eine Afrikanische Bundeslade, (Uppsala, 1952), 29; the author renders the name Maravi as 'die flammenden Ahnengeister'.

7 Chewa or Malawi Political Organization in the Precolonial Era

Harry W. Langworthy

The present traditional political organization of most of the Chewa, Mang'anja and Nyanja peoples, in a number of separate and more or less independent chieftainships—showing little evidence of a centralized political system—has not always been the case, as has been assumed with some justification by some. This present structure is largely the result of various factors, mainly of the nineteenth century, which encouraged the disintegration of much larger kingdoms, such as those of Kalonga, Undi and Lundu. It is the purpose of this paper to show what the probable structure of these kingdoms was, mainly by drawing on oral sources, but also using Portuguese sources to a certain extent. What is described is a somewhat static model which may not have existed in all of its parts at any one time, but it reflects the ideal structure which one can interpret is believed to have existed. Although this is largely an ideal reconstruction, factors of change as well as some of the changes in the political structure are considered.

In this paper I do not distinguish between the various names for the Malawi peoples, but use the term Chewa. I consider Malawi to be a term which largely applies to the rulers who immigrated from Luba country in Katanga. Nyanja, Mang'anja, Chipeta, Mbo, Ntumba, Chewa and other names I consider to be regional place names for the people of similar culture and language who came to be ruled by the Malawi kings and chiefs. The term Chewa is used here largely as most of the evidence is drawn from Undi's Malawi kingdom and its smaller neighbouring kingdoms of Chulu, Mkanda and the Mwases.[2]

This treatment of political structure owes much to the writings of Vansina, Lloyd and Southall who have considered various types of kingdom organization. Lloyd has suggested that one of the most important aspects of kingdom organization was how the rulers were selected. To a great extent the method of selecting rulers influenced the patterns of conflict and the degree of centralized power in a kingdom. The types of conflict caused political change, with which history is largely concerned. Other aspects of kingdom organization are both described and analysed in an attempt to show their significance for an understanding of history.[3]

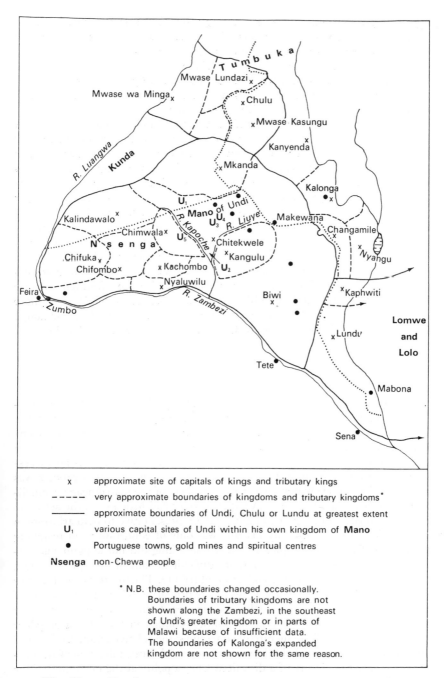

x	approximate site of capitals of kings and tributary kings
- - - -	very approximate boundaries of kingdoms and tributary kingdoms*
———	approximate boundaries of Undi, Chulu or Lundu at greatest extent
U_1	various capital sites of Undi within his own kingdom of **Mano**
●	Portuguese towns, gold mines and spiritual centres
Nsenga	non-Chewa people

* N.B. these boundaries changed occasionally.
Boundaries of tributary kingdoms are not
shown along the Zambezi, in the southeast
of Undi's greater kingdom or in parts of
Malawi because of insufficient data.
The boundaries of Kalonga's expanded
kingdom are not shown for the same reason.

7.1 The Chewa kingdoms

In addition to the methods of selecting rulers the other aspects of political organization which will be considered are relations between a king and his family, relations between a king and his subordinates and relations between a king and his council. These relations include considerations of bureaucratic organization, religious and spiritual affairs, the king's responsibilities for military protection, the administration of justice and the organization of and control over natural resources, tribute and trade.

Basically a kingdom can be distinguished from a chieftaincy by extensive territorial organization, a hierarchy of rule, delegated authority and a degree of centralization of power. In the Chewa kingdoms there could be four, three or two main levels of the pyramidal hierarchy of rulers: a king, in some cases tributary kings, chiefs who were subordinate either to a king or a tributary king and finally head men who were subordinate to a king, a tributary king or a chief. There were also councillor-officials at all levels. The distinction between kings and tributary kings is largely a matter of degree which partly depended on what period is being considered. The great kings were Kalonga, Lundu, Undi and possibly Chulu who had tributary kings under them. Some of the tributary kings under these great kings became independent kings at a later date. These included Kanyenda, Mkanda, Mwase Kasungu, Mwase Lundazi, Changamile and probably Kaphwiti. Undi seems to have been more successful in keeping his tributary kings relatively loyal. They included Chimwala, Kangulu, Kalindawalo, Chifombo, Chifuka and Nyaluwilo.

Selection of rulers

The method of selecting chiefs, tributary kings and kings for already established positions varied only slightly from area to area and from time to time. Generally a position was filled by unilinear inheritance, from within one matrilineage. The matrilineages of the different chiefs within a kingdom area were independent of each other and, unlike the Bemba, there was no succession from a junior position to a more senior one. The selection process was basically a local affair which concerned members of the matrilineage, councillors and subordinate headmen. A superior ruler had little say in the selection of a subordinate. Although he might send a representative to help arbitrate in a succession dispute, basically his role was only of confirming and installing the choice of the local people. The fact that a king did not appoint his subordinate rulers meant that it was more difficult to control them, to maintain their loyalty and to ensure the collection of tribute. The interests and loyalties of the subordinate rulers in a kingdom were primarily to both the members of their own lineages and the people in their area, both of whom had selected them. The most significant type of political conflict in the Chewa kingdom was between levels of the hierarchy concerning the relative amount of central authority which the king held. It was the successful decentralization of authority which gave the picture of a disunited Chewa polity at the beginning of the colonial era.

Although a king could not control the selection of his subordinates, it seems at least for a while in Undi's kingdom that Undi could unofficially make known whom he thought was the most qualified candidate, especially if there was a dispute at the local level. Another way in which a king occasionally could influence the selection of a subordinate was to create a new position in part of the area of the already established position in an attempt to diminish the power of the established position. In extreme cases it seems that it was possible for a king to remove a subordinate who was unsatisfactory. However, all of those attempts to influence the selection of a subordinate could only be successfully carried out with the cooperation of at least some of the people at the local level.

A King's Relations with his Family

The method of selecting the subordinate rulers in a kingdom was probably the most important aspect determining a king's power, the degree of centralization in his kingdom and the types of conflict which occurred. However, the succession patterns for the kingships were also important in the same terms of king's powers, degree of centralization and patterns of conflict. Whereas all Chewa kingdoms had basically the same methods of selecting chiefs, and so had similar conflicts over relative centralization of authority, the rules concerning a king's succession differed. The most senior and oldest kingdom, that of Kalonga, up to probably the late 1500s evidently had a system whereby any male who was a son of Nyangu, Kalonga's mother or sister, was eligible to succeed. Thus both younger brothers and sisters' sons were eligible to succeed. The selection of a new Kalonga seems to have been done mainly by his councillors, although there may have been competition among those eligible for the support of the councillors. An additional factor influencing the succession may have existed in this period, although possibly this did not become a rule until later. In order to be installed, the chosen Kalonga had to marry Mwali, who held the position of perpetual wife of Kalonga. While Kalonga was of the Phiri clan, she was from a local lineage of the Banda clan. This Banda lineage, which was linked in 'cousinship' with Kalonga's position, was probably that of Kalonga's senior councillor.[4]

The early succession to the Kalongaship probably was not particularly unstable, except that conflict within the royal family, particularly between generations, was possible. In the case of a prolonged dispute the absence of central authority could have been taken advantage of by subordinate rulers or external forces who wished to decentralize Kalonga's authority. Sometime, probably in the late 1500s, there was a succession dispute which in the long run seems to have had disastrous effects on Kalonga's central authority. The brother of the deceased Kalonga, Undi, was passed over and a young nephew was installed as the new Kalonga by the councillors. After continued quarrels Undi, who was probably the *nkhoswe* or guardian of the matrilineal segment, left Kalonga. Undi took with him Nyangu, the perpetual mother, and all of the female members of Kalonga's segment of the royal Phiri lineage. This meant that Kalonga had no means of ensuring his own succession. The

Kalonga from whom Undi departed may have been Kalonga Muzura, or Masula, who greatly expanded the kingdom into a short-lived empire in the early 1600s.[5] This secession of Undi almost certainly resulted in a very unsuitable succession for the Kalongaship, which is one of the main reasons for its decline.

After Undi's departure from Kalonga, to found his own kingdom, the senior royal Chewa matrilineage was controlled by Undi, not Kalonga. On the death of a Kalonga a successor had to be sought from Undi.[6] Although this would have entailed delays in installation, this feature of Kalonga's succession was not in itself detrimental to Kalonga's central authority. What was probably the main factor in the decline of Kalonga's powers was that as he did not have mothers and sisters to produce brothers and nephews, he did not have the vital continuing support of close royal kin in his capital. Instead he had the restrictions of the councillors who were of local Banda lineages and which included the family of his perpetual wife, Mwali. It is likely that by the local Banda councillors' insistence that a Kalonga-designate marry Mwali in order to be installed that they may have undermined much of the personal power of the Kalongaship. Perhaps they delayed recognizing a candidate sent by Undi until concessions had been agreed upon which were to their own local advantage. It seems most likely that the peculiar and unsuitable succession to the Kalongaship produced a situation which made easier the decentralization of the authority of the Kalongaship built by Masula. An important element in the decline of Kalonga's central authority could have been the influence of external agents, as suggested by Alpers.[7] An important pattern of conflict, over the succession to the kingship, compounded the potentially weakening effects of another type of conflict of the tendency towards decentralization which was inherent in the Chewa system.

It appears that the succession to the Undiship was not as stable as was Kalonga's. Perhaps the first Undi consciously established a pattern which could help to avoid the type of conflict and secession seen in the case of Undi's departure from Kalonga. Potential successors still had to be sons of the perpetual mother and sister, Nyangu, but it appears that brothers of the late Undi were excluded in favour of nephews. This eliminated a number of potential sources of conflict. In addition, while the kingdom expanded, Undi pursued a policy of sending many of his nephews, and potential heirs, to be chiefs of small areas. As these nephews were given new positions they were no longer eligible to compete for the Undiship. This system lasted until the middle of the nineteenth century. As a result of the stability of succession to the Undiship there seems to have been greater continuity of rule and less opportunity for subordinate rulers and external forces to take advantage of weakness and conflict at the centre of the kingdom, as was the case in so many central African kingdoms.[8]

Other lesser Chewa kings, such as Chulu, Kanyenda, Mkanda and Mwase Kasungu seem not to have had the institution of perpetual mother and sister. In some instances brothers were preferred over nephews for the succession, and in all cases the succession allowed brothers to succeed following the older pattern of the Kalongaship from which these positions were derived.[9] Although succession disputes are not generally remembered in Chewa history they seem to have been present from time to time in these small kingdoms. Little is known about succession and conflict either in the extinct position of Changamile in Dowa district or in the more important southern Malawi kingships or subordinate kingships of Kaphwiti and Lundu. In Fort Johnston district the important position of Nyangu continued as it was necessary for a woman to be there, who had the perpetual kin relation of mother to Kalonga, even if she was not the mother in real kin terms. This chieftainess was selected from the lineage of Changamile, as Kalonga was nominated from Undi's lineage.[10]

Although succession disputes within a royal family occurred which occasionally led to secession and other debilitating effects on a kingdom, in general the royal family supported the king. It was in the interest of members of a royal family to support the authority of the king which brought them power and wealth. Some of the royal family of a king hoped eventually to succeed to the kingship, while others hoped to be sent out as chiefs to new areas. The continual segmentation of the royal families of the various kings probably was responsible for most of the chiefs of the Phiri clan. The establishment of chiefs and tributary kings who are not of the Phiri clan was a more complex affair than segmentation as will be seen. As long as there seemed to be ample chance of assuming a position of political responsibility the members of the royal family were relatively content and probably did not cause too much conflict which might weaken a king's authority. However, it appears that especially during the middle and later nineteenth century, when the various powers of the kings had greatly declined and they were no longer able to provide new areas for their relatives, there was an increase in sorcery and other types of conflict within the royal families.[11]

Just where the royal families began and ended is not easy to determine and seems to have differed from area to area and from time to time. In some areas the royal family would include segments of the matrilineage which were related to the ruler's segment by virtue of having a common grandmother with the king. These more distant segments were in some instances considered royal as they could supply candidates for the succession to the royal position. However, in other areas, in terms of politics at the centre of the kingdom, the royal family was limited to the ruler's segment of the matrilineage with more distant segments rapidly becoming of commoner status unless given a subordinate position. This restricted conflict, as has been mentioned in connection with Undi's succession.

Although the royal family might in fact be relatively restricted in its membership, in theory it was very large and included all of the subordinate rulers, whether or not of the royal clan. All of the chiefs in an area were thought of as being linked by ties of perpetual kinship with the king. The Phiri rulers were thought of as either younger brothers or nephews of the Phiri clan king. In at least one instance a subordinate ruler, Chimwala, who helped install Undi and was an important tributary king, was considered to be a perpetual uncle of Undi. This extension of the royal family in terms of perpetual identity as Phiri rulers was important in terms of maintaining loyalty; however, it did not entirely prevent secession and disloyalty, especially during the nineteenth century.

Probably more important than perpetual kin relations among rulers of the royal clan were relations between Phiri kings and non-Phiri subordinates. The original real kin relationship which was perpetuated between the continuing positions was usually the result of the marriage of a king to a non-Phiri woman. Sometimes these marriages were political ones in attempts to gain control of an area. Chiefs of the Banda clan were thought of as perpetual sons or 'cousins' of a king. In some instances a king would give an area to a favoured son, while in other instances it appears that chiefs of the Banda gained areas as the result of compensation for litigation over a wrong done by a king or another chief to his wife's lineage.[12] Marriages between Phiri rulers and their sisters on the one hand and Banda women and men on the other hand usually did not have political motives in terms of expanding a kingdom although these marriages were politically important in terms of maintaining cousinship with the lineages of councillors. It is possible that the reciprocal relationships including marriage and cousinship between lineages of the Phiri and Banda clans in Kalonga's nuclear area represented an institutionalization of a compromise between immigrating Phiri rulers and older owners of the land as suggested by Hamilton.[13] However, similar relationships between lineages of the Phiri and Banda clans in the younger kingdoms, such as that of Undi, was the result of the migration of both of the clans into the area at the same time.

Much more political than the relations between lineages of the Phiri and Banda clans were the perpetual kin relations between the Phiri kings and their subordinates who were from clans other than Banda. These relations were particularly important with clans which were at least initially non-Chewa. Mkanda, of the Mbewe clan, and Kanyenda, of the Mwale clan, were tributary kings who claim to have been sons of Kalonga. Possibly their mothers were from local clans which had been conquered by the expansion of Kalonga's kingdom. The policy of marrying women of conquered peoples and making their sons chiefs may have been practiced by Kalonga and Lundu in the Makua and Lomwe areas of Mozambique. It was certainly practised by Undi in the expansion of his kingdom. When Undi conquered the independent Chewa king, Mkanda Mbewe, sisters were exchanged and perpetual cousinship started. Undi pursued the same policy when he conquered the Nsenga areas of Kalindawalo, of the Mwanza clan, in Petauke district and Chifuka, of the Lungu clan, in Mozambique.[14] The continuing relationship, with Undi marrying the sisters of his non-Phiri tributary kings, and the tributary kings marrying sisters of Undi helped to maintain a personal relationship which made disloyalty and attempts at secession somewhat more difficult. Although subordinate rulers were not really part of the royal family of a Chewa king the type of perpetual kin relations which were established did give a semblance of family identity to the rulers in a kingdom. Although most of the examples of perpetual kin relations are drawn from Undi's kingdom, from what little is known in other Chewa areas, it seems likely that the political organization in this respect was little different.

A King's Relations with Subordinates

The extension of perpetual kin relationships from a king's immediate royal family to include his subordinates was one aspect of a king's relations with his subordinates which attempted to counter the decentralising tendencies. In succeeding sections other aspects of a king's relations with his subordinates will be examined to show what made up a king's central authority. These aspects include the king's ritual and spiritual services, judicial services, economic services, military protection and control over tribute and trade. The basic principle governing the relations between a king and his subordinate tributary kings and chiefs was one of reciprocity of services from the king in return for goods from subordinates. Most traditional kings who had any degree of central authority outside of their capitals based their authority on this principle and their role as distributor kings.

Ritual, Spiritual and Religious Services

Among the most important services which a king either performed or arranged for were religious ones. The types of religious powers which a king exercised varied greatly from time to time and place to place. All kings had the ritual responsibility of either installing or giving approval for the installation of subordinate rulers. This legitimized the subordinate's authority and confirmed the delegation of authority from a king. However, installation was almost automatic and could not be denied in the Chewa system where the king had little control over the selection process of the rulers.

All kings had access to their ancestral spirits and could call upon them to protect an area and ensure its well-being. As a king was important in the kingdom the spirits of his ancestors were the most important and most effective spirits interceding with God. However, it appears that in terms of approaching ancestral spirits a king did not have a monopoly. In many areas of Phiri chiefs and kings it appears that a member of the Banda clan was in charge of the king's spirit house and had the responsibility of performing services, especially to call rain. Although the king controlled this type of religious service for the people he did not necessarily perform it. This division of religious responsibility was carried even farther as there were two important religious centres for the Chewa peoples which were so important that they were not really controlled by a king. It appears that at both of these centres, of Makewana in Lilongwe district for Undi and to a lesser extent for Kalonga, and of Mbona in Nsanje district for Lundu, there were spirit mediums who had a wide range of religious responsibilities and the ability to speak with God, not just ancestral spirits. As with the various spirit medium centres for the Shona in Rhodesia these two religious centres of Mbona and Makewana were allied with, to a certain extent dependent upon, but not necessarily controlled by, the kings.[15] It appears that when the kings were in a position to protect and maintain these centres, as well as effectively rule the areas surrounding them, then the separate religious institution worked to uphold the king's central authority.

However, it appears, at least for Undi's kingdom, that during the nineteenth century when the king's authority began to diminish and he was no longer able either to control the chiefs around Makewana's centre or to support and protect her court, then Makewana was unwilling or unable to use her religious powers to support Undi. It is probably significant that Undi played no part in the selection of a new Makewana. He could not expect as much loyalty as if he had appointed her from among his relatives or supporters.

It appears that at least the chiefs and kings of the Phiri clan were thought to have very great powers of sorcery.[16] This great power was more than what would be expected from one who had access to the most important ancestral spirits. This power of sorcery was used both to protect and coerce a king's subordinates. At least in Undi's kingdom local sorcerers were sent by subordinate rulers to Undi to be executed or kept as slaves. In other ways a king's powers of sorcery were thought to counter threats to his subordinates. For these and other services loyalty and tribute were expected by the king. If there appeared to be any reluctance on the part of a chief or tributary king to pay tribute it seems that the implicit threat of a king's great sorcery was usually sufficient to overcome any reluctance. However, it is possible that the threat of sorcery by a king to maintain loyalty and obedience might have been a dangerous weapon to use, particularly if subordinate rulers found that it did not work, or became convinced that in their own local areas their own sorcery was more powerful than was the sorcery of a distant king. When the religious services which a king was supposed to perform proved to be ineffective or unnecessary to a subordinate ruler then the vital cycle of reciprocity of goods for services which was basic to the maintenance of central authority was effectively broken. Religious ritual and spiritual powers of a king were the most important in maintaining some degree of loyalty and when decentralization and secession took place these ties were usually the last to be broken.

Judicial Services

It is not clear how important were the judicial services which a king gave. Like most other aspects of his authority a king delegated judicial powers to his subordinates. In some areas it is claimed that the cases which went to Undi were either those which the chiefs could not solve or which involved disputes between chiefs. In other areas it is claimed that as well as the former types of cases any cases which involved the king's ownership of the land and concern for the security of his people went to a king, such as either murder, sorcery, failure to report the death of certain types of royal animals which had either economic value, ritual importance or organs which provided poison, or neglect of or poor performance of local ritual duties.

In theory, and possibly in practice during the periods when the various kingdoms were at the height of their power, a king's judicial powers were considered to be great and he supposedly could intervene in disputes to maintain order and his own authority. In fact during much of the history of Chewa kingdoms it appears that a king's judicial authority can more accurately be considered as that of an arbitrator of disputes which were brought to him. His authority may have been what his subordinates would allow.

It seems likely that the judicial services of Undi, at least, and probably other rulers who were sent out into new areas from Kalonga's capital, were one of the more important reasons for the establishment of Chewa kingdoms in areas where people were already living. Before the coming of a state organization the local Bantu-speaking peoples seem not to have had a political organization beyond village headman. Although villages may have been linked by ties of kinship there was no effective institution for settling disputes between villages short of warfare. Chewa oral sources do not explicitly say that the arrival of Malawi chiefs and kings stopped feuding by the establishment of arbitration services. However, it can be inferred that the coming of impartial rulers and the establishment of a judicial system was welcomed.

Economic Services

As with the judicial services of a kingdom organization, it is also likely that the economic services played a part in the establishment and expansion of the various kingdoms. Furthermore, it was the economic aspects of the political organization which were most important in the vital cycle of reciprocity in terms of what the king received for his services. It was in return for the tribute received from the villages, through the chiefs and tributary kings, that a king gave his various services.

It seems likely that the establishment of some of the Chewa kingdoms, especially Undi's, as well as the expansion of most kingdoms, including that of Kalonga's kingdom in the early 1600s, was partly due to the ability of a king to distribute gifts of cloth and beads to headmen who previously had little opportunity to benefit from external trade. Economic services of redistribution were powerful inducements for the headmen to peacefully accept being included in a kingdom. The continuing pattern of distribution by the king back to chiefs and tributary kings of both items collected in tribute as well as imported trade goods gained from selling tribute goods helped to ensure loyalty and obedience. In addition this process of redistribution made the subordinate rulers to a certain extent economically dependent on the king. The king performed another economic service for his people of keeping large storehouses of grain which could be drawn upon in times of famine. It seems that the kings who lived in the cattle areas, such as Chulu, the Mwases and Mkanda, also kept cattle as insurance against famine. The performance of these economic services by a king presumed the efficient collection of tribute and a degree of control over external trade. In theory there was supposed to have been a monopoly of the collection of ivory tribute as well as a monopoly of its external sale. However, as will be seen, practice diverged from theory from time to time and from area to area. The successful decentralization of tribute and trade was probably the main factor in the decline of the central authority of the kings.

Military Activity

The military power of the kings and their service of providing physical protection for their peoples seems to have been relatively unimportant, compared with other aspects of power and services to maintain support. It is likely that military activities were of some importance in kingdom expansion, as is mentioned by Alpers for Kalonga's kingdom in the 1600s, and as is remembered in the traditions of Undi, Mkanda and others.[17] However, it is also likely that peaceful methods, such as the attraction of judicial services, economic gain, and perhaps spiritual powers were equally as important if not more so in expansion of Chewa rule. What military activity there was, either offensive or defensive, seems not to have been well organized, but was mainly a popular levy gathered from those areas which were willing to send troops. Most military activities took place during the dry season when harvesting had been completed and when travel was easier.

In theory, according to oral sources from Undi's area, a king had the responsibility of providing protection for his people. If his kingdom was invaded the king would call upon his chiefs to send men to deal with the problem. Likewise, if a king took offensive action he could expect the support of men from subordinates' areas. Troops from neighbouring areas of subordinate chiefs might also be used in disciplining other subordinates who were fighting each other or failing to pay tribute.[18] However, the successful military activities of a king depended on the co-operation of his subordinates who sent the men. This support became increasingly reluctant.

Most Chewa remember only the wars of the middle and late nineteenth century such as those of the Yao, Ngoni and Chikunda, depending on the area. These wars were largely responsible for ending the already greatly decentralized powers of most of the kings. By the time these external threats arrived most kingdoms were so disunited that the king of an area was able neither to command support from his subordinates to protect himself nor to provide protection for other parts of his kingdom which had been invaded. Memories of the most recent periods are largely ones of defeat with a few exceptions, the most prominent of which was Mwase Kasungu. Earlier military activities, some of which were presumably successful, probably more nearly approached the theory of what were the military services of the kings and the responsibilities of the people.

Court Organization

One aspect of a king's relations with his subordinates concerns the organization of his capital. In the village of the king lived his relatives, councillors, court officials and many slaves. The councillors and officials helped a king to operate the cycle of reciprocity of services for goods upon which his power was based. They enabled a king to carry out his services to his subordinates and were the vital contacts between him and his tributary kings and chiefs. They also organized the collection of tribute goods.

114

It appears that most of the councillors of Phiri kings were of 'cousin' lineages of the Banda or some other clan. As there had been intermarriage with families of the councillors and cousinship had been established the councillors were free to criticize and joke with the ruler. Councillors had a peculiar relationship with an individual king and his continuing position. Councillors might have more concern for the kingship than the king, for the institution than for the man. They might be considered as representing the people's interests against the arbitrary tendencies of a king. In a sense they provided a check on a king's powers and might be considered as an opposition. Ordinarily by representing their own interests they supported the institution while checking the individual holding the position. However, it appears that the councillors could be more of a check on the king than a supporter of his powers. This seems to have been the case both with the later Kalongas, who had no Phiri clan supporters, and with a late nineteenth century Undi who was faced with the destruction of his kingdom by the Ngoni.

Given the types of responsibilities which the councillors had it is difficult to see in what specific ways they may have opposed a king. They helped the king in decision-making and legal cases. In some areas it is claimed that they only advised the king who made up his own mind. In other areas it seems that there was discussion until a consensus was reached and a king could not go against a majority of his councillors. The councillors also had generalized administrative responsibilities in the capital of looking after the collection and storing of tribute, supervising trade and redistributing items of tribute and trade. They provided hospitality for visitors. They also acted as a clearing house of disputes, problems and reports from the subordinate areas. They represented the king on important missions to subordinate rulers to investigate conditions or to oversee the installation of a ruler. There are no known memories of councillors opposing a king, but it seems that they might have isolated a king or refused to co-operate fully in various duties. Whether councillors could be replaced or overruled by a king is not clear. As councillors were vital links in a king's relations with his subordinates their non-co-operation might have made easier the decentralization of power.

Apart from councillors there were other minor officials such as messengers, guards and personal attendants of the king. There seems not to have been a well organized bureaucracy with officials having specialized functions, as there was in the Shona, Lunda and Lozi kingdoms. Because of a relative lack of a well organized bureaucracy extending from the centre to all levels of the kingdom, and devoted to maintaining central authority, it seems that Chewa kingdoms were always relatively decentralized and that the delicate balance maintaining the king's authority and restraining conflict was easily upset by changing conditions. When a subordinate ruler wanted to deny the king's authority there was little which the king's officials could do to support the king. There was no central administrative institution representing the king to act as a check on the authority of a subordinate ruler in his own area, apart from fear of the king's religious and military powers and the loss of the king's services.

In the cycle of reciprocity, which involved the exchange of a king's services for his subordinates' goods and labour, the payment of goods was more than just an economic benefit for the king. It was a recognition of the services given by the king, an admission of his superiority and an acknowledgement both of loyalty and obedience of the subordinates and of their dependence on the king. The cycle of reciprocity of services for goods was the basis of a king's central authority. The cycle was a delicate balance, which in practice could easily be broken by the decentralizing tendencies in Chewa society and political structure.

The basic rationale for a king's collecting tribute was that he was the ultimate owner of the land and had given positions as local owners of the land to his subordinates. As owner of the land the king had certain rights and responsibilities, both to the land and to the people living on the land. These responsibilities or services have already been considered. From the successful performance of these responsibilities for the land and its people the king could expect certain rights, mainly the collection of tribute. Vansina distinguishes between types of tribute: tribute of allegiance and taxes, the former of which has little economic value and symbolizes the acceptance by the subordinate ruler of his subordinate position, the authority which he has delegated to him and his dependence upon the king. Taxation is supposedly based on assessment of the productivity of an area and parts of it are kept by the various subordinates who forward the rest to the king.[19] This seems a reasonable distinction, but there is some overlap in both the categories as well as the ritual significance in the types of tribute.

The tribute of allegiance which Chewa kings received included the red feathers of certain birds, at least the ground tusk of elephants, the skins of lions and leopards, and parts of other animals. A chief or his representative had to be present at the dismembering of lions, leopards, elephants and certain other animals to make certain that either poisonous parts of some animals or the tusks were forwarded to the king. A king received parts of these animals in recognition of his power, as in some way these animals were either powerful, or noble, or in the case of poisonous parts, the king had an obligation to protect his people by seeing to their disposal. The red feathers were connected to the symbolic significance of fire and blood. Another type of tribute existing at least in Undi's kingdom, which had more ritual significance, was the giving of mats which had been used in the girl's Chinamwali ceremony. In a sense this type of tribute, which had little economic value, was probably the recognition on the part of headmen and chiefs of the authority delegated to them to carry out the important ceremony. There does not seem to have been a similar type of tribute connected with the holding of Nyau initiation camps for men.

Although ivory and meat may have had some economic value, their symbolic value was possibly more important. The tribute in the form of taxation was primarily of economic value, although as most of it came from the land which the king owned it can be considered to have had some symbolic value as well.

The types of economic tribute varied greatly from area to area depending on what an area could produce. Areas near to a king's capital sent perishable goods, such as beer, meat, fish and fruits. Other areas sent iron implements, salt, chickens, goats, grain, tobacco, honey, pots, graphite for burnishing pots, baskets, wooden implements, drums and even poison used on arrows and spears. The fact that some areas claim to have sent both tusks of ivory, not just the tusk which touched the king's land, suggests that ivory was an item of taxation as well as of allegiance. Ivory which was not delivered to a chief to be sent as some sort of tribute to a king could either be sold by the hunter, theoretically only at a king's capital, or might be sold to the local chief who could send it to the king.

The tribute which was sent from the local chiefs or tributary kings to a king was used in a number of ways. Much of the food was used both to maintain the large number of dependents in a king's capital, as well as to provide hospitality for the constant flow of visitors. Some was stored as insurance against disasters. Much of the tribute was temporarily stored and then redistributed. The redistribution services performed by the king made his capital the centre of regional trade as shortages of goods in one area would be made up by surpluses sent as tribute from another area. As regional trade was theoretically directed towards a king's capital, instead of being organized directly between areas within a kingdom, the king was thought of as the provider for his people. In actual fact, there was regional trade among the areas in a kingdom, especially later in the history of the kingdoms when external traders became active.

In addition to the importance of tribute goods in terms of the internal regional trade in a kingdom, some of the goods were exported in long distance trade. The most important export during most periods was ivory. Of occasional importance were foodstuffs and iron implements which were not imported outside of Africa, but were involved in the regional network to which the foreigners trading with the Chewa had access. Slaves were rarely important in the export trade of Chewa kings in the early period. When the slave trade became important in the nineteenth century the power of most Chewa kings had become so decentralized that they did not benefit, with the exception of a few kings like Mwase Kasungu.

The export of ivory and other tribute goods by the kings was important in terms of the maintenance of their central authority as the imported goods were redistributed to the king's subordinates. Even more so than the redistribution of the internal tribute goods without a kingdom, the redistribution of the scarcer imported goods of cloth, beads, copper wires, Mpande shells and occasionally guns and ammunition was important in maintaining the economic dependence of the subordinates. Redistribution, as well as the other services of a king, encouraged the loyalty and obedience of subordinate rulers. However, much of a king's authority depended upon maintaining a virtual monopoly over the collection of ivory tribute and its sale to external traders. The breaking of this monopoly and the decentralization of the king's control over tribute and trade led to the general decline of the central powers of Chewa kings.

Until the nineteenth century most Chewa kings had been generally successful in maintaining their authority, particularly their monopoly over trade, in the face of the decentralizing tendencies within their kingdoms. It was only in the nineteenth century in most areas that external factors encouraged decentralization of the kingdoms. The exceptions where earlier decentralization took place were along the Zambezi, where there was contact with the Portuguese, and in Kalonga's kingdom. Occasionally Portuguese references before about 1800 give the impression of a monopoly being maintained. Kalonga is mentioned as restricting trade to himself and two other rulers at the end of the seventeenth century.[20] The early loss of central political authority by Kalonga can probably be seen as the result of a number of factors. The weakness at the centre caused by an unsuitable succession and the lack of relatives to support Kalonga was probably very important after the death of the great Kalonga Masula. A weakness at the centre could easily be taken advantage of by subordinates who either felt that they were receiving insufficient services or desired to control tribute and external trade to their own advantage. In the eastern part of Kalonga's kingdom, which was not Chewa, and so probably poorly integrated, the tendency towards decentralization would undoubtedly have been greater than in Chewa areas. Lundu's tributary kingdom, which evidently had previously been largely independent, probably felt little loyalty to Kalonga's central authority. In addition to the tendency towards decentralization, which was made easier by weakness at the centre, the fact that these areas had access to external trade contacts in their neighbouring areas undoubtedly further encouraged decentralization. Alpers mentions the developing Yao predominance on trade at Mozambique island as a factor later in the seventeenth century.[21]

As the eastern and southern parts of Kalonga's kingdom probably seceded in the mid or late seventeenth century, and as Undi had established himself independently to the south-west and west, including areas bordering on Tete, it would appear that Kalonga's economic position was greatly weakened. As well as having less tribute to redistribute in other areas to maintain loyalty, his access to Portuguese markets on the coast and along the Zambezi was denied him, thus making it more difficult to trade for cloth and other imports to redistribute to maintain his subordinates' allegiance. This would have further encouraged decentralization of the Chewa areas of his kingdom. It seems that some areas in Lilongwe district which had been in Kalonga's kingdom, probably had come under the control of Undi by the early eighteenth century. This may have been partly due to the greater ease with which Undi could distribute trade goods because he had access to the Portuguese trade at Tete and along the Zambezi.[22]

Little is known about the patterns of decentralization in Lundu's kingdom before the disruption of invading groups in the nineteenth century virtually destroyed his kingdom. It appears that there was decentralization especially along the Zambezi. Although largely independent, especially as he controlled the important religious centre of Mbona, Lundu developed more of a loyalty to Undi than to the increasingly weak Kalonga.[23]

The decline in power of Undi seems more complex, partly because there is more detailed evidence. Decentralization of Undi's authority seems to have begun in the areas farther from the capital where the temptations to trade directly with the Portuguese were greatest. In these areas along the Zambezi and in the Zimba area the local chiefs undoubtedly found Undi's services few and the possibility of successful spiritual or military coercement slight if tribute was not paid and Undi's monopoly of trade ignored. Particularly in the Zimba area north of Tete, where a number of small gold mines were located by the Portuguese in the middle of the eighteenth century, the settlement of the Portuguese and their slaves together with the passage of a large number of trade caravans encouraged decentralization. Whether Undi tried to do anything about the decline in his authority in the area during the late 1700s is not clear. It does seem that for a time he closed some of the gold mines and forced the Portuguese out of his area.[24] Evidently he tried to come to terms with the most important of the Portuguese families, for it seems that in the 1780s the head of the Pereiras married a daughter of Undi.[25]

Lacerda's account of his journey through the Zimba area and the potentially secessionist tributary kingdom of Mkanda in 1798 is not very informative about the degree of Undi's authority, but it does seem by the time Monteiro and Gamitto travelled through the same area some thirty years later that Undi's authority had declined.[26] The Zimba area was either subjected to the Portuguese or independent under Biwi and other chiefs. Mkanda had virtually seceded and in addition to tributary kings having decentralized Undi's authority the chiefs had also decentralized the authority of tributary kings.[27] It appears that Mkanda was able to secede from Undi's kingdom some time early in the nineteenth century. In addition to the fact that he had been an independent king earlier, and so was not so dependent on Undi for many religious and judicial services, he became less dependent on Undi's economic services as one of the east-west trade routes from Lake Malawi to Mwata Kazembe passed through his area.[28] The continuing activities of the Portuguese and their Chikunda retainers became increasingly detrimental to Undi's authority. No longer were the Portuguese content just to encourage decentralization of trade to their own advantage, but they began to conquer areas to include in prazoes and also employed hunters to roam through Undi's area seeking ivory. Hunting for ivory by well armed Chikunda further tended to erode the economic basis of Undi's authority. By the middle of the nineteenth century Undi's central authority had been greatly diminished in many areas. The areas to the south along the Zambezi had either been conquered or had successfully seceded due to the accessibility of trade with the Portuguese. To the east Mkanda's kingdom and areas in Lilongwe district, including Makewana's centre, seem to have seceded, or at least were less dependent on Undi for his services, due largely to the trade routes running through the area. Other areas of Undi's kingdom, including the Nsenga areas farther west, were still dependent on Undi for his economic and other services, and still occasionally sent tribute. When the Ngoni returned to the area in the 1860s Undi was in no position to protect his chiefs and the kingdom was rapidly dismantled as individual chiefs tried with little success to defend themselves.

The decline of Undi's kingdom does not seem to have been particularly due to either any weakness at the centre or conflict within the royal family, but seems to have been due to the natural tendency towards decentralization, or conflict between levels in the political hierarchy, which was inherent in the system. Without external factors operating to encourage decentralization the balance of power within the kingdom worked to maintain Undi's authority. When the various factors which worked to maintain central authority, such as economic benefit through redistribution, judicial services, religious and spiritual services and military services and threats, could be ignored by a subordinate rulers' desire to trade directly with external agents and cease paying tribute, then the vital cycle of reciprocity, upon which a king's power was based, was broken.

By the middle of the nineteenth century the decentralizing tendencies of the Chewa kingdom, encouraged by external agents, had fragmented and weakened the large kingdoms as well as many of the smaller previously tributary kingdoms. When the external forces changed from economic aggression to political aggression few of the kingdoms were able to survive successfully in their weakened state. The only strong Chewa centre to survive was that of Mwase Kasungu, whose area of control was severely limited. As it was, his survival was largely due to his having taken advantage of the new external factors to decentralize Chulu's kingdom.

FOOTNOTES

1 J. Vansina, *Kingdoms of the Savanna*, Univ. of Wisconsin Press, 1966, 4; J. Vansina, R. Mauny and L. V. Thomas eds, *The Historian in Tropical Africa*, O.U.P., 1964, 97.

2 Most of the material for this paper is the result of research done during 1964–65 in Eastern Zambia and Mchinji and Kasungu districts of Malawi. Most of this field research was concerned with the history of Undi's kingdom and was used in my Ph.D. dissertation 'A History of Undi's Kingdom to 1890: Aspects of Chewa History in East Central Africa' (Boston University, 1969). Field notes for this study, as well as for other Chewa areas, are deposited in the libraries of Boston University and the University of Zambia. Oral sources, which are not cited in this paper, are discussed and cited mainly in chapters 2, 3 and 9 of my dissertation.

3 J. Vansina, *Kingdoms of the Savanna* and 'A Comparison of African Kingdoms,' *Africa*, **32**, 4 (1962), 324–5; P. C. Lloyd, 'The Political Structure of African Kingdoms: An exploratory model,' *Political Systems and the distribution of Power*; ASA Monographs 2, London, 1965, 63–112; and A. W. Southall, *Alur Society, A study of processes and types of domination*, Cambridge, 1956.

4 Letter from W. H. J. Rangeley to T. C. Young of 25 June 1952 in Rangeley Papers in Society of Malawi Collection, file 1/2/1 (henceforth the Rangeley Papers are referred to only by the file number); S. Y. Nthara, *Mbiri ya Achewa*, Zomba, 1945.

5 The various spellings of the personal name of the presumed Kalonga who ruled in the early 1600s have been standardized by E. Axelson in *Portuguese in South-East Africa. 1600–1700*, Witwatersrand Univ. Press, 1960, as Muzura. It is just as likely to have been Masula in chiChewa. *Kumasula*: to loosen, unfasten or unbind, is the type of word which easily could have been used as a praise. See D. C. Scott and A. Hetherwick, *Dictionary of the Nyanja Language*, London, 1957, 272.

6 Apart from sources in Undi's area which mention Undi's control of the Kalonga succession, sources in Mankhamba, the area of the later Kalongas admit such: Kafulama, file 2/1/12; Mankhamba sources, 2/1/12; Mazengela, 2/1/1 and Rangeley to Young, letter of 25 June 1952 in files 1/1/3 and 1/2/1.

7 E. Alpers, 'The Mutapa and Malawi Political Systems,' 24–5 in T. O. Ranger, ed., *Aspects of Central African History*, London, 1968.

8 D. P. Abraham, 'Tasks in the Field of Early History,' *Conference on the History of Central African Peoples (C.H.C.A.P.)*, Lusaka, 1963, in note 19 mentions the intervention of the Mwene Mutapa in Undi's succession in 1755. This is doubtful and is not remembered in local Chewa sources.

9 Field notes from areas not in Undi's kingdom, corroborated to a certain extent by lineages collected by Rangeley and the lineage of Kanyenda, regarded as unreliable by Rangeley, in T. C. Young, *Notes on the History of the Tumbuka-Kamanga Peoples*, London, 1932.

10 Rangeley to Young, letter of 25 June 1952, file 1/2/1; Kalembo, file 1/1/3.

11 Oral sources and C. Wiese, 'Expedicao Portuguese a M'Pesene (1889),' *Boletin da Sociedade de Geographia de Lisboa*, 10, 8–9 (1891), ch. 3–4.

12 Rangeley to Young 30 April 1952, file 1/1/3; Chirunga, file 2/1/1 and oral sources.

13 R. A. Hamilton, 'Oral Tradition: Central Africa,' *History and Archaeology in Africa*, London, 1952, 21.

14 Although these relationships are not fully agreed on now by all parties concerned a number of independent sources support Undi's point of view. Forgetting the relationships is understandable in the light of their lack of function now and the patterns of indirect rule in ex-British colonial areas.

15 W. H. J. Rangeley, 'Mbona—the Rain Maker,' *Nyasa. J.*, **6**, 1 (1953), 8–27; and 'Two Nyasaland Rain Shrines—Makewana, the Mother of all People,' *Nyasa. J.*, **5**, 2 (1952), 31–50; T. Price, 'Malawi Rain Cults,' *Religion in Africa*, Edinburgh, 114–24; J. Fernandel, part of an untitled MS on Chewa history in the possession of A. Isaacman; A. C. P. Gamitto, *King Kazembe*, Lisbon, **1**, 1961 50, 76.

16 Gamitto, *Kazembe*, 1, 71–2; Wiese, 'Expedicao,' ch. 13, 554; and oral sources.

17 Alpers, 'Mutapa and Malawi,' 21–23 and oral sources.

18 Gamitto, *Kazembe*, 1, 70 and elsewhere mentions military activities.

19 Vansina, 'Comparison,' 326–7.

20 Axelson, *Portuguese*, 189.

21 Alpers, 'Mutapa and Malawi,' 24.

22 References to Undi's influence in Lilongwe come from sources within Undi's kingdom in Zambia as well as from Rangeley's notes, but are not corroborated by recent field research in the area.

23 Fernandel, MS, 14; J. P. R. Wallis ed., *The Zambezi Expedition of David Livingstone*, London, 1956 1, 172.

24 M. D. D. Newitt, trans., 'Ignacio Caeteno Xavier's Account of Portuguese East Africa,' *CHCAP*, 11.

25 Personal Communication from A. Isaacman, December 1968.

26 R. F. Burton, ed., *The Lands of Cazembe*, London, 1873, 35–8.

27 Gamitto, *Kazembe*, 1, 48 ff, 61, 69, 88–9, 109, 117, 141.

28 Burton, *Cazembe*, 35, 81.

8 The people of Bororo: a lexicostatistical enquiry

G. T. Nurse

In Portuguese chronicles and maps of the lower Zambezi valley during the sixteenth and seventeenth centuries there is frequent mention of the country of Bororo,[1] which lay to the north of the river and was often identified with the land of the Maravi.[2] This identification has sometimes been accepted without much question, but it seems to deserve closer examination. The name is itself suggestive. The land to the south was known as Botonga,[3] the country of the Tonga; it therefore appears that the initial element *Bo* represents the class fourteen noun-prefix, which is used in many Bantu languages to designate the lands of the people named in the radical following the prefix. Bororo would consequently be the land of the Roro, or Lolo, people.

The name Lolo is familiar in Malawi. It belongs to a section of that somewhat heterogeneous group of peoples who used to be known as the Nguru but are now collectively called the Lomwe. The Lomwe dialect cluster is closely related to Makua, which is spoken on the north-eastern coast of Moçambique and inland between the Lurio and Lujenda rivers.[4] The Lomwe cluster itself is readily divisible on morphological and lexical grounds into two main segments. The larger includes Mihavani, the commonest dialect of Lomwe spoken in Malawi, and Shirima, the commonest in Moçambique; for the sake of convenience I shall refer to it as Lomwe proper. Lolo is the collective name given to the dialects and peoples to the south of the main concentration of the Lomwe; among them are the Kokhola and the Cuabo.

In 1894, Alice Werner[5] interrogated a party of Lolo in Blantyre. They stated that they came from the region to the east of Lake Chilwa, and were 'subject to the Anguru'. She obtained from them a list of words which she later published as a vocabulary of the Lomwe dialect of Makua. Perhaps the most significant point about her list is that it is not Lolo: the words are distinctively Mihavani or Shirima rather than Kokhola or Cuabo, and some are borrowings from Chewa while others show phonological peculiarities not occurring in this cluster. It therefore appears either that some of the Lolo had even eighty years ago undergone linguistic resorption by neighbouring peoples (that they said they were 'subject to the Anguru' suggests a possible reason for this) or else that the original Lolo included the forebears of all who are now known as the Lomwe, and that the division into modern Lolo-speakers and speakers of Lomwe proper has happened since the seventeenth century.

Fortunately, we now have a very useful tool for determining the likelihood of the second of these alternatives. By no means everyone is prepared to accept the validity of all the claims made for glottochronology, but there seems to be little doubt that some of its results can provide useful hints or supporting evidences. It is based on the hypothesis, first developed by Swadesh,[6] that every language contains a number of semantic concepts which are basic and the words used to describe which undergo change or replacement at a universally regular rate. The hypothesis has been tested with regard to languages which have had a written form over a long period of time and in connection with languages whose approximate date of divergence from a common origin is known. It has been found to work well in many unrelated language families, though the formulae used for arriving at divergence times have so considerable a margin of error that no datings arrived at glotto-chronologically can be more than approximate.

Essentially the technique depends on the proper deployment of a standard basic list of words. The exact equivalents in commonest use in the languages or dialects under examination are collected; great care has to be taken to ensure that the words are those most familiar to native-speakers. The per-centages of those words which are cognate—i.e., which have an ultimate common origin—are determined; and the divergence time in millennia is calculated by dividing the logarithm of the percentage by the logarithm of the square of the estimated constant percentage retention rate over a millennium. The use of the square is indicated by the fact that the pair of languages being compared will have diverged in different ways from their common original; the unsquared rate is only applicable in the case of single linear development between earlier and later forms of the same language. It is obvious that there are several non-interdependent possible sources of error. The most important lies, of course, in the judgment of the observer; not everyone has the same criteria of cognation, and to provide a satisfactory scientific basis for these criteria a thorough phonological study of each language is, ideally, necessary. The choice of the words in the basic list is less mutable; certain lists have been found to give consistent results with widely different language families. Not all authorities are agreed on the best constant rate, though all of those proposed lie within consistently insignificant margins of error. The rate most generally favoured is eighty-six per cent per millennium, and that is the one I have used here.

I do not wish to exaggerate or minimize my sources or my capacities. As a linguist I cannot claim more than the status of an informed amateur, and my criteria of cognation, though strict, may be faulty. The word lists were, except in the instance of Makua, obtained directly by me from native-speakers, principally through the medium of the Chewa language. The Makua list was derived from Woodward[7], who does not give equivalents for all the words required; the percentages have been adjusted accordingly. The basic list used is the 100-word one drawn up by Swadesh.[8] It has some disadvantages—the presence of no less than five words for colours, one of them being yellow, introduces something of a cultural bias in the case of the Bantu languages, which do not always distinguish very clearly between colours, and tend to use borrowed or adapted words for yellow—but it has already been used to advantage in one local instance: information derived by means of it from Chewa and related languages has been shown to agree within permissible margins of error with traditional history and with archaeological findings respecting the migrations of the Maravi.[9]

The possibility that all the Lomwe might have been Lolo in the seventeenth century was tested by the comparison of modern Mihavani, representing Lomwe proper, with modern Kokhola, which was taken as the type-dialect for Lolo. These showed seventy-nine per cent of common cognates, which gives a divergence time of 782 years. As Hymes[10] has pointed out, the divergence times of glottochronology are minimal, which means that it is at least 800 years, and could be considerably longer, since the two segments of Lomwe began to diverge. We can exclude from the Kokhola list all those words which it has in common with Chewa but not also with Mihavani or Makua; we are then left with ninety-four words giving eighty-four per cent common cognation with Mihavani and a minimum divergence time of 578 years, which is still far too long. We may therefore conclude that the Lolo have been distinct from the other Lomwe since well before the seventeenth century, and that Alice Werner's informants may have been Lolo by descent but were not Lolo-speakers.

Several words in the Kokhola list differ completely from their equivalents in adjacent or related languages, and deserve investigation. Kokhola also has one phonological peculiarity which sets it apart from other Bantu languages: for the rough aspirate of Mihavani and Makua it substitutes an ejective glottal stop, as forcible as that found in Bushman but which could derive from contact with Arabs.[11]

There are seven words in the list of which cognates are found in Chewa and Mihavani but not in Makua. Two of them, representing the -ti root for 'to say' and the -sa root for 'to burn', are so standard in Bantu languages that it appears that their Makua equivalents, -himya and -parela, the latter of which is found in Mihavani with the slightly different meaning of 'to roast', must have acquired their present meanings since the split with Lomwe, rather than the Lomwe use of the standard roots representing borrowings. We have therefore eleven very probable borrowings from Chewa. To obtain what information we can from them about the dates of the Lolo, we can approach glottochronology from a slightly different angle. It seems reasonable to assume that words are acquired at the same rate as that at which they are lost; there is, after all, a simple one-for-one substitution. Assuming also that the basic vocabulary changes at a uniform rate, the borrowings may be taken to have been acquired at the same uniform rate. Here we are not examining a divergence between languages, but a linear process in the development of Kokhola, which we have taken as typical of the Lolo dialects. It is therefore necessary to use the unsquared rate. Moreover, we are dealing with retained cognates in a sense other than that in which we sought the date of a common origin; we are not looking forward, as it were, from a point of divergence but backward from a convergence; we are looking back to the time when the residua of the two languages, the parts which do not contain the borrowings in common, could have existed without them. What we are dating is therefore 100 − 11 per cent, or 89 per cent, of Kokhola. Dividing the logarithm of that by the logarithm of the rate, we obtain 771 years as the probable minimum period that Kokhola and Chewa have been in contact. This may appear to be a somewhat arbitrary and *ad hoc* method, but it seems sound enough. Applying a similar approach to Mihavani, only one word in the basic list, apart from those common to Mihavani and Kokhola, appears to be a borrowing from Chewa: *-birivira*, used here to mean 'to be green' but having, as does its Chewa equivalent, an additional range of meaning strongly modified by the universally wide semantic range of colour-terms in Bantu. This leads to a ninety-four per cent residuum for Mihavani prior to contact with the Maravi and 411 years as the probable minimum period of that contact.

It must be emphasized that these datings are only very broad approximations. Indeed, if they are regarded as more than that they become simply inconsistent. It would be difficult to reconcile the date of divergence of Mihavani from Kokhola with the periods of contact of both languages with Chewa; if the Lolo first encountered the Maravi only eleven years after splitting from

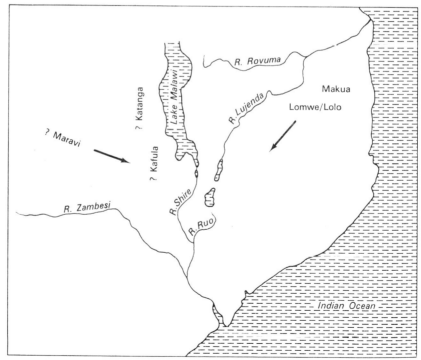

8.1   The people of Bororo, c. 800 A.D.

the Lomwe proper, it seems unlikely that some three and a half centuries would elapse before the latter also made contact. These are processes, not incidents. Again, comparisons with Makua give answers conflicting with apparent interrelations between the two; glottochronological counts suggest 1,182 years since Kokhola, and 1,044 years since Mihavani, diverged from a common tongue with Makua, yet 782 years ago they appear, on the same criteria, to have begun to diverge from their own common ancestor. It is consequently plain that the two languages ought not to be taken as single isolates, but as reference points lying in a spectrum of linguistic divergences. Bearing this in mind, we are able with modest assurance to postulate a gradual split, occurring between 1,200 and 1,000 years ago, between the two main segments of proto-Makua, that to the north and east developing into modern Makua, while the south-westerly division began to drift towards the Shire and the lower Zambezi. About 800 years ago the advance guard, the Lolo, first came into contact with the Maravi and began to develop linguistically along lines distinct from those of the later comers, the Lomwe proper. The

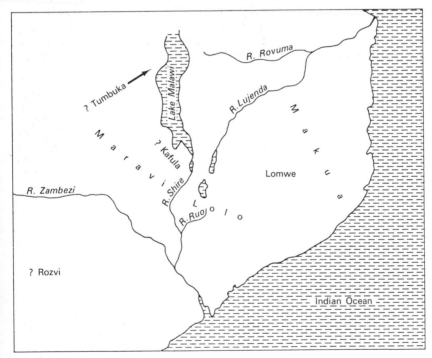

8.2   The people of Bororo, c. 1150 A.D.

Lolo settled along the Shire and Ruo rivers and stretched down to the north bank of the Zambezi while the Lomwe proper moved during the ensuing three of four centuries into a position adjoining the easternmost extension of the Maravi around the southern end of Lake Malawi.

Those are the main conclusions derivable from lexico-statistics. How well do they agree with what is known of traditional history, and with the early Portuguese accounts? The sparse traditions of the migrations of the Lomwe have been collected by L. D. Soka.[12] He describes the Lolo as originating from the neighbourhood of Quelimane and spreading along the trade-route between the coast and the upper Ruo valley. Here they came into contact with the Mang'anja, a Maravi people, who named them Kokhola after the wood-lands on the right bank of the Ruo where they settled. On the other side of the Ruo were the Thakwani and the Marenje, who differ very little from one another, and who are both named, as so many tribes seem to be, after hills. Along the rest of the route were the Cuabo or Chiwambo, people of the Fort, of Quelimane; and just to the north of them were the Manyawa and the Maratha, close in language and customs to the Lolo. These are, in fact, the regions which those branches of the Lolo occupy at the present day, and the account has a distinct flavour of having been constructed with this in mind. Reference to early Portuguese sources gives a somewhat different picture. When Vasco da Gama called at the mouth of the Quelimane river in 1498, there was no trading centre nearby,[13] though there were sailing vessels on the river and Arabs (Moors) among the people.[14] Rangeley[15] states, though without giving references, that the port of Quelimane was founded in 1544. About half a century later, dos Santos[16] described the mouth of the river

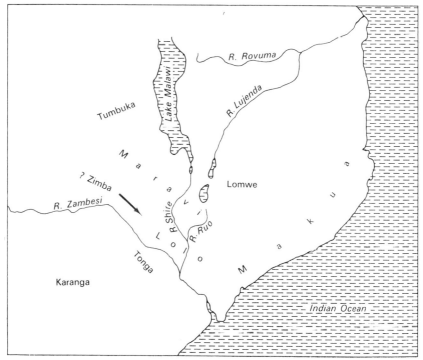

8.3 The people of Bororo, c. 1500 A.D.

without mentioning any large settlement at or near it, though a place called 'Quilinum' is shown in approximately the correct position in the 1592 map by Petrus Plancius.[17] The earliest reference to any permanent and official construction there appears to be in a letter of King Philip II of Portugal (Philip III of Spain) to the Viceroy of India, dated the 10 March 1618, and ordering the fortification of both the Luabo and the Quelimane mouths.[18] That the fort was built before 1635 we know from Pedro Barretto de Rezende,[19] who states that ships travelling four leagues up the river

'come to a fort which in the language of the country is called *chuambo*, and which we have erected on the lands of the right-hand bank, which are those of the Barorox'.

Chiwambo is a Chewa word, also found in Sena and Nyungwe, for a protective enclosure; it is a member of noun-class 7, the *ci-* being the class prefix. Noun-class 7 in Kokhola has, as is the rule in Makua and related languages,[20] fused with class 9; it either lacks a prefix or takes *e-*, as in Lomwe proper. In Makua the prefix is *i-*; in none of the languages of this cluster is it *ci-*. The name therefore indicates not only that that section of the Lolo calling themselves Cuabo achieved separate identity fairly late, but that they must have assumed that designation after they and the Portuguese had already been in contact with people speaking a Maravi language. Furthermore, the name Cuabo is accepted by those who bear it as a single ethnographically descriptive radical; they refer to themselves as aCuabo, their language as eCuabo, and so forth.

The early Arab traveller al-Idris referred to the people of the Mozambique coast as the *Wakwak*,[21] and this name is probably a version of 'Makua'.[22] One of the earliest mentions of Bororo is that in the account of the journey made by certain Jesuit Fathers[23] in the company of Francisco Barretto for the conquest of Monomotapa in 1569; on their return in 1572 they were prevented from traversing the country of the Mungazi and consequently had to cross the Zambezi into Bororo and make their way through it to Sena. In 1613 Diogo Simões became friendly with Sapoe, 'lord of the lands of Bororo', who allowed him to use a route through Bororo from Tete to Chicoa, which lies some sixty miles up the river.[24] It is tempting to identify this obliging gentleman with a forerunner of the modern Chief Nsabwe, in whose area in Thyolo district live most of the Kokhola of Malawi; but the presence of a village headman called Chicussy, who could not possibly have any connection with Chikusi Maseko, in the same area at the same time, warns us against any such easy onomastic equation. When Gaspar Bocarro made his famous journey in 1616, he crossed into Bororo shortly after leaving Tete.[25] At that time the delusive identification of Bororo with the Maravi lands held full sway; Maravi is described as the chief city of Bororo; and so the wide application of the name ought not, perhaps, to be taken too seriously.

In the light of this, it is interesting to compare the late sixteenth-century account of dos Santos with that of Rezende only some forty years later. Dos Santos, though he distinguishes throughout their length between the Bororo and Botonga banks of the Zambezi, describes the inhabitants of the north bank near the coast as Makua, and as being the same people as those inhabiting the mainland by Mozambique Island; while Rezende equally emphatically calls them Bororos, and ascribes the wars of the Portuguese with the Maravi king Muzura to the latter's assertion of hegemony over these people. It would appear therefore that the Lolo, far from having spread from Quelimane to the Ruo along a trade-route, were in fact moving in the opposite direction, and that it was their expansion from the Maravi periphery down the Zambezi in the early part of the seventeenth century which paved the way for that extension of the Maravi empire to the coast which was, during the ensuing two centuries, to cause so much trouble to the Portuguese, and to leave a linguistic-

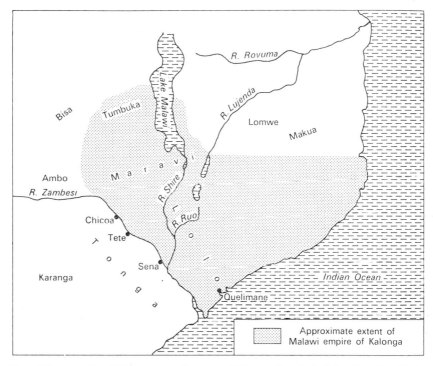

8.4   The people of Bororo, c. 1650 A.D. (The author is indebted to Dr E. A. Alpers for suggesting emendation of the original form of this map.)

ally and anthropologically confusing relic in the Maganjas da Costa.[26] In 1667 Manuel Barretto wrote that the Bororo nation adjoined the fort of Quelimane and extended for fifty leagues up the coast and fifty-two up the Zambezi to the river Embebe or Morumbara—presumably the old Murumbala bed of the Shire—which divided Bororo from the Maravi. He also stated that the Bororo chiefs were subjected by force to the Maravi, and that they had several times, using the name of Maravi, attempted to assault the settlement and fort of Quelimane.[27] The Makua must consequently by that time have been displaced northwards by Lolo moving down the Zambezi to the coast.

It is possible by judicious collation of our lexicostatistical results with these Portuguese records, and aided by the findings of the archeologists, to form a tentative picture of the migrations of the Lolo. At some time probably around A.D. 800 the forebears of both sections of the Lomwe began to separate from the main body of the Makua and move towards the south-west. About 400 years later the Lolo, forging on ahead, made contact with the Maravi. In this connection the evidence of archaeology is of great value, for the second phase of the Iron Age in Malawi began at about A.D. 1100, and some of the changes it introduced in pottery types are ascribed by Clark either to stylistic developments among the settled Katanga or to the incursion of an early group of Maravi.[28] The lexicostatistical evidence of Kokhola suggests that the latter was the more likely alternative. It was possibly pressure from the Lomwe proper behind them which caused the Lolo during the following 400 years to spread further to the south; the first contacts between speakers of the precursors of modern Chewa and Mihavani appear to have occurred more than 400 years ago, and the Lolo had reached the Zambezi at least by A.D. 1500. By the middle of the sixteenth century they were settled extensively along the north bank of the river, at least from the level of Chicoa to that of Sena. They had not, however, yet spread down to the sea, the shores of which were still peopled by the Makua. A hundred years later, after the devastating *völkerwanderung* of the Zimba, they were no longer to be found west of the Shire, but, as subjects of the conquering Maravi, they had occupied a large area of the coast.

Except in a few particulars, the position today appears to be much as it was at the beginning of the eighteenth century. Maravi occupation would have made it difficult for the Lolo to extend back up the Zambezi beyond its confluence with the Shire. The Makua had retired northward, but beyond them was the pressure of the Yao, and the Lomwe proper occupied the rest of the lands in the quadrilateral formed by the Lujenda, the Shire and Ruo, the Zambezi and the coast; and though a few Lolo might cross to the southern side of the Zambezi, the Tonga were themselves beginning to expand, and in the nineteenth century effectively displaced the Lolo in the Shire valley and some of the flat lands to the east of it, where they are known as Sena and Phodzo. At the present day, the Lolo are represented in Malawi mainly by the Kokhola, who live principally in the hills north and west of the confluence of the Shire and the Ruo, and by isolated pockets of Thakwani, Manyawa and Maratha, most of them in Mlanje and Chiradzulu districts. The three last-named peoples, together with the Marenje and the Nkusiyani, rather patchily occupy the area to the east of the Ruo, of Mlanje, and of Lake Chilwa, in Mozambique, where they are surrounded by and mixed with the Lomwe proper; while the Cuabo, who probably now outnumber all the rest of the Lolo put together, extend beyond them to Quelimane and its hinterland.

There can be little doubt that it was submission to the Maravi which enabled the Lolo to hold on to their lands and their identity. The history of a popula-

131

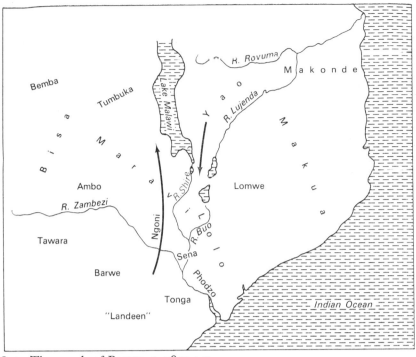

8.5 The people of Bororo, c. 1840 A.D.

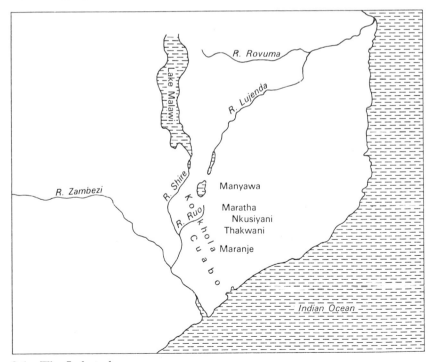

8.6 The Lolo today

tion of innocent bystanders, whose traditional way of life militates against the autochthonous centralization of power, and who lived, and still for preference live, in very small family-based communities, no innovators, modest farmers, small but dogged traders, warlike only as mercenaries, is naturally slender. The Lolo are not, never have been, and seem never to have wanted to be, notable or important; they are of much more interest to the linguist and the anthropologist than to the historian. An accident of geography secured frequent mentions of them in early Portuguese records; but for all that their image in those writings is a dim one. Yet their quiet and almost passive migrations do help, if only in rather a negative fashion, to cast some light on more assertive peoples. Not only must the cannibal Zimba have sustained themselves for at least part of their journey on a diet of Lolo, but the Malawi empire seems subsequently to have made use of their fighting qualities and given them the central authority which they themselves did not want, or were unable to develop. It is appropriate that modern Malawi should contain within its borders some remnants of a people who once made their own shy contribution to its ancestral glories.

SUMMARY

There can be little doubt that the name Bororo, frequently mentioned in early Portuguese records and maps of the lower Zambezi area, signified the country of the Lolo. Lexicostatistical comparisons of Kokhola, one of the extant Lolo dialects, with Makua and the Mihavani dialect of Lomwe proper suggest that the Lolo originally formed part of a south-western extension of the Makua which separated during the ninth and tenth centuries and made contact with the Maravi in the twelfth, at about the time that it began to be distinct from the Lomwe proper. The date of first contact with the Maravi may be evidence that the second phase of the Malawi Iron Age did not arise spontaneously but resulted from an early Maravi incursion. Spreading down the Ruo and Shire valleys, the Lolo must have reached the Zambezi by the late fifteenth century; when first mentioned by the Portuguese they occupied the north bank at least from Chicoa to Sena. After the Zimba disturbances the Lolo came under Maravi rule, and were instrumental in the thrust of the Malawi empire to the coast, where they displaced the Makua northwards. This centralization of authority apparently enabled the disorganized Lolo to retain their lands and their identity, which they have, with a few minor changes, succeeded in doing to the present day.

FOOTNOTES

[*RSEA* = Theal, G. M. *Records of South-Eastern Africa*. 1898–1903.]

1 Axelson, Eric, *The Portuguese in South-East Africa, 1600–1700*. 1964, 47,

52, 133. Teixeira, João, *Kingdom of Monomotapa*, 1630, map reproduced in Axelson, op. cit., facing 55.

2 Bocarro, Antonio, *Decadas*. Written 1613–1649, published 1876. *RSEA* 3, 324, 416.

3 Teixeira, *Kingdom*; Santos, João dos, *Ethiopia Oriental*, 1609; *RSEA* 7, 72, 254–5.

4 Bryan, M. A., *The Bantu Languages of Africa*, 1959, Map.

5 Werner, Alice, 'A Vocabulary of the Lomwe Dialect of Makua'. *J. Afr. Soc.*, 1, 1901–2, 236 et seq.

6 Swadesh, M., 'The Time Value of Linguistic Diversity'. Paper delivered at Viking Fund Supper Conference, New York, 1948.

7 Woodward, H. W., 'An Outline of Makua Grammar'. *Bantu Stud.*, 2, 1926, 269–325.

8 Swadesh, M., quoted in Samarin, W. J., *Field Linguistics*. 1967, 221–3.

9 Nurse, G. T., 'The Glottochronology of the Maravi Migrations'. In preparation.

10 Hymes, D. H., 'Lexicostatistics So Far', *Cur. Anthrop.*, 1 (1), 1960, 1–43.

11 Nurse, G. T., 'Anthropological Problems in Malawi'. Paper presented to the Southern African Conference on Sero-Anthropology, Johannesburg, 1969.

12 Soka, L. D., *Mbiri ya Alomwe*, 1963.

13 Goes, Damião, *Chronica do Felicissimo Rei Dom Emanuel da Gloriosa Memoria*, 1566; *RSEA* 3, 9–10, 76.

14 Barros, João de, *Da Asia*, 1552–1613; *RSEA* 4, 22–3, 169–70.

15 Rangeley, W. H. J., 'The Portuguese', *Nyasa. J.*, 17 (1), 1964, 48.

16 Dos Santos, op. cit. *RSEA*, 7, 71–3, 253–5.

17 Plancius, Petrus, *Delineatio orarum Manicongi, Angolae, Monomotapae, terrae natalis, Zofalae, Mozambicae, Abyssinorum &c. una cum vadis et sirtibus adjacentibus Item insulae magnae vulgo S. Laurentii alias Madagascar dictae inter maximas totius Orientis habitae*, 1592 or 1594.

18 Letter from Philip III, subscribed by the Duke of Villahermosa and the Count of Ficalho, to Dom João de Coutinho, Count of Redondo, Viceroy of India, dated 10 March 1618.; *RSEA*, 4, 134 and 138.

19 Rezende, Pedro Barretto de, *Do Estado de India*, MS in British Museum; submitted to Philip III in 1635; *RSEA*, 2, 383, 406.

20 Meinhof, C., 'Linguistische Studien in Ostafrika: Makua', *Mitteilungen des Seminars für Orientalische Sprachen zu Berlin*, 1907.

21 Rangeley, W. H. J., 'The Earliest Inhabitants of Nyasaland', *Nyasa. J.* 16 (2), 1963.

22 Nurse, G. T., 'The Name "Akafula" '. *Soc. Malawi J.*, 20 (2), 1967, 17–22.

23 Monclaro, Pe., S. J. *Relacao de Viagem q. fizerão os Pes. da Companhia de Jesus com Franco. Barretto na Conquista de Monomotapa no Anno de 1569.* MS in Bibliotheque Nationale, Paris; *RSEA*, 3, 19, 245.

24 Bocarro, op. cit.; *RSEA*, 3, 306–12, 398–406.

25 Bocarro, op. cit., *RSEA*, 3, 323–4, 416.

26 Dias, Margot, *Os Maganjas da Costa*, 1965.

27 Barretto, Manuel, *Informação do Estado e Conquista dos Rios de Cuama*, MS in Bibliothèque Nationale, Paris, dated 11 December 1667; *RSEA*, 3, 442, 470.

28 Clark, J. D., *Malawi Antiquities Programme*. 1968. 29–30.

9 Reflections on the Early History of North Malawi

Monica Wilson

During the past decade there has been a great increase in our knowledge of the history of north Malawi, and of the Corridor between the lakes, Malawi and Tanganyika. Anthropologists such as Dr Alison Redmayne, Mrs Beverley Brock and Dr R. G. Willis have written specifically on historical themes, and the historians, working from documentary material as well as oral traditions, have taught us much about pre-colonial trade, and something on the emergence and spread of chieftainship.[1] All this has added to our detailed knowledge of the evolving social structures and the succession of events in the Corridor especially during the nineteenth century, but there has not been any significant revision in the demarcation of cultural groups—what I call 'peoples'—set out in 1958, and what indicates them (see Fig. 9.1).[2] All the further evidence collected confirms that the Corridor was indeed an ancient crossroads of Africa, with movement of people from west, east, north and south. The recent work also confirms that there have been successive movements, resulting in layers of population with rather different techniques, customs and traditions; that chiefs and commoners are frequently of different stock, that among any one 'people' there are a number of chiefdoms, and the ruling lines of these different chiefdoms may be unrelated.[3] Only among one people, the Nyakyusa-Ngonde, do we find two proliferating lineages, claiming relationship, spreading over a large number of chiefdoms and even including groups speaking different languages.

The great change in perspective has come from the work of archaeologists: Professor Desmond Clark, Mr K. R. Robinson, Professor Brian Fagan, and others.[4] The change is in time depth. This has extended enormously.

The archaeological material is particularly exciting to me as an anthropologist, because it offers the possibility of relating oral traditions and genealogies collected by Godfrey Wilson and myself over thirty years ago, to radio carbon dates. These particular genealogies are instructive for three reasons: they are of two proliferating lineages giving many parallel lines; they are linked to generation celebrations held every thirty to thirty-five years; and they may, perhaps, be linked with pottery made from a particular clay, that

136

9.1 Peoples of the Nyasa-Tanganyika corridor

137

found near Pupangandu, on the north-east shore of Lake Malawi. Perhaps this sounds too good to be true. But if these genealogies can indeed be dated then we can deduce some sort of time scale for other traditions in the Corridor also. It is therefore worth taking a little time to examine the evidence.

I   AGE-ORGANIZATION AND ROYAL GENEALOGIES

The peoples of Ngonde, in north Malawi, had close cultural and historical connections with their neighbours across the Songwe, the Nyakyusa; they speak the same language, though with rather different accents, and there are clear oral traditions about the coming of the chiefs of both groups from BuKinga, high in the Livingstone mountains. Culturally, the Nyakyusa and Kinga differ considerably, and their languages are not mutually intelligible, but both parties agree that their chiefs spring from a common line, and this was reflected in the thirties by the celebration of communal rituals, celebrations which continued, at least sporadically, until the 1950s when I was last in BuNyakyusa.[5]

Like many East African peoples, the Nyakyusa had an age-organization. Every thirty to thirty-five years a great ritual was celebrated during which political power was handed over by fathers to sons, and the leaders of the fathers' generation, retiring, became priests. There was also a new deal in land, the sons' generation acquiring most of the best land, and a redistribution of cattle, sons acquiring at least part of their fathers' holdings. Unlike most East African peoples, the Nyakyusa had chiefs, and the generation celebrations were linked with a coronation, a coming out (*ubusoka*) at which the heirs to the retiring chief were publically recognized. Each chiefdom celebrated independently—timing was not co-ordinated from one chiefdom to the next. Usually there were two heirs who divided their father's country and might also extend the area of their rule by settling unoccupied land. Occasionally, there were more than two heirs, sometimes only one. Although the celebrations were linked to coronations they remained rituals for a generation, not for individuals, and if a chief lacked an heir, or an heir of the right age, the ritual nevertheless proceeded, someone—a man or girl—standing in for the heirs. Similarly, if a chief died young, the ritual was not celebrated again, but he was replaced by a brother, own or classificatory, who took his name and social personality. The ritual was tied to a generation, and the maturity of the generation as a whole determined the timing of the ritual. The chief and his heirs represented their respective generations. It is only when one delves deep that it may emerge that three men, bearing the same name, held office for a generation two of them dying young and being replaced.

Furthermore, the fact that the chiefdoms were expected to split in each generation, and usually did so, means that a number of royal lines developed simultaneously and the generation structure of each can be checked against the others. When Godfrey Wilson and I collected genealogies between 1934 and 1938 there were two major lineages, that of Lwembe's line and that of the

138

Kukwe, whose members supposed that they might have a common origin but could not trace the exact connection. The Lwembe lineage covered twenty-nine chiefdoms. Forty-six lineage segments were recorded, some having lost office or never acquired it, the Kukwe lineage covered twenty-four chiefdoms.

The informants on these lineages came from many different segments—no one man knew the whole of either major lineage. The informants were men with the reputation of being acknowledgeable about lineage history, and their names and positions are shown on the published genealogies.[6] The work was all done in KiNyakyusa, and genealogies were checked and rechecked. Of course there are probably some errors in detail, but I think that the Lwembe lineage may be taken as representing actual relationships or something near that, over ten generations. The preceding eleven generations represent a single line and are much more dubious, though the burial places of some of the chiefs mentioned are known. The Kukwe line is shallower, traditions of eight generations being consistent, but the previous six generations more uncertain.

In Ngonde the situation differed somewhat from that north of the Songwe. Everyone agreed that age-villages had once existed in Ngonde but the precise demarcation of generations, and the coming out ritual had lapsed before 1937 when Godfrey Wilson and I first visited there. The office of Kyungu was, however, still very important, and Peter the Kyungu, a man of great ability, took a lively interest in the history of his country. He spent many hours dictating what he remembered to Godfrey Wilson, and called in the notables famous for their knowledge of history and custom to the court at Mpata, where we were living.

According to Ngonde tradition, the first Kyungu, who settled on Mbande Hill (not far from the modern Karonga) came from BuKinga, and he was founder of the royal line in Ngonde. The name appears in the early, misty, generations of both Lwembe's line and the Kukwe line, and both these lines claim relationship with the Kyungu of Ngonde. Such connection is indeed likely, though the exact details are uncertain.

The personal name, Kyungu, became the title of an office, something that has happened repeatedly among the Nyakyusa-Ngonde people. The first Kyungu is described as a chief arriving with followers. His successors—his living representatives—were for many generations priests, or *divine kings*, living in seclusion. The office of Kyungu, like the corresponding office of Lwembe in BuNyakyusa, did not change by generation. The tenure of office by a divine king depended upon his health: if he fell ill he died—he was sometimes smothered—for an ailing divine king was thought to endanger the whole country. It would no longer be fertile; crops, stock, women would cease to bear and flourish; the army would be defeated, and so on. One cannot, therefore, count generations by counting Kyungus. Sixteen graves where Kyungus were buried were known in 1937, and Peter, who died on 30 August 1966 as a very old man, was thought to be the eighteenth in line,[7] but there may have been more than eighteen holders of the office.

However, since the first Kyungu appears in the genealogies (as I said, he is claimed by both Lwembe's line and the Kukwe line and the name appears in three successive generations in Lwembe's line), we can calculate generations back to the first Kyungu. He lived twelve to fourteen generations before 1937 depending upon which entry the calculation is based. Reckoning three generations to a 100 years, this brings us to between the late fifteenth and mid-sixteenth century. For ten generations the genealogy of Lwembe's line is based on the division of each chiefdom and a generation ritual which I believe provides reasonably accurate dating. Earlier generations are more doubtful, and here there might well have been telescoping of the genealogy.

The genealogies were published in 1958. I concluded then that the founders of the Nyakyusa lineage had arrived in the Rungwe valley between 1550 and 1650. Some people thought that I was putting the date far too early, but ten years later Professor Desmond Clark wrote telling me that he had a radio carbon date for Mbande Hill of 1410 $\pm$ 80. Mr K. R. Robinson showed firstly that a distinctive type of pottery found on Mbande Hill was similar in constitution to pottery from the Kisi pot-market at Pupangandu, and secondly that pottery from Mbande Hill resembled a pot illustrated by Fülleborn,[8] that came from the cave Palikyala, a ritual centre not far from the market. The Kisi chiefs who sacrificed not far from this cave also came from BuKinga.[9]

The questions at issue are: does the radio carbon date for Mbande Hill represent the occupation by the first Kyungu, or that of earlier people? And secondly, was Kisi pottery traded to Karonga before the arrival of the first Kyungu? We cannot yet be positive on either point, but it seems likely that it was the chiefs stemming from BuKinga who established links with the pot-market nestling against the mountains of BuKinga, and that the radio carbon date for Mbande Hill represents what traditions suggest was the first full settlement of Mbande Hill. Only further archaeological work can settle these points, but, taking into account all the present evidence, it is reasonable to postulate that the Nyakyusa chiefs reached the Rungwe valley and the Kyungu reached Mbande Hill sometime during the fifteenth century.

If this is true, then certain other things follow.

II   EARLIER OCCUPANTS

According to oral tradition (collected in 1937) the first Kyungu and his followers displaced Simbobwe, an elephant hunter and his men, on Mbande Hill. Simbobwe was a Fipa. Other peoples also were already in occupation when the Kyungu arrived. Descendants of the recognized leaders of these indigenous groups, such as the late Rheuben Mwenifumbo, were among our informants. The earliest occupants were Tumbuka-speakers, (including Wenya, Fungwe, and Yombe); Nyiha, including Lambya and Wandya; Nyamwanga and Iwa. The Kyungu is said to have circled westward and sojourned in the 'country of the Bisa' on his way from BuKinga.[10] According to Mr M. F. Thomas, the Bisa once occupied the present Kasama and Chinsali districts so Kyungu may not have travelled far west or south, but this tradition does imply that some Bisa ancestors, known by that name, were in what is now Zambia early in the fifteenth century. Thomas suggests that the Bisa royal line only came from Lunda about 1700, but he notes that the Chewa traditions mention a Bisa origin, and concludes that some people of Bisa stock may have moved east along with the Chewa, 'but are now governed by a ruling house that migrated from Lunda at a much later date.'[11]

As so often, traditions are contradictory on some points. For example, the Kyungu, Peter, told Godfrey Wilson in 1937 that the chiefs of Nyamwanga and Iwa were descended from brothers of the first Kyungu, and Nyondo, chief of the Lambya in Malawi, from his sister; but the Nyamwanga and Iwa chiefs themselves claim that their line originated in Luba country, their ancestor Mwemusi coming via Bisa country, and Nyondo, chief of the Lambya, told me proudly in 1954, 'Kyungu found us here', identifying himself with his people, and reasserting the very general view that the Nyiha preceded all the other present inhabitants of the Corridor. The Lambya are one section or 'dialect group' of the Nyiha[12] and the Safwa have now been shown to be another,[13] so both Lambya and Safwa may be regarded as part of the earliest layer of Bantu speakers in the Corridor.

We do not know how far north Tumbuka speakers stretched before the Kyungu came. The Henga section of the Tumbuka took refuge from the Ngoni by moving northward but some Tumbuka speakers were incorporated early in the Ngonde kingdom. Long ago Cullen Young suggested that the Tumbuka tradition of having come over 'a bridge of God' referred to the natural bridge over the Kiwira river in Rungwe district.[14] This is no more than speculation but it might be true. Evidence collected by Mr A. W. C. Msiska, a student of Chancellor College, indicates that the Phoka of the Nyika were a section of the Tumbuka-speaking people, and he implies that the people referred to as Nyika who live on the edge of the Nyika, were also Tumbuka-speaking. It seems likely that in this, as in several other contexts, Nyika refers to the environment in which a group live, not to their cultural characteristics, and the Nyika of the Nyika plateau may not be close in culture to the Nyiha of Mbozi.[15] Mr Vail argues that the northern Tumbuka were patrilineal even before the arrival of traders from across the Lake, and the Ngoni. If patrilineal descent and inheritance is indeed so ancient among the Tumbuka, it suggests that they have affinities with the Nyiha and other peoples of the Corridor, as well as with the Maravi peoples further south, who were matrilineal. Of course, forms of marriage and the rules of inheritance and descent often change when a people acquires stock, but linguistic evidence confirms the existence of northern connections for some Tumbuka (cf. paper 10), and pottery types may do so also.

It will be instructive to see how far a pattern of movement from west, north, and east are reflected in the archaeological record, and to compare the boundaries of the various cultures defined by archaeologists with those of contemporary peoples. Does the archaeological record show any division between the patrilineal peoples of the Corridor and the matrilineal Bemba-Bisa-Maravi peoples?

A fifteenth century date for the arrival of the Nyakyusa pushes back dates other than that suggested for the Bisa. If Kukwe traditions that Penja and

Lugulu were in the Nyakyusa valley ahead of them, and the Penja were an offshoot of the Bungu, then, even allowing that Kukwe occupation probably followed that of the Nyakyusa, the Bungu must have reached their present country at least by the fifteenth century, two centuries earlier than has been suggested.[16] It also implies that by the fifteenth century there were east to west movements of Bantu-speakers. A change in pottery styles at the salt pans of Ivuna is reported to have occurred in the mid-thirteenth century, and it may be that this reflects an east to west movement.[17] According to their own traditions, people who came from the east brought cattle with them to the Corridor, and of course cattle *must* have come from the north or the east; they could not have come from the Congo basin. The Ivuna excavations indicate the presence of cattle from the thirteenth century.[18]

The whole time-scale of the spread of Bantu-speakers from the Katanga areas, postulated by Guthrie and Oliver, is modified by the dates for iron tools in the Ngonde plain in the third century, and iron working at Kalambo[19] from the fourth century, so dates earlier than had been expected for secondary movements are hardly surprising.

III   TRADE

If the radio carbon date for Mbande Hill and the deductions drawn from the genealogies and oral tradition are valid (as I believe they are) then trade in ivory, cloth, metal, porcelain, and pots has continued at the north end of the lake uninterrupted since the fifteenth century. There have, however, been changes in the *direction* of trade and in the quantity and nature of goods traded. The earliest trade was doubtless very small in quantity.

According to Ngonde tradition the *first* Kyungu sent out ivory, and brought with him cloth which he distributed to leaders of earlier communities in recognition of office. Simbobwe who preceded Kyungu is described as 'an elephant hunter', and he had a stock of ivory, so the presumption is that he too traded. The oral tradition of trade to the Ngonde plain from before the time of the first Kyungu is confirmed by the discovery of trade glass beads at Mwamasapa dated to A.D. 1190 and at Mwenepera Hill dated to A.D. 1240.[20] A fifteenth century date for the ivory trade was queried at the conference by scholars working on trade from the coast; they had found no evidence of inland trade in ivory so early. Anthropologists are generally sceptical about the value of *absence* of evidence as an argument, but the point can only be settled by further archaeological and historical work.

During the period of the first ten Kyungus the ivory went north. The exact phrase of oral tradition recorded is 'north over the Ndali hills', but Mbande was at the entrance to the pass to the plateau, through which the Stevenson road was later built, and it is likely that carriers started up that pass, though once onto the plateau they might have cut eastward through Ndali. No-one knew for certain whether the ivory went eastward to the coast, or southward by the Bisa route: once on the plateau it would not have been impossible for the carriers to circle south to Bisa country. What is explicitly stated in Ngonde tradition is that trade southward across the Lake only began in the time of the tenth Kyungu. In traditions of the early period there is no mention of slaves or of guns: only of ivory going out and cloth, metal work, and porcelain coming in.

In view of the archaeological association of beads it is worth noting that the Nyakyusa-Ngonde did not use beads in any quantity, at least from 1890. What they used for decoration in 1935, as earlier, was copper wire to make body-rings, and white metal for anklets.[21] But during the same period (indeed even in 1955) their Lambya neighbours wore quantities of beads. The Safwa still trimmed their leather skirts with cowrie shells in 1938. In Tumbuka tradition there is word of early traders bringing beads, but not in Ngonde tradition.

As is shown in paper 10, Cullen Young described, nearly fifty years ago, traditions of a period in which the Tumbuka and Kamanga were 'using ivory as seats and bed props etc. without any idea of its trade value'. This was changed when a stranger, 'Mlowoka', came across the lake with a party of men and opened up the trade route to Kilwa. Cullen Young dates Mlowoka's arrival to about 1780. He thinks that he came 'eighty or ninety years' before the Ngoni. Elsewhere he says that: 'The Chikuramayembe line had held power for approximately sixty-five years before the Ngoni came.'[22]

The Ngoni in fact came earlier than Cullen Young supposed, and it seems likely that Mlowoka cannot have come later than the mid-eighteenth century. Looking back at the Ngonde and Tumbuka material I find no certain evidence to show whether it was Mlowoka or someone else who opened the trade across the lake with Ngonde; but it is perhaps significant that Ngonde tradition points to a crossing from Mwela (Manda or further north) to Karonga, and Tumbuka tradition to a crossing much further south. The *Lungwani* (Arab or half Arab) who came to Karonga brought cloth—red, white and dark, and body rings.

When one discusses trade in Africa it is as important as it is difficult to assess its quantity, and changes in quantity, and its exact distribution. The ivory trade in Ngonde goes back to the fifteenth century but the area from which ivory was drawn, the quantity of tusks exported was then very limited. The Nyakyusa valley remained sealed off from the trade by geographical barriers—high passes, a great marsh, and the squalls of the northern tip of the lake which even sank a lake steamer, the *Vipya*, in 1946. In 1883 Giraud, travelling through the Nyakyusa valley, noted that the Nyakyusa were the only people he had come across in Africa among whom the chiefs did not claim a tusk of every animal killed.[23] They did not do so because ivory was of negligible value. It was not yet exported. There was a tremendous development of the range and volume of the ivory trade in the Corridor after 1850 as Joseph Thompson makes clear.[24] This was linked to the spread of firearms and the use of slaves for transport.

A second example of the limitation of volume and range is in the use of metal. Though metal working at Kalambo dates back to the fourth century, still in 1938, an appreciable number of women and girls were still using wooden hoes for cultivation in BuNyakyusa a hundred miles away, because iron hoes were still expensive in terms of their resources. Repeatedly, I myself

143

saw wooden hoes in use.[25]

The Kisi pot-market at Pupangandu was already in full swing when the first European to reach the N.E. corner of the lake, Joseph Thompson, arrived in 1878. Sixty years later, when I was working in BuNyakyusa, pots were traded round the top of the lake by canoe, at least as far as Karonga, and northward by carriers as far as the Lupa gold fields. In 1932 the whole of the Nyakyusa valley was supplied with Kisi pots, though earlier pots had also been made by Penja in the hill country. The Kisi potters were specialists in their craft; lacking sufficient land to feed themselves by cultivation they sold pots for their fill in grain. The porters who hawked the pots through BuNyakyusa to the Lupa were usually Kinga.

The Corridor was a cross-roads, as I said, with people moving in and out in all directions. I believe that connections can be traced between Ngonde, and the Venda who live south of the Limpopo. The evidence lies in Venda oral tradition and the complex details of ritual which correspond on so many points to that of Ngonde that I do not think the correspondence can be accidental.[26] Quite independently Professor Inskeep of the University of Cape Town, reached the conclusion that pottery from Nkudzi and that of the Venda showed astonishing similarities.[27] The Nkudzi site is an eighteenth–nineteenth century cemetery. I am feeling around for some hypothesis which would draw together these two observations. Did the kingdom of Ngonde have any link with Nkudzi?

IV   QUESTIONS

A number of questions raised in the first draft of this chapter were answered in the valuable discussions at the conference, but the field for enquiry is still enormous. Three questions for historians and archaeologists strike me as particularly important.

1   How long has the Kisi pot market at Pupangandu been operating, what evidence is there of change in styles, and over what area were the pots traded? The Kisi pot market, is, I believe, the key to the early history of north Malawi.

2   What was the precise route of Bisa trade to the coast? Was Lacerda correct in saying that the Bisa themselves only began going to the coast in 1793 and before that the Yao were the carriers?[28] Is there any evidence on the extent of the area from which the Bisa drew ivory in the eighteenth century or earlier?

3   Did trade routes from the coast to the northern portion of the lake (Manda?) and to the central portion operate independently? Is there any indication from coastal sources of the date at which trade with Manda began?

Work by linguists and anthropologists in the country radiating from Mwenzo may still disentangle something of the ethnography of the Corridor. Questions to be investigated are:

4   What are the precise linguistic relations of Tumbuka with Nyamwanga and Nyiha?

5 What are the cultural affinities of Tumbuka with (i) Bisa (ii) Nyiha?
6 Are the people referred to as *Nyika* on the Nyika plateau in Malawi similar in language and custom to the *Nyiha* of Mbozi, or does the name *Nyika* merely refer to the type of country in which they live?

FOOTNOTES

1 A. Roberts (ed.), *Tanzania before 1900*, East African Publishing House, Nairobi, 1968. B. M. Sutton and A. D. Roberts, 'Uvinza and its Salt Industry', *Azania*, 3, 1968, 45–82. I. N. Kimambo and A. J. Tembu (eds), *A History of Tanzania*, East African Publishing House, Nairobi, 1969. R. Gray and D. Birmingham (eds), *Pre-Colonial African Trade*, O.U.P. London, 1970. A. Roberts, 'Chronology of the Bemba', *J. Afr. Hist.*, 11, 1970, 221–40.

2 Monica Wilson, *Peoples of the Nyasa-Tanganyika Corridor*, Communications from the School of African Studies, University of Cape Town, 1958. Criteria of 'peoples' and their dialect groups' are defined in this paper. Map 1 is a slightly amended version of that published in it.

3 Beverley Brock, 'The Nyiha of Mbozi', *Tanzania Notes and Records*, 65, 1966, 1–30; R. G. Willis, *The Fipa and Related Peoples*, International African Institute, London, 1966. G. K. Park, 'Kinga Priests'; the Politics of Pestilence' in M. J. Swart, V. W. Turner and A. Tuden, *Political Anthropology*, Aldine, Chicago, 1966. Alan Harwood, *Witchcraft, Sorcery and Social Categories among the Safwa*, Oxford University Press, London, 1970. G. Fortune, *The Bantu Languages of the Federation*, Rhodes Livingstone Institute, Lusaka, 1959.

4 K. R. Robinson, 'A Preliminary Report on the recent Archaeology of Ngonde, Northern Malawi', *J. Afr. Hist.*, 7, 1966, 169. K. R. Robinson and B. Sandelowsky, 'The Iron Age of North Malawi: Recent Work'. *Azania*, 3, 1968, 107–46. B. M. Fagan and J. E. Yellen, 'Ivuma: Ancient Salt-working in Southern Tanzania'. *Azania*, 3, 1968, 1–43. J. E. G. Sutton, ' "Ancient Civilisations" and Modern Agricultural Systems in the Southern Highlands of Tanzania'. *Azania*, 4, 1969, 1–13. B. M. Fagan, 'Radio-Carbon Dates for Sub-Saharan Africa' VI, *J. Afr. Hist.*, 11, 1969, 159–61. B. M. Fagan, 'Early Trade and Raw Materials in South Central Africa', in Gray & Birmingham, *Pre-Colonial African Trade*.

5 Monica Wilson, *Communal Rituals of the Nyakyusa*, O.U.P. London, 1958, reprint 1970.

6 Ibid., opposite 3, 27.

7 Godfrey Wilson, *The Constitution of Ngonde*, Rhodes Livingstone Papers, Livingstone, 1939, reprint 1969 Lusaka.

8 Wilson, *Communal Rituals*, 46–8. Robinson, 'Preliminary Report' J. *Afr. Hist.*, **7**, 172–84. F. Fülleborn, *Deutsch Ost-Africa*, Band XI, *Das Deutsche Njasse und Ruwuma Gebiet*, Berlin, 1906, Atlas plate 79.

9 Wilson, *Peoples of the Corridor*, 46–7.

10 Godfrey Wilson, *Constitution of Ngonde*, 10.

11 F. M. Thomas, *Historical Notes of the Bisa Tribe*, Rhodes Livingstone Institute, Lusaka, 1958, 8.

12 Monica Wilson, *Peoples of the Corridor*, 28–9.

13 Harwood, *Witchcraft*, 1.

14 T. Cullen-Young, 'Tribal Mixture in Northern Nyasaland' *J. Roy. Anthr. Inst.*, **63**, 1933, 9.

15 A. W. C. Msiska, 'An Account of Phoka History up to the coming of the Livingstonia Mission'. Unpublished History Seminar paper, Chancellor College, 1969/1970. cf. Robinson and Sandelowsky, 121.

16 Monica Wilson, *Peoples of the Corridor*, 9, 45. Roberts (ed.) *Tanzania before 1900*, 101.

17 Fagan and Yellen, 28.

18 Ibid., 31.

19 Fagan, 'Radio Carbon Dates. . . .' *J. Afr. Hist.*, 1969, 160.

20 Ibid., 161.

21 Fülleborn, *Atlas*, plates 70, 71. Monica Wilson, *Rituals of Kinship among the Nyakyusa*, O.U.P., London, 1957 plates 7 and 8; *Good Company* O.U.P., London, 1951, plate XIII. M. Gluckman and E. Colson (eds), *Seven Tribes in British Central Africa*, O.U.P., London,, 1951, plates XVIII–XIX.

22 T. Cullen Young, 'The Wa-Henga of North Nyasaland', *J. Afr. Soc.*, 1923–24, 190–2. T. Cullen Young, 'Intertribal-Mixture in North Nyasaland' *J. Roy. Anthr. Inst.*, **63**, 1933, 11.

23 V. Giraud, *Les Lacs de l'Afrique Equatoriale*. Hacette, Paris, 1890, 186.

24 J. Thompson, *To the Central African Lakes and Back*, Samson, Louw et al., London, 1881, 2 vols. II, 17.

25 Wilson, *Good Company*, plate VII.

26 M. Wilson and L. Thompson (eds), *The Oxford History of South Africa*, Clarendon, Oxford, 1969, I, 170–2.

27 Wilson and Thompson (eds), *Oxford History of South Africa*, I, 170–2.

28 F. J. M. Lacerda, *Lacerda's Journey to Cazembe*, 1798, Translated R. F. Burton, John Murray, London, 1873, 33–46.

10 Suggestions towards a reinterpreted Tumbuka History

H. Leroy Vail

The historiography of the Tumbuka-speaking peoples has long been dominated by two events. The first of these is the coming of the *Balowoka* traders from the east side of Lake Malawi in the latter half of the eighteenth century and the subsequent establishment of the Chikulamayembe dynasty centred in Nkhamanga, an event which has generally been interpreted as being instrumental in uniting the Tumbuka-speaking peoples for the first time.[2] The second major event is the advent of the Ngoni to northern Malawi, an arrival which is alleged to have destroyed the unity of the Tumbuka-speaking peoples through the destruction of the Chikulamayembe dynasty and its replacement by an Ngoni military and political elite. This emphasis upon only two events has naturally resulted in certain inaccuracies in the history of Northern Malawi and has permitted the formulation of certain myths about Tumbuka history. It is time to re-examine the history of the Tumbuka-speaking peoples in an effort to evaluate these myths and to rectify inaccuracies arising from their general acceptance in the past.

One such myth is what might be called the myth of simplicity. From our vantage point in time, we look back and postulate something called the Tumbuka people. This postulation is a great over-simplification, however. The reasons for this myth are two. First, in the colonial period it was natural for administrators and scholars alike to treat African peoples as *tribes*. The term *tribe* implied some sort of unity based on language and cultural traits, and, following from this synchronic unity, it was assumed that a particular tribe also had an historical unity. Hence, most works of the first half of the century, when dealing with various peoples' histories, sought for unitary origins of the peoples concerned. The results were histories of ruling clans that were accepted as the history of the entire tribe.

Usually, a common language was the dominant criterion for the decision that a particular group of people comprised a tribe. Thus Europeans were predisposed to see the non-Ngoni Tumbuka speakers as a unit, especially as little historical research was carried out in Malawi's Northern Region and as the little done tended to support the idea that the Tumbuka-speaking peoples

148

were a distinct unit.[3]

This notion of Tumbuka unity was strengthened by a second factor. This was the decision by the British colonial administration in 1907 to re-establish the chieftainship of the Chikulamayembe in Rumphi District. During the twentieth century the Chikulamayembe lineage has used history as a tool to strengthen its position. History has been employed to justify the chieftainship and establish its legitimacy, for, as is well known, the Chikulamayembe lineage is not an indigenous chiefly line, being as non-Tumbuka as any Ngoni chieftainship of Mzimba District. Because of this, there has been a certain measure of resistance to the Chikulamayembe chieftainship in Rumphi District by those people who see their ancestors and chieftainships as ante-dating the arrival of the Balowoka and the founding of the Chikulamayembe line. In reaction, supporters of the revived Chikulamayembe house have utilized history as a means of justifying its position, and in so doing they have created a second myth, the myth of the Chikulamayembe's state, a myth which has gone a long way to support the myth of simplicity.

From the point of view of Tumbuka historiography the decision by the Chikulamayembe establishment to set forth its own version of history has been an important one. This is so because the historiography of the Tumbuka-speaking peoples has been dominated by this official interpretation. The history of these peoples has been handled almost exclusively by early missionaries associated with Livingstonia Mission. Fraser and Elmslie, both associated with this mission, worked in northern Mzimba District in the late nineteenth and early twentieth centuries. Living in an area dominated by Ngoni chiefs and anxious to understand the dominant political forces in their area, their primary interests lay naturally with the Ngoni. Their books reflect only a passing interest in Tumbuka-speakers, and, at least in the case of Fraser, the information given about Tumbuka history and culture is often quite erroneous.[4]

The one missionary whose prime concern was the history of the Tumbuka-speakers themselves was T. Cullen Young. It is Young, who, through his many articles and books on Tumbuka history and culture, has set the tone for interpreting the history of these people. Today, when modern scholars approach the history of Northern Malawi, it is to Young's work that they turn.[5] Young's interpretation and presentation of Tumbuka history is largely the official interpretation provided by and associated with the supporters of the Chikulamayembe line. It is not insignificant that one of Young's principal sources of information while writing his *Notes on the History of the Tumbuka-Kamanga Peoples* was one Saulos Nyirenda, whose *History of the Tumbuka-Henga Peoples* which appeared in *Bantu Studies* in 1931, edited and translated by Young himself, is, in many places, little more than a glorification of and justification for the Chikulamayembe chieftainship.[6] Nyirenda's article was written, interestingly enough, at about the same time the British colonial administration was contemplating reviving the Chikulamayembe line in Rumphi area.[7] It is through Young's influence and his acceptance of the official history of the Chikulamayembe line, one part of which supports the notion of a unified Tumbuka people, that this particular interpretation has come to be generally accepted in Tumbuka historiography. Through his work the myth of simplicity and the mythology of the Chikulamayembe chieftainship have become standard for historians.

Obviously a fresh approach to the whole subject of the history of the Tumbuka-speaking peoples is needed to escape the assumptions that have moulded past Tumbuka historiography. My own recent research in northern Malawi suggests certain possible new interpretations.

First, and very briefly, I must touch upon the myth of simplicity. Until now I have spoken of the Tumbuka-speaking peoples rather than of the Tumbuka. This has been intentional, for from my research I have concluded that the assumed historical unity is a false assumption. The history of the pre-Ngoni Tumbuka-speaking peoples is not the history of a unified people but is rather the complex story of many different groups and clans. Thus, the Tumbuka-speakers fit the pattern that is becoming increasingly evident in the historiography of East and Central Africa.[8] Only through a detailed study of the history of these individual groups and clans will a truly accurate picture of Tumbuka history emerge.[9]

The scope of this paper excludes such a detailed analysis. One point worth mentioning, however, is that a very interesting pattern of culture seems to be emerging from my studies. There seem to be fairly distinct historical differences between the Tumbuka living in Mzimba, Nkhata Bay and Kasunga Districts, and in adjacent Zambian territory on the one hand, and those living in Rumphi and Chitipa Districts on the other. To the north, in Rumphi and Chitipa Districts, for example, the people seem for the most part to have followed historically a system of patrilineal descent and inheritance, whereas in the south a matrilineal system prevailed.[10] In addition, although this is less clear, the religious systems seem to have been markedly different, with the important spirit Chikang'ombe being fairly well-known in the south, but not known in the northern areas even though his home was Chikang'ombe Hill in Nkhamanga, deep into the northern zone. Lastly, the pre-Balowoka chiefly regalia, as described to me by informants, seems to have differed in the two areas.[11] It is likely that further distinctions will emerge with further research.

I attribute these cultural differences to the fact that the Tumbuka in the southern areas are derived from a mixture of matrilineal peoples from the West and, perhaps, the South with the autochthones of the area, people possibly related to the ancient Chewa peoples. On the other hand, evidence is strong that the northern zone was peopled either by groups who immigrated from patrilineal areas in Southern Tanzania and North-Eastern Zambia or by those who immigrated from matrilineal areas to the west at a relatively late date and adopted a patrilineal system of descent and inheritance. After moving into the area they mixed with the scattered Tumbuka-speakers of the region, absorbed certain aspects of Tumbuka culture, including language, and imposed upon the local people some aspects of their own culture and established themselves as politically dominant, usually in localized clan areas. While this interpretation is tentative, it is supported by certain linguistic evidence.

Generally speaking, people are quick to point out the relationships the Tumbuka have with the Chewa to the south.[12] In fact, Tumbuka people themselves often refer to these putative relationships. Having completed linguistic tests of ChiTumbuka, however, comparing it with ChiChewa on the one hand and ChiLambya and ChiNdali, two languages to the North of the Tumbuka zone, in northern Malawi and southern Tanzania, respectively, on the other, an interesting result was obtained. Using the Guthrie list of proto-Bantu starred forms as a point of departure, I compared 488 words in all of these languages.[13] Of these 488 words, 41·2 per cent occurred as cognates in both Chewa and Tumbuka, 45·7 per cent occurred in both Lambya and Tumbuka, while 42·3 per cent occurred in both Ndali and Tumbuka. Further, of the common words between Tumbuka and Chewa 30·3 per cent were unique to those two languages, not occurring in Lambya or Ndali, while 33·2 per cent were unique to Lambya and Tumbuka and 38·1 per cent were unique to Ndali and Tumbuka, not occurring in Chewa. These figures are significant, for while they show that Tumbuka and Chewa are linked from the point of view of vocabulary, they also give indication of an even closer relationship existing between Tumbuka and the languages to the north, at least on the level of lexis. It should prove interesting when further comparisons are made with the languages to the west of the Tumbuka zone, such as Lala, Lamba, Bisa and Bemba, to discover what links these languages have with Tumbuka.[14] If traditions I have collected for the southern Tumbuka zone are accurate, some firm linguistic link between Tumbuka and the languages to the west should be evident.

As I mentioned earlier, there are two myths to consider. As a total debunking of the myth of simplicity would require too much time and space, being based on detailed local and clan histories, I shall have to be content to have thrown some doubt on this myth and with having presented an alternative hypothesis of my own. Now I should like to turn to a reconsideration of the second myth, the myth of the Chikulamayembe chieftainship, the myth of the historical pre-eminence of Mlowoka and his successors. For reasons that shall become obvious as I continue, I shall for the most part henceforth restrict my discussion of Tumbuka history to my hypothesized northern culture zone.

The northern zone, roughly co-extensive with the present-day Rumphi District, is an area that in the period immediately preceding the coming of the Balowoka and the founders of the Chikulamayembe dynasty was subdivided into many small areas dominated by clan groups. Such clans would include the Luhangas, the Mkandawires, the Sowoyas, the Kachales, and similar groups, all names still well-known throughout Malawi. Therefore, to reconstruct the history of the area accurately, one must collect and analyze individual clan histories. The conclusion that one reaches after sifting through a mass of such clan histories is that in the early and mid-eighteenth century there was a sustained movement into the area by small groups of people from the west, the north, and the north-east, from Zambia and Tanzania. It was these immigrant groups that established themselves among the Tumbuka-speaking autochthones of the area and gained political pre-eminence over restricted territorial divisions.[15]

The traditions of the Phoka group, who inhabit the Nyika Plateau and the fringe lands between the Plateau and the Lake Shore, indicate that the

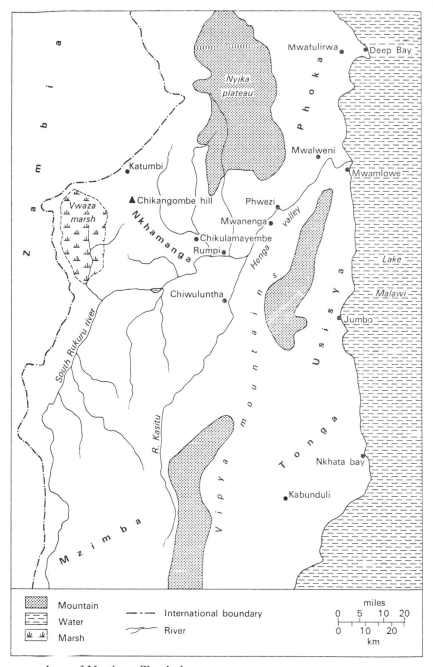

10.1   Area of Northern Tumbuka

original forbears of the Phoka migrated to the Nyika from the north, and the depth of genealogies that exist would indicate the first half of the eighteenth century, probably towards the earlier part, as the probable date of entry into the area. These Phoka traditions recall that other people lived in the area and became intermingled with the intruders, losing their own identity. Because the immigrants became politically and socially dominant, it is their history that is known today. It was through the intermingling and intermarriage of the Phoka immigrants with the indigenous Tumbuka-speakers that the Phoka came to adopt the Tumbuka language as their own, with only slight dialectical variations distinguishing it from the Tumbuka spoken elsewhere. Whether or not the indigenous people were matrilineal, it seems unquestionable that from the time the Phoka invaders arrived patrilineage was followed in the area.

At about the time the earliest Phoka were settling on the Nyika, a similar movement was taking place to the west, in the Nkhamanga area. It was at this time, as indicated by various Phoka traditions, that the first important clans of Nkhamanga, the Mkandawires and Luhangas, were settling there. Oral traditions gathered in Nkhamanga indicate that these clans were the first arrivals and that they entered from a generally westerly direction.[16] Soon afterwards, other clans followed, some from the north, others from the east and west.[17] Apparently the area was not crowded at this time, for traditions maintain that there was no warfare between the various groups. As with the Phoka, the people who entered Nkhamanga married the local people, established their own political dominance, and imposed a patrilineal complex upon the area.[18] An interesting tradition collected from an important member of the Luhanga clan, the dominant clan of the central Nkhamanga Plain in the pre-Balowoka era, asserts that when the founder of the clan arrived, the people that lived in the area ran away. According to the tradition, these people were called Tumbuka.

While new clans were entering Nkhamanga and Phoka country, so too were they entering the Henga area. The clans for which I have collected traditions in this area, such as Munthali and Harawa, do not claim a western origin, but are derived, in rather helter-skelter fashion, from the north and the east, that is from southern Tanzania generally. For example, traditions of the dominant Hango clan suggest a place of origin in the Ubena country of central southern Tanzania.[19] Other clans show similar points of origin.

So it is therefore that the area of present-day Rumphi District, in the period from about 1700 or so to the middle of the eighteenth century, experienced a steady influx of diverse groups from outside the area. It seems likely that the reasons for this movement of people into the area lie in the internal conditions of the regions from which they derived. For those who trace their origins to the west and north-west, the disturbances caused by Bemba expansion seem a likely explanation.[20] For those whose origins are traced to southern Tanzania, especially to the Ubena area, it is likely that they were encouraged by disturbances taking place in the Uhehe-Ubena area, although it is possible that trading possibilities prompted some.[21] It was from the time of these intrusions that I would date the divergence in culture of the peoples of Rumphi District from those to the south.

As has been mentioned already, the form of government in these areas in the mid-eighteenth century was chieftainship over restricted areas. It has often been asserted that these were clan areas only.[22] This is undoubtedly true for some Tumbuka areas, but it seems that in certain districts, as for example, Nkhamanga and Phoka country, there were chiefs who ruled loosely over the more narrow clan leaders. Thus, in Nkhamanga's central area, the Luhanga chief appears to have enjoyed a position of pre-eminence among the other chiefs of the area, while in Phoka country the chief who had prestige over all sub-chiefs was Mwacidika MwaPhoka.[23] From all accounts, however, in spite of the presence of a central chieftainship such as that of Luhanga or Mwacidika, complete with special insignia of office, it would be quite incorrect to say that strong chieftainship existed.[24] Instead, there seems to have prevailed a situation in which, because of the peacefulness of the region, little government was required. Cases in law were handled by the local chiefs, but there seems to have been nothing in the way of a centralized bureaucratic system, a military force, or collected taxes. Certain tribute was given to the chiefs, such as the skins of leopards or lions or portions of meat from a hunting kill, but by and large the chiefs do not seem to have been materially exalted above their countrymen. With the whole area divided in this fashion, it lacked political and military centralization.

It was into this situation that the Balowoka group intruded. According to traditions these people came as Arabs from beyond Lake Malawi as traders. We must now turn our attention to these Balowoka to gauge their impact upon the area in which they settled and to examine the official mythology that has become associated with them and their descendants.

Oral traditions taken in Rumphi District agree that the Balowoka arrived in the area soon after the clans who immigrated in the early eighteenth century had settled in. The traditions of the Luhanga family, for example, assert that it was during the chieftaincy of the second Luhanga chief, Mubila, that the most famous of the Balowoka, Mlowoka, arrived in Nkhamanga.[25] Similarly, traditions from Phoka country and the area around Hewe, to the West of Nkhamanga, also confirm that the Balowoka arrived in the second generation of chiefs for those areas. This would put the coming of these traders in the last half of the eighteenth century, probably between 1770 and 1780.[26]

According to tradition, the Balowoka were drawn to the area west of the Lake by rumours of an abundant untapped supply of ivory. It is likely that these traders were engaged in long-distance trade in ivory from the interior to the coast, probably to Kilwa. This is given support by the Swahili *History of Kilwa Kivinje* which Freeman-Grenville sees as clearly reflecting 'a trade connection with the region of Lake Nyasa' in the latter part of the eighteenth century.[27] It has been suggested by Young[28] and Alpers[29] that these traders were probably Yao, and I have discovered no evidence as yet to suggest otherwise.[30]

The people in Nkhamanga amongst whom the Balowoka came were favourably impressed both by the goods they were offered in exchange for ivory and leopard skins and by the generosity of the traders. The country abounded in elephants at this time and ivory was plentiful. It could be traded in great quantity for cloth, beads and similar merchandise that hitherto had been lacking in the region. The most prominent of this party of traders, Mlowoka, was an intelligent man who desired to ensure the supply of ivory for his long-distance trade dealings. He therefore adopted a friendly attitude towards the local chiefs and headmen, going through the countryside seeking out the politically powerful and making alliances with them by granting them gifts and crowning them with a dark blue or black cloth turban, a sign of their political power. By being associated in this way with Mlowoka the local leaders gained prestige and material goods. By associating himself and his group with the local leaders, Mlowoka ensured a friendly environment for his trading activities and the aid of the leaders with whom he was thus aligned in obtaining further supplies of ivory. In this manner, Mlowoka appears to have established an economic hegemony over the Nkhamanga-Henga-Phoka areas.[31]

Concerned with establishing a firm economic base in the area, Mlowoka married into the Luhanga clan, which dominated the central Nkhamanga Plain, an area rich in elephants and on a main trade route to Bisa country to the west. By marrying into this clan, and later into a branch of the Luhangas, the Kumwendas, Mlowoka assured himself of a geographical position to control a large part of the ivory trade, a position in the very heart of elephant country. In the years that followed, his compatriots likewise established for themselves similar economic bases throughout the area. According to Young and Nyirenda, the lieutenants of Mlowoka were established by him as follows: Katumbi received all the Hewe District, Kajumba the area to the north-west of Hewe towards Zambia's Bisa country, Chiwulunta the area to the south of Nkhamanga, Mwahenga and Mwalweni the region of the Henga Valley and Phoka country, Mwamlowe the area on the lake shore around the mouth of the South Rukuru River, Jumbo the coastal area to the south of Mwamlowe, and Kabunduli the area between the Dwangwa Valley in the south and Jumbo's territory in the north.[32]

This alleged territorial distribution of the Tumbuka-Tonga areas by Mlowoka to his henchmen as presented by Young and Nyirenda is the partial basis of the territorial claim of the Chikulamayembe chieftainship and is the version that one will hear today from supporters of the lineage. This territorial claim is the core of the mythology that surrounds the dynasty. But merely because it has been presented and accepted widely does not mean that it is necessarily accurate. In the first place, the Nkhamanga-based Mlowoka was not a political leader but a trader interested in securing his economic position in northern Malawi. As such, the distribution of his associate traders around the countryside in key locations would not mean necessarily an attempt to establish a political state with a territorial base. Rather, and considering his interests, far more likely, his main desire was to organize a far-reaching economic trading infra-structure to drain the country of ivory and to ensure the safety of the local trade routes, especially towards the west. Considering his interests, the claim that Mlowoka established a territorial state is doubtful.

More particularly, and more to the point, the status of certain of the lieutenants named in Nyirenda and Young is extremely dubious. Although it may be acceded that after the death of Mlowoka the areas of Katumbi,

Mwahenga, Mwalweni, and perhaps the areas of Kajumba, Mwamlowe and Jumbo, together with the Nkhamanga area itself, came to be associated loosely with the Chikulamayembe at Nkhamanga in a political way, the roles of Chiwulunta and Kabunduli are doubtful. Chiwulunta is alleged to have had control over most of what is now Mzimba District. Kabunduli is alleged to have had control over almost all the present-day Nkhata Bay District. From my field researches, however, I have not as yet uncovered a single scrap of evidence that would support the claim of Chiwulunta to all Mzimba District south of Nkhamanga. If Chiwulunta did rule an area south of Nkhamanga, it seems that it was very restricted indeed, probably to the northern fringe of Mzimba District around Lake Kazuni.

The position of Kabunduli's being a loyal compatriot of Mlowoka is likewise disputed. Kabunduli is generally seen, except in the official history of the Chikulamayembe house, as being in no way associated with the Balowoka, but rather with the Maravi invasions that took place centuries before the coming of the Balowoka.[33] Furthermore, traditions collected in Nkhata Bay District are consistent that neither Mlowoka nor the later Chikulamayembes exercised any sort of political power in the area, either directly or through the agency of Kabunduli.[34] It appears then, on all available evidence, that the claims of the official mythology to the areas of present-day Nkhata Bay and Mzimba Districts are grossly overstated and that these areas were not within any state of Mlowoka or the Chikulamayembes who followed him. At most, tentative trade feelers might have been sent to that area, but if this is the case, they were not followed up in later years by political control of any sort.

The official version of the history of Mlowoka and Chikulamayembe also maintains that the power of these men extended northwards from Nkhamanga all the way to the Songwe river, the border between Malawi and Tanzania.[35] As far as is known, there is absolutely no evidence available to substantiate this claim in any way. The Ngonde reject such a claim outright, and other groups South of the Songwe, such as the Lambya and Sukwa, have no tradition of political domination by Mlowoka or his successors.[36]

The territorial claims of the official history are inflated and have become historical myth, without a factual base. In actuality, the Chikulamayembe state, after the death of Mlowoka, was restricted to the band of territory stretching from the eastern part of Zambia in the west, across the Nkhamanga, Henga and Phoka areas, to the lake shore. The shape of this territory is instructive in that it forms part of a natural route from the rich elephant countries of eastern Zambia and Nkhamanga to the lake, and then across the lake to the routes to the coast. From the point of view of geography the area organized by Mlowoka and ruled over by his successors was a trade route, with lieutenants placed along the route at strategic points on an east-west line to protect the ivory trade and its Lake Shore embarkation points. What Mlowoka organized and what his successors ruled over was less a state than a trade route for ivory. This point will be amplified shortly. Mlowoka's action in organizing such a structure was a highly rational one, for, as a trader, he was content to ensure his economic well-being, and he did not divert himself vainly to acquire territory to the north and south of the area in which he had primary interests, an alleged acquisition that is an integral part of the official history of the Chikulamayembe line.

If this official mythology of which we have been speaking has a territorial facet, it also has a more overtly political aspect. According to Young and Nyirenda, and according to later historians who have followed in the footsteps of these two men, the advent of Mlowoka and the rule of his successors, the Chikulamayembes, established a unity hitherto unknown among the Tumbuka peoples. It is fair to say that this role as bringer of unity is used by the official history's supporters to justify the pre-eminent position that the Chikulamayembe today holds among Tumbuka chiefs. As we have seen already, however, Mlowoka and his descendants had no real power in most of Mzimba, Nkhata Bay, Chitipa or Karonga Districts. Now we must ask the evidence what power Mlowoka and his successors had in the area in which they were economically interested. Or, in other words, did Mlowoka and his successors actually establish a meaningful political unity, as has so often been claimed, or didn't they?

Looking back, we saw that the northern Tumbuka area was greatly divided in the period prior to the Balowoka's arrival. When he arrived, Mlowoka married into two of the leading clans of Nkhamanga, most importantly, into the Luhanga clan, a clan which claims to be one of the two oldest in the area. It was through this marriage policy that Mlowoka came to be connected with a real political force, but according to traditions, the Luhanga chief, Mubila, continued to rule even after the marriage of Mlowoka into the clan. Mlowoka is not himself held to be a chief in the traditions I have collected throughout Rumphi District. His own influence was based on his wealth as a trader and his connection with a leading political force in the area, not on any official political position he himself held.

When Mlowoka died, the first Chikulamayembe appeared. It was at this point that the son of Mlowoka, Gonapamuhanya, succeeded to the power and wealth of his father, Mlowoka, and to the political legitimacy of his grandfather, Mubila Luhanga, whose daughter had married Mlowoka. It seems that Gonapamuhanya's succession was irregular and resulted in the usurpation of power from the regular line of succession and the reduction of the Luhangas to the position of village headmen. It is from this irregular succession that we date the Chikulamayembe line as a true political force, and it can be dated to around 1805–10 or so. If we admit that after Mlowoka's death, political power in Nkhamanga passed to the Chikulamayembes, and if we admit additionally that Mwahenga, Mwamlowe, Katumbi, and the rest of Mlowoka's associates likewise established political power in their areas by combining a policy of well-advised marriages with great economic power through the control of the long-distance ivory trade, we are still left to assess the extent of unity that existed in the area ruled over by the Chikulamayembes.[37]

Applying traditional criteria of political structure to the Chikulamayembe's state, we find that it was very unsophisticated indeed. In the first place, within Nkhamanga itself the Chikulamayembes seem to have continued the general pattern of administration followed by the Luhangas before them, a pattern of extremely rudimentary and restrained government. On the judicial level, subchiefs and headmen continued to judge court cases and dispense justice. Only the most important cases were referred to the Chikulamayembe's attention. Under the Luhangas taxes in the form of tribute were paid in kind to the chief as a symbol of respect. This practice continued in the Chikulamayembe period, although one marked departure from past practice did occur. That is, the Chikulamayembes seem to have been able to exact a tribute or tax in the form of one ivory tusk for every elephant killed. This tax would, of course, bolster the Chikulamayembes' trading position immensely. Nor did the Chikulamayembes have either an army or an organized bureaucracy that could function to impose their will on potentially recalcitrant subjects. Finally, contrary to information found in Fraser and Young, there was no centralized religious system in Nkhamanga itself, let alone in all the area associated with the Chikulamayembes.[38]

Although worship was carried out at Chikang'ombe Hill, the place alleged to have been the central religious shrine for all the Chikulamayembes' territories, worship was also carried out at other places in Nkhamanga, such as Buma, Mang'weng'we, Nkonjera and elsewhere. Furthermore, the priests associated with these shrines, as far as I have been able to detect, were not chosen by the Chikulamayembes, but were instead selected from families with which the priesthood had been traditionally closely associated. They were not, moreover, associated with the priesthood of Chikang'ombe Hill. At Chikang'-ombe Hill the priest was chosen from the male line of the Kachale family, a clan related to the Mkandawire clan, and the office passed from father to son. This pattern of priestly succession was followed elsewhere throughout the Chikulamayembe's domains, although it is true that the Chikulamayembe himself sometimes led prayers addressed to the ancestor spirits. This custom, however, was merely a continuation of the custom of the country before the establishment of the Chikulamayembe chieftainship.

Although this is a very superficial review of the situation in Nkhamanga, it is adequate to show that the establishment of the Chikulamayembe dynasty was not a severe break with the past for the people of Nkhamanga. Justice, religion, governmental administration, all continued much as they had under the Luhangas and their sub-chiefs. It is natural that this should have happened, since, after all, the Balowoka did not constitute a conquering horde of invaders, but rather a very small elite without the power to change radically the society into which they came. The principal change they did bring was economic, not political or cultural. Perhaps it is due to the very fact that the Chikulamay-embes did allow the past ways to continue undisturbed that ensured that the people of the region would accept them and not overthrow their rule.

If this was the situation in Nkhamanga itself, what conditions existed outside the area? Was the Chikulamayembe's power stronger or weaker in the regions beyond? This particular subject still requires a great deal of fresh research, largely because in the past so much attention has been focussed upon the Chikulamayembe dynasty itself that consideration of the other Balowoka has been negligible. The assumption has always been that the other Balowoka rulers were loyal and subservient to the Chikulamayembe, and that he ruled the region through his compatriots. Although I have not been able to conduct research in all the areas allegedly under the Chikulamayembe, the research I

158

have done leads to a somewhat different conclusion.

The popular picture presented by the official history of the lineage is one of great political strength and unity, with the Chikulamayembe exercising power from the Dwangwa in the south to the Songwe in the north, from the Lake Shore to the Luangwa river in Zambia, an area of close to 20,000 square miles.[39] Apart from the matter of accuracy of territorial extent, which we have already covered, it seems that this picture is not correct and the reality of the situation was markedly different. For example, in the Hewe area the trader from the east, Mulindafwa, known as Katumbi, went his own way, establishing what seems to have emerged as a much more institutionalized and ritualized chieftainship than did the Chikulamayembe in Nkhamanga. This might well have been because the Chikulamayembe inherited legitimacy from the local owners of the land, the Luhangas, whereas from all accounts Katumbi was not welcomed in Hewe in a wholly friendly manner by the owners of the land there, Zolokere and Khutamaji.[40] As a result, it is likely that Katumbi felt the need to establish a chieftainship for himself and a well-developed official history of his own.[41] By so doing, he set himself apart from the Chikulamayembe. In the Henga Valley, Mwahenga followed a similarly independent course, setting up a distinct chieftainship and system of sub-chiefs without consulting with the Chikulamayembe. Further, the chief also gave himself a religious sanction by taking upon himself the role of priest at the local religious shrine at Phwezi.[42] Further investigations in the chiefdoms of Katumbi and Mwahenga, in addition to all the others of Mlowoka's compatriots, might well given additional evidence that the subsidiary chiefs of Chikulamayembe were, in fact, more independent than has been hitherto supposed. In any event, the two instances I have cited plus my investigations in Phoka country definitely indicate that central authority of the Chikulamayembe over local chiefs was not present to any marked degree.

Moving away from the relationship between the Chikulamayembe and his lieutenants, we must now consider his relations with the people in the outlying areas. Without doubt, the Chikulamayembe had some authority and influence in the lands beyond Nkhamanga itself. To deny this would be foolish. However, from all available evidence it appears that this influence was slight indeed. Just as in Nkhamanga itself, cases in law and the dispensing of justice were handled by local chiefs and headmen. Only very rare cases were referred to Nkhamanga. Moreover, taxes were not paid to the Chikulamayembe but rather to the local chief, such as Mwahenga or the Phoka chief Kachulu. It was up to these chiefs to send to the Chikulamayembe any tribute that was deemed appropriate. There were no officials from the Nkhamanga court exercising governmental control outside Nkhamanga, and government continued to be handled by local chiefs and head-men. Politically, then, the situation was highly decentralized. Religiously, each local area had its own centre of worship, generally associated with rain cults, and religious decentralization paralleled political decentralization. The extent of the Chikulamayembe's control in the outlying areas seems to have been in settling disputes between important leaders, as for example when he settled a quarrel between the Phoka leaders Mwacidika and Chaswela Mtimbaluji, later known as Kachulu, or in settling difficult or important judicial cases.

Apart from this lack of actual governing control, however, Mlowoka and the earliest Chikulamayembes exercised a real economic influence throughout the area, for it was in their hands and the hands of their lieutenants, politically independent though the latter might have been, that there rested a monopoly of the ivory trade and the distribution of goods from the coast. Basing their power on this economic factor, and not interfering in any meaningful way with the traditional life of the people they ruled, the Balowoka were viewed as benevolent and beneficial to the area as a whole. Because of its richness in ivory Nkhamanga and its adjacent areas came to be known throughout East Africa.[43] As far as the Chikulamayembes of this period were concerned, however, they were political leaders in Nkhamanga only, in the full sense of the term, and had very weak power beyond Nkhamanga proper, their real power in these places resting upon a trade monopoly.

This being the case, the Chikulamayembes, down to about 1850 or so, seem to have been militarily weak. According to tradition, for example, in the time of Chikulamayembe III, Pitamkusa, probably in the late 1820s, a new clan, the Nyirenda, came from across the lake and established themselves south of the Rukuru in the Henga Valley. In an attempt to dislodge this new clan, because of its interest in trade, the Chikulamayembe's forces were badly beaten, even though the Nyirenda could not have numbered very many people at this time.[44] Other traditions support the notion that the Chikulamayembe simply did not have enough force at his disposal to enforce his decisions.

With the strength of the Chikulamayembes resting upon economic control of the area, not political or military force, its position was necessarily a precarious one. Because of the abundance of ivory Nkhamanga's reputation grew and eventually acted as a magnet that quite naturally attracted other traders to the area, traders, who, if successful, would weaken the monopoly held by the Balowoka group. The fact that the Chikulamayembes had but little military strength nor any real political unity that could check fresh intrusions of traders is significant. From all indications, such a process of erosion of the trade monopoly did in fact occur. The instance already cited of the trader from across the lake, Kawunga Nyirenda, coming to the area and establishing himself permanently is but one case in point. Traditions collected from other clans in the hills south of the Henga area indicate that their forebears migrated to the district in the early nineteenth century to participate in the ivory trade and establish themselves in Chikulamayembe's domains.[45]

More important than this erosion of the economic dominance of the Balowoka's descendants, however, is the appearance at this time of a totally new type of trade and trader. This trader made a marked impact upon Tumbuka society in the pre-Ngoni period. In the early decades of the nineteenth century an increased demand for slaves on the Indian Ocean coast of Africa brought about a demand for slaves from the interior. During the time of Mlowoka and the earliest Chikulamayembes, the trade to the coast was in the form of ivory and other such exotic goods. Traditions from the entire area are unanimous that the Balowoka did not trade in slaves.[46] This lack of interest in slaves would harmonize with the fact that in the late eighteenth century and

160

the very early nineteenth the demand for slaves was fairly low.[47] However, as the demand for slaves grew, and as the fame of Nkhamanga as a centre for ivory spread, it was natural that long-distance slave and ivory traders should have made their appearance in the area.

And so it was that in the time of the later Chikulamayembes Swahili slave traders appeared on the scene.[48] Their arrival was a traumatic experience for Tumbuka society, not merely in the Chikulamayembe's area, but also in at least the northern two-thirds of Mzimba District. Circumventing the descendants of Mlowoka and his friends, now the holders of a much-weakened trade monopoly, the Swahili traders approached local village headmen and sub-chiefs with apparent impunity. These traders came by way of two main routes, one around the top of Lake Malawi from the north-east, through present-day Karonga District, and the other across the lake, landing near Nkhata Bay, and then striking inland.[49] Smashing the Balowokas' trade monopoly, these traders dealt with local village leaders who did not hesitate to sell slaves to the traders in exchange for cloth, beads, and other such merchandise. The slaves sold were generally criminals or those who had no protectors in the local society, such as orphans, but not always. By trading with the slave dealers, the local leaders could augment their position locally by gaining prestige and trade goods. This phenomenon aggravated further the already highly decentralized Tumbuka society by weakening the position of the major chiefs *vis à vis* local leaders and by encouraging rivalries among local leaders as to who should deal with the slave and ivory traders. So successful were these new traders that the traditions of the Chikulamayembe house maintain that the later Chikulamayembes did not trade at all, but were content to function as political leaders in Nkhamanga.

Faced with the loss of their trade monopoly and having failed to build up either a strong military system or a unified political structure beyond Nkhamanga, it is not surprising either that the Chikulamayembes, and probably the descendants of the other Balowoka, grew increasingly weak because of the activities of the new traders from the east. Taking this fact into consideration, it is not surprising that when the Ngoni arrived in the mid-nineteenth century they found a land that was politically and socially fissiparous, militarily weak, and an economy in an advanced state of decay because of exploitation by outside traders. Confronted by the strong military organization of the Ngoni, the Tumbuka peoples were easily conquered, and the lack of an organized opposition to the Ngoni led by the Chikulamayembe or his supporters is not really to be wondered at.

The dynasty founded by Mlowoka is an interesting one for what I see as a very paradoxical explanation for both its successes and its ultimate failure. In the first place, it was successful because it coupled economic strength through an ivory monopoly with an intelligent programme of amalgamation with, not conquest of, the local Tumbuka. Because the régimes set up by the Balowoka were tolerant of local customs, did not try to interfere greatly in local habits and institutions, accepted the religious cults associated with the area, were generous in their trade dealings, and did not attempt to remake the Tumbuka clan areas into a politically united empire, these régimes were accepted readily by the local Tumbuka. Yet such a system, although earning for itself a good reputation locally and developing the area's prosperity, could not survive indefinitely, given the changes that were taking place throughout East-Central Africa. It had within its structure the reasons for its own eventual easy destruction.

By not building up a centralized authority, with a strong military and political apparatus, and by relying upon trade alone as a base for their power, the Balowoka failed to provide for the future stability of their régimes. When other traders, such as Kawunga Nyirenda, moved in, the monopoly they enjoyed was weakened. With the arrival of the long-distance slave and ivory traders, the monopoly was broken entirely, leaving the Balowoka in a most unenviable position considering the imminent Ngoni attacks. When the Ngoni did arrive Tumbuka society was in much the same decentralized and militarily weak condition that it had been in some eighty years before, before the Balowoka's arrival. It was simply unable to defend itself effectively against the Ngoni *impi*. The outcome was a foregone conclusion, as the Tumbuka, although united in language and, to a certain degree at least, in culture, had no political or religious institutions capable of providing leadership for any resistance. It was not until some thirty years had passed that overt resistance did break out, and then it seems to have been the work of individuals of great character, such as Baza, Kanyoli and Kambondoma, rather than a revival of Nkhamanga or Tumbuka political institutions.[50]

The re-establishment of the Chikulamayembe chieftainship in 1907 by the British administration produced a wave of pride amongst certain elements of the Tumbuka, especially as it was viewed as redress, in part at least, for the defeat the Tumbuka had suffered at the hands of the Ngoni. But it also produced a mythology of the pre-Ngoni Chikulamayembe line that was geared to justify and legitimize the new paramount chieftainship through a recollection of its supposed past glories. It is, in some ways, most unfortunate that this particular interpretation of Tumbuka history gained the wide circulation it has achieved. The Chikulamayembe dynasty did much that was praiseworthy in its heyday, and it should not be condemned for its essentially humane attitude towards the Tumbuka over whom it established itself. Nor should its economic vigor in the late eighteenth and early nineteenth centuries be discounted, for it succeeded in making the name of Nkhamanga known far and wide as an area of prosperity and richness. Yet an acceptance of these virtues should not be transmogrified into an acceptance of such claims as that the dynasty controlled from the Songwe to the Dwangwa or that it established a strong political unity over the Tumbuka. The evidence does not support such an interpretation. Moreover, if it were true, it would be inconceivable that the Ngoni met with such little organized opposition from the Tumbuka as they did. By the time of the Ngoni arrival, the real base of the Chikulamayembe's power had been eroded and the Chikulamayembe dynasty was but a shadow of its former self, a self never, in any case, very strong politically or militarily.

The purpose of this paper has been to present some suggestions towards a reinterpreted Tumbuka history so that it can be seen not only in a more correct light than previously, but also as an integral part of the history of East-Central

Africa as a whole. The area was affected by phenomena from without, and these should be appreciated when approaching the history of the Tumbuka. Much further research needs to be done, especially in the southern and central parts of Mzimba District, where the Ngoni presence has masked the history of the pre-Ngoni inhabitants of the area to a great extent, and in the northern Mzimba and Rumphi areas, where far too little research has been done on the chieftainships of men such as Mwamlowe, Mwahenga, Katumbi and the others. Only when this additional investigation is done into clan histories and the histories of the less important chieftainships will a truly accurate picture of Tumbuka history emerge.

FOOTNOTES

1 The research upon which this paper is based has been carried out supported in part by a research grant from the University of Malawi. I should also like to acknowledge the useful comments on the material made by the Rev. Dr M. Schoffeleers, Professors E. A. Alpers, R. E. Gregson and Jan Vansina, and my colleagues at the University of Malawi. The interpretation here presented is strictly my own. Further, I should like to acknowledge the assistance I have received from my students at the University, without whose generous help my work would have been rendered much more difficult and less pleasant.

2 The term *Balowoka* means *those who have crossed over*, referring to people who have crossed from the east side of Lake Malawi. The singular of the term is *Mlowoka*.

3 Cf. Anonymous, 'The Tumbuka Tribe', *Aurora*, 5 (1), 1901, 2–3; Donald Fraser, *Winning a Primitive People* (London, 1914), 112–19.

4 W. A. Elmslie, *Among the Wild Ngoni* (Edinburgh, 1899); Fraser's information on the Chikulamayembes of the early nineteenth century is garbled, and his comments on the nature of Tumbuka religion, especially regarding the spirit Chikang'ombe, are inexact.

5 See, for example, Mary Tew, *The Peoples of the Lake Nyasa Region* (London, 1950), *passim*; Monica Wilson, *The Peoples of the Nyasa-Tanganyika Corridor* (Cape Town 1958), 38–40; J. G. Pike, *Malawi: A Political and Economic History* (London, 1968), 48–50; J. Omer-Cooper, *The Zulu Aftermath* (Evanston, 1966), 80–3.

6 T. Cullen Young, *Notes on the History of the Tumbuka-Kamanga Peoples* (London, 1932); Saulos Nyirenda, 'History of the Tumbuka-Henga People', trans. and ed. by T. C. Young, *Bantu Stud.*, 5 (1), 1930.

7 Nyirenda, *Henga*, 2.

8 Cf. R. Apthorpe, 'Problems of African History: The Nsenga of Northern Rhodesia', *Rhodes-Livingstone J.*, **28**, 1961, 47–67; Jan Vansina, *Kingdoms of the Savanna* (Madison 1966), 88; Andrew Roberts, ed., *Tanzania Before 1900* (Nairobi, 1968), passim.

9 Henceforth, for the sake of simplicity, I shall use the term Tumbuka instead of the term Tumbuka-speaking people except where the latter is preferable.

10 The over-simple interpretation presented by Young and embraced by others that a matrilineal complex changed to a patrilineal system because of the impact of the Chikulamayembe dynasty's patrilineality is invalid. Evidence taken from clan histories, genealogies, and oral traditional literature all attests to a patrilineal descent system before the advent of the Balowoka in the northern area, except among certain Nkhamanga clans.

11 For example, chiefs in the northern area were marked by a ritual axe (*kapopo*) worn over the shoulder, whereas this article is unknown as chiefly regalia in the southern area.

12 H. W. Langworthy, 'Understanding Malawi's Pre-Colonial History', *Soc. Malawi J.*, **23** (1), 1970, 38.

13 Cf. M. Guthrie, *Comparative Bantu* (London, 1967), I, passim.

14 Writing in 1891, Elmslie noted that from his experience in the country, it seemed that Tumbuka was most similar to Bemba and Bisa. W. A. Elmslie, *Notes on the Tumbuka Language as Spoken in Mombera's Country* (Aberdeen, 1891), v.

15 Why such groups were able to gain such political pre-eminence is unclear. It is possible that the invaders had a more highly developed sense of politics than the autochthones together with a superior material culture. It is most likely that this penetration was facilitated by a very thin population of Tumbuka-speakers, and that the immigration process was generally a peaceful one.

16 Cf. also Young, *Tumbuka-Kamanga History*, 155–8.

17 In writing of these clans it should be noted that the original 'clan' as described in tradition usually includes one leader, the eponymous founder, and a few relatives, usually male only. Thus, the term clan is perhaps an overly ambitious description of the intruding group.

18 Considering that the traditions of the dominant pre-Balowoka clans of Nkhamanga assert a Westerly origin for the clan forebears, the fact that
164

they adopted a patrilineal system poses a problem. It is possible that such was adopted because of the lack of women in the entering groups, although such an hypothesis is by no means a certain one.

19 A. K. Mhango, *The History of the Henga People* (Blantyre, 1970), Univ. of Malawi, seminar paper, mimeographed, 2.

20 Vansina, *Kingdoms*, 87–92; A. J. Wills, *An Introduction to the History of Central Africa* (London, 1964), 52–58.

21 Roland Oliver, 'The Interior, c.1500–1840', in R. Oliver and G. Mathew, eds, *History of East Africa* (London, 1963), I, 197. In certain clan traditions that I have collected that is evidence that at least certain clans were founded by people who came to the area to trade such things as salt and iron in the pre-Balowoka period. Cf. also Joseph Thomson, *To the Central African Lakes and Back*, (London, 1888), I, 272, for mention of disturbances in Bena country at a seemingly early point in time.

22 Young, *Tumbuka-Kamanga History*, passim.

23 The exact nature of the relationships between the main chief and the subsidiary rulers still needs to be worked out, but it seems to have centred around the main chief's acting as an adjudicator in disputes between subsidiary chiefs.

24 The precise situation that existed in Henga country still needs further investigation, although preliminary evidence indicates a situation similar to those of Nkhamanga and the Phoka area.

25 Mlowoka is not, of course, the person's proper name, but rather a praise name given to him because he had crossed the lake. Other names I have recorded for him are Kalakala and Kakala, while Young lists Sekulu and Nyirenda uses Chikulamayembe in his history. For the sake of simplicity I shall use Mlowoka.

26 *Midauko* (Livingstonia, Malawi, 1965), 5f.

27 Cited in G. S. P. Freeman-Grenville, *The French at Kilwa Island* (Oxford, 1965), 48f.

28 Young, *Tumbuka-Kamanga History*, 37.

29 Edward A. Alpers, *The Role of the Yao in the Development of Trade in East-Central Africa, 1698–c.1850* (Univ. of London, Ph.D. thesis, 1966), 206.

30 There is some suggestion that the Balowoka were not a united group

coming from one area or ethnic group. Thus, while some might have been Yao, others might have been derived from different areas. The solution of this problem awaits a detailed study of the clan histories of the Balowoka clans, something that has not yet been completed.

31 *Midauko*, 5f.

32 Young, *Tumbuka-Kamanga History*, 42f; Nyirenda, *Henga*, 8–10.

33 Cf. Young, *Tumbuka-Kamanga History*, 90–97; J. Van Velsen, 'Notes on the History of the Lakeside Tonga of Nyasaland', *Afr. Stud.*, **18** (3), 1959, 109; Pike, *Malawi*, 43.

34 Personal communication from Professor B. Pachai. See also Van Velsen, *Lakeside Tonga*, 111.

35 Nyirenda, *History*, 8; Young, *Tumbuka-Kamanga History*, 54.

36 For Ngonde, see Young, *Tumbuka-Kamanga History*, 62–80 and Godfrey Wilson, *The Constitution of the Ngonde* (Manchester, 1949), passim. For the Lambya and the Sukwa, personal communication with Mr O. Kalinga.

37 The role of Mwahanga and Mwamlowe as traders in ivory has not yet been proven, hence this admission must remain a tentative one.

38 Fraser, *Winning*, 121; T. Cullen Young, *Notes on the Customs and Folklore of the Tumbuka People* (Livingstonia, Malawi, 1931), 124, 131; Cf. also Mhango, *Henga*, 8f.

39 Young, *Tumbuka-Kamanga History*, 7; Nyirenda, *Henga*, 4.

40 *Midauko*, 6.

41 Cf. Malawi News Agency, *Themba Katumbi and Mulindafwa Celebrations*, (Rumphi, 1968).

42 Mhango, *Henga*, 7–9.

43 J. Rebman, *Dictionary of the Kiniassa Language* (St. Chrischona, 1877), v.

44 Young, *Tumbuka-Kamanga History*, 98–100; Nyirenda, *Henga*, 14.

45 Cf. also Young, *Tumbuka-Kamanga History*, 43, for mention of yet another clan who entered the Chikulamayembe's area to trade.

46 Cf. also Christopher St. John, 'Kazembe and the Tanganyika-Nyasa Corridor, 1800–1890', in Richard Grey and David Birmingham, eds, *Pre-*

Colonial African Trade, (London 1970), 217.

47 Edward A. Alpers, *The East African Slave Trade* (Nairobi, 1967), 8f. Cf.
also N. Bennett, 'The Arab Impact', in B. A. Ogot and J. A. Kieran,
Zamani: A Survey of East African History (Nairobi, 1968), 216–19.

48 By *Swahili* I refer to traders who dressed in the Swahili fashion, not
necessarily to traders from the coast itself.

49 In southern Mzimba District Kunda traders are also reported as active at
this time.

50 For the Henga revolt under Kanyoli and Kambondoma, see Nyirenda,
Henga, 36–52.

11 The Yao in Malawi: the importance of local research

E. A. Alpers

Before about 1860 there do not seem to have been any Yao-speaking people living farther south in what is today modern Malawi than the Mandimba, or Namwera hills, at the extreme southeast corner of Lake Malawi. Today, of course, the Yao are the dominant population group of the entire northern half of southern Malawi and they have exerted considerable influence on the history of Malawi since that date. Militarily powerful and commercially aggressive, the Yao dominated most of their neighbours for the remainder of the nineteenth century. When confronted by British imperialism, the major Yao chiefs led a bitter struggle to maintain their independence. But the Yao were by no means a single, undifferentiated ethnic group who were likely to respond similarly to the challenges of the times. Indeed, not only is it fruitless to generalize about the Yao as a whole, but it is also nonsensical to imagine that they were confronted with a similar set of circumstances at all times. This point is often obscured in treatments of the Yao in Malawi during the nineteenth century, but it emerges clearly in the twentieth century in the dichotomy between the rôles played by John Chilembwe and other Yao from the Shire Highlands and the Yao living around the south end of the lake. The underlying reasons for the differential responses of the several Yao groups to the challenges of colonial rule and independence have been admirably sketched by John McCracken, and I do not intend to repeat them here.[1] Rather, within McCracken's framework, with its emphasis on the economic variables and the relative unimportance of ethnicity in the Shire Highlands, and its stress on the rôle of Islam and the consequent lack of educational opportunities in the Liwonde and Fort Johnston districts, I wish to raise a number of questions regarding some of the more specific issues of Yao history in Malawi. All of these are questions that can be answered only through local investigation, including both field and archival research. Oral traditions, personal histories, and reminiscences, together with the rich archival sources, both official and unofficial, that exist in Malawi itself, provide an unrivalled fund for studying the history of the Yao.

The first set of questions that I wish to raise focuses on the migration of the

168

Yao into southern Malawi from the middle of the nineteenth century and has particular significance for the Yao who presently live in the Shire Highlands. We do not know very much about Yao-Maravi relations before the great Yao invasion that was witnessed in progress by members of David Livingstone's Zambezi Expedition (1855–63) and the first representatives of the Universities' Mission to Central Africa in the Shire valley (1861–64). But what we do know indicates that their relations were peaceable. Following the heyday of the Maravi empire in the seventeenth century, commercial relations came to be dominated by the Bisa from the west and the Yao from the east. The Maravi seem to have been in no position to dispute their neighbours' commercial dominance, and there is no indication of friction between them, although it cannot have been totally absent. Presumably, on the ill-defined borders of Yao and Maravi country people intermarried and exchanged ethnic identities as readily as people did anywhere in Africa. At Mozambique Island in 1804 the French slave trader, Epidariste Colin, was struck by the similarity between Yao and Maravi slaves and observed that they appeared to be 'related' to each other, 'above all in respect to customs'. A quarter of a century later, A. C. P. Gamitto remarked upon the close and amicable commercial relations between the Yao and the Maravi, who maintained firm control of the maritime trade across the south end of Lake Malawi. Livingstone noted the same economic cooperation between the Mang'anja and the Yao in 1859. And in the introduction to his compilation of vocabularies of African languages from Mozambique, W. H. J. Bleek noted in 1856 that the Yao and Maravi regularly intermarried.[2] We cannot say to which particular Yao group Bleek was referring, but most likely these were Mangoche Yao who were soon to become the reluctant vanguard of the Yao advance into southern Malawi.

Regrettably, Yohanna B. Abdallah, the only major Yao authority on Yao history, has little to add to this impressionistic picture of Yao-Maravi relations. Before their invasion of modern Malawi he records that the Yao exchanged trade goods from the coast, mainly cloth and beads, for cattle and salt with the Nyasa and Mang'anja. Their most important common market was at Ng'ombo, at the extreme southeast shore of the lake.[3]

Ng'ombo served as a collection point and market place for the translacustrine trade and occupied a position similar to Losewa (Losefa) to the north and to Nkhota Kota on the west-central lakeshore. According to Abdallah, Ng'ombo also developed as a centre for the ivory trade and when the demand for slaves at the coast percolated inland it soon became a slave market.[4] Despite Abdallah's unsupported implication that the Yao never enslaved other Yao-speaking people, the important point to note here is that they seem to have been content to trade for slaves with the Maravi at Ng'ombo, and presumably elsewhere. Slave raiding did not, apparently, become a feature of Yao-Maravi relations until after the Yao invasion was set in motion by a complicated and obscure series of events that lay beyond the control of both the Maravi and the Yao.

There are a number of similar, yet variant, accounts of the cause of this great Yao invasion of southern Malawi. One major point of agreement is that the Mangoche were not themselves the main actors in this migration, but were

169

as much victims of it as were the Maravi-speaking peoples of the Shire valley itself.[5] Rather, the centre of dispersal was somewhere in the heart of Yao country in northern Mozambique and keyed on the Machinga Yao, who now predominate around the south end of the lake. These Yao, so the various sources tell us, were attacked from the east by the Lolo, or Makua-Lomwe people, who were in the throes of a severe famine and were, in any case, great enemies of the Yao. Pressures deriving from the Arab slave trade to Madagascar may also have been a major factor leading to dislocation among the Makua-Lomwe peoples.[6] Livingstone, for his part, reported of the Yao that, 'wars among themselves, for the supply of the Coast slave-trade, are said to have first set them in motion.'[7] At least one source suggests that the Yao were also set upon by the Maconde of northern Mozambique.[8] The general pattern is the same, with Yao fugitives transformed into invaders as they swept into southern Malawi, but the details vary according to the source of information. Stannus, working in the far south, presents a rather different set of details than does Abdallah, whose information came from farther north.[9] The full history of the genesis of the Yao migration cannot be reconstructed, of course, until the liberation of Mozambique makes it possible for historians to carry out research among the Makua-Lomwe peoples. But in the meantime, there is clearly a need for greater precision in our knowledge of the way in which the migration took place in Malawi that can be gained by a careful investigation of the traditions of the Yao of Malawi.

Two other questions are worth raising about the causes of the invasion. First, what was the impact of the Maseko Ngoni migration north and south to Songea district in Tanzania, to the east of Lake Malawi? Most sources reject the idea that the Ngoni were a factor in causing the Yao to disperse, but it would be remarkable if they made no impact at all upon the Yao at this date. Fr Pierre Dupeyron, for one, working among the Yao of Tumbini by Mt Mlanje, recorded in 1894 that the threat of locusts and rivalries with the Ngoni were the cause of the migration.[10] Second, how were the Masaninga Yao affected by the Makua-Lomwe attack? Abdallah has a few notes to this point, but more evidence would be welcome, particularly in regard to the conditions in which the great Mataka dynasty arose. There is no clear answer to either of these questions in the existing literature, but it may be possible to get at them in the field.

Related to the question of why the Yao migration took place, and central to Yao studies in Malawi, is the matter of how it took place. In his monograph on the Machinga Yao, J. C. Mitchell found that chiefs and headmen were ranked as aborigines, invaders, and newcomers.[11] If the invaders were an overwhelmingly powerful force, how did indigenous chiefs manage to hold their own in certain cases? Was the decisive element simply one of power relations, or were there other factors, such as ritual control over the land, that came into play? Indeed, was there ever any need for the invaders to establish a *modus vivendi* regarding rights to the land with previous inhabitants? Mitchell provides brief answers to some of these questions, and remarks upon the fact that, 'the claims of Nyanja chiefs to rank because they had occupied the land first were recognized by the Yao who absorbed them into the social structure in positions of high rank,' but there is a clear need for a more detailed reconstruction here, as Livingstone's tantalizing account suggests.

'The usual way in which they have advanced among the Manganja has been by slave-trading in a friendly way. Then, professing to wish to live as subjects, they have been welcomed as guests, and the Manganja, being great agriculturalists, have been able to support considerable bodies of these visitors for a time. When the provisions became scarce, the guests began to steal from the fields; quarrels arose in consequence, and, the Ajawa having firearms, their hosts got the worst of it, and were expelled from village after village, and out of their own country.'[12]

This process still ranks as an invasion, to be sure, but it reveals an altogether more complex situation than is immediately suggested by an uncritical acceptance of Mitchell's term, 'invaders'. Moreover, whatever the value of Mitchell's classification for the region of his study, it cannot be applied willy-nilly to the whole of Yao-dominated territory in Malawi. Thus the question of interaction between the invading Yao and the pre-existing population becomes a crucial one wherever there was not total displacement of that population. In the far south it will be a story of interaction between predominantly Mangoche Yao and Nyanja, or Mang'anja, but nearer to the lake it will be a matter of interaction between Machinga and Mangoche Yao, as well as Nyanja. The distinction between different Yao sections is not an unimportant one, for it appears that it was not always agreed upon by Yao-speaking peoples as to who, exactly, was a 'true' Yao. Henry Rowley, who was a member of the ill-fated U.M.C.A. mission to southern Malawi, made a clear distinction between these two divisions of the Yao-speaking people in his references to 'the Machinka, who were neighbours of the Ajawa,' and to 'a mixed horde of Ajawa and Machinka' raiders in the vicinity of Magomero.[13] Duff Macdonald, the most authoritative early student of the Yao, collected a number of tales among the Mangoche that he noted as being recorded in the Yao language, and others in the Machinga language.[14] This may have been Macdonald's error, but together with Rowley's observations it gives additional substance to the belief that there may have been a considerable amount of ethnocentricity among the various Yao divisions, as does the whole chauvinistic tone of Abdallah's presentation of the history of the Masaninga Yao.

The passage cited above from Livingstone also raises an important question bearing on the role of firearms in the establishment of Yao domination of the pre-existing population in southern Malawi from the time of the initial migration. Their importance later in the century is not in question, but it has become commonplace to assume that firearms won the day for the Yao in the course of their invasion. Abdallah very explicitly states that when the Lolo attacked the Yao and launched what Livingstone liked to call their 'migratory afflatus',[15] 'the Walolo were armed with guns, and we Yaos had not yet got any,' a point which his editor, Dr Sanderson, disputed in a note to the text. In the process of the flight, Abdallah continues, the Machinga themselves became invaders and concomitantly acquired firearms from their Lolo enemies, a claim which is equally disputed by Sanderson.[16] Archdeacon W. P. Johnson of the U.M.C.A., who probably knew the Yao better than any European of his generation with the exception of Duff Macdonald, is rather more specific in asserting that the Yao possessed both English 'Tower muskets' and French muskets with carved stocks when they fell upon the Maravi.[17] However, Bleek, whose few references to Yao history must be dated to the mid-1840s until proved otherwise, plainly states that the Yao were 'a people without firearms.'[18] Rowley, on the other hand, gives an account that differs in several respects from all of these. According to his Yao informants, whose reliability is by no means to be accepted uncritically,

'They one and all declared that they left their own country on account of war; that the Avisa and other Makoa tribes defeated them, and carried away very many of them as slaves; that those who escaped came down to the Manganja country poor and hungry; that upon their taking food to keep them from dying, the Manganja took many of them and sold them to the slavers; that at last quarrels arose between them, battles were fought, and the Ajawa found themselves able to defeat the Manganja. Then the slavers came to them, gave them guns and gunpowder for men, women, and children, and urged them to continue the war against the Manganja, and take the whole country.'[19]

This account reads suspiciously like an attempt to justify their own slaving to the British missionaries, who were known to be opposed to the trade, but it does have the virtue of opening a whole new range of questions to be asked in the field. As for the identity of the gun-gifting slavers, Rowley elsewhere suggests that these may have been the Portuguese at Tete.[20] Indeed, given the many coastal markets to which they had access, the problem of dating and quantifying the acquisition of firearms by the Yao, or more accurately by different Yao-speaking peoples, will probably never be satisfactorily answered. For the history of Malawi, however, the major challenge is the accurate reconstruction of the use of these firearms that the Yao actually possessed in order to determine if from the beginning of their migration their military superiority over the Nyanja and Mang'anja was a function of firepower or of more traditional methods of warfare, perhaps augmented by the shock value of thunderously noisy but antiquated muskets.[21]

The clearest indication that conditions varied widely from one group of Yao migrants or invaders to another comes from the numerous and seemingly conflicting observations of Dr (later Sir) John Kirk, who served as Botanist and Medical Officer of Livingstone's Zambezi expedition. Kirk's first comments concern a cluster of Yao slavers whom he encountered by Lake Chilwa in April 1859 and who initially denied that they were, in fact, Yao. 'What settled the point was their running away when we took out a rifle to show the chief.' More generally, Kirk wrote that, 'guns are not used in this quarter but having been attacked by those who have, they are very much afraid of them.'[22] In September, now to the northwest of Mt Zomba, 'we heard of a people

172

called Batshinga who have guns and make forays, carrying off cattle and slaves.'[23] In July 1861, at Chibisa's village, near modern Blantyre, refugees from Zomba arrived to report 'that their village had been attacked and their people carried off as slaves. It is said to have been done by the Bajawa with guns.' Yet when Livingstone's party pursued these Yao and confronted them in their camp on the western slopes of Mt Zomba three weeks later, they were opposed by poisoned arrows, which the Yao fired 'with tolerable aim at 100 yards.' But the Yao were routed by the Europeans' firearms, although Kirk reports that at one point 'our party was quite surrounded. Had the Ajawa fought at close quarters, it would have been hard for our fellows to stand against them. The Ajawa outranged the Manganja with their arrows but their guns did nothing. They seemed to have 4 guns.'[24] A month later, at the south end of Lake Malombe, the expedition witnessed the great misery being caused by Yao raiders on the east bank of the Shire river. Kirk wondered: 'The Manganja flee before them and yet they seem to have neither numbers nor guns against them. The Ajawa are few and said to have only one gun.' A few days later, however, at the south end of Lake Malawi, he found that guns were common.[25]

There are no ready answers provided by these widely divergent sources on the significance of firearms in the establishment of Yao hegemony in southern Malawi. But they do enable us to see that the entire process of the migration, not merely the problem of firearms, was much more complex and particularistic than has previously been thought. Here again, only local research can provide the meaningful reconstruction that is so urgently needed. What is wanted is a careful reconstruction of the course of the invasion, with as much attention being paid to the human geography of southern Malawi before that great movement as afterwards. With the Yao invasion still little more than a century distant, a village by village co-ordinated research programme, utilizing student researchers from the Department of History of the University of Malawi, might well repay the effort involved.

The final problem that is raised by the Yao invasion concerns the dominance of Yao identity in much of southern Malawi, even where Yao-speakers themselves were adopting the Maravi language at the expense of Yao. Undoubtedly, the fact that the Yao were invaders accounts for this phenomenon to a considerable extent, but one wonders if that is the sum total of the answer. Most of the sources that point to Yao cultural ascendancy are, in fact, the narrowly ethnocentric writings of early European colonialists, who see in the Yao an earlier superior conquering race in some respects comparable to themselves. Yet I have found at least one case, regarding hut types, where it seems that the Yao may have adopted Nyanja architectural styles in preference to their own.[26] It also seems likely that the Yao in Malawi have incorporated the Kapirintiwa and Lake Bangweulu myths of the creation of Man from the indigenous Maravi-speaking peoples.[27] As McCracken argues, ethnicity was a relatively insignificant factor in the Shire Highlands during the colonial period, but southern Malawi as a whole offers one of the most ethnically mixed areas in all of Africa as a result of the events of the past century. Surely it is important both historically and sociologically to understand the various factors influencing the changing patterns of personal identity of its people.

The second set of questions that I wish to raise in this chapter relates to the history of Islam among the Yao in Malawi, a subject which I have begun to explore more broadly elsewhere.[28] In that paper I argue that the Yao chiefs Mataka and Makanjila, and by extension others like them, declared for Islam because they regarded it as the most amenable way of modernizing their societies, especially of acquiring literacy for their people. I stand by that argument, but clearly as much can be learned from the descendants of these men as from the occasional notes that were left, sometimes inadvertently, by European travellers, missionaries, and administrators. A closely related question concerns the way in which Islam was spread among the Yao. Here, again, I have inferred a number of tentative conclusions from the literature, but a wealth of information remains to be recaptured from the Yao themselves, and especially from their Muslim *waalimu*.[29]

Not all Yao are Muslims, of course, but the Yao have been pre-eminently identified as a people for whom Islam is synonymous with being Yao. Given the history of the Muslim Yao of Malawi, what can we learn about the relationship of Islam to ethnic identity and to colonial rule, indeed to central government from whatever quarter? Is Islam, after all, a significant factor in this respect, or have the basic problems facing these Yao in the twentieth century been primarily educational and economic? Hitherto, Islam has been singled out as the determining fact of life for these Yao by many outside observers. To what degree is this illusion, and to what degree reality?

Continuing in this vein, one of the obvious results of the Yao embracement of Islam is that they have rejected Christian missionary efforts, together with access to Western education.[30] But did they reject the idea of education and modernization from their own point of view? As I argue in my Islamic paper, the spread of Islam and the desire for education progressed hand in glove. Every Muslim village had its koranic school, and in 1911 Fr Russell of the U.M.C.A. noted that, 'the Mohammedans are both rich and flourishing, and have there [Malindi] (a thing I saw for the first time) a boarding school for boys.'[31] In their monumental study of the Chilembwe Rising, Shepperson and Price noted that, in Central African history, Islam had first offered a way of advance beyond rigid tribalism, and still provided a possible alternative for the African who sought some status of dignity *vis-à-vis* the European.'[32] The existence of a network of Islamic schools, including at least one boarding school, indicates that Islam certainly did provide an alternative social structure for the African under colonial rule, complete with its own standards of success and achievement. John Iliffe has argued this for Tanganyika under German rule; Fr Peirone's study of Islam among the Yao of northern Moçambique reveals that a similar Islamic social structure and educational system operated there before the liberation struggle offered them an alternate system operated there before the liberation struggle offered them an alternative means of self assertion against a repressive Portuguese imperialism.[33] What was the nature and extent of this system among the Yao in Malawi during the colonial period, and how has the coming of independence affected it? The answer to these questions could illuminate our understanding of the signifi-

174

cance of Islam in much of East Africa during the twentieth century.

The last topic that I wish to suggest is in need of investigation is the spread and significance of *tariqas* among the Yao. Both Mitchell and J. N. D. Anderson have noted that rival Qadiri brotherhoods, the *twaliki* and the *sukutu(i)*, were active in certain sectors of Muslim Yao society in the 1940s.[34] Yet nothing at all is known about the way in which they penetrated to Malawi, nor about their significance to the Yao. Were they, or are they now, more widespread than they appear to have been at that time? Were they at all effective as agents of social, political or economic mobilization? Or were they solely a reflection of more fundamental cleavages in Yao society, as Mitchell suggests? With the recent surge of interest in the history of the Qadiriyya *tariqa* in the Congo and Tanzania, it would be most useful to have a better idea of its activities in Malawi, as well.[35]

I have raised a wide range of related questions in this chapter. My hope is that these questions will serve to stimulate historical research in Malawi, and by Malawians, in this instance among the Yao, not to claim that these are the only or, somehow, necessarily correct questions. Those concerning Islam I am actively interested in trying to answer myself; those relating to the migration of the Yao into Malawi await the attention of other students of history, who find Malawi's past as rich and rewarding as I do.

FOOTNOTES

1 John McCracken, 'The nineteenth century in Malawi', and 'African politics in twentieth-century Malawi', in T. O. Ranger (ed.), *Aspects of Central African History* (London, 1968), 100, 105, 108–10, 190.

2 Epidariste Colin, 'Notice sur Mozambique,' in Malte-Brun, *Annales des Voyages de la Géographie et de l'Histoire* (Paris, 1809), IX, 322–3; A. C. P. Gamitto, *King Kazembe*, trs. I. Cunnison (Lisboa, 1960), I, 64–5; David & Charles Livingstone, *Narrative of an Expedition to the Zambezi and its Tributaries* (London, 1865), 125–6; W. H. J. Bleek, *The Languages of Mosambique* (London 1856), xiv. Bleek's remarks are based on the notes of Dr William Peters of Berlin, who resided at Mozambique from 1842 to 1848. For a glimpse of Yao-Mang'anja intermarriage in 1861, or earlier, see Henry Rowley, *The Story of the Universities' Mission to Central Africa*, 2nd ed. (New York, 1969; originally published in 1867), 153.

3 Most nineteenth century maps locate Ng'ombo farther to the southeast than the modern Cape Ngombo, usually in the bay formed by the eastward turning of the lakeshore just south of Cape Ngombo.

4 Y. B. Abdallah, *The Yaos*, trs. & ed. M. Sanderson (Zomba, 1919), 28, 30.

5 From the historian's perspective it makes much more sense to refer to the

Bantu languages that have previously been called Chinyanja or Chichewa as Chimaravi, and the people themselves as the Maravi-speaking peoples. While this is a deviation from official, popular, and linguistic practice, I shall introduce it here in the hope that it may yet gain wider recognition in Malawi historiography.

6 See J. F. Elton, *Travels and Researches among the Lakes and Mountains of Eastern and Central Africa*, ed. H. B. Cotterill (London, 1879), Part I, chs. 3–5, but esp. at 195.

7 Livingstone, *Narrative*, 497. But cf. Henry Rowley's account cited in the text below (footnote 19).

8 Jorge Dias, *Os Macondes de Moçambique* (Lisboa, 1964), I, 80, citing the testimony of Nañolo Antupa, of the Vachipedi lineage.

9 H. S. Stannus, 'The Wayao of Nyasaland', Harvard African Studies, *Varia Africana III*, ed. E. A. Hooton & N. I. Bates (Cambridge, Mass., 1922), 231–3; Abdallah, *The Yaos*, 35–6.

10 Federico José Peirone, *A Tribo Ajaua do Alto Niassa (Moçambique) e Alguns Aspectos da sua Peoblemática Neo-Islámica* (Lisboa, 1967), citing Dupeyron to Bishop D.A. Barroso, 17 May 1894.

11 J. Clyde Mitchell, *The Yao Village—A Study in the Social Structure of a Nyasaland Tribe* (Manchester, 1956), 61–8, quotation at 62.

12 Livingstone, *Narrative*, 497; cf. J. J. Stegman, 'Nyasaland Droughts,' *Nyasa. J.*, 4 (1), 1951, 68–9, for some impressions of the drought that marked the Yao invasion of the Blantyre region in 1860 and its effect on Mang'anja agricultural production.

13 Rowley, *Story*, 185.

14 See especially, 'On our home (A Yao's history of his tribe),' in Duff Macdonald, *Africana, or the Heart of Heathen Africa* (London, 1882), II, 334–6.

15 Livingstone, *Narrative*, 497.

16 Abdallah, *The Yaos*, 35–6.

17 W. P. Johnson, *Nyasa the Great Water* (London, 1922), 93.

18 Bleck, *Languages*, xiv.

19 Rowley, *Story*, 185. Rowley is the only writer who mentions the Bisa in 176

this context. That they were a major factor in setting off the Yao dispersal seems very improbable, but it may be that Bisa trading parties had a hand in attacking those Yao who were interviewed by him.

20 Ibid., 92

21 For a discussion of the role of firearms in a neighbouring region of Central Africa, see A. D. Roberts, 'Firearms in north-eastern Zambia in the nineteenth century', *Transafr. J. Hist.*, **1** (2), 1971.

22 Reginald Foskett (ed.), *The Zambesi Journal and Letters of Dr John Kirk, 1858–63* (Edinburgh & London, 1965), I, 191.

23 Ibid., I, 247.

24 Ibid., II, 349–50, 358.

25 Ibid., II, 365, 367.

26 E. A. Alpers, 'Trade, State and Society among the Yao in the Nineteenth Century', *J. Afr. Hist.*, **10** (3), 1969, 419, n.59.

27 See, e.g., S. S. Murray, *A Handbook of Nyasaland* (London, 1922), 48.

28 Alpers, 'Towards a History of the Expansion of Islam in East Africa: the Matrilineal Peoples of the Southern Interior,' forthcoming in T. O. Ranger & I. N. Kimambo (eds), *Historical Studies in African Religious Systems*.

29 An impressive beginning to the reconstruction of the history of the Mponda chieftaincy has been made in chapter one of a forthcoming study by Ian Linden, 'The Aroma: Roman Catholics in Protestant Nyasaland, 1889–1939'.

30 McCracken, 'African Politics', 190.

31 Cited in A. G. Blood, *The History of the U.M.C.A.*, II, 1907–1932 (London, 1957), 162.

32 George Shepperson & Thomas Price, *Independent African: John Chilembwe and the Origins, Setting and significance of the Nyasaland native uprising of 1915* (Edinburgh, 1958), 407.

33 John Iliffe, *Tanganyika under German Rule, 1905–1912* (Cambridge, 1969), 189; Peirone, *A Tribo Ajaua*, 97–101; see also, A. Sousa Lobato, 'Monografia Etnografica Original sobre o Povo Ajaua,' *Boletim da Sociedade de Estudos da Colonia de Moçambique*, **63**, 1949, 16.

34 Mitchell, *Yao Village*, 51–2; J. N. D. Anderson, *Islamic Law in Africa* (London, 1954), 169–70.

35 See Armand Abel, *Les Musulmans Noirs de Maniema* (Brussels, 1960); B. G. Martin, 'Muslim Politics and resistance to colonial rule: Shaykh Uways B. Muhammad Al-Barāwā and the Qādirīya brotherhood in East Africa', *J. Afr. Hist.*, **10** (3), 1969, 471–86. Mr August Nimtz, Indiana University, is presently completing a dissertation on the historical role of the Qadiriyya in Bagamoyo, Tanzania.

12 Ngoni politics and diplomacy in Malawi: 1848-1904[1]

B. Pachai

I

By 1904 the Ngoni of Malawi were widely distributed through a large part of the country with main and subsidiary settlements of both the Jere and Maseko communities or *tribal clusters*. These settlements had a number of common characteristics. The chiefs (with few exceptions) could all claim linear political descent from those who had led them through most of the way to the chosen land; they were now under British protectorate rule; each main settlement had an administrative system with central authority, executive authority, military and judicial authority, all of which were subsequently modified to suit the protectorate government from time to time; each had started off with little more than a simple kinship organization with leadership provided by a determined individual of a well-known clan fleeing for safety and security with a hard core of kinsmen; each tribal cluster had to work out its own immediate political salvation during the period of dispersion or at the point of permanent settlement. The difference between these Ngoni and those of the Northern and Southern Nguni was that political evolution in the case of the former was based on trial and error tempered by a transference of 'home' patterns of government far removed in both space and time. Things not only happened quickly; they happened very far from 'home'; they happened, too, without precedents at first. Before political patterns and social adjustments could evolve, external intrusions brought about compelling side-effects. In the end a political system emerged. Hammond–Tooke has defined a political system broadly 'as the system of power-distribution in a society'.[2] In looking at this power-distribution in the Ngoni society of Malawi a number of propositions constitute a good starting point.

How did the Ngoni leadership and its followers manage their affairs in Malawi after about a generation of trials and travels? When Zwangendaba died at Mapupo in Fipa country about 1848 he had already put together the nucleus of a state in which his senior kinsman, Ntabeni, junior kinsman, Mgayi and senior induna, Gwaza Jere, were placed in influential positions over his sons, and heirs to the Ngoni state, who ranged from about eight years of age to about fifteen years. Almost twenty years later, the Maseko Ngoni,

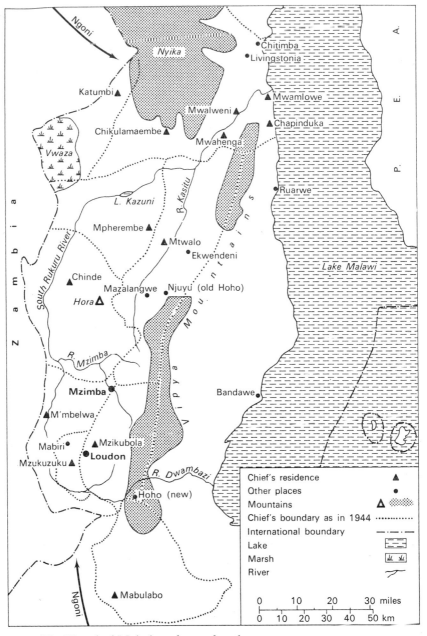

12.1 The Ngoni of Mzimba: places of settlement

who were led across the Zambezi and up to Songea by Mputa, came back to the Shire-Nyasa region under Mputa's brother, Chidiaonga, and settled first near Matope, then at Domwe, and finally in the Ncheu region of Malawi among mainly Chewa-speaking peoples. Chidiaonga was the Maseko regent; Ntabeni, brother of Zwangendaba, was the Jere regent. The term regent as used here refers to a senior kinsman who assumed leadership as the successor had not come of age to assume the chieftainship.

It was the regencies which made the first impact. Their failures and successes were due in part to the personalities of the regents as well as to the various internal and external circumstances of the time. Had succession disputes not taken place, the Ngoni would have been a more formidable force against all contending parties. When the regents had played their parts, for better or for worse, another influence entered the lives of the Ngoni in the form of the missionary factor. A third influence was that represented by alien African cultural groups. This local African factor was an important determinant of Ngoni policy. Finally, a most pervasive external influence was present in the form of the British political administration.

This article aims at tracing the operation of the Ngoni diplomatic and political machinery in its handling of all these four factors or influences. The review helps to set the scene for the vigorous and varied roles played later by the two Malawi Ngoni paramountcies during the colonial period: the capture, deposition and exile of Chimtunga Jere; the assertive and unique role of the M'Mbelwa African Administrative Council; the firm stand in internal and external politics of the greatest of the successors of Zwangendaba, M'Mbelwa II (1928–59); the contribution of that arch opponent of Federation, Inkosi Philip Gomani II (1924–54) whose politics of dissent ended with a fate reminiscent of that which had visited his father in 1896.

The evidence for all this has been obtained from missionary records; from official government despatches; from Ngoni historians; from African testimonies collected from the ruling and princely houses, as well as from non-Jere and non-Maseko Ngoni, and from Tumbuka, Tonga and Chewa peoples drawn into the arena of Ngoni politics. Because the Ngoni were an important political factor, the evidence is often coloured by what it hoped to achieve. At a given time Government administrators wanted to justify their attitudes and actions; missionaries had their own objectives; the ruling Ngoni classes had theirs; the affected African peoples reacted differently, depending on what they hoped to achieve. The more powerful the political factor the greater the number of interested parties involved. Due allowance must be made for the motivation behind every bit of evidence and this applies equally to oral traditions and testimonies as to documentary sources.

II

Succession disputes in the case of both the Jere and the Maseko Ngoni have been treated by historians as moments of crises, as no doubt they were. These were due not to the absence of laws of succession but to different interpretations placed on them by regents and indunas. Missionaries and colonial officials were often bewildered by the laws of succession, but the Ngoni, once all the interpretations had been submitted to the indaba or meeting and the roles of the holders of particular positions were explained and understood, took and accepted a decision. Besides their military prowess, the Ngoni are credited with the quality of being 'a disciplined people under a central authority'.[3] When this authority was questioned it was not that Ngoni society was disintegrating. Missionary letters give many instances of this. In 1884, for example, Mbelwa I would not allow the Livingstonia missionaries to call on his brother Mtwalo I because of some 'misunderstanding between himself and his brother, partly because he keeps us to and for himself and won't allow us to visit Mtwalo'.[4] Two years later the same chief found himself in a confrontation with his councillors. He was wise enough to recognize their strength and to propose concessions to the demands made to keep the missionaries out.[5] These two illustrations show a strengthening of the Ngoni political machinery. There were many crucial issues which gave rise to the challenges to his authority which the Paramount had to contend with. These will be considered later. The point is that Ngoni discipline did not break down under the welter of a variety of changing situations represented either in succession disputes or in the growing political sophistication of his subjects.

The durability of the political structure would gain by an acceptable resolution of succession disputes. There were many factors which determined the process of succession. First, there was the royal village system which apportioned different functional roles to the *gogo* and the *lusungulu* villages or houses. These houses were occupied by different wives of the chief and it was the rank of the mother which determined the successor. In the case of the Jere Ngoni the same succession pattern applied to the paramount as to his subordinate kinsmen of the royal clan. The first wife of a ruler or heir was the senior in time but not in rank. She was the *msulamizi*, known more commonly in Northern Malawi as 'muyesula msizi'—the redeemer. Her village (msizini) was the place of refuge for subjects in distress. She occupied the *gogo* house and had the function of being an important figure in the ceremonial and ritual life of the village. The *lusungulu* house was occupied by the chosen 'big wife' for whom lobola had been paid from the herd of the Queen Mother (the *inkosikazi* or main wife of the reigning paramount or chief who occupied the central hut or *indlunkulu* in the village of her son, the heir). There were other criteria which the occupant of the *lusungulu* house had to satisfy. She had to come from an important home or be the daughter of a chief; she had to be a good wife, of good behaviour, who cared for her husband. She had to come from a family of means so as to provide for *mungenisa khaya*, the beer offering that had to be brought to the husband's village from her parents' village in order that she would gain entry into her new village (*kungena khaya*). She was to be in a position to ask her parents to offer gifts on the occasion of the birth of the first child (*mbereko*) and meat for consumption (*dende*) as well as for women retainers (*vidandani*)[6]. It was from the *lusungulu* house only that a heir was chosen.[7]

This brief account of the Ngoni succession pattern would help to explain why Mbelwa, the youngest of the contending sons of Zwangendaba, assumed the mantle of successor to the Jere paramountcy between 1855 and 1857 and Chikusi the mantle of the Maseko paramountcy between 1868 and 1870. Historians are not agreed as to the legitimate candidate for Zwangendaba's throne. Cullen Young writes that Zwangendaba named Lomagazi as his successor and thus 'actually appointed Mbelwa'. Lomagazi was Mbelwa's elder sister and both were the children of Munene Mgomezulu. Since a daughter could not succeed, her full brother could step into the succession. Elmslie says that 'Mtwalo should have been chief, but he resigned in favour of Mombera'. Mtwalo was the elder brother of Mbelwa and son of Qutu Mgomezulu, younger sister of Munene. Y. M. Chibambo notes that Zwangendaba chose Ngodoyi, Ntabeni's son, and therefore his nephew 'because he was well grown and intelligent'. Cullen Young's further point against Mtwalo's accession was that 'he failed to achieve his puberty at the expected time'. Mpezeni, the eldest son, and Mtwalo, the second son, have their champions and Barnes, reviewing all these, says that what was important was that 'firstly there was a disputed succession, and secondly that present-day rival groups (i.e. in the 1940s) are still concerned each to show that its claimant was the legitimate heir'.[8]

On the face of it this was an inauspicious start to the Ngoni political history in the post-Zwangendaba period. None of the sons of Zwangendaba was old enough to be installed chief. Ntabeni was the undisputed senior kinsman and could assume the leadership temporarily. It was his politics that created a cleavage in Ngoni society. We have already noted the succession laws. To this information must be added the Ngoni custom that a chief was buried in the cattle fold of his *inkosikazi* in his *lusungulu* village. His son and successor could not be buried there as well because 'only one bull may rule a herd'. Once a chief was buried in his *lusungulu* village its status was altered to that of *gogo*. It was here that his spirit was guarded and future ceremonials performed. Hlatshwayo, father of Zwangendaba, was buried at Elangeni; Zwangendaba was buried at Ekwendeni. Earlier on, two years before the Zambezi crossing, Zwangendaba's *lusungulu* village was *Emveyeyeni* where his Nqumayo wives, the sisters Lompetu and Soseya, were placed. An unfortunate hair-in-the-beer incident led to the village being wiped out. Soseya was saved by a kindly act and kept in hiding until the birth of her son, Ntuto (Mpezeni). When he was some four years old Mpezeni and his mother were presented to a forgiving chief; they were allotted to the *gogo* village of Elangeni. The Mgomezulu sisters had in the interim occupied the new royal village or *lusungulu*; the senior was Munene. Her son was Mhlahlo (later Mombera, Mbelwa and M'Mbelwa). Mtwalo was the elder brother but the son of the junior Mgomezulu wife. He did not have to vacate his position as Elmslie has pointed out because 'being of a quiet disposition . . . (and because) he felt the burden of ruling such a jealous, discontented people as they had become would be too great for him'.[9] His position and rank did not entitle him to undisputed succession.

The northern Ngoni were not a jealous people tottering on the brink of total collapse in 1848. Ntabeni's policies very nearly led to that when he

183

named Mpezeni as the heir; Mtwalo as second in line and banished Mbelwa and his mother from Ekwendeni to start a new village. Chibambo is clear on the point that it was Ntabeni alone who brought on the catastrophe which followed.

'This was done by Ntabeni to bring shame on Munene. But we shall see that this brought trouble on the whole tribe and led to three or four secessions. When Zwangendaba changed the official head wife and the succession of Mpezeni, the royal house became, as we have seen, that of Munene. The first-born child here was a girl named Lomagazi, and because the Ngoni law does not permit a female to succeed, Mwambera the brother of Lomagazi had become Zwangendaba's real heir, despite Ntabeni's revengeful plans'.[10]

The decade after 1848 saw both a weakening and a strengthening of the Ngoni: four major groups were hived off; Ntabeni died. Mgayi and Gwaza took it in turn to bring the migrants to a settled home. Mbelwa was installed paramount chief of those Ngoni who were still part of the main host, in the Henga valley at Ng'onga, near present Phwampa in the Rumpi District on the road from Jakwa to Livingstonia, between 1855 and 1857. Rangeley describes this occasion as if it was pregnant with dire and explosive consequences, with the warring regiments armed to the teeth, 'with sweating hands gripping the razor-edged *Ijoyi*, not knowing whether the outcome of the meeting would be bloody affray . . .'.[11] The evidence points in the other direction. The man who had master-minded the details for the occasion was Gwaza Jere, Zwangendaba's loyal induna. He had a few years before made Mpezeni chief of his segment at Makukwe near present Tukuyu in Tanzania. To prevent civil war from breaking out when Mpezeni returned to the main host at Chidhlodhlo, Gwaza led Mbelwa and Mtwalo across the Nyika into the Henga valley. Here he offered the chieftainship to Mtwalo who promptly and firmly declined it. Mtwalo then took the feathers of the uluvi bird, 'which are worn only by the chief, and he strode out into the company, and stuck them on Mwambera's head, saying, "I choose you as chief, tomorrow you may if you wish it, make an end of me".'[12] The Gwaza stroke of diplomacy is clearly evident: he had earlier installed Mpezeni as chief of a group; he had then led the rest away from an explosive situation. The feathers of the uluvi bird were hidden on Mtwalo's person for some use. The words by Mtwalo were the final stroke in a diplomatic coup that has since then paid off in keeping the peace between the two senior groups of the Jere hierarchy. This understanding between the Mbelwa and Mtwalo segments has been one of the strengthening features of Ngoni politics in Malawi.

One other development tended to further strengthen the northern Ngoni: this was the departure westwards of Zwangendaba's eldest son Ntuto, more popularly known as Mpezeni. With him went along his younger brother Mperembe who after many exploits in Bemba and Bisa country returned to join the northern Ngoni in the 1870s. But Mpezeni never returned. He went on to settle in eastern Zambia from where his warriors raided deep into Malawi as far as the central lakeshore area. Two of his segments, led by the founders of the present Mlonyeni and Zulu chieftainships, settled at Mchinji on the Malawi-Zambia border. It is ironical that Mpezeni whose removal from the main Malawi Jere host did so much to prevent recurring friction between the sons of Zwangendaba was himself deposed in 1898 by troops from Malawi after his son, Singu, had led an abortive rising against the increasing European influences in his father's new home.[13]

It is not possible here to deal with the succession episodes of the succeeding chiefs. It is sufficient for our purposes to say that when the successor to Mbelwa I was being chosen between 1891 and 1896 there were three candidates and a few complications. The spear at the graveside was held by a brother in the absence of an immediate resolution of the succession. When Mtwalo I died the holding of the graveside spear was entrusted to his son Yohane of the *gogo* house. There was again a case of lack of unanimity as to the rightful candidate but this was sorted out in a few years when the legitimate candidate was ready to assume his position. In 1915 the protectorate government deposed the northern Ngoni paramount chief; sent him in exile from Mzimba to Nsanje and only allowed him to return in 1920 as a village headman. But throughout this period the northern Ngoni recognized him alone as their paramount chief. He died without being reinstated by the government but he was always the people's paramount chief. All these situations were successfully counteracted because of the lessons of the past; the roles of regents and rulers and above all by a fundamental respect for ordered discussion and discipline.

In the central kingdom of the Maseko Ngoni the paramount chief did not share his authority with any other member of his clan, though two clans were placed in a special functional relationship to the paramount. The Phungwako clan was the custodian of the paramount's 'medicines' and the Ngozo clan provided the paramount with a personal companion whom Margaret Read refers to as the royal shadow.[14] The succession to the chieftainship derived from the inheritance which devolved upon the eldest son. Other criteria had to be satisfied: he should be the most suitable in the eyes of the people of the tribe; he had to be the son of a woman for whom dowry had been paid. He was nominated at a private meeting of principal and village headmen (later referred to as the *alumuzana* and the *masenga*). The nominated ruler was then presented to a public meeting where he was accorded the royal acclaim of *Bayete*. Mputa, the first Maseko paramount chief, had two important wives at Songea. The first wife was Namlangeni whose two children were Makwangwala (who was captured by the followers of Mhalule Gama after Mputa's death and retained in Songea) and Manga who returned to Domwe under the regency of Mputa's brother, Chidiaonga. The other was Nachikhumba, mother of Chikusi, who was the *inkosikazi* who later occupied the *lusungulu* village of Liwisini, east of the Kirk Range.

The Maseko chieftainship question was not a complicated one. From about 1855 to 1870 Chidiaonga brought his people back from Songea to Njowe near the Matope area of Chinamvuu and finally to Domwe. When Livingstone passed through the Kirk range area in 1863 he did not report on Ngoni devastations as he was to do in the case of his observations in the more northerly area. The Jere Ngoni were by then settled in the Henga and Kasitu valleys; the Maseko were not yet back from their return journey from Amatengo country. Chidiaonga successfully attacked the Yao under Kawinga at Kongwe and made a good collection of cattle. The Maseko power was consolidated by Chidiaonga who even pronounced on the chieftainship shortly before his death around 1876.

> ' "Now I leave this country in the hands of the owner, because I was only appointed to keep it for him. This is your leader". He sent for Cikusi and gave him his father's spear, saying to him. "This country is yours". He said to Cifisi his own son, "You, my son, do not struggle with Cikusi. He is the only paramount here".'

The respondent went on to describe what happened after Cidiaonga's death.

> 'Cidyawonga we did not burn because he had cared for the Paramountcy. And when Cidyawonga died we put Cikusi in his place'.[15]

Yet almost immediately afterwards, Chikusi and Chifisi were at war with each other. Why should this have happened? Most writers mention a disputed succession;[16] that Chifisi claimed the throne. His descendants of the Kachindamoto family follow this tradition of explanation; the Gomani group do not see it as a disputed succession but put it down to a misunderstanding of the military role assigned to Chidiaonga and his successors, that of head of the mjokozera war division. It is true that at a later stage both groups sought alliances with the Yao, chiefly with Mponda, but as this was in the 1880s it does not explain the Chikusi-Chifisi cleavage of the 1870s. Could the rift have started fundamentally because the Maseko were becoming less Ngoni-oriented and ostensibly over the burial question?

The Maseko was one of two Swazi clans who did not bury their dead but cremated them "on flat stones near flowing water, and as the fire reached the head of the deceased chief, it is stated that a bird, the *umnguphane*, sacred to the clan, rose phoenix-like from the flames'.[17] The testimony cited earlier says 'Cidyawonga we did not burn because he had cared for the Paramountcy'. Did this mean that he was not cremated because he was only a regent or that he was such a good regent that burial and not cremation was decided upon? It is clear that not to cremate was a slight to the Maseko of that period. W. P. Johnson gives a dramatic account of the cremation of the Maseko Paramount, Mputa, at Songea:

> 'His funeral seems to have been the last united act of his people and the Angoni. It must have been impressive. They blocked the water of the upper Lihuhu with stones, put the body of the chief in the skin of a newly killed bull, and burnt it in the dry bed of the river. The Angoni stood in crowds on the banks, all silent till the heat of the fire made the bones of the corpse crack; then together they beat their shields with their spears.'[18]

186

The clashes took place mainly when chiefs died (Chidiaonga 1876, and Chikusi and Chifisi in 1891). When Chikusi, who succeeded to Chidiaonga's position, died, he was cremated. This is, at least, a more plausible reason for enmity than the frivolous explanation in another context that the unequal sharing of game one day during the march southwards in the post-Zwangendaba period had led to Mpezeni and Mbelwa dividing up the Jere kingship.[19]

Unlike the case of the northern Ngoni, there is no evidence that the regent Chidiaonga was responsible for the feuds which rent the Maseko Ngoni after his death. The fact that he held the regency for over ten years in an area where the Mtunda, the Ambo and the Ntumba were willing and eager to be Ngoni-ized because of lack of defences against the invaders did not help in the preservation of Ngoni customs and speech. The retention of the war machine was all that was necessary. The ease with which conquest was achieved did not necessitate the strengthening and projection of the Ngoni image. The first Ngoni characteristic to be lost was language. When R. C. F. Maugham accompanied the expedition against Gomani in 1896 he reported that the Ncheu Ngoni were all speaking Chinyanja. In 1901 a District Resident in the area observed as follows:

'I found then that the language of the Ncheu natives was entirely Chinyanja. A few natives could understand Zulu; they used some Zulu songs and many of them still retained the Zulu war dress which they elaborated with bead work and used for dances. There were no Zulu place names or personal names.'

The same resident had earlier been posted to Nkhata Bay in 1897 to start the West Nyasa District administration. Of that area he noted:

'I found that Zulu was the language of Mbelwa's country. The Atumbuka of course retained their own language but for the most part could understand Zulu. The place names of the villages of the important chiefs were Zulu. Each large chief had his impi of warriors in Zulu war dress. The paramount chief held his indabas in his great cattle kraal. He was always greeted with the Zulu salutation *Bayete*'.[20]

A smaller original following, a long period in the wandering stage among non-warring peoples who were docile and receptive, caused the language of the Maseko to go first. The succession dispute following Chidiaonga's death must have gained from both the burial episode and from Chifisi's belief, in largely non-Ngoni setting, that his direct filial descent combined with the long period of his father's regency entitled him to compete in the succession stakes when Chidiaonga died.[21]

That was the first time when the Maseko throne was competed for by the descendants of both Mputa and Chidiaonga. Chikusi got the position through the laws of Ngoni inheritance by which his house stood in the direct line of succession. He was supported by Chifisi on this occasion and for a number of years the Ngoni factions lived in peace with Chifisi enjoying the position of military leader of the mjokozera war division. The intrusion of the Yao factor was in time to lead to disruption of this harmony. When Kawinga from Mt Chikala attacked Pimbi's people in the Upper Shire, a place not far from the Maseko settlement, the Maseko answered Pimbi's summons for assistance and repulsed Kawinga in a united action.[22] A few months later developments among the Mponda Yao were to lead to ultimate division within the Maseko ranks. In July, 1889 the ruling Mponda died and a dispute over the succession broke out. Malunda, the elder of the two sons of the late Mponda, looked around for alliances to overthrow the newly-installed chief. Liwonde and Kawinga responded; Chikusi refused.[23] This earned him the gratitude of the ruling Mponda for future advantage. The attempt failed but it was the beginning of the rift between Chikusi and Chifisi as it afforded each the opportunity of ready-made rival camps in any future conflict. The opportunity came in 1891 when Chifisi died. Chikusi demanded the privilege of arranging for the funeral but this Chifisi's successor, Kachindamoto, refused; the indecisive battle of *Mwala wa Nkhondo* followed even before Chifisi was buried. In the same year Chikusi died and this time it was Kachindamoto's turn to attack Chikusi's successor, Gomani. After a series of campaigns which lasted three years and in which the fortunes of war fluctuated, Gomani's forces were victorious. The decisive battle of *Mlomo wa Nkhuku* on Dedza plateau spelt the end of the unity of the Maseko kingdom of Mputa. The assistance which Gomani received from the Yao of Tambala and Mponda no doubt contributed to his victory. Territorial spheres of influence were demarcated with Gomani holding sway from Domwe to Lizulu and Kachindamoto to the north-east from Ntakataka to the lakeshore. Captain Edwards of the Protectorate armed forces sealed the peace pact between the descendants of Mputa and Chidiaonga in 1894 in true British fashion by making Gomani and Kachindamoto shake hands in public. The royal salute of *Bayete* and with it the position of paramount chief remained in the keeping of the Mputa line.[24]

Fission of the two main groups had now taken place introducing permanent peace between them. Thereafter each followed its own way in all social and political affairs. Where larger issues of Maseko import were concerned the Mputa line as the keeper of the royal inheritance took precedence. When Chikusi of the Mputa line died in 1891, there were two candidates from this line from among the six sons of Chikusi (Nkwaila, Zintambira, Kabango, Ziwisani, Gomani and Mandala). By now the house system of residence and inheritance was declining. Primogeniture was the first qualification. This Mandala satisfied but the selection councils found that two other qualifications were not met, viz., the dowry question and the candidate's suitability on the grounds of character, temperament and personal relationship with subjects.[25] The Alumuzana and Masenga councils ruled in favour of Gomani (Chatamtumba). One testimony points to Gomani's victory at a public trial when the two candidates were made to stand each on one leg with the other foot resting on the knee, for the period of the cremation of Chikusi's body.[26] What is not disputed is that there were two candidates and that Gomani was adjudged to be the more suitable. Mandala is mentioned in the diplomatic intrigues which followed in the ensuing Gomani-Kachindamoto wars. He is reported to have

188

entered into secret negotiations with Kachindamoto and Bvumbwe to wrest the throne but the plot does not appear to have succeeded. Bvumbwe fled southwards and Mandala relented. Mandala's championship of the Gomani cause is listed as a decisive factor against Kachindamoto and his more substantial role was yet to be played when Gomani was killed in October 1896.

When Gomani I was shot by British troops at Dombole his son and heir, Zitonga, was two years old. He was born in the *lusungulu* village of Chikusi at Lizulu where the Queen Mother, Mai Namagagula presided. For a short while two regencies were set up comprising Gomani's wife, Namlangeni and his brother, Mandala. This was short lived because, when a border commission delimited the Portuguese and British territories, Namlangeni and Mandala fled to the Portuguese side of the kingdom. Here they tried to raise an army but failed and the immediate members of the Gomani family were all arrested. They included Namlangeni, and the brothers Mandala, Nkwaila, Zintambira, Ziwisani and Kabango. Except for Zintambira who later returned to head the Maseko kingdom in Portuguese territory (where his descendant today holds the imposing but powerless title of king of Angonia) the rest died in captivity. It was only in 1906 that the headmen detained with them were released and allowed to return to both the Portuguese and British sides of Central Ngoniland. An inter-regnum existed between 1896 and 1921 during which the great *mulumuzana* or headman Chakumbira Ndau assisted by Mambeya Moyo looked after the affairs of the Gomani state. Zitonga received a European-style education through the sponsorship of a European friend of his late father, a hunter by the name of Walker. Zitonga succeeded to the Maseko paramountcy as Inkosi Gomani II in 1921.[27]

In spite of the succession disputes, and partly because of them, the inheritors of the mantles of Zwangendaba and Mputa weathered the storms of the nineteenth and early twentieth centuries in admirable fashion. The system would have collapsed had its custodians been less resilient.

In the period covered in this article there were six different rulers and regents functioning at different times with varying degrees of success in the political life of the main Ngoni hosts in the north and south.[28] After 1875 those in office had to contend in their external relations with three important influences, viz., indigenous and neighbouring peoples, missionaries, and the advent of British administration. Of these the first powerful impact came from the Scottish missionary factor represented in the work of the Livingstonia and Blantyre missionaries. In 1878 Dr Laws and Mr James Stewart visited Chikusi where they were kept waiting for four days before Chikusi would see them, an experience which Dr Stewart was to live through when he visited Mbelwa the following year. The British Consul, Hawes, on the other hand, had a pleasant experience at Kujipore when he called on Chikusi in 1886. The Ngoni chiefs kept strict protocol in their dealing with Europeans. Where this was not respected by the visitors, as it happened in the case of the Chiwere Ndlovu Ngoni of Dowa district, the consequences were very serious. Dr Laws, who was kept waiting for days by Chikusi, was surprised when Jumbe came out of his village to meet him half-way at Nkhota Kota in 1879;[29] but this is understandable when we consider that Jumbe was saddled with internal disaffection led by his headman, Chiwaura, and external threats from the Yao. The Ngoni were in no hurry to seek political alliances with Europeans.

During the period of waiting, Chikusi's councillors wanted an assurance from Laws as to the motives of the visiting party; chiefly to ensure that there was no evil intention and that no harm would befall Chikusi. When the interview was finally granted, the councillors sat themselves in a protective row between their chief and the visitors.[30] The object of the visit was to announce the work of the missionaries and to promise to open a mission station in Chikusi's country when possible. Chikusi resisted missionary intrusion for many years but saw like his contemporary, Lobengula that the white men were the agents for bringing in material goods and that they could not be fended off for long.

Before Scottish missionaries could work in his area much had happened in the external politics of Chikusi's kingdom. In 1882 Chikusi's people invaded the Shire Highlands and Lowlands plundering the Yao, Chewa and Kololo lands. The Kololo chief, Kasisi, in an attempt to prevent another invasion, sent some of his headmen and vassals to form defensive posts and settlements at various fords on the Shire. This arrangement was reinforced by sending some of the Kololo themselves to live on the spot (one of whom was the chief Mlauli) and to forge alliances with Chewa chiefs like Gwaza and Mpimbi in the area above Matope, and Chigaru below Matope. The creation of these lines of defences did not hold the Ngoni of Chikusi in rein. Through shrewd diplomacy one of Chikusi's headmen, Nyamuka, entered into a pact with the Chewa chief, Gwaza, by which he promised not to attack Chewa settlements on the river banks in return for their neutrality and the right to pass unmolested on their way to the Shire Highlands. The objective seemed to be mainly Yao settlements.[31]

The area devastated was curtailed by missionary action. David Clement Scott, head of the Blantyre Mission since 1881, visited Chikusi in August 1884 to arrange about starting a mission at a future date. He reported that the meeting was successful 'though very weighty' and that he had seen the preparations for war. The visit was helpful to the missionaries for, as Scott reported, 'the Ngoni were instructed not to enter the territory of the white men'.[32] The raid took place later that month and Zomba, Cholo, Mlanje as far as Machemba, and the Blantyre areas of Malabvi, Mpingwe and Bangwe were raided. John Moir of the African Lakes Corporation and Henry Henderson of the Blantyre Mission met Nyamuka's invading party at Ndirande Hill about a mile from Blantyre Mission. Moir offered the leader a present of calico and extracted a promise that the area between Blantyre and Bangwe would not be molested. The invading party, estimated to be a thousand men, kept their promise. Henderson even reported that they 'professed to be friendly towards us'. Missionary intervention had led to salutary results. Consul O'Neill summarized this in his despatch to the Foreign Office:

'The most remarkable thing about the raid, and one I should think unique in the history of raids of such marauding tribes as the Angoni and Makanquara, is the manner in which the lives and property of the English and their dependents have been respected. A greater proof could not be given of the wholesome influence exerted by the Mission over the surrounding people—an influence based entirely on respect and affection, for none knew better than the Angoni how completely defenceless the Blantyre Mission is. It is very satisfactory also to know that not only were the people attached to the Mission spared (some 800 took shelter at Blantyre and Mandala), but that Mr. Scott was able to secure the safety of the people of the Ajawa Chief Kapeni (who has always been on the friendliest terms with the Mission) at Soche and others at Dirandi and Malabvi'.[33]

In this report Chikusi is said to have come under mission influence but this was not due to any evangelizing work being carried out in his area. Chikusi was at first reluctant to accept a mission station in his area. Laws had to make a number of representations and it was only in 1887 that he consented to a station being built at Livlezi to the east of his settlement beyond Chilobwe hill. Dr G. Henry and Mr McIntyre were the first missionaries. Afterwards they received permission to start a mission village at Mpondera's. It was only in the period of Gomani I that the Church of Scotland started mission work at Nthumbi, where Harry Kambwiri Matecheta spent many years; the Zambezi Industrial Mission at Ntonda, Chiole and Dombole; the Baptist Industrial Mission at Gowa. The White Fathers at Nzama (1901), Mua (1902), Ntakataka (1908) and Bembeke (1910) only began to gain support and adherents during the period of rule of Gomani II and Kachindamoto II, a period outside the scope of this article.

Chikusi was interested in the material aspects of missionary contribution. To him the missionaries and traders were alike. When the *Lake Nyasa* was abandoned at Matope awaiting repairs he made a point of removing the pressure gauge and other gadgets, no doubt to him symbolic of the white man's wealth.[34] Missionaries and traders were not drawn into the Ngoni politics in the south to the same extent as they were in the north. They acted more as remote controls.

In the north the Jere Ngoni subjugated by conquest or kept in a state of perpetual fear the Tumbuka, Tonga, Henga, and Phoka peoples. On the periphery, the other raided peoples mainly belonged to the Chewa and Ngonde societies. The village elders were allowed to live in their old villages in a form of patron-client relationship. The younger people were incorporated into the Ngoni society. In the Henga and Kasitu valleys where the Ngoni settled, the sixth paramount chief of an aggregation of peoples, many of whom did not recognize this paramountcy, was in office at this time (Chikulamayembe Bwati) and he offered no resistance to the Ngoni invaders, being himself more of a trade leader than a military leader. The Tumbuka observed patrilineal inheritance and patrilocal marriage but the chieftainship was inherited matrilineally. The Tonga were akin while the Henga and Phoka peoples, like the Ngoni, were thoroughly patrilineal. What the Ngoni did introduce in the area was martial organization and many more herds of cattle. The Ngoni did seem to be favoured for a more rapid increase of their line, as certain Nguni and Sotho lineages, described by Monica Wilson in the following words:

'I suggest that these were lineages which increased faster than the previous occupants because they commanded wealth, could marry many wives, and traced descent in the patrilineal line. It is in this fashion that a small group of cattle-owners establishing themselves among hunters or cultivators could increase fast. They married women of the group among whom they settled, and their offspring became part of the dominant group'.[35]

But within twenty years of Ngoni overlordship the younger generation of the subjugated peoples, reared in Ngoni communities and trained in Ngoni fighting methods, took up arms against the invaders.

This reaction was facilitated by the fact that the agglomeration of chieftainships in Tumbuka land was not destroyed by the mere fact of Ngoni settlement in their country. Traditional religion survived; traditional chieftainships survived. What the Ngoni in effect did was to foist upon the non-military peoples of the land a system of indirect overlordship, collecting tribute, absorbing local people where necessary into the military machine, and raiding neighbouring areas for food and serfs. Rev. Charles Chinula, Tumbuka educationist himself, has noted in his article on 'Baza's rebellion' that Baza, too, enjoyed a measure of freedom after the Ngoni advent:

'When Baza surrendered to Ng'onomo, the latter handed him to M'Mbelwa's head wife, Munene, and he soon became a great warrior and hero, and brought chief M'Mbelwa slaves, ivory etc., to show his loyalty. But although he was under the Ngoni, he retained his villages, and his authority over his subjects.'

The northern Ngoni had come to settle among Tumbuka-speaking peoples of whom the main groups were the Tumbuka proper, the Henga, the Kamanga, the Hewe and the Phoka. By the nineteenth century, when the Ngoni arrived, the Chikulamayembe dynasty had established its hegemony over a large part of a trading state called Nkamanga. There were, of course, other chieftainships among the Tumbuka-speaking peoples, most of whom had come into existence in the eighteenth century. The Tumbuka proper who had lived in the region many centuries before, probably before the arrival of the Malawi chiefly clans between the thirteenth and fourteenth centuries A.D., were themselves not organized under territorial chiefs. For this reason, they did not resist the eighteenth century traders from across the eastern side of Lake Malawi or the nineteenth century Ngoni invasion. As the original owners of the land, what claim would they have to the recognition of Tumbuka-proper chieftainships when the Jere kingdom inaugurated by the sons of Zwangendaba spread its rule over them?

In 1958, or about one hundred years after the Ngoni settled permanently in the country of Tumbuka-speaking peoples, a meeting was held in two places in the Mzimba district to discuss the claims put forward by two groups of Tumbuka proper for the restoration of Tumbuka chieftainships. The meetings were both held under the chairmanship of Inkosi Ya Makosi, M'Mbelwa II in the M'Mbelwa African Administrative Council. The claims put forward were for the restoration of the chieftainships of Baza Dokowe and Katumbi Chimjokola Jenjewe. The details of this manifestation of Tumbuka chieftainships are not properly the concern of this paper, but certain conclusions arrived at after full discussions at these meetings, at which members of the Tumbuka community were present, are important. The first was the admission that there were no Tumbuka chieftainships before the advent of the Ngoni, and the second that the pre-Mlowoka Tumbuka proper did not live in large villages but in small, scattered groups, under family or clan heads. These points, which were made by a prominent Tumbuka, were not disputed at the meetings. One of the Tumbuka was an old man born in the last quarter of the nineteenth century. The conclusion, by common consent, was that the Tumbuka proper were not politically organized in the pre-Ngoni period.

Other questions which were raised at the meetings were: what were the symbols of Tumbuka chieftainships? Where did the Tumbuka come from? These issues were raised by those who wished to have their claims ratified and the argument put forward was that the Mazirankundu beads were symbols of chiefly authority; that certain places like Jenjewe or Mbalale were the headquarters of certain Tumbuka proper chieftainships. The counter to these arguments was that the beads were a later introduction by Arab traders and that every Tumbuka was allowed to put them on; and as for migration and settlement of the Tumbuka, those who remembered their traditions claimed to have lived at different places at various times: Chitipa and Karonga in the north and in the south and east in Chewa and Tonga country. But many were not able to trace their movements, adding to the assumption that where traditions of settlements or movements are not clearly remembered, the reaction is symptomatic of the absence of a functional role: that of establishing claims to chieftainships. Traditions of burial places of ancestors are well remembered when the ancestors belong to a chiefly line so that the claims of descendants to chiefly positions could be supported.

Thus we see that a hundred years after the arrival of the Ngoni, it was difficult for the Tumbuka-proper to explain who their pre-Ngoni chiefs were. What seems probable is that provided survival was itself not threatened, the pre-Ngoni peoples tolerated a great deal of the Ngoni irritants whilst biding their time mastering Ngoni fighting methods. The Ngoni headman Mayayi Chiputula Nhlane, in whose village on the border of Ngoni-Tonga territory most of the subject Tonga lived, was looked upon by a large number of Tonga as the guardian of their interests, having himself married many Tonga women. His death, coupled with fears of a general purge of the aged and infirm, set off a series of revolts which ended in a consolidation of the Ngoni position. In a little over five years (1875–81) the Ngoni re-asserted their presence, this time largely through force of arms. It was not in every campaign that the Ngoni were victorious but in sum they were now more firmly in the saddle than they had been a generation earlier.

Their most formidable foes were the Tonga who were drawn into Ngoni society because the latter needed food (cassava) and people (to enlarge their villages and join their regiments). The Ngoni did not feel secure in new surroundings and sought to strengthen themselves. How did they set about

193

doing this? A young researcher has come up with this explanation:

'After subjugating the Tonga, they (the Ngoni) went from village to village asking for young men and boys, a system called "kuhola". They took these young men and boys, trained them in the art of war, and gave them an Ngoni identity. This they rightly thought would make their tribe big and great. We have no statistical data and demographic information to show how successful the Ngoni were at this system but one gets the idea that it all worked very well. When these young men and boys grew up they would fight for the Ngoni.'[36]

The Tonga struck first (1874–75), followed by the Nkamanga-Henga (1876) and the Tumbuka proper (1880), the last-named being not the rising it is made out to be but the culmination of a personal quarrel between Baza Dokowe and Ng'onomo Makamo. Agreeing with the version that the quarrel was over ivory, the Rev. Charles Chinula wrote in 1928: 'There is a great deal of misunderstanding in connection with Baza's rebellion.'

For the purposes of Ngoni politics and Scottish missionary intervention it is necessary to say that the rebellious Tonga fled to their pre-Ngoni homes in the lakeshore area of Chinteche and Bandawe. At Chinteche in 1876–77 the hitherto invincible Ngoni war machine broke down before a determined Tonga resistance led by one Kazizwa.[37] The débâcle at Chinteche was a bitter pill for the Ngoni to swallow. Each side sought revenge: the Ngoni to avenge their defeat; the Tonga to wipe out old scores of conquest and raids.

It is in this background that we should consider the activities of the Livingstonia missionaries who, in search of a more permanent and attractive site for their headquarters as well as for new spheres for mission work, set up two observation posts in 1878, at Bandawe, and at Kaning'ina near the present town of Mzuzu. The first of these was in Tonga territory; the second on the Tonga-Ngoni boundary. In 1881 the observation posts were abandoned when permanent headquarters of the Livingstonia Mission was set up at Bandawe with the gleeful consent of the harassed Tonga.

But the Ngoni were less gleeful of the missionary presence. When James Stewart visited Kaning'ina in 1879, Mbelwa would not see him. His headmen could not understand why the missionaries should have settled in Tonga country. What the Ngoni desired was an exclusive Ngoni-Missionary alliance. Stewart wrote home as follows:

'They have lost both power and prestige within the last two years, and may now be resolving to attempt to regain both. I heard later that there are two parties in their council. Mombera and Chipatula and their headmen are desirous of peace and to invite us still to come among them, while Ntwaro and Mperembe wish to keep us at a distance, and to recover their power by force of arms. It was in deference to the wishes of this party that Mombera would not see us. I may mention now that two months afterwards Ntwaro broke the peace and attacked and burned two Atimbuka villages, killing the inhabitants. I fully expect that soon the Atonga and Atimbuka in alliance will drive the Amangone out of the country.'[38]

Stewart's prediction was wrong, The Ngoni had come to stay. Whoever came between them and their objectives did so at their own peril. This was pointed out clearly to Dr Laws when he first met Mbelwa in January 1879 in the company of the Xhosa, William Koyi Mtusane, and Frederick Moir. Mbelwa requested the missionaries to live with them since they were the rulers of the land and the Tonga were mere subjects.

'Our children we must have back, and we would have gone and fought with the Tonga, and driven them into the Lake, had you not visited us and said war was bad. . . . You say there should be peace; send back our children and there will be lasting peace'.

The conditions laid down were difficult for the missionaries to fulfil. As Laws pointed out, the missionaries wished to maintain a position of neutrality and they needed a lakeshore outlet to receive their provisions. In the meantime, the Kaning'ina outstation was there to serve the Ngoni.[39] The position was unacceptable to the Ngoni. When Stewart visited the chief later that year he received the rebuff already mentioned. The Baza Dokowe incident of 1880 in the very heart of Ngoni settlement—a few miles from Mbelwa's headquarters near Hora Mountain—was attributed by the Ngoni to the Mission teaching of equality and righteousness. After Dokowe's supporters were ruthlessly crushed (the movement, since it started off as no more than a personal quarrel, lacked both support and organization), the Ngoni turned on the Tonga again, increasing the ferocity and the frequency of raids into Tongaland.

How did the Ngoni of the following generation see this epoch of missionary intervention? In his memorandum to the Royal Commission on closer union headed by Lord Bledisloe in 1938, Inkosi Mbelwa II made, *inter alia*, the following submission:

'Before the European advent in this country my grandfather Inkosi Mbelwa's kingdom extended as far as Lwangwa Valley, covering the following districts: Karonga, Kasungu, Chintechi and Lundazi or Senga-land, Mzimba being its centre. His mode of rule was not to root off people from their countries, but left them to rule over their people under him according to their custom and creed. He only collected young men who were trained as warriors, who after they were trained made some revolts and in most cases they were got back and to be got back; but the missionary intervened by preaching the Gospel which made peace for all'.

But before peace could come, Laws and his co-missionaries had to walk the tight-rope of dangerous diplomacy with the warring factions. As a first step Laws was compelled to take note of Ngoni sentiment and politics especially since the Livingstonia Mission had shifted its headquarters to Bandawe in 1881. The success of the mission depended on the existence of a peaceful Tongaland. In that same year Laws paid his second visit to Mbelwa. A big *indaba* was held at Njuyu followed by local discussions in which the chief's brothers, indunas and headmen participated. The result was that Mbelwa agreed to receive a mission at Hoho village, situated at the foot of Njuyu Hill, north of the Kasitu river, about twelve miles from present Ekwendeni, as from 1882. The missionaries left here were William Koyi and James Sutherland.[40] In 1889 a second station was started at Ekwendeni under Elmslie.[41] A third station, a branch of Njuyu, was started in 1893 with Peter McCallum as artisan-teacher and Dr Steele as medical missionary at Hora, near the mountain scene of the tragic Dokowe incident of 1880.

The opening of the Njuyu station in 1882 was no more than a symbolic gesture. The missionaries had no permission to teach the children or to preach to anyone at first. Their role was little more than that of hostages, as a two-way guarantee against attacks on or by the Ngoni and Tonga. Dr Laws paid a third visit to Mbelwa in 1882 and yet another in 1883 in an effort to get the restrictions lifted. He failed to obtain permission from Mbelwa to open schools. The only concession granted was that the missionaries could preach in Hoho village alone and this Koyi did by visiting people in their huts. The result was not altogether unrewarding but it was slow in coming. The Hoho village profited in other ways by being able to sell their produce to missionaries in exchange for calico, a point which was impressed upon Dr Laws as being unfair to the other Ngoni settlements. Mbelwa's objection to the opening of schools was that since he was unable to evaluate the type of instruction to be given, he should be taught first in order to ensure that missionary teachings would not undermine the structure of Ngoni society.[42]

For Mbelwa and his Ngoni, long accustomed to having their own way in all dealings based purely on martial strength, the political diplomacy which now followed altered the situation drastically in 1882. They were now saddled with the presence and interference of missionaries in their domestic and external relations. Mbelwa would not order the sacking of Bandawe while the missionaries were there. He had developed a respect and affection for Koyi and Laws. His brothers, indunas, headmen and warriors did not all have the same disposition toward the missionary intervention. Mbelwa had asked Laws to carry a message from him to the Tonga in 1881 conveying his terms for settlement. Laws agreed to act as an emissary on just that occasion and thereafter to wash his hands of active involvement. The Bandawe Tonga had received the representations in a spirit of negotiation and compromise and were prepared to pursue the matter; the Chinteche Tonga had scorned the representations and offered to settle old scores in the way the Ngoni had taught them. This was a powerful affront and two factors prevented Mbelwa from accepting the challenge: his respect for mission property and presence and doubts over whether he had the army to succeed in reversing the Chinteche disaster of 1876–77 though he is reported to have planned a defensive campaign on the lines of the fight at Hora Mountain in 1880. He had already committed himself to helping Mwase Kasungu against the Jumbe of Nkhota Kota in a quarrel in which these chiefs were involved. His dilemma over the Chinteche affair was resolved for him by the virtual annihilation of the Ngoni army which set out against Jumbe.[43] The stabbing spear was being superseded by

196

the muzzle-loader and now there were two scores to settle: the old one against the Tonga; the new one against the Jumbe.

With enemies all around him, Mbelwa had to make sure of the role the missionaries were playing at Njuyu. Were they in league with his enemies and working towards undermining his position and authority? He demanded to know in 1883. He sent a heifer to the Njuyu missionaries as a gift and as a token of his friendship with the missionaries. Koyi and Sutherland did not know what Mbelwa's motives were. They summoned Laws to come immediately to find out. Nobody else, they were sure, could discern Mbelwa's motives and nobody else would receive Mbelwa's confidence as Laws would. Sutherland told Laws: 'We have an opinion of the disposition of Mombera and the people that were you on the ground the country would lie before you'.[44] Mbelwa, upset by the personal tragedy of the death of his eldest daughter and of that of an invalid brother, moved towards a settlement with the missionaries. He attended their prayer meetings, participating in his own way and punctuating Koyi's sermons with 'Amacebo ako' ('your lies'). He offered the missionaries a deal in 1884. If the missionaries would allow him to sally north to raid for cattle as well as to punish those recalcitrant Tonga they could have his permission to open schools in Ngoni territory.[45]

The missionaries for their part tried to wield indirect pressures. First, they sought in vain the support of Mbelwa's councillors. After a whole day's parleying the missionaries reported that 'the only conclusion that they arrived at is that we must give Mombera the Kalata and he will teach the children himself'. Second, they sought and obtained at long last Mbelwa's consent to see Mtwalo on whom they had pinned their hopes and whose support the Ngoni paramount required in order to meet any criticism or opposition from his councillors.[46]

There were pressing reasons why Mbelwa should resolve the missionary question at home for it was being used as a lever by his councillors to extract various concessions, chiefly to go on raids. Another area of local disaffection was growing among the Tumbuka, who followed Tonga-Ngoni relations closely. When they received word that the Chinteche Tonga leader Kangoma was negotiating an alliance with the Jumbe against the Ngoni, here, they felt, was a fruitful opportunity for co-operation to settle old scores. A missionary informed Dr Laws of this.

'The Atimbuka are presently thinking of leaving the Angoni. And so there is a good deal of trouble in Angoniland. The Atimbuka protest against the slavery of the Ngoni and say the white men tell them not to have slaves. So they are to have freedom and speak of joining Kambombo. Perhaps nothing may come out of it. I almost wish they would leave as it would so weaken the Angoni that we might have peace. The Atimbuka are the fighting men for the Angoni.'[47]

What ultimately weakened the Ngoni and led to the extension of missionary activities in Mbelwa's country as well as eventually to the imposition of Protectorate rule in the area was not the existence and influence of local or external forces contributing to a debilitation of the Ngoni but to the super-vention of natural forces. Mbelwa's lands experienced recurring drought conditions since 1882. This was variously interpreted by the medicine men, indunas, councillors and the chief's brothers depending on what each affected group desired. Three main reasons were given by the witch doctors: that the Ngoni were not friendly to the whites and would not listen to them; the existence of enmity between the chief and his brothers; the refusal of the Ngoni to accept the white man's *kalata* (letter). The position became worse in 1886. No rain had fallen in the area between November 1885 and early May 1886. The warriors wanted to remedy the position by wiping out the mission-aries but they were severely admonished by Mbelwa.[48] An appeal was made to Dr Elmslie for rain at an ordinary Sunday prayer meeting as a last resort. The course of Ngoni and mission history in Mbelwa's country was altered by a freak of nature when the storm clouds broke benevolently over the parched lands a day after that appeal. Elmslie left for Bandawe almost immediately afterwards to look after the mission while Laws was away on leave. He repor-ted with justifiable pride:

'letters from the hills today bring the news that the Angoni as a tribe are to go to war no more—that the threatened insurrection of the released slaves is to be met by a union of Mombera and all his brothers, which has just been consummated, all old quarrels having been settled, that the brothers are to settle near Mombera, but best of all the councillors were sent to inform us that the children are ours to teach and that they desire us to do so and to preach through the length and breadth of the land.'[49]

The break-through was made even if the follow-up needed tact and toler-ance. A new era dawned in Ngoni history and the people were naturally slow and diffident to take quick advantage of the missionary presence. The Hoho people would not send their children to school. Until this happened there could be no formal opening. Mbelwa hesitated to open a school in his own village because this might arouse envy. He had all along been criticized for being too soft with the missionaries.[50] Now he wanted Laws to know that both climate and soil had combined to affect Ngoni politics. He pointed out that the Ngoni villages would have to move; that the soil was poor in the area of present settlement. Now that raiding was curtailed, peace could only be won and kept if there was plenty of food cultivated. He saw that it would soon be necessary to shift to the Mzimba river area. He asked whether the missionaries would follow the Ngoni villages. Such a decision only Dr Laws could take for the local missionaries.[51]

When Mbelwa was convinced that this would in fact be the case—as it certainly turned out to be in subsequent years[52]—he summoned an indaba in the great cattle kraal in December 1886. Here he declared unequivocally that the missionaries were free to teach any child from any district. With this public declaration the paramount chief of the northern Ngoni dispelled any doubt as to the status of the Scottish missionaries. The uncertain days since 1882 were over for the moment, though not altogether free of trouble for all parties concerned, as Elmslie noted in his report to Dr Laws:

'Chipatula [sic] was their and our "umtelele" or "go-between" and in the fewest possible words we thanked Mombera. . . The drought led to this new move because we know that some of the Councillors do not believe that we have power over the rain and they refused to join the party. Those who came believe that we keep away the rain because of their action in regard to schools. I am tired of being considered a god, but gladly accept whatever position I am called upon to fill. The position is plain. If rain comes to satisfy them now their belief in our powers to do good or ill as we choose will be strengthened and we will be gods for another year or till the next drought. If rain does not come then we will be speedily asked what more we wish and the crisis will have come as to what is to be done with us'.[53]

The crisis did come the following year when a party of Livingstonia missionaries and Tonga carriers was attacked by a band suspected to be Ngoni. The road from Chinteche to Mzuzu and Hora was closed. No Tonga carriers were willing to enter Ngoni land. The Tonga retaliated by striking at the nearest Ngoni base, that of Mtwalo. This embittered Mtwalo and he used pressure on Mbelwa to sanction an attack on the Tonga. Fortunately for the missionaries and the Tonga, Mbelwa was not prepared to break the pledge given. He was constrained, however, to ask for three things: the Ngoni children still with the Tonga should be returned; there should be more evidence of material wealth coming to his people as a result of missionary activities in his area; one white person only should man the Bandawe post and the rest should join the mission stations in Ngoni land. Elmslie lived through the turbulent days among Mbelwa's people, watching with trepidation the war preparations and growing impatience. Although he buried three-quarters of his medicine in preparation for a hasty retreat he took the view that Ngoni land was preferable to Tonga land but Laws did not agree. Elmslie even suggested the neutral port of Ruarwe to resolve the harbour argument but Laws remained unimpressed. Elmslie admitted that they were looking at the position with jaundiced eyes, 'You from a Lake or Atonga side and me from an Angoni side.'

Mbelwa pressed for a personal meeting with Laws in 1887, a request which was not met either because the Tonga refused to release him for the trip or because he was himself not prepared to evacuate his post. Mbelwa then made two moves. In the one he tried to cajole Elmslie into closing down the mission stations in Ngoni land and thus returning the Ngoni cattle given as pledge of good conduct by the Ngoni. This Elmslie would not do, realizing that such a move would play right into the hands of the Ngoni politicians. The second was to make a last-minute appeal to Laws to get out of Tonga land for the sake of his personal safety and thus be in a position to open more stations in Ngoni land. Elmslie supported Mbelwa and seemed convinced that his sincerest wish was to free Dr Laws from virtual captivity by the Tonga. 'Let us go', the Ngoni seemed to say, 'and give Robert peace'. To Elmslie, the mission headquarters would best be located in Ngoni land because the people were willing to receive missionaries; they were powerful and independent and their influence was felt hundreds of miles away; the area was healthy and the scope was wide. Laws did not budge; the Mbelwa proposals were not met. Local affrays continued but Mbelwa refused to give the command for war till the end. The crisis passed over when the Ekwendeni Mission was started in 1889. It was now seen that the pressure behind Mbelwa was generated by his brother Mtwalo. A mission at Mtwalo's headquarters turned out to be one of the shrewdest moves by the Livingstonia missionaries.[54]

It was only when Mbelwa died in 1891 that the war-hungry hordes made one last foray. The Tonga leader, Kambombo, for long a thorn in their path, was killed and the plunderers looted deep into Northern Malawi. One of Mbelwa's sons was not willing to join the warriors and when upbraided as a coward went to the missionary McCallum at Ekwendeni and said that he would go but that he would not kill. Another Ngoni explained that they were going out in search of cattle 'and then they will make peace with the white man'.[55] The white man referred to was Harry Hamilton Johnston, British Commissioner and Consul-General. With this a new dimension was now to enter into Ngoni politics. Up till now it had been a triangular affair involving mainly the Ngoni, Tonga and missionaries. Mbelwa and Laws were the heroes of this period, each supported by able lieutenants. Their wits and friendship were well matched. It is hard to say who was the more fortunately placed. To both must go credit for a measure of honest diplomacy. The more creditable performance was that of Mbelwa. To him negotiation and compromise were new attributes in the Ngoni repertoire. The fact that he resorted to them is an index of maturity of leadership; the fact that the Ngoni political system found room and use for them is a commentary on the flexibility of the system itself.

III

Consul Hawes visited Chikusi in 1886, staying for four days in the chief's meeting place at Kujipore (Chikusi's capital was at Liwisini a distance of about five hours' journey). The attitude he adopted was that he was dealing with an independent ruler on dignified and respectful terms. In his report he noted: 'I thanked His Majesty on behalf of Her Majesty's Government for the reception he had given me.' He gave Chikusi impressive gifts in keeping with the chief's status. At the talks held Chikusi promised to give every facility and protection to the Scottish Missions when established in Ngoni land; to discontinue raids in the Zomba and Blantyre areas and to set up a military town at Mpimbi on the Shire river to prevent his people from getting beyond this point. Chikusi gave a pledge to honour the undertaking—a pledge he never broke—in the following words: 'If I break my word, white man, you may come and spit in my eyes'.[56] The entire negotiations were conducted with the greatest decorum. The chief was not in the best of health and therefore not at his capital village. When he chanced to meet Hawes unexpectedly at Kujipore he accorded Hawes the dignity of his station, a point the Consul was not slow to grasp. Through an interpreter, Chikusi told Hawes:

'The King says he is very glad to see you. He has heard that you have come from the Queen of a great country. On that account he wishes to do special honour by coming out to meet you.'[57]

There is no reason to believe that Consul Hawes was anything but honest in his despatches. There was no good reason why Chikusi should have been presented in this light for flattery sake. The area was not yet in the arena of colonial dispute, nor was it involved in the Anglo-Portuguese rivalry at this time for treaties with African chiefs. Hawes reported on Chikusi as he found him. The tragedy which struck Chikusi's successor was due solely to the politics of Harry Johnston who saw his immediate programme in the following sinister terms:

'The general policy to be followed at first should be "Divide et Impera". Discount the personal interests of the various native chiefs and Arab Sultans as far as possible; discreetly encourage their mutual rivalries (stopping short, of course, of inciting them to civil war); bind over the more influential men to your interests by small money subsidies, and you will easily become the unquestioned Rulers of Nyasaland.'[58]

On his first treaty-making expedition in Malawi in 1889–1890, while still Consul at Mozambique, the only Ngoni chief with whom Johnston signed a treaty was Chiwere Ndlovu of Dowa. Either through ignorance or design he labelled Chikusi, Chiwere, Palankungu, Kanguru, Undi, Mpeseni, Mwase Kasungu and Mbelwa as leading Angoni chiefs.[59] He was to say very much the same thing at the beginning of 1896 when reporting the happy tidings of victory at long last against Mlozi, the Yao Saidi Mwazungu, and Mwase Kasungu. The latter was specially dubbed an Ngoni chief. Swann, District Resident at Nkhota Kota, reinforced this by informing Johnston who Mwase was. 'Mwasi himself is a stranger and an alien, of Zulu extraction'. After almost eight years in and out of the country, Johnston surely knew who the Ngoni were. His motives for confusing identities are not difficult to explain. By 1896 he wanted not only to show that he was the unquestioned ruler of Nyasaland but a legitimate ruler at that for

'these enemies whom we have recently conquered, like all with whom we have fought since our assumption of the Protectorate, were not natives of the country fighting for their independence, but aliens of Arab, Yao, or Zulu race who were contesting with us the supremacy over the natives of Nyasaland'.[60]

It was wrong for Johnston to say that the Ngoni were in this contest with the Administration. Chikusi had received three visits from Administrative Agents, one in 1882 by Montague Kerr, another by Consul Hawes in 1886 and the third by Alfred Sharpe in 1890. With Hawes he had made a gentleman's agreement; with Sharpe he had done the same but in neither case had he signed away his territory. The uniform 'treaty' which Sharpe negotiated with

Chiwere, Mwase and others in 1890 was no more than a printed form which stated that the chief concerned agreed to peace between subjects of the British Queen and himself; to British subjects building houses, and holding property 'according to laws in force' in the chief's country; to trading by British subjects; to an undertaking not to cede the territory to any other power without the consent of the British Government.[61] This was far from placing his country under British protection, as Johnston claimed.

In August, 1891, Chikusi died, almost a year after Sharpe's visit. Johnston reported that the youthful Chatumtumba (Gomani I) who succeeded him had sent an emissary to Zomba and placed himself under British protection, asking for assistance against the Chifisi-Mponda league against him. The present paramount, Gomani III, denies strenuously that any such pact was made. There is no documentary evidence of one. According to Johnston's own version he pursued the matter by calling on Mponda to desist and to pay reparations to the Ngoni. He was met by a solid phalanx of Mponda's and Chifisi's men, with the likelihood of Makanjira joining. No more was heard about his intervention on behalf of Chikusi.[62] It was not Chikusi's cause that Johnston was championing or furthering by this intervention.

Though he reported well of the Ngoni in 1894, calling them 'splendid fellows' and 'the backbone of British Central Africa', Johnston had no desire to allow the existence of states within a state and sounded the ominous alarm that 'we shall have to try conclusions (with them) some day'.[63] It is not mere coincidence that Johnston waited till 1896 to try his conclusions. In 1891 he entered into a treaty with Mbelwa by which he undertook not to tax Mbelwa's people or interfere with them in any way provided that they remained in the area then occupied by them, i.e. between the South Rukuru river in the north and Hora Mountain in the south and that they did not raid or molest the inhabitants outside their country.

It is true that the Livingstonia missionaries asked Johnston not to interfere with the northern Ngoni but it is equally true that the Livingstonia missionaries were helpless to enforce any conditions on the Ngoni. It was the power of the Ngoni themselves that deterred Johnston and his successor from taking precipitate action. Sir Alfred Sharpe admitted this as late as 1899.

'. . . They are a very independent tribe, and to have attempted to put in force the Hut Tax and any large measure of direct control hitherto would have meant disturbances, which I have been anxious to avoid'.[64]

British protectorate policy was to wait for the most opportune moment and at the same time to procure a *casus belli*. With the northern Ngoni they were very much restrained. When Chibisa fled to Hora after the fall of Mwase Kasungu in 1895 and received asylum from Mbelwa's great warrior Ng'onomo, the Administration was outraged. At this moment of administering the *coup de grace* to its surviving opponents it sought in turn the heads of Mlozi, Mwase Kasungu, Saidi Mwazungu, Chibisa and lastly Gomani I. Now only the last two remained and one of these was in hiding in the heart of Mbelwa's land where the missionaries were expected and requested to take up the

Administration's cause. District Resident Swann addressed the Ngoni regent and indunas through the missionaries, asking them to hand over Chibisa. At the same time he prevailed upon the missionaries to use their good offices to seek the arrest of Chibisa. Elmslie was careful not to involve the Ngoni in any way. He advised the rulers and their advisers to disown both Chibisa and Ng'onomo and thereafter to ask the Administration to take whatever punitive action it wished independently of mission or Ngoni involvement. This Swann was not prepared to do and Chibisa was allowed to stay unmolested until he left of his own accord later that year for Mpezeni's to whip up support.[65]

Johnston was not prepared to fight the northern Ngoni over the Chibisa affair. He was not prepared to do the thing for himself nor was Elmslie prepared to do it for him. The missionaries were at an advantage. They could do without the government but the government could not do without them. 'It is no doubt desirable', wrote Elmslie,

'to have them settled under British rule and I have no doubt all would act on our advice, but getting into political relations is not agreeable. Only so far as indirectly such things may help our work—our position is not dependent on the Government. . .'[66]

Another mission and a chief of a breakaway Ngoni community were placed in similar circumstances in 1895–96. The Dutch Reformed Church Mission[67] worked in the area of Chief Chiwere Ndlovu. The subjugation by the Administration of a number of African chiefs was a matter of growing concern to Chiwere. He was under great pressure from his head wife, indunas and headmen to expel or exterminate the missionaries. Like Mbelwa he resisted these demands but the word got round that the missionaries were in imminent danger. Zomba sent five Makua soldiers to guard the mission at Mvera without being requested by the missionaries to do so. The presence of uniformed policemen at the Mission aroused the hostility of Chiwere's people. Was the mission in collusion with the Administration? Was there any difference between one white man and another?[68] The point which worried Chiwere was how could W. H. Murray be his friend as well as the friend of the Administration which was anxious to take his land from him and turn him 'into a slave'.[69]

Chiwere and his followers came to the conclusion that the representatives of the Administration who were now trespassing in their area should be wiped out. But before carrying this out, Chiwere summoned a meeting of the D.R.C.M. missionaries and suggested a line of action:

'How will it be if I call up my warriors and drive out the white man who is now trying to come in here and we and you should stay on alone in the land? If you say yes we can clinch the matter here and now'.[70]

The missionaries took care not to offend Chiwere and his people and at the same time to point out to them the serious consequences of such a deed. Though disappointed in the advice, Chiwere accepted it and promised not to harm the Administration. When the Administration made a tactical blunder of convening a meeting with the Ngoni chief, Msakambewa at Kongwe, Chiwere took this to be an insult as Msakambewa was deemed to be junior to him, and he did not attend, concluding that the Administration was plotting with Msakambewa to undermine his authority. In this state of mind, the appearance of a government boundary expedition in his headquarters at Msongandeu was sufficient provocation for Chiwere to flee for safety to a small village called Mbindo from where he planned to attack the European forces which were closing in on him. The fact that he did not do so and finally agreed to accept Codrington and the British Administration in his area was due entirely to the intervention of and the assurance by W. H. Murray:

'If Mala (Codrington) were to arrest your chief he would have to arrest me too. If he kills Chiwere he will have to kill me too'.[71]

There was no killing on this occasion and one strong Ngoni community was now under effective British rule by missionary persuasion. When the second, the Maseko of Gomani I, suffered the same fate the event was immortalized by the tragedy which visited it. Gomani had a number of grievances. He was not in favour of the payment of tax by his people in his area, arguing that he had never asked for British protection. He objected to the employment of his subjects by the Administration or by the Zambezi Industrial Mission or other employers. On 6 October 1896 he and his indunas called on the missionary in charge of the Zambezi Industrial Mission at Dombole and demanded the release of those who worked for the Mission, suspecting that some of them had been responsible for plundering the goods of the African Lakes Corporation. The demand was refused. That night about 27 villages were burned down on Gomani's orders. This led to his arrest by Captain Ashton. On 27 October Gomani I was given a summary trial and ordered to be marched off to Blantyre. Refusing to walk further he was tied to a tree between Dombole and Chiole and shot.[72] Another strong Ngoni community was now under effective British rule and this time because of grievances against missionaries. Gomani I was condemned on the strength of testimonies by missionaries but fundamentally because the paramount chief believed that the area was his domain. He was not prepared to compromise as Mbelwa had done.

The last and largest Ngoni community in Malawi entered the administrative fold relatively quietly. A number of factors combined to bring this about. For long the Livingstonia missionaries had preached the sermon of protection alike for the raided and the raiders, more particularly to the former. The Mbelwa Ngoni were made to see the positive side of a protectorate government when their material wealth—their cattle—was protected from exploitation by traders who paraded as government agents. One such man was William Ziehl who was charged by the government with stealing 10 cattle and 10 goats and for waging war against the Ngoni of the north. For these offences he was given a sentence of £50 fine or 6 months' imprisonment in 1899. Capt. Pearce, who tried the case, was quick to point out the propaganda value of this occasion.

'. . . if I may venture to express my opinion, there will be few opportunities more suitable than the present for opening out this large and populated district, while the memories of the white man's trial and the event at Ekwendeni are impressed in their minds'.[73]

A further factor was the outbreak of rinderpest which virtually wiped out their cattle stocks in 1893. This development undermined much of the economic and social foundations of Ngoni society. It has been noted already that ever since 1899 there was talk of moving into new lands as the fertility of the old ones was fast diminishing. Lands became denuded of trees and fertile lands became wastelands. Even before Mbelwa died in August, 1891 his son Chimtunga (who was later to be enthroned as paramount chief in 1896) moved his village some 40 miles south of Hora Mountain and settled between present Loudon Mission and the Rukuru river on the east and west. This movement was interpreted by the Administration as a violation of the treaty obligations of 1891. One other factor was the incompetent rule of Chimtunga, the successor of Mbelwa I. He was unpopular with some of the amakosi, two of whom paid a call at the instigation of the Scottish missionaries, on the British Resident at Nkhata Bay, for the express purpose of seeking British protection which they were told by the missionaries would neutralize Chimtunga's incompetence. This move, however small, strengthened the hands of Commissioner Sharpe. A last contributory factor was an incident of 1904, when tax-collectors crossed over into Ngoni territory from Tonga land and began to collect hut-taxes in a non-authorized area. They burned down the villages of those who, rightly in the circumstances, refused to pay tax in the Ngoni sector. This incident had serious repercussions and the protectorate Government moved in using the pretext that since the 1891 treaty had now been abrogated by the Ngoni in one important respect the government was justified in taking this step.[74]

A fallacy about the coming of British Administration to northern Ngoniland is that it was due purely and simply to Dr Laws; that he had decided that the time had come and had therefore summoned Sir Alfred Sharpe to consummate the deed.[75] Laws does not himself make this claim. If anything, Laws wanted this to come about long before 1904 and had suggested it about 1896 when Elmslie had refused to do Johnston's dirty work for him in the Chibisa affair.

As early as 1901, three years before the cumulative effect was felt of the proverbial last straw that broke the northern Ngoni's back, the missionaries had begun to see that the odds were against the Ngoni. Some of the prouder ones among them were able and willing to tell the missionaries just what they had done to the Ngoni: 'You have spoiled the country', said Ng'onomo.

'You have just come from Marambo. The people there were once mine. There at Kusungu you see the people running to "the Consol" with tusks which should have been brought to me as of old. You have caused me and my country to die.'

Even the missionaries could not but reflect with admiration:

'But Ng'onomo had beaten others and he knows when he is beaten himself. It is such as he who are the only ones in Ngoniland that voice any sentiment of opposition to the Administration.'[76]

Had the missionaries the power of crystal-gazing they would have added that there was more of the warrior Ng'onomo yet to come after 1904.

On 24 October 1904 Commissioner Sharpe, in the presence of a number of Livingstonia missionaries (excluding the veterans Laws and Elmslie), two European ladies, and thousands of Ngoni, brought northern Ngoniland under British rule with the following assurances: the authority of the hereditary chiefs would be upheld; they would be able to decide minor disputes among their people; they would receive annual subsidies. The chiefs for their part undertook to act justly and rightly; not to accept bribes; to get their people to pay tax; to obey the Resident and to follow his advice.[77]

Since this article started off as an account of Ngoni politics in Malawi, let us leave the last word with Inkosi Mbelwa Jere II;

'Long ago in the time of my father before the Government took over my district there came a European from Northern Rhodesia who had to shoot, and rob people their property, and did all sorts of evil and damages to man and property, we were protected by the Nyasaland Government; this is one of the reasons that my father willingly placed himself under the Imperial Government Rule because the Deputy Commissioner, Mr. Pearce, had displayed justice and shewed great protection by fining that European and making him to pay all damages made to people. The second reason was that on occasions the Commissioners visited his country, they promised him that his kingdom will be as that of Khama and the Prince of Zanzibar, and that no European will have power over his country and over him, also that Her Majesty Queen Victoria will send a Consul to help him and to strengthen his power and that his people will pay taxes to him and not to Her Majesty the Queen. In course of time after Her Majesty the Queen died, Sir Alfred Sharpe came with the question of collecting taxes, this was refused at many times until 1904 when a treaty was made, and it was more favourable to us than it appears on the attached extract printed by missionaries at Livingstonia Mission.'[78]

The Maseko and Jere Ngoni of Malawi, who constitute the focus of this study, played an active part in the political affairs of their time. The quality of diplomacy is not measured solely by the success which attends it but by the vigour and vitality with which it is played. Between 1848 and 1904 these communities were not only presented with a series of succession disputes and a rather unfortunate spate of deaths of rulers in a series. Their political manoeuvres were of necessity those of migrant communities against mainly other migrant communities, both black and white. Traditional lore mixed with western lore; the cattle kraal competed with the school, church and classroom;

206

the assegai with the muzzle-loader and the cross; the heathen with the Christian; the Paramount with the Protectorate. It was a period when contradictions had to be reconciled and compromise solutions sought. If they lost a few wars and some rounds of diplomacy and one paramount chief, the Ngoni did not lose the battle for survival. They lived through the colonial interlude with greater adaptability than many. This was due in no small measure to the variety and vitality of their politics.

FOOTNOTES

1 This article is part of a larger study on the Malawi Ngoni for which I have received financial assistance from the University of Malawi with a small grant from the British Council. I wish to express my deep appreciation to them. In the field I have received assistance from the Paramount chiefs of the Jere and Maseko Ngoni, their amakosana and representatives; from District Commissioners and a whole host of informants at village levels. Mr Petros Moyo, Ngoni historian himself, accompanied me on many trips. I am grateful, too, for the opportunity to research in the Public Record Office, the British Museum, the Royal Commonwealth Society Library, the National Library of Scotland, the Church of Scotland Library, the Malawi Society Library and the National Archives, Zomba. The Librarian and his staff at the University of Malawi, Chancellor College, have been of greater help than I can acknowledge. I am grateful, too, for the helpful comments received from Professor Margaret Read, who pioneered studies on the Malawi Ngoni.

2 Hammond-Tooke, D., 'The "other side" of frontier history; a model of Cape Nguni Political Progress', in Thompson L. (Ed.) *African Societies in Southern Africa* (Heinemann, 1969) 235.

3 Fraser, Donald, *Winning a Primitive People*, (London 1914) 29.

4 George Williams to Dr Laws, December 1884. Missionary Letters, University of Edinburgh Library.

5 George Williams to Laws, 7 October 1886, U.E.L.

6 Research interviews conducted by Duncan I Nkhoma in the area of the Mzukuzuku chieftainship, 1968-9. Testimonies of Rev. P. Ziba, Rev. Charles C. Chinula, Petros Hlanzo Moyo.

7 For the village system and marriage customs of the Ngoni and Swazi see also Read, Margaret, *The Ngoni of Nyasaland* (London, 1955) 20-1 and 48-9 and Kuper, Hilda, *An African Aristocracy* (London 1965), 54-5 and 92-4.

8 Young, Cullen, T., *Notes on the History of the Tumbuka-Kamanga Peoples* (London, 1932) 113–17; Elmslie, W. A., *Among the Wild Ngoni*, (London 1899) 27; Chibambo, Y. M., *My Ngoni of Nyasaland* (London n.d.) 27; Barnes, A. J., *Politics in a Changing Society*, (London 1934) 21.

9 This evaluation belies the undoubted success of the Mtwalo chieftainships in the villages of Ekwendeni, Ezondweni, Emanqalingeni and Emchayachayeni. Mtwalo I ruled his own village from about 1855 until he died in October, 1890. His successor and son Muhawi Amon Mtwalo was born in 1873 at Uswesi, east of Coma Mountain. He was installed chief on 15 June 1896 and after a very long and successful period of rule he died at Ezondweni on 1 April 1970, having been in office for 74 years. A fuller account of Mtwalo II and M'Mbelwa II is under preparation.

10 Chibambo, 28–9.

11 Rangeley, W. H. J., 'Mtwalo', *Nyasa. J.*, 5 (1), 1952, 64.

12 Chibambo, 34–5.

13 T. W. Baxter, 'The Angoni Rebellion and Mpezeni', *N. Rhodes. J.*, 11, 1950, 14–24. Mpezeni was reinstated after being in exile for a year. He died on 21 October 1900. The brother who had accompanied him away from Malawi, Mperembe, died in October, 1909 and was the last of the sons of Zwangendaba.

14 Read, 61.

15 Read, 55.

16 Read, 55.

17 Kuper, 86, fn.1.

18 Johnson, W. P., *Nyasa The Great Water. Being a description of the Lake and the Life of the People.* (London 1922) 105.

19 Field, Annis, S., *Visiilano*, (1940) 16.

20 Cardew, A. C., the Resident, commenting in a letter to Ian Nance, District Commissioner, 8 November 1952. Cardew noted the testimony of an old man named Yakobe who was born about the time Chidiaonga arrived at Domwe about 1870. Yakobe obtained the information, which he passed on, from his parents and others who would have had first-hand knowledge of the position. 'Yakobe says that when Chidiaonga Maseko arrived at Domwe the natives of the Ncheu District were Amalawi, Ambo and Ancheu. These people never learnt Chingoni. When Chidiaonga came he

made war upon them and subdued them and ruled them from Domwe. He raided them occasionally for recruits for his army, slaves, wives, etc., but even people thus captured did not learn Chingoni. He did not put indunas in the Ncheu District and the Angoni did not settle in the District. He merely ruled the District from Domwe sending warriors to enforce his orders when necessary.' Cardew to Rangeley, 10 December 1952, Rangeley Papers M.S. of the Society of Malawi. These Papers are being edited by the writer by direction of the Society of Malawi.

21 One tradition states that Chidiaonga betrayed Mputa in the struggle with the Mhalule Gama in Songea and was responsible for Mputa's death, after which he seized the chieftainship. Chifisi's claim to succeed would be strengthened by this seizure.

22 Acting Consul Buchanan to Marquis of Salisbury, 29 January 1889. *Accounts and Papers*, Vol. 72, 1889, 285. P.R.O.

23 *Accounts and Papers*, Vol. 72, 213–14. The old Mponda who had ruled from 1886–89 had found it convenient to pay tribute to Chikusi as a guarantee for immunity against Ngoni raids. Hanna, A. J., *The Beginnings of Nyasa-land and North-Eastern Rhodesia*, 1859–1895, (Oxford, 1956) 73. On page 186 Hanna notes that from 1889 to 1891 there had been sporadic fighting between Mponda and Chikusi's Angoni. This could only refer to the support which was being given by different groups in the Chikusi kingdom to the factions which existed in the Mponda chieftainship.

24 Dedza District Notebook, Vol. I, 1907 and the Ncheu District Notebook, Vol. I, 1907, National Archives, for the details of the conflict.
The Manser-Bartlett Papers in the University of Malawi Library refer to the conflict and follow closely the version in the above named District Notebooks. The late Mr Bartlett must have referred to them. The information has been supplemented by personal interviews conducted in the Gomani and Kachindamoto areas.

25 Ncheu District Notebook Vol. I, 1907 records that Mandala, the eldest son of Chikusi, was passed over 'as the headmen considered him of too fierce and turbulent a nature to hold sway over them, for they were afraid that he would oppress and even slay some of his own people; Chatum-tumba on the other hand, was of a milder disposition, and on that account found favour with them.' N.A.Z.

26 This contest is not borne out by a testimony recorded by Margaret Read, which nevertheless gives details of Gomani 'standing on one leg with a shield in his hand'. Read, 57.

27 I am grateful to Inkosi Willard Gomani III and to his court historian, Bambo Kaizokaya Dolozi, for some of the details on which this section is

based.

28 See also G. T. Nurse, 'The Installation of Inkosi Ya Makosi Gomani III'. *Afr. Mus. Soc. J.*, **4** (1), 1966–67, 56–63.
In the North, Ntabeni, Mgayi, Gwaza (regents), M'mbelwa I, Mkuzo (regent) and Chimtunga; in the south, Chidiaonga (regent), Chikusi, Gomani I, Namlangeni, Mandala and Chakumbira Ndau (regents).

29 Laws, R., *Reminiscences of Livingstonia* (Edinburgh and London 1934), 67–70. Diary of Robert Laws. E. 62/15. Gen. 561–563, Drummond Room, University of Edinburgh, entry of 19 August 1878. He described Chikusi as having a bulk which surpassed any that Laws had seen in Africa. About two miles from Chikusi's village was the village of 'Gaomozi', otherwise known as Chifisi. He notes that the brothers were at war because Chikusi refused to give help to Chifisi in his losing battle with the Yao chief Pemba. As to relative size, Laws felt that Chifisi's village was larger and more compact.

30 Note Dr Laws' explanation given later when kept waiting to see Mbelwa on one occasion. 'We had to wait for some time to see him, that being a sign of willingness on his part to receive us. . .' Laws, *Reminiscences of Livingstonia*, (1934) 180.

31 Blantyre District Notebook, Vol. I, 1907. National Archives, Zomba.

32 Rev. David Clement Scott to Consul O'Neill, 8 September 1884, *Accounts and Papers*, 1884–1885, Vol. 73, 406–7, P.R.O.

33 Henry Henderson to Consul O'Neill, 7 September 1884; John Moir to Consul O'Neill 26 August 1884; Consul O'Neill to Earl Granville, 3 October, 1884, *Accounts and Papers*, Vol. 73, 406–7, P.R.O.
The Makwangwara was the name given to the Ngoni of Mhalule Gama and the remnants of the Maseko who did not return to Malawi but settled in Songea. In September, 1882 a large invading party attacked the U.M.C.A. mission at Masasi in spite of the efforts of the European missionaries to prevent it. Though no Europeans were killed, the mission property was utterly destroyed.
G. H. Wilson, *The History of the Universities' Mission to Central Africa*, (London, 1936) Chapter XII 'The Masasi Raid', 56–9. As Consul in Moçambique, O'Neill must have been aware of this incident when his despatch was written.

34 Harkess, African Lakes Corporation to Dr Laws, 28 March, 1885, Missionary Letters, U.E.L.

35 Monica Wilson, 'Changes in social structure in Southern Africa: the relevance of kinship studies to the historian' in L. M. Thompson, (ed.)

36 D. M. Manda, 'The Ngoni-Tonga Conflict: causes and aftermath', Chancellor College History Department Research paper, 1968–1969.

37 For the revolts, Mphande, C. Z., 'Some Aspects of the History of the Tonga up to 1934', History Seminar Paper, University of Malawi, Chancellor College, 1968–69; Saulos Nyirenda, 'History of the Tumbuka-Henga People', *Bantu Stud.*, 5, 1931, 1–75; T. Cullen Young, 118–36, Chibambo, 43–9, and C. C. Chinula, 'Baza's rebellion', *The Livingstonia News*, 15, 1928.

38 James Stewart, C.E. to Dr George Smith, Foreign Secretary of the Free Church of Scotland, 31 December 1879 in *Livingstonia Mission 1875–1900* kindly made available by Professor George Shepperson.

39 Elmslie, 95–8.

40 The first missionaries at Njuyu were William Koyi and James Sutherland. Walter Angus Elmslie arrived in 1884. Sutherland died on 29 September 1885 and Koyi died on 4 June 1886; his grave is in the neighbouring woods not far from the first mission. The first African converts in Ngoniland were Mawalero Tembo and Makara Tembo both of whom were baptized in 1890. (The first African to be baptized by the Livingstonia missionaries was Albert Namalambe in Bandawe in 1881. Namalambe spent most of his life in the Cape Maclear area.) The first women converts at Njuyu were Elizabeth Moyo, wife of Mawalero Tembo, and Ann Zivezah Sakara, wife of Chitezi Tembo, headman of Hoho village. Hoho village at Njuyu became the headquarters of the Nhlane family when they shifted from Kaning'ina shortly after 1879. The Livingstonia missionaries carried through the association with the Nhlane family now led by Ben Nhlane. Hence the meeting in 1881 at Hoho. In 1904 the Nhlane family shifted to Dwambazi which is the new Hoho.

41 The old Ekwendeni was nearer the Lunyangwa, about 1½ miles away from the present Edwendeni. On the old site and about 50 yards from the Lunyangwa are a number of graves of some pioneers of mission work in the area; the Rev. George Steele, whose tombstone inscription reads: 'Umfindisi wa Bangoni, Wazalwa November 30, 1861. Wafa June 26, 1895'; that of Ngoni historian and early minister, Rev. Yesaya Mlonyeni Chibambo, born 1887; died 6 August, 1943; that of Hezekiah Mavuvu Tweya, one of the first three ministers of the Livingstonia Mission to be ordained in 1914; died November 16, 1930.

42 Laws, 181–3; Chibambo, 55–7; Elmslie, 101–4.

43 James Sutherland to Dr Laws, from Njuyu, 2 October, 1882 and 17

November, 1882, Missionary Letters. U.E.L.

44 Sutherland to Laws 29 September 1883. It is worth recording that in 1879 Jumbe offered Mbelwa an alliance to defeat the Tonga. Mbelwa asked the missionaries at Kaning'ina whether he should accept. The missionaries advised against it. Miller to Stewart, from Kaning'ina, 8 June 1879.

45 Sutherland to Laws, 12 March 1884. By now Mbelwa had granted permission to Koyi to preach in his village and Mtwalo's head wife had expressed support for the Church. Peter McCallum to Dr Laws, 20 January, 1883.

46 George Williams to Dr Laws, December, 1884.

47 William Scott to Dr Laws 17 February 1885. M'mbelwa asked the missionaries for protection and even requested a revolver to be at his side at night. This the missionaries did not give him. Elmslie to Laws, 12 February 1885.

48 Elmslie to Dr Cross, 8 February 1886.

49 Elmslie to Laws from Bandawe, 10 May 1886.

50 Elmslie to Laws, 5 November 1886.

51 George Williams writing from Njuyu to Dr Laws, 2 October 1886.

52 In 1902 Hora Mission, which had opened in 1893, shifted to Luasozi about 2½ miles from present Loudon Mission which was started by Fraser in 1903. Hoho village shifted to Dwambazi in present southern Mzimba in 1904. Here Simon Nhlane was chief. His brothers Yobe Nhlane and Daniel Nhlane later shifted in 1909 to Mirenje. These villages are in Inkosi Maulau's area today.

53 Elmslie to Dr Laws, 12 December, 1886. The first school opened at Hoho village in Njuyu on 13 December 1883.

54 This section is based on a series of letters appearing under the classification of M.S. 7890 in the National Library of Scotland and detailed as follows: W. A. Elmslie to Laws 14 August 1887; 24 August 1887; 6 September 1887; 12 September 1887; 15 September 1887; 5 October 1887; 10 October 1887 and M.S. 7892. Elmslie to Dr Smith, 26 January 1889.

55 M.S. 7896. George Steele to Dr Laws from Njuyu, 31 January 1892.

56 *Accounts and Papers*, Vol. 78, 353–6, Consul Hawes to the Earl of Rosebery, 3 June and 1 July 1886. P.R.O.

57 Consul Hawes to Earl of Rosebery, 1 July 1886, *Accounts and Papers*, Vol. 78, 353–6. Hawes was very much impressed by the organization of the Chikusi state. 'I was much struck by the respectful manner of the people I have met with in Angoni Land. The whole country is under perfect control, and the greatest respect is shown to the King and to all officials. To the King's wives also the highest respect is shown on meeting them by kneeling down. This honour is paid not only by women and children but also by men.'

58 'Memorandum on the Administration of British Central Africa by a Chartered Company'. H. H. Johnston to Directors of the B.S.A. Company, 17 July 1890. F.O. 84/2052. P.R.O.

59 Report dated 17 March 1890, F.O. 84/2051.

60 *Accounts and Papers*, 1898, Vol. 58, Africa, Vol. 4, 1896, Correspondence respecting operations against slave-traders in B.C.A. c.7925, and c.8013.

61 F.O. 84/2052, Alfred Sharpe's treaties.

62 *Accounts and Papers*, 1892, Vol. 74 Africa No. 5, 1892.

63 Report by Commissioner Johnston of the First Three Years' Administration of the Eastern Portion of British Central Africa, 31 March, 1894, Africa No. 6, (1894) 24.

64 Sharpe to Salisbury, 16 June 1896, F.O. 2/209.

65 M.S. 7879, National Library of Scotland, Dr Elmslie to Dr Smith 9 April 1896; 24 June 1896, and 22 July 1896.

66 Elmslie to Dr Smith, 24 June 1896.

67 This started at Mvera in 1889. Its headquarters shifted to Nkhoma in 1912. By 1896 it had posts at Mvera, Kongwe, Livlezi and Nkhoma. The first superintendent of the Mission was the Rev. A. C. Murray.

68 W. H. Murray to his father, 25 December 1895, gives an account of these events. I am grateful to the late Mr Lou Pretorius of Nkhoma Mission for showing me these letters and for assistance in the preparation of an article entitled 'The Dutch Reformed Church Mission and Central Angoniland during the Turbulent Years, 1895–1896'. See also *Mbiri ya Misyoni ya D.R.C.* 48–52.

69 W. H. Murray to his parents, 4 May 1896 in which he notes that Codrington was building a house for himself near Chiwere's much to the chief's annoyance. On 30 June another letter states that the Ngoni, passive up till

now, might 'follow a different line'.

70 Murray, W. H., *Op Pad* (Suid–Afrikaanse Bybelvereniging, Cape Town, 1940) 82–3.

71 Murray, *Op. Pad.*, 92. Murray had earlier extracted a promise from Codrington that no harm would come to Chiwere.

72 Diary of W. Gresham, Zambezi Industrial Mission, Ncheu District Notebook, Vol. I, 1907. National Archives, Zomba.

73 F.O. 2/209, folio 168–9 and Capt. Pearce to Alfred Sharpe 15 June 1899.

74 Fraser, Donald, *Winning a Primitive People* (London 1914), 239–44, and given in greater detail in Fraser, Agnes R., *Donald Fraser*, (London 1934), 64–9.

75 See, for example, *The Nyasaland Times*, 15 May 1950.

76 *Aurora*, 1 April, 1901.

77 C.O. 525/66. Governor Smith to Colonial Office, secret despatch of 17 January 1916.

78 Memorandum submitted by Mbelwa II to the Bledisloe Commission, 1938. For an interesting account of the continuing stability of Ngoni states in Malawi and Zambia before the advent of Europeans, see J. K. Rennie, 'The Ngoni states and European Intrusion', E. Stokes & R. Brown, (ed.), *The Zambesian Past* (Manchester University Press) 1965, 302–31.

13 Religion and Politics in Northern Ngoniland, 1881-1904[1]

John McCracken

I

The impact of Christianity is one of the great themes in the modern history of Malawi. In one sense it involved a challenge to the cultural and political independence of the area more formidable, perhaps, than any that had taken place before. Christian missionaries from their earliest contacts with the country were active protagonists for the extension of colonial rule. European social beliefs and assumptions were brought sharply into conflict with the complex network of social beliefs already in existence. In another sense, however, the history of expanding Christianity is the history of African initiative. The varied response of different societies in the pioneer period to the opportunities provided by the missionaries are of crucial importance for an understanding of the educational and political patterns that were later to emerge. The growth of a Christian elite, composed initially of teachers and catechists, not only led to the evangelization of other societies, but also created the conditions in which new ideas could be successfully propagated and new men could emerge as the spokesmen for their people. Defined in the terms that C. C. Wrigley has used for Buganda it is clear that no Christian revolution took place in Malawi; there was no transfer of power within an existing society from a traditional ruler to a new dynamic body of converts.[2] Defined in a broader sense, however, it may be argued that such a revolution occurred. Spearheaded by the activities of the first generation of Christian converts, a profound change in the relations of the lakeside Tonga with the wider world took place in the thirty years before 1914. At the same time, and more unexpectedly, the active involvement of many of the northern Ngoni with the Livingstonia Mission meant that Christian teachers there also came to assume a role of considerable importance. The nature of these latter changes, and the process by which they were brought about, is the subject of this paper.

II

There is a sense in which the pattern of much of the later history of colonial Malawi was set in the 1870s and 1880s with the initial contact of African

215

societies and European missionaries. At that time the predominantly agricultural peoples of the country were coming under considerable pressure from a
series of intruders, notably the Yao at the south end of the lake and four groups
of Ngoni. What the full effects of these intrusions were it is not within the
scope of this paper to describe, but one broad distinction can be drawn. In the
southern districts the Yao and Maseko Ngoni came to dominate the Malawi
around the lake and in the Shire and Dedza highlands by the 1870s. In the
north, however, the reluctance of Arab or Swahili merchants to burden themselves with territorial responsibilities meant that, despite the expansion of the
northern Ngoni, considerable pockets of agriculturalists remained independent. Whereas in the south missionaries from the 1870s were to deal almost
exclusively with the new intruding political leaders, in the north they were to
make significant contacts with the old cultivators.

This factor is of importance in explaining the different ways in which
African peoples reacted to the presence of the Livingstonia Mission. For the
Machinga Yao at the south end of the lake the revolutionary economic
demands of the missionaries that they should abandon slave-trading and turn
to commerce along the lines of the Shire river were incompatible with their
deep involvement on the East coast trade. Only superficial use was made of
Livingstonia missionaries in the six years, from 1875 to 1881, they spent at
Cape Maclear, and subsequently the Machinga Yao turned increasingly to
Islam as a substitute historic religion.

For the lakeside Tonga, however, the situation was markedly different.
Preyed upon by Mbelwa's Ngoni from the 1850s, the Tonga retained their
independence by withdrawing into a number of stockaded villages, the most
important for our purpose being those of Marenga near Bandawe and of
Mankhambira at Chinteche. The defeat of an Ngoni impi at Chinteche in
1877 did not prevent the recurrence of raids in later years, and consequently
the Tonga welcomed the mission as a diplomatic ally, and used it partly as an
envoy through which negotiations could be profitably transacted, and partly
as a source of military strength, capable of using its contacts with the African
Lakes Company as a means of averting Ngoni attacks.

The transformation of this tactical alliance into a more fundamental relationship has been described sufficiently often to warrant only brief mention
here.[3] Driven by the internal competitiveness inherent in their society, Tonga
headmen by 1883 were seeking to obtain schools for their villages, firstly no
doubt as a means of cementing the alliance with the mission, but subsequently,
from 1888 at least, in order to obtain the skills they could utilize in a new
western-dominated economy. Meanwhile, the emergence of such an economy
in the Shire highlands encouraged the beginning of labour migration from
1886, and created the conditions in which the Tonga came to be regarded as
'the krumen of this protectorate'.[4] It is true that Christianity was regarded
with much greater suspicion than the educational skills also imported. The
first few Tonga converts were not made till 1889, and these were mostly
teachers and scholars of whom it was said, 'Some have been at school with us
at Cape Maclear, others joined us as occasional scholars soon after work was
begun at Bandawe'.[5] By the latter years of the nineteenth century, however,

216

the crisis of belief which appears to have affected the Tonga at this time was beginning to respond to the new evangelical methods of the younger missionaries, and the increased familiarity with the Tonga language which at least one of them now possessed. From 1895 to 1898, and again for several years from 1903, waves of popular religious enthusiasm swept through Tongaland with thousands of listeners attending church services and hundreds more coming forward in search of baptism. 'At village after village the attendance and interest gradually increased until the people were coming "according to their houses",' a missionary reported in 1903.[6] By 1906 Sabbath services were being held in ninety-eight centres, attended each week by over 14,000 hearers.[7]

If the contrast between Tonga acceptance and Yao rejection of mission activities appears to demonstrate the distinction between the response of indigenous agriculturalists and intruding traders, the reactions of other peoples within Livingstonia's sphere of work convincingly points to the dangers of taking any such blanket generalization too far. The northern Ngoni, for example, as one of those Nguni groups who formed centralized military states dominating the districts in which they came to rest, appear obvious candidates for rejection. Elsewhere individual missionaries and traders like Robert Moffat among the Matabele and Carl Wiese with Mpezeni's Ngoni might succeed in striking up personal friendships with Nguni chiefs, but their formidable military systems, as Moffat recognized, were too vigorous to be pushed aside by the challenge of Christianity,[8] while their need to raid or control subject peoples threw such hazards in the path of colonial plans for labour recruitment and economic exploitation that armed conflict with Europeans very often resulted.

To this general pattern northern Ngoniland provides an exception. Superficially Mbelwa's Ngoni differed little from their kinsmen to the south. They dominated at the height of their influence an area said to be 30,000 square miles in dimension, populated by Tonga, Tumbuka, Henga, Ngonde, Chewa, Bisa and others. Whereas 'in all the other districts the missionaries were hailed, so Elmslie claimed, 'as the friends and protectors of the people . . . (the Ngoni) needed not our protection as they were masters of the country for many miles around'.[9]

On a deeper level, however, the northern Ngoni were subjected to internal and external pressures which made them particularly receptive to missionary advances. In the first place, there is evidence to suggest that the balance of power in their favour, on which depended the continued vitality of the state, was beginning to tilt against them by the 1880s. Ngoni military successes were based on their powers of cohesion and the use of the short stabbing spear and oxhide shield. These had been sufficient to win them numerous striking victories during their northwards march, but they were less effective when pitted against agricultural peoples who had withdrawn into prepared stockaded villages, particularly if such peoples possessed the new improved firearms with increased velocity which were beginning to become available in East-Central Africa by the last two decades of the nineteenth century.[10]

The significance of these organizational and technical innovations first became apparent in the 1860s when the Chewa chief Mwase Kasungu defeated an Ngoni impi with the aid of guns sold to him by traders from Nkhota Kota.[11] Over a decade later Mankhambira's successful defence of Chinteche stockade against several attacks gave warning that Tonga villages were now less vulnerable than they had previously been.[12] The sharp reverse suffered by an impi in 1882 at Nkhota Kota where the Jumbe had accumulated up to 2,000 firearms, was further evidence that Swahili trading settlements were also too formidable to be raided with impunity.[13]

The Ngoni, it is true, still won victories from time to time in open warfare. Frequent raids were made on Tonga cultivating their uplands gardens during the 1880s, and a successful attack on the Bemba took place in 1887.[14] Nevertheless, a serious loss of confidence appears to have afflicted some leaders during the decade. Elmslie wrote in 1886 that the tentative move to the Mzimba district was a sign of relative decline in Ngoni power:[15]

'The end of the Angoni Kingdom as a maurauding tribe is not far distant. Hemmed in on every side they must give in soon and the fact that they are looking for an uncultivated country as a new settlement means a great deal in the history of a tribe which has never broken up ground for itself but swallowed up the gardens of other tribes.'

Even N'gonomo, the military commander, was pessimistic about his army's abilities when confronted by new forms of organization. According to Elmslie, he told Mbelwa that it was only through the aid of the Senga with their guns that the Bemba had been defeated. Without their support he refused to attack Chinteche in 1887.[16]

While these external pressures may have played a part in persuading Ngoni leaders of the need to adapt alternate functions to those integral to a raiding economy, certain internal divisions were probably of greater importance in explaining the nature of Ngoni response to the arrival of the missionaries.

First among these divisions was the tension created by those subject peoples who still felt themselves at odds with their captors. In most Ngoni societies, recent captives were efficiently assimilated by distributing them all over the country under Ngoni leaders in such a way that they were unable to retain their old loyalties, and turned instead to the new. In northern Ngoniland, however, many of the captives taken from neighbouring tribes were permitted to remain together in groups under their own local chiefs and following their own laws and customs.[17] This distinction which contributed to three breakaways of people of a common stock—Tonga, Henga and Tumbuka—in the 1870s remained an issue of importance on into the 1880s. In 1885, for example, Elmslie reported rumours of a forthcoming rising by Tumbuka which, though it came to nothing, caused 'a good deal of trouble in Angoniland'.[18]

A further source of tension was provided by the captives taken before or shortly after the crossing of the Zambezi. Because chieftaincies in the northern kingdom were reserved almost exclusively for members of the royal clan, the Jere, this group had little opportunity of rising to the highest political offices. On the other hand, the most able among them were highly prized as councillors by the chief of each segment—many of the true Ngoni being themselves

218

segment heads—and they were also in demand as diviners, an occupation practised by few of the original refugees from Shaka.[19] As lieutenants or councillors they were nominally dependent on the good graces of the chief. But because it was believed to be unfitting for the chief, the symbol of common unity within the segment or state, to interfere too frequently in domestic disputes, real power tended to slip towards the lieutenants. Consul Goodrich, who visited Mbelwa in April 1885, noted that 'the affairs of the country are managed by a council of indunas who merely notify to Mombera their decisions so that the chief himself has but little power'.[20] By the mid-1880s customs were being introduced by councillors, notably the secret sale of slaves to Arab traders, of which the true Ngoni were said to disapprove.[21] The position of the most senior chiefs, even of the paramount, was being put in question. According to George Williams, the last of the Africans from Lovedale to be employed by Livingstonia, 'the fact is that Mombera would really make friends with the mission, for the councillors are using all their power to undermine his influence in fact if it was in their power they would wrest the kingdom out of his hands'.[22] Elmslie saw matters in a similar, though possibly exaggerated, light. The councillors, he reported in February 1886,

'are freed slaves and hate us because they cannot get their ends attained in the downthrow of the Angoni since we and only we maintain the Jeri dynasty. Mombera is powerless . . . The Jeris give evidence of the great moral truths of the Bible. They made slaves till now not 200 remain of the Angoni and all the power is in the hands of these freed slaves.'[23]

Finally, tension existed between the paramount and his peers, the heads of the major segments within the state. As Barnes has shown, the snowball state system had a built-in tendency towards fission which did not necessarily presage its collapse or decay. In ideal circumstances each son of a segment holder created his own segment when he came of age drawn both from recent captives and from individuals from the older segments. Expansion thus continued at a great rate till the moment was reached when the paramount chief with the very slender central powers available to him would be unable to control the now unwieldy kingdom. One or more segments would therefore break away to found their own state, and the process would continue as before.[24] But if fission was a natural ingredient of the Ngoni state system, this did not prevent conflict between the paramount and his subordinate chiefs being almost endemic, particularly among the northern Ngoni where rivalry at the top took place within a single clan. Mbelwa not only had the example of the ominous break-up of the kingdom following his father's death constantly before him, he must also have been acutely aware that at least one chief, Mtwalo, had rights as good as his own to the paramountcy, while another, Mperembe, had actually broken away from the kingdom for a while before returning. As Mbelwa's own personal segment was smaller than those of some of the other chiefs, he had little reserve power at his disposal with which to maintain unity. Elmslie in 1885 spoke of enmity between Mbelwa and

Mtwalo and the fear that 'the tribe may divide as Mtwaro is trying to set up as chief'.[25] Mbelwa, he thought,

'seems going wrong as chief and irritating his people by disturbing them. He goes about alone now and he has recently taken cattle he had at kraals of Angoni and given them to the Atimbuka to keep.'[26]

Even the insignificant Chiputula segment found it possible to plan a breakaway to Mzimba when Mbelwa found judgment against it.[27]

It was against this background that Mbelwa faced Livingstonia during the 1880s. Clearly he regarded its agents as men of some importance not only because of their wealth and technical skills, but also because of certain supernatural powers they were supposed to possess. To the Ngoni who made extensive use of medicines to strengthen their army in battle and deprive the enemy of courage, Mankhambira's claim 'that the English had given him plants which would strengthen him for War' must have appeared as convincing as his second threat 'that the steamer was away for an English army and there was another coming by land to drive the Angoni out of the country'.[28] It was hardly surprising that Mtwalo in October 1879 asked Miller 'that I should wash his body with medicine to protect him from his enemies who wished to kill him'[29]—particularly as the missionaries, with doubtful propriety, had dangled before the Ngoni the claim that acceptance of Christianity permitted the believer to enter upon the fruits of western power. 'I showed them a Bible,' wrote Riddel of his first visit to Mbelwa,

'and told them it was it that made our nation rich and powerful . . . I then gave a sample of the Commandments and some of the leading virtues it inculcated. I said if they received it, it would make them wise and happy and teach them how to become wealthy by fair means and not by robbery.'[30]

Mbelwa was thus in no position to ignore the mission as a political force, even though the military nature of the Ngoni kingdom offered him few opportunities for utilizing it in the type of constructive role visualized for C.M.S. agents by Mutesa of Buganda. Instead he followed a policy in which two principles appeared of primary importance: the first the desire to isolate the mission from any potential rival, Tonga, Tumbuka-Ngoni or Ngoni; the second, the wish to prevent antagonizing others by making its material assets widely available.

In the earliest phase it was the first principle that dominated. Mbelwa encouraged the establishment of the pioneer station at Njuyu in 1882, but the missionaries there were refused access to other chiefs and were not allowed to open schools. The only instruction was that given, unsuccessfully, to Mbelwa himself: 'Whenever he comes I get him on to the A B C', wrote Sutherland sadly in December 1884, 'but before he goes any distance he tells me to . . . Get out of here, . . . Give me cloth and so on'.[31]

The breakdown of this policy of isolation appears to have arisen out of the social tensions which I have already described. By mid-1880s certain groups in Ngoniland were beginning to identify themselves with the mission. Although they were not allowed to open schools, the missionaries were not prevented from holding evangelistic services at their station, Njuyu, and these, while attended primarily by mission servants, began by August 1884 to attract a scattering of local villagers, most of them members of the Ngoni serf population. Others in groups of sixty or more came to work for three weeks or a month as labourers in the mission brickfield, and this became such a popular employment that by June 1885 the heads of the neighbouring village to the station were protesting that only their dependents should be given work, and not those from a distance.[32]

Further consolidation of the mission's role was provided in February 1886, when after the efforts of diviners had failed to break the long drought of that year, Elmslie was called upon by Mbelwa to give his assistance. Mbelwa's motives in this affair must remain a matter of speculation, but it is important to recognize the existence, as in other centralized societies where the secular ruler was trying to consolidate his power, of tension between the royal authorities and religious officials, emphasized in the case of the Ngoni by the fact that most of the diviners, like most of the councillors, came from north of the Zambezi. Under Zwangendaba recently captured diviners had used their power to kill off older established Ngoni of Tsonga origin, while Zwangendaba himself is credited, in a story identical in all essential details to one told of Shaka among the Zulu, of deliberately sprinkling blood on the doorways of his kraal in order to trick the diviners into giving false judgment, and then slaying those who fell into the trap.[33] It is not impossible that Mbelwa in turning to Elmslie was seeking to reduce his dependence on a social group which he saw as a threat to the stability of his kingdom. Certainly in subsequent months the missionaries regarded his alliance with Livingstonia as resulting largely from his desire for 'a safeguard for the future' against the councillors who, it was believed, were 'yearly increasing in power'.[34]

At all events, the rain episode when taken with other developments so increased the attractiveness of the mission to important new elements among the Ngoni that Mbelwa, whatever his original motives, could no longer continue with his policy of exclusion. The reaction of the Ngoni-Tumbuka who, following the rain episode, began to attend evangelistic meetings in crowds, was soon paralleled by the marked interest shown by some of the segment heads, anxious, both Elmslie and Williams believed, to win the support of the mission in any dispute with overmighty councillors. In danger of arousing hostility against himself by refusing easy access to the missionaries, Mbelwa now changed his plans, and after a meeting with Mtwalo, gave permission in May 1886 for them to teach through the length of his land. His only advice, expressed through members of his council, was 'that instead of confining our work to the people around one station we would open stations at each of the principal divisions of the tribe.'[35]

The suggestion in principle was warmly welcomed by Elmslie who only a year before had told the home committee of his desire to plant sub-stations throughout the more distant parts of the kingdom. The rapid expansion of European-manned stations elsewhere in northern Malawi meant, however, that no new recruits were available to supplement those already in the field. After William Koyi's sudden death in June 1886 had reduced the Ngoniland staff to two, Williams went to Chinyera, the outstation about 5 miles from Njuyu which he had temporarily opened the year before, and Elmslie started up a small school at the centre. But the key problem—the need to establish contacts with segments other than Mbelwa's was not met, with the result that opposition against any school being established at once became apparent. In November 1886 Elmslie reported the current situation:[36]

> 'Mombera does not now see that we can have a school simply on one side and though offer was made to open one at his place he did not seem willing for it as he is afraid of the jealousy of others, and until the chief is availing himself of the school the Hoho people will not send any children to be taught. If we could open a dozen schools in the country we could have one here but because we cannot do that we cannot have one.'

Only a tiny group of six or seven pupils continued to frequent the mission-house and receive lessons in secret.

Matters were now speedily moving to a head. In December permission to open a school was once more granted, and once more antagonism against Mbelwa for monopolizing the new asset was aroused. This time, however, the form it took threatened the whole position of Livingstonia. If agents could not be spared for Ngoniland while Bandawe thrived, it was logical for sub-chiefs to seek to force the whole staff to come up to the hills. Little was done till August 1887, as Laws' visit the month before was optimistically regarded as a prelude for more favourable changes. But after he had left empty-handed and particularly after Williams, now the only Lovedale man on the staff and a valuable go-between, had informed Mbelwa that he too was to leave, the dam broke with spectacular force. If Williams went, all the missionaries should leave, Mbelwa declared as a prelude to his most important demand: either they come up to him from Bandawe and leave the Tonga to the mercies of the Ngoni, or they must evacuate the country altogether.[37]

Besides the central issue of desire for access to the mission several other factors were of importance—all concerned with the increasing power of the Tonga vis-à-vis the Ngoni. During the 1880s the African Lakes Company had been extending its sphere of operations, setting up a central depot at Karonga in 1884 and a small store at Bandawe a year later. From the depot guns and ammunition were sold to Arab traders, in contravention of the Company's stated policy, and these traders in their turn, so the Ngoni contended, sold guns to the Tonga, thus building up the latter's supply of armaments.[38] Various incidents, moreover, notably the treaty negotiated by the A.L.C. with Tonga chiefs in 1885, gave colour to the Ngoni belief that the British were prepared to protect the Tonga against them, and these were exacerbated by the fact that Tonga carriers sometimes taunted their former masters with boasts of their newfound power, and that Tonga raids occasionally took place on Ngoni villages, as well as vice versa.[39] Underlying all was the feeling that the Tonga were gaining more than the Ngoni from the British connection;

222

that they received more employment and hence more calico, and even—an interesting point for the date, 1887—that they were sometimes paid in cash, thus permitting them to buy what they wanted, while the Ngoni only got cloth. As Elmslie declared, 'Jealousy of the Tonga is a big factor in the whole question and because it is so our difficulties are very great'.[40]

For two months, August to October 1887, the crisis continued to smoulder. Elmslie, already burdened by the need to care for his wife in the last stage of a difficult pregnancy, sent contradictory messages by every post to Laws at Bandawe. All the missionaries should leave Ngoniland, he declared in one letter; all those at Bandawe should join him in the hills, he advised in another. 'We cannot save the Atonga by staying among them or by going away. . . . There is ample room for us all here and it is as suitable a field as any on the west coast'.[41]

Laws, however, remained firm. On 27 October 1887 he attended a great meeting with Mbelwa's councillors, and after much argument reached a compromise agreement: the missionaries would remain at Bandawe but would not interfere with what the Ngoni did at Chinteche, the northern focus of Tonga power. A station would also be opened at Mtwalo's head-village as soon as possible.[42]

To Elmslie, a fervent admirer of Laws who had first sparked off his enthusiasm for Africa, there was no question as to how the drama had been resolved. In a much quoted passage written years later, he declared: 'Living, as I did, with Mombera for six years before he died, I never knew of his having stopped a single war party from attacking the helpless Tonga around Dr Laws' station at Bandawe because of his belief in God; but over and over again because of his attachment to Dr Laws he refused to sanction war'.[43] But personal affection at the best is a weak instrument in bringing about profound political change, and though Elmslie drew the parallel of Laws's friendship with Mbelwa and Robert Moffat's with Mzilikazi, it is clear from his correspondence that the two cases were distinct. Mbelwa never gave any sign of manifesting that strange, almost physical, affection for the European which Mzilikazi so frequently indulged in. His interest in Laws arose directly from the fact that the missionaries in Ngoniland were young and inexperienced, and referred everything to their senior colleague. As no firm decision could be made in his absence, Mbelwa was naturally eager that he should attend major conferences.[44]

The strength of the agreement thus lay not in personal factors but in the extent to which it coincided with the pressures and changes in power in the political structure—and particularly in the growing isolation of the Jere from their councillors on the one hand and of Mbelwa from the segment heads on the other. Aware for the first time of the imperative need for widening their base, the missionaries began to make strenuous efforts to spread their influence among the more distant parts of the kingdom. In November 1887 Elmslie made a pioneering visit to N'gonomo and Mtwalo in their villages, while Williams went to Mperembe's. Some delay followed during which Mtwalo sent several messages regarding the proposed residency. In July 1889, however, Elmslie visited Mtwalo again and got his ready consent for a station to be built near him, and in August this was finally established under the artisan McCallum close to Mtwalo's head village of Ekwendeni. Within a month of his arrival McCallum had over 140 pupils at school. By 1895 Ekwendeni had become Livingstonia's largest Ngoniland station.[15]

The mission's success came at an important moment in the history of the Ngoni. If one were to accept the supposition that all Ngoni groups depended inevitably for continued integration upon the assimilation of a steady supply of captives from beyond their kingdom, then they might all have been expected to continue raiding till they were eventually checked and crushed by superior forces. In fact each group differed from the other, in part according to the extent to which they had assimilated local peoples, and each, even before the European conquest, was capable of adapting institutions and customs for new functions, given that the pressures to change were sufficiently large and that alternative functions actually existed.

For the northern Ngoni, pressure to change was provided, as we have already seen, by the mounting capabilities of the peoples beyond their frontier to repel attacks. Despite the assurance from the mission that an attack on Chinteche would not involve them in a collision with the British, they still hesitated to move. In November 1887 Elmslie reported that the season was now too late for any assault to be planned. N'gonomo, the Ngoni war leader, refused to mount an attack without the support of Senga guns and unless the Tonga could be lured out of their stockade, and without his support those sections of the Ngoni nearest to the Tonga would take no action.[46] The year after, N'gonomo went north to raid for cattle.[47] Gradually the project faded out of mind and the Tonga were left in peace.

The failure to attack Chinteche did not, of course, mean the end of all Ngoni raiding. Because the missionaries, and later other Europeans, usually approached the Ngoni from Tongaland, there is a tendency to regard Ngoni-Tonga relations as the only ones of importance. But the Ngoni were surrounded by a variety of people—the Tumbuka, Henga and Ngonde to the north, Chewa to the south, Senga in the Luangwa valley to the west, and these latter in particular continued to be subjected to Ngoni raids well into the 1890s, despite Chibambo's claim that raiding had completely ceased in Ngoniland by 1893. According to Fraser, a more reliable witness on this point, national raids had ended by the time of his arrival in the country late in 1896, but attacks by members of an age-regiment within a single segment, notably those of Mperembe and N'gonomo, continued along with independent raids by groups of young men acting without orders.[48] These were small affairs, however, when compared with the nation-wide assaults of an earlier period, and they were largely restricted to areas where few Europeans had penetrated and none settled, an important consideration in the 1890s, when the *pax Britannica* was slowly being imposed on those regions frequented by the British.

Meanwhile, through Livingstonia, new functions and opportunities were beginning to emerge as alternatives to those integral to a raiding economy. The young men of military age were clearly those most deeply affected by the constraints placed upon their traditional activities, for many of them sought military success as a means of achieving upward social mobility, and looked

224

to the continuance of warfare in order to integrate themselves successfully within their society. During the 1880s it was men of this age-group who most insistently demanded of Mbelwa that he should give his authority for raids, attempting on one occasion to refuse to permit him to enter his new village till the order had been given.[49]

One possible alternative appeared to lie, as Mbelwa himself at one time seems to have recognized, in the educational facilities offered by the mission. As early as 1886 he told Elmslie that while small boys would have to be kept from school in order to herd the cattle, 'he could send us scores of idle young men' instead.[50] Mbelwa's acceptance of the missionaries, however, was motivated, if my analysis is correct, not by any desire to utilize them in modernizing the state structure, as in Buganda, or by establishing favourable contacts on a popular level with a larger society, as with the Tonga, but rather by the wish to remove a source of internal conflict by making the material assets of the mission widely available, and perhaps in the hope that with stations in every part of the kingdom, it would act as an integrating force in a splintering polity. The consequence was that the initial impetus towards education was relatively muted. Scholars at Njuyu amounted to nearly ninety in March 1889, and further schools were opened at Chinyera Mlima and Ekwendeni, so that by 1890 attendance in the whole of Ngoniland stood at the 500 mark, and at an average of nearly 600 three years later. At Njuyu, however, Elmslie was forced to follow the example of many other missionaries in Central Africa in providing presents for those who came regularly, while at Ekwendeni attendance fell by half within two months of opening.[51]

A crucial weakness of the mission's educational work was its failure to provide worthwhile benefits for those it wished to attract. In the absence of opportunities within the Ngoni state the only immediate beneficiaries were the small band of teachers—forty of them in 1893—employed at rates of up to five shillings a month.[52] Other Ngoni worked as labourers in the service of the mission, and one, Chitezi, received a contract to make and deliver bricks for mission buildings, though the rate at which he was paid—four shillings per 1,000 bricks—cannot have permitted him to accumulate considerable capital.[53] In the absence of any local market other than that provided by the mission, possible developments in this sphere were clearly very limited; and as with the Tonga, though with far greater geographical obstacles to overcome, enterprising Ngoni increasingly came to look for wage labour beyond their homeland. In 1894 it was reported that a large number of carriers employed on the expedition to seek a suitable site for the Livingstonia Institution came from Ekwendeni.[54] They formed the vanguard for a mass exodus of labour which by 1914 was to rival even that from Tongaland. New ladders for the ambitious were being created. Advancement was no longer to depend entirely on prowess in war.

As in other parts of the country, missionary influence where it penetrated deepest did so primarily among the weakest portions of the people and among those most intimately connected with the mission's work. The first pupils at Njuyu, two of whom became the first Ngoni converts, in April 1890, were three sons of a diviner from Senga country, Mawelero Tembo, Makara Tembo and Chitezi. According to their father in a statement reported and possibly embellished by Elmslie, 'We were nothing till you came—you have made us forget we are slaves as we are all treated alike by you.'[55] Several other early pupils at Njuyu were also slave children—Elmslie argued that they were quicker to learn than the true Ngoni; while at Ekwendeni, even during the first days of teaching when curiosity was at its height, the children of Chief Mtwalo were among the small number not attending.[56] The first pupils became in their turn the first teachers, and then the first converts. When Steele in 1892 performed the second baptismal service in Ngoniland, eight of the nine converts were teachers, and the ninth was the wife of Mawelero Tembo.[57]

Even in the 1890s, however, the ambiguity in the attitude of Ngoni authorities was beginning to wear thin. If members of the Jere clan were among the most resolute in opposing missionary advances as likely to destroy the integrity of the kingdom and undermine military values, they were also those most closely in touch with the missionaries—with the exception of the converts and teachers—and those whom the missionaries were most anxious to influence: 'if we can get teachers of a high "tshibango" (caste)', wrote Elmslie, 'so much the better'.[58] By July 1888 one member of the royal clan was serving as a cook at Njuyu. In November 1889 he became a teacher, and was baptized with the other teachers 2½ years later.[59] More significant, several of Mtwalo's children at Ekwendeni came under the mission's influence, notably Mzikuwola, who later took the name of Yohane, the eldest son of Mtwalo, though by a junior wife, and Muhawi, later known as Amon, the true heir. Both were attending school in October 1890 at the time of their father's death. In the succeeding interregnum the missionaries, under the misconception that Mzikuwola would succeed—or had succeeded—to the chieftaincy, quickly made him a teacher, a position not attained by his potentially more powerful half-brother till 1893. They also used their persuasion to such effect that Mzikuwola, though not yet baptized, began reading the Commandments to the people of his village, weighed his influence against the despatch of war-parties, and only agreed to go out on a raid into the Luangwa valley in 1891 on the private understanding with McCallum that he personally would kill no one.[60] Though only eleven converts existed in Ngoniland in 1892, the close alliance forged by the missionaries with some members of the ruling sector ensured that when the breakthrough did come it should have the effect of perpetuating existing privilege rather than of replacing it by a new political order.

There can be little doubt that the extension of British colonial rule in Malawi from 1891 offered a challenge to the northern Ngoni to which they could accomodate themselves only with difficulty. Despite the striking changes effected through missionary contact in the 1880s, the revolution in their society was not complete when H. H. Johnston took up the reins of administration and it was by no means clear whether as raiding military people they would be prepared peacefully to accept the suzerainty of an overlord. With the death of Mbelwa in August 1891 and the subsequent growth of disunity within the kingdom in the four years' interregnum before Chimtunga's accession to the paramountcy, the likelihood of direct confrontation appeared to most observers to be great.[61] A marked increase in sporadic raiding expeditions took place in 1892 and 1893, and these led even some of Livingstonia's agents to demand the destruction of the Ngoni kingdom.[62] That this was avoided in the early 1890s can be accounted by circumstances beyond the control of the Ngoni —the remoteness of their homeland from the seats of administrative and economic power and the fact that, unlike their southern cousins at Ncheu, they placed no obstacle in the path of labour recruitment for European plantations.[63] A further factor was the necessary embarrassment involved for any colonial régime in intervening forcibly in an area where mission stations were already well established. This latter point, according to Johnston, was uppermost in his decision after the defeat of the north-end Arabs, not to turn against the Ngoni at once but to deal with the Chewa chief, Mwase Kasungu, instead.[64] And when Mwase Kasungu had been defeated and his headman Chabisa had fled to N'gonomo for protection, it was only Elmslie's opposition to the plans of the Collector at Nkhota Kota for a punitive raid and his ability to get Ngoni chiefs to send letters to the Consul-General professing friendship that persuaded Johnston not to intervene unless directly provoked.[65]

In the breathing space thus provided the Ngoni witnessed repeated demonstrations of the superiority of British arms, not only in the campaign against the Arabs and Mwase Kasungu, but also against Gomani's Ngoni from Ncheu in 1896 and against Mpeseni's Ngoni two years later. Whether the lesson to be drawn from the expeditions was the futility of armed resistance or the need to resist on a wider scale than before was not at once apparent. While some chiefs, notably those in close contact with the mission, favoured conciliation, others, headed by Ng'onomo, looked instead, if the scattered and sometimes contradictory reports of Government and missionary agents are to be trusted, to the re-establishment of links between the various Ngoni groups, and particularly with Mpeseni.[66] But even at this stage Ng'onomo combined defiance with a desire to negotiate and in 1897 sent a present of ivory to the Collector at Nkhota Kota as a token of his friendship.[67] With the defeat of Mpeseni he repudiated any connection between them and turned decisively to a British alliance. So great was now the apprehension of the northern Ngoni that when Major Harding's expedition landed at Bandawe in June or July 1898 many feared that the Administration had designs upon them and sought to escape by fleeing to the lake and west to the Luangwa valley.[68] In involving themselves in a wage economy the young men of warrior age were implicitly rejecting raiding as a primary occupation, a point clearly made in the 1890s when, following Mpeseni's request to join him against the whites, a section among them proved to be the most resolute opponents of the resumption of warfare.[69]

The fact that direct conflict was only averted even at this period by the missionary presence is striking evidence of the importance of European attitudes in determining whether or not African societies would openly resist their advance. Hitherto the absence of European economic interests among them had gone far to explain why the northern Ngoni were left undisturbed. From 1898, however, a trickle of gold-prospectors and cattle-dealers, anxious to recoup the losses they had suffered in Southern Rhodesia, began to push into the northern highlands. They were followed, though at a distance, by

British administrative agents, who having established a government post at Nkhata Bay in 1897, circumscribed the Ngoni's freedom of action by refusing to recognize their rights of suzerainty over Tumbuka subjects spreading south in search of new land. From 1903 Ngoni and Tumbuka alike were authorized to bring their disputes direct to the *Boma* at the lake. The next year parties of Yao policemen were sent deep into Ngoniland to collect taxes and to burn the villages of those who would not pay.[70]

The inevitable reaction to the extension of the colonial frontier came in 1899 when the activities of the notorious trader W. R. Ziehl in commandeering cattle without payment so inflamed the Ngoni against him that only the swift intervention of Donald Fraser prevented an expedition being sent in pursuit.[71] Five years later further friction resulted from the attempt of police to raise taxes within the watershed of the Rukuru, and once again Fraser's intervention was required to dissuade the police from intervening further. By this time land under Ngoni control had become so wasted that thousands of them, headed by Tumbuka subjects, were beginning to move south beyond the boundaries previously established by H. H. Johnston. It was this move which created the conditions in which, on 2 September 1904, an agreement between the Ngoni and Administration was finally achieved.

At a time when the positive effects of resistance are being rediscovered it is well to emphasize the substantial benefits gained by the Ngoni from negotiation. On a purely negative side the 1904 treaty ensured that the transition of power would take place as painlessly as possible. Taxation was not to be commenced before January 1906; none of the old quarrels between the Ngoni and other peoples were to be pursued further; no Tonga or Yao police were to be used in Ngoniland; Ngoni police were to be recruited as far as possible; and six chiefs, headed by Chimtunga were to receive subsidies. More positively, the major interests of the Ngoni were largely respected. Cattle, Sharpe promised, would not be confiscated for offences; no sudden scattering of subjects beyond their chiefs' control would be allowed; the Ngoni would be free to hunt on the bend of the Rukuru river. Above all, land would be found for those who wanted it beyond the limits of their own now exhausted domain. The Ngoni people would be preserved as a nation rather than destroyed.[72]

Such a settlement could hardly have been achieved had the extension of formal rule not been taking place side by side with the massive popular response of many Ngoni and Tumbuka to the missionary message. During the 1890s two new factors helped to increase the attraction of the mission. The improved labour opportunities in the Shire highlands and elsewhere contributed to a new appreciation of the commercial value of education, which led in its turn to a marked expansion in attendance. From 1893 when 630 pupils were enrolled in ten schools in Ngoniland, numbers expanded so considerably that by 1898 the highest number attending in a day was 4,040. The introduction of school fees hindered the advance in the next three years, but in 1901 55 schools existed with an average of 2,800 pupils.[73] A few years later the southern sphere, organized from the station of Hora, and later from Loudon, was divided for administrative purposes from that run from Ekwendeni. So vigorously did it thrive that in 1904 it alone maintained 134 schools

228

with up to 9,000 pupils.[74] By 1909, 150 out-schools were open there with 12,000 pupils and Fraser, the missionary in charge, could question 'whether there is another mission in the world with so great school systems attached to one station as you will find in the Livingstonia Mission'.[75]

The other new factor was the spread of evangelical Christianity, influenced no doubt by the new approach towards problems of conversion that Fraser in particular introduced, but taking on some of the characteristics of a witch-craft eradication movement. Introduced in Tongaland as early as 1895, the wave of enthusiasm burst upon the Ngoni three years later. At Ekwendeni in May 1898 a four-day communion season was held which attracted congregations of between 3,000 and 4,000 and gave rise to intense evangelical fervour. 'Among some of the teachers God seemed to be moving mightily', wrote Fraser.

'At one of the evening meetings with them, after I had spoken of backsliding and the need for re-consecration, we had a time of open prayer. Man after man prayed making broken confessions of sin, some were sobbing aloud, others gave way to severe physical emotion and became hysterical.'[76]

Some teachers in the tradition of John the Baptist, spent nights in prayer out in the bush, and were rewarded with visions of 'bright angelic forms' which Fraser, now thoroughly alarmed, attempted to dispel through medicinal doses at the dispensary. In 1892 there had been only 11 converts in Ngoniland. In 1898, 195 adults were baptized in a day, and a year later 672 Church members took communion watched by crowds 6,000 or 7,000 strong.[77] By 1909 some 2,000 were applying for admittance to the Church at a single session, and 683 adults and children were being baptized in a day.[78]

The question of the wider effects of the popular explosion on Livingstonia's relations with the Ngoni can be answered only with diffidence in a work based largely on written material. From the 1880s missionary strategy had been dedicated to the spreading of influence over a wide area rather than to the creation of closed enclaves. The distinction between German missionaries among the Nyakyusa who sought to organize their converts into closed mission villages and the Scots in Ngonde who recommended that Christians should remain in their own homes to influence their neighbours has been pertinently made by Monica Wilson.[79] No schools for the sons of chiefs were specially established and so no formal alliance with particular Christian groups or tribal elites were expressly created. In practice, however, the breakdown of the isolated position of the missionary elite led in Ngoniland to the substantial identification of leaders within the traditional political structure with the newly-educated classes. In June 1897 Muhawi (Amon), now a mission teacher, officially succeeded his father Mtwalo as ruler over the Ekwendeni segment, while his half brother, Mzikuwola (or Yohane), also a teacher, became one of his sub-chiefs.[80] Impressed perhaps by Elmslie's warning that without education the sons of chiefs and councillors would decline to the level of slaves and carriers, Maulau, a further segment head, requested the teacher Makara Tembo in 1895 to reside at his village where his eldest son put away his wives

229

and was baptized two years later.[81] Mperembe, Mbelwa's half-brother, praised the work of the teachers, though gaining little himself from education, while Chimtunga, the new paramount, received a modicum of instruction and sent his own son to school.[82] By 1900 when at least four members of the Jere clan, including Muhawi, were teaching at Ekwendeni central school, the cycle had begun whereby members of the royal clan passed from school to institution and became teachers, before entering the tribal authority structure where the social pressures upon them, and particularly the need to take more than one wife, led to their suspension from church membership, as Muhawi was suspended in 1906.[83]

But whether missionary education was related to status, as to some degree it was among the Ngoni, or to earlier alliances made by the mission with particular villages, as was the case with the Tonga, the fact remained that the political importance of mission teachers in the north grew significantly as the European presence became more intense. Ngoni chiefs and Tonga alike, who formerly had sought the alliance only of white teachers, now turned to Africans to act as intermediaries in their relations with the wider world. Mawalero Tembo and his colleagues threw their weight successfully against the despatch of a military expedition following the coronation of Chimtunga in 1897; they were consulted on matters affecting the action of the Administration, particularly on doubtful court cases where an adverse decision could lead to Government intervention; and one of their number, David Zinyoka, acted as interpreter when Sharpe, in 1904, held discussions with Ngoni chiefs.[84] Moreover, they took a line on European intrusion that brought them into conflict from time to time with members of yet another new authority structure, the police, and which won them a reputation as trouble-makers among Government officials. In Tongaland between 1903 and 1905 the 'very great influence' of mission teachers was blamed for the failure of labour recruitment campaigns.[85] In Ngonde mission teachers were criticized for 'spreading foolish and false reports about the civil police, to whom they attribute every imaginable crime'.[86] In Ngoniland mission teachers personally expostulated with W. R. Ziehl when he tried to seize cattle from individuals who refused to part with them, and after 1904 spoke on occasions to the local magistrate H. C. McDonald about 'civil evils that were hindering progress' and 'plans for the people'.[87] No less than in the 1880s they attempted a secular role alongside their educational one; but whereas before their attempts at interference only underlined the isolation of their position, now and increasingly into the 1920s, they came to conceive of themselves, and to be accepted, as spokesmen to the colonial authorities and as representatives of their people.

III

Although it is difficult to generalize about the consequences of the missionary impact on northern Malawi, two points may be made with some confidence. Firstly, it is clear that the dynamic response of various northern peoples, when combined with Livingstonia's own exceptional concern for change, had the

230

effect of making the northern province the most advanced area in terms of educational activity of any in Central Africa. By 1904, sixty per cent of the pupils receiving education in Malawi did so in Livingstonia's schools, while almost all those obtaining post-primary training attended the Overtoun Institution. Despite the drastic fall in Livingstonia's proportion of pupils and schools by the 1920s, the pattern thus established continued unchanged in essentials.[88] Second, it can be argued that the involvement of some members of the Jere clan in mission activities is also a matter of considerable significance. The aim of most pre-colonial educational systems was to integrate individuals effectively within their society. Mission education, on the other hand, was divisive by nature, being open to some groups and closed to others. By associating themselves with Livingstonia, the Jere helped to create a certain continuity which had its effect on the political character of northern Ngoniland in the years after the first world war. Instead of opposing the paramount and his peers as conservative traditionalists, the new men of the 1920s were to ally themselves with Ngoni authorities, and to seek to further their cause against colonial pressures.

FOOTNOTES

1 This paper is based on research undertaken for my larger work, 'Livingstonia Mission and the Evolution of Malawi, 1875–1939', Cambridge Ph.D., 1967.

2 C. C. Wrigley, 'The Christian Revolution in Buganda', *Comparative Studies in Society and History* II (1959).

3 See particularly, J. van Velsen, 'The Missionary Factor among the Lakeside Tonga of Nyasaland', *Rhodes–Livingstone J.*, **26**, 1959.

4 A. Sharpe to Sir C. Hill, 14 January 1897, F.O. 2/127. Sharpe is of course referring to the Kru people of the Windward Coast, many of whom worked in European ships and trading establishments from the eighteenth century.

5 *Free Church of Scotland Monthly Record*, August 1889; April 1890, 106.

6 Ibid, October 1903, 457.

7 Livingstonia Mission Report 1906, 32.

8 Moffat's views are strikingly expressed in J. P. R. Wallis (ed.), *Matabele Journals of Robert and Emily Moffat*, London, 1945, 256–7.

9 W. A. Elmslie, *Among the Wild Ngoni*, Edinburgh 1899, 78.

10 R. W. Beachey, 'The Arms Trade in East Africa in the Late Nineteenth Century', *J. Afr. Hist.*, **3**, 1962, 3. A valuable article which stresses how unimportant firearms were in East-Central Africa up to the 1880s is Andrew D. Roberts, 'Firearms in North-Eastern Zambia before 1900', *Trans-Afr. J. Hist.*, **2**, 1970.

11 T. Cullen Young, *Notes on the History of the Tumbuka-Kamanga Peoples in the Northern Province of Nyasaland*, London 1932, 125.

12 *F.C. Monthly Record*, April 1878 p. 86; Diary of John Gunn, entry for 9 November 1878, National Library of Scotland mss 7906.

13 Bandawe Journal entry for 28 October 1885, N.L.S. mss 7911; Diary of Dr Laws entry for 20 Nov. 1882, Laws Papers, Edinburgh University Library.

14 Elmslie to Laws, 7 Nov. 1887, N.L.S. mss 7890.

15 Elmslie to Laws, 22 Nov. 1886, Shepperson Collection, Edinburgh.

16 Elmslie to Laws, 10 Dec. 1887, N.L.S. mss 7890; 13 May 1888, N.L.S. mss 7891.

17 J. A. Barnes, *Politics in a Changing Society*, London 1954 pp. 24–5. Y. M. Chibambo, *My Ngoni of Nyasaland*, London 1942, 39–41.

18 Elmslie to Laws, 29 Jan. 1885, Shepperson Collection.

19 Margaret Read, *The Ngoni of Nyasaland*, Oxford 1956 pp. 49–50, 137.

20 Goodrich to F.O., 24 April 1885, F.O. 84, 1702.

21 Ibid.; G. Williams to Laws, Dec. 1884, Shepperson Collection.

22 G. Williams to Laws 7 Oct. 1886, Shepperson Collection.

23 Elmslie to Cross, 8 Feb. 1886, Shepperson Collection. For a similar situation among Mpezeni's Ngoni see Barnes, *Politics*, 46.

24 Ibid., 57–61.

25 Elmslie to Dr Smith, 29 May 1885 quoted in *F.C. Monthly Record*, Oct. 1885.

26 Elmslie to Laws, 23 Dec. 1885, Shepperson Collection.

27 G. Williams to Laws, 27 Jan. 1887, N.L.S. mss 7890.

28 Kaningina Station Journal entry for 20 Dec. 1878, N.L.S. mss 7910.

29 Ibid entry for 1 Oct. 1879.

30 Ibid., entry for 20 Dec. 1878.

31 Sutherland to Laws, 23 Dec. 1884, Shepperson Collection.

32 Elmslie to Laws 9 June 1885, Shepperson Collection.

33 Chibambo, p. 23; Elmslie, *Wild Ngoni*, 23–24; Read, *Ngoni*, 179–80. For a dramatic rendering of the Zulu equivalent see E. A. Ritter, *Shaka Zulu*, London, 7 imp. 1962, 241–54.

34 Williams to Laws, 7 Oct. 1886, Shepperson Collection.

35 Elmslie to Laws, 10 May 1886 Shepperson Collection; Elmslie 25 June 1886, quoted in *F.C. Monthly Record*, Dec. 1886, 365.

36 Elmslie to Laws, 5 Nov. 1886, Shepperson Collection.

37 Elmslie to Laws, 10 August 1887, N.L.S. mss 7890; Elmslie 23 Aug. 1887 in *F.C. Monthly Record*, Feb. 1885, 45.

38 Elmslie to Laws, 10 Aug. 1887, N.L.S. mss 7890.

39 Elmslie to Laws, 15 Oct. 1886, 12 Oct. 1885; Elmslie to Cross, 8 Feb. 1886 Shepperson Collection.

40 Elmslie to Laws, 24 Aug. 1887, N.L.S. mss 7890.

41 Elmslie to Laws, 24 Sept. 1887 and 15 Sept. 1887, N.L.S. mss 7890.

42 See reports in *F.C. Monthly Record*, March 1887, p. 76 and in Laws to Smith, 8 Nov. 1887, quoted in *Scottish Leader*, 27 Jan. 1888, cutting in N.L.S. mss 7906.

43 Elmslie, *Wild Ngoni*, 94.

44 See Sutherland to Laws, 17 June 1885, Williams to Laws 2 Oct. 1886, Shepperson Collection.

45 McCallum to Laws, 16 Nov. 1889, N.L.S. mss 7892; Elmslie, 'Report for Ngoniland District', 1895, N.L.S. mss 7878.

46 Elmslie to Laws, 10 Dec. 1887, N.L.S. mss 7890; 26 Dec. 1887, N.L.S. mss 7891.

47 Elmslie to Laws, 13 May 1888, N.L.S. mss 7891.

48 Chibambo, *My Ngoni*, p. 53; Fraser to Dr Smith, 20 Oct. 1896, N.L.S. mss 7880; Donald Fraser, *Winning a Primitive People*, London 1914, 41.

49 *F.C. Monthly Record*, Sept. 1887, 271; Elmslie, *Wild Ngoni*, 166–7.

50 Elmslie to Laws, 15 Oct. 1886, Shepperson Collection.

51 Elmslie to Laws, 24 Nov. 1888, N.L.S. mss 7891; McCallum to Laws, 10 Dec. 1889, N.L.S. mss 7892.

52 Livingstonia Mission Report 1893–4, 8.

53 Elmslie to Laws, 18 Aug. 1888, N.L.S. mss 7891.

54 Livingstonia Mission Report July–Dec. 1894, 14.

55 Quoted in Elmslie to Cross, 8 Feb. 1886, Shepperson Collection.

56 Elmslie to Laws, 16 Dec. 1888, N.L.S. mss 7891; McCallum to Laws, 16 Dec. 1887, N.L.S. mss 7892.

57 Steele to Laws, 4 May 1892, M.L.S. mss 7896.

58 Elmslie to Laws, 17 July 1888, N.L.S. mss 7891.

59 Ibid; Elmslie to Laws, 22 Nov. 1889, N.L.S. mss 7892; Livingstonia Mission Report, 1893–4, 8.

60 W. H. J. Rangeley, 'Mtwalo', *Nyasa. J.*, **6**, 1952, 65–8; McCallum to Laws, 27 Dec. 1890, N.L.S. mss 7894, 17 Mar. 1891, 2 May 1891, N.L.S. mss 7895; Steele to Laws, 13 Jan. 1892, N.L.S. mss 7896.

61 Rangeley, 'Mtwalo', 67–8; Steele to Laws, 13 Jan. 1892, N.L.S. mss 7896; J. G. Phillips, 8 April 1896 quoted in *Central Africa*, Aug. 1896, 136.

62 See the remarks of Kerr Cross, *Central Africa*, April 1893, 50–52.

63 For a brief summary based largely on a chapter by Eric Stokes in *The Zambesian Past* see John McCracken, 'Malawi in the Nineteenth Century' in T. O. Ranger (ed.), *Aspects of Central African History*, London 1968.

64 *Report . . . on the Trade and General Condition of the British Central African Protectorate*, 1895–96, Cmd. 8254, 13.

65 Elmslie to Dr Smith, 24 June, 1896, N.L.S. mss 7879; Swann to Laws,

14 Feb. 1897, Laws Papers. Johnston's reply is quoted in Fraser, *Primitive People*, 239.

66 Swann to Laws, 14 Feb. 1897, Laws Papers. A survey of the evidence is provided in a footnote on p. 258 of my dissertation.

67 *Aurora*, June 1898, 24.

68 Ibid, Aug. 1898, 32.

69 Elmslie to Hetherwick, 27 March 1915, Hetherwick Paper, Zomba.

70 *Aurora*, April 1901, p. 4; Monthly Report Nkhata, 1 Jan. 1904, Zomba NNC 3/4/1; Fraser, *Primitive People*, 240.

71 *Aurora*, June 1899, 21–3; Fraser, *Primitive People*, 103–11.

72 The only full record of the agreement that I know is to be found in the Mzimba District Book dated 24 Oct. 1904. Another less detailed account appears in Sharpe to C.O., 14 Oct. 1904, C.O. 525/3.

73 Livingstonia Mission Report, 1901, p. 14, 1902, 31.

74 Ibid, 1904, 31.

75 Ibid, 1909, 23.

76 Fraser to Smith, 16 May 1898, N.L.S. mss 7881.

77 Ibid; 7 June 1899, N.L.S. mss 7882 Livingstonia Mission Report, 1898–1899, p. 111.

78 *F.C. Monthly Record*, Oct. 1909, 450.

79 Monica Wilson, *Good Company*, London 1951, 42.

80 Livingstonia Mission Report, 1897–98, 11–12.

81 Elmslie, 'Report on Ngoniland District', 1895, N.L.S. mss 7878; Livingstonia Mission Report July–Dec. 1895, p. 12; Jan–June 1896, 16; *Aurora*, June 1897, 22.

82 Fraser to Dr Smith, 20 Oct. 1897, N.L.S. mss 7880; Fraser, *Primitive People*, 49–50.

83 Livingstonia Mission Report, 1897–98, 1906, 24; Fraser, 'The Growth of the Church in the Mission Field', *International Review of Missions*, II

(1913), 238.

84 Livingstonia Mission Report, 1897–98, 12; *Aurora*, Oct. 1902, 86; Personal communication from Rev. Z. P. Ziba, 24 July 1964, Loudon; *F.C. Monthly Record*, Jan., 1905, 25.

85 Annual Report of the Collector, Nkhata, 1903–4, Zomba NNC 3/1/1; Monthly Report of the Collector, Nkhata, 1 Aug. 1904; 1 Dec. 1905, Zomba NNC 3/4/1.

86 Sharpe to F.O., 19 May 1902, F.O. 2/606.

87 Donald Fraser, *The Autobiography of an African*, London, 1925, 203.

88 According to my calculations, Livingstonia possessed 61 per cent of all schools in Malawi in 1904–5, 31 per cent in 1910, 16 per cent in 1924 and 10·18 per cent in 1934. In that year, however, 32·45 per cent of assisted upper and lower schools were run by Livingstonia.

14 The Maseko Ngoni at Domwe: 1870-1900[1]

Ian Linden

When the Maseko Ngoni settled in Domwe c.1870 their society had already been shaped by almost fifty years of warfare and migrations. The army, organized on an age-set principle, brought together 'captives from the march' with different tribal backgrounds. To avoid bids for power by close relatives of the paramount *alumuzana* and *izinduna*, who occupied the positions of political power within the state, were chosen not from the royal family but from members of the aristocratic Swazi clans.

'When the Ngoni were coming from the south they chose lesser chiefs and *izinduna* from the *amakosana*, who were the paramount's brothers, sons of his father and of his father's brothers. These amakosana were honoured next to the paramount. The *alumuzana* were for justice in the courts and for being the ears of the paramount in all the country. The change was made by Mputa because he saw that if the *amakosana* were given power they claimed to be big chiefs themselves. Therefore he chose for the courts and for leaders in war and for lesser chiefs the *alumuzana* and *izinduna* who were clever and whom he could trust.'[2]

Such leaders, chosen for loyalty to the paramount, extended his rule over assimilated groups and minimized the danger of local revolts. Religious office was held by members of minor clans and recently assimilated groups whose role in society was strictly circumscribed. In short, as the Maseko made their permanent settlement around Domwe mountain in the Dedza district of Malawi, they formed a tightly knit, centralized society based on the strength, both military and social, of a well-trained army.

The internal vigour and potential for expansion of this system was apparent during the heyday of Maseko power between 1870–85. Its weakness and inability to respond to changing circumstances became equally evident in the last fifteen years of the nineteenth century. The division of the period 1870–1900 into the categories 'rise' and 'fall' is simple, though unoriginal, but corresponds broadly with the facts.

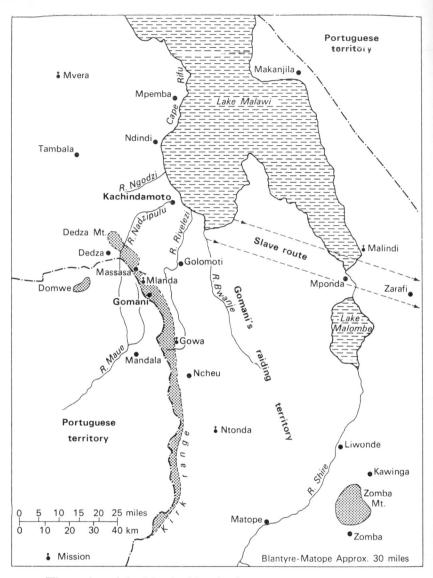

14.1   The region of the Maseko Ngoni, 1870–1900

The Dedza district formed the periphery of Mpezeni's raiding territory and there seems to have been an initial degree of overlap between the two Ngoni kingdoms. The Fort Jameson (now known as Chipata) Ngoni appear to have attacked Domwe at least once, and there is evidence that Magwambane, a cousin of Mpezeni, was killed during one such abortive raid.[3] The Maseko themselves were raiding mainly in an arc to the east of Domwe, extending from Nkhoma in the North to South of the Shire. Ntumba, Chipeta, Nyanja and Mbo villages were brought under Ngoni rule. Few Chewa villages managed to withstand the Ngoni onslaughts unless they were fortunate enough to occupy relatively impregnable positions, such as the top of Chirenje mountain where Chief Odete held out until dislodged by British cannon in 1898. The more gently sloping mountain opposite Chirenje, and rising above Kasina mission, known significantly by older people as 'Chidiaonga',[4] has the remains of a burnt-out village still visible on its summit.

Chidiaonga, the regent, died in the early 1870s and Chikusi, who had until then been in the care of Mputa's chief wife, Namlangeni, became paramount. By 1875 Chikusi was proving himself in raids across the Shire on Yao villages.[5] Already the area between Murchison Falls (now known as Kolombidzo) and Lake Malombe was beginning to show signs of depredations by the powerful Yao.[6] The force of the Maseko can be gauged by the response of the Kololo chiefs in the lower Shire; stockaded villages were built at the main fords on the Shire staffed by Kololo, or headmen drawn from their Mang'anja vassals. In 1884 Chikusi's raiding parties bribed their way across the river again to put the fear of God into the European population of the Shire highlands. The ostensible reason for this crossing was to offer assistance to Malemia at Zomba against another Yao chief, Kawinga.[7]

The impressive Ngoni advance, reaching even to the sacred groves of Buchanan's coffee plantation, was cut short at Mkanda hill, where a stand by the Yao, backed up with strong fire-power and watched by the Church of Scotland missionaries, had a group of the Maseko retreating through Blantyre. This massive trans-Shire raid was a harbinger of future events; in the face of superior Yao fire-power the Maseko could be thrown into disarray.

The Yao invasion of Malawi that gained momentum in the 1860s had dramatically altered the political and economic situation around the southern end of Lake Malawi. Slave caravans converged on the area of present-day Fort Johnston as the Yao chiefs in the Mlanje and Zomba districts became profitably involved as middlemen in the coastal slave trade. Although chiefs such as Mponda, Makanjila, Matapwiri and Zarafi had fewer followers than Chikusi, their possession of powerful Enfield rifles brought by Arabs from the coast more than offset the numerical superiority of the Ngoni. By the 1880s the southern end of the lake was ringed with Yao chieftainships, from Mpemba and Tambala around Cape Rifu to Makanjila opposite them on the other side of the lake. In the centre, by the Shire, was Mponda whose strength in 1884 can be guessed from the following entry in the diary kept by an employee of the African Lakes Company:

'He had sitting round him about 40 of those low caste arabs and all were armed with guns. . . . Mponda showed the captain a goodly number of Enfield rifles and as he showed them he boasted that now he had as many guns as the white man.'[8]

The Maseko found themselves on the edge of a major slave route that stretched from Mwase Kasungu's in the north to the coastal ports of Mozambique and southern Tanzania. This was not entirely to their disadvantage. The large numbers of Chewa-speaking groups falling under Ngoni hegemony from 1870 onwards risked swamping Maseko society with captives that could only be absorbed with difficulty. The slave trade with the lakeshore Yao and Chikunda middlemen from the Zambezi valley offered a convenient method for disposing of the unassimilable and the socially undesirable.

This pressure from Chewa groups with their alien traditions and social organization might account for the centralization of Chikusi's kingdom that began during this period; his capital, Liwisini, was to grow considerably in size.[9] This concentration of population may have been forced on the paramount by the few aristocratic Swazi-clan members at his disposal. Hawes observed in 1886 that: 'Of the real Angoni, with the exception of the King, his numerous wives and family, the Chiefs of districts and towns, and the Headmen of villages, but few exist.'[10] This aristocracy had to serve a kingdom that extended from Domwe to Mpimbi, on the Shire, and the edge of the Pirilongwe forest, as well as to an ill-defined extent westwards. To make his presence felt even more the paramount took up residence in each of his major villages for a period of the year.

Perhaps the most serious defect of the Maseko custom of passing over the *amakosana* in the choice of leading indunas was that disaffected members of the royal family were given little incentive to support the paramount. Coupled with this there was the problem of the regency; on the death of the regent his son was passed over in favour of the legitimate patrilineal heir to the paramountcy. For the son of Chidiaonga, a regent who had been in power during the long march from Songea to Dedza and had established the Domwe settlement, the sight of a young cousin as paramount must have been extremely galling. Chifisi, Chidiaonga's son, had every reason for disentangling his segment from Chikusi's jurisdiction.

These tensions were aggravated in the 1880s by the sheer success of the Ngoni raids. Unlike the situation on the march, once settled, the paramount found it impossible to restrain the build-up of local regiments belonging to particular indunas, defined territorially rather than by age-set. Such brigades were able to swell their ranks with captives from local raids to create formidable little armies not directly controlled by the paramount. This problem would have been more acute when a young paramount was surrounded with older, more experienced indunas, at the beginning of his reign. Chikusi's attempts to centralize his polity can also be understood in the light of this need to control the proliferation of semi-autonomous local regiments.[11]

There can be little doubt that before 1890 Chifisi built up such an army, the Njokozera war division, which became independent from, and a powerful threat to, Chikusi's paramountcy. At the same time the lakeshore Yao, as yet free from British punitive expeditions, were at their apogee, walled up in strong stockades through which a steady trickle of slaves passed. The lesson of Songea seems to have been salutary for both Chikusi and Chifisi began forming strategic alliances with the Yao.[12]

With fortified villages along the Shire and the Blantyre area dominated by the Church of Scotland missionaries, it is not surprising that both Maseko

240

leaders turned their attention to the old Mpinganjıla crossing between the two lakes, where the self-titled Mponda II had made his stockade.[13] This part of the Shire was not only a weak link in the slave route to Angoche but, owing to the Chungwarungwaru war between Mponda II and his relatives, a weak point in Machinga control of the southern end of the lake.

By 1889 Chifisi had made an alliance with Mponda who doubtless saw in this incipient Ngoni civil war a way to relieve himself of an annual tribute to Chikusi.[14] Chikusi, in turn, allied with Mponda's enemies, Malunda and Chungwarungwaru, so that the Ngoni and Yao succession disputes had, as it were, coalesced; a remarkable example of how much the need for well-timed alliances had been impressed on the Maseko by the débâcle at Songea. As a result of the alliance Ngoni troops moved into the Lake Malombe area and 400 of Chifisi's men under his war induna, Gwaza, became loosely attached to Mponda as mercenaries. On 22 January 1891, Chikusi with his Yao allies mounted a major attack on Mponda, This battle, if the word can be used, was recorded by the White Fathers who were living at Mponda's stockade. It is worth describing it here in some detail as symptomatic of the declining prowess of the Ngoni:

'At daybreak the king comes to the mission asking for guns which we lend him. All along the outer stockade the men are on watch, laughing and joking like troops in their trenches. We find the king under a tree where he had taken up his position next to the Yao banner which was hoisted on the inner stockade. Seven barrels of powder and a pile of musket balls are stacked up on his mat. We arrive just as the Msano[15] is going out with the sorcerer to make some war medicine. On every one of the termite mounds sentries are mounted. In a space no bigger than a third of the stockade we count 300 guns—(which means 1,000 guns overall not to mention men only carrying their bows). . . . At a distance of 300–400 metres we see the Angoni advancing. With our field-glasses we can make out individuals with their enormous massed head-pieces. They advance slowly, very many of them, like an ant-heap on the move; Chungwarungwaru's men are with them. The enemy moves in slowly and inexorably, destroying the fields of mapemba as they go. Finally at 10.30 a.m. there is a fusillade from the south-west corner of the village. Five minutes later we can hear the 'lou-lou's' from the women. The enemy had fled at the first volley carrying off their dead and wounded. What cowardice for the redoubtable Angoni.'[16]

Later in March, after raiding parties from Mponda's had been harassing Chikusi's outlying villages, taking slaves, it seems, almost at will, a major assault was mounted on Liwisini and the capital looted and razed.[17] The conservative military tactics of the Maseko, their use of the shield and short stabbing spear, bows, arrows, and clubs with a minimum of old flintlock rifles was no match for the Machinga raiding parties. The conclusions of the missionaries on this score, whose testimony, after two years of close contact with Mponda, must be taken to be reliable, can hardly be gainsaid:

'We are no longer in the time of Mr. Steere, who in his introduction to Yao Grammar informs us that the Yao were members of a tribe using bows and arrows, despised by tribes with clubs, axes and spears like the Angonio. Thanks to guns, which have replaced bows and arrows, the roles now seem to be reversed. It is the Yao who despise the Angoni at least as much as they used to be despised themselves.'[18]

These remarks can profitably be contrasted with those of occasional visitors to the Ngoni such as Johnston and Hawes. Johnston's preconceptions were surely clouding his judgment when he expatiated on how Chikusi was 'by far the most powerful chief between the Zambezi and Lake Nyasa'.[19] Similarly four years earlier in 1886 Hawes was writing: 'It is undoubtedly owing to the despotic sway of the King that Angoni Land is kept under such complete control. He has absolute power ...'[20] The fascination of both administrators and missionaries with what they took to be the Ngoni *übermensch* says a lot for the darker recesses of the Victorian mind.

The year 1891 was a turning point for the Maseko Ngoni. Chifisi died in March and Chikusi in August, the last of the leaders moulded by the rigours of the *Mfecane*. With the Portuguese threat countered and Johnston as official Consul, planters began to come into the Shire highlands at a steady trickle. The rate is conveniently reflected in the rising cost of land, from a penny per acre in 1890 to two shillings and sixpence in 1893 with some plots in Blantyre going for up to £20 per acre.[21] The few Ngoni labourers who had come down to build Blantyre cathedral in the 1880s became hundreds, working as porters up and down the Shire, or as seasonal plantation labour. The Maseko had begun to lose their credibility,[22] not only in the eyes of the Yao but, more insidiously, in the sight of their own Chewa bondsmen.

Chifisi was succeeded by his eldest son, Pasekupe, known as Kachindamoto, who was then barely fifteen years old, while an equally youthful Gomani was established as paramount. An attack by Gomani on Kachindamoto was repulsed on a hill at Masasa's along the Ncheu-Dedza road, called Mwala-wa-Nkhondo, but later in the year Kachindamoto's main village, Muchokozwa was successfully sacked.[23] Both chiefs had an immediate need to prove their capabilities in warfare before their people.

By the end of October 1891 British punitive expeditions had made Mponda limit his activities. The two branches of the Maseko now turned their attention to the next most likely allies in the region, the British with their Sikh and Tonga mercenaries. Gomani began to angle for an alliance with the British in early 1892 but it was ultimately Kachindamoto's men who were enlisted in Johnston's campaign against Zarafi. 'These men came down in hundreds to assist us in fighting Zarafi', Johnston wrote and, with his enthusiasm for the Ngoni abating somewhat, added that they did not turn out to be so brave as they looked.[24]

One advantage for the Maseko of the continuing warfare against the Yao, and even the civil war, was that their regiments were kept active and trained in combat. The heart of Ngoni society, the army, was kept ticking over, not with impressive victories, captives and rich herds as of old, but at least enough to keep up morale. There was no other alternative once the Kirk Range began to 'dry up' and raids became increasingly more difficult and less profitable. It was already a losing battle as more and more Chewa 'Ngoni' began slipping away in the Yao and European economies. Finding Ngoni society anything but invincible many people were looking to other centres of power and prestige.

Mponda's supernumerary gardens, part of the economics of slavery, used to provide food for caravans en route for the coast, claimed a certain number. A report by Nicholl, the Collector for Central Angoniland, gives a little evidence as to the importance of the Yao economy: 'A large party of Ngoni, numbering about a hundred people were met, each carrying a load of grain— (the pay it was said for ten days work). It is well known that numbers of Angoni hoed for Mponda's Yao and their Swahili guests, even when their friends and relations were fighting Mponda's people'.[25]

The pull of the European economy was certainly greater. According to the editor of the B.C.A. Gazette: 'The help which is afforded this country by the Spring rush of the Ngoni, who after the crops are finished come down here for three to four months' work, was well demonstated in 1893.'[26] The influx of Ngoni labour had, in fact, become essential to the coffee and tobacco planters; with wages at five to six shillings the Ngoni provided a pool of cheap labour for crops yielding a small margin of profit.

The drain of manpower from the Maseko army must have been unsettling for Gomani. As a greater percentage of young men left the villages for long periods, working Mponda's fields and then as porters in the Blantyre and Chikwawa areas, returning with salt, grain and maybe twenty to thirty shillings, Ngoni society with its traditional 'martial way of life' risked being undermined. Travellers through the Dedza district began reporting widespread *mwabvi* ordeals imposed by Gomani, a typical symptom in Bantu society of rapid social change. And it is perhaps in this light that the renewal of widespread hostilities between Gomani and Kachindamoto in 1894 should be seen; as an attempt to pull their regiments together again, reassert the traditional values, and stop the flow of men to the British and Yao. If this is a correct analysis then Gomani's tactics succeeded; strong complaints were made by the planters in the Blantyre area as the flow of men coming across the Shire on the Tonga ferries dropped virtually to zero in 1894.[27]

In January 1894 Kachindamoto attacked Gomani a second time and was pushed back to Dedza. Mponda, acting as usual as a weather-vane for forces around the lake, changed sides and aided Gomani in a successful attack on Kachindamoto at Mlomo-wa-Nkhukhu (the chicken's beak), a hill near Dedza. Kachindamoto was heavily defeated and sent fleeing to Mlunduni, and from there to Tambala's. Mponda, working on the principle of 'divide and rule', favoured by Johnston in a similar position of manpower shortage, predictably refused to goad Kachindamoto into attacking him, and retired from the fray. He had done remarkably well from the Ngoni civil war. When his stockade was finally taken by the British in the following year it was found that of his 378 slaves, 27 were Ngoni and 128 were Chipeta from the Dedza/Domwe district, Gomani's preserve.[28]

Lacking Mponda's guns to destroy Kachindamoto, Gomani allied with the

243

Mangoche Yao of Cape Rifu, Tambala and Mpemba. Kachindamoto was forced to retreat again into the area of Chimbulanga, a minor chief of Ndindi. Possibly as repayment for favours rendered by Chifisi at an earlier date, Chimbulanga moved one of his villages, N'goma's, so that Kachindamoto could settle by the lake between the Nadzipulu and Ngodzi streams.[29]

At this point, in desperation, Kachindamoto sent messengers to Fort Johnston to request British assistance. He had been forced out of the Dedza district in January before the harvest, and had failed to get any food at Tambala's. Many of his women and children had begun to die of the foul water by the lake. When Major Edwards arrived at Kachindamoto's in early October 1894 he found a very frightened eighteen-year-old limping around with bullet wounds in his legs from his old friend Mponda's Enfields. Surrounding him were an armed bodyguard of over one hundred men carrying ancient flintlock rifles. His available strength could hardly have exceeded 1,300 men including some men from Chimbulanga's, under the direction of his surviving indunas, Kanyesi, Chakachadza, Chantulo, Ngundadzuwa and Gwaza.[30] Ranged against him at Kanjobvu on the other side of the mountains was Gomani with an estimated force of 5,000 men.[31]

The presence of the British saved Kachindamoto. Mpemba who had been in pursuit held off and on 31 October Ndindi came in apologetically to explain that he had fought only through fear of Tambala. Not surprisingly Kachindamoto pressed for a fort to be built in his new villages at Ntakataka, and for Edwards to negotiate a ceasefire. After a visit to Gomani, 12 November was set as the date for a meeting and a reluctant and disbelieving Kachindamoto limped across the mountain to Masasa's in the Dedza plain with his remaining warriors. There a scene of colonial high force was enacted as the two young chiefs were obliged to shake hands in front of a crowd of over 6,000 warriors, and under the approving gaze of the Revs. Robertson and Murray of the Dutch Reformed Church.

The missionaries were far from being mere onlookers at the colonial spectacle. Mission stations had multiplied in Central Angoniland, with Europeans at Livlezi, Mvera, Goa, Ntonda, Chioli and Pantumba. Many of Gomani's villages were beginning to slip into the orbit of the missions. The Europeans presence meant a serious curtailment of further raiding and recruitment into the army.

Equally challenging for Gomani, the efficiency and extent of B.C.A. government tax collecting was improving throughout Nyasaland. The £790 collected as hut tax in 1892 had risen to £4,696 by the end of 1895.[32] At a rate of three shillings per hut this represented more than 600 medium-sized villages under British control; the tax, levied on many villages that had been under Ngoni jurisdiction for twenty-five years, could only be considered an improper tribute paid to the British.

Towards the end of 1895 reports were reaching Zomba that Gomani had been buying guns and gunpowder from Zambezi traders and harassing villages paying hut tax. After an attempt by Gomani to enlist the support of Chiwere, a neighbouring Ngoni chief to the north-east, had failed owing to pressure from Dutch Reformed missionaries, the attacks came on 6 October 1896 and were centred predictably on mission stations and villages that had been paying hut tax. In the words of Chief Gania of Kandeu: 'Chief Gomani was angry that the women who lived at the Goa mission wore "luvi" feathers in their hats. He went to the mission to tell them to take them off.'[33] If it is recalled that 'luvi' feathers in the head-dress were a symbol of the paramount's power, this account of events becomes delightfully analytic. Villages paying hut tax under mission influence were flaunting Gomani's authority. The two ladies at Goa were, indeed, a challenge.

The first reports that 600 Ngoni had been killing mission natives and asking for calico, sent in by Mr Barclay from the Zambezi Industrial Mission at Ntonda, reached a somewhat jittery government: 'In view of the events in Mashonaland it would be a dangerous course for me to delay any operations against Chikusi' wrote Sharpe.[34] Although Zomba had been genuinely shaken by the news of the Mashonaland risings, this was partly humbug. No European had been touched during the raids. With the Yao subdued, the Fort Jameson and Dedza Ngoni came into the front line of British pacification efforts. Johnston's vain hope in 1893 that Gomani would come to heel had been dissipated long ago, and some campaign was doubtless already in the offing.[35]

Given such an excellent excuse Sharpe did not waste any time. On 12 October, Captain Stewart left Zomba for Fort Liwonde and Dedza while Manning came down the lake from Tambala's in a gunboat. By 23 October, what meagre resistance there had been was crushed and Gomani was in hiding. Approached by the acting vice-consul at Blantyre, Mr Greville, Gomani explained that all captives from the raids belonged to him and that he saw no reason for handing them over to the British. On 27 October, Gomani, tricked into laying down his arms, was shot, raising a few complaints from the Church of Scotland.[36]

From the insignificant resistance put up by the Maseko, and Gomani's naïve insistence on his ownership of the people over which he had had traditional jurisdiction, it can only be inferred that the British assault came as a surprise. The attacks on the mission villages seem to have been a gesture by Gomani to his people and older indunas to show that the position of the Ngoni aristocracy over their conquered territory had not changed. This was, of course, not the case. A number of reports from the missions mentioned the discovery of such things as dummies with spears through them and magic gates after the attacks, further proof that Chewa influence on Ngoni society had extended to the practice of preventive magic in warfare.

With the paramount dead, many of the Maseko fled south and eastwards. Mandala, as elder brother of Gomani who was formerly rejected as paramount by the people on grounds of bad character, became chief in the Domwe area. The legitimate heir, Philip Gomani, still a baby, was brought with his mother Namagagula to the principal village of the Ndau clan, Maganga, where he found refuge.[37] Mandala, living up to his reputation, was seizing women and children from the villages of his sub-chiefs, Nkwaila and Njobvualema within two years of taking over. The captives were sold to a chief in P.E.A., Chemsinga, who was trading in slaves along the Zambezi.[38]

In April 1898 Msekandiwana, who lived on Domwe mountain itself, thirty miles to the north of Mandala, gathered together over 6,000 men and called on Mandala's assistance in what was to be the last desperate attempt of the Maseko to keep alive their former way of life. Mandala was unavailable, embroiled in a battle with Njobvualema and Nkwaila who had rebelled at the repeated abductions from their villages. Two companies of Tonga and Sikh troops converged on Domwe under the leadership of Pearce and Brogden, and, after meeting stiff resistance, put down the rising. From Lieutenant Brogden's fulsome report it is clear that the Maseko had, at last, learnt the value of heavy fire-power. 'They were armed almost entirely with guns and attacked up vigorously, advancing to within 20–30 yards and opening fire on us.'[39] But they missed their chance. The last resistance of the Maseko as an organized army ended when Msekandiwana shot himself through the chest to avoid Gomani's ignominious death by execution.

The other branch of the Maseko, by necessity rather than design, were already dependent on the British. In August 1896, Robert Codrington, the Collector, was 'most cordially received at Kachindamoto's and found him 'much inclined to European ways'.[40] In case the point had been missed, the young chief asked for, and was promptly dispatched, a red ensign. Two years later his policy of collaboration was clearly paying off: 'His villages appear to be increasing in size and the population has a well-fed look about them.'[41]

However, with an end to raiding came an end to the periodic influx of cattle into the chief's kraal. Like Mandala, Kachindamoto found himself without the old advantages of leadership in a martial society. He also resorted to the solution of selling off recalcitrant members of his villages to replace the booty of war. Makanjila, who continued slaving into the twentieth century, was a willing buyer.

'The dhows would come after dark. The Arabs had yokes put on the captives. I saw them talking round the fire with Chief Kachindamoto. They would put out into the lake and land further down the coast from where they went on foot. The captives would be terrified and think that they were on the other side of the lake.'[42]

By 1899 Kachindamoto had an impressive list of murders to his name including his chief induna, Gwaza, his grandmother hacked to death with an axe, and one of his wives, Nantini. His younger brother, Ndindi, who wanted to take over the chieftainship informed the Boma at Dowa. In September soldiers were sent to arrest Kachindamoto and he fled into the hills. Captured and pushed into a wicker cage on the pretext that he was insane, he refused to go to Zomba for trial and committed suicide with a bayonet.[43] In the subsequent succession dispute Ndindi was rejected in favour of an elder sister, Nyathei, who after suffering torture at Ndindi's hands, fled with the legitimate heir, Abraham Kachindamoto. Nyathei was shortly afterwards to become regent until 1912.[44]

And so with this wave of suicides, risings and executions the Maseko Ngoni passed from history as a martial society. No single factor was the cause of this rapid decline. Perhaps the most important had been the pressures from the

Yao and European economies with their slavery and wage labour. Behind the economies had been their techniques of warfare. Although the Ngoni appear to have known how to make crude muzzle-loaders,[45] and traded and captured a considerable number in the 1890s, it was only by about 1898 that they had learnt to use them efficiently. It is hard to know whether this was merely another instance of military crassness, a quality one might reasonably suppose to be universal, or a product of the essential conservatism of Ngoni society. This conservatism was most likely to be apparent in the army, the basis of the Maseko social system.

On the other hand, the Ngoni aristocracy were undoubtedly threatened by the grass-roots disruption associated with the assimilation of large numbers of Chewa captives. The influence of Chewa wives, with strong and fixed ideas on child rearing and family structure[46] had from 1870 a whole generation to take effect. A large percentage of young men fighting in the 1890s would have had Chewa mothers. This clash of matrilineal Chewa with the patrilineal Ngoni must have generated more tensions within society than the assimilation of the patrilineal northern Tumbuka by the Mbelwa Ngoni in the north of Malawi. The Ngoni aristocracy therefore had very good reasons for reacting conservatively. While the fragmented remains of the Maravi confederation presented no political and military threat—there were no risings as in the north—the aristocracy faced a far more insidious erosion of Ngoni society, culture and language. By 1898 Chingoni was rare in the Central Region.[47] Read's comparative study of Gomani's and Mbelwa's Ngoni provides impressive evidence of the degree to which the Chewa were successful in imposing their cultural patterns while remaining a 'conquered' people. An attitude of conservatism amongst the indunas was therefore entirely rational. It only became catastrophic when it was extended, as it was bound to be, to include military tactics.

The importance of the war divisions in resisting changes in Ngoni society cannot be underestimated. The last revolt of the Maseko was significantly led by the survivors of the Phungwako clan, the keepers of the war medicines, and Kachere and Msekandiwana played an important ritual role in warfare before 1898. Oral traditions seem to suggest that there were two forces at work in Ngoni society towards the end of the nineteenth century, an element that was willing to come to terms with reality and one that was fixed in a traditional mould. The use of Yao mercenaries may have represented a compromise between those who thought the pattern of warfare should change and those who would never agree to the use of rifles by Ngoni warriors.[48]

In oral traditions the choice between peace and continued warfare was presented as a choice between remaining Ngoni or becoming Chewa. The Maseko defeat at Songea was attributed to Mlangeni's decision to settle peacefully amongst the Chewa near Ncheu in the 1840s. The Chewa correlate of this theme is the often heard statement 'we defeated them with our women'. There seems to be little doubt that the last of the Karonga, Sosola, did accompany Chidiaonga to Songea and the gist of almost all oral traditions is how the Chewa repeatedly hoodwinked the Ngoni, firstly in alliances of convenience and then in vassalage. The conclusion that the leaders of the major Maseko war divisions saw continued warfare as a defence against Chewa-ization of their society is hard to escape.

If the comparison between the Mbelwa and Maseko Ngoni is instructive, a comparison of the two branches of the Maseko is more so. When Kachinda-moto's chief induna was murdered he lost the son of a captive taken around the south-west corner of Lake Malawi c.1845.[49] If Gwaza was typical of Kachindamoto's indunas his villages must have had next to no Swazi clan survivors. Gomani certainly had more. In 1902 Kachindamoto was living in a massive village of over 10,000 people with his other villages close-by,[50] a degree of centralization imposed by a shortage of 'pure' Ngoni. While Gomani was strong enough in the 1930s to crush the nyau cult in his area, Kachindamoto, despite the help of powerful and persistent Catholic missionaries, failed. He lived in constant dread of poisoning and was barely holding on to his more distant villages.[51]

The importance of Chewa religion, nyau and rain cults together with sorcery, in contributing to the Ngoni decline can only be guessed. The Nyau cult with its hierarchy of officials outside the jurisdiction of traditional village leaders, with a secret society initiation and code, has obvious subversive potential. Whether it in fact sustained Chewa culture in the face of Ngoni demands is hard to say.[52] The role of the sorcerer is equally difficult to ascertain, though the use of preventive magic during the 1896 rising would indicate some influence on the Ngoni aristocracy.[53]

Finally there comes the element of bluff. Just as the British, so the Ngoni succeeded in subduing a very large number of people with a minimum of direct rule. This depended to a large degree on a myth of invincibility. Once this myth was seen through, and here the Yao seem to have beaten the British by several years, the Ngoni faced what today might be called a 'credibility gap'. Add to this the temptation for indunas to deal privately with the Yao, the weakness of the regency, the proximity of the European and Yao economies, the divisive and debilitating civil war, and the rapid decline of the Maseko Ngoni after 1885 becomes almost inevitable.

This is not to say, though, that the Maseko disintegrated as a people as they entered the twentieth century. Before 1929 the heirs to the leaders of the previous century, Philip Gomani and Abraham Kachindamoto, had been converted to Christianity. Judicious support of missionaries and government officials allowed them to retain much of their former power. Nonetheless the years 1870–1900 demonstrate clearly how a combination of factors was able to destroy the way of life of a society that was, in the final analysis, more adapted to the rigours of the *Mfecane*, than to the problems of settlement close to the British and Yao guns and economies.

FOOTNOTES

1 All foreign office references have been taken from the microfilm collection, Chancellor College Library, University of Malawi. Oral testimonies were

taken down as notes during field work in the Dedza and Mchinji districts 1967–69. I am indebted to Mr J. K. Rennie for his scholarly criticisms of an earlier draft of this MS. Mission references are translated from the French.

2 M. Read, *The Ngoni of Nyasaland*, (London 1956), 97.

3 Oral Testimony from Nyathei, regentess at Ntakataka 1899–1911 in Manser-Bartlett papers, Chancellor College Library, University of Malawi.

4 Personal communication from Rev. J. Saffroy, W.F.

5 W. H. J. Rangeley, 'The Makololo of Dr Livingstone', *Nyasa. J.* **12** (1), 1959, 59.

6 E. D. Young, *Nyassa* (London 1877), 61.

7 Rangeley, 'The Makololo', 59.

8 A. C. Ross, 'Origins and Development of the Church of Scotland Mission at Blantyre, Nyasaland 1875–1926', Ph.D. thesis, University of Edinburgh (1968), 124.

9 As judged by the differences between Hawes to Roseberry, a description in 1886: F.O. 541/50 Hawes to Roseberry, 7 July 1886 and reports from Machinga Yao returning from raids: Mponda Mission Diary, 11 May 1891.

10 Hawes to Roseberry, 7 July 1886.

11 J. Omer-Cooper, 'Aspects of political change in the nineteenth-century Mfecane', L. Thompson (ed.), *African Societies in southern Africa*, (London 1969), 224.

12 The Maseko were defeated at Songea by the sons of Zulu, Hawai and Chipeta in alliance with the Bena, Nindi, Pangwa and other subject tribes. I. Linden, 'Some oral traditions of the Maseko Ngoni', forthcoming publication.

13 W. H. J. Rangeley, 'The Amacinga Yao', *Nyasa. J.*, 1962, 54.

14 Hawes to Roseberry, 7 July 1886.

15 Msano was the name given to the mother of the chief, who in the matrilineal Yao had considerable power.

16 Mponda Mission Diary, 22 January 1891. Bishop's Archives, Lilongwe.

17 Mponda Mission Diary, 1 May 1891.

18 Mponda Mission Diary, 25 March 1891.

19 F.O. 84/2052, Johnston to Salisbury, 10 June 1890.

20 Hawes to Roseberry, 7 July 1886.

21 F.O. 2/54, Johnston to Anderson, 21 January 1893.

22 I am indebted to Rev. Tom Price who when asked his opinion on the decline of the Maseko replied much to the point: 'Och, they just lost their credibility'.

23 Nyathei, Manser-Bartlett papers.

24 H. H. Johnston, *British Central Africa* (London 1897), 106.

25 *B.C.A.G.* 20 February 1894, Nicholl.

26 *B.C.A.G.* 15 July 1895 Editorial.

27 *B.C.A.G.* 15 July 1895, Editorial.

28 *B.C.A.G.* 1 December 1895.

29 Oral Testimonies. Chief Mpemba and Ndindi. Manser-Bartlett papers.

30 Oral Testimony. Samson Kachindamoto. Ntaka-taka, May 1969.

31 F.O. 2/68. Edwards to Acting Consul 31 October 1894.

32 *B.C.A.G.* 7 March 1894 and B.C.A.G. 1 June 1896.

33 I am indebted to Rev. H. Vernooy W.F. Kandeu Mission for this story.

34 F.O. 2/108 Sharpe to Salisbury 18 October 1896.

35 J. K. Rennie, 'The Ngoni States and European Intrusion', E. Stokes and R. Brown (eds.) *The Zambesian Past*, (Manchester 1966), 321.

36 *B.C.A.G.* 15 October 1896, *B.C.A.G.* 1 November 1896, Genthe.

37 Read, *The Ngoni*, 106.

38 F.O. 2/147 Manning to Salisbury 22 April 1898.

39 F.O. 2/147 Pearce to Manning 15 May 1898, Brogden to Manning 17 May 1898.

40 *B.C.A.G.* 15 September 1896.

41 *B.C.A.G.* 12 November 1898.

42 Oral Testimony. Pio Kupempha. Nyanja, Ntakataka, Jakobi Mbalule, Ntumba, Gwaza's Bembeke. May 1969.

43 Oral Testimony. Jakobi Mbalule. Eye witness. May 1969.

44 Mua Mission Diary 1902–1911.

45 Oral Testimony. T. Kabanga-Ndau. Chief Induna at Makwangwala's, Dzunje. October 1968.

46 M. Read, *Children of their Fathers*, (London 1959), 63.

47 Codrington, R. 'The Central Angoniland District of the British Central African Protectorate' *Geograph. J.*, **2**, 1898, 512.

48 I am indebted to Dr Andrew Roberts for this suggestion.

49 Kautsiri, Nyathei's husband. Manser-Bartlett papers.

50 Mua Mission Diary 14 September 1902.

51 Mua Mission Diary 1930–45.

52 J. M. Schoffeleers and I. Linden, 'The resistance of the Nyau cult to the Catholic missions in Malawi', Dar es Salaam Conf. June 1970.

53 W. E. Rau, 'The Ngoni diaspora and religious interaction in East and Central Africa'. Seminar paper, U.C.L.A.

15 Portugal's attitude to Nyasaland during the period of the partition of Africa

E. Axelson

On the eve of the scramble for Africa the Governor-General of Mozambique reported to his minister in Lisbon that Portuguese occupation on the coast of the province was virtually limited to the capitals of the district, and that dominion over the native peoples of the interior was purely nominal.[1] The military establishment to protect points along 1,440 miles of coastline and 500 miles up the Zambezi to Zumbo was only three battalions of troops, totalling 57 officers, 54 non-commissioned officers, and 1,233 troops. These battalions were 300 below strength; and most of the troops were *degredados*, or soldiers serving detention, or blacks as yet untrained.[2] Here, obviously, was no offensive force; but Portugal had succeeded in re-asserting authority over *prazo*-holders on the lower Zambezi,[3] while inland Portugal regarded a broad belt of country as reserved for her future expansion, as far as Angola if she so desired, by virtue of Portuguese discovery and prior interest.[4]

The departure from England in 1875 of Lieut. E. Young for the Zambezi to select a site for the Livingstonia mission of the Free Church of Scotland, accompanied by representatives of the Church of Scotland on a similar mission, threatened what Portugal regarded as her exclusive rights in the area. The party travelled with the blessing of the British government which hoped that the Livingstonia mission would 'promote commerce and civilization in those parts leading to the suppression of the Slave Trade' and which brought knowledge of the mission to the attention of the Portuguese government, with the request that it instruct its authorities in Mozambique to offer good offices and assistance.[5]

The liberal Andrade Corvo, Portuguese Minister of Marine and the Colonies, accepted that the mission would facilitate lawful trade and instructed his Governor-General, 'Should the said missionaries pass through Portuguese territory, any assistance they may stand in need of is to be rendered them, and especially that facilities should be given them for their journey to their place of destination.'[6]

But Corvo was fully aware of the possible implications of the mission, and he secretly instructed the Governor-General to choose a point on the banks of

252

the Shire and there place a garrison which would ensure Portuguese possession of the Shire as far as the Nyasa. The Governor-General promptly replied that he was much embarrassed by this request: Portugal enjoyed full dominion about the mouth of the Zambezi, but the Shire traversed land which was occupied by tribes which did not owe allegiance to Portugal. If the intention was to extend Portuguese dominion to the shores of Nyasa there was insufficient force in Mozambique, for only half of his small establishment was effective: such a force must be sent from either Portugal or from Portuguese India.[7] He warned that the missions would have to be closely watched. An Englishman, Faulkner, had been recently inciting the Kololo to attack Portuguese *prazos*, and he feared that these missionaries might induce tribesmen to revolt against the Portuguese, or provoke the tribesmen against themselves, and Portugal lacked the strength to protect them.[8]

The question of customs duties also disturbed the Portuguese authorities. Elton, the British consul in Mozambique, had warned that full imposts levied on the cost of the steam-launch, the boats, the merchandise and the provisions introduced by Young's party would cripple the finances of the enterprise, and it was because of heavy Portuguese customs duties that Bishop Steere was taking the Universities Mission to Nyasa overland from Lindi, beyond Portuguese jurisdiction.[9] The British government, 'fully conscious that they have no claim to exemption of these articles from Custom duties', nevertheless asked the Portuguese cabinet for its 'friendly consideration as proof of friendliness to a mission which may do much to benefit the Portuguese possessions.'[10]

Young did not pay customs duties for the simple reason that he entered the Zambezi by the Inhamissengo (Kongone) mouth, which was not recognized as a port of entry and therefore had no custom-house. The Governor-General was most concerned about this free and uncontrolled entry of merchandise, arms and gunpowder into Portuguese territory; he was quite convinced that the mission had ulterior political and economic motives.[11] The Governor-General was right. The trader Cotterill reported to the Secretary of State for foreign affairs in October, 1876, that there was fear among his countrymen lest the Portuguese force their way up the Shire and hoist their flag where the Union Jack had first been planted: there were now twenty-three British subjects at Livingstonia and 'we are all of the most decided opinion that no permanent good can be effected until the region of Lake Nyasa is placed under British jurisdiction. We have a right to the country by discovery, and by first occupation.'[12] Derby replied that the British government had no reason to believe that Portugal intended to assert claims of sovereignty over Nyasa, 'nor would they look with indifference on any attempt on the part of the Portuguese Government to take possession of that lake, or to interfere with the free access to and free navigation on it by British subjects.'[13] Young announced that his mission was now 'in possession of Lake Nyasa' and delivered such tirades against the Portuguese that Morier, the British Minister in Lisbon, was obliged to take him to task for his 'spirit of hatred, malice and uncharitableness against Portugal and the Portuguese' which was prejudicing Portuguese opinion against the mission. But the minister himself saw the day when the growth of commerce would lead to British jurisdiction, territorial rights and sovereignty.[14]

The Governor-General warned Lisbon again of British ambitions in the area, and that Britain was completely unscrupulous in the means she used to realize her designs.[15] Castilho, the capable and energetic Governor of Lourenço Marques, underlined to the Governor-General that the limits of Mozambique had never been defined in the interior and Portugal could in theory expand as far as Angola, but in practice Portugal was occupying only a few isolated and unhealthy points on the coast and on the Zambezi; it would be better by far, he urged, if Portugal could occupy high ground in the interior, as had been done by the Boers in South Africa, which would be better suited for settlement by whites.[16] It was not only Manica and Mashonaland that he had in mind, but the Shire highlands. But in the whole district of Sena there were only twenty-nine soldiers.[17] Portugal simply lacked the force to expand up the Shire, particularly since the missionaries were now supplying tribesmen hostile to Portugal with arms and ammunition.[18]

Corvo was responsible for a reform in the Mozambique tariff; import and export duties were reduced, and a transit duty introduced of only 3 per cent.[19] This encouraged the establishment of the Livingstonia Central Africa Company, soon to be known as the Africa Lakes Company, and plans to place a steam-launch on the Zambezi-Shire service.[20] But the application of a transit duty postulated not only a port of entry but a port of exit, and this involved the question of the interior frontier. It seemed prudent to the British authorities to suggest simply that the port of exit be at the confluence of the Zambezi and the Shire.[21] Morier negotiated a treaty concerned principally with Lourenço Marques in 1879, and he inserted in it a clause by which Portugal undertook not to hinder the free use of the Zambezi and its effluents 'as a great waterway for the commerce of central Africa' and to grant no exclusive concessions or monopolies for its navigation. This treaty, owing to change of government and circumstance, was not ratified,[22] and it remained uncertain whether the Portuguese government approved the principle of free navigation. A mining and industrial concession granted to Captain Paiva de Andrada was seen by some as a potential threat to the Protestant missions. This concession covered an area contained by two arcs, with a radius of thirty-six leagues, centred on Tete and Zumbo, joined by parallel lines; the area included part of the Shire valley and highlands. Andrada, as Morier admitted, was 'an enthusiast bitten with the belief that Africa can only be effectively civilized by means of industrial operations carried on in the interior with free negro labour. He believes that teaching the African new wants only to be satisfied by the earning of wages will alter the whole current of his life by inducing new habits and create a state of society before which the slave trade will die a natural death.' Andrada's ambition was to establish throughout the Portuguese possessions nuclei of free negro communities fed by European capital and directed by European managers. His proposals, in fact, were nearly identical to those of the Scotch missionaries and so aroused their jealousy and sharpened their desire to raise the British flag.[23] But Andrada turned to more profitable fields.[24]

The Church of Scotland was soon on the defensive, however, with the publication of *The Blantyre Missionaries: Discreditable Disclosures.*[25] Portuguese authorities appreciated more than ever the necessity for extending administration and justice to the area. But a new Governor of Zambezia reported most adversely on the situation on the lower Zambezi and, apprehensive of the strength of certain *prazo*-holders, he even ordered an escape route to be reconnoitred up the Shire to Blantyre.[26] His commissioner was most enthusiastic about Blantyre: 'Blantyre is a garden'; he praised the comfortable, well-furnished house in which he was lodged, the dahlias, carnations and other flowers which surrounded it, the clumps of bamboo and the closely-planted eucalyptus trees.[27] The Governor-General sent his secretary-general to hold inquiry into the exact situation on the Zambezi and then travel up the Shire, reporting on the Kololo on the way, to Blantyre; there he was to inspect the mission and report on whether Portuguese jurisdiction should be extended over it.[28] But the secretary-general was too attached to life even to begin this programme.[29]

The Portuguese authorities found it expedient to enter into alliance with some of the *prazo*-holders, and in 1882 Portuguese jurisdiction again became effective over Massingire, the *prazo* which controlled the lower Shire and where a military command became established.[30] Chief Chipatula, from his stockade at Chilomo, aggrieved that the Portuguese would not sell him arms and ammunition, raided into Massingire. These disturbances on the Shire caused the British government to accede to a suggestion made by the Livingstonia mission in 1880 that a consular officer be appointed on Nyasa, and in 1883 Capt. Foot, R.N., was appointed consul 'in the territories of the African kings and chiefs in the districts adjacent to Lake Nyasa'.[31] The Portuguese government, in granting him exemption from customs duties on his personal belongings, merchandise and arms, emphasized that Portugal did not abandon her rights to territories she had always maintained to be under her dominion and sovereignty.[32]

The murder of Chipatula by an Englishman brought crisis to the Shire. Followers of Chikuse, son of Chipatula, plundered the African Lakes Company launch, and fired on the Portuguese force which sought to intervene. The Kololo provoked revolt in Massingire, and the burning of the internal custom post further complicated communications on the Shire. Moir, the manager of the African Lakes Company, worked on rumours of a Portuguese advance into the area to persuade a number of Kololo to request a British protectorate over the area. A Portuguese expedition, under Augusto Cardoso, reached Nyasa overland from near Ibo, and persuaded Cuirassia and other chiefs to accept the Portuguese flag. The murder of an Austrian trader provoked further disorders and further expectation of Portuguese intervention. But Portuguese strength was inadequate, and Hawes, Foot's successor, proceeded systematically to visit chiefs over a widening area and to further British influence.[33]

The Portuguese government, anxious to assert sovereignty long claimed over the lower Congo and Cabinda, was prepared to make concessions elsewhere, and in a treaty signed between Portugal and Britain on 26 February 1884 Portugal recognized 'the entire freedom in respect to commerce and navigation of the Rivers Congo and Zambezi and their effluents for the subjects and flags of all nations,' and 'The claims of Portugal on the Shire shall not extend beyond the confluence of the River Ruo with that river'.[34] The treaty was not ratified because of protests by other powers, and the consequence was the Berlin West Africa Conference of 1884–85. A commission of the conference extended the free trade area to the Indian ocean; the southern limit was the mouth of the Zambezi, to a point five miles up the Shire from the Zambezi, and thence along the watershed between the Zambezi and the Congo. Serpa Pinto, one of the Portuguese representatives, immediately asserted Portugal's sovereign rights within part of this area. Another commission considered regulations for the free navigation on the Congo and the British representative suggested that Portugal should apply the principles applicable to the Congo to the Zambezi; Penafiel, the Portuguese plenipotentiary, exclaimed that Portugal had already introduced free navigation to the Zambezi; but the matter was outside the bases of discussion of the conference, and the Portuguese government reserved its rights to apply the principles which it judged to be the most suitable.[35] The map attached to the white book containing the Portuguese-German treaty of 1886 graphically illustrated the belt across Africa which Portugal regarded as reserved for her influence; it included the southern half of Nyasa.[36]

The Governor-General of Mozambique subsequently declared that he knew of no law which extended free navigation to the Zambezi[37] and this question became urgent with the outbreak of war between the African Lakes Company and Arabs in the Karonga area. The Portuguese were concerned at the effect this war had on their commerce,[38] still greater was their concern when the African Lakes Company demanded the right to import rifles, machine-guns and ammunition, rockets and dynamite, and when Hawes removed nineteen cases of ammunition from a custom-house without paying duty. To Castilho, now governor-general, this was an effront to Portuguese sovereignty: 'In my opinion the territories adjacent to the Zambezi, to the Shire, and at least to the southern part of Nyasa, very far in the interior, should be considered as ours.' He could only invoke a decree of 1885 which authorized governors to forbid the introduction of arms and ammunition into their districts in certain circumstances.[39] The Portuguese government demanded that its British counterpart stop the war[40] and it invoked regulations which prohibited foreigners from owning vessels operating on ports and rivers of the province, which caused the *James Stevenson* to be arrested.[41]

It was these circumstances which prompted the British Secretary of State for foreign affairs to require Sir E. Hertslet, the Foreign Office librarian, to prepare a memorandum 'as to the Right of a Power holding Possession of the Mouth of a River (both banks), to stop the Passage of Merchant Ships up that River wishing to reach Territory beyond its Jurisdiction'. Hertslet found something of a precedent in 1861 when the French had applied to the Governor of Sierra Leone for permission to proceed up the Sierra Leone river beyond the limits of Freetown. The Governor had refused, and the Queen's Advocate had confirmed 'where one nation was in possession of both banks of a river and commanded the navigable channel, which nation had not conceded the right of free navigation thereof, and where there existed no recognized "riparian" States higher up the river, there was no sufficient authority for maintaining

256

that any other nation could, irrespectively of Treaty or usage, lawfully enforce the right of navigating the river above its mouth, and beyond the territorial limits of the State owning both banks thereof.' Moreover, in 1858 a treaty between Peru and the U.S.A. gave the north Americans the right to navigate the Peruvian reaches of the Amazon. Brazil refused to allow American vessels to navigate the lower Amazon on their way to Peru. The U.S.A. claimed passage as a right, and appealed to the Declaration of Vienna, 1815, and the law of Nations; but the British government intervened and declared that the regulation laid down in 1815 applied only to European rivers. Hertslet also quoted from Sir Travers Twiss, *Law of Nations in Time of Peace*, section 145:

'A river, of which both banks are in the possession of one and the same nation, may be regarded as a stream of water contained in a certain channel, which channel forms part of the territory of the Nation.

Such water, accordingly, whilst passing through the territory of a nation, is subject, like all other things within its territory, to the empire of the nation, and those who navigate upon it are subject to the jurisdiction of the nation *ratione loci*.

The exercise of the right of empire over such a river by a nation, whilst it flows through its territory, does not in any way militate against the use of it as running water by other nations, or conflict with the exercise of their corresponding right of empire over it whilst it flows through their respective territories. We find accordingly by the practice of nations that a nation having physical possession of both banks of a river is held to be in juridical possession of the stream of water contained within its banks, and may rightfully exclude at its pleasure every other nation from the use of the stream, whilst it is passing through its territory, and this rule of positive law holds good whatever may be the breadth of a river.

Twiss continued,

'It may be observed, in regard to this right of exclusive use which a nation being in possession of both banks exercises over the stream of a navigable river, that a nation so established has a physical power of constantly acting upon the stream, and of excluding at its pleasure the action of any other nation, which power constitutes juridical possession. On the other hand, the stream, whilst it is included within the territory of a nation, cannot be considered to be destined by the Creator to continue open to the common use of mankind any more than the banks and adjacent lands, which have been appropriated and so withdrawn from common use.'

Hertslet's conclusion was that whilst modifications were possible by compact between nations no authority on international law would 'go so far as to say that a nation occupying the upper part of a river would have a right to demand, by international law, a passage for its vessels of commerce through the lower part of that river where both banks belonged to another Power, unless the navigation of that river had been declared to be open to the vessels of all nations, which is not the case with the Zambezi'.[42]

Hertslet's memorandum vindicated Portuguese rights, and the permanent under-secretary in the Foreign Office minuted to Salisbury that a state possessing a stretch of river and its tributaries could indeed forbid navigation to foreigners failing treaties to the contrary; but where states were established on the upper waters or effluents a different circumstance arose and they could acquire transit rights. There were obvious advantages in establishing a civilized administration on the upper Shire and in defining national limits. But there was little possibility of negotiation while Salisbury, rejecting Hertslet's arguments, was bringing heavy pressure to bear on the Portuguese government to admit more arms and munitions, and even artillery, for use by the African Lakes Company.[43]

A Portuguese expedition, however, caused Salisbury to reconsider his obdurate attitude. In July 1888, the King of Portugal put his signature to secret instructions to Lieut. António Maria Cardoso who was to lead an expedition, the principal aim of which was to establish a mission on Nyasa which would serve as a centre from which Portugal could enlarge her influence in that region 'taking advantage of the benevolence and respect which the peoples of those regions maintain towards the Portuguese name.' Cordoso was to establish a station in the territory of chief Cuirassia; this site promised comfort and security to the members of the mission and for future operation. He was to treat Cuirassia well, and manifest no hostility to other chiefs or tribesmen or foreigners. He was to assure the foreigners in particular that Portugal had no wish for conquest, but only to protect them and provide them with means to increase their commerce. The government intended to place steamers on the Zambezi and Shire, so Cardoso was required to survey those rivers. An amount of 25,000 milreis was made available for the mission.[44]

Maria Cardoso found Cuirassia to be without influence, but he persuaded numbers of other chiefs at the south-eastern end of Nyasa to place their marks on treaties in which they declared themselves to be vassals of the king of Portugal, and he was even to persuade Mponda, who controlled the source of the Shire, to make a similar avowal.[45] Cardinal Lavigerie, the influential founder of the Société de Notre-Dame d'Afrique, undertook to found churches, chapels and schools, and to supply five missionaries to propagate the Catholic faith.[46]

In these circumstances Salisbury decided to come to terms with Portugal. He named as negotiator not the British minister in London but the consul-elect to Mozambique, H. H. Johnston. Johnston had already published an article in *The Times* in which he urged 'a continuous band of British dominion' from South Africa to Egypt. It says much for his persuasiveness that he talked the Portuguese Prime Minister into abandoning Portugal's age-old claim to a belt of territory across Africa and into guaranteeing free navigation on the Zambezi. He had to offer powerful inducements; and his main *quid pro quo* was that Portugal should be allowed to annex the Shire highlands and the land around the southern end of Nyasa.[47] This proposal was unacceptable to Salisbury—and to many Scotsmen—and events took their course.

In July, 1889, a British gunboat with Johnston aboard forced the Chinde entrance of the Zambezi. Johnston indulged in treaty-making on the Shire, and

258

authorized Buchanan, the acting consul, to declare a protectorate over the area, which he duly did on 19 August 1889. On the lower Shire was an expedition led by Serpa Pinto who had been instructed to protect engineers surveying a railway line past the Shire rapids; he had also responded to a call by the local agent of the African Lakes Company for protection against Kololo who had fired on a Lakes' steam-launch. But Serpa Pinto had no desire to precipitate hostilities; he advanced his camp to Mpassa, and then sought new instructions. On 8 November, however, Mlauri and his men, instigated by Moir, attacked his camp, which was in the Massingire *prazo*, twenty-five miles south of the Ruo; the attack was beaten off. Reinforcements reached the Portuguese, including two armoured launches, and on 15 November Serpa Pinto advanced northwards. He occupied Chilomo and Lieut. João Coutinho continued to Katunga. The riverine chiefs announced their allegiance to Portugal.[48] Serpa Pinto, seriously ill, was carried to the coast from where, on 26 December 1889, he proudly cabled to Lisbon,

Shire occupied. The English flag taken in the *prazo* Massingire had been hoisted by the Kololo who attacked us in the lands of the crown but they were routed with great losses. In the campaign I granted the greatest protection to the English and their belongings, and I have letters of thanks from them. The people of Massingire on the Shire are occupying their old villages and cultivating their lands. The Kololo people, decimated in the fighting, are completely submissive. The route to Nyasa is secure for the commerce of all nations, and that great focus of slavery and iniquity which the government could not condone is ended. Kololo chiefs admit in public statement that they were sent there by the governor of Tete and by João de Jesus Maria in whose house Livingstone had left them and that they have always considered themselves Portuguese subjects; they had been instigated to revolt by the manager of the Lakes Company; but they admit that Rev. Scott, head of the Blantyre mission, had counselled peace and moderation. They declared apocryphal the treaties which the consul has made, and they refuse the English protectorate which they wanted to impose. My stay there is not necessary because I have established Portuguese authority and the country is occupied.[49]

But the Serpa Pinto expedition, misrepresented in various quarters, together with reports of renewed Portuguese activity in Mashonaland, stiffened Salisbury's resolve to act against Portugal, and that same Boxing Day Salisbury ordered the Channel and Mediterranean naval squadrons to concentrate at Gibraltar ready to over-awe Lisbon, and for a squadron to assemble at Zanzibar to seize Mozambique if need be. On 8 January 1890 the board of the newly formed British South Africa Company met in London to discuss plans for the occupation of Mashonaland, and on 10 January the British minister in Lisbon presented to the Portuguese government an ultimatum demanding that it send orders to the 'Governor of Moçambique to withdraw all Portuguese troops that are on the Shire, or in Kalolo country, or in Mashonaland.' The Portuguese government had no alternative but to yield.[50]

FOOTNOTES

1 Governor-General to Minister, 23/6/1875, Arquivo Histórico Ultramarino (in Lisbon), Moçambique, Pasta 29.

2 Governor-General to Minister, 31/12/1874, AHU, Moçambique, Pasta 29.

3 M. D. D. Newitt, 'The Portuguese on the Zambezi from the seventeenth to the nineteenth centuries', *Race*, April 1968, 477–98; Newitt and P. S. Garlake, 'The "aringa" at Massangano', *J. Afr. Hist.*, 1967, 133–56.

4 A. Teixeira da Mota, *A Cartografia antiga da Africa Central e a travessia entre Angola e Moçambique 1500–1860*, Lourenço Marques, 1964.

5 Derby to Lytton, 28/5/1875, Confidential Print 2915, 290–1; Bourke to Elton, 28/5/1875, CP 2915, 326.

6 Corvo, *portaria*, 28/6/1875, CP 2915, 295.

7 Governor-General to Minister, 16/9/1875, A.H.U. Moçambique, Pasta 29.

8 Governor-General to Minister, 27/9/1875, A.H.U., Moçambique, Pasta 29.

9 Elton to Derby, 20/7/1875, CP 2915, 354–5.

10 Derby to Lytton, 15/9/1875, CP 2915, 294; Lytton to Corvo, 30/9/1875, CP 2915, 296.

11 Governor-General to Minister, 23/12/1875, A.H.U., Moçambique, Pasta 29, and 24/1/1876, Pasta 30.

12 Cotterill to Derby, 30/10/1876, CP 3686, 174–5.

13 Pauncefote to Cotterill, 7/2/1877, CP 3686, 175.

14 Morier to Derby, 27/2/1877, CP 3686, 83–5; Morier to Young, 31/12/1877, CP 3928, 121–3.

15 Governor-General to Minister, 12/6/1877, A.H.U., Moçambique, Pasta 30.

16 Castilho to Governor-General, 26/2/1877, A.H.U., Moçambique, Pasta 30.

17 Antonio Martins Correa, Curador-geral, Relatório, 31/1/1878, A.H.U., Moçambique, Pasta 31.

18 Morier to Salisbury, 14/5/1878, CP 3928, 116, and 15/5/1878, 119–20.

19 Gould to Derby, 18/8/1877, CP 3686, 293–4.

20 Salisbury to Morier, 18/4/1878, CP 3928, 106–7, and 30/7/1878, 132.

21 Morier to Salisbury, 28/4/1878, CP 3928, 112–13 and to Corvo, 3/5/1878, 114–15.

22 A. J. Hanna, *The Beginnings of Nyasaland and North-Eastern Rhodesia, 1859–1895*, Oxford, 1956, 115–19. E. Axelson, *Portugal and the Scramble for Africa, 1875–1891*, Witwatersrand University Press, 1967, 20–37.

23 Morier to Salisbury, 5/2/1880, Public Record Office, Foreign Office 179/220.

24 *Portugal and the Scramble*, 126–36.

25 By A. Chirnside, London, 1880.

26 *Portugal and the Scramble*, 139–40.

27 A. d'Oliveira Barreto, Tete, 16/5/1881, Relatório . . ., A.H.U., Moçambique, 1 Repartição, Pasta 3.

28 Governor-General, instrucções to Almeida de Cunha, 11/12/1881, A.H.U., Moçambique, 1 Rep., Pasta 1; O'Neill to Granville, 25/1/1882, CP 4777, 64–5.

29 *Portugal and the Scramble*, 140.

30 Ibid., 141.

31 Ibid., 163–4.

32 Bocage to Baring, 8/11/1883, Necessidades, Soberania de Portugal na Zambezia 1 and CP 4914, 16.

33 *Portugal and the Scramble*, 164–70. For Cardoso's expedition see A. Lobato, 'Augusto Cardoso e o Lago Niassa', *Stvdia*, **19**, December 1966, 7–91.

34 *Portugal and the Scramble*, 61–3; E. Hertslet, *Map of Africa by Treaty*, London, 1894, 713–14.

35 *Africa No. 4 (1885)*, 126–51.

36 J. de Almada, *Tratados aplicaveis ao Ultramar, mapas apensos ao Volume V*, Lisbon, 1943, No. LXXIII.

37 Director-General to Sec.-general, 12/3/1888, Nec., Sob. Port. Zamb. 1.

38 Amorim to Sec.-general, 25/2/1888, A.H.U., Moçambique 2, Caixa 5.

39 Castilho to Minister, 3/3/1888, A.H.U., Moçambique 2 Rep., Caixa 5.

40 Min. to Min. Foreign Affairs, 2/3/1888, Nec., Sob, Port. Zamb. 1.

41 Dir.-general to Sec.-general, 12/3/1888, Nec., Sob. Port. Zamb. 1.

42 CP 5727, 16.

43 *Portugal and the Scramble*, 174–82.

44 Rei, instrucções, 5/7/1888, Nec., Sob. Port. Zamb. 1.

45 *Termos de Vassallagem nos territorios de Machona, Zambezia e Nyassa 1858 a 1889*, Lisbon, 1890.

46 'Fundação da Missão Religiosa de M'Ponda', Negocios Externos, *Negocios da Africa Oriental e Central*, Lisbon, 1890, p. 241–69.

47 Johnston to Petre, 8/4/1889, CP 5970, 52–6; R. Oliver, *Sir Harry Johnston and the Scramble for Africa*, London, 1959.

48 *Portugal and the Scramble*, 204–13.

49 Serpa Pinto to Min., 26/12/1889, *Negocios*, 1890, 167.

50 *Portugal and the Scramble*, 213–28.

16 Notes on the origins of the Arab War

H. W. Macmillan

The origins of what came to be known as 'The Arab War' have never been satisfactorily explained.[1] Most commentators have suggested that the underlying cause was commercial rivalry between the Arabs who settled at the north end of Lake Malawi during the 1880s, and the African Lakes Company who established a station at Karonga, as the base of the Stevenson road to the south end of Lake Tanganyika, in the same period.[2] The war can, according to this view, be seen as a straight-forward clash between the exponents of 'illegitimate' and 'legitimate' commerce. The European participants and their supporters in Britain found it useful, for propaganda purposes, to think of the war as a crusade in which one side was the representative of good, and the other of evil, but there was nothing so clear-cut about the background. The relationship which grew up between the contestants in the course of the 1880s was not one of commercial rivalry but one of partnership which proved extremely profitable to the Company, and was, presumably, also advantageous to the Arabs themselves. The purpose of this essay is to examine the changing situation at the north end of Lake Malawi during the 1880s, and to suggest possible alternative explanations for the involvement of the African Lakes Company, which aimed to bring about change in central Africa through the peaceful influence of commerce, in a conflict with its most important trading partners, in defence of the Ngonda people.

The north end of Lake Malawi was visited by E. D. Young and Robert Laws on their first circumnavigation of the lake in 1875. On this voyage they located and bought land at the Kambwe lagoon, which was thought to be a suitable site for a harbour.[3] The chief there, Karonga, welcomed Dr James Stewart and his party on their visit in 1877, giving them presents of food and a small tusk.[4] Herbert Rhodes was the first European to build a house in the vicinity. He was reported to have established the 'nucleus of a trading station' there early in 1889.[5] He used it as a base for his assault on the untapped supplies of elephants and ivory in the marshes to the north of the Songwe. Consul Elton had seen a herd of over 300 elephants there on his visit.[6] John Moir and James Stewart, C.E., established a station for the African Lakes Company, then known as the

263

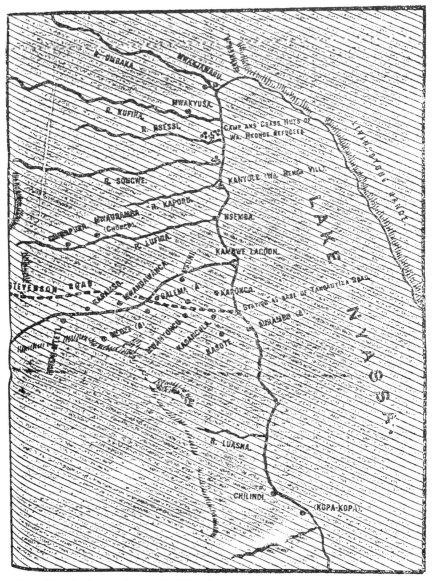

16.1 The Arab war (from the *Manchester Guardian*, 25 February 1888)

Livingstonia Central African Company, in October, 1879. John Moir bought land there but on account of the closing of the Kambwe lagoon by silt he moved in December to the Mbashi river at the far north end of the lake which provided, at that time, an excellent harbour. He bought land there and built a house which was used in the next two seasons as the base for the Company's hunting operations.[7] This place has come to be known as Mwaya; the name is said to be a corruption of Moir. Fred Moir was known there from an early date as *Miskita Moyo*.[8] It was originally intended that this station should be the Lake Malawi terminus of the Stevenson road, and James Stewart, C.E., began work on the construction of the road from there in 1881, but he was forced to abandon this route after the murder of nineteen of his workers in December of that year.[9] He moved his base south to Karonga where he built 'a large house with an enclosed verandah' which became the nucleus of the Company's store.[10] From early in 1882 Karonga became the headquarters of the Company at the north end. From here the construction work on the Stevenson road and the transport of the London Missionary Society's steamer, the *Good News*, was organized. There was, however, no permanent agent of the Company settled there until 1884.

The pre-existing political situation is obscure. The first visitors to the north end did not discriminate between the peoples who have come to be known as the Ngonde and the Nyakyusa; they referred to both as the 'Chungus', a name which was derived from the paramount chief of the Ngonde, the Kyungu.[11] Later on a distinction was made between the Wankonde and the Mwamba or Sankilis, who were thought to be separated by the river Songwe, which eventually became the boundary between the British and German spheres of influence, and, consequently, between Malawi and Tanzania. These two peoples were very close in terms of language and culture and were much intermarried and related. It is probable, though, that the Songwe marked the northern boundary of the sovereignty of the Kyungu. Among the Nyakyusa to the north of the river there was no acknowledged paramount, though there were several important chiefs.[12] The so-called Elephant Marsh may have formed a barrier between the two groups; the largest concentrations of Nyakyusa lived at the head of the lake and in the hills behind, rising rowards Tukuyu. It was, however, with those who lived in the plains near the lake that the Company was most concerned.

Arabs began to arrive in this vicinity almost simultaneously with the Company. They were attracted to the area by the abundant supply of ivory, by the possibilities of acquiring slaves which were presented by local feuds, and by the strategic importance of the lake crossing from Deep Bay to the east side which was opened up at this time. This crossing, which shortened the route from the Senga country, and the south end of Lake Tanganyika, to Kilwa, and Zanzibar, was made possible by arrangements which appear to have been made with the Songea Ngoni, or Gwangwara, as they were known. These people, who had been the scourge of most of the population of the east coast of the lake, raiding as far south as the Shire Highlands, seem to have become more settled during the early 1880s and were, like their cousins under Mbelwa, Chikusi and Mpezeni, beginning to enter into diplomatic and commercial relationships.[13] There is no written evidence of Arabs at the north end until 1881; Fred Moir met some at the Mbashi in August of that year. When he reached the Company's house there in July, no-one came out to greet the steamer, and he found the villages burnt.[14] There had apparently been a succession dispute following the death of a chief, Malaseka. Two other chiefs, Mwakyusa and Manjawarra, had called in some Arabs to help them with their guns against a third chief, Massewa. There was evidence that the Arabs had obtained slaves as a result of their assistance. Fred Moir wrote:

'The Arabs have kept very much out of my way, tho' I have not sought to avoid a meeting. One day they met us on the road with several small tusks they said they wanted to sell, as we were far from here they said they would come some other time. They have not come since. They have also been very careful to keep slaves away from here. [Moir had seen one woman who had escaped in a goree stick.] My boys on a road where they were not expected came on a gang of slaves bound southwards in gorees—it is most aggravating to know that people, some of whom have formerly welcomed us to their villages . . . are at the present moment being driven away south in slave sticks.'[15]

Moir felt that if he had arrived at the north end two months earlier the war could have been avoided 'for this year at least'.

'And when we came I would have undertaken to frighten out the dozen or two Arabs who were here, probably without firing a gun, but if there was a possibility of armed resistance we might have had to use our guns. I hear today that they have all cleared out but I cannot say if it is really the case.'[16]

It is probable that the same group of Arabs had been involved in an Ngonde war. Moir passed the burnt out remains of a village which they had occupied north of Karonga,[17] and the Kyungu, Mwafonga, was said to have been killed by Arabs in this year.[18] Neither this Kyungu nor his successor, Mwabalambo, appears to have been able to command the support of all the people; the ease with which the Arabs were able to establish themselves in the area was attributed to the weakness of the Kyungu. Mlozi, the leader of this group of Arabs, was implicated in some way in this dispute but his precise role is not clear. He was able to persuade the Ngonde to allow him to settle at Mpata about twelve miles west of Karonga, on the way to Tanganyika. He must have settled there between 1881 and 1883. He had come from the Senga Arabs to whom he continued to owe some allegiance.[19]

The situation was made more complicated by the settlement at Kaporo, about fifteen miles north of Karonga, at approximately the same time, of a group of Henga people under the leadership of Kanyoli. His followers were Tumbuka-speaking people who had been subjected and partially assimilated by Mbelwa's Ngoni. Following the successful Tonga revolt of about 1875, the Ngoni began to fear that the Tumbuka people might also rebel. Mtwalo, the brother and rival of Mbelwa, who took a consistently hard line on military and diplomatic questions, proposed that in order to prevent such an occurrence, and to consolidate the position of the Ngoni, the mature Tumbuka speaking Henga and Nkhamanga should be killed, leaving the children and youths to be brought up as Ngoni. The news that this plan was about to be put into practice provoked a rebellion in the Henga valley. Mbelwa called in Mwase from
266

Kasungu with his guns to help him put the rebellion down, but Kanyoli and some of his followers managed to escape.[20] This was in 1879, while John Moir was travelling west towards the Luangwa.

Kanyoli, who had been a commander in the Ngoni army, and whose men were at least partially trained in the regimental system, moved north where he was called in to help Massewa against his rivals among the Nyakyusa. He was allowed, or chose, to settle at Kaporo from where he continued to make raids to the north, especially for cattle. Ngonde sources stress that he had come to their country as a refugee and had been allowed to settle as a favour, thus making more pointed his later treachery, but it is probable that they were in no position to argue with him. They were said to have tried to persuade the Arabs to act against him, and his presence may have been part of the explanation for their reception of these otherwise unwelcome guests.[21]

II

There is no evidence of commercial contact between the north end Arabs and the Company until July 1883 when James Stewart, C.E. told James Stevenson:

'What is even stranger, the Arab visitors in the district are now well-disposed and have been selling supplies to Munro . . . and ivory to Monteith at the Lake.'[22]

John Moir reported to the Directors of the A.L.C. in January 1884 that a considerable trade had been done at Karonga during the preceding year, chiefly by Monteith.[23] Low Monteith Fotheringham and J. L. Nicoll were stationed at Karonga continuously from the latter months of 1884.[24] They were engaged alternately in leading caravans across to Lake Tanganyika with the parts of the *Good News*, and with goods and passengers for the L.M.S., and in supervising the Karonga store and developing the ivory trade there. Alexander Carson, the L.M.S. engineer, visited Karonga in May 1886 and left a detailed account of their activities. He makes it clear that Arabs had been attracted to the district in large numbers by the opportunity given for exchanging their ivory. They were said to be building villages in the vicinity and to have many people attached to them, including slaves of various types. The Company's steamer, the *Ilala*, was at this time taking regular cargoes of ivory south.[25] Carson saw her take 'a large quantity of ivory down with her and during the week I saw much more bought.' He described the business conducted at the station:

'Arabs arrive early in the day at the station with a string of men following, who carry elephants' tusks, hippo teeth, rhinoceros horns, guns etc. The chief is sometimes a tall and lanky man with cadaverous features, sometimes a portly man with bright black eyes and flowing beard. Some look shabby in their calico robes and fez, some dress in fine linen with embroidery and have silver jewelry. Their followers are dressed according to their rank, fez and robes or anything between that and a little piece of dirty cloth. They sit on the floor of the store, the chief in front, and followers behind according to rank, with ivory besides them. The agent of the A.L.C. sits in front, with his bales of calico, bags of salt, and cases of provisions around him. A tusk is presented for inspection, which is weighed, then an offer is made to the owner who looks demure and shakes his head, and states his figure. The agent raises the amount offered, gradually, and the Arab gradually lowers his until after a great deal of shaking of heads with downcast eyes and a few words the bargain is struck and the calico measured out, when another tusk is in like manner disposed of. Sometimes beads, salt, soap or vinegar are wanted as part payment when an equivalent in calico is returned by the owner. This goes on for days together and generally stops not so much for want of ivory as want of calico, for the Co. seems always behind in the supply of their stations as they are of the mission stations.'[26]

The latter comment was undoubtedly true. Fotheringham had made a special trip to Mandala in 1885 to attempt to get more cloth to keep the business going. He was constantly disappointed by the quantities which the steamer brought up.[27] Carson makes no reference to powder being given for ivory at this date; Lugard claimed that the Company had supplied some to Arabs, and there is evidence that limited quantities were supplied at a later date.[28] Here, as elsewhere, the refusal to sell powder and guns would have inhibited trade, and there must have been a temptation to allow some sales. The Company would not, however, sell powder to the Jumbe of Nkhota Kota in 1888, though it was his most insistent demand.[29]

III

The second function of the station at Karonga, as the base for organization of caravans to the south end of Lake Tanganyika along the Stevenson road, was made more difficult by the unwillingness of the Ngonde to carry loads further than the few miles between the Kambwe lagoon and the Company store, and by the unsettled political state of the plateau over which the route passed.[30] The first difficulty was overcome by the introduction of workers from elsewhere. Some of these were men on contract from Bandawe, and from the Shire Highlands, including some Yao, and, according to Carson, some 'Manganja'. Others were unrecruited volunteers, many of them Mambwe, who came over from the vicinity of Mbala, near the south end of Lake Tanganyika, in the hope of getting loads to carry back with them. Carson was glad to be able to employ a party of Mambwe who had come over for this purpose as they contracted to carry his loads all the way to their destination while other loads had to be carried in short stages across the plateau by different people.[31] On other occasions porters had to be sent for from Mweniwanda, about fifty miles up the road.[32] Throughout the history of the Stevenson road as a tenga-tenga route the vast majority of those employed as porters came from the areas

268

which are now in Zambia and Tanzania, with the exception of the Tonga who came from over a hundred miles to the south. It is remarkable that Mambwe should have come, apparently spontaneously, at such an early date over two hundred miles without any certainty of getting work. Like the Tonga they came to be known as energetic labour migrants.[33]

The political uncertainties on the plateau were due largely to the unpredictable nature of Bemba raids against which all the villages beyond Mweniwanda were heavily stockaded;[34] to conflicts between the Mambwe and the Nyamwanga; and to the ambivalent position of Kabunda, the most wealthy of the Arab traders in the area, who was settled on the Lofu river among the Lungu, whom he appears alternately to have protected against the Bemba and to have raided for slaves. The Bemba acted as suppliers of slaves to Kabunda and to the Senga Arabs, whose leader was Salim bin Nasur. Carson, on his journey in 1886, found much evidence of recent raiding though he noticed in one instance that a cache of tinned food which had been left at a village eighteen months previously by Fred Moir for the use of future Company caravans had been carefully set on one side by the raiding party.[35] Fotheringham had been much delayed on one of his journeys by a war between a 'renegade' Mambwe chief and some of the Nyamwanga.[36]

The precise role of Kabunda is difficult to analyze. He was a cultivated man from the Persian Gulf and received European visitors with considerable style. Fred Moir and James Roxburgh met him in September, 1883, near the Lofu river, when he was setting out on his way to Zanzibar with a caravan of over 3,000 people, most of whom were said to be slaves in sticks, many of them carrying loads. Fred Moir's description of the scene is so graphic as to be almost unbelievable but it is confirmed less dramatically by Roxburgh.[37] They found that most of the villages at the south east end of Lake Tanganyika, including those at Niamkolo, and Zomb's (on the plateau above the lake near the present town of Mbala, formerly Abercorn) had been destroyed. Moir attributed this destruction to Kabunda's preparations for departure, while Hore of the L.M.S. thought that it was the work of the Bemba.[38] Harry Johnston stayed with Kabunda for a week in 1889 and spent there according to his biographer, 'perhaps the most consciously enjoyed moment of his life'.[39] He regarded Kabunda as a reformed character, though it is clear from A. J. Swann's account that the Lungu were being raided, presumably on Kabunda's instructions, within weeks of Johnston's departure.[40] Kabunda is said to have declared himself Sultan of Ulungu in about 1887, and it may be that, as Hore believed, he provided some protection to the Lungu in the immediate vicinity of his settlement, but it would seem that the majority were at the mercy of his whim.[41]

The successful development of the ivory trade at Karonga undoubtedly led to an increase in the number of Arabs who were in the area, although it had not attracted them there in the first place. In addition to Mlozi, who was established at Mpata by 1883, villages were established in the next four years by Msalemu, at the point where the Stevenson road crossed the Rukuru about five miles from Karonga; by Kopa Kopa, about twelve miles to the south of Karonga, between there and Deep Bay, from where there was a ferry to

Capandansere's on the east coast; and by Salim bin Najim, about a mile and a half from the Company station, along the lake shore. The latter left for the coast in about September 1887 and was not involved in the war. He had left his valuables in the custody of Fotheringham and told his people to go to him in case of trouble.[42] Mlozi, Kopa Kopa and Msalemu were the three most important of the Arab protagonists.

Although the Ngonde were comparatively slow to respond to the lure of wage labour, partly because they had very little need of cloth which they rarely wore, the people in the vicinity of the store at Karonga had close relations with the Company's agents. They did some work on the station, and supplied food for the agents and for the imported employees. Fotheringham and Nicoll began missionary work among them, and the chiefs, Karonga, Kasingula and Mulilema, came to rely on the Company for mediation in disputes.[43] Karonga and Kasingula both signed petitions to Queen Victoria, asking for the declaration of a British protectorate in 1885.[44] These petitions, which were signed by many of the less powerful chiefs with whom the Company came in contact at this time, were intended to be used by the Company and mission pressure group in Scotland to influence the British government to declare a protectorate over the company's sphere of operations. For a variety of reasons they were never used for the purpose for which they were intended, but they were never repudiated by the Ngonde, nor by the Nyakyusa chiefs, Mwakyusa, Manajawara, and Mankenja, who also signed.[45] The signing of the petitions undoubtedly raised the expectation among the Ngonde of protection from the Company, and engendered an equal sense of obligation on the part of the Company's agents, Fotheringham and Nicoll, who were constantly in close contact with them. At the time that these petitions were signed there can have been little suspicion that the Company might be called on to defend the Ngonde against the Arabs in the area, with whom the Company's agents had equally close and cordial relations. The Ngonde had been encouraged to sign the petitions, not by fear of the Arabs, but by fear of the Ngoni, and of Kanyoli.[46]

It should be clear from the above account that commercial rivalry cannot be a sufficient cause of the war which eventually broke out in November 1887. The Company and the Arabs were not rivals but partners in the ivory trade, and the Company's agents had never made any attempt to interfere with the slave trade, which these merchants carried on as a discreet sideline. If this theory is excluded there remain two possible types of explanation: that the war was the culmination of a series of minor irritations between the Arabs and the Ngonde with the Company being called in as the protector of the latter; or that the war was the result of a premeditated political design by Mlozi, and the other Arabs, to drive the Ngonde from their fertile plain. If the latter alternative is accepted it has further to be asked: was this design conceived and carried out independently by Mlozi, and his friends, or was it the result of a move by Arabs all over central Africa to lay claim to 'effective occupation' of the interior after the European powers had staked out their claims to the coastline of Africa?

IV

An examination of the immediate background to the war provides evidence to support each of these explanations and it may appear difficult at this point in time to reach a positive conclusion between one or the other. Fotheringham gave some evidence to support the first view when he wrote:

'One great cause of trouble during the last two years at Karonga has been shortness of supplies, thus causing Arabs who have come long distances to wait in the district as long as three months before we could give them their goods. The Arabs always bring great numbers of people along with them: hence there have been continual quarrels between them and the natives about food, the Arabs invariably helping themselves ... Ramathan, one of the principal Arab leaders, a white Belooch, came down from Kabunda's with 1,500 lbs., of ivory. He could not be supplied with goods, and as he had seventy people with him and about fifty guns, the natives did not care for his presence.'[47]

The first incident in the sequence of events which led up to the outbreak of the war seems to have fitted into this category of friction. A headman, Kasote, of a village to the south of Karonga, was killed by a white Arab as a result of a trivial dispute. Fotheringham was asked by Kasote's superior, Kasingula, to recover the body of the dead man, which he did, and then met a deputation of two thousand Ngonde from the Karonga area who wanted to attack Salim bin Najim's village in retaliation. Fotheringham was afraid that this might lead to a general war in which the Ngonde would be at a disadvantage, and attempted to find a peaceful solution to the dispute. He was unable to persuade Salim bin Najim to hand over the murderer of Kasote to the Ngonde but he was able after four days of negotiation to persuade Salim to give, and the Ngonde chiefs to accept compensation.[48] This was in July 1887; there was no further incident until October, but in the meantime tension had been maintained by the continued presence of Ramathan, who was awaiting payment for ivory which he had sold to the Company, and by the arrival in September of a large number of *ruga-ruga*, presumably from the Senga Arabs, who, according to Mlozi, were going to be used in an attack on Mbelwa's Ngoni, who had killed one of his brothers.[49]

It was on the 4 October 1887, that a quarrel broke out at a village near Mpata, Mlozi's settlement twelve miles up the Tanganyika road, as a result of which a headman, Mwini-Mtete, was killed. As the people there were some distance from the station, and were not in close contact with the Company, there was no question of mediation by the agent. The Ngonde concerned attacked some of Mlozi's people who were buying food at the time of the murder, killing some and capturing others, including several of Mlozi's wives, according to his account.[50] The Arabs retaliated with attacks on the Ngonde villages near Mpata, and the destruction of all the villages between there and Karonga. Most of the inhabitants fled to Ngerenge, the headquarters of the Kyungu, about twelve miles to the north of Karonga. Fotheringham attempted to intercede with Mlozi to prevent the destruction of the villages of Karonga, Kasingula, and Mulilema which were close to the station.

In answer to his messages Fotheringham was told by Ramathan that the fighting would not stop until all the Ngonde had been killed or driven out; that 'the country was now the Arabs'' and that Mlozi was Sultan of Konde'; that if Fotheringham wanted workers he could employ Henga people who were 'the children of the Arabs'; and that if he ventured out from the station he might be shot as 'Ramathan means to have war'.[51] Mlozi was prepared in view of their friendship, and of the fact that Fotheringham had been in the area for longer than any of the Arabs but himself, to allow Kasingula and Mulilema to stay in their villages as 'children of the white man' if Fotheringham sent up thirty pounds of powder, two thousand percussion caps, one thousand flints and a supply of red cloth. Fotheringham consulted Kasingula and they agreed to reject this demand as acceptance would have recognized Mlozi's assumed position.[52]

Fotheringham saw Ramathan for the second time on 7 October and was told that Kasingula could stay if he recognized Mlozi as his chief, sent men to hoe his gardens, and women for his harem. Fotheringham replied that Kasingula would not recognize Mlozi, and that the situation would be reported to the British Consul at Zomba, and to John Moir at Mandala.[53] Mlozi then sent a message regretting his earlier demands and asking Fotheringham to arrange a *mirandu* (conference) with the Kyungu in order to settle his differences with the Ngonde. The Kyungu was sent for and came to the station but Mlozi did not keep the appiontment. Mlozi suggested that the Kyungu should stay at the station while he went to attack the Ngonde at Ngerenge. Fotheringham feared that if the Kyungu stayed at the station the rest of the Ngonde would come to be with him, that the station would be attacked, and the Company involved in the war. He asked the Kyungu to return to Ngerenge and at the same time began to build a brick wall around the previously unstockaded agents' house and store. He was careful to warn Mlozi that he was doing this. Mlozi replied that he had no objection, and Fotheringham learnt from Ramathan that the attack on the Ngonde had been delayed until reinforcements came from the Senga Arabs.[54]

Fotheringham met Mlozi and Salim bin Nasur, one of the Senga Arabs, at Msalemu's village on 15 October. It was agreed that Ramathan and his *ruga-ruga* should leave their village near the station as a preliminary to the return of Karonga, Kasingula and Mulilema. Ramathan left for Mpata's on the 16th but returned to Karonga on 17 October. The people of these three chiefs were told by the Henga at Kaporo that the way was clear for them to return to their homes; they came back as far as the Kambwe marshes, a few miles to the north of Karonga, and from there became involved in skirmishes with Arabs from Ramathan's, who were beginning to loot the food which was still stored in their villages. On 27 October the Arabs, together with the Henga, attacked the Ngonde who were taking refuge in the marsh, setting fire to the reeds, and shooting at the people who came out; many were also taken by the crocodiles which were numerous there. Some escaped to the Songwe river, about twenty miles to the north, where they were still liable to attack by

272

the Henga from Kanyoli's, which was a few miles to the south of that river.[55]

On 2 November the Arabs attacked Ngerenge, taking many prisoners and capturing many cattle. The rest of the Ngonde then fled north to the Songwe. Kopa Kopa's victorious war party passed the station on its return and Kopa Kopa himself warned that he intended to build his village at Karonga and that he would return to negotiate, which Fotheringham understood to mean dictate terms.[56]

It was on the evening of that day that the steamer arrived with enough goods to pay the Company's outstanding debts, and with a party of reinforcements. The party consisted of Consul Henry O'Neill,[57] from Mozambique; Alfred Sharpe,[58] who had been hunting as a freelance in connection with the Company; the Rev. Laurence Scott, brother-in-law of O'Neill, and brother of C. P. Scott, the editor of the *Manchester Guardian*; and Dr Tomory of the L.M.S. who had recently passed through Karonga on his way home from Lake Tanganyika but felt it his duty, as a doctor and missionary, to return to Karonga.[59] The steamer brought little ammunition to add to the thirteen Chassepot rifles and thirty-four cartridges which were all that were in the Company's armoury.[60] On 6 November J. L. Nicoll returned from a two month journey to Tanganyika, bringing with him about twenty men and eighteen guns, mainly breech-loaders. On the same day about sixty Henga people, who had formerly lived with Chief Karonga, came to ask for refuge; they claimed to have been threatened with attack by Kanyoli, the Henga chief, and that they had nowhere else to go. They were allowed to stay at the station, becoming the first refugees to be given protection by the Company. They had no food and were starving.[61] On 7 November Ramathan came to the station to settle his outstanding account. Fotheringham felt that the outstanding debt stood in favour of the Company: so long as it was unpaid an attack on the station was unlikely and the Company had some hold over the Arabs. The eventual attack followed almost immediately after the settlement of the last account, that with Salim bin Nasur.[62]

Meanwhile Consul O'Neill made several attempts to enter into negotiations but was unsuccessful. The Arabs began to cut trees to build stockades from which to attack the station. Karonga, Kasingula and Mulilema sent repeated requests that they should be allowed to return with their people from Kaporo, where they were suffering from attacks by Kanyoli, and where they had no food or shelter. On 17 November a party was sent to bring them back; they returned on 19 November with about 1,500 people, together with their cattle and goats. Fotheringham was then warned that there would be an attack on the following day. Last minute preparations were made, thorn bushes were piled up to extend the fort to the lake, which formed the east side of a rectangle. The first attack came on 23 November, when J. L. Nicoll was sent to the north end to summon the Nyakyusa chiefs to the Company's assistance.[63]

V

Fotheringham was certain that the murder of Mwini-Mtete in October had been premeditated, and that it had been done on the instructions of Mlozi in order to precipitate a war in which the Ngonde could be driven out, the Henga put in their place, and Mlozi proclaimed Sultan.[64] Mlozi himself argued that if the murder had been deliberate, he would have been careful to see that none of his wives were out at the Ngonde villages at the time.[65] Even if Mlozi's word is accepted it seems clear that he used the Ngonde reaction to the murder as an excuse for a bid to establish himself as a political power in the area on the model of the Jumbe at Nkhota Kota. The fact that he was prepared by attacking the Company's station to sacrifice an apparently advantageous commercial connection, suggests that political considerations were uppermost in his mind. He presumably felt that the eventual decision of the Europeans at Karonga to allow some of the Ngonde to take refuge at the station was a challenge to his newly asserted authority. Fotheringham was influenced in his decision to allow the Ngonde to return partly by the knowledge that they were likely to suffer extremely from starvation and attack by the Henga if they did not return; and partly by Mlozi's repeated protestations that he had no quarrel with the Company, and that he would not object to the return of the people of the villages close to the station.[66] Fotheringham had earlier shown his reluctance to become directly involved by asking the Kyungu to leave the station when Mlozi threatened to attack Ngerenge. The offering of protection to some of the Ngonde was the only provocation which the Company provided for the Arab attack. In view of the Company's association over eight years with the chiefs in question it would have been very difficult to reject their request. To do so would have seemed to deny the humanitarian foundations on which the Company claimed to have been based. It had, of course, to be presumed that at least some of the Ngonde who were captured as a result of the Arab attacks would find their way to the slave markets. While there could be no doubt that Mlozi and his associates were slave traders it does not seem that the attacks on the Ngonde fall into the category of straightforward slave raids. The declaration of the Sultanate, the attempts to gain recognition from the Company, and the chiefs under its protection, and the successful levying of tribute from the southern Ngonde chiefs, such as Kayuni, near Deep Bay, all suggest that the primary motives for the coup were political.[67]

If it is accepted that the attacks on the Ngonde and the Company were simply the result of an accumulation of friction, or of commercial rivalry, but rather of political design, it remains to be asked: was this design conceived and carried out by the Karonga Arabs as an independent venture, or was it, in the words of Robert Laws, 'no mere isolated spurt, but part of a concerted scheme for resuscitating the slave trade to more than its previous vigour'?[68] Laws, O'Neill, Fotheringham, and D. C. Scott, of Blantyre, all believed that the outbreak at the north end was related to other manifestations of Arab power in the Congo Free State and Uganda.[69] It preceded the resistance to the imposition of German government on the east coast, but was thought to be part of the same phenomenon. O'Neill was certain that it had been inspired from Zanzibar and that pressure should be brought to bear on the north end Arabs from there.[70]

VI

There is some evidence to suggest that the attacks at the north end may have been premeditated over a fairly long period and that they were concerted with other powers in the area. The active role of Ramathan, Kabunda's agent, in the attacks, and the gradual build-up of *ruga-ruga* at the Arab settlements in the months preceding them, together with the declared delay in the attack on Ngerenge until reinforcements came from Senga, all suggest that Kabunda and the Senga Arabs were implicated. The only independent African account of the war, written by a follower of Kanyoli, indicates that Mlozi and the other Arab leaders swore blood brotherhood with Kanyoli and his headmen before the attack and that it had been agreed in advance that the Ngonde should be driven out and the Henga put in their place.[71] An induna of Mhalule, the chief of the Songea Ngoni, told John Buchanan and W. P. Johnson in March 1888, that Mlozi had sent messengers to Mhalule a year previously asking for help against 'the English'. Mhalule was said to have refused to co-operate and to have advised Mlozi not to attack them. A representative was, however, sent to Mlozi to discuss a possible combined attack on the Nyakyusa; this fell through, and the independent attack on the Ngonde was said to be the result.[72] Robert Laws heard from Mbelwa's Ngoni 'that a compact existed between the Arabs and the Lo Bemba, whereby the latter were to proceed south along the Luangwa valley, while the Arabs were to execute a corresponding move along the lake shore and intervening ground.'[73] Laws never had any doubts as to the correctness of the Lakes Company's stand at Karonga and wrote in 1889 that he felt that

> 'the check they gave, and have kept up, on the Arabs, (has) . . . been the means of preventing Arab combination and aggression which would have secured their dominance on the lake, and which most probably Zomba, Blantyre, and Mandala would not have escaped.'[74]

On the other hand, during the two years that the war lasted, Mlozi received very little overt diplomatic or practical help from the other Arab powers in the area. Kabunda and the Senga Arabs, while they almost certainly gave some material assistance, were careful to appear strictly neutral; the Jumbe of Nkhota Kota similarly remained impartial.[75] Mlozi received some supplies from the east coast of the lake and seems always to have been well provided with ammunition, but he never mounted a serious offensive after his initial successes in the latter months of 1887. During 1888 there were rumours that he was bankrupt, and that he was unable to return to the Senga Arabs, because he was in debt to them.[76]

Probably recognition would have followed on success. Owing to the Company's refusal to allow him to subjugate the Ngonde, Mlozi was never able to claim complete success, even during the period of three months when the Company was forced to abandon its Karonga station. It seems probable that he had gambled on the Company's putting the valuable business which he and his fellow Arabs did with it before the interests of the Ngonde. When the Company, or its agent, seemed to be taking the Ngonde under its protection, he may have hoped that a successful attack on the poorly armed Europeans and their refugee allies would compel recognition of his claims. There is no evidence that he wanted the Company to cease its commercial operations in the area, which had clearly been of benefit to him, and to the other Arab merchants.

There is not, as yet, sufficient evidence to come to a definite conclusion as to the origins of the war. The suggestion that it was due to commercial rivalry was dismissed at the outset; the suggestion that the attack on the Ngonde was the unpremeditated reaction to a series of irritations seems also to be unsatisfactory in view of the evidence of planning, especially of the pact with Kanyoli. It is probable that Mlozi was making a deliberate effort to assert his supremacy over the Ngonde, and even over the Company itself, which cannot have appeared a very formidable opponent, represented as it was by never more than two agents. The extent to which his action was concerted with other Arabs in the area, such as Salim bin Nasur, and Kabunda, may never be known owing to the loss of Mlozi's correspondence, which was captured after his final defeat in December 1895.[77] It is very likely that they had some knowledge of his intentions. The role of Ramathan, one of Kabunda's men, must be significant; but it seems unlikely that Mlozi's attack was inspired from Zanzibar, as Consul O'Neill believed.

The origins of the war are of considerably greater interest for the political and social history of the Karonga area than the events of the war itself, which ended in stalemate after two years. Neither side could afford to fight to a conclusion. Its greatest significance lay in the propaganda value which was extracted from it by the Company, and the missions' supporters in Britain. There can be little doubt that the war played an important part in arousing the interest of the British public in the area, and in bringing pressure to bear on Lord Salisbury's government to declare a protectorate over the region which now comprises Malawi and Zambia. This was a consequence, which Mlozi could not have calculated on when he attacked the Ngonde in November 1887.

FOOTNOTES

1 The use of the word *Arab* poses a definitional problem. Low Monteith Fotheringham divided Arabs in central Africa into three categories: '. . . the Muscat, or white Arab, who is the true species . . . the Mswahili, or coast Arab, who is black, but is strictly Mohammedan in religion . . . and third, any up country native, who adopts the manners and customs of the Moslem.' (L. M. Fotheringham, *Adventures in Nyasaland*, London 1891,

12.) Fred Moir gave a similar definition: 'The so-called "Arab" may be divided into three classes: the true Arab, the Mswahili, and lastly any wild up country native who may have willingly, or unwillingly, joined the Moslem caravan, particularly if he can sport a garment and tie a dirty bit of turban around his head by way of turban.' (F. Moir, 'Englishmen and Arabs in East Africa', *Murray's Magazine*, London, November 1888, 627.) Of the Arabs referred to in this essay, Mlozi, Kopa Kopa, and Ramathan would have come into the second category, and might more correctly have been referred to as Swahilis, but it would be pedantic to insist on this. Kabunda, and Salim bin Nasur would have come in the first category.

2 Eg., R. Oliver, *The Missionary Factor in East Africa*, London, 1952, 114; M. Perham, *Lugard, The Years of Adventure*, London, 1956, 96.

3 J. Moir to A. Cunningham, Secretary of the B.C.A. Administration, notes on the history of Karonga, 8th November, 1898, Moir letterbook, number 3, The University of the Witwatersrand Library, Johannesburg, South Africa. The three Moir letterbooks in Johannesburg are afterwards referred to as L.B. (1), (2) or (3).

4 Dr J. Stewart to Dr A. Duff, 20 October 1877, Stewart papers, National Archives, Salisbury, Rhodesia.

5 Diary of J. Gunn, gardener at Livingstonia, 4th April; 7 August, 1879, press cuttings from *The Northern Ensign*, Wick, in MS 7906, The National Library of Scotland, Edinburgh. Herbert Rhodes was an elder brother of Cecil Rhodes.

6 F. J. Elton, *The Lakes and Mountains of Eastern and Central Africa*, ed. H. B. Cotterill, London, 1879.

7 J. Moir to A. Cunningham, 8 November 1898, L.B. (3).

8 F. Moir to father, 3 September 1880, L.B. (1).

9 J. W. Jack, *Daybreak at Livingstonia*, Edinburgh, 1901, 229–30.

10 J. Stewart, C.E., to Dr J. Stewart, 1 July 1882, Stewart papers, Salisbury.

11 E.g., F. J. Elton, *The Lakes*, 324.

12 E.g., F. Moir to father, 14 August, 1880, L.B. (1); see also F. D. Lugard, 'The fight against the slave traders on Nyassa,' *The Contemporary Review*, 56, September 1889, 334, on distinction between the Ngonde and the Nyakyusa and on the recent political history of the Ngonde.

13 E.g., Buchanan to Salisbury, 14 March 1888, F.O. 84/1883.

14 F. Moir to father, 29 July 1881, L.B. (1).

15 F. Moir to Miss E. Moir, 14 Auguxt 1881, L.B. (1).

16 Ibid., F.M. wrote 'two *years* earlier'; in the context he must have intended to write 'months'.

17 F.M. address illegible, 27 August, 1881, L.B. (1).

18 G. Wilson, *The Constitution of Ngonde*, Rhodes-Livingstone Papers, no. 3, 1939, 67.

19 T. C. Young, *Notes on the History of the Tumbuka-Kamanga Peoples*, London, 1932, 66–70.

20 T. C. Young, *Notes*, 122.

21 T. C. Young, *Notes*, 66, 71, 124–5, 131.

22 J. Stewart, C.E., to J. Stevenson, 2 July, 1883, in *The Proceedings of the Royal Geographical Society.*, N.S., **15**, 1883, 689.

23 J. Moir, to Directors, A.L.C. 21 January 1884, L.B. (1).

24 L. M. Fothcringham, *Adventures in Nyassaland*, 12–13.

25 Diaries of F. J. Morrison, A.L.C. engineer, Edinburgh University Library, 27 January, 11 March 1886.

26 A. Carson, 'From Quelimane to Niamkolo', L.M.S., C.A., Journals, box 3/35, ff. 40–1.

27 E.g., Hore to Secretary, L.M.S., 7 September 1885, L.M.S. C.A., 6/2/A.

28 F. D. Lugard, *The Rise of Our East African Empire*, Edinburgh, 1893, Vol. I., 27, 53. Peter Moore, an A.L.C. agent at Karonga, recorded in December 1890 that he was permitted to supply 5 lbs. of powder for every 35 lbs. of ivory bought from Arab traders, among them Mlozi and Kopa Kopa. He personally was reluctant to sell them powder but he agreed that it was difficult to answer their complaint: 'If we cannot get powder how can we kill elephants to get ivory?' 'Extracts from the letters and diaries of Peter Moore,' Part 2, 17, 24 December 1890, in *Nyasa. J.*, **2**, 1958, 64. The originals of these diaries which were in the custody of the Society of Malawi, have now been lost.

29 'A visit to a slave-trading chief,' by 'S', press-cutting, January, 1889, paper unknown, in National Library of Scotland, M.S. 7906.

30 A. Carson, 'From Quelimane', 63.

31 A. Carson, 'From Quelimane', 45–6.

32 Dr Tomory to the Secretary, L.M.S., 2 May 1887, in L.M.S., C.A. 7/1/D.

33 See W. Watson, *Tribal Cohesion in a Money Economy, a Study of the Mambwe People of Northern Rhodesia*, Manchester, 1958, 10, and Chapter III, 'The quest for wages', 36–71. He points out that the need for a payment by men on marriage provided a motive for Mambwe labour migrants. He correctly points out that the first Mambwe to work for wages were those employed on the transport of *The Good News*.

34 A. Carson, 'From Quelimane', 61.

35 A. Carson, 'From Quelimane', 71–2.

36 Fotheringham, *Adventures*, 17–19.

37 F. Moir, 'The eastern route to central Africa', talk to the Scottish Geographical Society, 3 February 1885, in *Scot. Geograph. Mag.*, 1, 1885, 110–11. See also J. Roxburgh to Secretary, L.M.S., 14 October 1883, L.M.S., C.A. 5/3/A.

38 E. C. Hore, *Tanganyika, Eleven Years in Central Africa*, London, 1892, 157, 232.

39 R. Oliver, *Sir Harry Johnston and the Scramble for Africa*, London, 1957, 167; also H. H. Johnston, *The Story of My Life*, London 1923, 270.

40 A. J. Swann, *Fighting the Slave Hunters in Central Africa*, London, 1910, 192.

41 R. Oliver, *The Missionary Factor in East Africa*, 112–13; the reference given here to Lugard, *The Rise of Our East African Empire*, Vol. I, 53, does not appear to be correct.

42 Fotheringham, *Adventures*, 32–43; see also map of the north end in *The Manchester Guardian*, 25 February 1888, with report from the north end, dated 10 December, and probably written by Consul O'Neill or the Rev. Laurence Scott.

43 E.g., Morrison diaries, 27th May, 1885.

44 Report on the Moir treaties, enclosed with J. Moir to Sir Percy Anderson, 22 April 1886, F.O. 84/1784.

45 The spelling of the Ngonde and Nyakyusa names in this paper is that used in the letters of the period, and has not been modernized. A great deal of detail about the Nyakyusa leaders can be found in S. Charsley, *Princes of Nyakyusa*, Nairobi, 1969. Much work remains to be done, however, on the oral tradition of the Ngonde and the Nyakyusa.

46 Report on the Moir treaties, enclosed with J. Moir to Sir Percy Anderson, 22 April 1886, F.O. 84/1784.

47 Fotheringham, *Adventures*, 35, quoting a letter of 23 May 1888.

48 Fotheringham, *Adventures*, 34–43.

49 Fotheringham, *Adventures*, 44.

50 L. M. Fotheringham to Consul Hawes, 16 October 1887, in Hawes to Salisbury, 16 November 1887, F.O. 84/1829.

51 Fotheringham, *Adventures*, 45–7, and Fotheringham to Hawes 16 October 1887, F.O. 84/1829.

52 Fotheringham, *Adventures*, 52–3.

53 Fotheringham, *Adventures*, 56.

54 Fotheringham, *Adventures*, 57–62.

55 Fotheringham, *Adventures*, 67–82.

56 Fotheringham, *Adventures*, 85.

57 H. E. O'Neill, entered Navy, 1862, H.M.S. *London*, Zanzibar, 1875–79; Consul at Mozambique, 1879–89; Consul at Leghorn, and later at Rouen, retired 1899.

58 Alfred Sharpe, born 1853, solicitor, acting magistrate, Fiji, 1885–86, hunting on commission basis for the Lakes Company, 1877, volunteer in Arab War, 1887–89, engaged on treaty making for H. H. Johnston and the A.L.C. and B.S.A. Companies, 1889–91; Vice-Consul, B.C.A., 1891; Consul, 1894, Commissioner and Commander in Chief, B.C.A., 1897; Governor, Nyasaland Protectorate, 1907–10; died, 1935.

59 J. L. Tomory, to Hawes, 14 January 1888, with Hawes to Salisbury, 16 January 1888, F.O. 84/1883.

60 Fotheringham to Hawes, 16 October 1887, F.O. 84/1829, by the date of the Arab attack the defenders of Karonga had 32 breech-loading rifles with

330 cartridges, and 12 percussion guns, together with a few sporting rifles and elephant guns. Fotheringham, *Adventures*, 90.

61 Fotheringham, *Adventures*, 87.

62 Fotheringham, *Adventures*, 87–94.

63 Fotheringham, *Adventures*, 89–92; L. M. Fotheringham and the Rev. J. A. Bain to Hawes, 17 October to 4 December, in Hawes to Salisbury, 16 January, 1888, F.O. 84/1883.

64 Fotheringham, *Adventures*, 46.

65 Fotheringham, *Adventures*, 71.

66 Fotheringham, *Adventures*, 89.

67 On the position of the southern Ngonde, see letter from W. P. Johnson, 23 April 1888, in *Central Africa*, Vol. VI, 1888, 97.

68 Quoted in O'Neill to Salisbury, 30 May 1888, F.O. 84/1883.

69 Fotheringham, *Adventures*, 33; D. C. Scott to J. Robertson, 10 May 1889, Edinburgh University Library.

70 O'Neill to Salisbury, 3 February 1888, F.O. 84/1901. For fuller consideration of this question, see R. Oliver, *The Missionary Factor in East Africa*, 96–116.

71 Andrew Nkonjera, 'History of the Kamanga tribe of Lake Nyasa', part 2, *J. Afr. Soc.*, **11**, 1911–12, 231. Nkonjera was a Henga living at Kanyoli's during the war. His opinion was confirmed in T. C. Young, *Notes*, 70; and in Hawes to Salisbury, 10 January 1888, F.O. 84/1883.

72 J. Buchanan to Salisbury, 14 March 1888, F.O. 84/1883.

73 Quoted in O'Neill to Salisbury, 30 May 1888, F.O. 84/1846. The Ngoni had heard this from captives whom they had taken from the Bemba as a result of a joint attack made on the Bemba with the Bisa and the Senga.

74 R. Laws to J. Buchanan, 30 May 1889, in J. Buchanan to Salisbury, 4 July, 1889, F.O. 84/1942.

75 Fotheringham, *Adventures*, 135–6, 138, 140. By November 1888 there was a rumour that the Senga Arabs had 'thrown in their lot' with Mlozi. If this was true it could have been due to the news of the rising against the Germans on the east coast which had begun by then, cf. M. Perham, op.

cit., 138. See also J. A. Bain to R. Laws, 22 August 1888, MS 7891, on the relations of Mlozi with the Senga Arabs, and J. A. Bain to Laws 14 August, 1888, MS 7891, on the risk of a junction between Mlozi and the Arabs at Mereres, (Tukuyu); this did not happen. National Library of Scotland, Edinburgh.

76 Robert Laws, *The Scottish Leader*, 27 January, 1888.

77 *British Central Africa Gazette*, January 1896. These papers were presumably lost in the fire which broke out in the Secretariat buildings in Zomba in 1919.

17 Politics of Collaboration-Imperialism in Practice

Anthony J. Dachs

In barely a decade scholars have transformed the study of African history. Above all they have revealed African societies as dynamic, subject to internal pressures and changes and engaged in the normal activities of foreign affairs and external trade. Into this situation both informal imperialism and colonial rule intruded. They did not operate within, still less exercise their will on, static societies. They were not free to mould circumstances, nor to pursue preconceived policies and strategies evolved in Europe. They worked within African situations and were limited by the means of those situations. Imperialism in practice was confined.

The most apparent confinement of the European imperialists was by assertion of the African peoples against them. Hence have followed scholarly studies of the risings by the Ndebele and Shona in Rhodesia, the Zulu in Natal and Maji-Maji in Tanganyika.[1] These have demonstrated above all, 'an interplay between European and African initiatives by showing that Africans were not the passive objects of colonial rule, unable to influence their fate or to respond rationally to new situations. . . . Many responses can . . . be explained as rational calculations of interest and probable consequence.'[2] Sometimes these ideas have been projected also into the future, to show a continuity of protest that provided a basis for modern nationalism or to show a loss of authority that opened the way for a new era under new leadership and with new tactics.[3] But such interpretations may threaten the normal concentration on the particular circumstances of each situation by encouraging general theory above unique studies. Each protest had its own nature, its own movement, its own cause and its own aim. But more than that each was itself complex. Each had some counterpoise in groups who either remained aloof from protest or who participated against revolt, sometimes turning the scales to favour the colonial administrator. Thus, as one would expect, there were not only rebels but also neutrals and collaborators. Each was a unique response to the local situation, a weighing of interests and a calculation of odds. Such a detailed picture is already emerging for the Shona uprising in Rhodesia.[4] It is also true, and with similar importance, for the whole field of imperial studies.

To maintain themselves colonial administrations depended on collaborators, whether their system was one of direct or indirect rule. In one case traditional leaders collaborated, in the other a new agency was employed. The need for collaborators and the method of using them were the same. Similarly, alien traders relied on the goodwill of those whom they visited for profitable exchange. So too missionary advance rested not only on the success of 'native agents' but from the start it depended on the reception of the chief and his headmen or of a faction able to protect their settlement. Administrator, trader and missionary needed more than co-operation, they required collaborators to support them and to make advance possible. In 1861 John Stuart Mill observed: 'Such a thing as government of one people by another does not and cannot exist.' African history has shown him right.

European imperialism, both formal and informal, aimed at altering African societies. In order to do so each sought and found African collaborators within indigenous politics to act as levers for bringing about the different changes that were desired. If the objectives differed from religious advance to commercial benefit or political influence, the method was the same. Each had to play tribal politics to break into, to establish himself and to do his chosen work in African communities. But more than that, tribal politics sometimes even determined the nature of the European presence. For example, both the centralized Ndebele and the more loosely congregated southern Tswana distinguished between the secular benefits and the socio political threat of permanent missionary settlement. Hence both conducted their diplomacy so as to obtain the advantages without paying for them by way of allowing preaching and teaching and conversion. The priorities of the African were of course the converse of the missionaries. But it was the tribal leaders who chose which missionary gifts to accept and which to reject and so dictated what the missionaries could and could not do. Ironically the missionaries in Matabeleland and southern Bechuanaland had at first to accept a material and secular role that was opposite to their purpose. The missionaries' policy was determined not so much by what their home societies or their consciences suggested it ought to be as by the role in tribal society that its leaders chose to allocate to them.[5]

Moreover, sometimes missionaries succeeded in winning even such restricted access only by using their material resources to play tribal politics. In the African circumstances they had to use the same techniques of informal sway through finding and rewarding collaborators within African polities as were normally employed by the trader, the consul and eventually the district commissioner in similar situations. Essentially the methods of winning influence employed by the religious expansionist were similar to those used by secular agents. Deliberately the missionaries offered the attractive commercial, technical, diplomatic and military resources of European secular civilization to create a faction in tribal politics that could be relied on to collaborate with their religious purposes, even though these allies might still reject the Christian teaching. But more than that, collaboration was dynamic and advantage was mutual. Having found collaborators, the alien strove to increase their power. Frequently this involved change in the tribal systems, sometimes even their

284

entire replacement by alien rule. Then collaboration could proceed on a new footing and European advance be more rapid.

Overall Imperial policy was often pragmatic.[6] Direction lay frequently with the local agent but his initiative was limited in practice by the circumstances in which he found himself. The European intrusion into African politics meant above all the arrival of a new and powerful group. So, according to Pringle, the Yao regarded the Blantyre missionaries as 'like themselves, a new tribe come to settle for their own pleasure or profit. They look upon them as wealthy colonists . . . who have plenty of calico to give as wages.'[7] Before the African lay the whole range of foreign policies from forceful rejection to glad welcome. Moreover, frequently policy and relations varied according to time and circumstance. Since the parties were often trying to make use of each other for opposite purposes, chiefs and headmen shifted between collaboration and resistance according to the political exigencies of the moment. This meant too that alien influence did not usually disrupt or divide tribal politics as much as might have been expected. African determination of the relationship prevented this. On such an understanding students of the Mwene Mutapa dynasty in Central Africa might avoid the attractive alliteration of referring to 'Portuguese puppets' to admit a varied foreign policy with Arab groups and Portuguese, missionaries and traders and even Changamire to preserve at least some measure of independent action.[8]

The Malawi situation during the second half of the nineteenth century favoured collaboration with the European missionaries and administrators. For these Europeans formed but one of several nineteenth century intrusions. Before had come Yao and Ngoni settlers with whom the local polities had already been obliged to establish a relationship, generally one of collaboration with the nearest powerful group. This experience was widespread and productive of 'a series of powerful and mutually hostile states'.[9] Before this could be fully accomplished the European intruded into a situation almost tailor-made for playing off rivalries and attracting alliances. Above all the alien administration was able to exploit 'the conflict of interests between the settled agricultural population and the military trading elements, especially among the Yao groups, where the conflict often corresponded to a large extent with the ethnic differences between the immigrant Yao and the indigenous Nyanja.'[10] Rivalries between collaborators with the Arab trade and those who did not participate made attractive the opportunity for collaboration with the strength and wealth of the white man. So the Kololo looked to the Blantyre Mission in their foreign policy both as an alternative to the slave trade and as a support against the Yao and the southern Ngoni. So too Kapeni invited the mission to settle in his country as a means of added power and a source of calico.[11] On account of the material weakness of his administration Johnston depended on such calculations in African politics. He relied on collaboration to make possible his policy of 'divide and rule'. This was encouraged by the Malawi situation and allowed by the tribal leaders, on whom rested the final word.

Inevitably the European missionary penetration of Malawi was secular as well as religious. The missionaries advocated secular change as well as religious conversion. They offered secular advantage and a secular relationship. They intruded into the realm of secular politics by their settlement, their display of skills and possessions and by their role for peace. Willingly or not, whether as a part of missionary policy or apart from this, they became a secular power in the country. Certainly they did not resist this role for it offered them an opening into African politics and a means of acquiring collaborators. So Riddell informed Mbelwa's Ngoni that it was the Bible 'that made our nation rich and powerful. . . . I said if they received it, it would make them wise and happy and teach them how to become wealthy by fair means, not by robbery.'[12] Deliberately secular wealth was offered and equally deliberately an alternative to raiding so that secular protection was conferred on the Tonga. Hence the missions upset the balance between the Tonga and Mbelwa's Ngoni, and within the Ngoni between Mbelwa and Mtwalo. As a result Mbelwa, while offended by the missionaries' support of the Tonga, himself relied upon the advantages of their connection against Mtwalo and his dissident section. So Mbelwa sought to reserve missionary contact and the advantages which flowed from it for himself, refusing access to the districts of Mtwalo, Mperembe and others.[13] The missionaries should serve the power of Mbelwa, collaboration should benefit the collaborator. The Gospel message was little welcomed. Instead the missionaries were 'pestered for medicine, guns and powder'.[14] Teaching was opposed for the Ngoni perceived the dangers of a missionary revolution: 'If we give you our children to teach, your words will steal their hearts; and they will grow up cowards, and refuse to fight for us when we are old; and knowing more than we do, they will despise us.'[15] The Ngoni defined the terms and conditions of mission settlement. Theirs was the power to do so.

Collaboration was secular. Mbelwa offered the missionaries a secular relationship that would confer prestige on his position: 'We are disappointed that you have not come and settled with us. . . . Why do you live at the Lake? Can you milk fish? . . . But if you come here we will give you cattle.'[16] Chipatula recognized the power of European firearms: 'The country is yours. . . . We are your children.'[17] Missionary power attracted also the Tonga, offering them protection and an improved position.[18] So too the strength of the missionaries' arms had gained for them access to the Kololo and the Nyanja. Before the first mission settlement at Magomero in 1861 Mackenzie's party had already repelled Yao in a raid on the Nyanja. Livingstone pledged the future of the mission as a place of refuge: 'I am going, but some will stay. They will stay here and make a strong place to which women and children may flee in case of attack.'[19] The price of the mission's protection was that 'these chiefs promised not to take part in the slave trade themselves in return for mission support against slave raiders.'[20] The Malawi situation provided a ready opening for the pioneer missionaries and offered to them ready collaborators. The price of collaboration was remarkably similar to that asked for by Johnston in his administration's search for peace and the destruction of Arab power. Later, in 1896, Laws admitted to Swann: 'We may not get the credit for it, but there is a preparation for British rule going on in Ngoniland which may yet make it the easiest transfer of power in British Central Africa.'[21]

If collaboration was secular, advance too was secular. For religious conversions were few, even among the protected Tonga. The Ngoni accepted the secular advantages of missionary contact without sharing in the religious. The Yao remained largely aloof, refusing to send their children to school at Livingstonia or their peoples to work there.[22] But secular advance prepared the way for religious success, particularly by making ready a class of western-orientated, pro-missionary tribesmen able to assume positions of influence under a European administration. The missionaries prepared the way for that administration and stood to benefit from it in their religious work.[23] They aimed at reducing Arab influence in Malawi and replacing the slave trade with that 'legitimate commerce' advocated by Livingstone. At their stations the missionaries trained clerks and artisans. They paid workers regular wages and through their guidance raised a group of small landowners.[24] They introduced an incipient cash economy and looked forward to the advent of a British administration that would assure their work. So the Blantyre Mission rejoiced at Britain's formal assumption of responsibility: 'There has dawned a new life upon this land. British protection was what we had hardly dared to hope for. . . . Nothing could exceed the heartiness with which we welcome what has been done.'[25] To the missionaries British administration meant order, peace and security out of raiding and uncertainty, such as would encourage advance in Christian religion and western civilization. That a further decade of conflict and warfare lay ahead was not apparent in 1891. Simply, the missionaries rejoiced.

Johnston, according to Holmberg, 'went out to South-East Africa not to implement a policy agreed upon in advance between himself, Rhodes and the F[oreign] O[ffice], but to keep all avenues open, in a situation fraught still with uncertainties.'[26] Yet Johnston was limited by the funds and materials he was granted. He was confined too by an Imperial Government reluctant for new responsibilities. Above all he was confronted by the prevailing situation in Malawi, the rivalries of groups and interests and by the need to suppress slave raiding. Although his personal control of funds, however limited, and his personal command of the administration's forces allowed a personal policy, both the situation and his means determined Johnston on a policy of 'divide and rule'. He needed, at least at the opening of his administration, collaborators within African politics.

The general tenor of his instructions in 1891 limited Johnston to control the external relations of the local polities. In practice, however, since control of external relations meant interference with trade and with the wealth and power of peoples dependent on trade, Johnston's administration inevitably challenged the position of chiefs and the relationships of peoples with each other. This coupled with the requirement that Johnston 'secure peace and order, and, by every legitimate means . . . check the Slave Trade',[27] launched the new administration on a career of interference. Handicapped by financial stringency and a weak military force Johnston had to find collaborators in African politics to work the social and economic revolution that his instructions demanded. He had effectively to protect the weak and, for the strong, to exceed the attractions of Arab trade by British peace. Since he could not at once succeed on economic grounds he became obliged to expel or overcome the

Arabs and their collaborators. To this he had no alternative. In 1895 Johnston justified his actions on three grounds: 'We have waged war against the Yaos and Arabs because they are (1) Not natives of the country, (2) They are rival aspirants with us to be the rulers of the country, (3) and because they are recalcitrant to all compliance with elementary regulations providing for peace and quiet and undisturbed commerce.'[28] The policy behind his actions was the creation of a peaceful British protectorate. Those who supported him in his endeavours gained protection, those who resisted eventually faced the force of his arms. But part of his policy was a search for collaborators whom his administration above all needed. This search provides some consistency to Johnston's actions apart from his expulsion of foreigners.

The Yao were not consistently attacked. Rather Mponda could for a while at least be contained within the British fold for he, 'having reflected . . . on the relative advantages of a Portuguese or English alliance, and not liking the Portuguese on nearer acquaintance, had decided to make a treaty with us and accept one flag.'[29] For a while collaboration served Mponda well for formerly his position had been 'rather uncertain. He had but little control over his people and his own tenure of power was menaced by rival and more legitimate claimants to the throne, besides the threatened attacks of the Angoni and the Makandanji clan. . . . our alliance gave him a more secure position in the country. He has certainly ever since been remarkably friendly and helpful.'[30] Eventually public feeling forced Mponda back to slaving and finally to an attack on the administration. Collaboration had come to an end. Mponda was deposed.[31] So too for a while Kazembe was preserved in power at Rifu for 'although rather a weak man, he has a good disposition, and, if properly supported, will probably prove a fair specimen of a native Ruler.'[32] In 1894 Kazembe too was deposed but his career provides an example of Johnston's willingness to preserve a native ruler as a bolster to his administration. So too Johnston looked within polities for collaboration. He did not answer Kawinga's refusal to cease raiding with immediate war. Instead he was 'content to make a separate peace with his sub-chiefs in the hope of detaching them from his control.'[33] The policy paid off. Piecemeal the Yao were divided and overcome.

To win collaborators Johnston had deliberately to court their support. For the weak his arms were sufficient attraction. So many Nyanja were tempted 'to welcome the British as a liberating power'.[34] So in 1891 Chikusi also sent a deputation to Zomba to pledge his allegiance to the British Crown and to request protection from Mponda.[35] But the powerful did not need protection, on the same grounds as Mpeseni in north-eastern Rhodesia 'could see no valid reason why he should grant special privileges to Sharpe and those whom Sharpe represented, since he had no need to invoke their protection against his neighbours—it was, on the contrary, his Chewa neighbours who needed to be protected against him.'[36] Yet prestige and protection were the reverse sides of the same coin. Assault was a reluctant recourse, as Johnston explained to Rosebery in 1893: 'If I find that it is possible to buy them out without a great expenditure of money, I prefer this course to a resort to arms.'[37] Deliberately Johnston aimed at attracting collaborators, and with some success. Jumbe, appreciative of the 'signal honour' of a personal letter to himself as Sultan of

Marimba from Queen Victoria under the Royal Sign Manual and read to him in Yao by Buchanan, pledged his assistance in 'maintaining law and order'.[38] So too Mlozi, out of ambition to be accepted as Sultan of Nkonde, wished to 'stand well in the eyes of the Queen of England' and 'be recognized by the English as a factor in Nyasaland politics'.[39] In the history of Malawi Jumbe's collaboration was crucial, so that Johnston claimed 'Jumbe's support . . . "turned the whole tide of Arab feeling in Nyasa and Tanganyika in our favour" ', avoiding Muslim political dominance in British Central Africa.[40] The capture of Jumbe's favour reduced the 'old British fear that Islam would unite the tribes of Central Africa against them'.[41]

Collaboration divided the peoples of Malawi for Johnston's administration, making possible a policy of 'divide and rule'. Like any other policy it also divided polities within themselves. So Jumbe found himself opposed by the Yao Ciwaura who saw opportunity to lead popular resistance to Jumbe's collaboration. Instead he looked to alliance with Makanjila as the main opponent of British administration.[42] Hence the power of Jumbe waned until his authority was practically confined to Nkhota Kota. Despite his loss of popular backing Jumbe was rewarded for his collaboration. As part of Johnston's campaign against Makanjila, Ciwaura was overcome and Jumbe restored to full authority throughout his country.[43] Similarly Kambasani was granted Makanjila country as a reward for her support for the administration since 1891 as part of an internal factional struggle with Makanjila.[44] Collaboration bore fruits for both parties.

Collaboration was a necessity in late nineteenth century Malawi. It was also a deliberate part of Johnston's policy. This was more than that charged by the Blantyre missionaries, more than simply 'to crush and destroy all native authority and independence'.[45] It was more than 'sweeping away with a firm hand the traditional political systems'.[46] Johnston aimed above all at establishing peace and replacing Arab power by British. For this he needed collaborators and he employed collaborators. Collaboration was part of his method and part of his policy.

FOOTNOTES

1 T. O. Ranger, *Revolt in Southern Rhodesia, 1896–7* (London, 1967); Shula Marks, *Reluctant Rebellion* (London 1970); John Iliffe, *Tanganyika under German Rule, 1905–12* (Cambridge 1969).

2 Iliffe, 5–6.

3 Cf., A. B. Davidson, 'African Resistance and Rebellion against the Imposition of Colonial Rule', in T. O. Ranger, ed., *Emerging Themes of African History* (London 1968); T. O. Ranger, 'Connections between "Primary Resistance" Movements and Modern Mass Nationalism in East and Central Africa', *J. Afr. Hist.*, **9**, 1968; T. O. Ranger, 'African Reactions to

the Imposition of Colonial Rule in East and Central Africa', in L. H. Gann, and Peter Duignan, eds., *Colonialism in Africa, 1870–1960*, vol. I (Cambridge 1969).

4 D. N. Beach, 'The Rising in South-West Mashonaland', Draft Ph.D. thesis, University of London, 1971.

5 For development of this cf., Anthony J. Dachs, 'Missionary Imperialism in Bechuanaland, 1813–1896', Ph.D. Thesis, University of Cambridge, 1968.

6 Cf., W. David McIntyre, *The Imperial Frontier in the Tropics, 1865–1875* (London 1967).

7 Cited in Ake Holmberg, *African Tribes and European Agencies* (Goteberg 1966), 234.

8 Cf., D. P. Abraham, 'Ethno-History of the Empire of Mutapa', in J. Vansina, ed., *The Historian in Tropical Africa* (London, 1964).

9 H. Langworthy and J. D. Omer-Cooper, 'The Impact of the Ngoni and the Yao on the Nineteenth Century History of Malawi', in B. Pachai, ed., *Malawi Past and Present* (Limbe 1967), 20.

10 Eric Stokes, 'Malawi Political Systems and the Introduction of Colonial Rule, 1891–1896', in Eric Stokes and Richard Brown, eds., *The Zambesian Past* (Manchester, 1966), 367.

11 Cf., Report by Pringle on Blantyre Mission, 1880, cited in Holmberg, 234.

12 K. J. McCracken, 'Livingstonia as an Industrial Mission, 1875–1900', in *Religion in Africa*, Proceedings of a Seminar held in the Centre of African Studies, University of Edinburgh, 1964, 90.

13 W. A. Elmslie, *Among the Wild Ngoni* (Edinburgh 1899), 129.

14 Elmslie, 135.

15 Elmslie, 128.

16 W. P. Livingstone, *Laws of Livingstonia* (London, n.d.), 162.

17 Livingstone, 156.

18 J. van Velsen, 'The Missionary Factor among the Lakeside Tonga of Nyasaland', *Rhodes-Livingstone J.*, **26**, 1959.

19 Owen Chadwick, *Mackenzie's Grave* (London 1959), 51.

20 B. Pachai, 'Christianity and Commerce in Malawi', in Pachai, ed., *Malawi Past and Present*, 25.

21 Livingstone, 284.

22 McCracken, 90.

23 Cf., Livingstone, 144.

24 Cf., McCracken, 87–8; van Velsen, 14.

25 Cited in A. J. Hanna, *The Beginnings of Nyasaland and North-Eastern Rhodesia, 1859–1895*, (Oxford 1969), 145.

26 Holmberg, 266.

27 Foreign Office to Johnston, 24 March 1891, F.O. 6178/9.

28 Johnston to Rhodes, 31 December 1895, cited in Hanna 155.

29 Hanna, 156.

30 Johnston to Salisbury, Zomba, 24 November 1891, F.O. 6337/74/1.

31 Stokes, 366.

32 Johnston to Rosebery, Zomba, 9 December 1893, F.O. 6537/31/1.

33 Hanna, 189.

34 Hanna, 201.

35 Johnston to Salisbury, Zomba, 24 November 1891, F.O. 6337/74/1.

36 Hanna, 156–7.

37 Johnston to Rosebery, Zomba, 1 September 1893, F.O. 6482/232.

38 Buchanan to Salisbury, Ngoto Ngoto, 17 March 1891, F.O. 6178/87.

39 Buchanan to Salisbury, Karonga, 29 March 1891, F.O. 6178/89.

40 George Shepperson, 'The Jumbe of Kota Kota and some Aspects of the History of Islam in British Central Africa', in I. M. Lewis, ed., *Islam in Tropical Africa* (London 1966), 198.

41 Shepperson, 201.

42 Johnston to Rosebery, Zomba, 9 December 1893, F.O. 6537/31/1.

43 Johnston to Kimberley, Zomba, 19 May 1895, F.O. 6784/15.

44 Johnston to Rosebery, Zomba, 9 December 1893, F.O. 6537/31/1.

45 McMurtrie to Salisbury, 24 March 1892, F.O. 6337/64.

46 Eric Stokes, 'Early European Administration and African Political Systems in Nyasaland, 1891–1897', Rhodes-Livingstone Institute, History of Central African Peoples Conference, 1963, 13.

18 Johnston and Jameson: a comparative study in the imposition of colonial rule[1]

Robin H. Palmer

I

It has become commonplace in recent years for the 'new Africanists' to stress, and perhaps overstress, the importance of the once neglected African factor in the history of Africa. For much of the colonial era African history was written almost exclusively in the context of European activity on the continent, and elaborate theories of Hamitic origin were evolved to explain anything which appeared, in European eyes, to rise significantly above the level of barbarism.[2] Today, as one might expect, such theories continue to flourish south of the Zambezi; the latest example of this literature of the absurd is entitled *The Arab Builders of Zimbabwe*.[3] But elsewhere these aberrations have been corrected, with the result that even the history of colonial Africa is now seen primarily in terms of African responses to European pressures.[4]

Indeed, we hear a great deal these days about African reactions, initiative and resistance. But the picture which tends to emerge is often very one-dimensional, for African reactions are all too frequently studied in a vacuum, and very little attempt is made to analyze the structure of the colonial societies in which they take place or to enquire how such societies actually functioned. The swing against colonial history has gone so far that it is often exceedingly difficult to ascertain precisely what Africans are reacting against. The whole concept of the new *African Voice* series is likely to prove somewhat artificial unless African voices are effectively integrated with the frequently very complex nature of local colonial administrations. Such administrations were never monolithic. In the case of Malawi, for example, we should need to know the precise roles of the Scottish missionaries and the Shire Highlands planters in both the formulation of government policies and in frustrating their implementation. For very often official policies bore no relation to reality. One reason for this was the existence of competing pressure groups, both black and white; another was the lack of unity even within the administration. The essential job of the man on the spot, for instance, was to collect taxes and keep his district quiet. This would often involve considerably watering down decrees from above which were liable to prove unpopular. As a result, such people were often held in higher esteem by their charges than their more remote, and often

293

ill-informed and unsympathetic, superiors.

Colonial governments would thus often go through the motions, usually slow motions, of passing legislation on such matters as land and labour which, given the prevailing economic conditions, stood absolutely no chance of being implemented in the manner intended. One thinks in this respect of Johnston's 'non-disturbance clause', of the numerous attempts to provide security for African tenants on European plantations in the Shire Highlands, and of the 1930 Land Apportionment Act in Rhodesia, which envisaged the movement, into already congested African areas, of at least 100,000 people within six years, as though it could be done by magic.

Historians of the colonial period need therefore to look rather more closely at the areas they are studying. On the emotive question of African resistance, it is perfectly understandable that academics wedded to the illusion that African nationalism was everywhere a dynamic, mass movement, should concern themselves with discovering, and sometimes even fabricating, the minutest manifestations of African resistance. But it is most arrant nonsense to suggest, as Mr Gwassa does, that it was psychologically impossible for any African polity to welcome the coming of the Europeans.[5] It requires very little imagination to recognize that some at least of the peoples subjected to Ngoni harassment were likely to welcome almost any outside force which could guarantee them some form of respite. Whilst it would be folly to deny the importance of African resistance, the role of non-resistance, collaboration and 'improvement' should not be ignored, for it may be that such reactions were more typical than is currently supposed.

II

This paper essays a comparative study of the imposition and establishment of colonial rule in Malawi and Rhodesia. It seeks to draw analogies where valid and to indicate significant points of difference, while taking as its focal point the almost exactly contemporaneous administrative careers of Harry Hamilton Johnston and Leander Starr Jameson.[6] It will be objected, of course, that such an approach is old-fashioned, not to say hide-bound, and that the careers of two expatriates are but peripheral to a proper study of African history.[7] But their careers will be examined principally with a view to showing how far they paid attention to African realities whilst constructing their embryo states, and to what extent they chose to ignore these realities, and whether it mattered if they did so. In the end Africa destroyed them both, at least temporarily, for Johnston broke down with his third attack of blackwater fever and retired to England, while Jameson went off his head,[8] invaded the Transvaal, and retired to Pretoria Jail.[9]

The establishment of a firm British presence in Malawi and Rhodesia bore almost no relation to pressures arising from African polities within the two territories. Lake Malawi was 'Livingstone's Lake', around whose shore six missions and the African Lakes Company peddled their wares. Vested interests, emanating almost exclusively from north of the Tweed, were being established, and strong and influential pressures were applied in the City of Westminster to prevent the land of Livingstone from falling under the sway of the Portuguese. In Rhodesia, the climactic event took place to the south, with the discovery of the Witwatersrand gold deposits in 1886. This portentous event threatened to dismantle the carefully woven fabric of British supremacy in South Africa, and so Rhodes looked north, dreaming of a second Rand and a British counterweight to the Transvaal. African realities intervened only to the extent that the pioneers skirted the Ndebele state and established themselves among the politically fragmented and militarily much weaker Shona peoples.

If occupation of the two territories took place largely as a result of non-African pressures, the whole ethos of the two administrations was very different. Rhodesia, in the years before the great risings of 1896, witnessed 'the age of the fortune hunters',[10] in which some 5,000 Europeans came flocking in, mostly looking for gold. Inevitably the efforts of the administration were largely directed to the problems arising from this sudden influx of Europeans, as the first seeds of a 'white man's country' were rapidly being sown. In the circumstances, it was scarcely surprising that at the end of 1896 the missionary, Carnegie, could write 'Up till now there has been really no native policy whatever.'[11]

Malawi presented a very different, and rather more typical, picture. Few fortune hunters arrived and there were never more than 400 Europeans resident in the country throughout the 1890s. Though Johnston was given to occasional flights of fancy, in which he saw Malawi as 'another Brazil',[12] it soon became obvious that the country had little to offer the British exchequer; indeed the whole process leading up to the establishment of a Protectorate was somewhat apologetic and half-hearted, quite different in character from the thrustful acquisitiveness of Rhodes' drive to the north. The early administration in Malawi was weak in numbers and resources, it could hope to establish its control over the country only slowly, and, as Dr Dachs has shown,[13] it desperately needed African allies, or collaborators, as they were once called, before the word became outlawed by the 'Dar school'. In short, then, whilst in Rhodesia comparatively little attention was paid to the possibility of African reactions, in Malawi the very weakness of Johnston's administration compelled him to enter the field of African politics and to attempt to outbid his rivals.

III

What, in brief, was the precolonial political situation on which Johnston and Jameson attempted to impose their wills? To take Rhodesia first. Two very different state systems co-existed, but not peacefully. In the northern, eastern and central parts of the country lived the indigenous Shona-speaking peoples, while in the south and west the newly arrived Ndebele had created a military state which was feared and respected throughout Southern Africa by Africans and Europeans alike.

The great days of Shona history had long since passed. Towards the end of the fifteenth century the empire of Mwene Mutapa had extended from north of the Zambezi to the Limpopo, and from the Kalahari almost to the Indian Ocean, while in the seventeenth century the armies of the Rozvi empire had defeated Portuguese forces on three occasions. But in the early nineteenth century, the *Mfecane* brought an end to the last vestiges of independent Shona power. In the 1820s, Soshangane settled his Shangaan people in Gazaland and began raiding the eastern districts of Rhodesia. He defeated his Ngoni rivals, Zwangendaba and Nxaba, who then turned and smashed the Rozvi settlements at Zimbabwe and Khami, and ended Rozvi resistance at Thaba zi ka Mambo, where the last *Mambo* hurled himself off the rock. The Ngoni hordes then moved north into the present Zambia, Malawi and Tanzania, but they were followed in the late 1830s by Mzilikazi's Ndebele, who finally settled at Bulawayo and began to establish their dominance over the surrounding country.

The result of all this upheaval was that by 1890 the Shona-speaking peoples possessed no centralized authority, and were scattered throughout Mashonaland and parts of Matabeleland, living in small, and often rival chiefdoms, in which coherent decision-making was rendered difficult by a complex collateral system of succession. Subjected in the south and west to Ndebele attacks, and in the east and north to periodic Gaza and Portuguese *prazo* raids, the Shona tended to confine their settlement to the rugged, granite *kopje* country,[14] though this 'stronghold complex' may well have predated the *Mfecane* and existed in the last, and far from tranquil days of the Rozvi empire. By 1880, however, a massive influx of guns had so strengthened the Shona that their capacity to resist the Ndebele had greatly increased, though this tendency continued to be offset by their lack of political unity. Many Shona paramounts in fact entered alliances with the Portuguese in 1889-90, in an attempt to secure greater protection against the Ndebele.[15] But though politically fragmented, the Shona retained, in the Mwari cult and through their spirit mediums, a degree of religious cohesion which was to prove of crucial significance during their great rising of 1896-97. To the early Europeans, however, the Shona appeared a cowardly, degenerate people, who could not conceivably have enjoyed a glorious past nor pose a serious military threat in the future. Since the Europeans were allegedly protecting them from the Ndebele, Shona allegiance could be taken for granted. The Shona were natural 'loyalists' whose feelings need not be taken into consideration.

The small and highly centralized military state of the Ndebele was situated on the Matabeleland highveld around Bulawayo. It was a rigidly hierarchical society, with no intermarriage permitted among the three main castes—not at all the type to conform to President Nyerere's belief in a golden, classless, precolonial world.[16] At the top was the king, Mzilikazi and then Lobengula, an absolute monarch with wide-ranging powers, commander of the army, law-giver and judge, subject only to advice, and not direction, from the three great councillors and the two councils, the *izikulu* and the *umpakati*. Beneath him was the aristocracy or *zansi*, consisting of 'pure' Ndebele who had begun the long march from Zululand. They occupied almost all the important offices of state and positions of command in the army, and they manned the leading regiments. Below them were the middle class, the *enhla*, who were mostly Sotho and Tswana captives incorporated into the snowball state in the course of its wanderings south of the Limpopo. They were obliged to swear an oath of personal allegiance to the king, and very quickly came to regard themselves as true Ndebele. They tended to despise the serf class, the *holi*, consisting mostly of Shona peoples captured after the final settlement at Bulawayo. The *holi* did most of the menial work, but they too felt a degree of loyalty to the state which had so abruptly adopted them, and many of them joined the Ndebele rising of 1896.

The Ndebele state was organized on a military basis and was littered with army barracks. Compulsory military service began at the age of fifteen. Unlike the agricultural Shona, the Ndebele were pastoralists. They made relatively little attempt to cultivate, but raided neighbouring peoples annually for food and cattle, as well as captives. They built up an enormous herd of cattle, somewhere in the region of a quarter of a million, which later attracted the envious attention of many would-be European ranchers. The Europeans respected and feared the capabilities of the Ndebele army, which campaigned as far afield as Lewanika's country to the north and Khama's to the south. The Ndebele were regarded as courageous and stubborn fighters, they basked in the high esteem generally reserved for pastoralists,[17] and were accorded something of the same mystique which Europeans in Kenya exhibited for the Masai, a mystique which betrays unmistakable signs of racialism.[18]

In Malawi the situation was somewhat more complex, though here too nineteenth century immigrants had wrought destruction and imposed an unhappy division between raiders and raided. But the raids were not confined, as in Rhodesia, to crops and captives for the Ngoni states, since Malawi witnessed the coming of the slave trade on a scale unrivalled elsewhere in East and Central Africa. Though Dr McCracken, of the famous 'Dar school', attempts to play down the accepted view of wholesale devastation, making the valid point that much of the evidence has been collected from the raided peoples rather than the raiders, even he is forced to admit that the general scene was a sombre one.[19]

Foremost among those who suffered were the once prosperous Maravi peoples of the southern end of the lake. Like the Shona, the Maravi comprised a group of different though related peoples, speaking various dialects of the Chewa cluster. For over half of the seventeenth century the Maravi had established an empire, built up on the ivory trade to Kilwa and Mozambique, which extended almost from the Luangwa in the west to the coast opposite Mozambique Island in the east. But following the death of the great *Kalonga*, Muzura, in about 1750, power passed into the hands of the Undi chieftainship, and a decline set in,[20] intensified during the eighteenth century by the coming of rival Yao and Bisa traders. Thus unity was lost, and the Maravi split once again into the original ten independent peoples, among them the Chewa, Nyanja and Mang'anja. Even the power of these local chiefs was on the wane by the beginning of the nineteenth century.

Among the people of the north, the Tumbuka, the Ngonde and the Tonga, the situation was rather different. Mr Vail, who is gently dissecting the 'myth of simplicity' woven around Tumbuka history, has shown how, around 1770, the Balowoka traders from the east entered Tumbuka country, attracted by large untapped supplies of ivory, and established a loose confederation under the Chikulamayembe dynasty at Nkhamanga, though the extent and power of this empire has often been exaggerated.[21] Similarly, among the Ngonde, the old *ntemi* chiefs, or *Kyungu*, whose functions had once been purely religious, were emerging as strong secular leaders, determined to take advantage of the ivory trade.[22]

The first of the three intrusive elements to burst upon nineteenth century Malawi were the Ngoni. Following the death of their leader Zwangendaba in Ufipa, at the southern end of Lake Tanganyika in about 1848, a great process of fission occurred, caused largely by the fact that none of his sons was old enough to be installed as chief. Within what is now Tanzania, the Tuta section moved north and finally settled to the north west of Tabora, while the Gwangwara moved south east to Songea and, after pushing the Maseko southwards, themselves split into two groups. Others turned south. Mpezeni's Ngoni eventually established themselves around Fort Jameson, now Chipata, in Zambia, while in Malawi the Maseko were driven into the Kirk Range of the Dedza district, the Mbelwa broke up what remained of the Tumbuka confederation and settled around Mzimba, and the Chiwere, a splinter group from Gwaza Jere, ended up near Dowa.

The second invaders, the Yao, were, with the Nyamwezi and the Kamba, one of the great long distance trading peoples of East Africa. From perhaps the very early eighteenth century the Yao had carried ivory from the area around Lake Malawi to the coast at Kilwa, and their influence gradually spread from their homeland in north west Moçambique to parts of Tanzania and Malawi. In the 1850s four Yao groups left Mozambique, perhaps as a result of internal disputes and defeat suffered at the hands of the Makua,[23] and settled among the Nyanja at the southern end of Lake Malawi, where they developed strong chiefs, perhaps for the first time. These chiefs were generally successful traders or soldiers, and their emergence may have been stimulated by the demands of the slave trade,[24] though this is still a matter of some controversy. Once in Malawi, the Yao entered into something of a symbiotic relationship with Arab and Swahili traders, and ivory very soon took second place to the trade in human beings. There was some element of free trade, since the Yao sold slaves to Arabs and Portuguese with notable impartiality. Some Yao adopted Islam and Arab-style houses and dress.[25]

Following Seyyid Said's decision in 1840 to establish permanent residence at Zanzibar, the new Arab settlers and the older coastal Swahili began their attempts to take over the long distance trade routes pioneered by the Africans of the interior. In Malawi they concentrated their attention on the northern shores of the Lake, and Mr Vail informs us that Swahili slave traders arrived among the Tumbuka before the Ngoni and did much to facilitate the subsequent success of the latter.[26] Occasionally the Arabs or Swahilis established permanent centres, as at Nkhota Kota in the 1840s and at Karonga in the 1880s. The combination of Arab and Yao slave raiding, plus the more 'traditional' Ngoni and occasional Portuguese *prazo* raids, was a formidable one which brought considerable hardship to the indigenous peoples, as the writings of Livingstone and others vividly testify.

Thus in the south the Yao and the Maseko Ngoni together dominated the Maravi peoples around the Lake and in the Dedza and Shire Highlands. These areas were obliged to endure regular raiding, the task of the Yao being somewhat facilitated by the earlier ravages of the Ngoni. But in the north a rather different situation obtained. Here the Arabs were not as a rule predisposed to make permanent settlements, perhaps they had no need to, and so, despite the presence of the Mbelwa Ngoni, it remained possible for the Ngonde, some of the Tonga and Mwase Kasungu's Chewa to retain a degree of political independence, and even on occasion to beat off Ngoni raiders. But the cost was often, as in Mashonaland, the emergence of a 'stronghold complex', since people were sometimes driven 'to the cliffs and escarpments bordering the lake, where they eked out a precarious existence on almost inaccessible crags or behind water falls'.[27]

Chronic insecurity was therefore a very widespread feature of life in nineteenth century Malawi; for example, 'The Nganja peoples of the Shire valley caught between the Ngoni and the Yao were reduced to a pitiable plight.'[28] The Ngoni, like their cousins in Rhodesia, raided both for food and captives, principally among the Chewa, Tumbuka and Tonga, though these people were not assimilated as successfully as the Ndebele captives. However, as Dr Linden points out, the slave trade may well have offered the Maseko 'a convenient method for disposing of the unassimilable and the socially undesirable.'[29] But the Yao were even more formidable, since they managed to procure a vast number of rifles from the Arabs, and it was this virtual monopoly over guns and slaves, and their complete economic dependence upon the slave trade, which made a confrontation between them and the British administration highly probable. The Ngoni too were likely to find great difficulty accommodating themselves to the arrival of Johnston, but among the raided people, the Maravi, the Tonga and the Tumbuka, Johnston might reasonably hope to attract people who would be willing to serve in some capacity as agents of imperialism.

IV

Such, in rather simplified terms, was the political situation confronting the first proconsuls in Malawi and Rhodesia. What sort of men were they? Harry Johnston was blessed with immense ability but a rather absurd appearance. He was perhaps a little too conscious of both. He was not subjected to the customary upbringing of his contemporaries, public school, Oxbridge and muscular Christianity, and his African career began in a most singular manner, as an artist in Tunis. Aggressive, hypochondriac, snobbish, fastidious, demanding clean tablecloths, silver cutlery and cut glass at dinner in the middle of the bush, Johnston was 'a thoroughly unlikeable person',[30] 'the little, prancing Proconsul'.[31] But he was teeming with energy, a man in a great hurry,[32] something of a walking encyclopaedia, and a prolific and verbose writer. All in all, perhaps not a bad man to turn a 'paper protectorate' into a solid reality.

Johnston's instinct was to smash tribal authority where it appeared to pose a threat, assert his own control and then look around for pliant substitutes. In Nigeria he had deposed the famous Ja Ja, but in Malawi, as Professor Stokes has shown, he was obliged to tread with a good deal of care,[33] though he was still too inclined to use the heavy hand, to 'overkill' in today's jargon. Finally, he felt continually frustrated by the very mild limitations imposed on his powers by his superiors—the telegraph did not reach Blantyre until 1895—and he was inclined at times to over-optimism. 'Only give me a free hand in British Central Africa [Malawi] for the next five years,' he wrote early in 1891, 'and if I do not hand you over at the end a settled, prosperous, mapped, known, governed, cultivated territory in the full swing of cheerful industry, it will be because I am buried under one of its baobab trees.'[34]

Starr Jameson was a man in a somewhat similar mould. Popularly known as 'Doctor Jim', Jameson, like Rhodes, came to South Africa for his health and stayed to make a nuisance of himself, Unlike Johnston, he was a man of immense personal charm, which he paraded particularly for the benefit of Lobengula. Gallant, impulsive, gun-runner and chain-smoker, he was 'a born gambler: life to him was like a game of whist'[35] His adventurousness turned to recklessness as his gambles succeeded one by one, and it was this deceptively sweet smell of success which led him to the Raid, and to Pretoria Jail, Wormwood Scrubs and Holloway. Yet even then he showed remarkable resilience and emerged ultimately to become Prime Minister of the Cape and President of the British South Africa Company.

Jameson despised both red tape and Colquhoun, his short-lived bureaucratic predecessor, and was given to enforcing laws which were still in the first stages of drafting.[36] He was 'the instinctive surgeon: he could operate, with a few swift cuts, not only on people, but on history.'[37] But he was never his own master, for he fell under the looming shadow of Rhodes, became his devoted admirer and shared his vision of a British South Africa and an Empire stretching ultimately to Cairo. It was only red tape which prevented him acquiring the port of Beira for Rhodesia. He was in many ways the ideal man on the spot, 'admirably fitted for the period in which rough justice was appropriate'.[38] And rough justice was certainly what he dispensed. He saw Rhodesia as a white man's country, believed in giving the settlers their head and so became something of a white Rhodesian folk hero. He behaved as though Africans were not a factor to be taken into consideration, a belief greatly strengthened after the easy overthrow of the Ndebele in 1893. It was an oversight which was to cost a great many white lives.

v

So much for the men and the situations confronting them. We need to look now at some of the ways in which colonial rule was imposed on the African societies we have discussed and to what extent conditions within these societies moulded such imposition. Clearly a detailed account of the administrative policies of the two men would be both tedious and unnecessary, since this has already been done a good many times, perhaps most successfully by Oliver and Stokes, and by Ranger and Gann.[39] What we shall attempt here is a comparative study, looking first at general policy and then at those themes which dominate nearly all early colonial contact with African societies: taxation, labour and land.

Firstly we must remember the very different material resources which were at the disposal of the two administrations. The Rhodesian Pioneer Column comprised a Pioneer Corps of 180 and a police force of 500 Europeans, representing 'an exercise of European power quite without parallel anywhere else in East and Central Africa.'[40] Moreover, Jameson had at his disposal 'the expansive energies of the South African economy and the private fortune and personal dreams of Cecil John Rhodes'.[41] Johnston on the other hand had a police force of 70 Indians and 150 Zanzibaris and Makua under a single European officer. 'No other administration in what became British tropical Africa started out with such slender financial and military backing', writes Stokes. 'The subsidy of £10,000 a year from Rhodes, free transport by the Lakes Company steamers and consular salaries met by the British Treasury, provided no more than shoe-string government.'[42]

Inevitably this wide disparity in resources shaped the policies which Johnston and Jameson were able to pursue. Whilst 'whites in Rhodesia, whether settlers or administrators, did not pay that cautious respect to African military potential which characterized colonial regimes to the north',[43] Johnston was writing, at the end of 1890, that 'Our policy in Nyasaland in our present state of weakness must be "Divide and Rule",'[44] and he was inevitably committed to a 'spoiling policy of weakening, dividing and wearing down every indigenous political system that possessed any capacity to menace or resist.'[45] Indeed, it can of course be argued that the lighter the occupying force, the more destructive might be the end result for African societies.

Thus we find Johnston in 1891 beginning his step by step conquest of Malawi, attempting, rather frenetically, to impose his authority and to rake in some taxes to help meet the costs of his administration. The situation, as we have seen, was ripe for 'divide and rule', and in another chapter Dr Dachs has shown how the missionaries had already been playing this role, often unconsciously.[46] Though Johnston had been expressly advised not to interfere unduly with the chiefs and to attempt to use them as allies, he 'launched out immediately . . . with a whirlwind campaign of punitive expeditions.'[47] He aimed initially at using the Shire Highlands as his base, and then extending his control up the Shire to the Lake before taking on the really powerful lakeside raiders. He conveniently ignored polities which he was powerless to subdue, like the Maseko and Mbelwa Ngoni, though he never confessed his impotence, while with the Arabs at Karonga and Nkhota Kota he made cynical compacts which would last just as long as a relatively equal balance of power obtained. For a while he even toyed with the idea of using the Arabs as allies, though he quickly abandoned it.[48]

Johnston began confidently enough against the Yao chief Mponda and his allies, but the damaging reverses suffered at the hands of Makanjira and Zarafi (Jalasi) quickly brought home just how weak his position really was. He was forced to go cap in hand to Rhodes, who dipped into his purse and pulled out £10,000 for the 'Makanjira Fund'. With the aid of this windfall, Johnston was able by the end of 1893 to break the back of Yao power, though there was a strong revival early in 1895 and both Makanjira and Zarafi continued to operate as migrant warlords within the Portuguese sphere until as late as 1900. But the years 1895–96 saw Johnston's administration in a comparatively strong position, both financially and militarily, and he was at last able to mop up the central and southern Ngoni, Mlozi and Mwase Kasungu, under a variety of pretexts. Thus the British were finally in the saddle, though the process of gaining control had been a slow and arduous one, in which the need for temporary, and expendable, allies and the neutralization of others through treaties had played a significant part. 'Piecemeal the Yao were divided and overcome', writes Dr Dachs,[49] and in general Johnston had made skilful use of the inherent rivalries between the settled agricultural communities and the parasitic raiders. In doing so, he had seen fit to depose many rulers and replace them with more pliant creatures, with the inevitable result that the chiefs came to rely more and more heavily on the British and hence lost much of their popular support.

Jameson in Rhodesia was little concerned with such problems. His administration felt itself secure and its immediate objectives were rapid economic development combined with extensive European settlement. So little were Rhodes and Jameson concerned with security that in 1892 they cut the police force to the very bone, partly because it had become too expensive but also because it was believed to be unnecessary. The Europeans despised the Shona and feared no reaction from them. Those who had given the matter any thought believed that the Shona regarded them as deliverers from the Ndebele. Jameson's abundant energies were mostly taken up with what he considered larger issues: the economic development of Mashonaland, expansion towards Gazaland and Beira, the Company's rights in Barotseland and Botswana, and the problems posed by Paul Kruger's Transvaal. For Jameson, the only role for African societies was to become tame suppliers of labour.

The 'native problem' was thought to concern only the Ndebele, with whom Jameson was at first anxious to avoid conflict. He tried to prevent Europeans crossing a tacitly accepted boundary between the two spheres of influence, while Lobengula, though not abandoning his claims to parts of Mashonaland, also endeavoured to restrain his young men from raiding near the European centres. This *modus vivendi* worked surprisingly well on the whole; there were few serious incidents between the two powers. But things began to change in 1893, when it became clear that Mashonaland was not to be a second Rand, that the Company was close to exhausting its capital and the value of its shares began to drop alarmingly. In the circumstances Jameson seized the opportunity afforded by the Victoria Incident of July to push matters to a head. 'We have the excuse for a row over murdered women and children now', he wired the Company's Cape Town secretary, 'and the getting Matabeleland open would give us a tremendous lift in shares and everything else.'[50] Perhaps

Matabeleland would be the promised second Rand, certainly it was rich in cattle and ideal ranching country, while the warlike Ndebele would no doubt make excellent labourers,[51] and not run away like the cowardly Shona. Hence the Matabele War and the absurdly easy Company victory, aided considerably by 'abominably bad' Ndebele generalship.[52] After the war and the death of Lobengula, Jameson took a leaf out of Johnston's book and refused to appoint or recognize any successor. The victory was important not simply because it apparently removed the last potential threat to European domination of Rhodesia, but also psychologically, since it left the whites with a dangerous belief in their invulnerability and a conviction that Africans were not a factor meriting serious consideration.

Such an attitude had already taken root in Mashonaland. Jameson had envisaged no need for a 'native policy' and a Native Department was not established until the end of 1894, its primary function being to facilitate the collection of the hut tax. This policy conformed very much to his own inclination, though it also stemmed from a number of directives from Imperial officials, telling the Company that 'the natives and chiefs should be left to follow their own laws and customs without interference from the officers of the administration'.[53] But though the theory may have had much to recommend it, in practice it proved far from realistic. It was impossible for a thousand or so Europeans suddenly to decamp in the middle of Mashonaland, and then rush around digging for gold and pegging large farms without making any contact with the Shona, more especially as most European enterprises desperately needed a supply of labour. As Johnston noted in Malawi, there was an urgent need to 'introduce the native labourer to the European capitalist',[54] rather as though it were a school dance.

Jameson was a confirmed believer in the doctrine of *laissez-faire*, of leaving the settlers to administer their own, and frequently very brutal, methods of justice. Predictably, this led to disastrous consequences, as the well known Guerold, Moghabi and Ngomo (Nenguwo) incidents testify. At the last of these, even the normally quiescent Imperial authorities were moved to protest. Twenty-three Africans were killed in retaliation for the alleged theft of goods from a trader's store, a punishment which was considered to be 'utterly disproportionate to the original offence',[55] while the Colonial Secretary observed that 'Captain Lendy acted in this matter with recklessness and undue harshness.'[56] Following these rebukes, Jameson made more strenuous efforts to prevent a recurrence of such incidents. The Resident Magistrate at Victoria, for example, was told: 'It is absolutely necessary for the preservation of peace in the country that the natives should be allowed to settle their own disputes . . . among themselves in their own way.'[57] Things did improve a little, but in the absence of any formal administrative structure and any means of channelling grievances, arbitrary justice inevitably continued, and this could not help but influence African attitudes towards the Europeans. Thus, as Professor Ranger has noted, sins both of omission and of commission were perpetrated.[58]

Perhaps the thorniest problem facing early colonial administrators in their relations with Africans was that of taxation, since the paying of tax necessarily implied submission to and recognition of alien rule, and the loss of political sovereignty. It had of course done so in precolonial days as well; the great West African empires of Ghana, Mali and Songhai, and the more recent structures created by Mirambo and Nyungu ya Mawe in East Africa, had all imposed some form of tribute over their subject peoples, while in Rhodesia some Shona chiefdoms had paid tribute, usually in cattle, to the Ndebele and had thereby bought immunity from raiding. Thus the principle of giving tribute to one's overlord was well understood, but the major innovation of the European demand was that it often called for payment in cash, which most African societies simply did not possess. Hence it imposed, as it was meant to do, an obligation to work in order to earn the necessary money. Taxation and labour were thus intimately linked in nearly all colonial societies, nowhere more so than in Malawi.

As early as May 1892 Rhodes, who was beginning to feel the pinch, suggested that a tax be imposed in Mashonaland, but Jameson rejected the idea on the less than philanthropic grounds that he did not possess an administrative structure capable of collecting the tax.[59] The matter was raised again in the following year, the Company gently suggesting that taxation would 'to a certain extent furnish an incentive to labour which might otherwise be wanting'.[60] But the British government would have none of it, pointing out that the tax amounted to a 'charge for the occupation of their own lands',[61] and that it would arouse 'great antagonism on the part of the natives or of Lobengula or of both'.[62] And indeed it would, since Lobengula continued to regard the Shona as his vassals, while the Shona themselves had neither ceded, nor been asked to cede, any authority to the Company. The dispute was not pushed to a conclusion, and the Matabele War intervened. This radically altered the whole situation, since the Company now regarded itself as master of Rhodesia by right of conquest, though this claim was to be refuted in the Privy Council in 1918. At the time however the Imperial government was in no position to dispute the assertion, and it allowed the Company to begin collecting tax in 1894. Characteristically, Jameson jumped the gun and began collecting six months before he was legally empowered to do so.

The hut tax of ten shillings per annum was imposed only in Mashonaland; tax in Matabeleland was collected by way of confiscating the greater part of the Ndebele cattle. But as far as the Shona were concerned, they had still ceded no authority to the Company. As Ranger points out, 'Nothing had happened to make the Shona feel any more subject to the whites; certainly they did not feel themselves to have been conquered. The notion that the downfall of the Ndebele monarch whose sovereignty many of the Shona paramounts had never accepted involved their own submission to British authority was incomprehensible to the Shona and had it been comprehended would certainly have been repudiated.'[63] It was scarcely surprising, therefore, that the Shona reacted violently to the imposition of taxation.

The early, illegal collection of tax proved so difficult that towards the end of 1894 it was decided to create a Native Department specifically for the purpose of tax collection—a scarcely auspicious beginning to Rhodesian 'native policies'. The tax could be collected in cash, or in grain, cattle or labour, usually of two months' duration. A deliberate attempt was made to encourage payment by cash through the simple expedient of pricing cattle and grain below their market value, and refusing to give credit for the following year when more than 10 shillings' worth of goods was handed in.[64] By 1895 the Department was managing to collect about £5,000, while in some districts as much as one-third of the Shona cattle, sheep and goats were rounded up, often by force.[65] The young and inexperienced Native Commissioners were unwisely allowed great latitude, and were given no definite instructions on how to go about collecting the tax. Inevitably highly arbitrary methods were used; N/Cs and their African messengers roamed the country like Ndebele raiders, and some N/Cs even pocketed the tax for themselves. Such actions provoked strong resistance from the Shona paramounts and their people, resistance which for the most part the N/Cs deliberately concealed from Jameson. No attempt was made to follow the Malawi pattern of allowing the chiefs to collect the tax for the very good reason that they would have refused, since they had not acknowledged European overlordship. In short, the tax question was badly handled, extensive powers were delegated to incompetents and brigands, no thought was given to assessing possible Shona reaction, and no attempt was made to ameliorate the situation when that reaction was often found to be one of armed resistance. Delusions of white invulnerability persisted.

Though Ranger has argued that the demand for tax took place much earlier in the colonizing process in Mashonaland than elsewhere.[66] this is not entirely true, for in Malawi Johnston was imposing tax barely a year after assuming control. Unlike Jameson, he had no legal troubles to worry about, but he certainly had military and financial problems which did much to shape his thinking on the tax problem. We have already seen how the weakness of Johnston's administration forced him to adopt a gradualist and destructive policy in imposing his control over the country, and he was naturally not in a position to impose taxation until people acknowledged, or were forced to acknowledge, his authority. Early in 1894 Johnston wrote to Rosebery, informing him that 'As we extend the scope of our Administration more directly over the Protectorate, so no doubt we shall be able, acting with prudence and gentleness, to extend the taxable area.'[67] Prudence and gentleness are perhaps not the words that immediately spring to mind when one thinks of Johnston's activities in Malawi, but the gradualist approach was certainly forced on him by circumstance.

In 1892 Johnston decided to impose a hut tax of six shillings per annum in those districts over which he held effective control, arguing that he had few other possible sources of revenue, that his military campaigns against the slavers were extremely expensive, and that it was only right that people should pay for the peace and stability he had brought them. Later he was to argue that the money collected would make him less dependent financially on the

BSA Company. This marked the beginnings of his *cause célèbre* with the Blantyre missionaries, in which intemperate words and accusations were tossed about on both sides.[68] Almost as soon as Johnston began to collect the tax, the missionaries started attacking him, claiming that the amount was excessive in view of the fact that the average monthly wage was only three shillings, that Africans had not been consulted beforehand, and that it was often collected in an arbitrary manner. These criticisms evidently found their mark, for at a meeting in Blantyre later in the year with missionaries and settlers, Johnston agreed to reduce the tax to three shillings. The missionaries were not altogether satisfied, and offered the rather unhelpful suggestion that the tax be deferred for two or three years, so that Africans could come to appreciate the benefits bestowed on them by British protection.

The expansion of the taxable area was a slow process. People were generally obliged to pay either following military defeat or when their leaders felt they were no longer strong enough to withstand the administration, and sometimes after leaders had surrendered sovereignty in return for British protection against the raiders. Occasionally there was trouble when people, who were still regarded as vassals by one of the independent warlords, started paying tax, and thus by implication transferred their allegiance.[69] The tax was first collected in the Lower Shire, Blantyre and Zomba districts, and was gradually extended up the Shire to the Lake. By 1894 tax was being collected in eight districts; Lower Shire, Ruo, Mlanje, Blantyre, West Shire, Upper Shire, Zomba and South Nyasa. The remainder of the country was not brought to heel until after the successful campaigns of 1896, and even then the northern Ngoni were not incorporated until 1904. Taxation as with the restoration of the Bourbons, came in the van of military conquest, the amount collected rising from £790 in 1891-2 to £4,696 in 1895-6.

As in Rhodesia the tax at the beginning was collected either in cash or in kind, and the methods employed were often arbitrary because of the lack of a suitable administrative structure. Thus we find Collector Bell razing a village in Mlanje, while in the same district, though some years later, people fled across the Portuguese border until the collectors had gone. A solution was found to this problem by collecting the tax during the rainy season, when people were unwilling to abandon their gardens. Elsewhere, individual defaulters sometimes had their huts burnt down and their wives held as hostages. Johnston also hit upon the useful idea of getting the chiefs to collect the tax in some areas, and allowing them to take a ten per cent rake-off, which often amounted to £50, though, as Dr Tangri suggests, this may well have been an expedient forced upon him by the paucity of resources at his disposal.[70] In any event, Johnston's successor Sharpe found that the authority of the chiefs was crumbling too fast, and that this new role was undermining what little prestige they retained, so he was forced to abandon the idea and to use his own officials to collect the tax.

In general, however, brutality was the exception in Malawi, while in Rhodesia it was very much the rule. This was at least partly because on the whole Africans in Malawi were more ready to pay the tax, since they had either been conquered or had ceded their authority, which was not the case with the Shona. But as soon as both regimes felt themselves to be firmly entrenched, they promptly doubled the tax, in Malawi in 1901 and in Rhodesia two years later.

Turning now to the closely related problem of labour, we find at this time the most marked contrast between the two countries. In Malawi a good deal of deference was exhibited, while the administration itself was never in a sufficiently strong position to inflict forced labour. How different the situation in Rhodesia, where forced labour proved to be the most brutal of the many repressive policies conducted by Jameson's under-supervised administrators, and where almost no attempt was made to sympathize with the difficulties inevitably confronting Africans who were usually working for Europeans for the first time.

The emphasis placed on rapid economic development meant that European miners and farmers needed an immediate supply of labourers. It goes without saying that this supply was not readily forthcoming, and hence highly arbitrary methods were employed. Forced labour was widespread both in Mashonaland, and, after 1893, in Matabeleland. To begin with, private individuals went about 'recruiting' labour, but this did not prove very successful, and from 1894 the task was undertaken by the new Native Commissioners, whose lack of ability we have already considered. The N/Cs thus had the dual task of procuring local labour and collecting the hut tax, which had of course been designed specifically to increase the flow of labour.[71] And so we find the N/C Hartley writing, 'I am at present forcing the natives of this district to work surely against their will, using such measures as I think desirable.'[72] Prominent among such measures was the use of the hated native police, who roamed the country in armed bands, paying off old scores and dragging people off to the N/Cs for despatch to the mines and other centres of employment. The police were particularly unpleasant in Matabeleland, where they had deliberately been recruited from the former top regiments of Lobengula's army.

Conditions of work were generally appalling. Not only was there widespread recourse to the *sjambok*, both by employers and N/Cs—the N/C Mazoe 'had a reputation for flogging indiscriminately'[73]—and numerous fatalities in the extremely primitive mines, but many employers also deliberately picked quarrels with their workers near the end of the month, with the predictable and intended result that they fled their employment unpaid.[74] Severe punishments were also handed out to recalcitrants; one headman who failed to deliver the required quota of labourers was given fifty lashes, fined six goats and three head of cattle, and had his rifle confiscated.[75] Not unnaturally, with the use of such methods, labour became scarcer and people took to fleeing at the approach of the police, which in turn provoked even greater brutality.

There was strong and overt resistance to such policies in Mashonaland, as there was to the imposition of the hut tax, while in Matabeleland, where the N/Cs tended to regard themselves as *conquistadores* and acted in a most overweening manner, there was no active resistance, though any belief that the Ndebele had permanently accepted the new order of things was soon to be rudely shattered. A nice comment on labour conditions was expressed by the fact that many Africans in Rhodesia preferred to leave for the Transvaal to earn money for their taxes rather than work nearer home.

Little of this type of activity was seen in Malawi, largely because the scale of white economic enterprise was so much more limited, and was almost entirely confined to the Shire Highlands. Although some mining and land speculators entered Malawi from about 1885 and bequeathed Johnston something of a land problem, the number of European employers of labour remained extremely small, compared to Rhodesia, throughout the 1890s. There were naturally instances of ill-treatment, deriving from the widespread assumption that Africans would only respond to the iron hand, and from the fact that settlers in Malawi were not very different from their kith and kin in Rhodesia, described by one Colonial Office official as 'adventurers and nobodies'.[76] There were even cases of the Rhodesian practice of intimidating workers shortly before the end of the month, while many of the coffee and tobacco planters were constantly bemoaning the natural tendency of Africans to return to their own lands during the rainy season, and asking the administration to do something about it. But a number of factors combined to prevent, for the moment, the emergence of a situation in any way comparable with Rhodesia.

First the hut tax, at three shillings, was comparatively low, which meant that large numbers of people were able to pay their tax in kind without the need to seek employment. The fact that Johnston tried to prevent the incorporation of African villages within European estates was also important, at least in the early years, since it meant that estate owners frequently did not have Africans readily available whom they could threaten to evict if they failed to turn out for work. Both these factors tended to encourage the emergence of migrant labour. The coffee planters, who enjoyed a short-lived boom in the 1890s, found themselves unable to offer wages comparable to those paid by the administration or the transport firms, and coffee failed at least partly because of the recurrent shortage of labour during the rainy season. The coffee boom did however stimulate considerable activity in the field of transport. The lack of a railway meant there was a great demand for human porterage, and this became a comparatively popular form of employment, since the duration of the work was generally short and it was relatively well paid. But with wages everywhere usually in the region of three to five shillings per month, there was little incentive to work for long, and the general tendency was for people to work short periods only, either to pay off their taxes or to acquire calico or other prestige goods. One result of the very low wages offered and the limited range of employment opportunities was the emergence of migrant labour, now an integral part of Malawian life. In the early days workers generally moved south, to the mines of South Africa and Rhodesia. This situation sometimes encouraged a reverse process, as when planters in Cholo and Mlanje, finding it difficult to secure adequate local labour, encouraged a massive immigration of Lomwe from Moçambique. Sometimes the labour demand placed great stress on societies which had not yet succumb-
308

ed to Johnston. In the case of the Maseko Ngoni, for example, we find the Chewa subject peoples becoming one of the main suppliers of labour to the Shire Highlands, partly no doubt in an attempt to break away from Gomani's control. Gomani reacted violently in 1895, but the administration was unwilling to see itself deprived of such a valuable source of labour, and he was overthrown in the following year, resulting in a great influx of labourers, an estimated 5,000 working in the Shire Highlands in March 1897.[77] The other main migrant labourers were the Tonga, many of whom moved south to escape the threat of Ngoni raids, and worked as porters and in the police and on the European plantations. An estimated 2,000 were working in the Shire Highlands in May 1894.[78]

In 1894 Johnston, no doubt stirred by missionary pressure, acted decisively in an attempt to prevent the exploitation of labour. His labour regulations of that year stipulated that all Africans wishing to work had to register, those leaving one district to work in another had to possess a labour pass from a magistrate stating that they were not engaged to work elsewhere, and those employed outside their home districts had to have a written agreement with their employer, drawn up before a magistrate, stipulating the wage to be received and that the period of employment should not exceed one year. If the worker did not re-enlist at the end of the year, the employer was obliged to pay his passage home. In addition, magistrates were supposed to make sure that employers were in a position to pay and feed their workers. Other provisions dealt with housing, feeding, sanitary arrangements, medical care and the payment of wages to heirs in the event of death at work.[79] Not surprisingly these regulations were bitterly attacked by the white employers, to whom they must have smacked of communism, but a few of the more enlightened came to realize that appeals to a magistrate could be beneficial both to themselves and their employees. Naturally, with the slender resources of the administration and the general African ignorance of their rights, the regulations proved almost impossible to implement, but at least the philosophy behind them was totally alien to that prevailing in Rhodesia, and Johnston deserves some credit for his endeavours in this field.

VIII

Finally we come to the question of land, which again affords an illuminating contrast between the two countries, for while in Malawi some attempt was made to protect African land rights, in Rhodesia, typically, they were ignored altogether.

The Jamesonian era, which witnessed the alienation to Europeans of almost sixteen million acres of land, nearly one-sixth of the whole country, was of crucial importance in shaping the pattern of a land policy which was subsequently to be the greatest source of racial friction in Rhodesia.[80] Things did not begin too badly, for Colquhoun, during the brief period in which he held authority, endeavoured to prevent conflict with the Shona by confining provisional grants of land to Europeans to a relatively uninhabited area between the Hunyani and Umfuli rivers. But Jameson, who very soon assumed full control, showed no such regard for African interests. Though he did stipulate that 'no land was to be taken which was used by the natives for their villages and gardens',[81] he made no attempt to enforce this policy, which was almost universally ignored, especially by the missionaries, who played a prominent part in the early land grabbing and made a point of selecting land adjacent to, and sometimes including, African villages. Each of the pioneers was entitled to a free farm of 1,500 morgen (3,175 acres) in Mashonaland, and in 1891 they persuaded Rhodes to grant them title free of any occupation clause, a concession which began a long tradition of absentee landlordism. In Matabeleland they did even better. In August 1893 the settlers in Victoria refused to fight, though they were under an obligation to do so, unless they were granted certain concessions. These were incorporated into the Victoria Agreement, which stipulated that everyone who took up arms was to be entitled to a free farm of 3,000 morgen (6,350 acres) with no obligation to occupy the land. They were also guaranteed gold claims and a share in the loot—the Ndebele cattle. These terms applied both to the 414 men who invaded Matabeleland from Victoria and to the 258 men of the Salisbury column. Clearly the settlers had every reason to be grateful for Jameson's informal methods of administration.

In Mashonaland land was alienated principally around the main centres of Salisbury, Umtali and Victoria, at Enkeldoorn, where a large number of Transvaalers had settled, and in the Melsetter district after the 1893 Moodie Trek, where Europeans 'were allowed to peg off farms whenever they chose, and apparently without respect to the rights of the Natives. In fact, the very spots on which the Natives were most thickly situated, were, to a great extent, selected as farms.'[82] In Melsetter, where the Free State trekkers were rewarded with farms of 6,350 acres, Dumbar Moodie carved out for himself a huge estate of over 60,000 acres and, in the words of his successor, appeared 'entirely to have studied his own interests at the expense of those of the country'.[83] In Matabeleland the situation was even worse. 'Within a few months of the European occupation', a senior official of the Native Department subsequently wrote, 'practically the whole of their most valued region ceased to be their patrimony and passed into the private estate of individuals and the commercial property of companies. The whole of what their term "*nga pakati kwe lizwe*" (the midst of the land) conveyed became metamorphosed . . . into alien soil'.[84] The settlers wasted little time enforcing their conquest of the Ndebele; 'before many weeks had passed the country for sixty miles and more around Bulawayo was located as farms',[85] and by January 1894 over 900 farm rights had been issued and half of them pegged out.[86] The lands of the Ndebele, located within this sixty mile radius of Bulawayo, had been expropriated virtually *in toto*. Later in the year a Land Commission was appointed to make amends; it assigned two remote and virtually uninhabited areas, the Gwaai and Shangani Reserves, which, as Jameson's successor admitted, the Ndebele regarded as *cemeteries* not Homes'.[87] A Colonial Office official later confessed that 'the proceedings of the Land Commission were a farce'.[88]

What were the practical effects of such ruthless alienation? In the short term they were rather less than might be supposed, principally because so much of the 'European' land remained unoccupied. In Mashonaland, for example, only 300 farms were said to be occupied by October 1892,[89] and this is almost certainly an optimistic figure. The Shona who found themselves living on these farms were not often displaced, for very little active farming was undertaken. Without adequate equipment and labour, the European farmers were forced to work on a very small scale, much in the African manner, and they frequently purchased food from their African neighbours. They had no reason to compel Africans to move, and in any event there was ample room for movement on a farm of 3,000 acres or more. Whilst it is certainly true, therefore, that the future tenure of the Shona was prejudiced, their immediate tenure was largely undisturbed. There was also something of a fortunate difference of soil preference which allowed the Shona to escape the fate of the Ndebele, for in general the Europeans took up land on the heavy red soils, while the Shona preferred to work the lighter, and more easily manageable sandy soils.[90] Evidence that the immediate effects of land alienation were not severe comes from the fact that no direct correlation can be drawn between the extent of land alienated and the decision to join or stay out of the Rising of 1896–97, since some paramounts who had suffered great loss of land did not join the Rising, while others who had lost no land came out in revolt. Even in the case of the Ndebele one must remember that European absentee landlordism was the rule rather than the exception, so that by March 1895 a mere 900 acres were said to be under cultivation by Europeans.[91] Moreover, no attempt was ever made to force the Ndebele to move into the Gwaai and Shangani Reserves, for they were far too greatly prized as a potential labour force for such a scheme to be contemplated. Of course the Ndebele had numerous grievances at this time— they were treated as a conquered people, nearly 80 per cent of their cattle was expropriated, forced labour flourished and the police acted with great brutality—but the loss of land was generally not immediately felt. However, the long-term effects of this conquest settlement were to prove colossal.[92]

Once again, the situation was very different in Malawi. Here Johnston cast himself in the role of protector of African land rights, in contrast to Jameson, the arch expropriator.

Several European speculators entered Malawi before the declaration of a Protectorate, and a number of them claimed to have bought land from African chiefs, often by the disreputable and grossly fraudulent methods typical of the time. Fred Moir of the African Lakes Company, for example, purported to have bought some ten million acres from the Yao chief Makandanji for the princely sum of six pounds! In fairness, one should add that in some cases Europeans were welcomed as potential protectors from the Yao and Ngoni. Johnston was fully alive to the dangers of transactions like Moir's, and almost immediately on arrival he announced that no more sales of land were to be conducted without his prior approval. He finally got down to tackling the whole problem in the rainy season of 1892–93. He made a thorough investigation of all purported sales, enquiring into the price of land, the area granted, whether the granter was the rightful chief, and whether the chief had understood the full implications of the transaction. In reality, few could have done so, since African and European concepts of landholding differed so widely, and Johnston never asked himself the awkward question whether or not any African chief had the right to alienate his peoples' land. He did, however, reject all claims which bordered on the absurd, modified others where the price was too low or the area granted excessive, sometimes offering Europeans land elsewhere, and ratified only those which appeared reasonable and genuine. In the case of all ratified grants, he issued Certificates of Claim, preventing existing African villages from being included within all but the smallest European estates, and often informing people in the vicinity that they were under no obligation to pay rent to the new landowners. He was also particularly severe in dealing with the claims of would-be absentee landlords. Such attitudes would have been anathema to Jameson. Even in the case of the African Lakes Company, by now a subsidiary to the BSA Company, Johnston whittled their exorbitant claims down to 55,000 acres in the Shire highlands and a vast grant of 2·7 million acres in North Nyasa, which was never taken up and was finally relinquished in 1936. Such meticulousness earned him the displeasure of Rhodes.

But severe as he was with fraudulent claimants, Johnston firmly believed that the future lay in a plantation, rather than a peasant, economy, and that some land should be given to European, and even Asian, settlers, who would promote the development of export crops such as coffee, tea and tobacco. These beliefs, by no means untypical of the time, led him to declare Crown Land all the land of chiefs who had signed treaties ceding sovereignty, and to regard the lands of the defeated Yao chiefs as being at the disposal of his administration.[93] He also regarded unoccupied land as Crown Land, and was prepared to lease, on a fourteen to twenty-one year basis, up to one quarter of this to non-Africans, holding the rest in trust for future African needs.[94] Johnston was also influenced by the belief that the Crown should be the largest landowner, so that it could use the profits for the development of the country, and prevent large areas of land falling into the hands of speculative companies,[95] as had already happened in Rhodesia. All in all, almost one million acres in the Shire highlands, nearly half the total area, was alienated to Europeans, though, as in Rhodesia, only a minute proportion of this land was actually utilized. Finally, Johnston encouraged the development of African individual tenure, a remarkably progressive attitude for the time, and something which the Rhodesian administration did everything it could to prevent.

There were, however, a number of serious weaknesses in Johnston's land policies. Quite apart from the fact that he could not afford a proper surveyor, only villages existing at the time grants were confirmed were protected from incorporation within European estates. This ignored the fact that Africans practised shifting cultivation methods, and hence villages split up and re-grouped and people moved about their tribal lands with scant reference to Johnston's land division. Many people therefore subsequently moved onto European estates, thereby losing all their original rights, and from the 1900s found themselves liable to rent or labour services. African land rights 'were in fact left in great ambiguity, which made their position insecure and created difficulties for the future.'[96] Johnston also regarded chiefs ruling in 1891 as the

312

real owners of the land, ignoring the fact that in many cases immigrant Kololo had usurped Mang'anja chieftainships, and had given away land to which they did not feel deeply attached. Such magnanimity was resented and repudiated by the indigenous people. It was also inevitable that as the number of settlers increased, so the pressure on land became greater. In the last years of his administration, Johnston granted Certificates of Claim which included African villages, and this tendency increased under his successors, with the result that the early years of the twentieth century witnessed the emergence of serious land and labour problems in the Shire Highlands, which were to become an important ingredient in the Chilembwe Rising of 1915.

IX

What conclusions, if any, can be gleaned from this somewhat peripatetic paper? We have observed how the Rhodesian administration acted as though Africans were not a factor worthy of consideration when formulating policies, an attitude intensified after the overthrow of the Ndebele state, and we have compared this with Johnston's almost perpetual state of warfare and his removal of potential rivals one by one until his supremacy was finally established. Curiously, however, it was in Rhodesia, where the European presence was so much stronger and the abuses much greater, that Africans retained the greater capacity to resist. And this was a direct result of what, from Jameson's point of view, was a great sin of omission. For unlike Johnston, Jameson had tampered very little with the structure of tribal authority, and had made no attempt to depose potential trouble-makers, precisely because he entertained no expectation of African resistance. Thus we find in 1896 the Shona paramounts and the Ndebele aristocracy still retained sufficient authority to bring their people out, albeit aided by religious leaders who were able to increase the scale of commitment, into the greatest African rising of its type, a rising which very nearly cost the Company its charter and which cost it over seven million pounds in hard cash.[97] Resistance on such a scale was not possible in Malawi, where Johnston had effectively neutralized most of the chieftainships, and where serious precolonial rivalries and clashes of interests had been even further intensified by 'divide and rule'. Here at least, Johnston's preoccupation with African realities, a natural concomitant of the weakness of his administration, proved decisive, for his constant meddling in African politics had critically affected the African capacity to resist. And when resistance finally emerged, it came from that archetypal 'new man', John Chilembwe.

In short, Johnston had been obliged to tread carefully and colonial rule made its impact in a typically gradual manner by slow absorption, without appearing to offer an immediate, revolutionary threat to traditional society. But Jameson had foolishly ignored the implications for African societies of his type of administration, and this almost incredible indifference produced a strong reaction, as did similar attitudes in Tanzania and South West Africa. The sudden social, political and economic revolution, with its great pressures of taxation, labour and land, which confronted the African peoples of Rhodesia, was too abrupt to be digested painlessly, and with traditional rulers left virtually unscathed, the reaction took the form of a violent and very wide-spread attempt to overthrow the whole colonial structure.

Perhaps one should conclude however, not by emphasizing the difference between the two countries, but rather by drawing attention to important similarities, for 'In many respects the Shire Highlands was a microcosm of Southern Rhodesia.'[98] This was particularly true after 1900, when conditions, at last, began to improve in Rhodesia, while in Malawi they showed a marked deterioration. In Rhodesia the outbreak of the 1896–97 risings impelled the hitherto acquiescent Imperial government into action. An Imperial resident, Sir Richard Martin, was sent to Salisbury to direct operations against the 'rebels' and to take charge of the post-war settlement. Martin's successors continued to act as the eyes and ears of the Imperial government until 1923. Among other things they were responsible for ending forced labour, for assigning native reserves throughout the country and for defeating the Company's attempts to reacquire much of this land between 1908–14. In addition, the attempt in 1903 to quadruple the hut tax was defeated and the appointment of Native Commissioners was much more closely controlled than hitherto, thus ensuring some degree of regular and ordered administration and an end to 'the age of the fortune hunters'.

Malawi witnessed no such age of improvement. Vested interests in the City of London, Johannesburg and Salisbury ensured that the primary function of colonial Malawi was to provide labour for the mines of the south,[99] though there were recurrent battles between South Africa and Rhodesia concerning who was to be the principal recipient of this labour. Hence no encouragement was given to the development of African cash crops, and the lack of any serious economic development in the Northern and Central Provinces obliged people to work far from home to pay their hut tax. This was intensified in 1901, when those who did not work for at least one month in the year had their tax doubled from three to six shillings. Thus we have the supreme irony, given the situation in the south, of Africans in the Northern Province demanding the introduction of (non-Rhodesian) European settlers, in the hope that they would be able to provide employment in the area.

In the southern province, and particularly in the Shire Highlands where half of the land was in European hands, conditions were very different indeed, and Shepperson and Price have drawn attention to the importance of land grievances in producing a climate of discontent which was eventually to find expression in the Chilembwe Rising of 1915.[100] As early as 1903 the Land Commission noted that European planters 'have already assumed the tone and privileges of the feudal seigneurs of the native occupier', and that 'no tenure is recognized in the native, who is treated as a tenant at will, and who is frequently subject to the arbitrary demands of an often autocratic and some-times uneducated master. . . . No lease is granted in any case, no compensation for disturbance is awarded, and the native tenant tends more and more to become the serf or villein of the European owner.'[101] Many tenants in fact found themselves obliged to work for one month to pay their tax and a further month to pay rent to their landlord, the more unscrupulous of whom equated

314

one month with six weeks of labour. There was little good land not already in European hands, and Africans were often moved from one estate to another and forbidden to grow their own crops or to cut timber. On the Bruce Estates frequent recourse was had to the whip. The choice was often one of enduring considerable hardship or facing instant eviction.[102]

The European planters played an important political role. Unlike their kith and kin in Rhodesia, they were never sufficiently numerous to achieve complete control, but many of them did possess direct access to top government officials, and were frequently able to bypass the 'democratic' channel of the Legislative Council, and to amend bills prior to their introduction or to modify them after promulgation. In short, they were able to veto any attempt to improve fundamentally the position of their African tenants, with the end result that twentieth-century African politics in both Rhodesia and southern Malawi tended to be dominated by the twin problems of land and labour.

FOOTNOTES

1 *Note on sources*: except where stated, archival sources refer to the National Archives of Rhodesia. Regrettably, the National Archives of Malawi remain closed. The prefix C.O. and F.O. refers to records of the Colonial and Foreign Offices, now held in the Public Record Office, London.

2 E. R. Sanders, 'The Hamitic hypothesis, its origin and functions in time perspective', *J. Afr. Hist.*, **10**, 1969, 521–32.

3 J. E. Mullan, *The Arab Builders of Zimbabwe* (Umtali 1970).

4 For example, J. B. Webster and A. A. Boahen with H. O. Idowu, *The Revolutionary Years: West Africa since 1800* (London 1968); T. O. Ranger (Ed.), *Aspects of Central African History* (London 1968), 154–272.

5 G. C. K. Gwassa, 'The German intervention and African resistance in Tanzania', in I. N. Kimambo and A. J. Temu (Eds), *A History of Tanzania* (Nairobi, 1969), 90.

6 Johnston was appointed British Consul at Mozambique in January 1889, which office he used to establish a British sphere of influence in Malawi. In February 1891 he became Commissioner and Consul-General to the British Central Africa Protectorate (Malawi), and finally left the country in May 1896. Jameson travelled with the pioneer column which reached Salisbury in September 1890, and though without a formal title, was appointed by Rhodes to take charge of 'political' affairs. In September 1891 he became Chief Magistrate, Mashonaland, and in September 1894 Administrator of 'Southern Rhodesia', being relieved of his post when

he landed in Pretoria Jail in January 1896 after the ill-fated Raid which bears his name.

7 In the recent 'peoples' history' of Tanzania, for instance, we find no mention of Governors Cameron and Turnbull: Kimambo and Temu, *Tanzania*. An interesting attack has recently been launched on the 'Dar school': D. Denoon and A. Kuper, 'Nationalist historians in search of a nation: the "new historiography" in Dar es Salaam', *African Affairs*, **69**, 1970, 329–49.

8 Hist. MSS. MI 1/1/2, Milton to his wife, 25 September 1896.

9 The Colonial Office presumed that the Company would 'at once remove from office . . . their present Administrator (who is lodged in Pretoria Gaol) and will appoint a properly qualified and prudent person in his place'. The words in brackets were excised at the request of Chamberlain. C. Palley, *The Constitutional History and Law of Southern Rhodesia, 1888–1965* (Oxford 1966), 149 n.3.

10 T. O. Ranger, 'The last word on Rhodes?', *Past and Present*, **28**, 1965, 122; R. H. Palmer, 'Aspects of Rhodesian Land Policy, 1890–1936', *Centr. Afr. Hist. Assoc.*, Local Series **22**, 1968, 6–12.

11 Hist. MSS. LO 6/1/5, Carnegie to Thompson, 12 December 1896.

12 F.O. 84/2052, Memo by Johnston, 29 December 1890.

13 See chapter 17.

14 R. H. Palmer, 'Red Soils in Rhodesia', *Afr. Soc. Res.*, **10**, 1970, 747–58.

15 Personal communication from Dr D. N. Beach, who submitted his Ph.D. thesis, 'The rising in south-western Mashonaland, 1896–7', to the University of London in 1971.

16 J. K. Nyerere, *Ujamaa—the basis of African Socialism* (Dar es Salaam, 1962).

17 J. E. G. Sutton, 'The settlement of East Africa', in B. Λ. Ogot and J. A. Kieran (Eds), *Zamani: A Survey of East African History* (Nairobi 1968), 97.

18 B. A. Ogot, 'The role of the pastoralist and the agriculturalist in African History: the case of East Africa', in T. O. Ranger (Ed.), *Emerging Themes of African History* (Nairobi 1968), 126.

19 J. McCracken, 'The nineteenth century in Malawi', in Ranger, *Aspects*,

97–111.

20 For possible reasons for this decline, see H. W. Langworthy, 'Chewa or Malawi political organization in the precolonial era', University of Malawi, Conference on the Early History of Malawi, July 1970. Chapter 7.

21 See chapter 10. Perhaps the same is true of many African 'empires' which have been brought to European light via obscure documents or eccentric missionaries, and 'over-written' in a desperate, but quite unnecessary, endeavour to prove that Africans too could build empires.

22 McCracken, 'The nineteenth century', 98; B. Davidson, *East and Central Africa to the late nineteenth century* (Nairobi 1968), 245–6.

23 E. A. Alpers, 'The Yao in Malawi: some suggestions for further research', University of Malawi, Conference on the Early History of Malawi, July 1970, 3–4. Chapter 11.

24 E. A. Alpers, 'Trade, State and Society among the Yao in the nineteenth century', *J. Afr. Hist.*, **10**, 1969, 407.

25 McCracken, 'The nineteenth century', 100.

26 Vail, 'Suggestions', Chapter 21.

27 J. K. Rennie, 'The Ngoni States and European Intrusion', in E. Stokes and R. Brown (Eds), *The Zambesian Past* (Manchester, 1966), 308.

28 H. W. Langworthy and J. D. Omer-Cooper, 'The impact of the Ngoni and the Yao on the nineteenth century History of Malawi', in B. Pachai, G. W. Smith and R. K. Tangri (Eds), *Malawi Past and Present* (Blantyre, 1968), 19.

29 I. Linden, 'The Maseko Ngoni at Domwe, 1870–1900', University of Malawi, Conference on the Early History of Malawi, July 1970, Chapter 14.

30 O. Ransford, *Livingstone's Lake* (London 1969), 189.

31 R. Oliver, *Sir Harry Johnston and the Scramble for Africa* (London 1964), 240.

32 Salisbury once observed that 'Johnston is in too much of a hurry. Rome was not built in a day.' F.O. 84/2052, Minute by Salisbury on Memo by Johnston, 29 December 1890.

33 E. Stokes, 'Malawi Political Systems and the Introduction of Colonial

Rule, 1891–1896', in Stokes and Brown, *Zambesian Past*, 352–75.

34 F.O. 84/2140, Johnston to Anderson, 9 February 1891.

35 O. Ransford, *The Rulers of Rhodesia* (London 1968), 185.

36 Palley, *Constitutional History*, 103.

37 S. G. Millin, *Rhodes* (London 1937), 258.

38 R. C. Tredgold, *The Rhodesia that was my life* (London 1968), 61.

39 Oliver, *Sir Harry Johnston*; Stokes, 'Malawi'; T. O. Ranger, *Revolt in Southern Rhodesia, 1896–7* (London 1967); L. H. Gann, *A History of Southern Rhodesia* (London 1965).

40 T. O. Ranger, 'African reaction and resistance to the imposition of colonial rule in East and Central Africa', in L. H. Gann and P. J. Duignan (Eds), *Colonialism in Africa 1870–1960. Vol. I The History and Politics of Colonialism 1870–1914* (Cambridge 1969), 294

41 Ranger, *Revolt*, 46.

42 Stokes, 'Malawi', 358–9.

43 Ranger, *Revolt*, 47.

44 F.O. 84/2052, Memo by Johnston, 29 December 1890.

45 Stokes, 'Malawi', 360.

46 Dachs, 'Politics', Chapter 17.

47 Stokes, 'Malawi', 359.

48 Early in 1890 he wrote of the Arabs that 'by a little tact and patience . . . we may skilfully make use of them and turn their dispositions to good account in the development of Africa. I think the Swahili as colonist and soldier may turn out to be a very useful ally'. F.O. 2/55, Johnston to Salisbury, 17 March 1890.

49 Dachs, 'Politics', Chapter 17.

50 Rhodes House, Rhodes Papers, MSS. Afr. s.228, C. 3B, Jameson to Harris, 19 July 1893. It has generally been assumed that Jameson and Harris were bosom friends, but Jameson once felt constrained to observe that 'Harris means well in Cape Town but is really a muddling ass—on

the surface a genius; but under the crust as thick as they are made.' Hist. MSS. JA 1/1/1, Jameson to Sam Jameson, 11 August 1892.

51 Thus we have Frank Johnson, the organizer of the pioneer column, lamenting that 'we have excellent labourers in the Matabele, and from the mining and commercial point of view I regret the loss of the 2,000 odd Matabele killed in the late war very much.' In A. R. Colquhoun, 'Matabeleland', *Proc. Roy. Col. Inst.*, **25**, 1893–94, 98.

52 Hist. MSS. SE 1/1/1, Selous to his mother, 15 November 1893.

53 C.O. 417/72, Imperial Secretary to Company, 5 June 1891. See also C.O. 417/72, Knutsford to Loch, 15 May 1891; Colonial Office to Company, 29 May 1891; High Commissioner's Proclamation of 10 June 1891.

54 F.O. 2/106, Johnston to Salisbury, 29 April 1896.

55 *African (South) 426*, Imperial Secretary to Company, 26 April 1892.

56 *African (South) 426*, Colonial Office to Company, 31 May 1892. Compare these comments with the reaction of Gifford, one of the Company's directors: 'I am thundering glad you gave the Mashonas a lesson they will not be so cheeky in future'. A 1/3/4, Gifford to Jameson, 1 April 1892.

57 DV 1/3/1, Assistant Secretary, Law Department, to Resident Magistrate, Victoria, 23 December 1893.

58 Ranger, *Revolt*, 53.

59 A 1/5/10, Memo of a conversation between Rhodes and Jameson, 15 May 1892.

60 *African (South) 454*, Company to Colonial Office, 7 July 1893.

61 *African (South) 441*, Imperial Secretary to Company, 29 August 1892.

62 *African (South) 441*, Colonial Office to Company, 29 June 1893.

63 Ranger, *Revolt*, 69.

64 J. J. Taylor, 'The origins of the Native Department in Southern Rhodesia, 1890–98', (unpublished 1968), 10.

65 D. N. Beach, 'The Politics of Collaboration: South Mashonaland, 1896–97', (unpublished 1969), 19.

66 Ranger, *Revolt*, 87.

67 F.O. 2/66, Johnston to Rosebery, 22 January 1894.

68 A. C. Ross, 'The African—a child or a man', in Stokes and Brown, *Zambesian Past*, 332–51.

69 Linden, 'Maseko Ngoni', Chapter 14.

70 R. K. Tangri, 'African reactions and resistance to the early colonial situation in Malawi, 1891–1915', *Central Africa Historical Association*, Local Series, **25**, 1969, 5.

71 Fairfield, a Colonial Office official sympathetic to the Company, pointed out that 'Rhodes' argument that the necessity of paying the tax will compel the Mashonas to work for the mining industry is all well enough in a Stock Exchange Luncheon Room, but it is hardly a *parliamentary* argument.' CT 1/3/1, Fairfield to Hawksley, 29 July 1893.

72 N 1/2/2, N/C Hartley to CNC Mashonaland, 30 November 1895.

73 C. G. Chivanda, 'The Mashona Rebellion in oral tradition: Mazoe District', (unpublished 1966), 7.

74 J 1/1/1, Resident Magistrate, Victoria, to Public Prosecutor, Salisbury, 23 October 1894; *C.8547*, Evidence of Carnegie to Sir Richard Martin, June 1896.

75 DS 1/1/1, Mining Commissioner, Mazoe, to Resident Magistrate, Salisbury, 8 & 16 March 1893.

76 C.O. 417/61, Minute by Wingfield, 28 July 1891.

77 Stokes, 'Malawi', 369.

78 F. E. Sanderson, 'The development of labour migration from Nyasaland, 1891–1914', *J. Afr. Hist.*, **2**, 1961, 260.

79 F.O. 2/87, Foreign Office to Sharpe, 25 January 1895.

80 I have dealt at greater length elsewhere with land policies in the 1890s: R. H. Palmer, 'War and Land in Rhodesia', *Transafr. J. Hist.*, **1** (2), 1971.

81 W. H. Brown, *On the South African Frontier*, (London 1899), 120.

82 NUE 2/1/2, Report of the N/C Melsetter for the half-year ending September 1897.

83 L 2/2/95/22, Magistrate, Melsetter, to Acting Administrator, 12 April 1896.

84 N 3/16/9, S/N Bulawayo to CNC, 1 June 1920.

85 A. Boggie, *From Ox-Wagon to Railway* (Bulawayo 1897), 26.

86 C. L. N. Newman, *Matabeleland and how we got it* (London 1895), 147.

87 Rhodes House, Rhodes Papers, MSS. Afr. s.228.1., Grey to Rhodes, 26 May 1897.

88 C.O. 417/219, Minute by Graham, 26 June 1897.

89 British South Africa Company, *Report on the Company's proceedings and the condition of the Territories within the sphere of its operations, 1889–92*, (London 1893), 25.

90 Palmer, 'Red Soils'.

91 British South Africa Company, *Report 1894–5*, 67.

92 In short, Native Commissioners after the Rising of 1896 found it impossible to assign adequate reserves in central Matabeleland, the Morris Carter Land Commission of 1925 was unable to implement territorial segregation on the Matabeleland highveld because there was nowhere to put Africans then living on European farms, while Ndebele political activity, when resumed in a new era, was based squarely on the issue of land. Palmer, 'Aspects' and 'War and Land'; T. O. Ranger, *The African Voice in Southern Rhodesia* (London 1970), 30–41, 64–87.

93 Ross, 'The African', 348.

94 F.O. 84/2197, Johnston to Rosebery, 13 October, 1892.

95 B. S. Krishnamurthy, 'Land and Labour in Nyasaland, 1891–1914', University of London, Ph.D. thesis, (1964), 123–4.

96 Krishnamurthy, 'Land and Labour', 128.

97 Ranger, 'African reactions', 298.

98 J. McCracken, 'African Politics in twentieth-century Malawi', in Ranger, *Aspects*, 196.

99 The Colonial Office, for example, turned down Sharpe's proposal to check the growth of migrant labour by introducing a pass system, observ-

ing that 'pass regulations ought not to be turned into an engine for preventing those who may be lawfully seeking employment elsewhere, from taking their labour to the best market.' F.O. 2/669, Colonial Office to Foreign Office, 2 November 1900.

100 G. Shepperson and T. Price, *Independent African* (Edinburgh 1963), 127–263.

101 F.O. 2/748, Land Commission to Pearce, 6 May 1903.

102 It is worth noting that many of the white planters came originally from the Scottish Highlands, where they had long been used to the practice of evicting tenants from their estates.

18.1   Sir Harry Hamilton Johnston

18.2 Sir Leander Starr Jameson

20.1 The twin islands of Likoma and Chisumulu, 1895, showing S.S. *Domira*

19 The Development of the Administration to 1897

C. A. Baker

I THE EARLY CONSULS

During the second half of the nineteenth century Great Britain appointed to Eastern and Central Africa a series of Consuls whose work gradually focused more and more clearly on the Malawi area, until the focusing became crystal clear with the declaration of the Nyasaland Districts Protectorate in 1891. Although it was only with this declaration that a central administration was set up and the machinery of central government was created, it may be profitable for us briefly to trace the way in which—from a legal and administrative viewpoint—Great Britain assumed responsibility for the executive government of the area.

If we wish to trace the origins of and legal authority for the executive power of Britain—both internal and external—we must turn back the pages of history, through nine centuries, to the Norman Conquest. William I, and subsequent sovereigns of Britain, ruled under the authority of the Royal Prerogative—the inherent right of the king to govern his people. This authority originated in the king's supreme position in the feudal hierarchy, and at first differed only in degree from the powers exercised by other feudal lords. Originally the Royal Prerogative was unrestricted, and covered legislative, judicial and executive powers, but as time passed it became limited to executive functions. Over the centuries the formerly unlimited executive powers have been diminished by statutes which have completely abolished some parts of the prerogative, have modified others, and have given yet others to persons or bodies other than the Sovereign. The prerogative has not, even now, however, completely disappeared, and in Britain the important remaining aspects, from a public administration point of view, are the powers to organize the executive work of government, to appoint public officers and—for our present purposes—to acquire territories overseas. Other prerogative aspects range from the power to declare war to the right of the Queen to demand from fishermen the sturgeon which they catch! All these powers, great and small, may be exercised by the Crown without the authority of Parliament. This is important in considering the early development of the Administration in what is today Malawi, because all the important early steps were taken under the legal authority of the prerogative, and not with express parliamentary sanction: the declaration of the Protectorate, the setting up of Departments and of the district administration, the appointment of officers, and the whole organization of the executive work. These tasks fell to Harry Johnston, but he was only one of a series of British Consuls appointed to this part of Africa.

David Livingstone was appointed Consul in February 1858, and his area of jurisdiction was vaguely defined as 'the Eastern Coast of Africa and the independent districts in the interior.' He travelled in Malawi in the late 1850s and early 1860s; and although the functions of his consular expedition were scientific rather than political or administrative, at least, John Kirk appears to have considered its members to have been in a position analogous to civil servants;[1] and the results of Livingstone's work—particularly the suppression of the slave trade, the establishment of missions, and the introduction of 'legitimate commerce', in Central Africa—were factors which helped to bring about the eventual declaration of a Protectorate. Livingstone's consular appointment was terminated in 1863.

It was not until 1875 that another Consul, James Frederic Elton, was appointed, and his jurisdiction was limited to 'the Portuguese possessions on the east coast of Africa', with his headquarters at Mozambique. Unlike Livingstone, his consular area did not include the interior, but his earlier post of Vice-Consul at Zanzibar made him familiar with, and deeply interested in, the slave trade, and he was given permission by the Foreign Office in 1877 to visit the interior and to enquire into that trade. His visit to the Malawi area added to his personal experience of the slave trade, and he formed the opinion that 'an immensity of good might be effected by a commissioner, whose aim should be to detach the chiefs from the Arab slave trade influences, and attach them to a policy of legitimate commerce and progress.'[2] His visit, however, was fatal, since having travelled the length of Malawi he died on his way back to the coast on 19 December 1877.

Two years later, in 1879, Henry Edward O'Neill was appointed Elton's successor to Mozambique. He had previously served as a lieutenant on a cruiser off the East Africa coast, and, like Elton, he was permitted to travel inland to investigate the slave trade. In the second half of 1883 and the early part of 1884 he travelled in Malawi, and, again like Elton, recommended the appointment of a slave trade commissioner in the interior. This recommendation was, in effect, adopted by the British government when they appointed Captain Charles Edward Foot as Consul.

Foot had commanded a British cruiser off the east coast of Africa for a number of years and had taken part in the blockade by warships trying to check the export of slaves.[3] He was, therefore, familiar with the slave trade—like Elton and O'Neill. Unlike them, however, his appointment was specifically to the Malawi area: to 'the territories of the African Kings and Chiefs in the districts adjacent to Lake Nyassa'; as Hetherwick later remarked, this was 'a commission wide enough to occupy the attention and energies of any man'.[4] Foot arrived in Blantyre with his wife, two children and Lawrence Goodrich, his assistant, early in 1884, and intended to settle in Blantyre, but he died on

16 August 1884, at the age of 43.[5]

Goodrich acted in Foot's place for fourteen months until A. G. S. Hawes arrived as Consul. Hawes decided to settle not at Blantyre, but at Zomba, so as to be nearer to the slave caravan routes, and thus took a step in the northward move of the administrative headquarters of the country a later stage of which is to be seen in the buildings of the new capital site at Lilongwe today.

When Hawes left at the end of 1887, John Buchanan took over as Acting Consul, and he continued to hold this post until Johnston set up his Protectorate Administration in 1891. In 1889 he declared a Protectorate over the 'Makololo, Yao and Machinga Countries'.[6]

During the period spanned by the consular appointments of Livingstone, Elton, O'Neill, Foot, Goodrich, Hawes and Buchanan, European immigrants entered Malawi and gradually established themselves. First, in 1861, the Universities Mission to Central Africa set itself up at Magomero, but after a relatively short time moved to Chikwawa, then to Morambala, and early in 1864 left the mainland of Africa to settle at Zanzibar. Then, in 1875–76, the Free Church of Scotland Mission established itself at Cape Maclear, and later at Bandawe and Livingstonia; and the Church of Scotland Mission set itself up at Blantyre. In 1878 the African Lakes Company arrived, and as the years passed established a chain of trading stations in the country. Planters, such as John Buchanan, Eugene Sharrer and John Bowhill began to cultivate in Zomba, Blantyre and Mlanje; by the end of the 1880s there was a significant British community in Malawi.

Simply stated, Malawi was an area at that time allocated to no external power; the Portuguese threatened from the south, the Germans from the east and north, and the Congo Free State from the west; inside the area the slave raiders threatened, and the missions and planters were pressing for British protection. These pressures, internal and external, began to build up in the late 1880s. Just at this time geographical and financial points of entry were found—the Chinde mouth of the Zambezi, and Rhodes' willingness to finance the administration of the area.

It was upon this scene that there entered the person who was to create and develop the early administration of the country: Harry Johnston. His work can be divided into three parts: his visit as Consul of Mozambique, his first tour as Commissioner and Consul-General, and his second—and final—tour in that capacity.

II THE VISIT OF JOHNSTON AS CONSUL AT MOCAMBIQUE

Johnston's first, but indirect, contact with the affairs of Central Africa was in 1884, when, having recently returned from the Congo, he was asked by the Foreign Office to give an opinion on a draft treaty with Portugal, which, had it been ratified, would have then confined the Portuguese political influence to the area south of the Shire-Ruo confluence.[7]

His second, and again indirect, contact with Malawi was in July of 1885 when, after he had returned from Kilimanjaro, he asked the Foreign Office to give him a consular appointment in some part of tropical Africa. In reply he was asked if he would be prepared, if the post became vacant, to go to Mozambique 'with a view to observing the progress of events in Nyasaland'.[8] Johnston agreed but the post was given to Hawes, and Johnston was appointed instead as Vice-Consul for the Oil Rivers and the Cameroons, where he stayed for nearly three years. This was a valuable training period for him: he acted as Consul for over a year when Consul Hewett was ill; he travelled widely through his consular area; he experienced the debilitations of an attack of blackwater fever—the first of six which he survived; he had time to think about and make recommendations on the political apportionment of Africa; he surveyed and mapped large areas of the Rio del Rey; he wrote detailed reports on, and made recommendation as to the future administration of, the country; he was forced to work under great pressure to deal with the work which accumulated whilst Hewett was ill; he made extensive biological collections; he had to deal with a complicated and dangerous affair which involved a major chief and a powerful Scottish trading company.[9] All this experience was to stand him in good stead when he served in Central Africa.

He left the Oil Rivers and Cameroons in July, 1888, and whilst on leave he was interviewed by Lord Salisbury, and as a result of a conversation at Hatfield he wrote an anonymous article which was published in *The Times* entitled 'Great Britain's Policy in Africa'.[10] In these ways he gained Salisbury's confidence and support. In November 1888, he was formally appointed O'Neill's successor as Consul to Mozambique, although it was clear that he was to have dealings in the Malawi area which Hawes had left and which was being looked after, in an acting capacity, by Buchanan.

After a very short time at Mozambique Johnston travelled inland, sailing through the recently-discovered Chinde mouth of the Zambezi delta at 7.30 a.m. on Sunday 28 July 1889, in H.M.S. 'Stork', the largest vessel then to have crossed the bar.[11] By so doing he claimed, for the first time physically, the right of free navigation on the Zambezi, and demonstrated quite clearly that the Royal Navy could reach the Shire River and be in a position to protect the settlements in the Shire Highlands.

His visit to Malawi in 1889 and early 1890 was to enable him to 'report on the troubles which had arisen with the Arabs [at Karonga] and above all with the Portuguese [on the lower Shire]; and . . . [to] take measures to secure the country from abrupt seizure by other European powers, by concluding treaties of friendship with the . . . chiefs, in which they bound themselves not to transfer their governing rights to any European Power without the consent of Her Majesty's Government.'[12] Johnston and John Lowe Nicoll (whom he had met at Quelimane) made treaties on the western shore of the lake and on the Tanganyika plateau; Buchanan made treaties in the Shire highlands; and Alfred Sharpe (whom Johnston had met in the Elephant Marsh) made treaties in what later became north-eastern Rhodesia.

Whilst Johnston was away with Nicoll in the north, the Portuguese under Major Serpa Pinto advanced up the Shire river, and threatened to occupy the Shire highlands. Buchanan, acting on instructions given to him earlier by Johnston, thereupon declared a British Protectorate over the 'Makololo, Yao
326

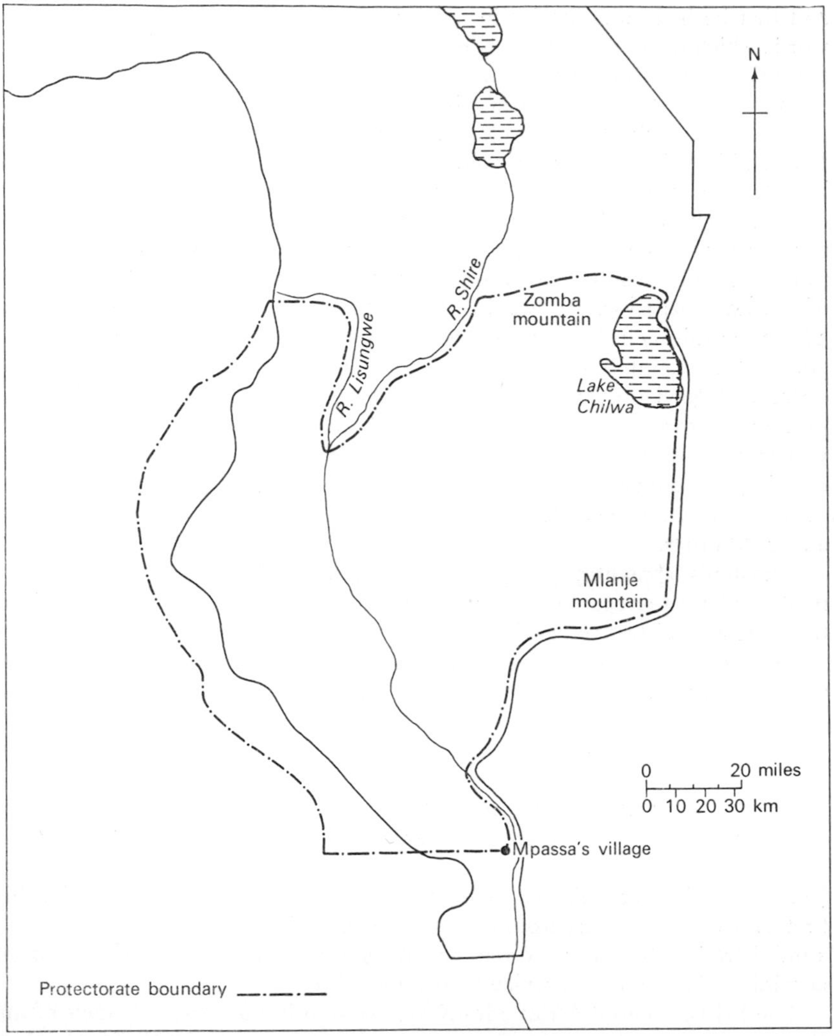
N
R. Shire
Zomba
mountain
R. Lisungwe
Lake
Chilwa
Mlanje
mountain
0 20 miles
0 10 20 30 km
Mpassa's village
Protectorate boundary

19.1 'Makololo, Yao and Machinga countries' Protectorate, 1889

and Machinga Countries' on 21st September 1889.[13] We do not know for sure whether Johnston had authority from the British government to instruct Buchanan to declare a Protectorate, but it seems that such authority may have been given. A clue lies in Johnston's account of his discussion with the governor of Mozambique in July 1889. 'The Governor asked me pointedly if I intended to proclaim a British Protectorate, and I told him I was authorized to do nothing of the kind, so long as Major Serpa Pinto or other Portuguese explorers took no political action outside Portuguese territory.'[14] It is, of course, quite possible that Johnston was deliberately using ambiguous language and that he had no authority in any case to declare a Protectorate, but the words which he used are, none the less, consistent with his having been given authority to act if Serpa Pinto moved too close to the Shire highlands.

Johnston returned to Mozambique early in 1890, and in May received permission to return to England. In August he was made a Commander of the Bath and later in the year was told by Lord Salisbury that he was being sent back to 'the Zambezi regions, to organize them into a Protectorate'.

On 14 February 1891—whilst Sharpe was only just ending his treaty-making journey in Central Africa—Johnston was formally appointed to be Commissioner and Consul-General to the territories under British influence north of the Zambezi river. He was instructed to consolidate the Protectorate; to advise the chiefs on their external relations with each other and with foreigners—but not to interfere unduly with their internal administration; to secure peace and good order; and to check the slave trade.[15] This appointment preceded by three months the declaration of the Protectorate to which Johnston was appointed: the Nyasaland Districts Protectorate. The notice broadly defining the boundaries of this Protectorate added that 'Measures are in course of preparation for the administration of justice and the maintenance of peace and good order.'[16]

Johnston's appointment—like the declaration of the Protectorate—was made under a prerogative Order in Council, and he was thereby authorized to create administrative districts and to appoint officers to reside in them. He was generally entrusted with the task of setting up a complete administration and bringing law and order to the country.

III   THE FOUNDATION OF THE ADMINISTRATION: JOHNSTON'S FIRST TOUR AS COMMISSIONER AND CONSUL-GENERAL

Johnston arrived at Chiromo on 16 July 1891, and the main tasks during his first tour of duty—apart from the military expeditions—were to build up an administrative staff, to settle the land question, to create a system of district administration, and to organize a postal service.

The British Central Africa administrative staff in the very early days of the Protectorate—that is, during the second half of 1891—consisted of fewer than twenty officers. With no grant-in-aid from the British Treasury, and depending almost entirely on the funds provided by Rhodes, Johnston was severely restricted in the way in which he could recruit his staff: some were 'picked up by the wayside and appointed on the spot',[17] others were on secondment from the army, and only one—Alexander Whyte—was recruited in a manner which would be considered proper today, that is through public advertisement and interview by a relatively impartial board.[18] Before 1895 Johnston 'was thrown entirely on his own resources to provide the necessary personnel, and . . . his choice was an extremely limited one'.[19] He was forced, therefore, to recruit many of his early officials locally or through friends and acquaintances.

The dangers of this rather free and haphazard form of recruitment were

328

obvious and could have led to the appointment of a number of undesirable men. Some such men were, in fact, attracted to British Central Africa in the hope of finding a job with the administration. For example, Alston records that a travelling-companion 'had been dismissed from the navy through drink and was now on his way to Zomba "on spec" to see if he could get command of one of the gun-boats',[20] and Maugham tells a similar story of another man, a Scot, who asked of him, 'Could ye no speak a word for me to the Commeesioner? Ah'd weel like wark i' the Government', and added, anxiously, 'there'd be a pension, wad there no'?'[21] There is no evidence that either applicant was successful in obtaining employment in government service. Johnston, no matter how short-staffed, had no time for layabouts and, for example, refused re-employment to a former commander of a river gun-boat, Hewitt, who had been dismissed for drunkenness,[22] and he dismissed Chalmers Duff for slackness.[23]

Despite the dangers of appointing unsuitable men which the limited finances forced upon him, Johnston, in fact, seems to have succeeded in appointing a group of hardworking, competent and realistic administrators. Save possibly for two—Allan Blair Watson, who was a drug-addict,[24] and George Hoare, who had eight African wives and drank a good deal[25]—their personal behaviour seems to have been good. The early administrators came from a great variety of backgrounds, and a number were very well-connected; for example, Edward Alston, who was a favourite godson of Queen Alexandra, and the son of Sir Francis Alston, Chief Clerk at the Foreign Office; Gordon, a cousin of the Earl of Aberdeen; and Gilbert Stevenson, a cousin of Robert Louis Stevenson. Some, such as Sharpe, Crawshay and Marshall had been big-game hunters. Some had served with the Missions, for example, Swann and Nicoll, and others with the African Lakes Company, for example Stevenson, Bainbridge, Nicoll and Kydd. Yet others, G. E. Jones, G. H. Tuckett and Ranald McDonald, had for many years been civil servants in other countries; and some came from the Army, for example Alston, Manning, Greville, Beeching and Crawshay, often from distinguished regiments. Their educational backgrounds also varied a great deal; some came from the great English public schools (McMaster from Harrow, Rhoades from Rugby, Sharpe and Beeching from Haileybury, Best from Cheltenham, Codrington from Marlborough, and Hunt from Eton) whilst others were not very well educated and in their written work displayed shortcomings of learning. Only a few—Best, Hunt, Hamilton, Hearsey and Blair Watson—were university graduates.

One of the most important matters with which Johnston had to deal, and one which has had lasting consequences, was the settlement of land claims and the working out of land policy for the Protectorate. From the mid-1870s onwards a number of Europeans had acquired land by various means, and this acquisition increased in pace after the declaration of the Protectorate. During a period of about eighteen months, beginning in the second half of 1892, Johnston, Sharpe and Sclater between them enquired into every claim to alienation of land in the country, and the story is best told in Johnston's own words: 'Admissible claims were divided into two kinds: claims to mineral rights, and claims to land with or without mineral rights. In the case of treaties conferring mining rights the investigation was relatively simple. The chief or chiefs alleged to be the grantors of such concessions were examined and if they admitted making the grants, and it could be shown that they had received fair value for same, the mining concessions were confirmed. In regard to land, long occupation and improvements were regarded as almost the best titles. These qualifications, however, applied to very few estates in British Central Africa, as in most cases the settlers had only arrived after the proclamation of the Protectorate. Only in cases of very lengthy occupation and much cultivation or building were claims sanctioned which were unsupported by properly executed documents. Even when land had been purchased, and the sale on the part of the chief was not repudiated, and the deed of sale was authentic, the concessionnaire was required to show what consideration had been paid, and if the grantor was not considered to have received fair value for his land the grantee had either to supplement his first payment by another, or the area of his estate was reduced to an extent fairly compatible with the sum paid. As land was of very little value before the establishment of the administration, and as undoubtedly the settlers had conferred great benefits on the country by clearing and planting, land was not rated at a high value in these settlements. Threepence an acre was the maximum, and this only in exceptionally favoured districts like Mlanje and Blantyre. Sometimes the value of the land was computed at as low as a half-penny an acre. Except on very small estates the existing . . . villages and plantations were exempted from all these purchases, and the [villagers] were informed that the sale of the surrounding land did not include the alienation of their homes and plantations . . . One of the results of the land settlement, therefore, was [the] restoring to them of the inalienable occupancy of their villages and plantations. Moreover, in sanctioning the various concessions in the name of the Government we reserved to the Crown the right to make roads, railways, or canals over anybody's property without compensation; the control of the water supply; and where mining rights were included in the concession, a royalty on the produce of the mines. In each deed (the deeds were styled *Certificates of Claim*) the boundaries of the property were set forth with sedulous accuracy, and it was provided that all these deeds should be eventually supplemented by an authoritative survey made by a Government surveyor . . . Throughout the whole settlement I believe I am right in saying that only one dispute regarding boundaries was brought into Court and not settled amicably and informally in my office. When all these claims had been arranged I concluded, on behalf of the Crown, treaties with all the chiefs of the Protectorate, securing Crown control over the remainder of the land, which [the chiefs] were henceforth unable to alienate without the sanction of the Commissioner. In some cases large sums of money were spent by the Government in buying up the waste land . . . where it was deemed advisable that a complete control over its disposal should be exercised. Except over a small area of land which is absolutely Crown Property, a percentage on the selling price or the rent is paid to the . . . chief when portions of the Crown lands are let or sold.'[26]

We have seen that when Johnston was appointed on 14 February 1891 he was instructed firstly to consolidate the Protectorate over the chiefs, secondly to advise the chiefs on their external relations with each other and with foreigners, thirdly, to secure peace and order, and fourthly to check the slave trade. It is clear that these instructions could not be carried out unless the administration was decentralized and representatives of the government were sent out into the rural areas of the country. The solution, it seemed to Johnston, was to create a system of district administration, and this he did.

By the end of 1892 Johnston had divided the country into four very large and not very precisely defined administrative districts: the Lower Shire; South, West and North Nyassa Districts.[27] The following year he re-divided the country into administrative units under the provisions of the African Orders in Council, 1889 and 1893—still under the prerogative. To each of the twelve districts which he now created he appointed a Collector of Revenues whose duties were to collect customs duties, to assess and levy taxes, to direct the police force of Sikhs and Zanzibaris, to administer justice, to act generally as political officers, and, in many cases, to be responsible for the postal services.[28]

A widely-meshed network of administrative stations, or *bomas*, was set up, first in the south but later spreading to the north of the country. They varied from the very small stations like Mpimbe, a mud and thatch fort built in 1893, to much larger centres such as Zomba and Blantyre.

Another very significant aspect of Johnston's work during his first tour of duty was the organizing of the postal service. In the early days outgoing letters were usually conveyed by African Lakes Company steamer to the Vice-Consul at Quelimane, accompanied by money for the postage; the Vice-Consul then affixed the stamps and sent the letters through the Portuguese Post Office at Quelimane.[29] In the middle of 1891 Johnston gave very clear instructions on his postal duties to Hugh Charlie Marshall, the Collector at Chiromo; he was to receive all outward mails and to sort them into three lots: the northern mail (Europe and the East); the southern mail (Europe, South Africa, West Africa and the Americas); and mail for Portuguese East Africa. He was also to receive all incoming British Central Africa mail, sort it and distribute it 'in the manner which seems best and safest'.[30]

In the middle of 1893 the postal service was organized by Ernest Edward Harrhy who, at Johnston's request, was seconded for a year from the Cape Town Post Office by Sir Somerset French, Postmaster-General of Cape Colony. Soon after his arrival he established a service of mail runners from Port Herald to Mpimbe, via Chiromo, Chikwawa and Blantyre, with a number of intermediate connections; regular weekly mails between Chiromo and Blantyre; a thrice-weekly service between Blantyre and Zomba; and weekly mails between Blantyre, Mlanje, Mpimbe and Fort Johnston.[31]

During December 1893, Harrhy set up the Post Office at Chinde, and thereafter the sorting and distributing of the mails, formerly done at Chiromo by Marshall, were carried out at Chinde.[32] At this time the postal service was said to be a financial drain on the administration, chiefly because incoming mails were paid for by the country of origin only as far as Chinde,[33] and Johnston could afford to write of those who used the service, 'If you don't like it, ... send your letters some other way.'[34]

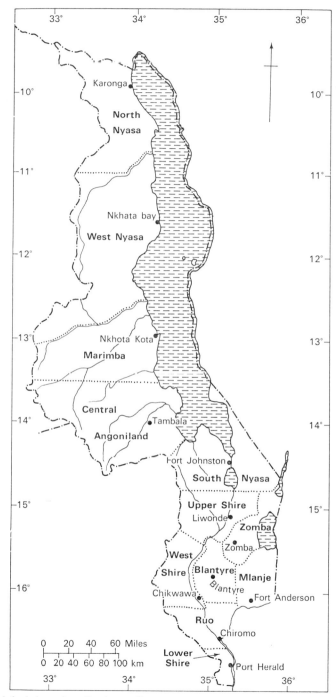

33° 34° 35° 36°

10°

Karonga

North
Nyasa

11°

Nkhata bay

West Nyasa

12°

13°

Nkhota Kota

Marimba

Central

14°

Tambala

Angoniland

Fort Johnston

South Nyasa

15°

Upper Shire

Liwonde

Zomba

Zomba

West
Shire

Blantyre

Blantyre

Mlanje

16°

Chikwawa

Fort Anderson

Ruo

Chiromo

0 20 40 60 Miles

0 20 40 60 80 100 km

Lower
Shire

Port Herald

33° 34° 35° 36°

19.2 Administrative districts, 1894

Harrhy returned to South Africa in 1894, and he was succeeded as Post-master-General of British Central Africa by J. E. McMaster, who came to the country in 1893 and worked for Sharrer's Zambezi Traffic Company, but soon joined the administration and was appointed Collector at Blantyre, Vice-Consul, Registrar, Judicial Officer and Postmaster-General. McMaster was succeeded as Postmaster-General by J. T. Gosling in 1897. Despite complaints to the contrary, expressed at public meetings in Blantyre,[35] the postal service grew and improved a great deal during Johnston's time until in 1897, in addition to the Postmaster-General, there were two Special Postmasters, one at Zomba and one at Blantyre, a Head Postmaster at Chinde, and twenty-seven Collectors and Assistant Collectors acting as Postmasters.[36] There was also at least one honorary Postmaster, McKinon at Cholo;[37] and one Postmistress, Mrs Jane Sazuze at Pangomani, Mlanje.[38]

Johnston's first tour of duty in British Central Africa was almost three years long, and he left for furlough in England in April, 1894. Much of his first three years was taken up in military campaigns—which I have not dealt with here because they are very fully covered elsewhere, and could be said to be merely the means whereby the civil administration was established—but, none the less, he was able to lay fairly sound foundations for his Administration. Despite very limited financial resources he had been able to gather round him a number of competent administrators; he had settled the land question in a skilful and timely fashion, and had prevented further alienation of tribal land; he had created a system of district administration which enabled him to fulfil the directions given to him when he was appointed—and, equally important, to collect revenue with which to pay his administrators; and he had organized the Postal Service.

He had much with which to be satisfied, but he was, none the less, a worried man. He had quarrelled—as it proved, irreparably—with Rhodes who had so far provided most of his funds. He was in deficit over the first three years of his administration, to the extent of £20,000, and the deficit was increasing at the rate of over £1,000 a month. The period of secondment to British Central Africa of the troops and officers of the Indian Army was drawing to a close, and he was still short of administrative officers. There had been a number of deaths: Maguire, Boyce and Piele.[39] He himself had been very ill, he was tired and was looking forward to a much needed rest.

IV   THE CONSOLIDATION AND DEVELOPMENT OF THE ADMINISTRATION:
     JOHNSTON'S SECOND TOUR OF DUTY

Despite his worries, Johnston was able to put to good use the twelve months during which he was away, and his efforts during this period were critical to the progress which he was able to accomplish during his second tour of duty. These efforts—strenuously and successfully made—were directed towards securing more staff and more money for his administration. Without men and money he would be unable to consolidate and develop the administration which he had founded.

Whilst on leave he produced a Blue Book in which he told the story, often in characteristically great detail, of the first three years of his administration. This report was widely read and served to make British Central Africa and his work there better known. He interviewed a number of people in England who wished to join his administration,[40] but he was much more successful in obtaining the services of additional men when he visited India, where he recruited over 200 Sikh soldiers and a number of officers.[41]

More important even than the recruitment of personnel were the financial arrangements which Johnston was able to enter into with the British Treasury. Hitherto, most of the money for administering British Central Africa had come from Rhodes and the British South Africa Company. In fact, the British South Africa Company had begun to finance the administration of the country some time before Johnston's arrival. In the middle of 1889 Lugard proposed to Rhodes that the slave trade in the area could be suppressed by the presence of an armed trading steamer on the lake and the establishment of a land force nearby. Rhodes agreed to pay a lump sum of £20,000 together with £9,000 a year for these purposes, and Lugard was to select his own officers and be directly responsible to the Board of the British South Africa Company. Lugard, however, heard no more about the proposals and Rhodes appears to have ignored or forgotten his agreement.[42]

In the same year the British South Africa Company bought a controlling interest in the African Lakes Company and agreed to provide up to £9,000 a year, from 1 January 1890 to the African Lakes Company, to maintain law and order north of the Zambezi, and to protect the mission stations.[43] The African Lakes Company received £13,500 during the eighteen months when they were at least supposed to be administering the country. Sir Percy Anderson, Head of the Africa Department at the Foreign Office, very firmly told the British South Africa Company that the £9,000 a year for administrative purposes was illegal, since the African Lakes Company was unchartered and had no rights and powers administratively, but he suggested that it would be both legal and advantageous to pay the sum to 'the real administering body, the Government'.[44]

On 3 November 1890, the Secretary of the British South Africa Company proposed to Johnston that he should take over the administration of the Company's sphere of influence north of the Zambezi. Johnston made it clear that he would not give up his Foreign Office appointment, but an arrangement was made whereby he became Commissioner and Consul-General of the British Central Africa Protectorate, responsible to the Foreign Office, and at the same time Administrator of the British South Africa Company's sphere of influence, responsible to the Board.[45]

So far as the British South Africa Company's contribution to Johnston's administration is concerned, Rhodes had given Johnston £2,000 in 1889 as 'something to start with for the Expedition and Presents to chiefs' in Central Africa; only £1,700 of this was spent, and the remainder was returned.[46] Early in 1891 the Company agreed to pay to Johnston for a period of 3 years, renewable at the British Government's discretion for a period not exceeding a further two years, the sum of £10,000 a year as a subsidy for maintaining the Police Force of British Central Africa. How he spent this sum was to be entirely Johnston's affair, and the Company did not wish to regulate the expenditure, Rhodes merely cautioning the Commissioner, rather mildly, '. . . be careful not to exceed your estimate'.[47] The British South Africa Company, through their controlling interest in the African Lakes Company, also agreed that Johnston should 'be empowered to make use of material of war belonging to the African Lakes Company in case of necessity, and to use free of charge . . . for administrative purposes the steamers belonging to that Company, due precaution being taken against unreasonable interference with their employment for the Company's trade'.[48] It appears that the British South Africa Company agreed to pay £2,500 a year to the African Lakes Company for this privilege although, much to Johnston's indignation, the African Lakes Company submitted to the Commissioner bills for the use of their steamers. Furthermore, the British South Africa Company agreed to pay the travelling expenses of the Commissioner and his Assistant when travelling within the Company's sphere of influence outside the Protectorate.[49] It seems also that the Company agreed to pay for the expenses of Alexander Whyte although Johnston later claimed that he personally paid most of the Scientific Department's expenses.[50]

Subsequently, the British South Africa Company allowed Johnston an extra sum of £5,000 'to meet the extra cost of introducing Indian troops and opening up stations in the northern part' of the Company's sphere. The Company also authorized Johnston to draw up to £10,000 for the Makanjira Campaign; of this sum only £4,000 was actually spent.[51]

In May of 1893, at Johnston's request, Rhodes agreed to increase his subsidy to £17,500 a year in exchange for the withdrawal of the free water transport agreement and for the conveying of all Crown rights in land in the Protectorate to the British South Africa Company.[52] The new agreement was to be for five years but this was later amended by the Foreign Office, in the formal agreement, to ten years; as a consequence of this apparently unilateral amendment and the erroneous inclusion of the free transport clause, Rhodes, in a fit of mixed anger and bitterness, withdrew the extra £7,500 agreed upon.[53]

The termination of the Company's contribution was brought about by an agreement signed by Rhodes on behalf of the British South Africa Company, and by Anderson on behalf of the Foreign Office. This agreement provided that the Commissioner should cease to administer the Company's sphere of influence not later than 30 June 1895, and that the Company's subsidy should not be paid after the end of that year.[54] From then onwards the full burden of outside support fell upon the Treasury.

The contribution of the British Treasury to the public finance of British Central Africa had grown sporadically over the years. The Treasury had paid the expenses of Consul Livingstone's 1859 expedition, and the salaries and travelling expenses of subsequent Consuls to Central Africa, although O'Neill had paid for his own journey to the interior in 1883, and Sharpe's treaty-making journeys in 1889-90 had been very largely at his own expense. It also paid the salaries and travelling expenses of the Consul-General and his deputy. The British government had provided the money to erect the Residency in Zomba, and £1,000 for its completion and improvements;[55] £1,200 to compensate the Makololo for their losses during the Portuguese invasion in 1889–90; £2,500 for presents to chiefs and the purchase of land; £9,200 for guns, rifles and ammunition for the Police Force; and £1,100 to the African Lakes Company for compensation in the Makanjira incident. The Admiralty also provided the gun-boats on the Lake, the Shire and the Zambezi.[56]

Johnston estimated that up to the end of March 1893, the British Treasury had contributed nearly £25,000 to British Central Africa. It seems, then, that by securing the initial financial support of Rhodes, by obtaining intermittent financial assistance from the British Treasury, and by incurring a substantial deficit, Johnston was able to increase his expenditure and expand the activities of his Administration until they reached a point at which the British government found it exceedingly difficult not to take over financial responsibility. This was a dangerous, even if calculated, risk, but not totally irresponsible, since Johnston did all that he could to increase internally-raised revenue, and was prepared to meet dishonoured official cheques from his own private means, even if the whole of his means were exhausted.

During Johnston's second tour of duty in British Central Africa the country received from the British government nearly £20,000 a year in grants-in-aid,[57] but extracting these grants was an unpleasant and extraordinarily difficult task, for as Duff said, 'the Treasury was uncommonly closefisted', and added that 'the British Treasury of those days always fell into a cold sweat at any suggestion of a grant-in-aid . . . we had to go to the Treasury, hat in hand, "with bated breath and whispering humbleness", to get the bare minimum required for essential public services. The . . . estimates . . . would have made a modern administrator rub his eyes.'[58]

Johnston, grateful as he was for the Treasury's support, believed that British Central Africa 'must justify its existence by eventually supporting itself on its locally raised revenue',[59] and he made great efforts to raise revenue internally to support the work of his Administration. He had been exceedingly quick off the mark, for example, in charging postal fees, since he announced Postage Rates in a notice dated 20 July 1891, at Chiromo, only four days after his arrival in the country.[60]

Another early source of local revenue was the Hut Tax. Before 1891 the Portuguese had been in the habit of levying a poll tax in the lower Shire area of about 2 shillings and 6 pence per person, irrespective of age and sex. The chiefs of the area asked Johnston what tax would be levied in the future by the British, and indicated that they preferred a hut tax, if possible at a lower total rate. Estimating the average number of occupants of a hut at three persons, Johnston decided that a tax on each hut of six shillings a year would be a reasonable sum, and it seems that this was acceptable to the people of the lower Shire area. It was clear, however, that taxation ought not to be confined to the extreme southern part of the country but should extend to other areas either where the inhabitants sought the establishment of administrative posts because they were unable to protect themselves, or where their conduct

336

obliged the administration to assert itself; and it was upon this basis that the Hut Tax was imposed.[61] The tax in 1892 was a poll tax on adult males, but thereafter it became a hut tax and the rate, originally six shillings a year, was reduced to three shillings as a result of representations made by the chiefs, missionaries, traders, and planters at Blantyre and Zomba late in 1892 and early in 1893. It seems that in bowing to the pressure of the public Johnston planned to do so only temporarily, since in a despatch of 12 June 1893, he said, 'I propose ... to levy (for the present at any rate) only 3s.od and not 6s.od. In time, as the [Africans] become wealthier, we shall, no doubt, be able to raise the Hut Tax to the original 6s. od. a hut.' It was not until four years after Johnston's departure, however, that the rate did return to six shillings. The tax was at first collected over the whole of the southern part of the Protectorate except Domasi where the missionaries had advised the chief not to pay. The Hut Tax Regulations of 1894 applied to the Lower Shire, Ruo, West Shire, Blantyre, Mlanje, Zomba, Upper Shire, and South Nyassa Districts. By the end of 1896 tax was collected in all parts of the country except the Northern Angoni area of the West Nyassa District where the Administration had not yet established itself. The tax was supposed to be collected by the chiefs in return for an allowance amounting to about ten per cent of the tax collected, but there is no evidence that the chiefs did, in fact, receive any share, and it is probable that the Hut Tax was collected by the Administration officials almost from the beginning.[62]

The administration had a much more difficult task legally to raise revenue by the imposition of customs duties, because the Berlin Act of 1885, to which Great Britain was signatory, had prohibited import duties in a large area including the whole of British Central Africa; and this Act was still in force when Johnston became Commissioner. Article III of the Act provided that 'Wares, of whatever origin, imported into these regions, under whatsoever flag, by sea or river, or overland, shall be subject to no other taxes than such as may be levied as fair compensation for expenditure in the interests of trade.'[63] Although this prohibition was removed by a declaration attached to the Brussels Act, 1890, the declaration was not ratified until 1892. Even so, the removal was not complete, since the Brussels Act declaration permitted the imposition of 'duties on imported goods, the scale of which shall not exceed a rate equivalent to 10 per cent ad valorem at the port of entry.'[64] It was not until well into 1892, therefore, that Johnston was able to impose import duties, although he had imposed an export duty on ivory rather earlier.[65]

Johnston also introduced a number of licence fees at an early date, covering for example fire-arms, big game hunting, importing alcohol, selling alcohol, and trading; and in 1895 he further extended his range of taxes by imposing stamp duties.[66]

From these five sources—postal duties, hut tax, customs duties, licensing, and stamp duties—together with the proceeds of the sale of Crown land, Johnston derived two-thirds of all his internally raised revenue.[67] A number of smallish sums seem to have been received by way of tribute or compensation from chiefs; these were often paid in ivory, for example £63 from Chikumbu and Chingomanji;[68] £316 12s 6d from Mponda, Makandanji and

Kawinga;[69] and ten tusks valued at about £65 from Kazembe.[70]

Although he had completely lost the financial support of Rhodes, Johnston made full use of the new British grants and of his increased local revenue, and these more extensive funds enabled him, during his second tour of duty, to consolidate and develop his administration.

This consolidation and development took the form of improved communications, extra buildings, the establishment of more *bomas*, and particularly the expansion of the Civil Service and central government departments.

A network of roads was essential to the administration of rural Malawi, and the beginnings of this network were made during Johnston's first tour. The object was to link the 'ports' of Chiromo, Chikwawa and Mpimbe with the main centres at Blantyre, Zomba and Mlanje, and to link these centres each with the others. During his first tour Johnston had improved the Chikwawa-Blantyre road and had constructed the Blantyre-Zomba, Zomba-Mlanje, and Zomba-Mpimbe roads. In 1895 and 1896 he extended and improved this basic pattern; Cavendish and Fletcher constructed the Chiromo-Zomba road, Devoy and Fletcher made the Zomba-Chikala and Zomba-Fort Liwonde roads, and others built the Blantyre-Cholo road, so that by the time Johnston ceased to be Commissioner the Shire Highlands area was well supplied with roads.[71]

A good deal of government building took place during 1895, 1896 and 1897: a new and permanent Army barracks,[72] a new hospital,[73] government headquarters offices[74] and the Survey Office[75] were all built in Zomba during this period. New or improved *bomas* were also erected at Karonga, Gowa, Dedza, Fort Alston, Tambala's, Nkhata Bay, Fort Hill, Chiwere's, Fort Johnston and Fort Maguire.[76] All this physical progress was made in an attempt to extend the area under the direct influence of the administration, and to improve conditions in some of the longer-established parts.

The number of officers in the administration continued to increase, and Johnston was now able to appoint to his staff such specialists as surveyors,[77] auditors,[78] doctors,[79] an architect[80] and a lawyer.[81] The official *Gazettes* during this period contained frequent notices of the appointment and arrival of new officers.

The extent of the physical development of the administration up to the time when Johnston handed over office to Alfred Sharpe can be measured by the facts that there were in 1897 nearly 400 miles of roads suitable for wheeled traffic, there were some forty administrative-military stations, the postal services were running well, the official revenue of the country exceeded £40,000, a system of courts had been created and the foundations of the district administration, the Civil Service, and the central government departments had been established.

The essential core of the work of modern government embraces law, order and defence; the collection and control of revenue with which to maintain and develop the other work of government; the administration of justice; communications; and the provision of social services, which is a fairly recent development.[82] Each of these functional areas received Johnston's early attention, and by the time he left each was the responsibility of a separate

338

23.1   Rev. Harry Kambwiri Matecheta

23.2 Rev. Wylie Pilgrim Chigamba

23.3 The new church of the Providence Industrial Mission: the sixtieth anniversary celebrations in 1960. John Chilembwe's successor, Dr Daniel Sharpe Malekubu, appears in the centre foreground

department of the central government.[83]

Law, order and defence were the responsibility of the Police Force, the Army, and the Naval Service, which together employed over 1,300 persons, 1,100 of them being Malawians. Revenue was raised by the twenty-seven members of the district administration, and was controlled centrally by the eight officers of the Treasury. Justice was administered by the Judicial Officer, and eight Collectors to whom were granted judicial warrants. Communications were looked after by the postal service, with its four officers, assisted by the members of the district administration who also acted as Postmasters, and by the Public Works Department, which was in charge of roadmaking and had fifteen officers. The social services were limited to health work; a meeting had been held in Blantyre as early as October 1894, to discuss the building of a public hospital, and the establishment of a public medical service,[84] and although only three medical officers were employed in 1897, they were the beginning of a medical service which in later years grew rapidly. In addition, there were a number of other governmental functions which were carried on by one or other of the departments, for example, the Government Print, surveys, and the registration of births, marriages and deaths.

All these activities of government were co-ordinated and controlled in the Commissioner's Office and in the Secretariat, which between them employed nine officials.

The handful of senior officers of the British Central Africa Administration who had served under Johnston in 1891 had by 1897 grown in number to over eighty. But it is not merely the increase in numbers and the expansion of the activities which they supervised which are impressive and important. What is important is that the administration, founded and consolidated over six brief years by Harry Johnston, provided the foundation upon which later heads of government have built, and are still building, the administration of Malawi. As James Stewart remarked of Johnston, 'If he did not satisfy everyone, he left good administrative results behind him'.[85]

FOOTNOTES

1 R. Foskett, Ed., *The Zambezi Journal and Letters of Dr. John Kirk*, Vol. 1, 255.

2 J. F. Elton, *Travels and Researches among the Lakes and Mountains of East and Central Africa*, 239.

3 A. Hetherwick, *The Romance of Blantyre*, 47.

4 A. Hetherwick, *The Romance of Blantyre*, 47.

5 A. J. Hanna, *The Beginnings of Nyasaland and North-Eastern Rhodesia*, 67.

6 E. Hertslett, *The Map of Africa by Treaty*, 3rd. Ed., 286.

7 H. H. Johnston, *British Central Africa*, 80.

8 H. H. Johnston, *The Story of My Life*, 150.

9 R. Oliver, *Sir Harry Johnston and the Scramble for Africa*, Chapter 4.

10 *The Times*, 22 August 1888.

11 Johnston's Journal, July 1889.

12 H. H. Johnston, *British Central Africa*, 81.

13 E. Hertslett, *The Map of Africa by Treaty*, 3rd ed., 386.

14 H. H. Johnston, *British Central Africa*, 82.

15 F.O. to Johnston, 24 March 1891.

16 E. Hertslett, *The Map of Africa by Treaty*, 3rd ed., 286.

17 F. Debenham, *Nyasaland, Land of the Lake*, 111.

18 H. H. Johnston, *The Story of My Life*, 289n.

19 R. C. F. Maugham, *Nyasaland in the Nineties*, 23.

20 E. Alston's diary, 24 January 1895.

21 R. C. F. Maugham, *Africa as I have Known it*, 49.

22 E. Alston's diary, 12 August 1895.

23 E. Alston's diary, 1 April 1896.

24 I. M. Graham, 'A Quarrel at Lake Mweru, 1896–1897', *N. Rhodesia J.*, 4 (6), 1961, 552–6; E. A. Copeman, 'Memories of Abandoned Bomas, No. 7, Shaloba', *N. Rhodesia J.*, 2 (5), 1955, 35–6.

25 E. Alston's diary, 13 February 1896.

26 H. H. Johnston, *British Central Africa*, 112 and 113.

27 A. J. Hanna, *The Beginnings of Nyasaland and North-Eastern Rhodesia*, 207.

28 H. H. Johnston, *British Central Africa*, 118, 119 and 153.

29 F. Melville, *British Central Africa*, 12.

30 Johnston to Marshall, 31 July 1891.

31 F. Melville, *British Central Africa*, 12f.

32 F. Melville, *British Central Africa*, 16.

33 *Brit. Cent. Afr. Gaz.*, 4 February 1895.

34 Johnston to Weatherley, 22 October 1892.

35 *Cent. Afr. Plant.*, November 1895, 38.

36 H. H. Johnston, *British Central Africa*, 152.

37 *Cent. Afr. Plant.*, November, 1895, 38.

38 *Nyasa. J.* **9** (2), 1956, 25.

39 *Brit. Cent. Afr. Gaz.*, 1 February 1894.

40 R. C. F. Maugham, *Africa as I have Known it*, 1.

41 A. Johnston, *The Life and Letters of Sir Harry Johnston*, 149.

42 F. D. Lugard, *The Rise of our East African Empire*, 158–9.

43 Rhodes and Cawston to Ewing, 5 June 1889.

44 R. Oliver, *Sir Harry Johnston and the Scramble for Africa*, 184–7.

45 A. J. Hanna, *The Beginnings of Nyasaland and North-Eastern Rhodesia*, 179ff.

46 Johnston to Rhodes, 8 October 1893; H. H. Johnston, *The Story of my Life*, 236.

47 Rhodes to Johnston, July 1891, cited in R. Oliver, *Sir Harry Johnston and the Scramble for Africa*, 196.

48 Johnston to Weatherley, 22 October 1892 and Rhodes to Johnston, 7 February 1891.

49 Johnston to Weatherley, 22 October 1892.

50 Johnston to Salisbury, 24 November 1890 and Johnston to Canning, 18

March 1894.

51 H. H. Johnston, *British Central Africa*, 97n.

52 Rhodes to Johnston, 30 April 1893.

53 Referred to in Johnston to Rhodes, 8 October 1893.

54 Agreement signed by Rhodes and Anderson, 24 November 1894.

55 Johnston to Canning, 10 March 1894.

56 A. J. Hanna, *The Beginnings of Nyasaland and North-Eastern Rhodesia*, 262.

57 *Brit. Cent. Afr. Gaz.*, 1 June 1896.

58 H. Duff, *African Small Chop*, 21–2.

59 H. H. Johnston, *British Central Africa*, 111.

60 *Nyasa. J.*, 1 (1), 1948, 21.

61 H. H. Johnston, *British Central Africa*, 110–12.

62 E. Smith, *Report on Direct Taxation*, 6–7.

63 E. Hertslett, *The Map of Africa by Treaty*, 472.

64 E. Hertslett, *The Map of Africa by Treaty*, 517.

65 A. J. Hanna, *The Beginnings of Nyasaland and North-Eastern Rhodesia*, 224–5.

66 A. J. Hanna, *The Beginnings of Nyasaland and North-Eastern Rhodesia*, 225.

67 *Brit. Cent. Afr. Gaz.*, 1 June 1896.

68 Johnston to Salisbury, 24 November 1891.

69 Johnston to Salisbury, 16 December 1891.

70 Johnston to Salisbury, 24 November 1891.

71 *Brit. Cent. Afr. Gaz.*, 1 June 1895, 1 March 1896, 15 June 1896, 1 October 1896.

72 *Brit. Cent. Afr. Gaz.*, 1 May 1896.

73 *Brit. Cent. Afr. Gaz.*, 1 May 1896.

74 *Brit. Cent. Afr. Gaz.*, 1 August 1897.

75 *Brit. Cent. Afr. Gaz.*, 1 December 1896.

76 *Brit. Cent. Afr. Gaz.*, 1896, 1897.

77 *Brit. Cent. Afr. Gaz.*, 1 February, 1896.

78 *Brit. Cent. Afr. Gaz.*, 15 January 1896.

79 *Brit. Cent. Afr. Gaz.*, 1 October 1896.

80 *Brit. Cent. Afr. Gaz.*, 15 August 1895.

81 *Brit. Cent. Afr. Gaz.*, 1 December 1896.

82 E. Sharpe, *J. Inst. Pub. Admin. Can.*, **10** (3), 1967.

83 H. H. Johnston, *British Central Africa*, 152–3.

84 *Cent. Afr. Plant.*, September 1895, 9.

85 J. Stewart, *Dawn in the Dark Continent*, 238.

20 A note on the Universities' Mission to Central Africa: 1859-1914

The Rev. Philip Elston

The subject of this paper is the early history of the Anglican mission in Malawi during the period 1859–1914. Although the emphasis throughout has been to give a descriptive rather than an analytic account of the mission's development during the period, I have departed from this procedure at various points. Thus, I have dealt at some length with the first mission led by Bishop Mackenzie, since it seems to me that the failure of the Mackenzie mission (and the nature of its failure) was traumatic in its effect and a profound influence upon the subsequent policy of the mission. Similarly, I have devoted some attention to the choice of Likoma Island as headquarters of the Nyasa Mission, since its pivotal importance in the strategy of the mission is often neglected or underrated nowadays.

Because most missions direct their energies into the three main activities of evangelism, education and medicine, I have for convenience brought together material under these headings for separate treatment. In the preparation of this paper I have made use of the mission's own publications (which promoted the work of the mission amongst its supporters in England), while the diaries, letters and station records consulted have provided valuable complementary insights. As far as possible I have tried to record the letter and the spirit of the mission's experience—a record of the cost involved in planting Christianity on African soil.

The costliness of the work is one of the features which marked the development of the mission's activity in Nyasaland; a development that was painfully slow in its earlier stages. Within the compass of a few thousand words it is not possible to give more than a brief sketch of that half century of activity which links the tragic mission of Bishop Mackenzie and his companions, with the well-established diocese that found itself disturbed by the Kaiser's War and the first rumblings of African discontent.

The main outline of the mission's work is well-known, and can be studied in the U.M.C.A.'s own three-volume History. For the purpose of this paper I propose to divide the period into three parts—to correspond with three phases of growth in the progress of the mission. The first phase will be con-

344

cerned with the twenty-five years of the mission's work in Central Africa from the departure from England in October 1860 of the small party led by Charles Mackenzie, to the choice of Likoma Island in August 1885 as the headquarters of the Lake Nyasa mission. The second phase, carrying the story forward to 1900, will deal with the establishment of mission stations around the shores of Lake Nyasa, served by the first of the mission steamers, the *Charles Janson*. The final phase, which covers the early years of the twentieth century —a period marked by further extension and the consolidation of existing work—is given in summary form.

I   THE PERIOD 1859–85

Studying the words spoken and written by churchmen in the mid-nineteenth century, one may discern two distinct strands of thought which were to influence the course of events in Central Africa. One was the conviction that the Gospel could and must be preached to all mankind; the other was a sense of guilt which sensitive Englishmen felt about the treatment of Africans arising from England's past share in the slave trade. In the light of these observations we may see David Livingstone's famous appeal and invitation of December 1857 to the English Church as the catalyst in a process which had already been a number of years in the making. Both strands of thought were brought together by Samuel Wilberforce, Bishop of Oxford, in his address to the Oxford and Cambridge Mission in November 1859 when he declared that, 'England can never be clear from the guilt of her long continued slave trade till Africa is free, civilized, and Christian.'[1]

The recital of events begins on New Year's Day 1861 when Charles Frederick Mackenzie was consecrated as first 'Bishop of the Mission to the tribes dwelling in the neighbourhood of the Lake Nyasa and River Shire' in St. George's Cathedral Cape Town. By early February the party was off the Kongone entrance to the Zambezi where they met up with Livingstone. Livingstone announced his intention of abandoning the Zambezi approach in favour of entry via the Rovuma river 450 miles further north (and outside Portuguese control). With great reluctance the Bishop bowed to the experience of the Doctor, so losing three months and a large part of the mission's stores in a fruitless attempt to navigate the Rovuma.

The *Pioneer* re-entered the Kongone mouth on 1 May, but despite confident predictions of a three weeks' passage to Chibisa's they encountered frequent obstacles, and it was mid-July before they gained their objective. They also met with obstruction from Mankokwe, an important Mang'anja chief whose authority extended as far north as Lake Chilwa. Mankokwe politely but firmly moved the party on, and was evidently unwilling to have the mission settle anywhere within his immediate jurisdiction, doing his best to persuade Chibisa to adopt a similar policy.[2] Chibisa was more than ready to accommodate the white man 'my brother', and the village became a temporary store depot. From Chibisa's the party set off for the highlands, where on

345

19 July they established themselves at Magomero; recommended to them by Livingstone for its advantage as a defensive site. Such a consideration was necessary, since they had already met the slave-raiding activities which were to be the cause of so much frustration in the following months. The encounter was important for the changed attitude towards bearing fire-arms; a subject much discussed by the Bishop and his companions. The problem, around which so much bitter feeling was to gather, was how far they should interfere with the slave trade going on all around them. Livingstone was evidently of the opinion that the realities of the situation called for decisive action, whatever the claims of Christian ethics might be. Mackenzie, overcoming his own misgivings, took part in what he later labelled 'the Ajawa Wars'.[3]

Whilst reassuring one another as to the rightness of their actions, the party seem to have been worried by the fear that these might be misinterpreted by their supporters in England. The official History is predictably hesitant on the same issue. Although venerating Mackenzie as the shepherd who had given his life for the sheep, it dissociated itself from the policy he adopted, while admitting the circumstance which made it necessary—'If we do not adopt their line, we can admire and follow their spirit.'[4] Three days after their arrival at Magomero they were obliged to make use of their weapons to drive off a Yao party fresh from raiding a Mang'anja village, and the mission took on the aspect of a refugee camp, so that by the beginning of October the Bishop had a flock of nearly 160 liberated slaves.

Although the ready-made congregation had been no part of the mission's design, it provided a focus for activity, and there began in the closing months of 1861 the work of fashioning a peaceful and ordered community. The primary role of the mission was, of course, a religious one, but this had to be set aside while the missionaries grappled with the business of acquiring a Mang'anja vocabulary, since Mackenzie was determined not to implant false or crude ideas of the Christian faith based upon a faulty knowledge of the native language. He was confident that although direct teaching was not yet possible, the pattern of life and conduct displayed by the missionaries themselves would be its own witness; meantime there was much building to be done, the sick to be cared for, and gardens to be prepared and planted. The provision of food for the community became a major anxiety as the mission noted the grim evidence of famine throughout the area, and the unsatisfactory means of communication with the outside world upon which it depended for vital supplies. The situation might be improved if an overland route between Magomero and the mouth of the Ruo river could be established. A reconnaissance expedition ran into trouble with some hostile villagers, and the Bishop led a reprisal raid—the project was abandoned.

Early in January 1862 Mackenzie, with a recent arrival, Henry Burrup, made his way down the Shire to meet his sister at the Ruo mouth. On the journey they lost their supply of medicine, and were then obliged to wait for three weeks at the rendezvous where they were to meet Livingstone. Both men were suffering from diarrhoea and fever, and on 31 January 1862 Bishop Mackenzie died, and was buried on the left bank of the Shire, at Chiromo. Burrup died three weeks later, after a nightmare journey back to Magomero.

346

Deprived of their leader, the party remained as determined as ever in their main task, although increasingly aware of their isolation, and pressure grew to withdraw to a healthier and more accessible site.

A renewal of tribal warfare hastened their decision, and on 25 April the mission evacuated Magomero and five days later arrived at Chibisa's where a second settlement was founded. During this period they gained some mastery of the native language and were able to reduce it to writing, translating the Lord's Prayer and some Scripture passages into Mang'anja. The mission remained at Chibisa's for nearly fifteen months, although it was soon evident that the site was unsuitable. Not only was it proving to be as unhealthy in its own way as Magomero had been, but in addition, they were greatly troubled and embarrassed by the presence at Chibisa's of Livingstone's Kololo, who were making a general nuisance in the area.

As it happened, the decision to withdraw was not theirs to make. Reports of their militancy at Magomero had led to hostile criticism and the loss of some influential support. More serious for their immediate situation was the news that Livingstone's expedition had been recalled. When the new Bishop, William Tozer, arrived in June 1863 to assume control of the mission's affairs, it was to order its withdrawal downstream to Mount Morambala in Portuguese territory. To the surviving members of the original party (two more had died at Chibisa's), such a withdrawal was tantamount to abandoning the work altogether, and the sense of failure was heightened by the awareness that Bishop Tozer and those whom he represented were critical of the way matters had been handled by the Mackenzie mission. This criticism revolved around two points already referred to: the interference in the slave trade, and the failure of the mission to impart any substantial religious teaching.[5] The move to Morambala was made in August 1863. Of the three sites occupied by the mission, Morambala was the least suitable, and Tozer stayed only long enough to decide that complete evacuation was unavoidable.

On 18 January 1864 Bishop Tozer left the area, having notified the home committee of his decision to remove the mission to the island of Zanzibar. Tozer did not wait confirmation of his decision, but with his friend Edward Steere left for Zanzibar where they landed on 31 August 1864. There the mission laid new foundations upon which to build; there it recovered its confidence, its support, and its determination to launch a second bid to open up the region around Lake Nyasa to missionary influence. It was to be more than 20 years before a new mission could be established, and in the interval Livingstone had met his death in the swamps of Bangweulu, and a new approach to the lake had been made by the Free Church of Scotland which had established a mission at Cape Maclear named in honour of the one who had inspired it, the *Livingstonia Mission*.

In the drama that had just been played out, each of the principals had his critics and advocates. Livingstone (it was said) had misled the mission and its supporters into supposing that entry into Central Africa would be a relatively simple matter giving unlimited opportunities for promoting Christianity and Commerce; whereas it had proved barren, and wasteful of human lives and money. Mackenzie had compromised his church by using force—how was it

347

possible to preach the Gospel of Peace with a bishop's crozier in one hand and a double-barrelled gun in the other? For his part, Tozer had betrayed the trust of those poor unfortunates who had found refuge with the mission and were now to be deserted; he was condoning the evils of the slave trade by his refusal to resist.

Friend and foe alike, the mistake that most people made about Livingstone was to forget that although he was capable of superhuman feats of endurance, he was human: liable to human errors of judgment, and apt to minimize difficulties in order to win support for his cause. It was sheer misfortune that the settled conditions which prevailed in the Shire Highlands during Livingstone's visit of 1859 had given way to the violence that the Mackenzie mission encountered. Mackenzie, in the handling of this violence, was confronted by a dilemma as old as Christianity itself: am I to withhold assistance when my neighbour is the victim of attack? Nor should his moral and material dependence upon Livingstone be overlooked. Bishop Tozer inherited the consequences of false or faulty judgments, and showed his own brand of courage when he decided not to attack the interior directly where communications were hazardous in the extreme, but to advance by a gradual process; slower but more sure. For this purpose it would be necessary to educate and train native teachers so that the work would not have to depend on the lives of a handful of white men to whom the climate had already proved so disastrous.[6]

It is no part of my brief to record the work of the Universities' mission at its Zanzibar base, and for the remaining years of Bishop Tozer's episcopate, no further attempt was made to renew work in Nyasaland. The mission's situation at Zanzibar was made secure, and fresh work begun on the mainland opposite. Bishop Tozer retired in 1872, and was succeeded as Bishop by his friend and fellow-worker, Edward Steere. Bishop Steere thought the time had come for a new attempt to reach the lake, and within a few months of assuming control he set out, adopting the route suggested by Livingstone in 1861, but following the Rovuma on foot.

Steere landed at Lindi, 300 miles south of Zanzibar, and walked across country to strike the Rovuma river on his way to Mwembe, Mataka's village, which was only seventy miles from the lake. The bishop noted during the course of his journey meeting nine caravans which represented between 1,500 and 2,000 slaves—perhaps 10,000 for the whole year.[7] The Bishop reached Mwembe early in December 1875 where he was persuaded to remain for two weeks. The delay ruled out any possibility of reaching the lake, since he was anxious to hurry back to the coast before the rainy season set in. Bishop Steere arrived back at Zanzibar in February 1876 and there, a few months later, welcomed two new recruits destined to be the architects of the Nyasa Mission, Chauncy Maples and William Percival Johnson. In October 1876 a second venture into the interior was made with the purpose of creating a Christian village composed of freed slaves (liberated at Zanzibar), who had already been baptized or were under instruction. Thus was established the first staging post on the way to the lake.

Five years later Johnson was back at Masasi on his way to the lake, taking

348

with him Charles Janson, with the intention of establishing a station on the lake shore. Janson's death at Chia in February 1882 was a sad blow to Johnson—'I went on up the coast alone in that Lenten season'.[8] Johnson pressed northwards to Chigoma, where it was known that a Nyasa chief called Chiteji lived, and made the village the base for his subsequent travels. He visited the Gwangwara (an off-shoot of the Ngoni) and was visited by the *Ilala*, although he was less happy to get a bill for £5 from the *Ilala*'s captain for a pleasure-trip to Chizumulu.

For nearly two years Johnson moved around the Lake, tracing the course of the Rovuma, and its main tributary, the Lujenda. The *Ilala* carried him north to Karonga where he met the Ngonde people, before he set out to make contact with the Nyaka-nyaka (or Bena) to the north-east. Returning along the east coast and skirting the Livingstone Mountains of S.W. Tanganyika, Johnson came across the temporary pile-villages of refugee communities.[9] By the time he returned to Chigoma Johnson was very ill, and was nursed back to health by the Scottish mission which had now moved to Bandawe, due west across the lake. Throughout this period Johnson was building up his knowledge of the Nyanja language into which he rendered the Gospels. Having recovered, Johnson left Bandawe and paid his first visit to Blantyre where, as he says, 'Dr Scott and his party gave me a royal welcome, and so did Mr John Moir, of the African Lakes Company.' From there he made his way back to the south-east end of the lake, and 'as usual I preached at places on the way, showing the people my credentials, as it were.'[10]

It was the result of Johnson's experiences during this period of isolated travel, including the timely assistance rendered him by the *Ilala*, that convinced him that the work of the mission could only be put on a secure basis in the Nyasa area if it had a small steamer 'which may be used as a Mission Ship and as a Training Home for African Teachers.'[11] In Johnson's view such a steamer would pass up and down the lake, serving the various stations, maintaining contact with the outside world, and acting as a floating headquarters (and refuge, if necessary). Once the initial expense had been met, less men would be needed, less risk to health involved, and less time wasted visiting the mission centres.

Johnson returned to England after an absence of seven years and, having secured approval for his plans from the home committee and the newly-appointed Bishop, Charles Smythies, spent the first half of 1884 raising money for a mission steamer. The money was subscribed readily, and Johnson returned to Africa in November 1884 with the steamer *Charles Janson* in 380 separate packages. The steamer was re-assembled at Matope, where, on 5 September 1885 it was launched; to serve the needs of the mission for the next fifty years. The launching of the *Charles Janson* gave the mission a new freedom as well as a new character, since it was now possible to select a suitable site to act as permanent headquarters.

The mission had already established friendly relations with Chiteji, the Nyasa chief at Chigoma, and Bishop Smythies now entered into an agreement with him for the building of a station on the island of Dicomo (opposite Chigoma village), over which Chiteji and his neighbour Mataka exercised authority. The agreement was ratified on 24 August 1885 and Chipyela ('place of burning'), where witches had formerly been burned alive, became the site of the new station being purchased according to native law. Sometime later, acting on Vice-Consul Buchanan's advice, a formal agreement was made with Chiteji settling the limits of the mission area, granting it exclusive rights over the adjacent harbour, and prohibiting the burning of witches on the island. It was not until 1895, and on his own initiative, that Harry Johnston made over the entire island to the mission in perpetuity, during the course of an official visit. Although there had been competition amongst the local chiefs as to who should accommodate the mission, support for a 'British presence' in the area was by no means unanimous, and the Commissioner's visit to Likoma brought a sharp protest from Mataka who demanded to know, 'Why do you English come here at all?—I don't want my land interfered with.'[12]

In the first part of this paper I have confined myself to sketching in the background history of the mission up to the point when it entered Malawi to begin work on the lake. For the rest of the paper I shall modify this procedure, since although the historical narrative will be given to provide a framework of reference, I shall break off at appropriate points in the narrative to discuss in greater detail various topics that are of special importance or significance.

The first topic to be treated in this way, is the choice of Likoma Island as the headquarters of the Nyasa Mission. The name itself is significant, for although it means 'beautiful', 'pleasant', 'desirable', Chauncy Maples attributed this to 'the safe asylum it affords from the incursions of marauding tribes'. With the wisdom that comes from hindsight, it is tempting to criticize the choice of Likoma as a suitable base of operations, having regard to a physical isolation exaggerated by the concentration of commercial and administrative activity in the south. But such a view ignores a number of important factors. For more than half a century Likoma Island was to be the centre of a missionary effort that embraced both sides of the lake. A map published in 1899 lists no fewer than seventeen stations on the eastern shore, compared with five on the western side. Further, the international boundaries delimiting German and Portuguese territory were still to be drawn, and as late as 1889 Chauncy Maples was hopeful that a British Protectorate would include the mainland opposite Likoma.[13] But all of this was in the future; the immediate arguments that favoured the island were: that it offered a much-needed refuge against the attacks of slave-raiders and hostile tribesmen; it was a relatively healthy place for expatriate workers, and (as Bishop Smythies noted) was in easy reach of the Bandawe Mission if needed.

II THE PERIOD 1885–1900

We may regard 1885 as a turning point in the progress of the mission; certainly the importance of the *Charles Janson* in the overall strategy cannot be over-estimated. The laborious and often dangerous overland route from

Zanzibar could be abandoned, since the steamer had access to Matope, on the Shire, where stores were taken on, and to Bandawe where Dr Laws was able to provide medical care until such time as the mission could fend for itself. This new security of communications meant that women could be recruited for the work, and towards the end of 1885 the Rev. George Swinny, with his wife Mary, was placed in charge of the Likoma station. He soon established a mission boarding school for some two dozen boys, being assisted by native teachers who had been trained at St Andrew's College, Zanzibar. Swinny died of fever in May 1887; his wife in 1888.

Meanwhile, Chauncy Maples, who had spent ten years working first at Masasi, and later at Newala, was brought to Likoma to strengthen the station staff, in July 1886, and in September was appointed Archdeacon of Nyasa with responsibility for the lakeshore work. For almost ten years, Maples built up the station at Likoma, while his friend Johnson continued his itinerant ministry using the *Charles Janson* as his base. It was a period of quiet, steady work which saw the creation of a chain of schools stretching along the eastern shore of the Lake from Ngofi to Msumba, and an ambitious programme of building on Likoma itself.

The opening up of the lakeshore towns and villages to Christian influence usually followed a regular pattern.[14] The missionary first paid an exploratory visit to the new area, perhaps taking some cloth for presents and barter, and sounded out the chief or headman as to establishing a school in the village. If the response was favourable, a married teacher would be sent to begin work. Maples writes of 'several teachers and their wives here now, ready to be "planted out" at the large towns on the shores of the Lake which the steamer visits'. School would be held outside the borrowed hut that was the teacher's house, with a minimum of school equipment—black- board, slates, chalk, an ABC sheet, and a *Hearer's Catechism*. Work with the women and girls of the village would be undertaken by the teacher's wife. If the work flourished a school would be built; otherwise the teacher would be withdrawn to another area. It is important to remember in this connection that the function of these schools was religious rather than educational, thus —'For the few years that he comes under the influence of the Mission what the child is taught of religion is vastly more important than that he should know how to read and write.'[15] The boys who were regular in their attendance became Hearers, and were expected to come on Sundays for instruction. After about a year they would be ready to enter the Catechumenate, when they would be given a small metal cross as an outward sign of their new allegiance. As soon as a teacher had established a catechumens' class a dormitory was built, since it was a general rule in the mission 'that all Christian and cate- chumen boys and young unmarried men shall sleep on the station, the teacher being responsible for them'. Only after a teacher had acquired a congrega- tion, and the first baptisms taken place, would the question of building a church be raised; in the interval the school would be used for church services.

While this lakeshore work was in progress the staff at Likoma was augmen- ted by the arrival in 1888 of two ladies, a nurse and a teacher, to work with the women and girls, and to supervise the girls' school which had been started

351

three years earlier by Mrs Swinny, and inherited by Archdeacon Maples. This work was of critical importance for the mission since the young men came forward more readily for instruction than the girls, which meant that there were not enough Christian or catechumen girls for the boys to marry, the mission having set its face against marriage between Christians and heathen. Although it was possible in later years to enforce this rule by the exercise of spiritual sanctions, at this juncture it was unrealistic even though Maples did everything he could 'to get the girls who are engaged to be married to various boys in the school, to come and be taught here and prepared for baptism'.[16]

Although steady progress was made the work was not without incident, as Mr Johnson discovered to his cost and discomfort when he agreed to land with Buchanan, the Acting-Consul, at Makanjila's, at the southern end of the Lake, in order to establish British intentions in the area. Both men were seized while attempting to address the crowd, manhandled, and placed under guard. The *Charles Janson*, helpless to intervene, returned the following day, and the prisoners were released after a ransom of paint, oil and calico had been sent ashore. The mission was also involved indirectly in the flare-up between Europeans and Arabs in 1887, when Monteith Fotheringham was holding Karonga against Mlozi. Chauncy Maples was approached for assistance and was able to supply, 'a large quantity of native food, some powder, caps, bullets, my Martini-Henry rifle and 280 cartridges . . . and have written to say that as soon as the *Charles Janson* comes back from the South I will urge Johnson to allow her to be sent North . . .'[17] However galling it may have been for those exposed to the evils of the slave trade, the mission did not rescind its policy of non-interference. Yet although direct intervention was ruled out, on a number of occasions the mission ransomed people from slavery, and soon after his arrival at Likoma, Maples rescued a young girl in this way. In 1887 he visited the Gwangwara with the express intention of ransoming some women taken captive during a Gwangwara raid on Masasi five years earlier.

On a happier note was the relationship between the mission and other churches working in the area. There are frequent references to the kind welcome given at the 'Scotch Mission' at Bandawe where mail was collected once a month—and when one of Cardinal Lavigerie's White Fathers called at Likoma he compared notes with Johnson and Maples as to missionary methods. . . . 'We did not waste time in controversy, I can assure you. He said of us, "You of your mission are very near to us in doctrine and practice".' But if Chauncy Maples had high regard for fellow-workers of other churches, this did not extend to all expatriates. . . 'Now that so many Europeans are flocking into the country we missionaries are bound to do what we can to keep up a high standard of morality. Englishmen do deteriorate so terribly fast when away from home . . .'

By 1891 it was evident to Bishop Smythies that the existing area in his charge was too great for one man to administer. The rapid expansion of the work in Nyasaland since the launching of the *Charles Janson* and the growing importance of the country to Britain, coupled with the difficulty of maintaining effective pastoral care over an area that stretched from Zanzibar to Lake

Nyasa led him to press for a division of labour by the creation of a separate diocese of Nyasaland. Bishop Smythies made his appeal for funds to endow the new diocese at the Annual Reunion in June, 1892, and by October £9,000 had been raised by direct giving, and a further £2,000 donated by S.P.G. and S.P.C.K. The first Bishop of Nyasaland (although fifth in the succession to Mackenzie) was Wilfrid Hornby, one of the founder-members of the Oxford Mission to Calcutta. The new Bishop arrived in his diocese in June 1893, but after about eight months' work at the Lake was invalided home and, on medical advice, obliged to resign his diocese. [1]

On the advice of Bishop Hornby the vacant bishopric was offered to Chauncy Maples, whose first reaction was to decline the offer, until Johnson persuaded him to take further advice before making a final decision. Maples went to England early in 1895, and in April accepted the vacant office, with the title Bishop of Likoma. Maples was consecrated Bishop two months later and soon afterwards began the return journey to Likoma. The account of his death in the waters of Lake Nyasa (the result of his determination to get to Likoma as quickly as possible), is too well-known to need further recital. The tragedy was doubly unfortunate, since it not only robbed the diocese of a leader who was known and respected by all, but could have been avoided if the Bishop had been less hasty and impatient. As it was, the diocese was without effective leadership (from Bishop Smythies surrender of authority) for nearly three years. Following hard on this tragedy came news of the death of one of the Likoma clergy, George Atlay, murdered by a party of Ngoni while on holiday in the hills behind Likoma. It seems that Atlay was mistaken for a German political agent; a loaded but unused rifle was found beside his body. A few weeks later the Rev. Arthur Sim died of fever at Nkhota Kota. This last loss was a grim reminder of the fact that although death by drowning, or at the hands of hostile tribesmen might be a necessary hazard of mission life, by far the most lethal killer was the climate itself.

Sim had begun his work in September 1894 at the invitation of the British Resident, Mr Nicholl. Nkota Kota was the town of the slaver chief Jumbe, and a depot for the trade before the slaves were shipped across the lake on their way to the coast. Under Arab influence the district had become a centre of Islam, and although Jumbe was deposed soon after Sim's arrival, and the Arabs had departed, the religion of the Prophet remained as their legacy to the town. Although Jumbe was willing for Sim to provide education, it may be wondered why the mission evangelized predominantly Muslim areas like Mponda's and Nkota Kota where there could be little hope of many conversions. The answer is twofold: the success of the Scottish Mission in the highland and animist parts of the country had left a vacuum along the Islamic lakeshore which the mission, with its Zanzibar background, felt able to handle; apart from which it saw itself as being at war with Islam in the battle for people's souls. [18]

353

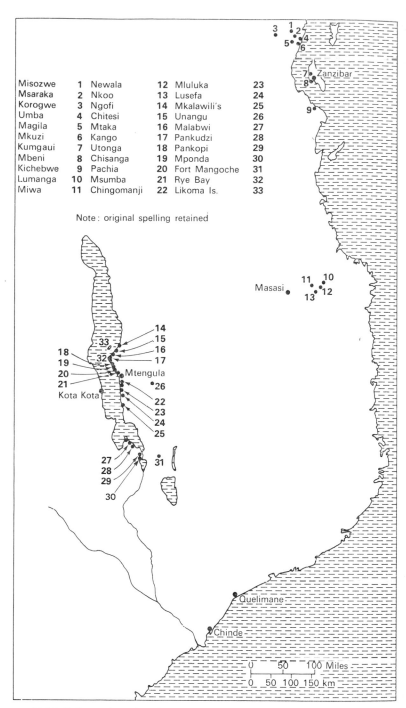

Misozwe	1	Newala	12	Mluluka	23
Msaraka	2	Nkoo	13	Lusefa	24
Korogwe	3	Ngofi	14	Mkalawili's	25
Umba	4	Chitesi	15	Unangu	26
Magila	5	Mtaka	16	Malabwi	27
Mkuzi	6	Kango	17	Pankudzi	28
Kumgaui	7	Utonga	18	Pankopi	29
Mbeni	8	Chisanga	19	Mponda	30
Kichebwe	9	Pachia	20	Fort Mangoche	31
Lumanga	10	Msumba	21	Rye Bay	32
Miwa	11	Chingomanji	22	Likoma Is.	33

Note: original spelling retained

20.2 U.M.C.A. stations in 1899

Medical work

The original mission had included a doctor in its number, but from the return to Nyasa in 1885, most of the medical work had been undertaken by nurses based at the larger stations and assisted by 'dispensary boys'; while most of the missionaries were adept at the diagnosis and treatment of simple ailments. The medical work of the mission was placed on a sound footing with the arrival in 1899 of Dr Robert Howard. Although Howard's main task was to superintend the medical services, he had been given another charge of almost equal importance: to check on the health of the missionaries themselves.

The number of deaths in the entire Universities' Mission, during the period 1860–1914 was ninety-eight. Of that number, only four died violent deaths: two by drowning (Chauncy Maples and Joseph Williams), and two murdered (George Atlay and Arthur Douglas). The death-toll reached a peak in the decade 1889–98 when no fewer than forty-five missionaries died. In Nyasaland there were twenty-two deaths and twenty-two invalidings between 1887–1903, in a staff varying from twelve to thirty-five.[19] The following extract from a missionary's diary provides a telling comment on missionaries' health at this time:

> Friday 19 October 1900
> '12 noon. Just as we began Litany the "C.J." arrived. After a short while the Bp., Mr Smith; and Mr Eyre came ashore. The Bishop gave me a sad story of the Archd's condition; there was no probable hope of his recovery. Together we went to the chapel and there chose the site for the Archd's grave (in the nave, near the Sanctuary step) in case of his death. Arrangements were also made in case of my breaking down in health; the Bishop said he would send Hancock (from Malindi).'[20]

The final irony lies in the fact that at the time of the Bishop's reassurance the Rev. Herbert Hancock had been dead two days—from appendicitis, not malaria.

With the limited knowledge about the prevention and control of malarial fever (thought to be due to exhalations from swamps or the damp night air) and other tropical diseases, and the overwork that had contributed to the early deaths of so many missionaries, the mortality rate was high. But there was also reason to suspect that an unwise asceticism was a cause of debilitation, and before leaving England Howard was instructed to check on any extreme ascetic practices which he considered harmful to the health and well-being of the mission staff.

Dr Howard worked in the diocese for ten years, and it was during his time that, 'every hospital and dispensary in the diocese has been built, mostly from his own plans and under his supervision.'[21] Medical work was closely wedded to evangelism, and the medical mission existed, as Howard wrote many years later 'to demonstrate practical Christianity . . . to all who come to it'. But getting people to come was often the most difficult part, as the medical reports often pointed out. Suspicion of the dispensaries and hospitals and the white man's 'magic' associated with them was commonplace—and the villagers at Chindamba's warned the daughter of a local chief that if she visited Malindi Hospital for treatment 'they' would cut off her leg and give her a wooden one.[22]

With the establishment of permanent hospitals at Likoma and Malindi the beginnings of a training programme for African medical staff began to take shape and the 'dispensary boys' were prepared for increased responsibility.

The period of uncertainty was brought to an end with the appointment of Dr John Hine (who had done much pioneering work at Unangu, in Yaoland) as successor to Bishop Maples. Dr Hine arrived at Likoma in March 1897 and one of his first acts as Bishop was to appoint William Percival Johnson as Archdeacon of Nyasa. He also instituted the first Diocesan Conference, and this became a regular feature of the diocese, giving opportunity for the mission staff to consult together, and formulate future policy. The subjects discussed ranged from indentures for apprentices and prices to be paid for mission goods by natives, to the admission of polygamists to the catechumenate and the marriage of christians and heathen (although these questions were reserved for discussion by the clergy).

Up to this time the clergy had been entirely expatriate, but in the closing years of the nineteenth century a native African ministry began to emerge. The first African to be admitted to Holy Orders was a Yao, Yohanna Abdallah, made deacon in 1894 and ordained priest in 1898, when two more Africans entered the diaconate, Augustine Ambali, a Nyamwezi, and Eustace Malisawa, another Yao. The first Malawian to be ordained was Leonard Kamungu, who entered the ministry in 1901. He died, most probably from poisoning, at Msoro in Zambia in 1913, having worked for a number of years at Nkhota Kota. At this time there were no facilities in Nyasaland for training a native clergy—such training was given at Kiungani, Zanzibar. Not until October 1905 when St Andrew's College, Nkwazi (on Likoma Island) was opened, could men undergo a regular course of study for the ministry in Nyasaland.

Education

We have already seen that the primary objective of the mission's educational work was the conversion of people to Christianity; to which the demands of secular learning took second place. Although this remained an important consideration it was evident from the turn of the century that, 'medical and educational work came to be viewed no longer as auxiliaries of evangelism but as means of consolidating the Christian life among those who had already been baptized.'[23] Later writers made it clear that the aim of the mission was 'to educate African children for their future vocation in life', and observed with some pride that the mission had taught 'many Africans to earn respectable livelihoods by printing, carpentry, masonry, laundry and agricultural work, and turned out many excellent schoolmasters and Government servants, interpreters, etc.'[24]

Some account has already been given of the functioning of the village schools. Their syllabus was necessarily dictated by the aims of the mission and the abilities of the teachers, most of whom could teach 'arithmetic up to fractions, reading and writing, a little very hazy geography, and a smattering of English . . . though some of the cleverer ones know Swahili as well as Chinyanja and Yao, and have a very fair knowledge of English.'[25] At the larger centres a more formal teaching programme could be adopted, and the following account of the girls' school at Mponda's gives the flavour of school-life in the 1900's: 'We are not ambitious, but our great aim is at present, to get out of Standard II. According to the Diocesan syllabus, the work of Standard II is as follows:— Reading: Æsop's Fables, with meaning. Writing: transcribe from blackboard or from book. Punctuation, capitals, double lines. Arithmetic: first four rules (short division only), multiplication and division, 1–6 and 10. Numeration and notation to 1,000 with easy problems. Singing: sol-fa rounds, three hymns from memory. Geography: plan of school and neighbourhood. Scripture: learn one Psalm, one hymn, and five verses of Scripture each quarter. . . . We can do all these things, but none of them very well, and arithmetic is certainly very poor.'[26]

The brighter boys from the different stations were encouraged to enrol as students at St Michael's College which was located at Msumba, until the murder of its Principal, Arthur Douglas, in 1911 necessitated its removal to Likoma. St Michael's, opened on a temporary basis in 1900 until the *Chauncy Maples* could train teachers on board, became a permanent institution in the following year, and offered a course of training intended to last four years. The first two years were spent at College, the third in teaching under European supervision, and the final year back at St Michael's (not all students attained this ideal). For those with a vocation to the priesthood, theological training was available from 1905. Such was the educational ladder that was open to the boys.

The girls were less fortunate, once their own schooling was completed, since there were no further education facilities available to them of comparable scope. Those wishing to make a career in teaching obtained their training and recognition under the pupil-teacher system. In order to improve both their status and proficiency, a common scheme of in-service training was drawn up for the diocese by which a five-years' syllabus for women teachers was introduced which included annual examinations and the award of graded certificates.

Such is a brief summary of educational work in the diocese, and although manual skills were by no means neglected, nevertheless the type of education provided by the mission had a strong academic bias, and was sometimes criticized on this account. 'What ultimate benefit', it was asked, 'does an African child gain from such an education?' The same question was often asked (with equal force) of the popular education provided in England by Mr Forster's Act of 1870.

Apart from the 'civilizing influence' attributed to Western education, it carried economic benefits, even though Canon Broomfield (for many years General Secretary of the Mission) has indicated that in the years preceding

357

the First World War there were very few openings for educated Africans outside the mission. As early as 1902 the flow of migrant workers seeking employment in other parts of southern Africa had begun, and it is interesting to conjecture how much of an advantage (or handicap) a knowledge of English and the ability to read and write may have been.[27]

Meanwhile, whatever the young men might do, 'the girls were to be taught reading and writing and the school subjects, not in order that they might be able when they left school to take up work such as that of a clerk, but that when they married they might be able with their husbands to make good Christian homes where their children would be cared for and brought up in the Christian faith.' The object of the mission was to civilize and christianize the people and education was part of the civilizing process; we now turn to study the second objective.

Evangelism

The aim of the mission's evangelistic work was to convert the people of the lake to Jesus Christ and to the new life which he offered. This evangelism was founded on the Dominical charge to preach, teach, heal and baptize— and was given its expression in the public preaching, the setting up of schools, the works of mercy traditionally associated with Christianity, and the establishment of a Church into which the newly-baptized could be admitted. This was the positive and most important aspect of the mission's work in Central Africa. But evangelism has a negative aspect, since before these activities become fully effective old ideas and ways of life that are hostile to them, or in direct conflict with them, have to be overcome.

Writing of the attitude amongst missionaries working in Africa at the end of the nineteenth century, Fr Adrian Hastings writes, 'what struck them, undoubtedly, was the darkness of the continent: its lack of religion and sound morals, its ignorance, its general pitiful condition made worse by the barbarity of the slave trade. Evangelization was seen as a liberation from a state of absolute awfulness and the picture of unredeemed Africa was often painted in colours as gruesome as possible the better to encourage missionary zeal at home.' Although acknowledging that this attitude was not universal, Fr Hastings adds, 'Nevertheless the negative approach has been very strong'.[28]

There can be little doubt that the promoters of the Universities' Mission shared this outlook—most of the mission literature of the period speaks of 'a battle . . . fought against the powers of darkness' or has emotive titles written in the same key. The obstacles to evangelism came from two directions: the traditional beliefs and customs of the people; and the growing influence of Islam in certain areas. Both of these subjects deserve better than the scanty treatment that I am able to give, nevertheless, whatever qualifications are admitted, it is clear that the mission was hostile to both influences, and inclined to dismiss them as positively harmful, or at best, as having little value.

Mohammedanism was regarded as the great rival of the Gospel, partly because of its aggressive character, but also because government officials were inclined to favour it as being better than heathenism. It was a commonplace amongst many colonial officials that the religion of the Prophet was suited to the African, and the next best religion to Christianity.[29] There was also an inevitable conflict between the mission and Islam arising from the Arab involvement in the slave trade and all the misery that this entailed. A further objection arose from the conviction that the Islam of Central Africa was syncretist: that the Muslim faith had been adulterated to accommodate African custom and practice.[30] But probably the chief source of hostility resulted from the fact that Islam was a proselytizing religion, and therefore in competition with the mission in seeking to make converts.

As often as not such competition manifested itself in the refusal by a village chief or headman to allow the mission to establish a school, or as the result of poor attendance to force the closure of an existing school. Sometimes more aggressive tactics were adopted.

Although the mission showed little sympathy for the traditional beliefs and practices of the native population, it would be misleading to suggest that it made a wholesale attempt to suppress the culture. What it was anxious to suppress were those features which it regarded as being incompatible with the Gospel and Christian standards of morality. But even if their attitude was often negative the missionaries were willing to acknowledge that 'there are many things that are "broken lights" of God', and that 'there are social customs and individual characteristics that are wholly admirable.'[31]

But such admiration did not extend to certain traditional dances, the practice of polygamy, or witchcraft. It should be made clear that not all dances were the subject of condemnation, which was reserved chiefly for certain of the initiation ceremonies in which dancing was a prominent feature. Such dances were said to be full of indecencies and immoralities, and debasing of the sexual instincts.[32] Although Chauncy Maples saw education rather than prohibition as the best weapon against this aspect of African life, one of the Likoma clergy went in person to withdraw a girl, the wife of a mission teacher, from the *nkole ya mimba* (i.e. initiation of the first pregnancy) while she was dancing.

Whatever arguments might be brought forward in defence of polygamy as part of the existing social structure, the mission saw it as contrary to the teaching of the New Testament and the direct injunction of Jesus. But, as in other parts of Africa, in its handling of this problem the mission sometimes left much to be desired in the realm of Christian love, although undoubtedly the demands of the law were fulfilled. A station labourer employed by the Malindi mission had to choose between his job and his three wives. It must have been small consolation to be given a four shilling loan to pay off the unwanted pair. The mission defended its position not only on grounds of the divine will, but because it saw polygamy as a devaluation of womanhood, and the place of women in society.

Any discussion of witchcraft is so open to objection and must be so hedged with qualifications that it is almost impossible to say anything of value outside a separate paper on the subject. It is important to distinguish between the

359

sing'anga (medicine man) and *mfiti* (witch or wizard). Writing of the medicine man Dr Howard observed that while some of his remedies were far from curative, 'His scientific outfit is a curious mixture of empirical knowledge and superstition. He knows a little about herbs and household remedies, and has some commonsense ideas about massage and first-aid, counter-irritation, cupping, etc.'[33] According to Chauncy Maples nearly everyone lived in daily dread of witchcraft ('ufiti'), to which many, if not most, natural deaths were attributed. . . . 'The ramifications of witchcraft—trial by ordeal, and the like —run through the whole of social life, such as it is, of these people, creating fear, and suspicion, and mistrust on all sides, breaking up families, severing friendships . . .'[34]

For traditional religion as a whole, there was scant respect, and it is variously described as 'a set of unconnected superstitions' and 'an unreasoned and blind fight against the gods of ill-luck and circumstance'. Confronted with such beliefs, the role of the mission was to be 'Lux in Tenebris'.

III   THE PERIOD *1900–1914*: A SUMMARY

By the turn of the century the progress of the Universities' Mission had more than justified Johnson's appeal for a steamer. But although the *Charles Janson* had done sterling work in making the lakeshore area accessible to the mission, it was proving inadequate for the increased volume of work which now included regular calls at twenty stations, as well as the transport of stores, mail, and passengers. Johnson began to canvass support for a new steamer, conceived in the grand manner as a floating mission station complete with chapel/lecture room, post office, sick bay, printing shop and passenger accommodation. Named *Chauncy Maples*, the new steamer was launched in June, 1901.

Apart from Likoma and the villages on the eastern lake shore, stations were active at Unangu, Nkhota Kota, and Mponda's and new work was begun at Malindi where engineering shops were erected to maintain the mission's growing fleet. Work on the Shire was extended in the Matope area, and work begun at Likwenu which by 1914 had developed into an important station. The period also witnessed much permanent building to replace the temporary structures which had previously done service. In 1900 a permanent church was built at Unangu, followed a year later by one at Nkhota Kota. This programme of permanent building became possible with the arrival in 1899 of a qualified architect, Mr Frank George. In addition to the churches already mentioned, George was responsible for those erected at Malindi and Mponda's. His crowning achievement was the Cathedral Church of St Peter on Likoma Island, built according to his design and under his direction by the men he had trained on the smaller churches. Like its Scottish counterpart in Blantyre, Likoma Cathedral remains as a tribute to the ingenuity and skill of its builders. Begun in 1903, the completed Cathedral was consecrated in 1911.

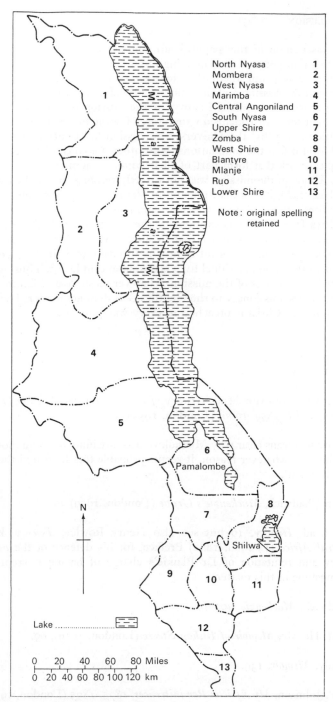

North Nyasa   1
Mombera   2
West Nyasa   3
Marimba   4
Central Angoniland 5
South Nyasa   6
Upper Shire   7
Zomba   8
West Shire   9
Blantyre   10
Mlanje   11
Ruo   12
Lower Shire   13

Note : original spelling
       retained

Pamalombe

N

Shilwa

Lake ....

0   20   40   60   80 Miles
0 20 40 60 80 100 120 km

20.3 Districts of Malawi in 1906

In the presentation of this paper I am conscious of having failed to get a quart into a pint pot, and of neglecting important areas of discussion such as the reaction of the people themselves to the mission's activities, or the relationship between the mission and the colonial administration. I am conscious also of giving more of an 'official history' of the mission than critical comment upon that history. In conclusion therefore. I want to say something of the contribution made 'by' the Universities' Mission 'to' Central Africa. At the material level it laid the foundations, with other missions, of the educational and medical work that form part of their common heritage to the people of Malawi. Although the mission was not directly responsible for the extinction of the slave trade, it was instrumental in showing, by precept and example, that 'the brotherhood of man' was not a pious phrase but a viable alternative to tribal warfare. In any assessment of the spiritual value of the mission's work, it is as well to remember that to quote the numbers baptized or the annual increase in communicant figures is to give only half the picture; the impact of Christ upon individual lives is the significant factor. Thus, whatever the faults or limitations of the mission; whatever its success or failure—in the words of the first missionary to the Gentiles—'It does not matter. I am happy —just so long as Christ is preached in every way possible.'

FOOTNOTES

1 A. E. Anderson-Morshead, *History of the Universities' Mission to Central Africa, Vol I (1859–1909)* (London, 1955), 5.

2 It is by no means clear why Mankokwe was unwilling to accommodate the mission; for whatever reason, it seems probable that he feared the risk of 'involvement'.

3 Owen Chadwick, *Mackenzie's Grave* (London, 1959) 59.

4 Morshead, *History*, 16 but see also Henry Rowley, *Twenty Years in Central Africa* (London, 1881) Preface, for his defence of the mission's policy and refutation of Dr Blaikie's charge of having misrepresented Livingstone in this matter.

5 Chadwick, *Mackenzie*, 202–6.

6 R. M. Heanly, *Memoir of Bishop Steere* (London, 1909), 69.

7 Heanly, *Memoir*, 139.

8 W. P. Johnson, *My African Reminiscences, 1875–1895* (London, 1924), 84.

9 Evidently the refugees were safe (as Likoma was) since the Ngoni had a superstitious fear of water. I am indebted to Mr Francis Bell for this information.

10 Johnson, *Reminiscences*, 109–10.

11 *Central Africa, Vol II* April 1884, 55.

12 D. Y. Mills, *What We Do In Nyasaland* (London, 1911), 17.

13 Ellen Maples, *Life and Letters of Chauncy Maples* (London, 1898), 308.

14 Mills, *What We Do*, 197–204 for a detailed account, but the book is a gold-mine.

15 Canon Duncan Travers in *The Reason Why*, D. Y. Mills (London, 1929), 53.

16 Maples, *Letters*, 279.

17 Maples, *Letters*, 289.

18 On this see *Life and Letters of Arthur Fraser Sim* (London, 1901).

19 A. G. Blood, *The History of the U.M.C.A., Vol. II (1907–1932)* (London, 1957), 31.

20 From the unpublished *Diary for 1900* of the Revd Caradoc Davies, U.M.C.A.

21 Blood, *History*, 31.

22 Extract from *Malindi Station Book, 1900–1911*, 129.

23 Canon J. V. Taylor in *Africa Handbook* (ed. Colin Legum) (London, 1969), 610.

24 Mills, *The Reason Why*, 13 and 49.

25 Mills, *What We Do*, 99.

26 Mills, *What We Do*, 106.

27 Extract, *Malindi Station Book*, 83 mentions men on ulendo to Fort Salisbury.

28 Fr Adrian Hastings, *Church and Mission in Modern Africa* (London, 1967),

60. The best assessment of the Christian Church in Africa to appear in recent years.

29 Godfrey Dale (ed.), *Darkness or Light* (London, 1925), 50 *et al.*

30 The Revds A. M. Jenkin and W. B. Suter in *What We Do*, 243–4 *et al.*

31 Donald Fraser, *The Future of Africa* (London, 1911), 116.

32 See H. S. Stannus, *Notes on Some Tribes of British Central Africa* (London, 1910) and reprinted from the R.A.I. Journal for a dispassionate account of such dances.

33 Dr Robert Howard in *Darkness or Light* (ed. Dale), 238.

34 Ellen Maples, *Journals and Papers of Chauncy Maples* (London, 1899), 171–2.

The following books not cited above were also consulted in the preparation of this paper, and contain a great deal of useful material:
Towards Freedom (U.M.C.A. Centenary Book) Canon G. Broomfield (London, 1957).
The Fortunate Few (Education in E. and C. Africa) A. G. Blood (ed.) (London, 1954).
A Time to Remember Mary McCulloch (London, 1959).

21 An introduction to the history of the Dutch Reformed Church Mission in Malawi 1889-1914

J. L. Pretorius

In 1884 and 1885 the Dutch Reformed Church in the Cape Colony was stirred by a deep religious awakening and in 1886 a group of ministers formed a ministers' missionary society. Every member undertook to contribute £10 annually and in this way enable the Society to support a missionary abroad, i.e. outside the Cape Colony.[1] At the same time a Students' Missionary Society was formed at Stellenbosch, near Cape Town, and the young secretary of this Society, Andrew Charles Murray, felt called to become a missionary. He started a correspondence with Dr James Stewart of Lovedale, who mentioned Nyasaland and its great need.[2]

After considering several possibilities, among them China and areas in the Transvaal Republic, the M.M.S. decided to send its lone missionary to Nyasaland for the following reasons.[3] Firstly, the Free Church of Scotland, offered them a vast area in Nyasaland whereas in South Africa most areas were already covered by missionary societies from Britain and Europe. Secondly, it would be impractical to send one single man to a remote area while in Nyasaland the Free Church was willing to take the D.R.C. Missionary under their wing.[4] Lastly, there was a need to awaken greater interest in the church in mission work. A mission outside South Africa would bring the D.R. Church into contact with a completely pagan society, untouched by Christianity or civilization. This would widen the vision of the Church and stimulate interest in mission work.

So in 1888 the young Rev. A. C. Murray sailed for Nyasaland. After a two month journey he arrived at Bandawe where Dr and Mrs Laws took him into their home. On the advice of Dr Laws, Rev. Murray, accompanied by a Rev. Bain, set out northwards to look for a suitable area among the Ngonde of northern Malawi and southern Tanzania. At Karonga they were delayed by the threat of an attack by Arab slavers but eventually reached Kararamuka where they hoped to start a mission station. They suffered continuous attacks of fever and in November 1888 Rev. Murray got sunstroke and almost died. He made a miraculous recovery and was sent to Njuyu, on the highlands, where he stayed for several months with Dr and Mrs Elmslie in order to regain his health.

This enforced delay had a great deal to do with the subsequent success of the D.R.C. Mission. The Elmslies' example and advice enabled him in later years to avoid many mistakes and gave him an insight into the methods the Livingstonia Mission had so successfully employed. The Dutch Reformed Church was greatly indebted to the Livingstonia Mission for the encouragement and help it received so unstintingly during those early years.[5]

I   THE PIONEER YEARS, 1889–99

In July 1889 Rev. A. C. Murray was joined by Rev. T. C. B. Vlok. Because of the unsettled conditions in the north, Rev. Murray had to abandon his hope of starting a mission among the Ngonde, and on the advice of Dr Laws Revs Murray and Vlok set out to look for a suitable mission field in the present-day Central Region. At that time the area was dominated by three warrior chiefs, the Chewa Chief Mwase of Kasungu, and the two Ngoni Chiefs, Chiwere[6] and Chikusi, while along the lakeshore there were several enclaves of Yao slavers. Their meeting with Mwase did not go well and they continued southwards until they reached Msakambewa, an important sub-chief of Chiwere. From there they went to Chiwere who welcomed them and agreed to allow them to start a mission station near his headquarters.

II   RELATIONSHIP BETWEEN THE FIRST MISSIONARIES AND THE CHIEFS

Although Nyasaland was declared a Protectorate in 1891 the *de facto* situation was that the central region chiefs were independent and regarded themselves as independent until British military might asserted itself locally between 1896 and 1897.

The mission policy was to recognize the chiefs and to approach them as independent rulers.[7] No mission station was started unless it had permission from or had been invited by the chief within whose area of jurisdiction the station would be sited.[8] This was particularly true of Mvera station (in Chiwere's area), Kongwe station (under Msakambewa), and Nkhoma (under Mazengera).

The chiefs' motives in allowing the missionaries to settle near their capitals seem to have been threefold: firstly, they saw the missionaries as valuable instruments in their foreign policies. They regarded the presence of a missionary as protection against neighbouring tribes. This was the reason cited by Mazengera for asking for a missionary at Nkhoma in 1896.[9] During the middle 1890s, especially, the chiefs saw the missionaries as valuable advisers and go-betweens in the chiefs' dealings with the steadily expanding British influence.[10]

It is clear from W. H. Murray's accounts, for instance, that Chiwere saw

British protection as involving the loss of his independence, threatening to turn him into a vassal chief of the British and constituting a threat to his life —i.e. he feared that the British would kill him if he surrendered.[11]

Both Chiwere and the British administration accepted W. H. Murray as a reliable go-between, even though Murray was himself reluctant to become involved in affairs of state.

For many months in 1896 Chiwere's Ngoni debated the coming of the British. In the end they decided to submit peacefully, partly on W. H. Murray's advice (who told them that even if they wiped out the local ones many more would come from overseas), and partly (probably) because of the example of Chikusi's fate.[12]

A similar debate apparently took place in the war councils of Chiwere's sub-chief, Msakambewa, and the missionaries whose lives at Kongwe were more than once threatened, but in the end here, too, it was decided to spare the missionaries, who were at the mercy of the warriors.

The second reason why the missionaries were accepted was that the chiefs saw in the presence of a missionary valuable insurance against the plotting of ambitious councillors. There is repeated evidence of instability and rivalry within the chiefs' councils, particularly among the warlike Ngoni[13] and the chief often found it useful to enhance his prestige by the presence of a missionary.

Thirdly, and closely connected with the previous factor, the missionaries were seen as persons with enormous powers to manipulate supernatural forces, i.e. they were regarded as a sort of super medium-men, in spite of their repeated protests to the contrary.[14]

The missionaries felt bound not to act unilaterally against the slave trade, except in isolated instances where only one or two individuals were concerned, in spite of their bitter opposition to the slave trade. They took the same attitude with regard to the malpractices surrounding the poison ordeal (*mwabvi*).[15] They took this moderate attitude because they recognized that they were obliged to accept the chief's authority. But it seems from W. H. Murray's letters that pressure was put on the British administration by the missionaries to stop the slave trade. He complained that the administration was reluctant to deal with the slave traders in his letters of 9 March and 24 May 1895.[16]

III   THE FIRST MISSION STATION

On 28 November 1889, A. C. Murray and T. C. B. Vlok pitched their tent under a *mkuyu* tree near Chiwere's village, 26 miles west of present-day Salima. They named their station Mvera (obedience). During the following eighty years the mission influence was to spread over the entire Central Region so that today the Nkhoma Synod of the C.C.A.P. has an estimated 300,000 adherents.[17]

But during that first decade the small mission repeatedly faced extinction by the Ngoni warriors, almost exactly in the same way as the Livingstonia Mission. There was the same ultimatum that they should 'make' rain (followed by the same miraculous answer to their desperate prayers); the same accounts of long, watchful, prayerful nights, as they huddled behind the wattle-and-daub walls of their primitive little houses, while the Ngoni warriors danced around their fires and the old councillors debated the fate of the white strangers. But time and again their lives were spared.[18]

The first task the two men set themselves was to gain the confidence of the headmen and people, but it was a long and uphill struggle. In 1890 the first school was started at Mvera under an African teacher named Tomani, who had been trained at Cape Maclear. At the same time a school was also opened at Ndindi on the lakeshore. Later four of the best pupils were sent to Livingstonia for training as teachers. (One of them, Amoni Ndiwo, became the first African ordained minister in the mission.)

By the end of 1894 there were five schools, apart from the schools at the south end of the lake which the Livingstonia Mission had handed over, and which were under the supervision of a former slave, Albert Namalambe, the first Malawian Christian.

During these first five years, five more missionaries joined Murray and Vlok, among whom were Rev. Robert Blake (1892) who started Kongwe station in 1894; Rev. W. H. Murray (1894) who took over Livlezi station from Livingstonia in 1895 and became head of the Mission until 1936; Mr A. v. d. Westhuizen, who laid the foundation of the mission's agricultural teaching, and Miss Martha Murray who started the first boarding school for girls in 1895.

At all three mission stations the missionaries were still occasionally threatened by the Ngoni, and slave raiding continued until the twentieth century, but the work expanded slowly. At the end of five years A. C. Murray baptized two men, but they soon reverted to their old way of life. There were many other disappointments. In 1895 Rev. Vlok returned to Malawi with a bride. Within a year she died of black water fever, followed by Mr Koos du Toit at Nkhoma, soon afterwards. A. C. Murray was savaged by a wounded leopard and had to leave the field and in 1898 J. S. Cridland died. Malaria was decimating the small band in the same way as it had decimated the U.M.C.A. and the Livingstonia missionaries in previous decades. Of the first twelve missionaries four died and several others had to leave the country for health reasons.

The death of Koos du Toit marked the turning point in the missionaries' long struggle to break through to the hearts of the people. On 10 December 1897, fourteen men and five women were baptized. They were a remarkable group of whom one, Mrs Sara Lingodzi Nabanda, is still alive today (1970).

In 1896 Livlezi station was vacated and by invitation of the Chewa chief Mazengera, who was living on the top of Nkhoma mountain, a mission station was started on the eastern slopes of the mountain. Mazengera's only aim was to protect himself against the slave raids of the warlike Yao chief Tambala and Chiwere's Ngoni, and not because he had any interest in the Gospel.[19]

By the end of the first decade there were eighteen missionaries on three stations, Mvera, Kongwe and Nkhoma, while the remarkable African evangelist, Albert Namalambe, looked after a network of fourteen schools, forty-eight teachers, 1,300 children and led a band of twenty-one baptized members and fifty-nine hearers, in the area south-west of the lake.

Details of The D.R.C. Mission in 1899[20]

	Mvera	Kongwe	Nkhoma	Livlezi	Total
Adult Church members	233	32	21	92	378
Baptism Class members	263	150	59	107	579
Evangelist-teachers	43	9	14	15	81
Assistant teachers	82	17	48	48	249
Schools	40	12	14	15	81
School children	3,206	1,200	1,313	1,555	7,274
Adults not yet allowed into Baptism Class	380	—	240	—	620
Collections, etc.	£69	£34	£33.2.6	£33.8.6	£169.11.0
Pagans in regular contact with the mission	8,000	4,000	2,500	2,460	16,900
Out-patients	3,650	4,015	4,745	—	12,410
Christian marriages	26	3	3	16	48
Half Christian marriages	12	2	5	—	19
Children christened	53	12	12	29	106

IV YEARS OF TROUBLE, 1899–1904

In 1899 the Anglo-Boer War (1899–1902) broke out in South Africa. At the same time alleged Government malpractices in connection with the collection of the three shillings tax on males led to a serious deterioration in the relations between the D.R.C. Mission and the government of the Protectorate. Both events had a far reaching effect on the work and strategy of the D.R.C. Mission in the twentieth century.

(a) *The Anglo-Boer War 1899–1902*
One of the most remarkable chapters in the otherwise bitter history of this war, the effects of which are still with us in 1970, is the story of the great religious awakening in certain Boer commando as well as in the prisoner-of-war camps in India and Cape Town, and in St Helena, Bermuda and Ceylon. A Boer general, Beyers, started the Men's Missionary Society and 175 Boer prisoners offered themselves for missionary work when they returned to South Africa after the end of the war.

In spite of the fact that thousands of Afrikaners were completely ruined and many thousands more were in desperate straits, the mission work of the D.R.

369

Church received a tremendous stimulus, and within a few years missionaries were working in six countries outside South Africa.[21] In Malawi the number of workers doubled between 1899 and 1903, from fourteen to twenty-eight and another fifty-three joined the mission between 1903 and 1914.

At the same time, however, relations with the British government in Malawi grew rapidly worse as the Anglo-Boer War progressed. In 1899 the youngest brother of Dr W. H. Murray, head of the mission, was treacherously shot dead after he had joined the Boer forces, and under the circumstances it was natural for the Protectorate government to view the South African missionaries with suspicion.

In spite of this suspicion, which severely hampered the mission's expansion in Dedza District as well as in the area west of Lilongwe in the period up to 1904, the influx of new missionaries made it possible to realize A. C. Murray's dream of a large field. In 1902 Mlanda was founded followed by Mphunzi (1903) and Malingunde (1907), both the latter after a long struggle with the local British authorities. In 1907 a missionary was placed at Malembo, on the lake, in 1910 Chinthembwe was founded and in 1914 Mchinji, on the western borders of the Central Region.

But at the end of 1900 all this was a long way away. The war news from South Africa was depressing, mission funds had reached a low point, there were very few new workers, and in the midst of all this the trouble about the tax on male adults broke out.

(b) *The Hut Tax*

In 1892 a hut tax of 3s. was imposed on every African male adult, a measure which was bitterly opposed by the Blantyre Mission as well as other missions. By about 1897 this tax was extended to the Central Region. There was no money in the Central Region and the tax measure was used to force adults to go and work on the estates around Blantyre. Tax defaulters were taken to Blantyre where they had to work for three months. One month's pay (3s.) was taken in lieu of tax and the remainder they received in cash or cloth.

There were many complaints:

On 25 December 1900, Dr W. H. Murray, then head of the Mission, wrote home from Mvera:

'Things are very unsettled in this district and natives are being subjected to much injustice and irregularity in the drastic measures that are being taken to compel them to work. . . . And so with the Xmas joy there is much to make one sad.'

A month earlier he had written:

' . . . Things have lately taken place that might shame any Savage, if committed by him, and that in the name and by the instruments of the Govt. Because men refuse to pay their taxes (on account of the hardships entailed

370

in going to work 200 miles away from their homes, where there is a great scarcity of food) women and little children have been ruthlessly shot down by native policemen, and we've still to see what's going to become of it.'

As a result of the methods employed,[22] a series of troubles broke out which ended with the Dutch Reformed Church Mission being charged with inciting the Africans not to pay their taxes or volunteer their labour, and Rev. Robert Blake was charged with using the pupit at Kongwe for the furtherance of his objections to the Administration's policy of labour and taxation.

The D.R.C. Missionaries were accused of lying by the magistrate for Dedza District. 'The whole version, as rendered, is a transparent act of petty revenge on the part of the Dutch Mission for their recent loss of wrongfully assumed jurisdiction over the natives,' was the official verdict of the Protectorate government.

More research is needed before we can adequately judge the rights and the wrongs of the dispute and the outcome of the court case against the Mission has not yet been traced.

However, it is clear that the missionaries had never assumed any form of jurisdiction over the tribes among whom they worked. It is true that Dr W. H. Murray and Robert Blake rendered valuable service to the Protectorate government in persuading Chiwere, Msakambewa and Mazengera to accept British protection, but their advice was only given at the request of the chiefs concerned and in fact had undermined their influence among many Ngoni indunas.[23]

There can be no doubt that in Dedza District, at least, government askari on occasion abused their position of authority. In July 1897, Rev. Vlok wrote:[24]

'We arrived early at Dedza. . . . It filled us with sorrow to see how the people ran away. They thought we were a government party. Some of the native government soldiers treat the poor wild natives in such a manner that now when any traveller approaches the entire village is deserted.'

In 1900 Rev. Vlok wrote about the migrant labourers (echoing Swann's letter almost word for word): ' . . . when they arrive home (they look like) walking skeletons'.[25]

As far as we know the Mission was acquitted but the whole episode had a fundamental effect on the basic strategy of the D.R.C. Mission in the twentieth century.

The mission had from the beginning seen its task as primarily to build up an independent Christian nation, built on the foundation of a self-supporting, self-governing church, expanding from its own inner strength.[26] But it now saw Western civilization without Christianity as the greatest threat to this ideal; and the Chimbulanga episode inspired them to attack the migratory labour problem from several sides.

'What really corrupts (the Africans) morally is the irreligious atmosphere

371

in which they are placed. They are influenced by whites who are without religion and who do not always set a good example. . . . To their pagan sins they then add the sins of a depraved civilization, and man is worse than he was, and further away from God.

'The people are threatened by moral decay ever since they were placed under the hut tax three years ago . . .'[27]

V YEARS OF GROWTH, 1904–14

In order to deal with this threat of 'moral decay' the D.R. Church embarked on an ambitious programme which amounted to nothing less than a full-scale, frontal assault on migrant labour.

Up to now the mission had merely followed as far as its funds allowed the methods taught them by Livingstonia Mission; after the trouble over the Chimbulanga expedition's activities blew over, the mission launched what today would be called a mass-literacy campaign as well as a comprehensive community development scheme. With the arrival of three new agricultural missionaries in 1904, a doctor and a nurse in 1900 and 1904 respectively, and several lady workers the mission was set for its 'great leap forward'.

While it is correct to say, as the Phelps-Stokes Commission said in 1924, that the main object of the D.R.C.M. schools was 'to instil a thorough knowledge of the Word of God into the minds of the scholars, old and young, and to raise a Bible reading people', it should also be added that the D.R.C.M. regarded the Christian family as the only true basis for a truly indigenous church, and this view explains many aspects of the D.R.C.M.'s policies in the years 1900 to 1914 (and after).

In order to achieve its aim of building up a self-supporting, self-propagating church, and to persuade the men to stay at home, the Mission mounted a three-pronged attack:

(a) *Rapid expansion of village schools*
The network of village schools, called 'outposts', was rapidly expanded. In the six years from 1904 to 1914, an average of 111 new outposts were opened each year so that at the outbreak of World War I there were 66,700 pupils in 750 'outposts', manned by 1,400 teachers and teacher-evangelists.[28] No-one, except in exceptional cases, was allowed to become a church member unless he or she could read. These outposts were visited regularly at least four times a year by a missionary 'inspector'. They formed the basis of the D.R.C.M.'s work in Malawi. A training school for teachers was started at Nkhoma in 1904.

(b) *Village industries and agriculture*
This venture formed the heart of the D.R.C.M.'s attempt to combat migrant labour and its attendant evils. The Phelps-Stokes Commission described it as follows:

'A feature of the Dutch Mission [sic] is its insistence on agicultural and

372

simple village industries. In these two important respects it has not its superior in all the Nyasaland schools. . . . The agriculture is . . . the 30-acre wheat field, the even larger maize field, the cane field, the orchards, the arrow root plantation, the flower and vegetable garden of a real farm. The mistake of making the agriculture more refined than the Natives are able to carry out on their own land has not been made. While the possibilities of new crops, new fruits and improved types of stock are always being considered, the aim (is) to produce something which the Natives can themselves imitate successfully in their own homes.'

'The same . . . outlook is seen in the *industries* taught. Instead of elaborate woodwork shops and . . . industries . . . which almost compels the Native to go to the European center to find an opportunity to practise his craft, the work at Nkhoma is planned to fit the men and women to become home workers. Nowhere in Nyasaland has the Commission seen a finer exhibit of home industries. Here were specimens of *wood and iron work, bark cloth, wool* and *linen*-weaving, *basket* and *mat* work of at least twenty kinds; leather work, including *bootmaking, sandal* and *harness making*, the treatment of the skins of animals, soap and oil making, bricks and tiles, machine and hand sewing and many other kinds of village industry. Natives are taught to use . . . the materials at their doors . . .

'Another piece of equally successful informal education is seen in the model Christian village. . . . The missionaries have shown the Natives how a model village may be laid out . . . (and) taught them how to build two and three-roomed huts out of pise de terre with thatched roofs . . .'[29]

In an effort to stimulate local trade each Mission station had its own store, weekly markets where village produce and products could be bartered were introduced and because money was virtually non-existent the Mission introduced its own currency (date unknown). The coin was a tin disc the size of a penny, punched with two holes and stamped MM (Mvera Mission).

One disc was worth about 2d (half a yard of cotton) and was soon known as *Chamkono*. They were withdrawn in 1909.[30]

A start was made with the importation of cattle with a view to improving local herds; among these were Poll Angus, Shorthorns, Herefords, Africanders, Frieslands and Jerseys. None of these lasted for many years but in several areas they did make a contribution towards improving local herds.[31] Great efforts were also made to encourage tree planting, but few were properly looked after.[32]

(c) *Christian wives and mothers:*
In 1895 the first boarding school for girls were started. By 1910 there were 300 girls in these boading schools. The prime object was to provide the young church leaders with Christian wives, who would spread the Gospel and improve the standard of living in the villages. To this end they were taught house craft, such as washing, ironing, cooking, making starch, soap and candles, as well as things they were traditionally taught, such as clay pot making.[33]

The Chewa are matrilineally organized and the initiation of girls (*china mwali*) plays an important part in their social organization. In order to loosen the hold of this ceremony (and of the old women who run it) over the young girls, an annual Christian initiation ceremony (*Chilangizo*) was introduced modelled on the traditional ceremony but with a Christian content. In addition, literacy and sewing classes (sometimes numbering over 200) for women were held regularly.

In this way the missionaries strove to improve the status of the women and to foster Christian family life without destroying the traditional tribal organization.

VI LITERATURE

As in the other missions great importance was attached to literature. The first book to be written in Chichewa at Mvera was *Mkhweri* by A. C. Murray, a little reader for the schools. The second book was *Mwambi wakale* by Robert Blake, still popular today after more than seventy years under the title *Mbiri Yakale*—a collection of stories for children from the Old Testament.

The Mission could not afford to provide readers for the large number of pupils and a series of twelve large spelling charts was produced—one for each class. If a pupil had mastered the last chart he or she could go on to *Mkhweri*. The first hymn book was printed in 1900 (at Blantyre).

The greatest literary contribution the Mission made in those early years was its major share in the translation of the Bible into Union Nyanja. On two occasions Dr W. H. Murray was selected to lead the translation of first the New and afterwards the Old Testament, between 1903 and 1918. He worked with Dr Hetherwick, Rev. Napier and three Africans, Mr Mathan Sunday from Blantyre, Mr Ismael Mwale of Ncheu and Mr Willebes Chikuse of Mvera.

Apart from the translation of the Bible, perhaps the most significant step was the founding of a magazine in 1909, of which Dr W. H. Murray remained the editor until 1936. The magazine, called *Mthenga*, and today called *Kuunika*, was never spectacular, and perhaps one of its most outstanding features has been its ability to survive; nevertheless, it played a most important part in encouraging the lonely out-school teachers, enriching their lives and binding the migrant workers to their home church.

Twenty years after its inception Victor Murray described the little magazine as follows:

'It is published six times a year at a penny per issue and has a circulation of 3,000. . . . One copy . . . included five Biblical and religious articles as well as others on—
   drink
   how to choose mealie-seed
   whirlwinds
   proverbs

374

our lungs
how to dry tobacco
the Nyasaland census
the journey to Salisbury
the custom of singing at funerals
and a letter to the editor on tribal names.
'There were six columns of general news covering China, South America
and the founding of Achimota College, the death of Sir Apolo Kagwa and
the celebration of the Railways' centenary.
'There is also a page for mothers and other issues include a serial story. It
is the best magazine of its kind I have seen in Africa . . .'[34]

In 1907 the D.R.C.M. received its first little printing press. Mr Anderson
Kadzichi, who had been taught to type by Mrs W. H. Murray, became the
first printer. (In later years he became the head African printer in the Lusaka
Government Printing Works.)[35]

VII EXPANSION INTO OTHER MISSION FIELDS

From its small beginnings in the Central Region the D.R.C.M. spread into
Zambia (1899), Rhodesia (1912) and Portuguese East Africa (1909).

The Work in Zambia

In 1897 Rev. A. C. Murray applied for permission to start work among
Mpezeni's Ngoni in Eastern Zambia but was told to wait. In 1898 a British
force defeated Mpezeni who was taken prisoner. From his jail he sent word
to Rev. Murray inviting him to send missionaries to his people. First Rev
Murray sent two evangelists to confirm if the Ngoni's request was in earnest,
and upon receiving affirmative reports Revs P. J. Smit and J. M. Hofmeyr
together with two African evangelists were sent out to start work in Zambia
in 1899, the first station being Magwero. The work in Zambia was the
responsibility of the D.R. Church in the Orange Free State but until 1908
the mission was directed from Malawi. In spite of the devastation caused by
the Anglo-Boer War—or perhaps because of it—the Orange Free State's work
expanded steadily and by 1914 had a string of six stations stretching westwards towards Lusaka—Magwero, Ft Jameson, Madzimoyo, Nyanje, Nsadzu
and Hofmeyr.[36]

The Work in Rhodesia

The imposition of a hut tax forced many Africans to go abroad in search of
work.[37] In 1905 a delegation of Malawian workers in Rhodesia walked on

375

foot to Mvera to ask for a missionary to look after their interests in Rhodesia, but only in 1911 could a suitable person be found in the person of Rev. T. C. B. Vlok who went to Salisbury in 1912—the beginning of one of the more unusual churches in Africa which today has eight ministers and 6,000 members in Rhodesia.

The Work in Portuguese East Africa

As early as 1902 Rev. A. G. Murray investigated the possibility of extending missionary work into Portuguese territory north of the Zambezi.[38] After several attempts had failed, the General Mission Secretary and the moderator of the D.R. Church in the Cape Colony appealed to the Prime Minister of the Cape Colony to obtain permission from the Governor-General of Moçambique for the D.R.C. to start mission work in Portuguese Angonia. The Prime Minister did so in 1906.[39]

However, no answer was forthcoming until 1908. Meanwhile, the missionaries in Nyasaland continued to exert pressure on the Portuguese authorities. In 1907 Rev. A. G. Murray went to see the Governor of Tete province, Kapitao Bettincount.[40] The main result of this meeting with the Governor was that the Governor cajoled the Roman Catholic mission which had been at Tete for 300 years to extend their work northwards and a government proclamation appeared in April 1908 which proclaimed virtually the entire Angoniland closed to all churches except the Roman Catholic Church.[41]

In June 1908 Rev. A. G. Murray went to see the Governor-General personally in Lourenço Marques and was given permission to start a mission station outside the area reserved for the R.C. Church, and subject to the new proclamations of 14 December 1907 in connection with schools, which laid down strict regulations with regard to such matters as standard of school buildings and medium of instruction.[42]

In 1909 the first station at Mphatso was started and a few years later permission was granted to open a second at Mwenzi, followed by a third at Benga and a fourth at Chipitu, in 1914. A fifth station at Matenje was opened in 1915.[43]

The reason why the Dutch Reformed Church Mission succeeded initially in expanding its work was probably due, at least in part, to the fact that Portugal became a republic in 1910. The new constitution established the principle of freedom of religion, and church and state were separated by a decree of 1911.[44] Furthermore, it seems as if the Portuguese viewed the German R.C. order who moved into Portuguese Angonia before World War I with almost as much suspicion as they viewed the South African Protestants.

After the rebellion in Barue in February 1915, for example, when missionaries were detained everywhere, the German priests were also jailed.[45]

Throughout the period of their work in P.E.A., the D.R.C. missionaries had to contend with continuous problems with the administration. They tended to blame the Roman Catholic Church for most of their troubles, but it does seem as if political factors played as great a role in determining the

Portuguese attitude. First, there was the fact that they came from Nyasaland, a territory which had been taken away from the Portuguese largely as a result of the presence of Protestant missionaries on the Shire Highlands. Second, the sugar estates were given the right to use 'forced labour' which seems to have caused some kind of conflict between the missionaries and the estate owners, which needs further investigation, and, third, the Portuguese mistrust of South African politicians rubbed off on the D.R.C. Mission. There is a letter by lawyer Ribeiro, written in 1914, which blames General Beyers' activities in the Cape for the worsening relations[46] and, after 1918, Smuts's desire to exchange Tanganyika for Moçambique south of the Zambezi alienated the Portuguese.[47] In addition, there were three local rebellions during the war years which increased Portuguese hostility towards missionaries: the Chilembwe Rising in Nyasaland (which the Portuguese regarded as proof of the subversive influence of missions[48] and the risings in Barue and Chiputu.[49] In 1916 the Portuguese arrested all the evangelist-teachers (sixty-five in number). About this Rev. A. G. Murray wrote:[50]

'We went to the Boma to hear what it means. They said they had been arrested because they don't obey the law—they don't learn Portuguese. In vain we pleaded and reminded them of the seventeen who had in fact already received their certificates. They were sent in shackles to Tete and from there to Mozambique Island. Some escaped en route, others died along the way, others died in Mozambique—some of pure maltreatment. Some were kept there from two to six years and were then returned, but four of them are still missing to-day (28 Feb. 1923). Their wives and little children are still faithfully waiting for them. That at least one is still alive is certain. Recently his wife received a letter from him. He wrote from Panjim, Portuguese India, and said he is being detained there. Where his 3 companions are he doesn't know but he had heard two years ago that they were to be sent to another Portuguese island, Timor.

We have often tried to do something for the four, but the Portuguese take no notice of our letters. When we talked to the High Commissioner, Dr Brito Comarho, about it, he only said that it was impossible that they would be exiled for such a long period.' (One of the four eventually returned in 1926 with an Indian wife.)

In 1914, however, at the end of the period which is the subject of this survey, all the later troubles were still far away. There were good relations with the local administrators and the local population, and after six years of work there were 129 full members and almost 400 hearers.[51]

VIII CONCLUSION

When World War I broke out the D.R.C.M. had over 11,000 adult church members. A school for evangelists with a two year theological training course had been started the previous year with twenty students—all chosen for their outstanding qualities as leaders. There were nine stations. Every Sunday about 4,000 lay Christians were preaching the Gospel to about 60,000 Africans in over 2,000 villages. Yet a spiritual deterioration was plainly visible and Dr W. H. Murray wrote that the position demanded much prayer.[52]

Then the Great War broke out, and the Christian faith received a blow in Africa as well as elsewhere from which it never completely recovered. The Dutch Reformed Church Mission experienced the full force of the changes that came with the First World War. Although many of the changes became apparent only several decades later there can be no doubt that they had their origin in the events inspired by or related to the First World War.

There is much to admire in the breadth of vision, the dedication to duty and sheer rugged perseverance that characterized those early pioneers. So much so that one hesitates to criticize. However, it is perhaps fair comment to say that the D.R.C. Mission policy as it took shape during those first two decades carried within it the seeds of what later became critical issues. There was, for example, their preoccupation with the preserving and development of the traditional tribal structures, and their strict code of social segregation. While they lived close to the people, and while there was no highly educated elite, these policies as well as their paternalistic attitude were of little or no hindrance—in fact, in several respects they fitted in well with the traditional tribal attitudes. But with the emergence of an educated elite among the African church members grievances and friction increased; however, that should be the subject of another paper. By 1914 the foundations had been well and truly laid, not only of an indigenous church but also of a spirit of co-operation and unity between most of the Protestant missions in Malawi, which led to the formation of a united indigenous Presbyterian church in 1924, by the two Scottish Missions and the Dutch Reformed Church Mission in Malawi.

FOOTNOTES

1 *De Zending Crisis*, A.Z.C. der N.G. Kerk, Kaapstad, 1918, 18.

2 G. F. Hugo, 'Inleiding tot die Geskiedenis van die N.G. Kerk in Malawi'. Unpublished notes, 3.

3 G. Hugo, 'Inleiding'.

4 Although the D.R.C.M. worked independently it did so under the guidance and protection of Livingstonia during the first twelve years.

5 J. L. Pretorius, 'The Story of the D.R.C. Mission in Nyasaland'. Unpublished notes, 1.

6 The correct rendering may be Kawere.

7 Retief, M. W., *William Murray of Nyasaland*, Lovedale, 1958, 10.

8 Retief, M. W., *William Murray*, 10.

9 Appendix I, 381-3.

10 W. H. Murray's letters to his parents during 1896, also Retief, 29, 36, 40.

11 W. H. Murray's letters to his parents during 1896.

12 W. H. Murray's letters, 1896. See also Pachai, chapter 12.

13 W. H. Murray's letters, 1896.

14 Retief, 12. Cf. a similar development among the Northern Ngoni, Pachai, chapter 12.

15 W. H. Murray's letter to his parents, 13 April 1897.

16 Ibid., Appendix I and II, 381-3.

17 I.e. adults as well as children.

18 There are several interesting accounts of these meetings in M. W. Retief, *Oorwinnings in Christus*, and W. H. Murray, *Op. Pad.*

19 T. C. B. Vlok, *Elf jaren in Midden Afrika*, Wellington, 1900.

20 T. C. B. Vlok, *Elf jaren*, 72.

21 Prof. J. du Plessis summed up 'the lessons of the war' as follows:
   '1 The War taught us true interest.
   2 The War taught us the meaning of earnest prayer.
   3 The War taught us to give freely.'
   (See T. C. B. Vlok, 101-4).

22 B. Pachai, 'Christianity and Commerce in Malawi' in B. Pachai *et. al.* (eds.) *Malawi Past and Present*, C.L.A.I.M., Blantyre, 1971, 62-4 for a letter from Alfred J. Swann on this matter.

23 J. L. Pretorius, 'The Story', 2.

24 T. C. B. Vlok, *Elf jaren*, 26.

25 T. C. B. Vlok, *Elf jaren*, 84.

26 J. L. Pretorius, 'The Story', 1.

27 T. C. B. Vlok named three reasons for starting agricultural and industrial teaching on a large scale. The most important was the 'moral decay' caused by the hut tax. See *Elf jaren*, 83–5.

28 J. W. L. Hofmeyr, *Attie Hofmeyr van Nyasaland*, Administratie Bureau, Stellenbosch, 1921, 47 and 50.

29 Dr Jesse Jones: *Education in East Africa*, Phelps–Stokes Fund, New York, 1925, 212–13.

30 J. L. Pretorius, 4.

31 J. L. Pretorius, 3.

32 J. L. Pretorius, 3.

33 Report of the Third General Missionary Conference, Mvera, 1910, 42–54.

34 Victor Murray, *The School in the Bush*, London, 1930, 89.

35 J. L. Pretorius, 2.

36 J. M. Cronje, *Kwayera*, Bloemfontein, 7–25.

37 A. C. Murray, *Ons Nyasa Akker*, Stellenbosch, 1931, 202.

38 Botha, P. B., Verslag aan die Ad Hoc Komitee van die Federale Raad van N.G. Kerk aangaande argiefstukke oor die N.G. Sendingwerk in Mosambiek. (Report to the Ad Hoc Committee of the Federal Council of D.R. Churches re archival sources with regard to D.R. mission work in Mozambique.) Unpublished.

39 Botha, Verslag, 1967, 4.

40 Page, H. T. S., Die N.G. Kerk Aanslag op P.O.A. (Mosambiek), 1908–1922. Unpublished, 1963, 39.

41 Page, Die N.G. Kerk, 41, for an account of meeting between Governor Bettincount and R.C. Church.

42 Botha, P. B., Verslag, 5.

43 Page, H. T. S., Die N.G. Kerk, 41–59.

44 Page, Die N.G. Kerk, 46.

45 Botha, P. B., Verslag, 9.

46 Botha, P. B., *Verslag*, 37. It is not clear what Gen. Beyers did in the Cape which antagonized the Portuguese authorities.

47 Hancock, W. K., *Smuts: The Sanguine Years*. Cambridge, 1962, 408.

48 Botha, P. B. *Verslag*, 37.

49 Botha, P. B. *Verslag*, 37. The Chiputu rebellion had especially serious consequences for the Mission.

50 Page, H. T. S., *Die N.G. Kerk*, 72.

51 Today there are over 2,000 members, albeit without pastoral care.

52 M. W. Retief, *William Murray of Nyasaland*, 117.

APPENDIX I

Letter from W. H. Murray to his Parents, Mvera, 9 March 1895

'Slave raiding is just as little a thing of the past as I am, and our men are afraid of being caught by that M'Pemba I wrote of some time past, or some other petty chief, the more so after what happened last week. Last Wednesday I sent off two men with a rather important letter to Livlezi. They never got there. With great difficulty they got ferried across the Lintippe in Mpemba's district. A little further on near where we have a school going, these two mail-men got their letter and parcel and their gun taken from them. They called the teacher, who interfered, but the letter was torn up, a soldered tin box battered and the gun taken. The teacher got caught, beaten and threatened with his life, but managed to recapture the gun and escape with the other two to our port at Maganga's. . . . Now we hear that our teacher has had the pluck to return to his post, burn the houses of the evildoers and coolly continue his work.

What the end of this is to be, we don't know. We greatly regret his action and fear this may bind our hands with the administration or involve us in some trouble if they do take up the case. This silly administration (some people) fondly fancies and flatters itself with the thought that slave trade is suppressed on the lake while we know that numbers of slaves are still sent over the lake and river under their very noses. And what makes it worse is that they don't seem anxious for information into the matter at all.

I shall need wisdom in passing that place next week. Of course I shall enquire into the matter, of course I shall be angry—may it be without sinning. That it takes grace not to think hard thoughts of these vile slave-traders I need not say.

Only yesterday I had a brush with one of them, and as follows: The day before yesterday, towards evening, a poor woman came seeking our assistance. The headman of her village had sold her child to some of these lake folk, old slave traders. Her husband was threatening suicide from grief. We promised to see about it the following morning, she leaving her two boys with us to show us the way next morning. At 7.30 I started with the donkey, . . . the two church members and our gardener. One of them had my gun, the other two had a gun each. I had a revolver at my waist. All this was with a defensive object of course, in case it were needed. It took me $\frac{3}{4}$ of an hour to get to this village. As we got into the court I demanded of the 3 or 4 worthies "where is the headman of the village?" "Over there"—pointing to some huts 50 yards off beyond some high grass. "That's a lie", I said, suspecting one of them was he. "No indeed", they say, I was assuming a high hand from the start and they were just in mortal fear. Especially when the donkey at a touch of the lash almost went over one of them.—Off to the next huts I post, unfortunately not leaving one of the boys to watch these 4 chaps. At these huts . . . they told us one of these we had just seen was the headman. In a few seconds I was there again—to find the placed cleared. We searched high and low as fast as possible but found no headman anywhere nor anyone who could give information. I now asked for the mother and father of the child. He seemed off his head, the mother sat wailing along side her hut taking no notice of anything. I decided to follow up the slavers. They were to be found at a village more than an hour further on, on the way to the lake. The father refuses to accompany us having utterly lost heart. I made him get up and lead the way. We ran on as fast as we could, the donkey, a fine creature, getting more shambuk than she deserved. . . . At last we got to the village, a big one whose headman has long worked in league with the slavers on the lake. I got our little party together and gave the strictest injunctions that no shot is to be fired without my orders. I moreover decide to act in a most high handed fashion from the outset. We were in the outer court before the folk were aware of us. They were scared. "Where are the men of Kachulu", I demanded, "In there," one says and points to an inner court with a high fence. The donkey was through the doorway in a jiffie with the 3 boys at her heels. On one side a little way off I saw a group of men and made for them at once. They were too taken by surprise. I was on them before they could think what it meant.

"Are you the men from Kachulu", I asked with as *savage eyes* and as *commanding voice* as I could manage. "Y-es", they say. "Bring me that little girl at once!!" They try to explain, get up, their guns are alongside them against the hut. I draw my revolver and cover them with it and demand that the girl be brought without a second's delay. I felt instinctively I was master of the situation and had to make immediate . . . use of my chance. The revolver muzzle was too much for those men. As it looked at them with its little hollow black eye, their guns were useless, and hurriedly one said to another, "Bring the girl, bring the girl". Out of the hut a poor little creature of 5 or 6 years old was brought at once and handed over. The father convulsively caught the child, the child clutched its father's legs and together they wheeled around in ecstasy. My revolver went back into its pouch. The raiders sat down frightened as could be. But the leader had slipped off just as I arrived on the scene . . .

. . . I asked for the mother and sat down. The people were gathering around. I looked up and saw a woman approaching in bent position casting handfuls of loose earth over her head and face. As she reached me she threw herself on the ground neither looking at me nor saying a single word, only rolling about at my feet and brining her hands softly together.

On my questioning it now appeared that the headman had ordered this little girl to be given in exchange for a gun he owed the Kachulu men. He had offered another gun but they refused it and demanded a *girl*.'

APPENDIX II

Letter from W. H. Murray to Parents, Mvera 24 May 1895

'This slave raiding or slave buying we are unfortunately hearing a good deal of still, and the Chief (Chiwere) practically declines to interfere. People are coming here repeatedly asking for our interference where a wife or a child has been caught and sold. The administration don't want us to interfere and it's altogether a difficult matter. I sometimes don't know what to do. Mr Blake hears even more of it up at Kongwe than we do here.'

22 Economic policy, land and labour in Nyasaland, 1890-1914

B. S. Krishnamurthy

I

In his survey of Nyasaland's economic policy during 1918–39, W. K. Hancock draws the conclusion that its economic problems 'arise from the comparative policy of her resources, not from racial privileges of possession and profit' and that its policy was inspired by the ideals of the missionaries who followed Livingstone. 'Nyasaland, more than any other African colony,' he says, 'is a creation of the missionaries' frontier . . . Nyasaland does not belong in spirit to the sphere of South Africa and Southern Rhodesia.'[1] In this paper I propose to test this conclusion for the first twenty-five years of colonial rule in Nyasaland.

At an early date in the Protectorate's history, Sir Harry Johnston, the first Commissioner and Consul-General, showed interest in the organization and development of land which was Nyasaland's great economic asset.[2] The question whether development should be undertaken through the agency of Africans or Europeans did not arouse much debate at the time. Although Johnston believed that the future of Nyasaland belonged to the African, yet he under-estimated the capacity of the African to make any contribution to the development of the Protectorate in the immediate future. He was of the opinion that Nyasaland would be developed by Europeans without whom 'Central Africa would be of no value'.[3]

Johnston based these assumptions on certain pragmatic considerations. Firstly, the Protectorate was in urgent need of finding its own sources of revenue. It is well-known that when the Protectorate was established it depended on a subsidy from the British South Africa Company but after Johnston's assertion of his independence from the Company, the Protectorate's expenditure was met by grants-in-aid from the British Treasury. The grants were, however, not expected to last for a long time and the Protectorate government was under constant pressure from the Treasury to make itself self-sufficient. Secondly, European settlers who had preceded the establishment of the Protectorate had already acquired large amounts of land and had also developed a coffee culture which promised to provide Nyasaland with a viable export.

384

They clamoured for the promotion of their interests and were able to mount virulent attacks on him both at home and in the Protectorate whenever his policies hurt them. 'The settler', Johnston reported to Lord Rosebery, the Secretary of State for Colonies, in 1892, 'usually treats me to a series of abusive letters, threatens me with a full exposure of my tyrannical proceedings in *Truth*, and no doubt forwards to the Foreign Office a highly coloured version of his own views of the case.'[4] Johnston was in no mood to antagonize the settlers whose presence in the country he valued.

The aim of his land settlement, therefore, was to encourage European enterprise. He confirmed the claims of those who had previously obtained concessions from local rulers and issued to each claimant a 'Certificate of Claim', which the claimant regarded as having given him freehold title to land. The Certificate of Claim was subject to certain conditions, the most important of these being that no African village and plantation situated on land at the time of the transfer should be disturbed. Apart from this, he did not pay attention to the complaints of Africans and their supporters in the Blantyre mission about the rights of chiefs to sell land for he thought that 'the question had gone too far ahead for any kind of restitution to take place without causing much clamour of excitement'.[5] Altogether about 3·5 million acres of land, including 2·7 million acres in North Nyasa for the British South Africa Company were alienated, most of this land being in Shire Highlands.

He, then, acquired on behalf of the Crown all 'waste and unoccupied' land which he proposed to use for the development of the country. He laid down rules for making grants to intending settlers on leasehold tenure only as he was strictly opposed to speculative interests.

He made no special provision for African participation in the development of the Protectorate, except that he was prepared to encourage those who were willing to buy or lease Crown land on an individual basis. On the whole, Johnston meant to confirm Africans in their existing holdings actually cultivated for subsistence purposes. In other words, Johnston did not envisage the African as anything more than a subsistence cultivator.

The issue of African peasant production came to the fore after 1903 as a consequence of certain important developments within the Protectorate: firstly, the migration of African labour to South Africa and Southern Rhodesia, secondly the growth of British demand for cotton and lastly African initiatives in the production of cash crops. The protagonists of African production headed by the Blantyre missionaries pressed for opportunities for Africans for the cultivation of cash crops as an alternative to migration when they saw that the British demand for cotton had stimulated not only European but also African production.[6]

Although the government declared that it would support both European and African interests, yet throughout the period before the outbreak of the War, policy-makers vacillated between the two interests.

In 1904, Sharpe, who had succeeded Johnston as Commissioner, started by giving tax rebates to encourage African cotton-growers, but he soon encountered a number of difficulties.[7] First of all, he was unable to supply all the seed demanded by African growers. He applied for a free supply of seed from the British Cotton Growing Association but was told to obtain it from local planters. The planters gave what was left over after meeting their own demands and the seed was often of poor quality.[8] Both Simpson, the cotton expert, and the British Cotton Growing Association suggested that an experimental farm should be opened and the Association was prepared to meet half the cost of the farm but Sharpe was not willing to spend more than £100 because he had no trust in the cotton expert.[9] There were also difficulties in finding buyers for the cotton.[10] Above all, Africans had to walk several days to reach the nearest European ginnery. Lack of transport was one of the main reasons for the neglect of remote districts especially in the north.[11] Sharpe was reluctant to incur additional expenditure to provide either seed or experimental farms.[12]

African industry therefore depended on the goodwill of the planters who opposed some of the measures taken by the government to encourage African cotton cultivators. The settlers wanted all facilities for themselves. They argued that there was no future for the European trader because of Indian competition in East and Central Africa and that the region's economic system should be based on European production.[13]

Whether government intended to encourage European or African production depended on its land and labour policies. As the economic objectives of the government can be discerned by the way it used the Crown lands we shall consider these first.

Sharpe's declared policy was to reserve as Crown lands the parts required for African use and to alienate land not required by them.[14] Although Africans living on Crown land had no legal title to land, yet the government allowed free use of land for food-planting and 'other purposes', which included a site for hut and, where possible, for cultivation of cotton within 'reasonable limits'.[15] The average size of an African farm was about two acres but in Ruo and West Shire districts, where cotton growing was popular with Africans, it was grown on small plots of a half to one acre, which gave the cultivator just enough money for his taxes.[16] This compares unfavourably with Uganda where the Ganda and others who practised intensive cultivation had an average holding of eight acres of which three acres were devoted to plantain, three to cotton and two to subsidiary crops while those who practised shifting cultivation had an average holding of five and a half to eight acres per family.[17] It should also be noted that Uganda, unlike Nyasaland, had two planting seasons. In Nyasaland, shifting cultivators who had only one planting season during which they had to grow crops to last them for the whole year, needed a larger area than in Uganda if they wanted to grow cash crops in addition to their subsistence cultivation. There were Africans who wanted to take up large areas. Hetherwick mentioned that forty-seven African peasants applied for land in 1910 but the government rejected their applications. The only way open to Africans who wanted more land than the government allowed them was to buy or lease it in competition with Europeans. But as Hetherwick complained, auction fees, lawyer's fees and other costs made it impossible for many Africans to acquire land in this manner.[18]

One of the arguments which government officials frequently used to explain their inability to solve the problem of African settlement was that the amount of Crown land was scarce.[19] Sharpe was conscious that alienation of land to non-Africans should be restricted, but did not enforce the principle. While reluctant to alienate large blocks of land to speculative interests, he wanted to encourage genuine settlers with moderate means.[20] There were already speculative interests who combined in 1902, to form powerful concerns to develop agriculture on capitalist lines. Besides, in the same year, Sharpe was asked by the Foreign Office to set aside about 360,000 acres as subsidy to one such concern, the British Central Africa Company, which undertook to build the railway in Nyasaland.[21] In addition, Sharpe alienated roughly about 100,000 acres to both old and new settlers. At first, Sharpe intended to grant leasehold tenures only but under pressure from the local planters, he introduced into the title-deeds an 'Option of Purchase' clause which entitled the lessees to convert their leases into freeholds after the expiry of the first term of tenure. Sharpe further provided that if the lease was converted before the expiry of the term, the lessee had to pay the original upset price whereas if conversion took place after the expiry of the term, the rent paid would be counted towards up to fifty per cent of the purchase price. The terms, as Sharpe said, were made very favourable to encourage intending settlers.[22]

Both the subsidy and alienated lands were known to be good for cotton. The Railway Company was to choose 260,000 acres in selected areas of Shire Highlands and the rest in Lower Shire valley while the planters obtained their land not only in Shire Highlands but also mostly in the districts of Lower Shire, West Shire, Upper Shire and Central Angoniland.

The Blantyre missionaries warned the government that alienations restricted the area available for cultivation by Africans who were becoming apprehensive about their security on land. Hetherwick told the Legislative Council in 1910 that if Africans were to be induced to remain on the soil, they should be given security and an adequate amount of land. The government allowed them free use of Crown land and excluded their villages and plantations from alienation, yet they were not assured. Hetherwick mentioned instances of Africans being moved from one place to another to make room for Europeans.[23] The grievance was widespread in relation to the subsidy lands, and Africans submitted two petitions questioning the right of the government to transfer land occupied by them.[24]

Alienation together with the influx of immigrants increased the pressure on Crown land in the Shire Highlands but except probably in Blantyre District there was no real shortage of land for African settlement. The Blantyre district, for instance, comprised an area of 1,064,155 acres of which about 588,000 acres had been alienated. Of the remaining 458,155 acres, the government set aside 49,203 acres in the Chiradzulu subdivision of the district and 7,142 acres in Ndirande subdivision for the railway, which left 401,810 acres with the government. Since, according to the government, about one third of this was cultivatable, there were 134,000 acres which at the rate of eight acres per hut could accommodate a population of 50,250 on the official estimate of an average of three persons per hut. According to the estimates, Blantyre district contained twice this number of people in 1909. This figure might have included migrant workers from outside the district; nevertheless, it confirms an impression of over-population by prevailing standards of land usage. Many Africans may have therefore been forced to live on private estates. However, in Zomba and Mlanje districts, the position was less critical. Zomba district had about 272,000 acres available for cultivation which could provide for 102,000 persons while its estimated population in 1909 was 57,000. In Mlanje district where 98,406 acres were assigned for the Railway Company, about 257,620 acres were available for cultivation, which meant that about 96,600 persons could be provided for as against its estimated population (for 1909) of 53,300 approximately.[25]

Sharpe's obligation to the Railway Company placed him in an awkward position because the blocks which the Company claimed in Blantyre and Mlanje districts were heavily populated by Africans. The contract with the Company contained clauses preserving the rights of Africans residing on the blocks but, as African settlements had increased since the signing of the contract, Sharpe feared that the Company might refuse to recognize any obligation to the newcomers. At the same time, as mentioned earlier Africans residing on these blocks were sorely troubled. Sharpe realized that it would cause great discontent if he attempted to move them and he asked the Colonial Office to persuade the Company to surrender the promised blocks in return for land elsewhere.[26] But the Colonial Office insisted that Sharpe should keep enough lands in the Highlands to honour the bargain with the Company. Sharpe consented under pressure to move 'a certain number of immigrant natives' to government land in other districts if the Company insisted on choosing its subsidy lands in Blantyre and Mlanje districts.[27]
any obligation to the newcomers. At the same time, as mentioned earlier

For these reasons, the Nyasaland government neglected the problem of African requirements. An additional factor was the prospect that the settlement scheme contemplated in the contract with the British Central Africa Scheme would materialize; and it was also likely that more settlers would follow the railway. Sharpe himself was interested in encouraging small settlers. He was not able to decide on African settlement until he was sure of European requirements.

In the meantime, Africans were allowed to grow small quantities of cotton for tax purposes in Lower Shire, Ruo and Mlanje districts. This was not encouraged in Blantyre and Zomba because of the opposition of the settlers.[28] More facilities became available to African cotton-growers after 1910, when the Colonial Office made a grant of £10,000 for 5 years on condition that the money should be spent on the development of cotton in the Protectorates.[29] A Cotton Ordinance, on the same lines as the Uganda Cotton Ordinance, was enacted in the same year to regulate the industry. It gave the government powers to supervise the distribution of seed.[30] The British Cotton Growing Association provided a free supply of seed, built ginneries in Port Herald, Chiromo and Karonga, and made arrangements for buying African cotton.[31] Manning, who succeeded Sharpe in 1911, instituted cotton markets to counteract traders who visited the villages and bought cotton for less than the market price.[32]

388

Finally, Manning tried to commit the British Cotton Growing Association to a policy of promoting cotton growing as an African peasant industry.[33] The Association, under pressure from local planters, refused to encourage cotton-growing near European centres. It also abandoned its earlier proposal to establish a ginnery and an experimental farm near Blantyre and Zomba.[34] In the Northern Districts, where it was possible to develop cotton, tobacco or dairy farming, according to the suitability of the soil, the government was said to be not in a hurry to undertake development because of transport difficulties.[35]

Manning adopted a pragmatic approach to economic development. His deputy, Pearce, told the Legislative Council that the government would hold the balance between both Europeans and Africans and that 'while ensuring full justice to the native as owner of the land, it [the government] must at the same time formulate a policy so as not to stifle the bona fide European enterprise'.[36] Manning proposed first of all to tackle the land question.

As the railway subsidy lands had been one of the major obstacles to land settlement, Manning secured control of the blocks by taking a firm stand against their transfer to the Company. The Company was compensated by a cash payment of £180,000 which the British government loaned to the Protectorate at an annual interest of four per cent.[37]

Manning's main concern was to secure 'a sufficiency of agricultural land' for African needs and he, therefore, intended to stiffen the conditions for alienation particularly in the Shire Highlands. Instead, he wanted to accommodate intending settlers on private estates. He levied a tax of a halfpenny an acre on all undeveloped land held by private estates in order to induce them to release land. He further issued a notice in 1912 abolishing the 'option of purchase' concession granted by Sharpe to lessees and thus made it clear that the government would adhere strictly to leasehold tenures.[38]

The government's policy on alienation of Crown lands was formulated in the Crown Lands Ordinance of 1912. It stated that leaseholds would be granted for short periods of seven, fourteen or twenty-one years at a reassessed rental of five per cent of the value of undeveloped agricultural land; that freeholds of not more than 250 acres would be granted only in exceptional circumstances; and that the site of 'any existing native village, settlement, plantation or pasture land' would be excluded from alienation and would be calculated at the rate of eight acres per hut.[39]

The Colonial Office held different views on the policy to be pursued in Nyasaland and was not very pleased with the Ordinance, which suggested that Manning wanted to keep the unalienated Crown land in the Shire Highlands as a reserve for Africans, and to close the door to European settlement. He was asked to modify the Ordinance so as to allow for longer leases of ninety-nine years for slow-maturing products on condition that a certain multiple of rent should be spent on development instead of a proportion of land as suggested by Manning; and, secondly, that compensation should be paid at the end of the tenure if the lessee did not wish to renew his lease. The Colonial Office instructed him to observe whether the Ordinance deterred intending settlers from taking up land.[40]

The final Ordinance which was passed by the Legislative Council in November 1912 contained the modifications suggested by the Colonial Office. Hetherwick, the only member who opposed the bill, remarked that it was 'a very fair and equitable measure by which settlers might get a position in the country.'[41]

Manning proposed to leave Africans undisturbed with an assurance that their land would not be touched or alienated. He considered that the scattered nature of African settlements was a serious obstacle to a policy of concentrating the people in reserves and decided, instead, to create Crown Land Reserves which 'would not be leased or disposed of until the government was in a position to know what the future requirements were as regards native needs and European immigration.'[42]

The Colonial Office, however, was not satisfied and insisted on 'ample reserves' for Africans which would leave the rest of the country for European immigration. The idea of reserves had been rejected in the past as savouring of segregation. Though it appealed to the Colonial Office as the only possible way of accommodating both African and European interests, the situation in the Shire Highlands militated against its adoption.[43] The differences of opinion between the Colonial Office and the Nyasaland government remained unresolved when Manning retired and, the new governor, Sir George Smith, who assumed office in 1913, shelved the land question.

Smith believed that the Protectorate would be developed by European settlers and not by Africans.[44] He wanted to be free to dispose of the Crown lands 'for suitable purposes and on suitable terms as occasion arises'.[45] He also objected to a policy of demarcating reserves, and suggested that the existing system which enabled Africans to use Crown land met their needs. Smith's policy was, therefore, to keep the Crown lands open for European settlement and to postpone the question of settling Africans who, he believed, would be nothing more than subsistence farmers for a long time to come.[46] The Colonial Office, however, warned him not to leave Africans without the protection of reserves since European immigration would probably follow the extension of the railway to the coast.[47] While Smith and the Colonial Office were debating these issues, the war intervened and the land question was postponed.

Thus, up to the outbreak of the war, the Nyasaland government was undecided as to a policy concerning the development of the land resources. As most policy-makers shared the view of the settlers that development should be undertaken by Europeans, they could not agree on the status of Crown lands until they had ascertained the nature of European requirements. Africans were allowed to use Crown lands for subsistence cultivation or the cultivation of cotton but the government could not make up its mind whether to provide incentives in the form of adequate provision of land to those Africans who were responding to economic opportunities. In the meantime, large speculative interests were also holding up land. In 1914, out of nearly a million acres of alienated land in the Shire Highlands, about 50,000 acres only had been developed.

These events and considerations may account for the government's policy or lack of one in the south but do not explain why it did not take up the settlement of Africans in the northern districts where the pressure of European demand did not exist. Perhaps the answer to this lies in its labour policy.

II

Let us now examine the government attitude to labour, an indispensable element of production for both Africans and Europeans. Subsistence cultivators employing traditional equipment needed ample supply of labour and land. This was not an uneconomic use of resources at the prevailing level of technology. While, therefore, Africans needed labour for themselves, there was competition for the same labour from Europeans not only within the Protectorate but also south of the Zambezi.

Planters and traders within the Protectorate, who were the largest employers of labour, made the most noise about their difficulties in getting men to work and expected the government to support them. They argued that Africans were lazy, lacked an economic urge to work, and would work only under compulsion. On the other hand, the Blantyre missionaries refuted the settler's assumptions. 'Does a "European colonist imagine that the native is unwilling to work and that he can be made to do so by presents and threats? Let him go and see the plantations of Buchanan Bros at Michiru, Lunzu, Chiradzulu and Zomba or the buildings at Mandala, Blantyre and Zomba. These are the products of free labour. The African can work without compulsion of any kind.'[48] All the missions were, in fact, of the general view that there was no dearth of voluntary labour in Nyasaland.

Africans who had even in pre-European days shown a keen desire for trade goods from the outside world were willing to work when they realized that labour could be exchanged for calico and other consumer articles. Many of them took advantage of missionary education to acquire skills which were in demand. Missionary influence also stimulated a desire for new wants, so that the Livingstonia mission was able to claim with, perhaps, a bit of exaggeration that 'the first impulse to sustained labour came to the native through mission work.'[49] By 1897, African workers were not content with calico but wanted cash in order to buy articles other than cloth.[50] But the problem was that the planters offered work in the wet season when Africans were busy planting their food crops and the conditions of work were not attractive.

The methods used to obtain labour varied. From the beginning, planters called upon Africans resident on their estates to work for them on pain of eviction or destruction of their crops. Claiming to have taken over the Chief's prerogatives together with his land, the settlers demanded *thangata*, labour services rendered to chiefs in the traditional society. In response to missionary objections to this 'crude method of exploitation', Johnston had, as we mentioned earlier, made it a condition of transfer that no African village or plantation on the estate should be disturbed, the implication being that African residents would not be obliged to work as 'serfs' or 'tenants' of the planters. However, as African 'villages' and 'plantations' were not clearly

391

defined, the planters were still able to exploit their residents for labour on the contention that the African residents, who practised shifting-cultivation, had moved to land within the alienated area. Furthermore, as Johnston allowed the planters to pay taxes on behalf of their 'labour-tenants' they felt entitled to reimburse themselves by asking their residents to work for them in lieu of taxes advanced.[51]

Where Africans lived on Crown lands, settlers either bribed the chiefs to supply workers or sent African capitaos whose methods of recruitment did not exclude intimidation.[52]

Migrants from the northern districts and from Portuguese East Africa formed an important source of labour. Mission-educated Tonga and Ngoni workers had been coming down for wage-employment from the earliest days of European enterprise and had also settled down on or near the estates.[53]

Similarly, the Lomwe who found better opportunities in the Shire Highlands than in their own country were also trickling in across the border. When it became difficult to attract African workers from the Shire Highlands who were able to earn cash by selling the surplus products of their garden plantation, settlers began to depend on supplies from the north. Recruiting, therefore, developed into a lucrative business. Recruiters obtained squads of labour for the employers and left the surplus for whom no jobs could be found to fend for themselves.[54]

The planters complained that the flow of labour was sporadic and that recruitment was costly. They wanted the government to provide labour for them. Johnston sympathized with their demands but did not want the government to be directly involved. He imposed a hut tax of six shillings in 1891, which was reduced to three shillings in 1893, insisted on its being paid in cash and instructed officials to direct tax-defaulters to employers.[55] District Officers used their 'moral influence' which amounted to compulsion. As new administrative districts were opened, Collectors assisted recruiters or sent tax-defaulters to planters who applied for them. This became a well established practice and after 1895 most workers were drafted from the densely populated Central Angoniland district.[56]

Johnston also introduced Labour Regulations in 1894 to control 'the supply of labour as a speculative trade'. Employers were required to enter into written contracts with workers recruited from outside their districts, and to pay wages and conduct money in cash in the presence of a magistrate at the end of the contract. Conditions were laid down for sanitation, food and housing and each engagement had to be registered on payment of a fee of one shilling.[57]

Although the government was satisfied that the measures were producing an increased supply of labour, the planters complained that there was no improvement in the situation. Plenty of labour was actually available in the dry season when the planters had no use for it but there was scarcity in the wet season. Many workers were also deterred from going to the Highlands because of food scarcity. In spite of government's repeated warning to planters that they should make provision for food and housing, workers were paid a small allowance for food in calico which they were unable to exchange for food. The Labour Regulations were not observed by planters who had opposed it since its introduction.[58] Workers were employed without written agreements and this led to serious complaints that they were not paid regularly. In 1900, there was a big decline in the production of coffee which the planters ascribed to labour shortages without regard to other factors such as drought and the saturation of the world market by Brazilian coffee. At a conference with Sharpe in 1900, they suggested that to increase the supply of labour, the government should raise taxes for men who did not work for Europeans for at least one month in a year and, secondly, that planters should form a Labour Bureau to take over the collection and distribution of labour among its members.[59]

Sharpe fell in line with their demands as they seemed to be convenient from the administrative point of view. As there was a good deal of disorganization in the methods of recruitment, he hoped that the Bureau might conduct things in a responsible manner. The district administrators sent all tax-defaulters to the Bureau which began its operations in 1901.[60] The Bureau paid the taxes of the workers and issued them with certificates showing the period of work done and tax-papers on which the amount of tax paid was entered.[61] Sharpe also issued new regulations in 1901 which imposed a double tax on all those who were not able to produce certificates to show that they worked for a month for Europeans.[62]

Although the new tax system resulted, as government reports said, in a 'largely augmented supply of labour', yet the basic character of the problem remained the same.[63] Both the government and employers were agreed in spite of their controversy over the amount of labour available that there was 'surplus' in the dry season and 'shortage' in the wet season. Also the Foreign Office disapproved of the system of taxes being paid by the Labour Bureau.[64] Sharpe himself saw that the planters used the system to extract forced labour from the estate population. In 1904, therefore, Sharpe issued new regulations replacing those of 1895.[65] The regulations abolished the practice whereby the government sent workers to the Bureau but the payment of taxes by employers was not altogether abolished. The regulations further laid down that in the Shire Province employers would be free to recruit without any permit, whereas in the Lake Province recruitment could be carried out only under permits issued by the government to approved recruiters, who would sign a bond for a prescribed amount to guarantee good behaviour. Labour from the Lake districts would be employed under written contract signed in the presence of a magistrate and registered by him at the rate of sixpence per labourer engaged. Employers would be obliged to provide transport, food and housing during the journey and while in employment. Several reasons can be suggested for the adoption of the revised regulations. The arrangement whereby officers recruited workers was an embarrassment since the government could not guarantee employment. Moreover, the government decided in 1904, to confine recruitment for the South African mines to the northern districts.

The settlers who had strongly attacked the government's policy on migration were further antagonized by the new regulations. Their relations with the government were never so bitter as during the period 1903–10, when they complained that Sharpe did not meet all their demands. They complained during 1905 and 1906 that registration fees, transport, and recruitment had raised the cost of labour; that as the Labour Bureau had closed down after the stoppage of the government's facilities, individual employers were unable to employ their own recruiters and that African workers abused the certificate system by collecting tax certificates from different employers, the certificates being then sold to men who did not work. The settlers demanded that the government should resume the practice of directing tax-defaulters to a new Labour Bureau and enforce the payment of taxes during the wet season when workers were most needed. Further, labour certificates should be issued only for work done in the wet season; and collectors should issue passes to work-seekers, which would be kept by the employer until the end of the contract period when he would deliver the pass to the collector who would discharge him of his tax obligations.[66] All these proposals amounted to forced labour and were rejected by Sharpe with one exception. He agreed that tax-defaulters should be handed over to the Bureau. A government notice issued in June 1907 stipulated that persons engaging labour should insist on seeing the worker's tax-papers, which the employer was to sign after confirming that it bore the same name as the possessor's.[67] Another notice issued in August 1907 provided that taxes would be collected as from 1 April of every year, which was what the settlers had demanded.[68] Sharpe made another concession in 1909 by relaxing the conditions for recruitment in the Lake districts. He was willing to instruct the Collectors to assist planters if they were prepared to organize a Labour Bureau and appoint recruiters, but the planters insisted that government should take the entire responsibility for supplying labour by organizing its own Labour Department.[69]

In the meantime, several planters had begun to depend on African residents on their estates. In 1902, some of the estates merged to form big companies which had the advantage of containing a large number of African villages with a potential labour force. The Tax Regulations of 1901 and the permission which Sharpe gave the planters to advance taxes on behalf of the resident villagers enabled the planters to demand services from the residents.[70] During 1902–3, the proprietors of these companies signed agreements with the chiefs and headmen of the villages that in consideration of their 'tenancy' their followers would work for two months in the wet season, one month for tax and one for wages. The employers allowed them to live rent-free and in most cases they did not pay wages. The agreements were made in the presence of District Residents who did not raise objections although the agreements were extended to all villages irrespective of whether they were original residents or new-comers.[71] The rights of the original residents to their village sites had been protected by Johnston in the certificates of claim but the newcomers were in a different position because they had migrated to the estates in search of work.

However, in 1903, Nunan, Chief Judge of the High Court of Nyasaland, set aside the agreements on the grounds that landholders were not entitled to compel African residents to work for them as tenants unless they were able

394

to prove that the tenants were not original residents.[72] The Land Commission of 1903, whose appointment followed this decision, recommended as a compromise that one tenth of the undeveloped land of the estates should be set aside in blocks of not less than eighty acres and not more than 3,200 acres within which Africans should be accommodated on the basis of eight acres per hut. Africans who would pay a rent of four shillings for each of their allotments should be free to work for anyone they pleased.[73] Accordingly, an Ordinance called the Native Locations Ordinance of 1904 was promulgated but the estate-holders refused to provide locations for immigrants.[74] As a result, the Ordinance was not enforced.

Sharpe, however, permitted the landholders to make agreements with their residents without prejudice to the 'legal claims of any particular native or class of natives'. The agreements which were made in the presence of the District Residents required every resident irrespective of whether he was an original one or an immigrant, to pay an annual rent of three shillings, which he was free to earn by working for the landholder or for any other person or by the sale of his produce in any market he wanted. Residents who refused to sign the agreement could move to Crown land on a date fixed by the District Resident.[75] But, in 1906, Sharpe made a further concession by giving the settlers freedom of contract and by instructing District Residents that they need not insist on any special conditions as both parties were 'quite free to make such agreements as they wish.'[76]

Thus a 'tenant system' of an oppressive type developed on the estates of the landholders. No money rent was collected but the residents were compelled to work for two months, one month's work being counted against tax and another month's against rent. By various devices the residents were made to work for longer periods. 'If a boy finished only 3 rows and did not finish the 4th row', Mwalimu, a resident of Magomero estate, told the Chilembwe Commission of Enquiry, 'it would be written as nothing in the book and next day he would be given 4 rows again.' Another witness, D. B. Ritchie, manager of the Likulezi estate, mentioned that a labourer had to do two months' work in order to fulfil his one month's obligation. African residents were moved from one estate to another, were not allowed to grow their own crops or cut timber for building their huts and were on certain estates beaten and whipped if they slackened in their work. Most African residents were forced to accept these hardships; otherwise they were liable to be evicted from the estates and the Crown lands where they could move to were densely populated.[77] In most cases, agreements were verbal and there was no law to enforce written agreements. Africans, therefore, had no legal protection.[78] In 1914, Smith wanted the Legislative Council to adopt an Ordinance for Compulsory Written Contracts between employers and African residents on their estates but it was strongly opposed by A. L. Bruce, an unofficial member of the Legislative Council, who said that the bill would 'upset the labour position' and 'retard development and extension of lands for plantation etc. . . .'[79] Bruce, it must be noted, was one of the large estate-holders who made only verbal contracts with their residents. On the suggestion of both Bruce and Dr Laws the bill was postponed and was not taken up until 1917. The

Government, thus, hesitated to do anything which might upset a major source of labour supply to planters.

III

Now we must turn to the other side of the demand for Nyasa labour. From the early days of European settlement in Southern Rhodesia, mission-educated Nyasaland workers with skills and a desire for an improved standard of living found in the colony a better market for their labour than in Nyasaland. There was, equally, an appreciation of Nyasa workers among settlers in Southern Rhodesia. By about the end of the nineteenth century when mining development in the colony created an increased demand for labour, recruiters and labour touts who operated on behalf of individual miners engaged Nyasa workers who crossed the border into North East Rhodesia which was the British South Africa Company's territory. It was not difficult for the recruiters to send African touts across the border into villages in Nyasaland to entice workers, in spite of the Nyasaland government's Native Labour Regulations of 1898 which required recruiters to obtain the sanction of the Commissioner before engaging labour for work outside the Protectorate. By 1903, it was estimated that about 6,126 Nyasa workers crossed the ferry at Feira to go south.[80] Because of protests from settlers in his country, Sharpe proposed, in 1900, to check the exodus by means of the Pass system but the Colonial Office to whom the matter was referred advised the Foreign Office that 'Pass laws ought not to be turned into an engine for preventing those who may be lawfully seeking employment elsewhere, from taking their labour to their best market.'[81] Sharpe tried in vain to get the co-operation of the authorities in north-east Rhodesia. Therefore, in 1903, he instructed the District Collectors of labour-supplying districts in the north to take steps to restrict the movement of workers across the border but this raised a storm of protest from the Company's servants in north-east Rhodesia, who complained that the 'boycotting' of the British South Africa Company's territories was 'opposed to the English conception of free trade and deprived the native of his natural right to sell his labour in the market of his own selection.'[82] With the inability of the Nyasaland government to control it, the exodus grew into large proportions in subsequent years.

In South Africa, the expansion of the mining industry after the cessation of the Boer War, created a big demand for labour. Both the Colonial Office and Lord Milner, the High Commissioner, depended on the mining industry for the implementation of their post-war resettlement scheme which was intended to establish the predominance of British interests in South Africa, for the payment of war debt, for revenue, and, above all, for a further loan of £30 million which the British government wanted to raise in connection with the resettlement scheme.[83] Both the mining industry and Lord Milner exerted pressure on the Colonial Office that the industry would not be able to support the schemes without an adequate supply of labour. Initially, the mine-owners asked for the importation of Chinese labour but as there was strong opposition to it from the Boers in South Africa and from the Liberals in Britain the British government did not permit it till 1904. Meanwhile, the demand fell on British Protectorates north of the Zambezi.[84] The Foreign Office, which was responsible for the Protectorates, took the same stand as the humanitarian critics of the Empire at the time who opposed the indenturing of Africans to further the interests of capitalists in South Africa.[85] However, Chamberlain ultimately prevailed upon the Foreign Office to permit the Witwatersrand Native Labour Association, the recruiting agency of the Chamber of Mines, to recruit labour in Nyasaland.[86]

Sharpe who was himself under the pressure of African demand for employment defended the policy of the Colonial Office against the opposition of the settlers in Nyasaland. He, certainly, had an alternative which was to absorb the 'surplus' dry season labour by encouraging peasant production as suggested by the missionaries but it is doubtful whether he could actually exercise such a choice in the face of the British government's decision.

WNLA was allowed to recruit 1,000 workers in 1903 and this was extended to 5,000 workers in 1904. The high mortality rate among the workers aroused humanitarian opposition in Britain but it was not until after the Liberals had come to power in 1907 that recruitment was suspended.[87]

The ban did not put an end to unauthorized migration. The Rhodesian Native Labour Bureau, the recruiting agency of the Southern Rhodesia Chamber of Mines, set up a recruiting post at Fort Jameson in 1906 when it was refused permission to recruit in Nyasaland and engaged Nyasa workers from there.[88] Similarly, the WNLA which wanted to re-open recruitment in Nyasaland warned the government that if official permission was refused, it would open recruiting posts at the border.[89] Sharpe realized that he was not in a position to control unauthorized migration without the co-operation of the other governments concerned. He, therefore, negotiated an arrangement with the British South Africa Company under which the Rhodesian Native Labour Bureau was forbidden to recruit in Nyasaland whereas the Nyasaland government undertook to issue passes to men who wished to go to Southern Rhodesia and would forward them to Fort Jameson where an agent of the Rhodesian government would take charge of them. It was also agreed that the Rhodesian Government would be responsible to the Nyasaland Government for the payment of the migrant's taxes and wages, half of which would be deferred until the end of the contract, and for their repatriation.[90] Although Southern Rhodesia accepted the terms at first, it refused in 1909 to make the government responsible for labour recruitment and wanted Nyasaland to deal with the RNLB.[91] Sharpe was displeased and refused to meet the representative of the RNLB who visited Nyasaland to arrange for the supply of labour. However, the Colonial Office intervened to ask Sharpe to supply 2,500 workers for farms and 1,500 workers for mines in Southern Rhodesia. Similarly, arrangements were made with WNLA to supply 3,000 workers for the mines in South Africa.[92] The new policy was given effect by the Employment of Natives Ordinance of 1909, which prohibited recruitment for employment outside the Protectorate and brought migration under the control of the pass system.[93]

The pass system was not successful. There were so many inconvenient conditions attached to the system that African workers were deterred from going to the Magistrate to obtain passes. Passes were issued to those who had paid their taxes and had made provision for the maintenance of their families. Intending migrants had also to sign a contract stating that they were engaged for a period of twelve months after which they would be repatriated and that half their wages be paid after their return. There was one Pass Officer who was available in the months of July to January only. Most African workers went without obtaining a pass. The government, therefore, did not succeed in bringing the movement of workers under its control.[94]

There was a strong suspicion among Sharpe's critics that he had not really banned recruiting for employers outside Nyasaland. So long as recruiting agents stationed within the Protectorate obtained labour from the District officials, it was difficult to dismiss these suspicions as baseless. In 1910, Sharpe responded to the pressure by asking the recruiting agencies to close their business within the Protectorate. This, in turn, gave rise to unauthorized migration and the situation, as the Ag. Governor, Wallis, reported, went back to what it was before.[95]

In 1911, Manning enforced strict measures to control unauthorized migration. Out of 1,535 workers who returned in 1911, he fined 1,368 men and imprisoned another 167 workers for short periods of 2 to 6 weeks for having left the country without obtaining passes.[96] He also amended the Employment of Native Ordinance of 1909 to make it possible for him to introduce penalties for inducing men to leave the Protectorate and obtain work outside the borders.[97] Finally, in 1912, he sought the permission of the Colonial Office to prohibit migration altogether.[98] In the meantime, however, the South African Government itself had passed a law prohibiting the recruitment of workers north of latitude 22° south. Manning then took the opportunity to terminate the arrangement with the RNLB when it refused to engage workers on the deferred-payment system.[99] But the prohibition of recruitment did not stop the flow of workers. Manning found that in spite of his measures, unauthorized migration went on unabated.

CONCLUSION

Nyasaland's economic policy cannot be understood without reference to the forces which acted upon the government during this period. These forces were the missionaries who were interested in the development of African commercial farming, the settlers and the big business interests represented in South Africa and Southern Rhodesia who wanted an ample supply of cheap labour. So far as Africans were concerned, some of them adapted themselves to the demands of cash economy but the majority of them resisted attempts to force them to work at the expense of their subsistence cultivation. Although the Nyasaland government wanted to maintain a fair balance of all these interests, European interests, particularly those of big business in South Africa and Southern Rhodesia, dominated its policy. The sinister pressures of the capitalists who were supported by the Imperial government prevented Nyasaland from taking control of its labour to protect the interests of the local settlers and of Africans. Nyasaland, in effect, became part of the economic system of the South deriving its revenue from its exports of labour. Neither missionaries nor Africans had any effective influence on the government's economic policy. While African economic development was a slow and difficult process, the Nyasaland government was unable to encourage it because of its commitment to supply labour to Europeans. We may therefore conclude that Nyasaland was not simply a missionary frontier; it was also the frontier of the white settlers and of the capitalist interests represented in South Africa and Southern Rhodesia.

FOOTNOTES

The argument of this paper is based on my thesis *Land and Labour in Nyasaland, 1890–1914*, London, 1964. Individual references to the thesis have been avoided. I would like to acknowledge my debt to Prof. Roland Oliver who supervised my thesis and to Prof. G. Shepperson for his comments. My thanks are also due to Dr H. J. Simons, University of Zambia, for his very detailed comments on the style of this paper.

1 Hancock, W. K., *Survey of British Commonwealth Affairs*, Oxford University Press, 1942, Vol. 2 Part II, 120–1.

   For the sake of historical accuracy, I have used throughout this paper 'Nyasaland', the name by which the modern state of Malawi was described during the colonial period.

2 See for details of Johnston's Land Settlement: Johnston to F.O. 14 October 1893 F.O. 403/185; Oliver, R., *Sir Harry Johnston and the Scramble for Africa*, London, 1964. 219–23; Hanna, A. J., *The Beginnings of Nyasaland and North Eastern Rhodesia*, Oxford, 1956.

3 Johnston, H. H., *British Central Africa*, London, 1899.

4 Johnston to F.O. 13 October 1892 F.O. 84/2197.

5 Johnston to F.O. 10 March 1892 F.O. 84/2197; Johnston to Anderson 21 January 1893 F.O. 2/54; For missionary view see *Life and Work in British Central Africa*, February 1892, March 1892.

6 *Life and Work* August 1902; February 1903; April 1903; Zambezi Industrial Mission, August, September, October 1903.

7 Sharpe to C.O. 8 November 1904 C.O. 525/3.

8 Annual Report for 1904–5 C.O. 525/8.

9 Sharpe to C.O. 2 July 1906 C.O. 525/13.

10 Annual Report for 1905–6 C.O. 525/13; Simpson to Sharpe 11 July 1906. Enclosure in Sharpe to C.O. 14 July 1906 C.O. 525/13.

11 Annual Report for 1906–7 C.O. 525/18.

12 British Cotton Growing Association to C.O. 9 May 1906 C.O. 525/16.

13 *British Central Africa Times*, 20 January 1906.

14 Sharpe to C.O. 20 October 1904 C.O. 525/3.

15 Sharpe to C.O. 6 March 1909 C.O. 525/28.

16 Report by the Director of Agriculture, 31 July 1911.

17 Thomas and Scot, *Uganda*, Oxford, 1935, 113–15.

18 Proceedings of the Legislative Council, January 1910.

19 Pearce to F.O. 10 April 1903 F.O. 403/336.

20 Sharpe to C.O. 20 October 1904 C.O. 525/3.

21 Memorandum on the British Central Africa Railway by the Crown Agents Office C.O. 525/4.

22 Sharpe to C.O. 20 July 1908 with inclosures C.O. 525/24.

23 Proc. Leg. Council January 1910.

24 Sharpe to C.O. 12 February 1910 with inclosures C.O. 525/32.

25 For population figures and area of districts; the *Handbook of Nyasaland*, Zomba, 1910, 104.

26 Sharpe to C.O. 12 February 1910 C.O. 525/32.

27 Minutes on above C.O. 525/32.

28 McCall to B.C.G.A. in B.C.G.A. to C.O. 525/41.

29 Wallis to C.O. 10 September 1910 C.O. 525/33.

30 Ibid.

31 Report on operation of B.C.G.A. in Nyasaland by McCall in Manning to C.O. 525/36; Report on B.C.G.A. 10 August 1912 in Manning to C.O. 10 August 1912 C.O. 525/43; Report on B.C.G.A. 21 January 1913 in Pearce to C.O. 1 February 1913 C.O. 525/46.

32 'History of a Movement to establish Govt. Cotton Markets' by McCall 9 April 1913 C.O. 525/48; Memo. By McCall 30 August 1913 C.O. 525/50.

33 B.C.G.A. to C.O. 20 March 1912 C.O. 525/45.

34 B.C.G.A. to C.O. 26 March 1912 C.O. 525/46; Minutes of a meeting of the Executive Committee of the B.C.G.A. 19 March 1912 enclosure in above; B.C.G.A. to C.O. 6 February 1913 C.O. 525/53.

35 Simpson to B.C.G.A. 24 February 1906 C.O. 525/19.

36 Proc. Leg. Council September 1912, June 1912.

37 Manning to C.O. 8 April 1911 C.O. 525/36; Manning to C.O. 10 June 1911 C.O. 525/37; C.O. to Treasury 2 October 1911 C.O. 525/37.

38 Manning to C.O. Secret 7 October 1911 C.O. 525/38; Proc. Leg. Council May 1911.

39 Manning to C.O. 5 August 1911 C.O. 525/37.

40 C.O. to Manning 21 October 1911 C.O. 525/37.

41 Proc. Leg. Council September 1912.

42 Manning to C.O. 16 November 1912 C.O. 525/44.

43 C.O. to O.A.G., Nyasaland. 24 January 1913 C.O. 525/44.

44 Smith to C.O. 6 December 1913 C.O. 525/51.

45 Ibid.

46 Ibid.

47 C.O. to Smith 18 February 1914 C.O. 525/51.

48 *Life and Work*, March 1892.

49 *The Aurora*, October 1899.

50 Report and Trade and General Conditions of the British Central Africa Protectorate 1 April 1895 to 31 March 1896, *Africa No. 5* (1896).

51 *The Nyasa News*, May 1894.

52 Report by Best, Collector of Blantyre Dt in Sharpe to F.O. 19 May 1902 F.O. 2/606.

53 *Life and Work*, June 1888; *British Central Africa Gazette*, April 1895.

54 Johnston to F.O. 12 January 1894 F.O. 2/66; *Life and Work*, November 1893.

55 Johnston to Anderson Private 24 March 1896 F.O. 2/106.

56 Duff, H. L., *Nyasaland Under the Foreign Office*, London 1903, 349–50.

57 *British Central Africa Gazette*, February 1894.

58 *British Central Africa Gazette*; February 1896; December 1896; September 1896; May 1896.

59 *Central African Times*, 5 May 1900.

60 *Central African Times*, 25 May 1901.

61 Sharpe to F.O. 12 March 1903 F.O. 2/746.

62 *British Central Africa Gazette*, December 1901.

63 Sharpe to F.O. 14 October 1902 F.O. 2/607.

64 Sharpe to F.O. 12 March 1903 and Minutes F.O. 2/746.

65 *British Central Africa Gazette*, November 1904; Sharpe to F.O. 8 February 1904 C.O. 525/1.

66 Sharpe to C.O. 19 March 1906 and enclosures C.O. 525/12.

67 *British Central Africa Gazette*, January 1907.

68 *British Central Africa Gazette*, August 1907.

69 Sharpe to C.O. 11 May 1909 C.O. 525/28.

70 *British Central Africa Gazette*, 10 March 1900.

71 Judge's Notes on Casson vs Blantyre and East Africa Company Ltd, 28 April 1903 F.O. 2/743; Duff, H. L. Report on Zomba Dt in Sharpe to F.O. 19 May 1902 F.O. 2/606.

72 Casson vs B. & E.A. Co. Ltd, 28 April 1903 F.O. 2/743.

73 Report of Land Commission 1903. F.O. 403/336.

74 *British Central Africa Gazette*, November 1904; Wemyss to Sharpe 13 November 1903.

75 *British Central Africa Gazette*, August 1903.

76 Sharpe to C.O. 22 June 1906 C.O. 525/13; Circular by Ag. Secy to Residents 26 July 1906 in Smith to C.O. Confidential 17 January 1914 C.O. 525/55.

77 Report on Nyasaland Native Rising 1915, Zomba, 1916.

78 Smith to C.O. 17 January 1914 with inclosures C.O. 525/55.

79 Proc. Leg. Council, March 1914.

80 Codrington to Sharpe 25 June 1904 N.E.A. 3/7–4 Lusaka archives.

81 Sharpe to F.O. 15 March 1900 and minutes F.O. 2/669.

82 Administrator, N.E.R. to Commr, Nyasaland 24 April 1903; Sharpe to Codrington 7 June 1904; Codrington to Sharpe 25 June 1904; Beaufort, L. P. Judge of the High Court, N.E.R. to Codrington 4 August 1903 N.E.A. 3/7–4 Lusaka archives.

83 C.O. to F.O. 4 December 1920 F.O. 2/789.

84 C.O. to F.O. 4 December 1902 F.O. 2/789.

85 F.O. to C.O. 29 August 1902 F.O. 2/789.

86 C.O. to F.O. 19 March 1903 F.O. 2/789, Hansard 19 March 1903, 1243.

87 Correspondence on the Migration of Nyasaland labour to the Transvaal and Southern Rhodesia, London, H.M.S.O. Cd. 3993.

88 Report on Nyasaland Natives in Southern Rhodesia, Casson to C.O. 23 November 1907 C.O. 525/22.

89 Knipe, WNLA to Manning 11 January 1908 in Manning to C.O. 18

January 1908 C.O. 525/23.

90 Sharpe to C.O. 16 January 1908 in Manning to C.O. 18 January 1908 C.O. 525/27.

91 Administrator S.R. to Gov. Nyasaland 30 April 1909 in Sharpe to C.O. 3 July 1909 C.O. 525/29.

92 C.O. to Sharpe 29 May 1909; Sharpe to C.O. 10 August 1909. Minutes C.O. 525/28.

93 Proc. Leg. Council, November 1909.

94 Casson's Report 19 September 1910 C.O. 525/35.

95 Memo. by N.A. Chamber 24 March 1910 C.O. 525/32; Proc. Leg. Council, November 1910.

96 Manning to C.O. 11 March 1911 C.O. 525/36.

97 Manning to C.O. 23 September 1911 C.O. 525/38.

98 Manning to C.O. 9 March 1912 and 16 March 1912 C.O. 525/41.

99 Manning to C.O. 25 May 1912 C.O. 525/42.

23 The place of John Chilembwe in Malawi historiography

George Shepperson

Historiography meant originally *the writing of history*. With the increasing professionalization of history in the twentieth century, historiography has acquired a second meaning, *the study of the writing of history*, which has come to overshadow and often to supplant entirely the original meaning of the word. Indeed, in the United States of America today, there are professional historians who believe that it is more realistic and profitable to teach students historiography in this second sense than to require them to study history in the conventional manner. To such academicians, it is futile to follow the traditional objectives of historians: the description and analysis of what happened in the past. To them, there can be no certainty in history: all that one can be sure of is that different historians have approached the study of the past in different ways; all that one may legitimately teach, therefore, is the changing and often conflicting interpretations of the past.

This is not a point of view which is likely to commend itself immediately to African historians. The study of the African past has been dominated for too long by the Hegelian view that Africa had no history that was worthy of consideration until the coming of aliens; and it is understandable that historians of today should strive to find the solid ground of the facts of the past rather than to struggle in the shifting sands of the varied and vying interpretations of history. Nevertheless, there are signs that historians of Africa are becoming increasingly interested in historiography in the second meaning of this word; and while it is unlikely that they will ever be captured by the relativist, almost solipsist view of history which fascinates many historians of the West, they cannot avoid being challenged by the different ways in which it is possible to interpret the events of the past. The study of historiography, of their own countries as well as of the world beyond, has a claim for consideration in academic research and curricula by African historians.

The papers of the 1967 and 1970 Conferences which have been organized by the Department of History at the University of Malawi indicate that there is no lack of themes in the history of Malawi which are capable of varying

405

interpretations, according to the discovery of new evidence and the changing standpoints of historians. Amongst these themes, the phenomenon of John Chilembwe and the so-called 'Native Rising within the Nyasaland Protectorate' in 1915 is clearly of major significance, not only for the discussion of its place in the history of Malawi but also because, by its dramatic nature, it presents within a relatively short compass most of the main questions which must be asked in the study of history and of historiography: the role of the individual in history; the problem of inevitability; the function of accident in a historical situation; the inter-relationship of internal and external factors; the part played by ideas in society; the meaning of class and culture; etc.

In this paper, the emphasis will be placed not on the study of John Chilembwe and his milieu in the period after the Second World War when the break-up of European empires, the rapid growth of nationalism amongst their subject peoples, and the turning of professional historians towards the once-neglected field of African history combined to create a new interest in Chilembwe. It will be placed largely on the attempts by Africans as well as Europeans in the two decades after the Rising to explain the events of 23 January to 4 February 1915 when John Chilembwe and his followers challenged European power in the Nyasaland Protectorate. These explanations, often in the form of memoranda rather than explicit pieces of historical writing, ought not to be neglected in the study of the historiography of the Chilembwe milieu. Historiography, however defined, is not the private preserve of professional historians—and those of them who claim that it is will find, at least in the case of Chilembwe, that they neglect at their peril the kind of proto-historiography which was produced in the twenty years after the Rising.

During the period and aftermath of any notable sequence of events in history, participants or those closely concerned with it often—indeed, one might say, usually—ask questions about it which anticipate the inquiries made subsequently by professional historians. This was true, for example, with the American Civil War; it was the case with Chilembwe and the 1915 Rising. Of the six fundamental groups of questions which have been asked about them, only one was not raised at the time. This is the problem of the growth of the myth of John Chilembwe: why it assumed the forms that it did after his death and what has been its function in Malawi since then. And even this problem was partly raised in the two decades after the shooting of John Chilembwe, albeit in a mythological form itself, when the belief was widespread that he had not died and the question was asked by many Africans, at home and abroad, where had John Chilembwe escaped to and when and how was he coming back home?

The other five fundamental groups of questions, however, in the historiography of John Chilembwe and the 1915 affair were all apparent shortly after the Rising. The first of them concerned Chilembwe himself. Why had he acted as he did? Was he a self-conscious martyr? Was he a hero and a patriot or a pathetic, frightened creature who struck out wildly, overcome by personal and political frustrations? Did he really know what he was doing?

The second group of questions stemmed logically from the first. Was the

Rising of purely local significance? Was it little more than the outcome of a vendetta between John Chilembwe and his followers and William Jervis Livingstone, the manager of the A. L. Bruce Estates at Chiradzulu, and his European staff?

Thirdly, if the Rising was not localized in significance, what was the extent and the nature of the support which it drew from other parts of the Protectorate? Why did men like Filipo Chinyama, John Gray Kufa Mapantha and David Kaduya throw in their lot with Chilembwe? Was not John Chilembwe, in spite of his key position in the African society of the Shire Highlands, just another member of an ambitious and frustrated African petty bourgeoisie in Nyasaland? Would the Rising have occurred if the First World War had not broken out; and what was Chilembwe's relationship with the Germans in East Africa? How much of the inspiration of the Rising came from outside of Nyasaland and what effects, if any, did it have beyond the Protectorate?

A fourth group of questions concerned intimately one of these queried external forces: Joseph Booth, the radical British missionary, who had taken Chilembwe to the United States and had remained in touch with him and many of his followers long after Booth was deported from British Central Africa. Could the Rising have taken place without Booth? And if he had any influence on it, what forms did this assume and how were they transmitted to the Protectorate?

The fifth and final group of questions was, perhaps, the most fundamental of them all. Was the Rising the end of the old order in Malawi or the beginning of the new? And, in this context, the 'old order' could be considered in two very different ways: the traditional, African order; or the British Empire itself. And, in its turn, the 'new order' was capable of two interpretations in this question: a new order of African accommodation to British rule in Nyasaland; or the ultimate emergence of independent African nationhood in Malawi. Was, indeed, the Rising forward or backward-looking; or was it something which in no sense marked a turning-point in the history of Malawi but, by its very religiosity, spanned three epochs: the traditional African order; the period of tutelage under British colonialism; and the emergence of a new, independent nation-State?

In one way or another, all of these five groups of questions are represented in the proto-historiography of Chilembwe and the 1915 Rising in Malawi.

It is not to be wondered at that Africans produced some interesting and instructive writing on the Rising, largely within the two decades after it. It had taken many Africans by surprise as much as Europeans. And those who had not been taken by surprise had to justify and explain their prior knowledge of the possibility of the Rising in the face of a Government Commission of Inquiry and a largely hostile and aggrieved European population.

Furthermore, there were several Africans in the Protectorate at this time to whom historical thinking was not an alien habit. To be sure, it could be argued that forms of historical thinking antedated European rule in British Central Africa. This view seems to have been implicit in a note by the Blantyre missionaries in their magazine for January 1893, although their manner of expressing themselves assumed something of the form of southern African whites:

'The natives have the clearest and most consistent knowledge of relationship, boundary of land or influence, and laws of succession; but diligent investigation is needed to get at it, if one would learn the truth. The history of the Yao conquest, the conquering chiefs, the divisions of the conquered land, are as clearly written in the memories of old men round about us, as was the Iliad upon the heart of the Homeric bard. Kaffir history would, if it were written out, be a Kaffir epic as truly as the Sagas of the North or the poem of Camoens were the pride of birth to German or Portuguese. It is strange that we should have come into contact with just such a dignity created by just such memories.'[1]

To this natural historical bent was added, for those Africans who had come under the influence of the Scottish-directed Christian missions at Blantyre and Livingstonia, the encouragement towards historical thinking about their own problems which some of the missionaries seem to have given them. At the Third General Missionary Conference of Nyasaland in 1910, this was reflected in the remarks of the Livingstonia missionary, W. A. Elmslie, on the place of history in the curriculum:

'The history course should not be confined to British history but should include and even start from the history of their own land and lead up to foreign history. It is one of the most valuable subjects which we can teach. The native thinks our life and institutions were all framed *en bloc* and handed over to us in some way, and nothing will awaken him more to the possibilities within the reach of the tribes than to learn the evolution of nations and national laws and institutions. The philosophy rather than the facts and dates of history should receive the greatest attention.'[2]

A similarly broad view of history in the African curriculum was taken by Alexander Hetherwick of Blantyre at the 1910 Conference:

'History should be on a broad basis, dealing with wide movements of races, tribes and nations in their effect on each other and on the history of the world. What could be more inappropriate than having a class engaged for a whole year's work on a bit of English or Scottish history?'[3]

Indeed, at an earlier missionary conference at Livingstonia in 1900, Hetherwick had underlined the importance of the teaching of English for helping the Africans of Malawi to understand those 'wide movements of races, tribes and nations' which were now engulfing them:

'I believe it to be good policy to teach English as widely as possible. Such a course will (1) open up to the native a vast region of thought and interest that otherwise would be closed to him; (2) it will prepare him to meet the tide of European thought and influence that is fast flowing into this land.'[4]

408

Before the twentieth century opened, there were many Africans in the Protectorate who had come under such influences. The journalism which emanated from the Blantyre and Livingstonia Missions, in English and the vernaculars, and from the secular interests of the Protectorate, was helping to produce in the African Christian converts men who were aware of political currents in the world around them and of the opportunities which the civilization and technology of the nineteenth century offered to people everywhere. What these were was revealed in the January 1890 issue of the Blantyre Mission's *Life and Work*, in the challenging and characteristic prose of David Clement Scott:

'A New Year has dawned and the 9th decade of the Nineteenth century has passed away. This era, so full of advance, so different from the grey dawn of the eighteenth, with such names as Darwin and Carlyle, Victor Hugo and Ernest Renan, Newman, Gladstone, the Emperor Nicholas and Chunder Sen; such phases of political change as the Liberal and Radical revolution; the balance of power in Europe; the advance of Russia; the development of the Empire of India; affairs in Egypt, and the Suez Canal; the Slave Trade; the meeting of the Powers in the vast stretches of Africa with such weapons as "spheres of influence", "effective occupation", delimitation by conference, "arbitration", "annexation", native signatures and Missionary appeal, passes quickly to the hive of all the centuries. . . . We wait for great development and new things. . . .'[5]

From such sources a habit of historical thinking had developed amongst many Africans in the Protectorate which was to find in the Chilembwe Rising an exercise for its talents. Indeed, when John Chilembwe sent to the *Nyasaland Times* in November 1914 his moving letter entitled 'The Voice of African Natives in the Present War'[6] there was more than an echo in it of what Elmslie had called 'the possibilities within the reach of the tribes (through a study of) . . . the evolution of nations and national laws and institutions'; of what Hetherwick had seen as 'wide movements of races, tribes and nations in their effect on each other and on the history of the world'; and of David Clement Scott's 'great development and new things' as the nineteenth century drew to a close. Chilembwe had the seeds of historical thought in him, too. It is hardly surprising, then, that those literate Africans who tried to interpret the significance of his Rising shortly after its *débâcle* may be considered contributors to the proto-historiography of Malawi.

Within six months of the failure of the Rising, five of them had written historical essays, of varying magnitudes, on its nature and problems. Not only do these essays add to our knowledge of John Chilembwe and the 1915 Rising but they represent the beginning of the study of Chilembwe in the history of Malawi and are themselves very minor but not insignificant pieces in the African historiography of Central Africa. It is not clear whether they were written independently or whether they were the result of encouragement—perhaps even of threats—by the members and their staff of the Governmental Commission which had been set up on 28 April 1915 to inquire into, amongst other things, 'the origin, causes and objects of the native rising in the Shire High-lands and elsewhere within the Nyasaland Protectorate, instigated by John Chilembwe.' Whatever stimulated them in the first place, they are all to be found in the evidence gathered by this Commission.[7]

The first essay was by Robertson Namate,[8] a Yao from Namilongo village, a clerk and typist in the Secretariat, and an elder of the Church of Scotland Mission in Zomba. Namate wrote from no personal knowledge of Chilembwe; but he clearly had definite opinions about him. It is in Namate's brief essay that the interpretation of Chilembwe's motives along the martyr-complex lines—which is likely to be a perennial source of controversy in the historio-graphy of the Rising—makes an early (perhaps a first) appearance. Linked to this was the interpretation of the localized as opposed to the general nature of the Rising: another basic element in the study of Chilembwe and his followers, across which the historiographical pendulum has already swung in opposed directions and is not likely to cease swinging in the future. As Namate put it in his erratic but energetic English:

'It may come across someone's mind or thought that the origin of the late John Chilembwe rising, I might call it, as I do not well see why it is called "Native Rising". It is not native rising generally but it was only a particular or Magomero or Chiradzulu native who rose in arms.'[9]

To Namate, the cause of the trouble was simply 'a total misunderstanding between Magomero Europeans and their native tenants'. But, he went on, instead of taking their grievances to the Boma, the African tenants of the A. L. Bruce Estates at Magomero

'might have thought it best to lay the whole of their burden to Chilembwe of whom, they must have regarded him, it appears somewhat great person and powerful who could do great deeds of deliverance.'[10]

In conclusion, Robertson Namate balanced the advantages and disadvantages of British rule. Slavery had been abolished and there was obvious techno-logical progress: 'Fire is kindled and without sticks rubbing against each other. No native blacksmith is now trying his best of making those blunt and sharp-ened hoes and axes etc.'[11] But against this must be set the indignities which Europeans had often heaped on the African. At this stage, Namate introduces the anger which many Africans felt at being forced to take their hats off when they passed a European, without receiving in return a similar salutation from the white man. The curt command which Namate renders as *Chosa chipewa and gwira pa manja ako*[12] (Take your hat off and hold it in your hand) together with the frequent use of the *chikoti* (whip) by Europeans were the main griev-ances he listed against them. Namato's statement on Chilembwe and his milieu was succinct but it has in it the germs of future historical studies.

The second essay was by the Rev. Stephen Kundecha, one of the first ordained African ministers of the Church of Scotland at Zomba. Kundecha, in fact, provided two statements: 'The Grievances of the Natives' and 'Notes on John Chilembwe's raiding and on education'. In his examination on 8 July 1915 before the Commission of Inquiry into the Rising, Kundecha revealed that he had known Chilembwe since 1900 when Chilembwe had gone to Zomba to see about land for his mission station at Chiradzulu. Kundecha's relations with Chilembwe were obviously close. Both men had tried to bring each other into their respective spheres of influence; and it is clear that Chilembwe had made an approach to Kundecha to throw in his lot with him when the Rising was imminent. It is this closeness of relationships between the two men which gives Stephen Kundecha's two statements a special authority. Nevertheless, Kundecha's statements are more than historical evidence. He showed genuine powers of historical thinking.[13] In his first statement, for example, he draws a picture of the Africans of the Protectorate as men of two worlds, marginal men, caught up in a perplexing situation of culture contact:

'. . . they are not quite sure whether their generations will stand on. Their experiences with the circumstances of the new life show them as if they were going only to die . . . They take the comparison on the old life before the Europeans came in and that of the new life after they are in . . . Long ago they all had their proper homes which they chose by themselves . . . They now seem confounded and in great perplexity as if they were strangers in the country. These cause them grieve, and make them think that they have no good development for facing the new life.'[14]

In this statement Kundecha listed under carefully-chosen headings the grievances felt by Africans: (1) the ones mentioned in the quotation above; (2) 'Their disappointments and disturbances in their efforts in business'; (3) 'Their want of different definite proper arrangements of respects of their superiors' (an important anthropological point which Kundecha had some difficulty in expressing but by which he meant that all Europeans, irrespective of their social standing, expected to be paid the same level of respect by Africans whereas, in traditional society, Africans gave their respects, from the Chiefs downwards, 'in a very definite manner according to their different standards of people'); (4) 'Their want of comfort whenever criminals' sentence of death is passed' (a plea for open courts of justice in the old, African manner); (5) 'Their want of careful observation on Natives Petitions'; (6) 'Requirement of native meeting' (a plea for a regular forum for the discussion of ideas which Africans wanted to put to the Government); (7) 'Their want of translated laws in native tongue'; and (8) Grievances associated with the manner of paying hut tax. Kundecha's list of African grievances[15] was a comprehensive one and it is likely that it assisted the Commissioners in setting out their section on *Native Grievances* in the report which they published on the Rising.[16]

As one reads Kundecha's statement of African grievances, one begins to feel that, unlike Robertson Namate, he is coming to the conclusion that the Chilembwe Rising was of general rather than localized significance. But he comes out definitely against this view at the beginning of his second statement which concerns Chilembwe directly:

'I do not see evidence that John Chilembwe's raiding was a general thing by the natives here, and I think it is not right to say so. Perhaps our Masters would think that people here say "we did not know", after they were asked, because they were afraid of being punished. But I would say that it is not so at all.'[17]

In this respect, Stephen Kundecha indicated that he had taken his own sampling of evidence from workers on the Magomero Estate.

In both of his statements, Kundecha shows that this sampling of evidence, at Magomero and presumably elsewhere in the Protectorate, was leading Africans to associate the European way of life with the extension of war: a process in which, they felt, the Christian missionaries played a part. Kundecha's quotation of African opinion here is somewhat over-succinct and hence inclined to be cryptic. But, taken with other remarks in his evidence at the Commission of Inquiry, it can be made to bear this interpretation. The Africans, according to Kundecha, believed that 'Adzungu [Europeans] are nothing but they are Nkhondo [war]';[18] and 'it is a general belief that "The Adzungu wa Boma [the Government] cannot make war without the missionaries".'[19] Stephen Kundecha obviously had the historian's instinct for the collection of evidence, not only in those instances of opinion about the Europeans but in other examples which he gives of the feeling of John Chilembwe's followers: for example, their belief that, as in the Book of Revelation at the end of the Bible, the Azungu were 'zirombo [pests] from the water'[20]—probably an association with and an extension of the first verse of Chapter 13 in Revelations, 'And I stood upon the sand of the sea, and saw a beast rise up out of the sand of the sea . . .'

Kundecha, however, had acquired this statement from another African minister: Harry Kambwiri Matecheta: one of the original seven candidates for the deaconate of the Blantyre Mission and the first ordained African minister of the Church of Scotland in 1911, who died in 1964 at the age of 91. It was the Rev. Matecheta who supplied the third essay to the Commission of Inquiry which he entitled 'The Origin of John Chilembwe Rising'. Harry Kambwiri's essay was probably written as much—if not more—to satisfy his own need for setting his thoughts in order as for the enlightenment of the Commissioners. He had gained the feeling of writing in his work as a compositor at the Blantyre Mission press in the late 1880s; and he had made his *début* as an essayist when, in response to an inquiry by Sir Harry Johnston for information on the products of Malawi, he had written a piece which had won him a prize of two pounds and a copy of Johnston's *British Central Africa*.[21] In his essay on the origins of Chilembwe's Rising, Harry Kambwiri showed not merely a literary bent but a clear, if rudimentary historiographical tendency. He began by a blunt statement which showed that he realized how complex the whole matter of John Chilembwe and the Rising was: 'This is a difficult question.'[22] His approach, while not lacking analysis, was chronological rather than thematic. This was to some extent forced upon him because Harry Kambwiri Matecheta's career had paralleled Chilembwe's own: they had been to school together, although Matecheta had been in the senior class;

412

Matecheta had known Chilembwe's mentor, Joseph Booth; he had seen Chilembwe return from America and had preached at the Providence Industrial Mission in its early days; he had been associated with Chilembwe in the project of the Natives Industrial Union of 1909; and, as with the Rev. Stephen Kundecha, Chilembwe had tried to get him to join a single pro-African church and to throw in his lot with Chilembwe's movement.[23] One sympathizes with Matecheta's chronological approach: it seems essential if the twists and turns of events which resolved themselves eventually in the denouement of 23 January 1915 and the attacks by Chilembwe's followers on the Europeans at Magomero are to be appreciated in their full drama.

And yet there was some proto-sociology in his essay. Like Kundecha, his essay contained a separate section on 'Native Grievances'—prompted, no doubt, by the terms of reference of the Commission which included an examination of 'any alleged grievances of the natives which may have conduced to the rising.' But within this section he discussed three factors which appeared to him to be very relevant to the Rising: the hut-tax (he gave a useful brief history of this from the days of Harry Johnston, the first Commissioner and Consul-General in the Protectorate); the changing social composition of Chilembwe's following, on which he commented that, when Chilembwe could not get 'educated natives' to join his Mission, 'he began to teach his own converts, many of whom were Angulu, Ampotola, and Angoni, who are newly come into the country and are raw natives';[24] and the sharpening of the colour line (Matecheta used this expression) within the Protectorate which he attributed to external factors such as the pro-Negro teaching of the Afro-American missionary at the early P.I.M., L.N. Cheek.

From an examination of Chilembwe's movement, chronologically and, to some extent, thematically, Harry Kambwiri parted company with Robertson Namate and Stephen Kundecha who had seen the Rising largely as a local vendetta against W. J. Livingstone and the Europeans at Magomero. Harry Kambwiri declared that Chilembwe did not attempt the Rising only because of 'Magomero oppression'.[25] To reinforce this view, he drew upon personal experience of a discussion which he had with John Chilembwe on the significance of the seventeenth verse of the second chapter of the First Epistle of Peter: 'Honour all men. Love the brotherhood. Fear God, Honour the king.' According to Kambwiri, Chilembwe had manifested his general rather than his particular feeling against Europeans in the Protectorate by declaring that ' "The King is not our King, but Azungu's King".'[26]

Kambwiri, furthermore, showed something of an interest in comparative history by referring to William G. Blaikie's *Personal Life of David Livingstone* (London 1880) from which he quoted the great explorer's anti-slavery sentiments.[27] Kambwiri's implication was obvious. The Europeans had freed the slaves in Malawi; they had then set up a regime which, in the abuse of Africans by some Europeans, amounted to re-enslavement. According to Kambwiri, Chilembwe had echoed European abuse of Africans: ' "Ufuna chikoti, or I'll take a stick to you, with such words as *Nyani* [baboon], Niger, etc." '.[28] To Kambwiri, this could only mean 'slaves', and he commented, clearly with an eye on the outcome of the Chilembwe movement, 'We natives have this

413

custom, never call your slave again when you have made him a free man, if you do he will leave you or be against you.'[29] He developed his extended, anti-slavery metaphor in the context of the problems of *tangata* on the European estates and concluded 'To one like John who had heard about the slaves in America, these things gave him great grief indeed.'[30] It was an approach which implied that John Chilembwe had something of Abraham Lincoln about him; that he was a liberator and a patriot and not the exponent of a vendetta.

Harry Kambwiri's 'The Origin of John Chilembwe Rising', in spite of its brevity, its obvious lapses of English style, and its rudimentary historiography, not only supplies important evidence for future historians of the Chilembwe milieu but it also provides a picture of an early African historian grappling imaginatively with essential historical problems. Later in his life, Harry Kambwiri Matecheta was to show that he had not lost his historical interests when he produced a pamphlet entitled *Blantyre Mission, Nkhani za Ciyambi Cace* in 1951. Here again his interest in origins manifested itself; and he revealed that he believed that the Rising was something of a turning-point in the history of Malawi by including a short chapter on the year 1915 ('Caka ca 1915'). It added little to his statement on Chilembwe and the Rising that was made in that year, apart from a reference to Chilembwe's boyhood interest in hunting elephants.[31] However, Matecheta left a number of manuscripts, some of which were used in a short biography of him, as yet unpublished, by his son, Clement, entitled *The African Missionary* and completed in the 1960s. Once again, a short section was provided on 'The Chilembwe Rising'. One wishes very much that Harry Kambwiri Matecheta could have expanded his ideas and information about John Chilembwe and the Rising into a book. It would have been worth reading.

The written statement that was presented to the Commissioners in 1915 by M. M. Chisuse, senior printer at the Blantyre Mission and the 'African Photographer' who took the striking picture of Chilembwe, his church and flock,[32] is very brief and, at first sight, seems almost a footnote to Harry Kambwiri Matecheta's 'Origin of John Chilembwe Rising'. Indeed, the two men were good friends, as Matecheta's son has pointed out; and it is possible that they discussed Chilembwe and the Rising frequently and cross-fertilized each other's ideas on it. Chisuse, to be sure, provides a memory of Joseph Booth which accords well with Matecheta's anti-slavery interpretation of Chilembwe:

'One day I met him [Joseph Booth] in Chinde when he was taking John Chilembwe away to America, and sitting on the sand near the Indian Ocean, he said, "I love the sea, because the sea does not tell any lies. Years ago we Europeans used to sail in this Ocean on to the coast and got you Africans as slaves and sold you in America: but now the Europeans have got another plan of just coming to take the land away from you and make you slaves together with the land.'[33]

And, in another place, Chisuse, like Matecheta, traced Chilembwe's feelings on what Chisuse called the 'colour question'[34] to American influences; and supplies the valuable information for any biographer of Chilembwe that he read such books as *Uncle Tom's Cabin*. Chisuse seems to have been more interested in anecdote than in interpretation; and he offers no estimate of such essential questions of the 1915 Rising as its scope and extent.

The same could not be said of the writer of another historical footnote on the Rising which was presented to the Commissioners in 1915. This was Elliot Kamwana, the disciple of Joseph Booth in his Watch Tower days, who had touched off a socially-conscious, apocalyptic, revivalist movement in the Tonga country of western Malawi in 1908–9 that led to his deportation from the Protectorate. Kamwana had been allowed to return to Mlanje after a period of exile in South Africa, and he was in political detention there on the eve of the Rising. It is now clear that he was in touch with John Chilembwe,[35] although the exact degree of his complicity in Chilembwe's movement is not yet clear. The Commissioners viewed him as a highly suspicious character. This may have had the effect of making Kamwana not exactly frank in his oral evidence to them. But in the written evidence which he supplied to the Commission he 'pulled no punches'. His interpretation of the scope of the Rising appears to have lain between that of Stephen Kundecha and Harry Kambwiri: on the one hand, it was carried out by 'particular classes of natives'; but, on the other, it 'was against Europeans generally'. Kamwana, who was well read in Pastor Charles Taze Russell's millenarian *Studies in the Scriptures*, did not lack a historical sense, some of which may have derived from the chiliastic chronology of the Russellite interpretation of the Bible and some from the acuteness of his observation and the breadth of his travels in southern Africa. If Chisuse's historical footnote was largely anecdotal, Kamwana's was interpretative in its nature. For one, too, who is often considered as the preacher of a verbose, chiliastic creed, he showed remarkable powers of succinct expression in his statement to the Commissioners. It reads:

'(1)   The said rising was to particular classes of natives, John Chilembwe was the instigator. The discontentment of the intelligent and emigrant natives did help the rising.

'(2)   Some grievances of the natives are these: Little wages, no liberty or franchise. Overtax, injustice, no pension or allowance for children, wife or parents of the dead soldiers in the war. Jealousy and hatred of particular classes of Europeans against the natives. The rising was against Europeans generally.

'(3)   The information can be obtained through those who are well acquainted with all classes of natives. The state of natives feeling can be obtained by one who has malice toward none, but love toward all. And he must know and understand the people.

'(4)   The Christian religion as a whole, had good and evil effects. Education in the colleges and seminaries has bad effect on natives mind for any people.

'Knowledge is power, but very few can use knowledge properly for general interest.

'Recommendations. I submit that if possible wages should be increased.

'Jealousy and hatred of particular classes of Europeans should stop.

'Pension and allowance for children, wife or parents of the dead soldier in the war should be considered. Liberty should be given to some extent.

'Native tax-collectors and policemen should stop to extort and ravish in the Districts.

'There should be no respect of persons in judgment.'[36]

In the five statements by Africans to the Commissioners of Inquiry into the Rising of 1915 which deserve to be considered as proto-historiography of and about the Chilembwe milieu, two of them, Kundecha's and Matecheta's (especially the latter), have the character of genuine, although rudimentary historical essays. The others (Namate, Chisuse and Kamwana) are footnotes to history, although the essential functions of historical writing, the collection and interpretation of information, are present in various ways throughout them. Taken together, the five statements indicate that historical thinking by Africans on John Chilembwe and the Rising of 1915 began early in Malawi. It is possible that further research will reveal other historical essays of this kind which were written by Africans from Malawi about Chilembwe and his supporters in the months and years which followed quickly on the Rising. Although discussion of the Rising and of Chilembwe were discouraged by the Government of the Nyasaland Protectorate at this time, it was a subject of such fascination to Africans of Malawi descent, in the Protectorate itself or in the countries to the south to which so many of them emigrated, that it is always possible that essays, even pamphlets or small, unpublished books were written by Africans, as private aids to the understanding of their position in an increasingly complex world or as documents for discrete circulation to small groups. As far south as the tip of Africa, Clements Kadalie, then coming to the peak of his power as leader of the Industrial and Commerical Workers Union of South Africa, could write home to a correspondent in Nyasaland in 1921:

'Yes, I [have] heard [about] that African patriot John Chilembwe and I am indeed proud of his name. It was a few days ago that I was relating his adventures to my staff at this office and they were indeed inspired. Further particulars about him will be much appreciated as I would like to obtain this information for [the] future history of Africa as I believe that white men will not preserve the genuine history of the black man.'[37]

The thirst for information on Chilembwe and his world thus existed at home and abroad within a few months of his death. It is hardly, surprising, therefore, that in 1931–2 George Simeon Mwase should have devoted two-thirds of his book entitled *A Dialogue of Nyasaland Record of Past Events, Environment & Present Outlook within the Protectorate* to John Chilembwe and the Rising of 1915.[38] The seeds which were to flower in Mwase's fascina ing little volume had been planted during the previous decade and a half by Namate, Kundecha, Matecheta, Chisuse, Kamwana and other Africans whose names and writings most probably await discovery. Unless this is realized, Mwase's work may too easily appear as exceptional and exotic.

Within the context of its times, however, it has an obvious value, not only for what it has to say about Chilembwe and the Rising but also for Mwase's historical method. Mwase obviously went to considerable pains to gather information about Chilembwe and to write an engaginga nd often cogent narrative, particularly on the organization and events of the Rising. He clearly realized, however, that the best historical writing must be something more than a chronicle: it must interpret as well as recount events. Mwase's approach was in the Thomas Carlyle tradition. John Chilembwe was a hero—an interpretation which Mwase interpreted again in terms of the Patriot Martyr. In terms of broader social forces, Mwase was less sure of himself, as appears in his ambiguous statement on the intention of the Rising: 'I must strongly say that John had no intention of rebelling against the Government, but as the Government is the head of everything and . . . [is held] responsible for any cause or reason, therefore I say he revolted against the Government.'[39] Mwase was more at ease in comparative history and his little book contains some interesting instances of genuine comparative historical thought. They range from his comparison of Chilembwe to John Brown and the abortive anti-slavery insurrection at Harper's Ferry, Virginia, in 1859; through an analogy with William Prynne and his battles with the English Established Church in the 1630s; to Mwase's striking parallel between Chilembwe in 1915 and Sir Roger Casement's attempt to stir up rebellion in Ireland the following year.[40]

Mwase's *Dialogue of Nyasaland* provides, in itself, a fascinating contrast between the methods of the medieval chronicler, with his uncritical acceptance of any fragment of evidence about his subject and his habit of putting words into his characters' mouths, and the modern historian with his reluctance to commit himself to generalizations until he has assembled an impressive and incontrovertible body of evidence. On the one hand, Mwase has no hesitation about putting into Chilembwe's mouth a long speech to his army on the morning of 23 January 1915 which may, perhaps, contain the substance of his meaning on that occasion but is most unlikely to be in the actual words he used or even in his style, as is indicated by the use of Latin tags which are clearly the addition of the stylistic Mwase. On the other hand, when relating the outcome of the Rising, Mwase makes it clear that he is writing from his own opinion rather than others' evidence: 'As the matter lies open like that, for someone to put in his opinions, I voluntarily take up the risk of entering in what I think. . . . would have been done. I do not mean I am correct.'[41] Mwase's work is likely to occupy an important place not only in the historiography of John Chilembwe and of Malawi but also in the evolution of writings by Africans about Africa in the age of colonialism.

It is interesting to contrast Mwase's dramatic representation of Chilembwe's speeches to his followers with the reporting by one of them, Mr Andrew G. Mkulichi, brother of Chilembwe's headteacher, Stephen Mkulichi, who was killed in the Rising. In the early 1950s, Mr Andrew G. Mkulichi wrote for Mr Thomas Price a forty-page account entitled *Maziko a Prov. Ind. Mission. Chiradzulo. Nyasaland. 1900 A.D.*[42] ('The Founding of the Providence Industrial Mission . . .'). It has none of the historical sophistication of Mwase's work but is, nevertheless, a rudimentary piece of institutional history in its own right as well as a valuable account of Chilembwe and the fifteen years before the Rising. Mr Mkulichi put only very brief speeches into Chilembwe's mouth. With one exception these were in the vernacular. This exception was the following representation of three memorable sentiments of Chilembwe's which are all given in English: '1. "I hear the crying of my Africans." 2. "My people are destroyed through lack of knowledge." 3. "It is better for me to die than to live."' Whether the use of English was for emphasis or whether Chilembwe actually used English in some of his speeches is not clear. Elsewhere, however, Mr Mkulichi reverts to the vernacular; and, unlike Mwase, indicates Chilembwe's habit of Biblical quotation. Typical of this is his reporting of Chilembwe's speech to his followers after the Censor had refused to permit *The Nyasaland Times* to publish Chilembwe's letter criticizing African embroilment in the First World War. The passage in question reads:

'. . . anayamba kuphunzitsa mwa mphamvu, nati Limbikani musafoke mu Mzimu ngakhale mudzaone. Pakuti ambiri adzafika mdzina la Kristu, nadzati ife ndife a Kristu. Ndipo anaphunsitza macitidwe 20: 29–32. Iye analimbikitsa ndi mau akuti Tiyenera kumva zowawa cifukwa omwe anali patsogolo pathu anamwa zowawa cifukwa cace ndifulumizani inu nonse kuti mukondane wina ndi wina, ndiku wapempheranso iwo amene anakuzunzani inu mwa Ambuye.'

(He [Chilembwe] began strong teaching. He said, 'Be strong. Don't be wearied in the Spirit even in the face of trouble. For many will arrive in Christ's name and will say we are of Christ.' And then he taught Acts chapter 20, verses 29–32. He strengthened them with these words, 'We ought to experience hardships because those who went before us had bitter experiences. That is why I urge you all that you love one another and pray to the Lord again for those who have been cruel to you.')

It is this mixture of religion and politics which brings Chilembwe and his followers close to what has been called in European history the 'Radical Reformation'.

Mwase, in his comparison of John Chilembwe and William Prynne, approached this parallel between Chilembwe's movement and the forces which had been unleashed by the Reformation of the Church in Europe. But neither he nor any of the other African writers on Chilembwe in the two decades after 1915 developed the idea. Both Kundecha and Matecheta had studied Church History in English when they were working for ordination into the ministry of the Church of Scotland. But if the parallel between the Chilembwe movement and ecclesiastical elements in the Reformation in European history occurred to them, they kept it to themselves.

Echoes, indeed, of Reformation controversies occurred in the writings by Europeans in the twenty years after the Rising. The most immediately important of these was the 1916 *Report of the Commission . . . into . . . the Native Rising*. Between their appointment on 28 April 1915 and the completion of their report on 14 January 1916, the Commissioners questioned a sequence of witnesses, African and European, and examined a mass of evidence, written and printed, which reminds one of a historical enquiry. Although their report was written in curt, numbered paragraphs in an official style, they sought, as all historians must do, answers to questions; and, according to their lights and, most probably, to the best of their ability, stated the truth, as they saw it, of an extremely complex situation. Subsequent evidence may lead one to disagree with some of their conclusions, but they do not appear to have concealed unpleasant facts: for example, in spite of attempts by representatives of the A. L. Bruce Estates at Magomero to show conditions there in a relatively favourable light, the *Report* brought out clearly that 'the treatment of labour and the system of tenancy on the Bruce Estates . . . were in several respects illegal and oppressive.'[43] Thus, although the report was not written in the form of a narrative, it can be construed as a contribution to the historiography of the Chilembwe milieu.

There was, of course, no attempt to portray Chilembwe as a martyr or a patriot; this was hardly to be expected of those who wrote from the standpoint of the colonial regime. Although the Commissioners showed some hesitation about Chilembwe's role in the events of early 1915 by saying that he 'appears to have instigated and organised' the Rising,[44] they were clear on its religio-political objects: 'the extermination or expulsion of the European population, and the setting up of a native state or theocracy of which John Chilembwe was to be head.'[45] The process behind this was the creation of independent African churches in the Protectorate. Chilembwe planned to 'form a union between their various sects and his own Mission . . . [and] succeeded in acquiring an ascendency over a number of native Churches particularly in the Zomba and Upper Shire Districts, which he turned to political account.'[46] To this internal religio-political factor, the Commissioners added an external one: that fusion of religion and politics which, in the first decade and a half of the twentieth century in southern and central Africa, had come to be known as Ethiopianism. 'A few emigrant natives had come into touch with Ethiopianism and shared Chilembwe's aims. The rising may be said to have been an ebullition of the form of Ethiopianism which has as its watchword 'Africa for the Africans'; and aims at securing for the native sole political control.'[47]

Apart from the nature of the evidence at their disposal which enabled them to draw religio-political conclusions of this nature, the Commissioners had amongst their number a cleric who brought a real touch of the days of the Reformation, with its concatenation of religion and politics, into their midst. He was A. G. B. Glossop, High Anglican Archdeacon of the Universities Mission to Central Africa at Likoma. At one stage in the taking of evidence by the Commissioners, a theological debate broke out between him and the Rev. Robert Hellier Napier of the Church of Scotland Mission who had known Chilembwe well and whose correspondence with the leader of the P.I.M. was adduced as evidence.[48] Glossop subsequently set down his views very clearly in words which hark back to the Erastian opponents of the insurgent peasants and the Anabaptist elements in their midst in early sixteenth century Germany:

> 'The overwhelming majority of the boys led away by John Chilembwe [said Glossop] . . . were the type which prints and proclaims as chief doctrine, "the Bible the sole guide of truth and doctrine". This means that every half-educated native who can just read the Bible in the vernacular proceeds to prove everything and anything he likes from Ezekiel and Daniel. As a logical result, in practice, each teacher secedes from the other on any little pretext and forms a new so-called Church upon any private quarrel, and proves that he is right from Isaiah and the Apocalypse. The rebel easily proves to his own satisfaction—which is all that is required—that the powers that be are to be destroyed, that a new reign, when Christ will reign upon the earth, is immediately at hand, and there will be no Government and no taxes and no white man control'.[49]

What, of course, Glossop did not mention here was that, as with Europeans and Americans, the Bible, with its documentation of two intrinsically historical religions, Judaism and Christianity, has often been the start of historical study looking beyond tribal boundaries amongst the Africans of Malawi and elsewhere. Certainly, this was the case with Chilembwe. As Joseph Booth wrote to him about their early days together in Malawi in the 1890s: 'Have you forgotten the marvellous and unthinkable greatness of the promise of God to you in Isaiah 60 v. 22 which you rushed to show me, in your canoe, as I came up river to Katunga long ago?'[50] The Biblical verse in question, with its overtones of development and destiny, reads: 'A little one shall become a thousand, and a small one a strong nation. I the LORD will hasten it in his time.'

It would be wrong, however, to give the impression that the 1916 *Report* dwelt only on religio-political factors. Its succinctness conceals the many complicated issues which it saw behind Chilembwe and the 1915 Rising. A cursory reading of the *Report* might give the impression that, by saying that 'The rising was not general' and 'was not conduced by any general native grievance,' it was expressing the 'localized vendetta' interpretation of the Rising.[51] But it did indicate that Chilembwe's influence reached beyond the simple bounds of the Magomero section of the A. L. Bruce Estates. In sum, the 1916 *Report* is a complex work which well repays study, against the documentation of it which is now becoming available, not only for what it has to say about the Rising but as a contribution to the study of the place of John Chilembwe in Malawi historiography.

The same can hardly be said about the official history of the Protectorate which was attempted in the two editions of *A Handbook of Nyasaland* (London, 1922 and 1932) compiled by the Chief Clerk of the Government, S. S. Murray.

420

The government of Nyasaland, which had been eager to get at the truth of the Chilembwe Rising during an anxious period of war against the Germans in 1915, had, in the post-War period, consigned it to the category of things best forgotten. There were but three brief mentions of it in the two editions of the *Handbook*. The religious element, however, again featured in this official account: it was called 'the semi-religious rising in January, 1915'[52] and was declared to be 'promoted by a native religious sect professing Ethiopianism,'[53] although Ethiopianism was never explained. But the *Handbook* did provide one detail which was not mentioned in the 1916 *Report*: it declared that the attack on Magomero 'was intended to synchronize with similar action on the part of the adherents of this sect in other parts of the Protectorate.'[54] It is probable that this is a reference, amongst other things, to the abortive rising under Filipo Chinyama at Ncheu—which still remains one of the most difficult and important questions of the Rising awaiting detailed study.

From the point of view of the government, therefore, the history of the Chilembwe Rising had not received the treatment it deserved in the two decades after 1915. (For all its value, the *Report* of 1916 had not been primarily historical. Indeed, it seems that it, too, attempted to cover up what had happened, although the urgency of doing something about clearly manifested African grievances in a time of war meant that much of historical and historiographical significance leaked out in the Commissioner's *Report* in 1916.) It was left to an ex-government servant, in the aftermath of the Rising, to supply the most considered account and analysis of it which was to be published until the period after the Second World War.

He was Dr Norman Leys, a Government medical officer. Leys served from 1905 in the East African Protectorate but was transferred from there to Nyasaland in 1913 because of his attempts to prevent alienation of Masai land to white settlers.[55] The action was typical of him. During his five years in the medical service in Nyasaland he noted the clash between European and African interests; and he made use of his observations after the war when, in 1924, he produced the first edition of his book *Kenya* in which he warned of the troubles to come for the colonial regime if it did not prevent the entrenchment of white settler privileges and did not open up educational and economic opportunities to Africans. Leys had served in Nyasaland throughout the period of the Chilembwe Rising; and he looked upon it as a warning of what was to come in Kenya if the system under which colonialism operated were not changed. He devoted a brief chapter of ten pages to it in his *Kenya* under the title of 'A Minor Rebellion in Nyasaland'. In spite of its brevity, his account of the 1915 Rising was based on thorough research. In addition to his own socially-conscious observations, particularly his interviews with many of the survivors of the Rising who were in prison in Zomba, Leys drew upon the 1916 *Report*; and 'got most valuable information' from the Rev. Robert Hellier Napier 'who knew Chilembwe better than any other European.'[56] Leys obviously used Napier's evidence in a very different way from Archdeacon Glossop on the Commission of Inquiry. Indeed, the different approaches to Napier by the two men, as reflected in the 1916 *Report* and in Leys' Chilembwe chapter, are in themselves interesting minor episodes in the study of the place of Chilembwe in Malawi historiography.

Leys saw the Rising as something very different from the traditional tribal rising against European authority. After a brief account of the growth of European estates in Nyasaland and a succinct note on Chilembwe and his trip to America, Leys discusses his growing embitterment at the treatment he received from Europeans on his return home. Leys then proceeds to describe the growth of Chilembwe as a 'deliverer' of his people on Old Testament lines. (Leys' emphasis here on the Old Testament is, no doubt, true in the main. But it does disguise Chilembwe's use of liberatory aspects of the New Testament— at least, as he envisaged them: for example, as Stephen Kundecha indicated, his employment of John VIII, 32, ('Ye shall know the truth, and the truth shall make you free',) to sound out Kundecha as a possible supporter in his conspiracy.)[57]

Leys' account of the organization and course of the Rising contains, in addition to the usual details, a number of interesting points. He speaks of Chilembwe's sounding 'some of the chiefs of the surrounding tribes, many of whom seem to have promised support without intending to give it':[58] an assertion which has never received the detailed examination that it deserves. Unlike the 1916 *Report*, Leys does not display Chilembwe as set on the total extinction or expulsion of Europeans in the Protectorate. 'A few, men and women, were to be allowed to remain as teachers, but without political authority.'[59] And he concludes his account of the Rising with something approaching a picture of the frustrated Chilembwe which seems to look forward to what could be a trend in the future historiography of the Rising: the attempt to interpret Chilembwe and his followers in psychological terms.[60] At the end, says Leys, 'Chilembwe himself, old, nearly blind and, some say, insane, was shot down in the long grass with most of the ring-leaders.'[61]

Like most writers on the Rising, in his day and since, it could be argued that Leys seemed to find some difficulty in deciding what the Rising was all about. He speaks of Chilembwe's having a 'plan to get the people on the estate to murder their masters, and then to bring about a general rebellion.'[62] Towards the end of his chapter, however, he supplements, if he does not contradict this claim, in his remark that Edmund 'Burke's statement that rebellion does not arise from a desire for change but from the impossibility of suffering more is by no means always true of rebellion in Europe, but it is certainly true of rebellion in Africa.'[63]

Unfortunately, Norman Leys was writing his account of the Chilembwe Rising in order to throw light on possible future developments in Kenya. With his undoubted knowledge of the contemporary Nyasaland scene, one regrets that he did not write more directly on the Rising, and that he did not, apparently, leave any papers on it. Leys did, however, write on 7 February 1918 a thirty-three-page, foolscap, closely-typed letter to the Secretary of State for the Colonies in London[64] which adumbrates his book, *Kenya*, of four years later. In the sixth section of this letter, he wrote an account of Chilembwe and the Rising which, although it anticipates some of Leys' remarks in his Chilembwe chapter in *Kenya*, is an independent statement which also has its place in the early historiography of the Rising. In his unpublished account, Norman

Leys indulged a taste for comparative history which does not appear in his book. Speaking of the decapitation of the manager of the A. L. Bruce Estates, Leys declares that Chilembwe 'mutilated his chief victim, and although this would suggest criminal lunacy in a civilized community, it is more likely to have been a reminiscence of certain incidents in the Old Testament, or even possibly of such State executions in our own history as the execution of Sir Thomas More or of the Earl of Strafford.'[65] Leys, furthermore, comes out with a statement on Chilembwe's motives which partially anticipates George Simeon Mwase's picture of the martyr-patriot: 'Chilembwe's attraction to his followers was, his ability aside, his claim to be a Christian and a patriot. It is highly probable he believed himself to be both.'[66] And towards the end of his long letter, Norman Leys provides a personal anecdote, not to be found elsewhere, which is well worth a place in the history of the Chilembwe milieu:

' A certain officer once told me [writes Leys] that he had a correspondence with John Chilembwe. Misled by the style of the letters he at first answered them as he would have answered the letters of a European. But, as he told me, when he learned who his correspondent was, he soon put him in his place. That officer had his share in the rising. There are few of us who have lived in these parts who have not had some share.'[67]

At the conclusion of this 1918 letter, Norman Leys, signing himself off as 'Medical Officer, Nyasaland', wrote a poignant paragraph which seems to look forward not only to the new historiography of John Chilembwe and the 1915 Rising, which started as colonialism in Africa was drawing to its close, but which may be construed as casting an eye towards Frantz Fanon and the therapeutic theory of violence in the Third World of the 1960s:

'In a standard book upon Nyasaland the native is described as a person most wisely treated like a dog to which one has the friendliest of feelings, wayward, quarrelsome, but happy when fed, obedient under discipline, submissive to direction because incapable of self-direction. It would be a hypocrisy to pretend that such a conception of native mentality had not been influential and even prevalent among those who have hitherto had the direction and shaped the policy of our governments. In permitting it to continue to influence events our country encourages the one means that, unfortunately, man can always use to prove that he is not canine but human, not slave but free, the murder of his master. To that expiation the war has brought our countrymen in these parts very near.'[68]

With the production shortly after the Great War of Norman Leys' accounts and analyses of the Chilembwe Rising, and the picture of it and its leader in George Simeon Mwase's book written on the eve of the Depression of the 1930s, two decades of perusing and probing into one of the most complicated and fascinating movements of transitional Africa and emergent Malawi came to a close. As I have suggested, we can see in these early historiographical attempts not only records but also interpretations of the Chilembwe milieu and what it would come to mean for the Malawi of the future. They indicate the emergence of a controversy in the historiography of Malawi similar to that which has been growing in Canadian historical scholarship around the figure of the métis leader, Louis Riel, since he organized his provisional government in Manitoba at the beginning of 1870; executed a white man two months later; was driven into exile by British military forces; and, after returning to lead a rebellion in Saskatchewan in 1885, was captured and hung. Will Malawi historians of the future say of Chilembwe, as a Canadian historian has declared of Riel, that he 'was not a great man; he was not even what Carlyle would call a near great. Nevertheless, he became, in death, one of the decisive figures of our history'?[69]

FOOTNOTES

1 *Life and Work in British Central Africa* (Blantyre), **47**, January, 1893, 4.

2 *Report of the Third General Missionary Conference of Nyasaland held at Mvera, 30th July to 7th August, 1910,* (Blantyre, 1910), 20.

3 Ibid., 27.

4 *The Nyasaland United Missionary Conference. Report of the Meetings held at the Livingstonia Missionary Institution, British Central Africa, October 12–20, 1900* (Livingstonia, 1901), 51.

5 *Life and Work. Blantyre Mission Supplement*, January 1890, 2.

6 George Shepperson and Thomas Price, *Independent African* (Edinburgh 1958), 234–5.

7 Because of the fifty-year rule then operated by the Public Record Office, London, this evidence was not available to George Shepperson and Thomas Price, when they were making their study of John Chilembwe in the 1950s. It is, however, now available in C.O. 525/66. *Nyasaland 1916. Vol. 1:* Nyasaland Native Rising. Commission of Inquiry, 217–664. Unfortunately this is a copy only of the oral evidence and some written statements presented to the Commissioners and does not contain the supplementary documents, (papers, books, pamphlets, magazines, etc.). It is likely that these were destroyed in the Secretariat fire at Zomba in 1919.

8 In the transcript of evidence in C.O. 525/66. *Nyasaland 1916. Vol. 1,* op. cit., Namate's name is mis-spelt as 'Namato'. I am grateful to Professor B. Pachai, whose researches have established beyond doubt that the real surname is 'Namate', for drawing my attention to this error.

9 C.O. 525/66, op. cit., 412.

10 Ibid., 412.

11 Ibid., 413.

12 Ibid., 413.

13 These suggest that it would be worth attempting to trace any of his papers and publications, however casual. Kundecha published a short series of notes entitled 'Mohammedanism in Nyasaland' in *Life and Work* (Edinburgh), **34**, May 1912, 153; and he may well have other short but significant publications to his credit.

14 C.O. 525/66, op. cit.,

15 Ibid., 458–61.

16 *Report of the Commission . . . to inquire into . . . the Native Rising within the Nyasaland Protectorate* (Zomba, 6819, 1916), 6–7.

17 C.O.525/66, op. cit., 462.

18 Ibid., 460.

19 Ibid., 464.

20 Ibid., 454–5.

21 Harry K. Matecheta, *Blantyre Mission. Nkhani za Ciyambi Cace* (Blantyre 1951), 26. Harry Kambwiri's essay (translated into English by Alexander Hetherwick) appeared as 'An essay on the Useful Trees of British Central Africa' in Harry H. Johnston's *British Central Africa* (London 1898), 227–232. Johnston graciously acknowledged it in the preface (xi) where he said, 'It is pleasant to think that one of my collaborators in this work is a native of British Central Africa.'

22 C.O. 525/66, op. cit., 531.

23 For sources of Harry Kambwiri Matecheta's life, see ibid., 524–37 and 563; Matecheta, op. cit.; and Clement Harry Matecheta, *The African Missionary* (unpaginated, unpublished copy in the possession of George Shepperson).

24 C.O. 525/66, op. cit., 534.

25 Ibid., 536.

26 Ibid., 536.

27 The influence of the life of—and lives of—David Livingstone on Africans of the generation of Harry Kambwiri Matecheta and John Chilembwe is a subject worthy of study. John Chilembwe is known to have possessed another popular biography of Livingstone: H. G. Adams, *David Living-stone. The Weaver Boy Who Became a Missionary* (London 1895). It was given to him shortly before he left America to return home by a 'Miss Bailey', presumably one of his teachers at the Afro-American Virginia Theological Seminary and College. It may be significant for the subsequent, tragic career of John Chilembwe that, in her inscription to John Chilembwe on the fly-leaf of this life of Livingstone, Miss Bailey referred to 'John 15.12–14,' verse 13 of which reads, 'Greater love hath no man than this, that a man lay down his life for his friends.' (I am grateful to Mr P. V. Turner, librarian of the Malawi Society, for drawing my attention to this book which was found in John Chilembwe's house by Aubrey M. D. Turnbull, Assistant Chief Secretary, Nyasaland, in 1915.)

28 C.O. 525/66, op. cit., 536.

29 Ibid., 536.

30 Ibid., 537.

31 Harry K. Matecheta, op. cit., 27.

32 For Chisuse's photographs of the Chilembwe milieu see Shepperson and Price, op cit., Plates 3, 10, 13(a), 14, 15(a), 16, 17 (a) and (b), 18, 19, 21, and 25.

33 C.O. 525/66, op. cit., 641.

34 Ibid., 641.

35 See the questioning of Kamwana by the Commissioners on 15 July 1915, C.O. 525/66, op. cit., 565–79, especially 574–5.

36 Ibid., 664.

37 George Simeon Mwase, *Strike a Blow and Die. A Narrative of Race Relations in Colonial Africa* (Cambridge, Mass., 1967), edited and introduced by Robert I. Rotberg, 5.

38 Ibid., 1–80.

39 Ibid., 29. Compare here the perceptive review of Mwase's book by Mr A. Atmore in *African Affairs* (London), 69, 276, July 1970, 303.

40 Ibid., 80.

41 Ibid., 58.

42 Cf. Ibid., 22. The original is in the possession of George Shepperson. It is handwritten and unpublished.

43 *Report*, op. cit., 6.

44 Ibid., 4.

45 Ibid., 6.

46 Ibid., 5.

47 Ibid., 6.

48 C.O. 525/66, op. cit., 477–80: Napier expressed himself strongly by saying 'I am sent here as a messenger of the Reformed Church.'

49 *Central Africa* (London), **34**, 1916, 178–9.

50 Public Record Office, London, C.O. 525/61: in letter of Joseph Booth to John Chilembwe, Sea Point, Capetown, Dec. 10, 1911, enclosed with Governor G. Smith to Secretary of State for the Colonies, Zomba, 29 May 1916.

51 *Report*, op. cit., 6, paragraphs 15 and 21.

52 1922 edition: 23; 1932 edition, 34.

53 1922 ed.: 269; 1932 ed., 422.

54 Ibid., 269 and 422 respectively. The third reference was purely a tribute to the work of the European Volunteer Force in February 1915 in helping to put down the Rising: 263 and 429 respectively.

55 See G. H. Mungeam, *British Rule in Kenya, 1895–1912* (Oxford, 1966), 261; George Bennett, *Kenya. A Political History* (Oxford 1963), 33–4 and 58; P.R.O., London C.O. 533/330: E. D. Denham, Colonial Secretary of Kenya, 27 March 1925.

56 Norman Leys, *Kenya* (London 1924), 327. To appreciate this statement by Leys, one must go to C.O. 525/66, op. cit., to the corpus of Napier's evidence given to the Commissioners on 5 July 1915 (466–485) and not to the best-known source on Napier: Alexander Hetherwick, ed., *Robert Hellier Napier in Nyasaland* (Edinburgh, 1925), where there are only three

brief references to Napier, Chilembwe and the Rising (69, 91–3 and 97). Hetherwick seems to have been concerned in the two decades after 1915 with playing down public discussion of Chilembwe and the Rising. Hence, he may be considered to qualify only negatively in any examination of his role in the historiography of Chilembwe at this time: compare his book, *The Romance of Blantyre* (London, undated), 213–14, for a brief account of the Rising in which Chilembwe is not even mentioned by name.

57 C.O. 525/66, op. cit., 454. Compare the reference to John's Gospel in 27 above.

58 Leys, op. cit., 328–9.

59 Ibid., 329.

60 The importance of psychology for the study of Chilembwe was emphasized by D. A. Low in 'Studying the Transformation of Africa', *Com. Stud. Soc. Hist.*, 7 (1), 1964, 26; and has recently been developed by Robert I. Rotberg in 'Psychological Stress and the Question of Identity: Chilembwe's Revolt Reconsidered,' *Power and Protest in Black Africa* (New York 1970), edited by Robert I. Rotberg and Ali A. Mazrui, 337–373.

61 Leys, op. cit., 329.

62 Ibid., 329.

63 Ibid., 333.

64 The letter is headed with the address, 2 Clarence Drive, Glasgow. Leys probably had a typed copy or copies of it made to circulate to persons on whom he wished to impress his anti-colonialist views. I am grateful to Professor D. A. Low of the University of Sussex, who was given a copy of it by the late Canon Hooper of the C.M.S., for providing me with a copy of this valuable document.

65 Leys letter of 7 February 1918, Hooper copy, 22.

66 Ibid., 22.

67 Ibid., 32.

68 Ibid., 33.

69 G. F. G. Stanley, *Louis Riel: Patriot or Rebel* (Canadian Historical Association Historical Booklet No. 2, Ottawa, 1967), 24.

24 Development and change in the history of Malawi

M. L. Chanock

> '*Yet I doubt not, thro' the ages one increasing purpose runs*'
> Tennyson.

I

The argument of this paper is that an overemphasis on unilinear development and directional change in recent writing on African history has produced an historiographical model which is not applicable to Malawi.[1] African historians pride themselves on being *au fait* with many related disciplines, in particular the social sciences, and this is clearly one influence which directs us to the study of change. In addition, Christianity and Commerce have given way to Nationalism and Development as the catchwords which embody Africa's goals, and the language of the economists, with its insistence on 'growth' and 'development', has come to have a pervasively dominant position in our thoughts. But the most important reason for this emphasis is that late Victorian Imperialism and its colonial aftermath gave rise to an enormous body of evolutionary writing about Africa. African society was judged and found wanting; it was static; it had not climbed the ladder of progress as the Anglo-Saxons had done; only the colonial era inaugurated a period of civilizing transformation. That there should have been a reaction against this kind of writing is not surprising. What is surprising is that there has been an acceptance of the premises on which it was based—an insistence that there was just such a pattern of indigenous African evolution. The new history is not satisfied with events, it seeks for, and finds, patterns of purposive and directional change. African history books are illustrated by pictures of pre-colonial towns, by examples of the complexity of African manufactures, by the regalia of African states; and the literature of African political science is adorned with pictures of irrigation projects, schools, industries and polling stations. We insist upon a rich and complex past and we desire a 'modernized' future. As historians we know the importance of continuity. What is more natural than that the new history should present a story of steady evolution emphasizing those modernizing elements whose historical role it is to carry Africa into an industrial future?

II

'History', writes Davidson, 'is the story of change and development.'[2] The notions of change and development are closely interlinked. When Trevor-Roper wrote of '. . . the unrewarding gyrations of barbarous tribes in picturesque but irrelevant corners of the globe'[3] he was not denying that Africa had a past but that it had a history which was significant and relevant to the modern world, that it had a history of progressive growth. Change might well be constant but it was not meaningful unless it was 'purposive movement'. Similarly Marx, when approaching the problem of Asian history, would give weight only to progressive change. Events were continually happening but history was not. Asian states show, he wrote '. . . an unchanging social infrastructure coupled with an increasing change in the persons and tribes who manage to ascribe to themselves the political superstructure.'[4] This meant that 'Indian society . . . has no history at all, at least no known history. What we call its history is but the history of the successive invaders who founded their empires on the passive basis of that unresisting and unchanging society.'[5]

Both Marx and Trevor-Roper thus combine stasis with anarchy in their description of the pre-colonial past of non-European societies, and both were at least clear that this class of happening was not history. African historians have rejected this picture of the past but their rejection has not been one which questions the connection of change with development—the hierarchy in which some history is historical and some is not. They have accepted this particular definition of history. What has been done rather is to assert the progressive nature of change in the African past. Examples of this kind of approach are easy to find. Omer-Cooper writes of the *Mfecane* that '. . . far from being a matter of whirling bands of barbarians . . . it was essentially a process of positive political change.'[6] He is praised for this approach by Marks who avers that 'Omer-Cooper, who is attuned to current African historiographical approaches . . . has been able to see behind the destructive impact of the *Mfecane* many of its remarkable and positive achievements.'[7] Roberts writes: 'In place of the old myth that the African past was more or less static, or at best repetitive, we have to acknowledge a continuous process of social and political innovation, economic improvement and technical change.'[8] Iliffe says that 'The re-appraisal is part of an attempt to re-establish the reality and meaningfulness of change in the African past.'[9] 'Reality' and 'meaningfulness' are linked by Ogot with a developmental process which culminates in 'civilization'. Africa used to be regarded as a dark continent, he writes, 'Isolated from the stream of world history it was supposed life had no meaning and purpose . . . (historical events) were unco-ordinated and purposeless, and consequently there was no development and hence no civilization.'[10] The new view is of course the reverse of this: events in the African past had co-ordination and purpose which led to development and civilization.

What this civilization is, and what constitutes modernity, the goal of development, is clearly enunciated by Davidson when he remarks of pre-colonial Kenya: 'This was very far from being a modern civilization. It had no machines, or factories, or modern methods of production.'[11] Involvement with current efforts to produce this kind of civilization has also led to an instrumental approach. Ranger has called for a developmental history in order to give an historical dimension to developmental studies and which would concentrate on change because this would show what '. . . history has to teach about the cultural flexibility of African peoples.'[12]

There is also a strong strand of evolutionism which is not only universalist and unilinear but also competitive. As there is but one path of human development history can be looked upon as an inter-societal race for progress. Oliver appears to be a competitive universalist. The Islamic African world, he writes, 'was ahead of' medieval Europe but in the seventeenth and eighteenth centuries Europe 'drew ahead'.[13] Things do sometimes go wrong—'many technical as well as political advances spread southward into tropical Africa . . . the trend was not always, however, progressive'—but there is little doubt that there is a right direction—'. . . the things of Europe triumphed because they represented the mainstream of human progress.'[14] Both technical and political changes seem to be measurable by the same progressive yardstick. This is an attitude akin to that of the Victorian evolutionists and to that of the development economists. Hunter, for example, writes '. . . there is a single direction of change which is applicable whether the process is far advanced or barely started, and for all the variations of custom and environment and influence, it always moves one way.'[15]

Two further general trends in African historiography must be noted before I turn to Malawi. The first is the still sturdy survival of the fascination with large scale states and the acceptance that their development is a stage in a common line of progression. Drum and trumpet history, from which the late Victorians were already freeing themselves, has been reborn. Davidson talks of the 'main lines . . . the lines of major change and development, of the rise and fall of states, of the folly and wisdom of Kings.'[16] The fact that new West African history was written before new East and Central African history was clearly a factor in shaping the course the writing of the latter would take. 'It is always a pleasure,' Burton wrote, 'after travelling through the semi-republican tribes of Africa, to arrive at the headquarters of a strong and sanguinary despotism. Only those who have lived in Africa can understand how it is so.'[17] Many historians have obviously shared Burton's pleasure. Conquest states, military states, or trading states, based upon a ruling warrior class or an elite whose power grows through control of trade are all, it seems, on the side of progress, and the oppression or exploitation which their activities involved, though not ignored, is of secondary importance to their 'achievements'.

The reason for this appears to be a concentration on present problems and future possibilities. Iliffe writes '. . . a modern and effective African society must also be one enlarged in scale.'[18] Enlargers of scale were therefore making 'political advances' because they were on the side of modernity. This emphasis is an integral part of a broader evolutionism. Ogot, for example, writes 'We see thus that one of the major results of the intrusion of the Bantu in East Africa was the gradual replacement of the hunter by the cultivator . . .' (so far so good) '. . . that is their arrival marked the transition from the hunting stage to the cultivating stage of civilization.'[19] This leap from statement to

431

theory is made in order to demonstrate that the triumph of the cultivators represented not only an economic change but also a political advance: the creation of 'larger and more integrated societies with more complex social institutions', and this was of importance (and we are back to present values) because African capacity to resist and withstand colonialism was strengthened. Marks interprets early nineteenth century Zulu history in terms of Shaka's achievement in state building, and Thompson remarks of subsequent developments that the '. . . Ndebele and Ngoni kingdoms regressed in different ways towards the decentralized norms of the traditional Nguni political system.'[20] State building therefore, by Nguni and even British imperialists, is a progressive development. Oliver concludes the *History of East Africa* by writing: 'For the integration of Africa with the general progress of man in the world outside, a drastic simplification of the old political diversity was an inescapable necessity.'[21] This process is seen finally as the forerunner of an indubitably progressive nationalism. As Davidson puts it—the new nations would be 'much more able to make progress' than the small communities of the past.[22]

A second factor on which comment should be made is the uniformity of the new history. There is a search for 'unifying themes' which does not of course involve writing out the differences between different historical situations, but is defined as a '. . . unity of approach (which) can be achieved by asking the same questions rather than by obtaining the same answers . . . a whole series of questions are asked again and again.'[23] By asking the same questions, by presupposing that the same problems are relevant, one is clearly imposing a pattern on the answers and in many situations highlighting artificially chosen factors. Part of the reason for uniformitarian pattern making is the lack of adequate 'subjective' evidence. '*Verstehen*' is missing. We often lack, therefore, a real sense of causality and historians have taken to manipulating their subjects into comprehensible and coherent patterns. Gray remarks that concentration on African initiative as the key to African history '. . . is the hardest to manipulate'.[24] The imposing of a pattern is very common in the historiography of African nationalism. Coleman, for example, starts with some '. . . fundamental assumptions. One is that the people of Nigeria are essentially not unlike other peoples. Another is that the most fruitful method of enquiry will be to look first for those underlying social changes that have precipitated nationalist movements in Europe and Asia. The discovery of uniformities and recurring patterns is not only of historical significance; it is also the fascinating aspect of the study of history.'[25] All historians do organize their material thematically: what is to be noted here is the need to show that African political development has followed the same lines as that of Europe and Asia. The notions of uniformity and social evolution are one; as Davidson has it '. . . the same basic lines of growth and expansion run through all these centuries.'[26]

The portrayal of an indigenous progressive developmental pattern in precolonial Africa means regarding the colonial period not merely as an 'administrative interlude' but as a pathological interruption. Of the nineteenth century crisis in East and Central Africa, Davidson writes that new forms of peace and unity would have been found if the colonialists had not come '. . . breaking into African development for more than half a century.'[27] Discussing the problem of state formation in nineteenth century Malawi, Langworthy and Omer-Cooper tell us that 'This process was not permitted to proceed to its logical conclusion.'[28] Whether the logical conclusion was increased anarchy or new forms of peace and unity is not clear from this text but in some cases analysis includes explicitly directional values. As Ajayi remarks '. . . the colonial regime tended usually to ally with the most conservative elements in society and to arrest the normal process of social and political change.'[29]

Ajayi sees the new history in terms of 'an ideological answer to Imperialism.'[30] But writing history in terms of progress and development is a European and not an African thing to do. African historiography tended to be narrative, annalistic or cyclical[31] and Hegelian canons and modernizing values are part of the colonial heritage, not a part of Africa's view of its past. This adoption of 'modernization ideals' is not limited to African historiography. Myrdal notes how in post colonial South Asia the intellectual elite has searched the past for indigenous cultural roots and manipulable nationalist symbols. 'Knowledge of pre-colonial history is usually so shaky,' he writes, 'that it lends itself even better to a rationalisation of modernisation ideals.'[32] The new history arises from the existence of the new nation states, legitimizes the claims of their ruling classes to power and justifies the policies they wish to pursue.[33] It is a result also of a general rejection of both the recent past and the present. The new nationalism wants two things: first 'roots'—a sense of historical continuity; secondly, change—towards an economically developed future. An evolutionary history meets both these needs. Rejection of the present and desire for a past and a future combine to produce a picture of evolutionary progression.

The role of history in European culture as a legitimizer of nation states and rulers has long been recognized. History has also been, more often than not, the most conservative of the social sciences, concerned with continuities and survivals and emphasizing these as a weapon against social engineering—a means by which to demonstrate the impossibility of the changes demanded by those who want to upset the *status quo*. African history however must serve those who want change. This has been called a 'transition from colonial to radical history'[34] but change can be a ruling class interest as much as conservation can be. Radical history in Europe is, among liberal historians, the history of injustice and oppression, among Marxists, working class history. Radical history in Africa is rather different. I have noted the concentration on the skills and achievements of state builders rather than the travails of those built upon. But more important is the evocation of continuity, not to emphasize the need to preserve, as in European conservative history, but to underline the need for change. Lonsdale writes: 'the recapture of the past is essential to the building of the new society' and talks of 'modern African states reaching back . . . to recover elements of a former political dynamic.'[35] The desire of the radicals to give their modernizing ideology indigenous roots is all the more comprehensible since the transformation they desire involves to a large degree a continuation and intensification of the alien pressures introduced by European domination.

The result has been the concentration of historians on the 'modernizing'

433

elements, the 'new men', the precursors of today's rulers. The colonialists, say Oliver and Atmore, '. . . ignored the new men on whom the future of Africa was really to depend.'[36] This 'mistake' is no longer made. The identification of change and 'modernization' have led to a ransacking of the past for predecessors, a concentration on the groups which appear to have been pointing in the right direction. In colonial times modernization used to be defined in terms of progress towards individual land tenure and the acceptance of the moral value of work—especially work for Europeans on farms or in mines or industry. It is still defined in terms of acceptance of industrial society though if and when socialism succeeds capitalism as the most modern of goals is never clear. On occasion political as well as economic values are part of the definition. Lonsdale writes that we must not assume that only acculturated Africans desired modernization but must regard it as a more widespread desire. Moreover it is not merely a desire for modern goods but '. . . modernisation means the broadening of popular participation in the decision making process.'[37]

There is then a certain pattern evident in the history of Africa which has been published in the last decade—a pattern which is found in works on Malawian history. By drawing attention to the emphasis on evolutionary change I have not, I think, merely produced a catalogue of innocent use of metaphor. Our understanding of recent Malawian history is out of focus. We focus on the role of the educated elite in a peasant dominated country; on the influence of urbanization in a country with no cities; on the influence of industrialization in the most rural part of Central Africa. The same kind of historical writing has been evident in the huge body of literature on Nigeria and Ghana which failed to give due weight to those social forces whose values were not the same as those of the historians. To understand the historical processes in this part of Central Africa we need to look at what has happened without interpreting it in the light of what we would like to come about.

III

Like other areas of Africa Malawi was judged and found wanting by the colonial evolutionists. Examples from the main 'authorities' will suffice. Hetherwick wrote 'Africa stood still while the great human world outside was generation upon generation developing.' He was a firm believer in the total inability of Africans to innovate and in the static and unchanging tenor of life in the African village, (though it is a pleasant relief to note that the monotony of village life was broken by 'recurrent saturnalia').[38] He found in Malawi a 'stagnant pool' in which minimum use of resources was made; in thought, culture, arts and crafts he judged Malawians to be quite unfit to meet 'the coming changes' in their environment. The new converts alone made efforts, 'pathetic in their simplicity', to approach 'a civilized way of life'. Examples of evolutionary thinking by other missionaries are not hard to find—(it was even suggested that 'For centuries past . . . the trend of the Negro has been a retrograde one . . . a backward rather than a forward movement . . .')[39]—and

434

their views were shared by the administrators. Harry Johnston's views are well known. Africans '. . . wallow in their half animal existence'; the task of the colonial rulers was '. . . deliberately (to) raise the races of our backward fellow men out of the Stone Age into the Age of Steel.'[40] Ross says that the Blantyre Mission and the Administration had fundamental differences of principle. He explains: 'The issue of principle was twofold: first, was the African of the day capable of becoming a responsible and civilized individual, and secondly, was African culture capable of being the foundation of modern development?'[41] How to promote progress was at issue, not a difference as to what progress was. Not only Europeans held these views. Others also believed that colonialism was bringing about a desirable transformation. In 1920 Yesaya Chibambo saw the country as being '. . . in a new era with a new life, new knowledge, new resolutions, new laws and new customs which can be learnt through education . . .' and went on '. . . it would be foolish and ridiculous if the people of this country dislike the new civilisation.'[42]

Views of this sort are to be expected of missionaries, pro-consuls and deracinated new men but it is strange to find present day historians of Malawi with similar attitudes. Books on Malawi have been judged according to whether or not they contribute to a general evolutionary picture. For example Hanna is criticized for contending that before the colonial era people '. . . were making no progress towards evolving a civilization of their own' not by questioning the assumptions behind the statement but by counter assertion. The same critic praises Wills because '. . . the picture of hard fought development that he presents is far closer to the findings of modern scholarship than the stereotype of pre-colonial stagnation which has previously been presented in some works of this kind.'[43] The belief that Christianity and Commerce were roads to progress still runs through the writing of the history of the colonial era. Referring to the so-called diaspora Pachai writes 'Whether one speaks of race relations, of culture contacts, of economic development, of social mobility, of political social and occupational sophistication, one sees generally in the men who return from a spell of work outside . . . the stamp of progress.' He then goes on to give two typical examples of what he feels to be 'the agency of progress; these are Chilembwe's attempt to enter the field of European Commerce and D. S. Malekebu's ('. . . his words re-echo the soundings of continuous progress') conversion of 17,000 souls between 1926 and 1938.[44] Pachai's adoption of Livingstone's criteria of advancement is complete and explicit.

The present general scenario of Malawian history is one of innovating precolonial society forming states, engaging in long distance trade, set back a little by colonial conquest which, however, planted the seeds of its own undoing because the missionaries and migrant labour system gave rise to a new forward looking class which sired Malawian nationalism. A caricature perhaps but it outlines the elements of the current interpretation. In the colonial era the missions and the system of migrant labour are generally seen as the most important of the modernizing agencies. Ross writes of the early part of the century 'there was . . . a great deal of change. By the early 1920s Malawi society had settled into a new shape. The dominant group by then was a new elite of

educated clerks, teachers and pastors, all with Protestant Church backgrounds
... although few towns grew to any size in Malawi the impact of urbanization
on life was early and widely felt ...'[45] This kind of analysis, the result of an
evolutionary framework which has given rise to an historiography of optimism
(the latter itself a most Victorian characteristic) is an impediment to the understanding of the political processes of twentieth century Malawi. Could we not
construct an alternative model: one which would not force the changes which
have taken place into a value based version of modernity; one which would
de-modernize the Christians, de-politicise Independency and stress the cohesion which the migrant system helped to preserve. We would then be able to
regard the nationalist movement, for example, for what it was—a mass movement in a peasant country—and to depart from our fascination with the
rhetoric of the 'new men' and examine the reactions of the 'old'.

We are still, *au fond*, victims of the image which the missions had of themselves and accept the missionary assumption that Christianity was a 'modernizing' religion. To Oliver the missions were both agents of and handmaidens
to inevitable change: 'Christianity had not so much to drive out the old gods,
which were already doomed, as to temper by industrial and religious education
a social and economic revolution inexorably pressing in from the outside at a
rate which threatened to be physically and morally overwhelming.'[46] Oliver
and Atmore write: 'The mission school soon emerged as a clear avenue for
advancement along which the ambitious could escape from the narrow discipline of village life into a wider world ... (missions) were introducing Africans
into the modern world into which they were now entering.'[47] For most in
Malawi, of course, a rural mission school provided bare literacy and the 'escape' was to the Rhodesian farm or mine compound. How much wider a world
this was is worth thinking about. Historians of Malawi's missions have concentrated on the role of the Scots missions in producing an 'elite'. The Catholic
and Dutch Reformed missions which did not play this role have been ignored.

McCracken has written that the lakeside Tonga turned in the 1880s 'to the
education supplied by Livingstonia in order to obtain the necessary techniques
for grappling with the new Shire highlands based western economy.'[48] In
highlighting this motive McCracken is emphasizing the degree of comprehen-
sion of the new environment which Malawians had and this, according to his
account, is followed by increasing efforts to control this new environment—the
'new men' 'taking the process of betterment into their own hands.'[49] The
emphasis, then, on the reception of both Christianity and education is that it
was a part of a forward looking understanding of modernity. The religion of
the missionaries, however, was one among many and I think it worth looking
more closely at the spirit in which the old superstitions were rejected for new
ones. Livingstone observed that 'Many expected to be transformed at once
into civilized men possessing the clothing, goods, arms, horses and waggons
of the more favoured portions of humanity.'[50] Many missionaries have testi-
fied that many converts regarded the Bible as a magical key to a new life and
indeed it was not unusual for missionaries to present the Bible as a talisman.
'I showed them a Bible,' wrote Riddell of his first visit to Mombera's Ngoni,
'and told them that it was it that made our nation rich and powerful.'[51] This
436

was not the approach only of an isolated missionary. Lord Clarendon, then Her Majesty's Secretary of State for Foreign Affairs, gave to Livingstone before he set off on the Zambezi expedition an official letter in which Clarendon advised chiefs that 'as we have derived all our greatness from the divine religion which we received from heaven, it will be well if you consider it carefully when any of our people talk to you about it.'[52] A new magic which promised greater wealth or power, or understanding of the supernatural, was embraced in place of the old: for many Christianity was thought to be a more powerful war medicine, for others 'pressure of dreams' and the desire for their interpretation was an important motive for conversion.[53]

Traces of a similar attitude towards writing, books and education can also be found. Gamitto comments of the Marave that 'they think that our method of communication by writing is magic.'[54] Donald Fraser, describing the visit of a headman to the mission house wrote: 'As he passes through the study and sees the shelves filled with books he is silent as in the presence of potential magic.'[55] While not insisting on the literal truth of this sort of testimony I think that we must reconsider the motives for embracing Christianity and education and ask whether instrumental motives are the right ones to emphasize. Education was a part of the missionaries' package; the main purpose of education was conversion; church and school usually occupied the same building and, particularly in the villages, a solitary mission teacher/evangelist combined the spiritual and temporal roles. How far then did people really distinguish between these component parts? Religion, and its book, the Bible, promised immediate spiritual, and in the eyes of many, material, benefits. Education and its books seemed to promise the same benefits with the same immediacy. People could not have understood how very far down the ladder of civilization the colonial world view placed them. They expected a rapid transformation and disillusionment showed itself as early as the 1890s and contributed to the growth of Independency, and years later even among those who had persevered—leading to accusations that Europeans '. . . frame[d] elaborate and complicated adverse systems as a means of retarding their deserved developments.'[56]

The rapid growth of Independency, instead of being regarded as a proto-nationalist reaction can be understood in these terms.[57] Ajayi has pointed out that the European conception of religion had become limited in the sense that religion was 'confined only to a special area of a man's life.'[58] But the Scots missionaries in particular transgressed the boundaries between the spiritual and the temporal; they acted as if Christian precepts regulated society and encouraged this belief in their converts. This was of course not the view of the men—the soldiers, administrators, planters and mine foremen—who moulded the world into which the converts moved. The converts found European institutions 'too cheaty, too thefty, too mockery'[59] because they failed to understand that Europe did not expect Christian principles to order the building of society. The profligation of churches, the splintering and mutation involved in the acceptance of the alien doctrine show both the trust in doctrine and the degree to which it was misunderstood. What can we say then of the 'first Christian generation' if we look at the Protectorate and the generation as a whole? A brief and intermittent acquaintance with a rural mission school and a puzzling and bruising contact with Christian hypocrisy did not produce men objectively capable of 'taking the process of betterment' into their own hands.[60] Perhaps the substance of what remained from contact with learning by rote, church discipline and biblical doctrine was a respect for the many new rules which had to be observed to achieve the promised rewards within the authoritarian structure of colonial society, rather than the provision of an ideological base for innovators.

In addition both churches and sects attracted large numbers of women. A good deal of the recent history of Africa has been written as if half the population did not exist, which is a curious feature in a body of literature so focussed on social change. We have so far been told little of the presence or absence of the progressive 'new women' in Malawi. The educational opportunities open to women were even more restricted than those for men. Women remained at home without that limited experience of a 'wider world' which migrancy gave some men—hedged around by an additional code of rules to which to conform. McCracken reports the observation of Major C. A. Edwards in 1897 that the girls school at Livingstonia '. . . called up visions of housekeepers and female servants in the days to come.'[61] Even the most innovating of missions did not make a startling attack on the position of women in society.

It was the most common of commonplaces among the colonial administrators and white regimes in Africa that the old order was disintegrating and usually this was regretted because it meant a decline of authority generally. (The various laments of Smuts and Lugard are good examples of this.) The recent history of Malawi has been written on the assumption that colonialism did have a disintegrative impact particularly because of the volume of migrant labour and this assumption acts as a baseline for interpretations which stress not only changes in village life but the important role of a diaspora in creating and spreading the new ideas of the new men. Audrey Richards testifies to an early hypersensitivity to the impact of colonialism: 'We had an extraordinary sense of haste,' she recalls, 'a feeling that the whole of an interesting social organization would be lost if we were not there quickly enough.' Extensive experience of societies under the impact of colonialism has made her think otherwise. 'To view colonial administration as a force attacking native society,' she writes, 'has perhaps caused too great a concentration on the disruptive processes and too little on the forces of integration which are also at work.'[62] I suggest that this last remark is apposite to the effect of labour migration in Malawi. Migration did contribute to economic change—but in those parts of Central and Southern Africa to which the migrants went—not in Malawi. A large proportion of the migrants, especially those from the central region, were men of little education who were migrant agricultural labourers; those who went to the towns found themselves in a most hostile environment where the lack of social and economic security perpetuated their attachment to the land from which they had come.[63] That the returning migrants had different ideas is no doubt true but South African mines and Rhodesian farms have, historically, shown little evidence of being radical hatching grounds. Even if the new ideas were eagerly innovatory rather than cautiously with-

438

drawing it seems an error to overemphasize peripheral new ideas at the expense of central old ones especially as the basis of the old society, production methods and land tenure, remained relatively unaffected. Soper wrote that one advantage of the migration system was that the men came back as 'agents of progress' but, as Sanderson points out, in peasant terms progress could only mean improved crop production and access to wider markets, which was precisely what the structure of which migration was a part prevented.[64] We have been taught to appreciate the complexity of the pre-colonial economy; given this complexity a slow influx of cash and new goods could easily be accommodated. Indeed the new goods which did come into the village were by and large cheaper and more convenient versions of things already in use and contained little of a transformatory nature.[65] Van Velsen points out the chronic internal labour shortage in Malawi in colonial times and remarks on it being paradoxical. But regular labour implied a commitment to a new life which people neither wanted nor needed, a commitment which was more unlikely to be made where it involved the low wages and unpleasant working conditions which Malawians found. Cash needs were more easily met through migrancy—from the refuge, as Watson puts it, the peasants raided the cash economy for goods.[66] As with religion we should not therefore overemphasize migrancy as a factor leading to a modernizing transformation. Migrancy impeded economic change and did not necessarily lead to new ideas replacing old ones. As Marwick pointed out the reverse could occur: where migrancy did lead to economic differentiation the resultant tensions bred an increase in belief in and accusations of sorcery.[67]

If we do not find transformation through external economic impact, what of indigenous evolution? Evolutionism is clearly apparent in the first stirrings of serious economic history of pre-colonial East and Central Africa. Gray and Birmingham write that the pre-colonial African economy was made up not of 'the inward looking units of a subsistence economy'—which they contrast with 'vigorous' modernity—but that in its complexity one can '. . . begin to discern a series of innovations which together constitute a mode of economic organisation midway between subsistence and a fully fledged market economy.'[68] Powerful metaphor accompanies their description of the stages through which African economies pass. In susbsistence economies 'The impulse towards innovation and economic specialisation is continually suppressed and shackled' while the professional trader, like the Victorian entrepreneur, is the hero of the economic past: 'Their achievements more perhaps than any other set of facts should effectively destroy the stereotype of a pre-colonial Africa prostrate and passive before the forces of the outside world.'[69] We ought to be very much on guard against creating an oversimplified straw model of a 'subsistence economy' and then regarding all elaborations on it as signs of evolution to a 'midway' stage. Livingstone related of Mang'anja economic life that 'In addition to working in iron and cotton and basket making they cultivate the soil intensively . . . Iron ore is dug out of the hills and its manufacture is a staple trade. Each village has its melting house, its charcoal burners and blacksmiths.'[70] Gamitto observed 'The Marave busy themselves for the most part with agriculture from which they gain their livelihood. Weavers, smiths and basket makers and those that practice other trades do so mostly for amusement rather than as a way of life.'[71] Both these descriptions show a complex economic life; both point to the centrality of agriculture; neither show the existence of a class whose prime activity was divorced from agriculture and neither observe a process of capital accumulation and investment. It could be that they describe a 'midway' stage but it is not clear how Gray and Birmingham would know that this is so. Marx was able to describe the very specialized Indian village economy without postulating that it was, of its own internal dynamic, in motion towards what he regarded as the next necessary stage.[72] However, as Gellner observes, the world at present is divided between the industrialized and '. . . the other people whose main characteristic is their capacity of becoming such.'[73] Some African historians therefore feel a need to demonstrate the capacity of nineteenth century African societies to industrialize. I do not think that this is something that a historian can do; we can deal only with what we know to have happened—the impact upon Africa of an alien form of industrialization based upon an alien technology. For industrial Africa *nos ancêtres* are *les Gaulois* and not *les Africains*.

Marx wrote to Engels in 1853 that the break up of Indian village life was the *sine qua non* for Europeanization (i.e. for change and development). 'Alone the tax gatherer was not the man to achieve this'; he wrote, 'the destruction of their archaic industry was necessary to deprive the villages of their self supporting character.'[74] Like any good evangelist we can build upon this piece of writ. In Malawi the nineteenth century invasions did not achieve it; nor did the slave trade; nor did religion; nor did education; nor did migrant labour. The new men—migrants, clerks and communicants—were not a new class. They formed a small group, many of whom were forced outside of the Malawian economy to make use of their new skills; and fascination with their mystified groping with the new world should not displace a sense of proportion as to their historical importance. The heart of the transformatory process lies elsewhere. It lies in the villages with the gradual change from a 'subsistence' to a market oriented peasantry.

The impatience of the new history has led it to concentrate its search for continuity on a continuing revolutionary tradition. We could look for it in more obvious areas. Authority also continues. Stokes has noted that the colonial government '. . . made radical changes only at the level of the paramountcies. At the level of local headman or local chiefs little disruption occurs.'[75] We must concentrate not on phantom ideologies but on the emergence of political attitudes related to what has actually taken place. For example, the prestige carried by age was not entirely disrupted by the missions. Price writes that '. . . the Christian community fitted into the social category of dignified seniors from the first.'[76] Macdonald writes that the Livingstonia schools preferred as its teachers not young men with mere academic ability but older men with prestige and strong character. The 'Three Hearth Stones' of the Jeanes Schools—'Health, Work and Character'—help to emphasize the strand of stabilizing discipline which runs through the educational system.[77] The soldiers and the police who served the colonial government were trained to uphold the authority of government and we could look for continuity in

440

their roles. Finally, we must look at the connections between the new elite and the old. Barnes remarks that 'Clerks aspire to become headmen when they retire, while headmen aspire to be the fathers and fathers in law of clerks.'[78] The colonial government created not one set of clerks but two and the clerks who serviced the Native Authority bureaucracy were not an agency which disrupted the authority of the old elite. Colonialism was above all a law and order system, and this legacy, even if it upsets a scheme which places radical politics at the culmination of political development, should not be ignored.

FOOTNOTES

1 I have, I hope, benefited from discussion of this paper with participants at the conference at which it was presented, my colleagues in the History Department and Lois Chanock, Ian Linden, Brian Phipps and Landeg White of the University of Malawi.

2 Davidson, B., *East and Central Africa to the Late 19th Century*, London, 1967, Study note 1,2.

3 Quoted in Fage, J. D. *On the Nature of African History*, Birmingham, 1965, 1.

4 Quoted in Avineri S. *Karl Marx on Colonialism and Modernisation*, New York 1969, 10.

5 Ibid.

6 In Thompson, L., ed., *African Societies in Southern Africa*, London 1969, 207.

7 *J. Afr. Hist.*, **8** (3), 1964. 'The Ngoni, the Natalians and their History'.

8 Roberts, A. ed., *Tanzania Before 1900*, East African Publishing House, 1968. Preface.

9 Iliffe, J. *Tanganyika Under German Rule 1905–1912*, Cambridge, 1965, 1. He is referring to the re-appraisal of colonialism which accompanied independence.

10 Ogot, B., in the preface to Davidson, B. *East and Central Africa*.

11 Davidson, B. *East and Central Africa*, 190. Admittedly this is a school text but it hands down the university approach in a pithy form.

12 Ranger, T. ed., *Emerging Themes in African History*, London 1968, **20**.

13 Oliver, R. ed., *The Dawn of African History*, London 1961, 97.

14 Ibid., 98–100 and 102.

15 Hunter, G. *The New Societies of Tropical Africa.*

16 *East and Central Africa*, 40.

17 Quoted in Elmslie, W. A., *Among the Wild Ngoni*, 3rd ed. London 1970, 105.

18 Iliffe, J., *Tanganyika Under German Rule*, 149.

19 Ogot, B., in Ranger T., *Emerging Themes*, 126 et seq.

20 Marks, S. in Oliver, R. ed., *The Middle Age of African History*, London 1967, 90–1, and Thompson, L. in Thompson L. ed., *African Societies in Southern Africa*, 16.

21 In Oliver, R. and Mathew, G. eds, *A History of East Africa*, Oxford, 1965, Vol. 1, 456.

22 *East and Central Africa*, 205.

23 Ranger, T. in Ranger, T. ed., *Aspects of Central African History*, London 1968, XIII.

24 In his review of 'Aspects of Central African History' in *J. Afr. Hist.*, **10** (1), 1969. Oliver once remarked 'We can only walk round the perimeter wall of African History, peering in wherever there is a window.' *Dawn*, 96.

25 Coleman, J. S., *Nigeria: background to Nationalism*, California, 1965, 6–7.

26 Davidson, *East and Central Africa*, 119.

27 Davidson, *East and Central Africa*, 219.

28 In Pachai, et al. ed. *Malawi Past and Present*, Malawi, 1967. 'The Old Order Changeth', 20.

29 In Ranger, *Emerging Themes*, 195.

30 Ajayi, J., 'The Place of African History and Culture in the Process of Nation Building South of the Sahara'. In Wallerstein, I., ed., *Social Change: the Colonial Situation*, New York 1966, 612.

31 Wilks, I. in Fage, J. D. ed., *Africa Discovers Her Past*, London 1970, 7.

32 Myrdal, G., *Asian Drama*, London 1968, Vol. 1, 73–77. Some nineteenth century English historians responded to change in the same way. E. A. Freeman, for example, wrote: 'Let ancient customs prevail; let us ever stand fast in the old paths. But the old paths have in England ever been the paths of progress.' See Williams, E., *British Historians and the West Indies*, London 1966, 41.

33 In 1956 Hodgkin remarked that one of the distinguishing marks of this class was 'the importance attached to the idea of progress'. Wallerstein, *Social Change*, 361–2. I think it worth remarking that the new South African history is the freest of all of evolutionary metaphor because there is, as yet, no new state and no new rulers at the culmination of the process.

34 Wright, M. reviewing Iliffe, *Tanganyika Under German Rule* in *J. Afr. Hist.*, **10** (3), 1969.

35 Lonsdale, J., 'The Emergence of African Nations' in *African Affairs*, **67** (266), 1968. See, too, Nisbet, R., *Social Change and History*, New York, 1969 for comments on '. . . the integrative-prophetic function of the metaphor of growth', 250.

36 Oliver, R. and Atmore, A., *Africa Since 1800*, Cambridge 1967, 159.

37 Lonsdale, J., *Emergence*, 14 and 16. The ethnocentric contrast between primitive and civilized has at last disappeared from African history. Lonsdale has proposed the outlawing of the word 'traditional' (*Emerging Themes*, 216 f.n. 11) and that 'modern', disguising as it does the value judgments involved, should be banished with it.

38 Hetherwick, A., *The Gospel and the African*, Edinburgh 1932, 13–14, 28, and 124–7.

39 Johnston J., *Robert Laws of Livingstonia*, London 1935, 178.

40 Quoted in Stokes, E. and Brown, R. eds., *The Zambesian Past*, Manchester 1966, 356.

41 In *Zambesian Past*, 351.

42 Quoted in the *Zambesian Past*, 383. Chibambo was the author of *My Ngoni of Nyasaland*. Van Velsen's article shows that these views were fairly common among the Native Association leaders.

43 *J. Afr. Hist.*, **1** (11), 1961 and **0** (2), 1966. R. Gray, reviewing Hanna, A. J.

The Story of Rhodesia and Nyasaland, and Wills, A. J. *Introduction to the History of Central Africa.*

44 Pachai, B., *The Malawi Diaspora and Elements of Clements Kadalie,* Central Africa Historical Association Local Series, 24, 9.

45 Ross, A. C. in *Witchcraft and Healing,* University of Edinburgh 1969. In the discussion following, Dr. Willis put his finger on the problem by remarking that Ross's account of past and present 'doesn't hang together.'

46 Oliver, R., *The Missionary Factor in East Africa,* London 1952, 16. This passage is cited with approval by Ross in *Religion in Africa,* Edinburgh, 1964.

47 *Africa Since 1800,* 157.

48 McCracken, J., 'Livingstonia Mission and the Evolution of Malawi 1875-1939', Cambridge Ph.D. 1967, 10.

49 Ibid., 358.

50 Quoted by Shepperson, G. in *Religion in Africa,* 50.

51 Quoted by McCracken in *Religion in Africa,* 90. Later Elmslie had to discourage the 'superstitious belief about a mere book'. McCracken 'Livingstonia Mission', 172.

52 Quoted in Blaikie, W. G., *The Life of David Livingstone,* London 1916, 196.

53 See Chadwick, O. *Mackenzie's Grave,* London 1959, 73 and Ross, A. C. 'The Origins and Development of the Church of Scotland Mission, Blantyre, 1875 1900'. Ph.D. Edinburgh 1968. 135.

54 Gamitto, A. C. P., *King Kazembe,* Lisbon 1960. Trans. I. Cunnison, 79.

55 Fraser, D., *African Idyll,* London 1923, 21.

56 Quoted in Macdonald, R., 'A History of African Education in Nyasaland 1875–1945'. Ph.D. Edinburgh 1969, 457.

57 See Shepperson, G., 'Ethiopianism Past and Present' in Baeta, C. G. *Christianity in Tropical Africa,* Oxford 1968, 262-3, where this point is strongly made though for different reasons.

58 Ajayi, J., *Christian Missions in Nigeria,* London 1965, 1-2.

59 The words of Charles Domingo, a product of Livingstonia and Lovedale, who became an active separatist. Quoted by McCracken in Ranger

60 My inarticulate major premise, if articulated, would be that men can make their own history only when they are conscious of their objective position in society and history.

61 McCracken, 'Livingstonia Mission', 251.

62 *African Affairs*, **66** (262), 1967 'The Presidential Address', quoted by Pratt in Low, D. A. and Pratt, R. C., *Buganda and British Overrule*, Oxford 1960, 169.

63 See Sanderson, F. E. 'Nyasaland Migrant Labour in British Central Africa 1890–1939'. M. A. University of Manchester 1960, 149, and van Velsen, J., 'Labour Migration as a Positive Factor in Tonga Tribal Society', in Wallerstein, *Social Change.*

64 See Sanderson, F. E., 'Nyasaland Migrant Labour', 149 where he quotes Soper, T. from the *J. Afr. Admin.*, **11** (2), 1959.

65 According to *Report on . . . the British Central Africa Protectorate 1902–3*, Cmd 1772, goods being purchased by Africans were cloth, cheap leather belts, knives, matches, salt, cheap lamps, looking glasses, snuff boxes, leather purses, tinned foods, waistcoats, cheap iron hoes, tin boxes and locks. McCracken, 'Livingstonia Mission', 263, f.n. 3.

66 Quoted in Hunter *New Societies*, 196. Considerable 'conservatism' survives in Lesotho, a society in which there has been widespread acceptance of Christianity: it has a high degree of literacy and a migrant labour system.

67 Marwick, M., *Sorcery in its Social Setting*, Manchester 1965, 51.

68 Gray, R. and Birmingham, D., *Pre-colonial African Trade. Essays on Trade in Eastern and Central Africa before 1900*, London 1970, 1.

69 Ibid., 3 and 13.

70 Quoted in Wills, A. J., *Introduction*, 91.

71 *King Kazembe*, 68.

72 See Avineri, *Marx*, 92–3.

73 Gellner, E. *Thought and Change*, London, 36.

74 Quoted in Avineri, *Marx*, 456.

75 In *Zambesian Past*, 372.

76 Price, T., 'The Missionary Struggle with Complexity' in Baeta, G., *Christianity*, 110.

77 See Macdonald, R., 'History of African Education, 1875–1939'. Ph.D. University of Edinburgh, 1969, Chapter III and Chapter VI, 334.

78 Barnes, J. A., *Politics in a Changing Society*, 2nd ed. Manchester 1967, 156.

Index

454